NEW ORLEANS
CITY GUIDE

1938

WITH A NEW INTRODUCTION BY LAWRENCE N. POWELL

Garrett County Press Reprint Edition 2009

For more information address:
GARRETT COUNTY PRESS
www.gcpress.com

Cover Photo Courtesy of The Historic New Orleans Collection,
acc.no.1979.325.4628.

Cover Design by Kevin Stone
Publisher's Note: Previous reprints of the New Orleans City Guide (reprinted in
1952 & 1983) were facsimiles of the original 1938 edition. For this book, the
manuscript was typeset by Kevin Stone. Whenever possible we used the original
photographs from the 1938 edition. Original photographs came from the collection
at the State Library of Louisiana, and are noted by the initials "SL" on the
illustrations content page. Photographs and illustrations that could not be located
were scanned from a first edition copy.

The text is set in Slimbach.

Library of Congress Cataloging-in-Publication Data

New Orleans city guide / written and compiled by the Federal Writers Project of
the Works Progress Administration for the City of New Orleans ; illustrated. --
Garrett County Press 1st ed.
     p. cm.
Originally published: Boston : Houghton Mifflin Company, 1938.
Includes bibliographical references and index.
ISBN 978-1-891053-08-5 (alk. paper)
1. New Orleans (La.)--Guidebooks. 2. New Orleans (La.)--Social life and cus-
toms--20th century. 3. City and town life--Louisiana--New Orleans--History--20th
century. I. Federal Writers' Project (New Orleans, La.)
F379.N5F34 2008
917.63'350462--dc22
                                        2009001238

LYLE SAXON AND THE NEW ORLEANS CITY GUIDE
BY LAWRENCE N. POWELL

Reminders of Franklin Roosevelt's New Deal are hard to miss in many American cities and towns. They are visible in Georgian-style post offices, and in huge train station murals splashed with the autumnal colors of rustic America bringing in the crops. The Great Depression did more than spur the rise of the modern American regulatory state; it also saw the federal government take some ownership of the country's historical and cultural memory. After years of squabbling that its melody was beyond the register of ordinary people, for example, Congress in the 1930s finally made the Star Spangled Banner the national anthem. A few years later Washington established the National Archives as the final resting place for federal records. And from 1935 to 1941 the WPA (Works Progress Administration), that most storied of New Deal alphabet agencies, brought forth the American Guide Series. Its roughly 400 volumes encompassed every state as well as the territories of Alaska and Puerto Rico, and the District of Columbia. There were thematic and regional volumes, too, such as *The Oregon Trail*.[1] Produced by an agency of the WPA called the Federal Writers' Project (FWP), the guides were widely praised. The critic Alfred Kazin extolled them as a symbol of the "reawakened American sense of its own history." Lewis Mumford, another cultural mandarin and a historian of cities, described the collected volumes as "his generation's 'finest contribution to American patriotism.'"[2]

And then there were the guides to major cities: New York and San Francisco, Chicago and Atlanta, to name but a few, which also appeared in the American Guide Series. The *New Orleans City Guide*, first published in 1938 and reissued in 1952 and 1983, was one of the marquee productions. A writer in a highbrow New York review described it as "perhaps the masterpiece of the whole [guide] series."[3] You need only thumb through the New Orleans volume to understand the critical acclaim. Its pages crackle with the nervous energy of good writing. No tour guide, before or since-and there have been several good ones-has done a better job mapping the Crescent City's fabled enjoyment culture. It surveys most of the music and art scene from that period, paints vivid pictures of carnival pageantry, and evokes New Orleans' love of fun and whimsy. The city's storied restaurants, several of them still in business, get proper

---

1. Michael Kammen, *Mystic Chords of Memory: The Transformation of Tradition in American Culture* (New York: Alfred A. Knopf, 1991), 444-6, 474-6.

2. Jerre Mangione, *The Dream and the Deal: The Federal Writer's Project, 1935-1943* (Boston and Toronto: Little, Brown and Company, 1972), 365 (for the first quotation); Kammen, (for the first quotation); Kammen, *Mystic Chords*, 464 (for the second quotation). See also Christine Bold, *The WPA Guides: Mapping America* (Jackson, MS: University Press of Mississippi, 1999), 7.

3. Quoted in Ronnie Wayne Clayton, "A History of the Federal Writers' Project in Louisiana" (Ph.D: LSU, 1974), 190. That high opinion was shared by the national office too, where it was regarded as one of the series's "literary gems." Mangione, *The Dream and the Deal*, 92.

billing; so do legendary recipes. Even the history it serves up is entertaining, although some chapters have to be taken *cum grano salis* (of which, more later).

There have been a lot of changes in the cityscape since the New Orleans guide was first released. Upriver from the French Quarter the skyline has become mini-Manhattanized, anchored by that trademark blister on Poydras Street that Saints fans call the Superdome.[4] Canal Street has seen its shopping emporiums shut down or decamp for the suburbs, while several Royal Street antique shops have fled to Magazine Street. Interstate highways have disfigured if not destroyed too many New Orleans neighborhoods, the bulk of them traditionally black. In the Warehouse District, where the clangor of drays and aroma of roasting coffee had once filled the air, locals and out-of-towners now stroll past art galleries, trendy eateries, and boutique hotels and condos. One change was long overdue: the uprooting of segregation (though not the racial face of poverty), with its "colored only" drinking fountains, restrooms, streetcar seating, and other vestiges of separate-but-hardly-equal affronts to dignity. Yet despite the onslaught of urban renewal; the rise of the suburbs; the collapse of the oil patch; the constant churning and turnover of restaurants, bars, and nightclubs; despite all this and more, including the decline in population and the shrinkage of New Orleans' footprint, the urban community surveyed in these pages a lifetime ago remains startlingly recognizable. Change in these latitudes has often been more of the same. Which is why this WPA guidebook deserves placement in the ranks of the permanently useful. You can still follow one of its recommended automobile tours and not feel so much as three minutes behind the times.

Nationwide the American Guide Series was a collective enterprise. Copy flowed from local researchers to state scribes thence upward to national editors, who wrestled the clichés into acceptable prose and sent the text back down the pipeline to state directors. But in Louisiana, and particularly on the New Orleans volume, one man alone, Lyle Saxon (1891-1946), did most of the writing and editing. (He also did most of the heavy lifting for the other book-length volumes produced by the Louisiana Writers' Project: *Louisiana: A Guide to the State* and *Gumbo Ya-Ya*, a collection of Louisiana folklore.) For a program ostensibly aimed at helping professional writers weather the economic turbulence of the 1930s, few from those ranks were put in charge of state offices. Several alumni, such as Ralph Ellison, who worked on the New York City guide, and Saul Bellow and Studs Terkel went on to distinguished literary careers. But you can count on one hand the number of writers given high administrative responsibility. Saxon was one of them, and maybe the most highly regarded of the lot. On several occasions Washington called for his assistance to troubleshoot guide work in nearby states where bottlenecks were choking off

---

4. To echo novelist Tom Piazza: *City of Refuge* (New York: Harper Collins, 2008), 7.

progress. The central office brought him to DC to work on the national desk. They even kept him on the payroll after the Federal Writers' Project began winding down in the 1940s, one of only four state directors so favored.[5]

A Baton Rouge native who had been a reporter for various New Orleans newspapers before cutting loose to write popular histories, short stories, and one novel, Saxon hosted the literary bohemians who descended on the *Vieux Carré* in the 1920s, turning it into a "poor man's Paris."[6] He himself had moved to the French Quarter just before World War One, when most of its denizens were people of color, first and second-generation Italian immigrants, or the occasional white Creole.[7] His reportage on the *Vieux Carré*, its colorful personalities, and particularly the artist colony that soon congregated there helped spur the preservation movement largely responsible for sparing this historic district from the bulldozer revolution soon to scar many American cities. Saxon's appreciative writing also drew to the Quarter in the early 1920s such major American writers as Sherwood Anderson, William Faulkner, and John Dos Passos, even Edmund Wilson breezing through on a busman's holiday. John Steinbeck was married in a French Quarter townhouse owned by Saxon. Tall and thin, with grayish blue eyes, Saxon looked off-kilter among these raffish, often scrubby literary men. He inclined toward tailored suits, was polished and fastidious in his manners. Anderson and Faulkner liked to make fun of his affectations, even as they appreciated his friendship and generosity. Faulkner stayed at Saxon's New York apartment when he traveled to Gotham seeking a publisher for *The Sound and the Fury*. Yet Saxon always stood apart, in but never of the crowd. A masterful raconteur and an exceptional listener, gracious even toward admiring strangers who shoved their way into his privacy, he concealed a basic unhappiness behind a self-effacement that discouraged intimacy. "He was a very strange person," George Healy, Jr., his former editor on the *Times-Picayune* remembered. "Bill Faulkner was an oddball, but once you knew him, you knew him. I never did know Lyle Saxon."[8]

Some of Saxon's oddness was that of a frustrated novelist who could never find comfort in his own skin (except in a Mardi Gras costume, the more absurd, the better). His adult life seemed a never-ending battle against depression, self-loathing, and alcoholism. Permanent scars had been left by a journalist father's abandonment shortly after Saxon's birth.

5. Clayton, "Federal Writers' Project in Louisiana," xiii-xiv, 36-43, 148-55.

6. Chance Harvey, *The Life and Letters of Lyle Saxon* (Gretna, LA: Pelican Press, 2003), 63.

7. The word Creole in Louisiana has had a tangled lexical history. Originally denoting anyone or anything native to Louisiana, by the time of the Civil War and increasingly afterwards white Creoles had launched a campaign to prove that Creoles were pureblooded Europeans, in order to disprove the evidence of everyone's eyes that racial mixing had taken place between Latin whites and people of African descent. Today the term generally refers to Afro-Creoles.

8. Harvey, *Life and Letters*, 19-69, 109-14 (the quotation is on 48).

Most of all, there was his bisexual orientation, which he tried to hide even from bohemian associates. Nearly everyone who has written about Saxon agrees that he sought inner peace and a new identity by writing his life story into the cultural heritage of the plantation South. His romantic histories, beginning with *Fabulous New Orleans,* and followed quickly by *Father Mississippi* and *Old Louisiana,* all authored during a literary sojourn in New York City in the late Twenties, were more anecdotal reinvention than anything else. It is impossible to read them without concluding that Saxon had spent an idyllic childhood on this or that plantation riding horses and swimming with black playmates, helping hand out gifts to cane cutters every Christmas. Critics from the national media who didn't know better hailed him as "the new chronicler of the South." But it was all myth and magnolias. Saxon hadn't even been born in Dixie, but Washington State. His family background was Baton Rouge shopkeeping. His single mother pinched pennies by scribbling reviews for the local paper. Even his grandmother-an early suffragist in New Orleans known for her outspoken antislavery opinions-belied the plantation myth. But the more that Saxon's self-fashioning diverged from reality, the harder he strove to cultivate the image of having been to the manor born.[9]

Beginning in 1924, Saxon made long sojourns at Melrose plantation in the Cane River region of Natchitoches parish. The invitation came from Cammie Henry, the chatelaine who turned this famed former property of Afro-Creole slaveowners into an artists' retreat. Here he took up, at intervals, writerly residence in an old slave cabin, installing the de rigueur four-poster bed and lining the study with floor-to-ceiling bookshelves crammed with his collection of "pre-Civil War Portraits of Negroes." He'd write for a spell, amble down sun-latticed paths shaded by live oaks and crepe myrtle, maybe visit the Negro quarters, and then drink alone at night. Late in life he sank a small fortune into a 16-room French Quarter townhouse, donning the mask of urban sophisticate. It was as if he were striving to recreate the lifestyle of planter patriarchs who used to divide their time between big houses in the country and Creole mansions in town, or perhaps to relive the days when French chevaliers and Spanish dons lorded it over Louisiana. After Saxon shifted his lodgings to the grand old St. Charles Hotel, where he lived the last dozen years of his life, he hired a black valet and chauffeur named Joe Gilmore. The move to the St. Charles came during Saxon's stint as director of the Federal Writers Project in Louisiana. Part major-domo, part Rochester to Saxon's Jack Benny, Gilmore's principal tasks seem to have been preparing strong coffee in the morning, mixing absinthe frappés at night, and remaining on stand-by for jovial companionship. He became known as the "Black Saxon."[10]

9. Ibid., 21-56; Rosan Augusta Jordan and Frank De Caro, "'In This Folk-Lore Land': Race, Class, Identity, and Folklore Studies in Louisiana," *The Journal of American Folklore,* 109 (Winter, 1996), 46-9, 143-5, 161, 165.

10. Saxon tells this story in his posthumously published *The Friends of Joe Gilmore* (New York: Hastings House, 1948), 3-9; also 19. See also Harvey, *Life and Letters,* 180-8.

Saxon's infatuation with the romance of the Old South found plenty of scope for expression in the New Orleans guide. The history he really cared about were the glamour decades prior to the Civil War, when New Orleans blossomed overnight from a backwater of empire into a veritable Calcutta of cotton and slavery. Other periods in the city's past seemed squalid in comparison, especially Reconstruction. Saxon dismissed it as "the blackest [time] in the history of New Orleans," a judgment sharply at variance with modern scholarship or sensibility. Moreover, it's hard to stifle winces when he slips into black dialect and other expressions of "affectionate paternalism." They are hard to miss in "local color" passages on voodoo and black spiritual churches, here dubbed "Negro cults." But these sacred institutions, rooted as they were in the culture of West Africa and the Caribbean, were part of a significant religious movement, a fact that a cursory check of the local black press would have revealed.[11] Readers need to approach these sections of the New Orleans volume with a healthy dose of skepticism. And yet, this can't be the whole story. For what stands out about the *New Orleans City Guide* are not the traces of racial condescension, but the willingness of a southern white man to devote serious attention to black subjects during the 1930s.

Some of Saxon's openness was owing to pressure from the Washington headquarters on local and state offices to be culturally inclusive in their coverage. It led to a constant tug of war between the metropole and the Jim Crow provinces, with the latter often refusing to budge. The Mississippi guide described the typical black inhabitant as "a genial mass of remarkable qualities...carefree and shrewd....As for the Negro question – that, too, is just another problem he has left for the white man to cope with."[12] Other southern volumes in the series were not much better. Saxon was never this crude. The New Orleans staff took seriously the charge to be of help to the "Negro traveler" by delineating African American entertainment venues and institutions, and by taking note of black cultural and artistic contributions. They brushed aside complaints from university music department heads that "too much credit was being given to the colored people and their type of music and too little to musical culture among white people." The New Orleans group were not afraid to take risks. The talented visual artist Caroline Durieux, who did many of the line drawings for the guide, palmed herself off as a pickpocket in order to gain entry to a black demimonde otherwise closed to average whites. Apparently, so did Saxon himself-but under the cover of a mask during carnival season.[13]

11. For examples in the *New Orleans City Guide*, see pages 24 (for the quotation) and 210-211. See also Harvey, *Life and Letters*, 173; Claude F. Jacobs, "Folk for Whom? Tourist Guidebooks, Local Color, and the Spiritual Churches of New Orleans," 114 (Summer, 2001), 309-330; and Anthony J. Stanonis, *Creating the Big Easy: New Orleans and the Emergence of Modern Tourism*, 1918-1945 (Athens and London: The University of Georgia Press, 2006), 224-6.

12. Quoted in Jerrold Hirsch, *Portrait of America: A Cultural History of the Federal Writers' Project* (Chapel Hill: UNC Press 2003), 127. See also Bold, *WPA Guides*, 3-36 and *passim*.

13. Clayton, "Federal Writers' Project in Louisiana," 159 (for the quotation) and 180. See also Jordan and Frank De Caro, "'In This Folk-Lore Land,'" 50.

In one area Saxon needed little nudging from northern liberals: the expectation that local FWP directors would seek out folk material. The populism of the 1930s brimmed with optimism about bridging the divide between high culture and popular folkways. That zeitgeist brought literary expatriates home from Europe, spurred the new regionalism in the visual arts, encouraged the folk craft movement, inspired appreciation for vernacular music, and galvanized the documentary photography of Walker Evans and Dorothea Lange.[14] Collecting African-American folk material was nothing new in Louisiana. White New Orleanians, many of them academics and society matrons, had been gathering up trickster tales and work song lyrics since before the turn of the twentieth century. But the motivation was elitist, even reactionary, a kind of anthropology for scoring deeper the line of color. They used African-American folk material to mark off their identities from that of "superstitious" field hands, while indulging nostalgia for plantation yesteryears. Saxon descended from this tradition. The discoverer of black folk painter Clementine Hunter, he too used the vast storehouse of vernacular lore and lyric amassed over a lifetime to validate his bona fides as a white person.[15] But he went further, doubtless due to his own keenly felt marginality. He comes close to identifying with his African-American informants. His sole novel, about the tragic circumstances of "mulattos" in the Cane River area, evinced this sensitivity. So did a racist self-characterization in a letter to a friend that he regarded himself "a poor but honest nigger." It was a revelatory slip that gave away more than Saxon probably intended.[16]

And then there was his peculiar posthumously published autobiography, *The Friends of Joe Gilmore*: a memoir wherein the white Saxon completes himself through his relationship with his alter ego, the black Saxon. Where the writer is meek, Joe is imperious, a veritable "Emperor Jones" toward black servants and market vendors. He learns to mimic Saxon's voice on the phone, recites Saxon's poems to dinner guests, manages his wardrobe, announces when it's time to drive to the country. "Boss, I think we both needs some air." And always Joe stands ready to pour a drink: brandied coffee, mint juleps, Ramos gin fizzes, high balls, and of course absinthe frappés. On weekend trips to the "Shadows on the Teche" in New Iberia, a plantation owned by the bachelor painter Weeks Hall, white bosses and black valets and yardmen lounge before the fireplace sharing drinks, gratifying an interracial bonhomie that bent but never breached the barriers of racial custom.[17]

The final verdict on Saxon's racial sensibilities should probably rest with the black intellectuals with whom he came into frequent contact. From all

14. Kammen, *Mystic Chords*, 407-8, 419-21, 426-36, 443.

15 Only a fraction of the material appears in the New Orleans guide; the bulk of it was published in *Gumbo Ya-Ya*.

16. Jordan and Frank De Caro, "'In This Folk-Lore Land,'" 31-59 (the quotation is on 49). See also Harvey, *Life and Letters*, 182-5.

17. *Friends of Joe Gilmore*, 54 (for the quotation).

accounts, their interaction was of the unself-conscious variety. Marcus Christian, who directed the Negro Division of the New Orleans Writers' Project based at Dillard University, long remembered the handshake on the evening Saxon offered him the job: "that impulsive outward swing of his hand that nearly described an arc, but an arc that in its downward swing, hesitated just long enough to give your hand time enough to rise slightly and meet his in a gesture of genuine fellowship ... a clasping of hands in an expansive, mellow, hail-fellow mood." The poet Langston Hughes and the renowned sculptor Richmond Barthé likewise respected the genial head of the Louisiana FWP. *The Louisiana Weekly*, New Orleans only black newspaper, published a glowing obituary when Saxon died in 1946. This is hardly the sort of recognition run-of-the-mill racial paternalists receive from men quick to pick up on white condescension. In Saxon's troubled soul, black intellectuals obviously saw something out of the ordinary.[18]

It is a melancholy fact that Saxon, the frustrated novelist, never relaxed into his achievements in non-fiction. He was scornful of the popular histories authored at the height of his career, even after they garnered critical acclaim. He was even more dismissive about his work for the WPA. "I'm right back where I started from six and a half years ago," he complained in 1942. "And all I've got to show for those years is the sad fact that I'm much older, and my eyes are bad now, and I've published some guidebooks ... What the hell?" In his declining years, as he grew fatter, struggled with the aftermath of a ruptured appendix, and descended ever more deeply into the haze of alcoholism, he morphed into a tourist attraction for out-of-towners who had prepped for their visit by reading his romantic glosses on state and city history, and it intensified his ruefulness: "I started out as a writer, and I end as a souvenir," went another of his laments.[19] But of all of Saxon's contributions to Louisiana literature, the *New Orleans City Guide* may end up enjoying the longest shelf life of all.

Saxon was a person of his time and place, and his guidebook to the Crescent City must be read bearing that fact in mind. But readers would do well to remember that what separates us from him is not superior enlightenment but time and circumstances. It's a gap worth bridging, if only to appreciate arguably the most serviceable guide to the city's culture and history appearing to date.

18. Harvey, *Life and Letters*, 33-4; Clayton, "Federal Writers' Project in Louisiana," 141. For more on the remarkable Dillard Project, see Ronnie W. Clayton, "The Federal Writers' Project for Blacks in Louisiana," *Louisiana History*, 19 (Summer, 1978), 327-35; and Joan Redding, "The Dillard Project: The Black Unit of the Louisiana Writers' Project," in ibid., 32 (Winter, 1991), 47-62.

19. Harvey, *Life and Letters*, 203 (for the first quotation) and 214 (for the second quotation).

AMERICAN GUIDE SERIES

NEW ORLEANS CITY GUIDE 1938

Written and compiled by the Federal Writers Project of the Works Progress Administration for the City of New Orleans

ROBERT MAESTRI, MAYOR OF NEW ORLEANS, CO-OPERATING SPONSOR

Illustrated

GARRETT COUNTY PRESS – NEW ORLEANS

HARRY L. HOPKINS
ADMINISTRATOR

The greatest power against which the city of New Orleans
has had to pit its strength has been also the source of
its life: the Mississippi River. The struggle to use
and control it has resulted in brilliant feats of
commerce, engineering, sanitation, and medical research.
The writers of the Federal Writers' Project of
New Orleans have, I think, succeeded in conveying the
quality of their romantic and powerful city; the sense of
its strength and destiny, as well as its gaiety, ease and
its art of living.

What this book does for the city of New Orleans, the
American Guide series aims to do for the life and times
of the forty-eight states and a number of important
American cities and towns -- probably the most ambitious
attempt as yet made to portray honestly and completely the
history, struggles, and triumphs of the American people.
If the Federal Writers manage to complete this job in the
same competent manner evidenced in their publications made
available to date, we can expect the series to become a
standard reference collection for students of almost every
aspect of American life.

Harry L. Hopkins
Administrator

WORKS PROGRESS ADMINISTRATION

HARRY L. HOPKINS, *Administrator*

ELLEN S. WOODWARD, *Assistant Administrator*

HENRY G. ALSBERG, *Director of Federal Writers' Project*

CITY OF NEW ORLEANS
OFFICE OF THE MAYOR

The New Orleans City Guide is the first major accomplishment of the Federal Writers' Project of Louisiana. More than a conventional guidebook, this volume attempts to describe the history and heritage of New Orleans, as well as its numerous points of interest.

As Mayor of New Orleans, I am greatly pleased that this publication is being made available to the public.

Robert S. Maestri
Mayor of New Orleans.

PREFACE

THE New Orleans City Guide has been compiled and edited by the workers on the New Orleans division of the Federal Writers' Project of Louisiana, and is one of an extensive series of American guides being compiled by the Federal Writers' Project of the Works Progress Administration. Its purpose is to present as complete a picture as possible of New Orleans within the limits of a volume that is not too unwieldy. For generous co-operation in supplying information, offering advice and suggestions, and for other assistance during the preparation of this volume, grateful acknowledgments are due to many persons and institutions, both public and private. We are particularly indebted to the following four people who have read and criticized the manuscript as a whole: the Reverend Harold A. Gaudin, President of Loyola University; Mr. Robert Usher, Librarian of the Howard Memorial Library, who in addition wrote the paragraph on the founding of New Orleans which has been incorporated in the French Quarter Tour; Mr. Richard Kirk of Tulane University; and Mr. Hermann Deutsch of the *New Orleans Item*.

We are also indebted to a number of people who read and criticized parts of the manuscript dealing with their own special fields, including Mr. Nathaniel Curtis and Mr. Moise Goldstein — Architecture; and Mr. Stanley Clisby Arthur — French Quarter Tour.

We are likewise indebted to the libraries, museums, and newspaper offices of the city and to the Association of Commerce for their consistent co-operation. Other acknowledgments are made in the text and in the bibliography.

We are indebted for certain of the photographs to the New Orleans Association of Commerce, the *Times-Picayune*, and the Historic American Buildings Survey. Most of the photographs, however, and all of the drawings are the work of staff artists and photographers.

Although few cross-references have been used in the text, the detailed index should make it simple for the reader to find whatever he is looking for.

LYLE SAXON, *State Director*
EDWARD P. DREYER, *Assistant State Director*

CONTENTS

III. SECTIONAL DESCRIPTIONS AND TOURS

ILLUSTRATIONS

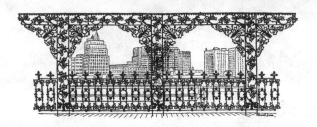

NEW ORLEANS OLD AND NEW

HAVE you ever been in New Orleans? If not you'd better go.
It's a nation of a queer place; day and night a show!
Frenchmen, Spaniards, West Indians, Creoles, Mustees,
Yankees, Kentuckians, Tennesseans, lawyers and trustees,
*   *   *   *   *   *   *   *   *   *   *
Negroes in purple and fine linen, and slaves in rags and chains.
Ships, arks, steamboat, robbers, pirates, alligators,
Assassins, gamblers, drunkards, and cotton speculators;
Sailors, soldiers, pretty girls, and ugly fortune-tellers;
Pimps, imps, shrimps, and all sorts of dirty fellows;
*   *   *   *   *   *   *   *   *   *   *
A progeny of all colors – and infernal motley crew;
Yellow fever in February – muddy streets all the year;
Many things to hope for, and a devilish sight to fear!
Gold and silver bullion – United States bank notes,
Horse-racers, cock-fighters, and beggars without coats,
Snapping-turtles, sugar-houses, water-snakes,
Molasses, flour, whiskey, tobacco, corn and johnny-cakes,
Beef, cattle, hogs, pork, turkeys, Kentucky rifles,
Lumber, boards, apples, cotton, and many other trifles.
Butter, cheese, onions, wild beasts in wooden cages,
Barbers, waiters, draymen, with the highest sort of wages.

THIS was written more than a hundred years ago, when New Orleans had
already passed its first century mark, by one Colonel Creecy, a man of parts
and of gusto. New Orleans today, with a population of nearly half a million,
the largest city south of the Mason-Dixon line, and one of the largest ports in
the United States, is remembered with pleasure by countless travelers who have
taken the colonel's advice. Alligators, to be sure, are now seldom encountered outside of curio stores; but cotton speculators are still at large. Sailors and pretty girls,
horse-racers and cock-fighters are always with us, to say nothing of the pimps and
the imps and the shrimps. And there are the Mardi Gras, the French Quarter, the
cemeteries above ground, the river, the lake, the food, and the drinks.

Traditionally the city that care forgot, New Orleans is, perhaps, best known for
its liberal attitude toward human frailties, its 'Live and Let Live' policy. To the
tourist the city is first of all a place in which to eat, drink, and be merry.

Generations of gourmands and tipplers have waxed fat on gumbo and bouilla-baisse and pompano, and gay on gin fizzes and absinthe drips and Sazerac cock-tails; many of them, Thackeray and Mark Twain included, have communicated their appreciation of the 'American Paris' to the world. Generations of revelers have gone their joyous way through Carnival Season to Mardi Gras, that maddest of all mad days when every man may be a king, or, if he prefers, a tramp or a clown or an Indian chief, and dance in the streets. Generations of dandies and sports and adventurers have, with their 'ladies,' played fast and loose in the gam-bling-houses and 'sporting' houses of the 'American Marseilles.' Ever since the middle of the eighteenth century, when the Marquis de Vaudreuil attempted to set up in Nouvelle Orléans a miniature Versailles, a reputation for gaiety and aban-don has persisted. These, then, the joys of the flesh, the traveler first remembers.

But there are other memories in that strange jumble of recollections which the visitor to New Orleans takes away. For New Orleans is likewise a pious and virtuous city. For a hundred years Catholicism was the religion command-ed by law, and the Catholic Church still controls the largest congregation in the city, adding, with its processions and feasts and rituals, color to the lives of even non-Catholics. Other religious denominations have, of course, long since established strong followings. New Orleans today is a city of much faith and of many faiths, where people still pray and where the personal columns of the newspapers give daily evidence that prayers are still answered.

And then there is the French Quarter, that Vieux Carré or 'Old Square' which lies below Canal Street and along the Mississippi River. Once the walled city of Nouvelle Orléans, it remains today one of the most interesting spots in the United States.

Here one finds the narrow streets with overhanging balconies, the beau-tiful wrought-iron and cast-iron railings, the great barred doors and tropical courtyards. Many of these fine houses are more than a century and a quar-ter old, and they stand today as monuments to their forgotten architects. For it must be remembered that New Orleans was a Latin city already a centu-ry old before it became a part of the United States; and it was as unlike the American cities along the Atlantic seaboard as though Louisiana were on another continent. Louisiana was closely allied to France and Spain, and had almost nothing to do with the American Revolution; it became a part of the United States through purchase. Even today New Orleans – American city though it is – still retains a definite Latin quality.

Dividing the older downtown section of the city from the uptown or American section lies Canal Street, a magnificent thoroughfare, one of the widest streets in the United States, and reputed to be one of the four best-lighted streets in the world. In winter it is full of the usual urban bustle of the American city, but in summer, when life becomes slow and lazy, Canal Street at night presents a charming picture. It is rather like a slow-motion moving picture as white-clad men and women stroll along the brightly lighted thoroughfare, stopping to imbibe the ever-popular iced drinks, then continuing the evening promenade.

Going uptown (or south) from Canal Street, one reaches the Garden District, bounded by St. Charles, Jackson, and Louisiana Avenues and by Magazine Street. Built nearly a hundred years ago, it is a beautiful section today, recalling an earlier, happier, and more leisurely period. Here stand large, handsome houses built by the first Americans who came to Louisiana after the Purchase in 1803. The houses are set deep in gardens; there are broad verandas (called 'galleries' in Louisiana) and the large white columns of the Greek Revival. There are graceful cast-iron railings, white doorways bright through vines and palm trees, and high brick walls enclosing gardens which blossom with magnolias, crêpe myrtles, oleanders, azaleas, and gardenias. There is scarcely a day in the year when flowers cannot be seen.

Continuing uptown beyond the Garden District, we find more broad avenues lined with great trees and well-kept lawns and gardens. This section extends for miles. St. Charles Avenue is the main thoroughfare, and the adjoining streets are filled with pleasing houses and gardens. The residential district is full of charm. Even the humbler homes have flowers and well-kept hedges; and there are large and beautiful parks. New Orleans is a city that lives outdoors in summertime.

St. Charles Avenue eventually reaches Carrollton Avenue, and this neighborhood was once the separately incorporated town of Carrollton. Near the river-front above Canal Street is the old American business section, in some ways very much like the French Quarter, which lies below Canal Street. Nowadays it is given over to wholesale dealers near Canal Street, and to a poor neighborhood as one goes farther uptown. This section is known today as 'The Irish Channel' because of the numbers of Irish families who once lived there. It bears the reputation of being 'tough,' but it is probably no tougher than other localities lying along the docks.

The visitor to New Orleans is always interested in the Port and in the docks, which extend for fourteen miles along the river. Here are vessels which sail the Seven Seas, and flags of all nations flutter at the mast heads. Ferries cross and recross the Mississippi, which is approximately a half mile wide at New Orleans. Sea gulls follow the ships, searching for food, and make the visitor realize that the Gulf of Mexico is not far away.

The wharves are divided into sections, each with its particular use; there are grain wharves, cotton sheds, and, most interesting to the visitor, the wharves where the great green bunches of bananas are transported from ships to freight cars. When a banana ship is in port, the wharf presents a scene of great activity; hundreds of laborers carry the fruit to the waiting cars. Old Negro women, fat and wearing snowy turbans on their heads, move about in the crowd selling sandwiches and sweet cakes. Those who taste their wares find the dainties both appetizing and toothsome. All day long the groaning conveyors lift bunches of bananas from the hold of the ship, and all day long the men continue to move in a line carrying them. Darkness falls and the lights flash on; there are long swaying shadows, and the fruit is doubly green in the artificial light. The hours pass by and the men continue at their labor. Then there is a shout and the great conveyors stop. The ship is empty. The line breaks, the men scatter, forming another line before the paymaster.

The coffee docks, the cotton docks, and the molasses sheds all present interesting scenes of activity during the working day. But as a rule it is only the banana wharf which presents an interesting activity in the evening.

Across the river from the foot of Canal Street lies Algiers, a part of New Orleans, but connected directly with it by ferry traffic only, and preserving to a considerable extent the atmosphere of a small Louisiana town. Gretna, Harvey, Marrero, and Westwego are other towns which line the river above Algiers and are likewise reached by ferries. Nine miles above the city the Huey P. Long Bridge, the twenty-ninth and one of the finest spans across the Mississippi, gives New Orleans an unbroken highway to the west.

Toward the northern boundary of the city lie the suburban districts – Gentilly and Metairie – and beyond them is Lake Pontchartrain, which plays an important part in the social life of New Orleans in the summer. One of the largest lakes in the country, its water is somewhat salty, as it connects with Lake Borgne, which, in turn, connects with the Gulf of Mexico. Here the city has erected a sea wall for protection from the high waves of tropical storms; and here, off the wall from West End to the Industrial Canal, the people of New Orleans swim. On Sundays and holidays many thousands spend the day at the lake. There are also amusement parks, restaurants, and open squares with palms and flowers. In addition to the lake shore, there are Audubon and City Parks, each equally lovely and well kept, and each provided with large swimming pools, tennis courts, and golf links. A pleasant feature is night swimming and tennis, as pools and courts alike are illuminated. At present (1937), both parks and the lake shore are being beautified by the Federal Government through Works Progress Administration projects.

Throughout a tour of the city one cannot fail to be impressed by streets whose names are derived from saints, soldiers, authors, and astronomers, from classical mythology and Indian legend, from fish and fowl, and from the heavenly bodies. And should the visitor be too startled by Calliope's journey from Jefferson Davis past the Spanish Governors, Miro and Galvez, and eventually to Tchoupitoulas, or by St. Claude's meeting first with Piety and then with Desire, or too puzzled by words such as *Creole, lagniappe,* and *banquette,* a brief account of street names as well as a glossary of unusual words and phrases in constant use in New Orleans has been added at the back of the book.

GENERAL INFORMATION

Railroad Stations: Union Station, 1001 S. Rampart St., for Gulf Coast Lines, Illinois Central, Southern Pacific, and Yazoo and Mississippi Valley; Terminal Station, 1125 Canal St., for Gulf Mobile, and Northern and Southern Railway; 701 South Rampart St. for Louisiana and Arkansas; foot of Canal St. for Louisville and Nashville; 1125 Annunciation St. for Missouri Pacific and Texas and Pacific.

Steamship Piers: Poydras St. for Delta Line; Galvez St. for Luckenbach Line; Louisa St. for Standard Fruit; Thalia St. for United Fruit. Bienville St. for Morgan Line (Southern Pacific).

Bus Stations: 1520 Canal St. for Teche-Greyhound Lines; 207 St. Charles St. for Missouri Pacific Trailways.

Airport: Shushan Airport, 9 miles from city on Lake Pontchartrain; Eastern Air Lines and Chicago and Southern Air Lines; 20 minutes from Canal St. Taxi, $1.50 per passenger each way.

Ferries: Canal St. Ferry to Bouny St., Algiers; Jackson Avenue Ferry to Huey P. Long Ave. (Copernicus St.), Gretna; Louisiana Ave. Ferry to Destrehan Ave., Harvey; Napoleon Ave. Ferry to Barataria Road, Marrero; Walnut St. Ferry to Westwego. All except Louisiana Ave. Ferry give 24-hour service.

Excursions: River excursion steamer, leaving from the foot of Canal St., makes day and night harbor trips from October to May. Several weekly excursions via Harvey Canal are made to Grand Isle. For information and schedules consult Grand Isle Chamber of Commerce, Carondelet Building.

Taxis: Fare 40¢ (1 or 5 passengers) within city zone (roughly the metropolitan area west of the Inner-Harbor Navigation Canal), with proportionate increase beyond. Have understanding with taxi-driver before making out-of-zone trips.

Street-cars: Trolleys and motor-busses serve all sections of the city. Fare 7¢ with universal transfer. All lines except Napoleon Ave. start at Canal St.

Traffic Regulations: Care must be taken to observe the signal lights and direction signs at street intersections. These signs are either in center of street or on sidewalk. Many one-way streets, indicated by arrow signs at every intersection, will be encountered throughout the city; all cross-streets between Decatur and Rampart on Canal are one-way streets. Watch for 'No Left Turn' signs. When left turn is permitted in business sections, get into traffic lane on extreme left and turn on red light. 'Stop,' 'slow,' and red arrow signs at dangerous corners must be obeyed under penalty of arrest. Persons under 16 years of age not allowed to drive. Secure a visitor's permit, without cost, from the License Examiner before 12 o'clock noon of the day following arrival; good for 30 days. For parking consult signs or traffic officer.

Street Order and Numbering: Streets are numbered uptown and downtown (north and south) from Canal Street, beginning with 100. Corners and sides of streets are described as uptown or downtown (upriver or downriver) and as river or lake (woods). Streets running from river to lake are numbered away from the river. Even numbers are on river and uptown side of street, and odd numbers on lake and downtown side. Note that streets crossing Canal between North and South Peters and North and South Rampart have different names on opposite sides of Canal St.

Accommodations: Hotels and boarding-house rates vary according to season and occasion. Accommodations in private homes are obtainable during Mardi Gras and Mid-Winter Sports Carnival. Tourist and trailer camps are located on US 90 and 61. Consult Association of Commerce, or daily newspaper bureau. (*See Hotels and Restaurants.*)

Information Service: Association of Commerce and all leading hotels and newspaper offices.

Theaters and Motion-Picture Houses: Twelve motion-picture theaters (some admitting Negroes) in business section, including one exclusively for Negroes; occasional road shows; concerts, ballets, and operas at Municipal Auditorium.

Concert Halls: Municipal Auditorium, Jerusalem (Shriners) Temple, and Dixon Hall (Newcomb College). Concerts, plays, etc., are also held at school auditoriums such as McMain High School and Rabouin Trade School.

Sports and Recreation: See *Recreational Facilities, Amateur Sports Events, and Professional Sports Events.*

CHURCH GUIDE

Adventist
Seventh Day Adventist, 1500 Camp St.
Seventh Day (Negro), 2412 Delachaise St.

American Old Catholic
American Old Catholic, St. John Chapel, 3151 Dauphine St.

Assembly of God
First Assembly of God, 1033 Friscoville Ave.
Spain Street, 1017 Spain St.

Baptist
Calvary, 802 Olivier St., Algiers
Canal Boulevard, 5324 Canal Blvd.
Carrollton Avenue, 2428 Carrollton Ave.
Central, 129 S. Jefferson Davis Pkwy.
Coliseum Place, 1376 Camp St.
Emmanuel, 1017 N. Dorgenois St.
First, 3436 St. Charles Ave.
First, Opelousas Ave. and Seguin St., Algiers
Franklin Avenue, 2515 Franklin Ave.
Gentilly, 5141 Franklin Ave.
Grace, N. Rampart and Alvar Sts.
Lakeview, West End Blvd. and Polk Ave.
Napoleon Avenue, Napoleon and S. Claiborne Aves.
St. Charles Avenue, 7100 St. Charles Ave.
Valence Street, 4626 Magazine St.
Zion Travelers' (Negro), 404 Adams St.

Catholic
All Saints, 1419 Teche St., Algiers
Annunciation, 1221 Mandeville St.
Corpus Christi (Negro), 2020 St. Bernard Ave.
Holy Ghost (Negro), 2001 Louisiana Ave.
Holy Name of Mary, 418 Verret St., Algiers
Holy Name of Jesus, 6363 St. Charles Ave.
Holy Redeemer (Negro), 2122 Royal St.
Holy Trinity, 725 St. Ferdinand St.
Immaculate Conception (Jesuits' Church), 132 Baronne St.
Incarnate Word, 8316 Apricot St.
Mater Dolorosa, 1226 S. Carrollton Ave.

Our Lady of Good Counsel, 1307 Louisiana Ave.
Our Lady of Guadalupe, 1101 Conti St.
Our Lady of Holy Rosary, 3368 Esplanade Ave.
Our Lady of Lourdes, 2406 Napoleon Ave.
Our Lady of Sacred Heart, 1728 St. Bernard Ave.
Our Lady Star of the Sea, 1901 St. Roch Ave.
Our Mother of Perpetual Help Chapel, 2523 Prytania St.
Sacred Heart of Jesus, 3226 Canal St.
St. Alphonsus, 2043 Constance St.
St. Ann's, 2125 Ursuline Ave.
St. Anthony of Padua, 4630 Canal St.
St. Augustine's, 1210 Gov. Nicholls St.
St. Cecilia's, 4219 N. Rampart St.
St. Dominic's, 224 Harrison Ave.
St. Francis de Sales, 2209 Second St.
St. Francis of Assisi, 631 State St.
St. Henry's, 812 General Pershing St.
St. James Major, Lotus nr. Gentilly Blvd.
St. Joan of Arc (Negro), 919 Cambronne St.
St. John the Baptist, 1139 Dryades St.
St. Joseph, 1810 Tulane Ave.
St. Katherine (Negro), 1509 Tulane Ave.
St. Leo the Great, 2916 Paris Ave.
St. Louis Cathedral, Chartres St. bet. St. Peter and St. Ann Sts.
St. Mary of the Angels, N. Miro and Congress Sts.
St. Mary's Assumption, Josephine bet. Constance and Laurel Sts.
St. Mary's Italian, 1114 Chartres St.
St. Matthias, 4224 S. Broad St.
St. Maurice, 605 St. Maurice Ave.
St. Michaels, 1526 Chippewa St.
St. Patrick's, 716 Camp St.
St. Peter Claver (Negro), 1919 St. Philip St.
St. Peter and St. Paul, 2317 Burgundy St.
St. Rita's, 2620 Pine St.
St. Rose of Lima, 2541 Bayou Rd.
St. Stephen's, 1007 Napoleon Ave.
St. Theresa Little Flower of Jesus, 9002 Quince St.
St. Theresa, 1109 Coliseum St.
St. Vincent de Paul, 3049 Dauphine St.

Christian Science

First, 1436 Nashville Ave.
Second, 630 Common St.
Third, 2333 Fern St.

Church of Christ

First, 2919 Camp St.

Church of God

First, 4967 DeMontluzin St.

Church of the Nazarene

Church of the Nazarene, 8518 Oak St.

Congregational Church

University (Negro), 2420 Canal St.

Disciples of Christ

Carrollton Ave. Christian, 4540 Carrollton Ave.
St. Charles Ave. Christian, 6200 St. Charles Ave.

Episcopal

Christ Church Cathedral, 2919 St. Charles Ave.
Church of the Annunciation, 4515 S. Claiborne Ave.
Church of the Holy Comforter, 4481 DeMontluzin St.
Grace, 1501 Canal St.
Mount Olivet, 530 Pelican Ave., Algiers
St. Andrew's, 8021 Zimple St., cor. Carrollton Ave.
St. Anna's, 1313 Esplanade Ave.
St. George's, 4600 St. Charles Ave.
St. John's, 800 Third St.
St. Paul's, 1127 Gaiennie St.
St. Philip's, Henry Clay Ave. and Chestnut St.
Trinity, 1329 Jackson Ave.

Evangelical

Bethany, 3712 S. Broad St.
Bethel, 2205 Franklin Ave.
First, 1829 Carondelet St.
Jackson Avenue, 705 Jackson Ave.
St. John, 8439 Belfast St.
St. Matthew's, S. Carrollton Ave., cor. Willow St.
St. Paul's, 5901 Patton St.
Salem, 930 Milan St.
Trinity Evangelical, 4439 Canal St.

Evangelical Lutheran

Christ Church, 714 Caffin Ave.
Emanuel Evangelical, N. Broad and Iberville Sts.
First English, 1032 Port St.
Grace, 3845 Iberville St.
Redeemer, 1314 Alvar St.
St. John's, 3937 Canal St.
St. Luke's, 2400 Onzaga St.
St. Paul's, Burgundy and Port Sts.
Zion, 1924 St. Charles Ave.

Greek

Greek Orthodox, 1222 N. Dorgenois St.

Jewish Orthodox

Ansche Sphard, Cardondelet St., bet. Jackson Ave. and Philip St.
Congregation Beth Israel, 1616 Carondelet St.
Chrevra Thilim, 826 Lafayette St.

Jewish Reform

Congregation Gates of Prayer, 1139 Napoleon Ave.
Temple Sinai, 6221 St. Charles Ave.
Touro Synagogue, 4238 St. Charles Ave.

Latter Day Saints

Mormons, 642 North St.

Lutheran

Colored Lutheran, 1720 Holly Grove St.

Hope Chapel, 1810 Adams St.
Mount Calvary, 2900 Grand Route St. John
Norwegian Seamen's Chapel, 1722 Prytania St.
St. Matthew's, Franklin Ave. and Wisteria Sts.
Trinity, 440 Olivier St., Algiers

Methodist Episcopal

Church of the Redeemer, 601 Esplanade Ave.
Eighth Street, 834 Eighth St.
Grace (Negro), 2201 Iberville St.
Napoleon Avenue, 2524 Napoleon Ave.

Methodist Episcopal South

Algiers Methodist, 823 Opelousas Ave., Algiers
Carrollton Avenue, Carrollton Ave. and Freret St.
Chalmette, 3625 N. Galvez St.
Epworth, 4140 Cana St.
Felicity Street, 1218 Felicity St.
First Methodist, 1108 St. Charles Ave.
Rayne Memorial, 3906 St. Charles Ave.
St. Mark's, N. Rampart and Gov. Nicholls Sts.
Second, Burgundy St., bet. St. Roch Ave. and Music St.

Presbyterian

Canal Street, 4302 Canal St.
Carrollton, 2100 S. Carrollton Ave.
Claiborne Avenue, 1659 N. Claiborne Ave.
First, Lafayette Square
First Street, 821 First Street
Gentilly, Gentilly Blvd. and Franklin Ave.
Lakeview, Polk Ave. and Catina St.
Napoleon Avenue, St. Charles and Napoleon Aves.
Prytania Street, 2101 Prytania St.
St. Charles Avenue, St. Charles Ave. and State St.
Third, 2540 Esplanade Ave.

Presbyterian in U.S.A.

Bethel, Burgundy St., near Tupelo St.
Westminster, 3102 St. Charles Ave.

Rosicrucian

Rosicrucian Study Group, 429 Carondelet St.

Spiritualist

First Church of Divine Fellowship, 823 Spain St.
First Church of Spiritual and Psychic Research, 720 Girod St.
Sacred Heart Spiritual Church, 1734 Amelia St.

Theosophical Society

Brother Lodge, 2504 Esplanade Ave.
Crescent City Lodge, 315 St. Charles St

Unitarian

First, 1800 Jefferson Ave.

Unity

Unity Society of Practical Christianity, 3rd floor, 604 Canal St.

HOTEL AND OTHER ACCOMMODATIONS

ALTHOUGH New Orleans normally possesses ample hotel and other facilities for the many thousands who come yearly to enjoy its mild climate, romantic atmosphere, Mid-Winter Sports Carnival, and worldfamed Mardi Gras, to prevent possible inconvenience or disappointment it is suggested that visitors write or wire in advance for accommodations desired, especially during the winter months.

Hotels

DeSoto Hotel, 420 Baronne St. ; 226 rooms – all with hot and cold running water, and 175 with private bath; rates $1.50 up, European plan; garage 50¢ extra; convention hall, writing-room, restaurant (lunch 60¢, dinner $1), coffee shop, and bar.

Jung Hotel, 1500 Canal St.; 700 rooms, all with private bath, running ice water, ceiling fans, servidor, and outside exposure; rates $3-$4, European plan; parking lot 15¢ extra; roof garden, three convention halls, dining-room, coffee shop, bar, Turkish baths, barber shop, and beauty parlor.

Lafayette Hotel, 628 St. Charles St.; 80 rooms, all with running water and ceiling fans – 55 with private baths; rates, $1.75 up, European plan; garage 50¢ extra.

LaSalle Hotel, 1113 Canal St.; 100 rooms – 70 with ceiling fans, and 50 with private bath; rates, $1.25-$2.50, European plan; garage 50¢ extra.

Monteleone Hotel, 214 Royal St.; 600 rooms – 540 have radios, 500 have private baths, and all have hot and cold running water and ceiling fans; rates $1.50-$3.50. European plan; garage 50¢, parking lot 15¢; convention hall, dining-room, coffee shop, bar, and beauty parlor.

New Orleans Hotel, 1300 Canal St.; 275 rooms, all with private bath and ceiling fan; rates $3 up, European plan; garage 50¢ extra; convention hall, air-conditioned dining-room and coffee shop, writing-room, and barber shop.

Roosevelt Hotel, 123 Baronne St.; 700 rooms, 400 air-conditioned; rates $3.50 up. European plan; garage 50¢ extra; convention halls, diningrooms, coffee shop, bar, cocktail lounge, beauty parlor, Turkish baths, etc.

Senator Hotel, 208 Dauphine St.; 115 rooms – 68 with private baths; rates $1 up.

St. Charles Hotel, 211 St. Charles St.; 600 rooms with hot and cold water, and radio all with private bath; rates $3 up; European plan; dining-room, bar, barber shop, beauty parlor, writing-rooms, etc.

Apartment Hotels

Carol Hotel, 3628 St. Charles Ave. (St. Charles car from Canal and Baronne Sts.), thirty-six blocks from Canal; 42 rooms, each with private bath and ceiling fan; rates by the day $1.50 up, lower by week or month, à la carte or table d'hôte dining-room service.

Pontchartrain Apartment Hotel, 2031 St. Charles Ave. (St. Charles car from Canal and Baronne Sts.); 80 efficiency apartments in four sizes, all with private baths; rates $3 per day up, $85 per month up; garage 50¢ day, weekly and monthly rates available.

Y.M.C.A. and Y.W.C.A.

Y.M.C.A., 936 St. Charles Ave. (Lee Circle); 40 rooms for local and visiting members only. Central floor bath; recreational facilities available.

Y.W.C.A., 929 Gravier St.; accommodations for 53 private rooms, double rooms, and dormitories (4 beds); central baths, coffee shop, recreational facilities; rates 75¢, $1, and $1.50; weekly and monthly rates available.

Tourist Camps

A number of tourist camps are located on US 90, 61, and 65; rates $1 per day up.

Accommodations for Negroes

Page Hotel, 1038 Dryades St.; 15 rooms all with hot and cold shower baths, running ice water; rates 75¢ to $1.50, European plan; no extra charge for auto parking and telephone.

Patterson Hotel, 761 S. Rampart St.; 26 rooms, all with baths; rates 75¢ to $1.50.

Y.M.C.A., 2220 Dryades St. (Freret car from Canal and St. Charles Sts.); room list available; transients placed in private homes.

Y.W.C.A., 2436 Canal St. (Cemeteries or West End car from any place on Canal St.); accommodations for 36 transients; central bath; meals served on request; rates $1.50 week up.

Additional Information

There are many other small hotels, tourist camps, tourist homes, and boarding-houses which may be found listed in the telephone directory, or easily identified while driving about the city by the signs displayed. St. Charles Avenue above Poydras Street as far up as Jackson Avenue is lined with small hotels and rooming houses, as likewise are Canal from Claiborne to Broad, Esplanade from the river to North Galvez, and Royal from Ursuline to Canal. Mention is made of these particular streets largely because of their accessibility and profuse accommodations; however, there are many other thoroughfares upon which such facilities may be found.

NIGHT LIFE

NEW ORLEANS, traditionally the 'city that care forgot,' offers to lovers of night life an unusual and varied number of night clubs and bars, ranging from the more expensive ones in the better hotels, to the 'Harlem' clubs and honky-tonks of the less select sections of the city. There is to be found entertainment to suit every taste, with a corresponding range of rates.

At the arrival of dawn, disciples of the night turn to the French Market, where society matrons and truck-drivers sit on stools and drink coffee in friendly proximity. Another well-known place for ending the evening is the all-night 'poor boy' stand of the Martin Brothers (2004 St. Claude Ave.), where appetites otherwise insatiable can be appeased for ten cents.

In New Orleans, as elsewhere, clubs and bars move, change names, go out of business, or, from time to time, are closed by the police. This is particularly true of the 'hotter of the hot spots.' The places listed below are those at present in operation (autumn, 1937). For later developments, ask the cab-driver. Telephone for reservations and information concerning minimum and cover charges.

Clubs and Bars on or Above Canal Street

The *Blue Room*, a night club and cocktail lounge, is located on the first floor of the Roosevelt Hotel (122 Baronne St.). It offers, by way of entertainment in its nightly floor show, dance numbers by nationally known teams. Syncopated music is furnished by such orchestras as those of Phil Harris, Smith Ballew, and Frankie Masters. The Blue Room is frequently redecorated. Here may be found a circular bar, whose pride is the 'Ramos Gin Fizz' made from the original recipe of the famous Ramos Bar. Dinner is served from 6 to 9 P.M.; music is furnished by the same orchestra which plays for the dancing from 10 P.M. to 2 A.M. Cocktail hours are from 2.30 to 5.30 on Saturday and Sunday afternoons.

Crescent Billiard Hall, 117 St. Charles St. (second floor), was one of the first billiard halls opened in New Orleans. In addition to pool and billiard rooms, cocktail lounge, and bar, there is a room devoted to games.

Halson Cocktail Lounge, in the Pontchartrain Apartment Hotel at 2031 St. Charles Ave., is open to the public from 11.30 A.M. until 12.30 A.M. In addition to stronger drinks, light refreshments are served. Cocktail hours are from 4 P.M. to 9 P.M.

Roosevelt Bar, one of the better-class bars of the city, is a rendezvous in the Roosevelt Hotel. Here, as in the Blue Room, the specialty is the 'Ramos Gin Fizz'; all of the nationally known drinks as well as southern favorites are available. The doors are open from 8.30 A.M. to 2 A.M. customarily, though during the Mardi Gras season the bar remains open all night.

St. Charles Bar (St. Charles Hotel), 211 St. Charles St., is classed among the oldest and best-known bars in the city. A wide variety of drinks is served, especial pride being taken in its 'Planter's Punch' and 'Old Fashioned' cocktail. Cocktail hours, at which there is music, are from 4.30 to 7 P.M. and from 9.30 until midnight. The bar is open from 7 A.M. to 12.30 A.M. ; during the Carnival season it remains open all night.

St. Germain Cocktail Lounge, 1753 St. Charles Ave., is open from 1 P.M. until 'the last customer leaves.' Bridge groups and parties are especially catered to.

Sazerac Bar, 300 Carondelet St., is the only bar in the city where the famous Sazerac Cocktail is mixed from a famous recipe. The doors are open from 8 A.M. until 9 P.M. Ladies are served only one day a year – Mardi Gras.

French Quarter Clubs and Bars

Absinthe House Bar, 400 Bourbon St., has the original marble-topped bar formerly housed at 238 Bourbon St. (the old Absinthe House) which at one time was famous for its *absinthe frappé.* The bar is open from 6 A.M. to 3 A.M.

Club Plantation, 942 Conti St., is open from 10 P.M. to 5 A.M. An orchestra furnishes music for dancing, and floor shows are presented at 2 and at 4 A.M. The club was formerly operated by Pete Herman, blind exbantamweight champion (1922); the specialty is 'Planter's Punch.'

Dog House, 300 North Rampart St., is open from 9 P.M. until 4 A.M. Both jazz orchestra and floor show are colored, and three performances are given nightly, 11 P.M., 1.30 and 3 A.M. A 'high-class place,' says the proprietor, 'for middle class people, and one where they can have freedom of body and soul.' The taxi girls bring their lunch.

La Lune, 800 Bourbon St., is one of the more popular spots of the French Quarter. The establishment is conducted in Mexican style, with Don Ramon and his orchestra furnishing music for dancing. Excellent Mexican dinners are served and *tequila* may be had. The club is open from 9 P.M. to 6 A.M.

Monteleone Hotel Bar, located in the Monteleone Hotel at 214 Royal St., serves sandwiches and drinks. The specialty is the 'Vieux Carré Cocktail.' The bar is open from 7 A.M. until midnight.

New Silver Slipper, 426 Bourbon St., has three floor shows nightly – 11.30 P.M., 1.30 and 3 A.M.

Nut Club (Café de L'Opéra), 507 Bourbon St., open from 10 P.M. until 5 A.M., presents floor shows nightly at 1 and 3 A.M. Music is furnished by the 'Nut Club Ensemble,' and dinner is served from 5 to 10 P.M.

Original Absinthe House, 238 Bourbon St., was erected in 1798, and has served as a place of revelry almost continuously ever since. The doors are open from 9 P.M. until 4 A.M. There are two floor shows nightly, 12.30 and 3 A.M.

Pat O Brien's, 638 St. Peter St., is at present one of the most popular of the small bars of the Quarter and on Saturday and holiday nights is apt to over-flow with tipplers of every description.

Prima's Shim Sham Club, 229 Bourbon St., is open during the winter months from 10 P.M. to 5 A.M. There are three floor shows nightly, 11.30 P.M., 1.30 and 3.30 A.M.

Sloppy Jim's is located at 236 Royal St., just below the Monteleone Hotel. The specialty here is the 'Sloppy Jim Cocktail.' A wide variety of other drinks is served. The bar is open from 9 A.M. until 12 P.M.

Also in the Vieux Carré, amid the somewhat distinctive atmosphere and odors of the French Market, are several Decatur Street 'hot spots' whose names are perhaps indicative of the type of entertainment to be found. One is greeted by such names as the *King Fish,* where 'Ya Man' and his colored orchestra produce sizzling jazz, the *Silver Moon, Guestella's,* and *Rudy's,* the former names of which were *Popeye's,* the *Rose Bowl,* and *Mama's Place,* respectively. At these places the floor shows are marked by the utmost abandon, to say the least. The performers range in color from a 'high yaller' to ebony. Floor shows are at 11.30 P.M., 1.30 and 3 A.M.

Suburban Night Clubs

Chez Paree, 8502 Pontchartrain Blvd., is one of the best of the suburban clubs. Music is furnished by a local orchestra, and floor shows are pre sented at midnight and at 2 A.M.

Cotton Club, 2935 Jefferson Highway, is open from 10 P.M. to 3 A.M. Entertainment is furnished by a local orchestra and there are two floor shows nightly, 12.30 and 2.30 A.M.

Pirates' Den, Avenue A and 38th St. (near Pontchartrain Blvd.), serves drinks and sandwiches. The place remains open at night as long as the crowd lingers; the bar is open all day.

Prima's Penthouse, West End, especially popular during the summer because of its proximity to Lake Pontchartrain, is open from 10 P.M. until 2A.M.

Gambling

Beyond the city limits in the adjacent parishes of Jefferson and St. Bernard are several large and elaborately appointed gambling-houses: the *Old Southport* and the *Original Southport* in Jefferson Parish (taxi 40¢ within a half block of either place), and the *Jai Alai, Arabi Club,* and *Riverview* in St. Bernard Parish (taxi 75¢). All may be reached by street-car. Although gambling is, strictly speaking, illegal, these places are usually open for business from dusk to dawn.

Pleasure Boats

There is nightly dancing on Mississippi River boats from September through the following June; the 'Capitol' in the earlier part of the season, the 'President' later. Both boats leave the foot of Canal Street at 9 P.M. and return at 12.30 A.M.

Negro Night Clubs

The Negro night clubs of New Orleans are patterned after those of Harlem. The proprietors visit Harlem to study the color schemes and acquire the atmosphere of night clubs there, because 'it serves well along publicity lines.' Even the music and floor shows are handled in the Harlem manner – nothing less than 'red hot.' The tunes are loud, but have the 'swing' that causes Negroes to move their bodies and tap their feet. 'They b'lieve in mugging.' All kinds of whiskies are served; champagne or any kind of cocktail may be purchased. 'When a colored man steps out he is out.'

Negro night clubs open at present include: the *Tick Tock Tavern*, 235 S. Rampart St.; the *Rhythm Club*, 3000 Jackson Ave.; the *Cotton Club*, 1301 Bienville St.; and the *Japanese Tea Garden*, 1140 St. Philip St. Special programs and floor shows vary. White persons are admitted to these night clubs at any time. Reservations may be made by telephone.

RECREATIONAL FACILITIES

Audubon Park (Magazine car from Canal and Magazine Sts. or St. Charles car from Canal and Baronne Sts.) has 247 acres of gardens, lagoon, zoological exhibits, and recreational facilities. Tennis courts, baseball diamonds, football gridirons, picnic grounds, playgrounds (including merry-go-round, etc.), bridle path, swimming pool, band stand, 18-hole golf course, boating, and fishing are recreational facilities to be found in the park. (*See* respective sports for hours, reservations, and admission charges.)

City Park (Esplanade bus from Canal and Burgundy or City Park from Canal and Bourbon Sts. go to different entrances; Cemeteries car from any place on Canal – transfer to Carrollton bus at Carrollton Ave.), the sixth largest municipal park in the United States (extension work under the Works Progress Administration is raising its rank) affords the most extensive recreational facilities to be found in the city. Facilities, including those now under construction, will eventually provide a stadium with a seating capacity of 25,000, a yacht basin, 12 baseball diamonds, 33 tennis courts, two 18-hole golf courses, football gridirons, picnic grounds, bridle paths, play grounds, a swimming pool, a bandstand and boating and fishing. (*See* respective sports for hours, reservations and admission charges.)

Lake Pontchartrain Shore (West End car from any place on Canal St. to West End; transfer to Robert E. Lee bus at West End to go to Pontchartrain Beach; to reach Milneburg take Frenchmen bus from Canal and Chartres Sts. and transfer to Milneburg bus at Frenchmen and Gentilly Road; taxi fare to Beach is 70¢) has miles of sandy bathing beaches from West End to Milneburg. Extensive work under the Works Progress Administration will provide tennis courts, baseball diamonds, horseshoe courts, wading pools, etc. Cruisers, skiffs, and other craft may be rented at various places along the lakefront. An amusement park is located at Pontchartrain Beach.

New Orleans Athletic Club, 222 N. Rampart St., has a fully equipped gymnasium, boxing arena, swimming pool, baketball court, baseball diamond, squash court, double bowling alleys, solarium, cinder running track (on roof), rifle range, and two indoor and two outdoor handball courts. All facilities are restricted to members and their guests.

Young Men's Christian Association, 936 St. Charles Ave., has a swimming pool, well-equipped gymnasium, basketball court, two handball courts, two ping pong tables for men and two for boys, billiard table, pool table, cue roque table (for boys), and a volley-ball court. All facilities are restricted to members and their guests.

Young Women's Christian Association, 929 Gravier St., has facilities for basketball, tennis, badminton, volley ball, indoor baseball, impressionistic, tap, and social dancing, tumbling, and calisthenics. The Y.M.C.A. and St. Mark's Community Center Pools are used for swimming. Picnics, outings, wiener roasts, etc., are held in season. Membership is not necessary for the enjoyment of the Y.W.C.A. recreational facilities. Charges are the same as those asked of members.

Young Men's Hebrew Association, 1205 St. Charles Ave. (St. Charles car from Canal and Baronne Sts.), offers members and their guests recreational facilities including a swimming pool, two basketball courts, outdoor soft-ball diamond, two handball courts, four pool tables, two billiard tables, and a small gymnasium.

Colonial Country Club, Jefferson Highway (US 61), is located about ten miles above New Orleans (follow S. Claiborne Ave. and US 61). The 18-hole golf course (6279 yards) is restricted to members and their guests. Professional instruction is available.

Lakewood Country Club (formerly the West End Country Club), Pontchartrain Blvd. beyond Metairie Cemetery (West End car from any place on Canal St.), is composed largely of Jewish members. The 18-hole golf course and four tennis courts are restricted to members and their guests.

Metairie Golf Club, Metairie Ridge (taxi 70¢), is an 18-hole course (6711 yards) restricted to members and guests. Professional instruction is available.

New Orleans Country Club, 6440 Pontchartrain Blvd. (West End car from any place on Canal St. to Pontchartrain Blvd.; walk four blocks to the left), has an 18-hole golf course (6466 yards) restricted to members and their guests. Professional instruction is available. A swimming pool and eight tennis courts are other recreational facilities.

Baseball

Audubon Park has four diamonds; free on weekdays, $2 per game on Sundays and holidays. The diamond having the grandstand is rented on Sundays and holidays for $3; 10¢ admission is charged for viewing the games.

City Park has 8 soft-ball diamonds ($1 per game) and a standard-size field ($1.50 per game).

Numerous playgrounds and empty lots afford playing facilities for 'scrub' games.

Billiards

Crescent Billiard Hall, 117 St. Charles St. Eight pool and four billiard tables.

New Orleans Athletic Club, 222 N. Rampart St. Three pocket-billiard tables; available to members and their guests only.

Royal Billiard Hall, 115 Royal St. Ten pool and eight billiard tables.

Y.M.C.A., 936 St. Charles Ave. One pool and one billiard table; available to members and their guests only. Boys may play cue roque.

Boating

Audubon Park. Canoes and skiffs may be rented for boating in the artificial lagoon; hours 9 to 6 daily. A 'Swan' boat carries passengers.

City Park. (See above.) Canoes and skiffs may be rented for boating in the lagoon; hours 9 to 6 daily.

Lake Pontchartrain Shore. Cruisers, skiffs, and other craft may be rented at various places along the lakefront.

Southern Yacht Club, West End, Pontchartrain Blvd. (West End car, any place on Canal St.), has yachting and other facilities available for members and their guests.

Bowling

Deutsches Haus, 200 S. Galvez St. (West End or Cemeteries car from any place on Canal St.; walk two blocks uptown). Guests of members only.

Germania Lodge, F. & A.M., 4415 Bienville Ave. (West End or Cemeteries car from any place on Canal St. to Alexander St.; walk two blocks downtown). Alley is rented to the public for $5 per night (attendants and service included).

New Orleans Athletic Club, 222 N. Rampart St. Admission to double bowling alleys by guest card only.

Bridge

Roosevelt Hotel, 123 Baronne St. Games played every day beginning at 2 and 7.45 P.M. Instructions in contract offered every afternoon and on Tuesday and Thursday evenings. Duplicate tournaments held.

Chess

Paul Morphy Club, 625 Common St., has facilities for chess, checkers, billiards, and bridge. Complimentary memberships are extended to visitors.

Fishing (See Hunting and Fishing.)

Golf

Audubon Golf Club, 473 Walnut St. (St. Charles car from Canal and Baronne Sts. to Walnut; walk three blocks toward river). The 18-hole course (5718 yards) is open to guests of members and patrons of leading hotels. Professional instructions are available.

City Park Golf Courses (walk along bayou at Esplanade entrance and turn right after crossing railroad tracks) are the only public links in the city. Two 18-hole courses are available; No. 1 (6445 yards) and No. 2 (5500 yards) have a 50¢ fee, which entitles the golfer to play an entire day. On No. 1 it is necessary to engage a caddy (75¢). Books entitling the purchaser to play as often as desired may be obtained for $3, exclusive of caddy fees. Professional instruction is available.

Colonial Country Club. (See above.)

Lakewood Country Club. (See above.)

Metairie Golf Club. (See above.)

New Orleans Country Club. (See above.)

Gymnasiums

Behrman Public School Gymnasium, 2800 Prytania St., corner of Washington Ave. (St. Charles car from Canal and Baronne Sts.), is operated as part of the recreational activities of the Orleans Parish School Board for basketball games and swimming classes. All school children, from both public and parochial schools, are permitted to enjoy its facilities free of charge.

Marullo's, 343 Baronne St. (private gym for men); 316½ St. Charles St. (for women).

New Orleans Athletic Club. Available to guests of members only.

Y.M.C.A. Classes are held at 12.15 P.M. Mondays, Wednesdays, and Fridays, and at 5.30 P.M. Tuesdays and Thursdays; available to guests of members only.

Y.M.H.A. Available to guests of members only.

Y.W.C.A. Morning classes are held on Mondays, Wednesdays, and Fridays at 10. Evening classes are held on Mondays, Tuesdays, and Thursdays at 6.15. Gym facilities are available to non-members.

Riding

Audubon Riding Club, Audubon Park.

Airport Riding Academy, Milneburg (Frenchmen bus from Canal and Chartres Sts.); taxi 70¢.

Golden Spur Riding Academy, 3000 Jefferson Highway (out S. Claiborne Ave. and US 61); taxi $1.50.

Bridle paths are located in Audubon Park and City Park, along the levee above Audubon Park, and along the lake-front at Lake Pontchartrain.

Swimming

Audubon Park Natatorium, open from 6 A.M. to 10 P.M. daily from May to September, is divided into two 75 X 225-feet sections graduating in depth from three to nine feet. A children's wading pool, diving boards, chutes, etc., are among the facilities.

City Park Natatorium, open from 6 A.M. to 10 P.M. daily from May to September, is a 75 X 200-feet pool graduating in depth from two to nine feet. Suits and towels may be rented.

Lake-front swimming may be enjoyed along the Pontchartrain sea wall from West End to Little Woods. A Negro beach is located a short distance west of Shushan Airport. Signs indicate the depths at various intervals along the sea wall. At Spanish Fort a beach (Pontchartrain Beach) has been made by pumping in sand from the lake.

Masonic Temple Natatorium, 333 St. Charles St., open from 7 A.M. to 10 P.M. from May to September, is a 17 x 42-feet pool graduating in depth from three to six feet. Suits and towels may be rented.

New Orleans Athletic Club Pool (20 X 40 feet), open from 9 A.M. to 11 P.M. daily, is fed from a salt-water well and graduates in depth from 3½ to 7½ feet. Only members and their guests are admitted.

New Orleans Country Club Pool, measuring 40 X 120 feet and graduating in depth from three to ten feet, is open from May to September. Only members and their guests are admitted.

Y.M.C.A. Natatorium is a 20 X 60-feet pool graduating in depth from two to nine feet. Only members and their guests are admitted.

Y.M.H.A. Natatorium, open from 9 A.M. to 10 P.M. daily, is a 20 X 60-feet pool graduating in depth from four to eight feet. Only members and their guests are admitted.

Tennis

Audubon Park has a total of 23 all-weather courts, 19 of which are illuminated for night playing. The ticket office is located in front of the Natatorium. Reservations must be made in person unless the player possesses a ticket book entitling him to telephone reservations for day or night. Reservations may also be made through Dunlap's Sporting Goods Company, 138 Carondelet St.

City Park has a total of 30 tennis courts for day and night playing. Reservations must be made in person at the ticket office near the Dumaine St. entrance.

Lakewood Country Club has four courts for the use of members and their guests.

New Orleans Country Club has seven courts for the use of members and their guests.

The New Orleans Lawn Tennis Club, 4025 Saratoga Street (Freret car from Canal and St. Charles Sts.), has enjoyed an uninterrupted existence since December 15, 1876, the date of its organization. The use of the eight courts and a comfortable clubhouse is restricted to a membership of 140. Club tournaments are held regularly, and an annual citywide tournament is played on the courts.

Trap Shooting

Jefferson Skeet Club, opposite the Colonial Country Club on Jefferson Highway (out S. Claiborne Ave. and US 61), is open on Saturdays and Sundays.

NEGRO RECREATIONAL FACILITIES

Young Men's Christian Association, 2220 Dryades St. (Freret car from Canal and St. Charles Sts., or Jackson car from Canal and Baronne Sts. to Jackson Ave.; walk one block uptown), has recreational facilities including an outdoor tennis court, soft-ball diamond and basketball court, four pool tables, ping pong table, and tables for bridge, whist, chess, and checkers. Guests of members have access, free of charge, to all facilities.

Young Women's Christian Association, 2436 Canal St. (West End or Cemeteries car from any place on Canal St.), permits guests of members to have access, free of charge, to all the facilities which include an outdoor tennis and volley-ball court, and bridge tables. Tap and ballet dancing, along with stunts, form a part of the entertainment on Activity Day every Thursday from 5.30 to 9.

Billiards

Autocrat Social and Pleasure Club, 1725 St. Bernard Ave. (St. Bernard bus from Canal and Burgundy Sts.). Three pool tables; available to members and their guests only.

Pelican Billiard Hall, 303 S. Rampart St. Eight pool tables.

Y.M.C.A., 2220 Dryades St. Four pool tables; available to members and their guests only.

Gymnasiums

San Jacinto Club, 1422 Dumaine St. (City Park car from Canal and Bourbon Sts.). Gym (facilities for calisthenics and boxing) for members and their guests only.

Swimming

Lake Pontchartrain. The section of the sea wall reserved for Negroes is located a short distance west of Shushan Airport.

Thomy Lafon Pool, Sixth and S. Robertson Sts. (Freret car from Canal and St. Charles to Sixth St.; walk one block right), measuring 60 X 30 feet and graduating in depth from four to seven feet, is an outdoor pool open from 9 A.M. to 10 P.M. Admission for night and Sunday swimming is 10¢; free during the day.

Tennis

Y.M.C.A. Two courts available to members and their guests.

HUNTING AND FISHING

US 90 traverses the tidal pass and lake districts along the Louisville and Nashville Railroad from New Orleans to Pearl River, a favorite hunting and fishing area close to New Orleans. At Chef Menteur, Lake St. Catherine, and Rigolets there are ample accommodations. Both black bass and salt-water fish are found at all these points. Duck and snipe shooting is usually good.

A popular hunting trip out of New Orleans is to the State shooting grounds at Pass-à-Loutre in the delta of the Mississippi River, an excellent duck-shooting locality. Reservations and necessary information may be secured at the office of the Department of Conservation, New Orleans Court Building, Chartres and Conti Sts. Mallard, canvasback, pin-tailed, and other choice ducks abound in the thousands of acres set aside here partly as a public shooting grounds and partly as a bird refuge.

La 1 and 31 lead to the hunting and fishing territory of St. Bernard Parish and the upper and central parts of Plaquemines Parish. Some of the more important points are Reggio, Yscloskey, Delacroix Island, Pointe-à-la-Hache, and Buras. Duck and snipe are generally plentiful throughout this territory in the hunting season.

Down Bayou Barataria (cross on the Napoleon Ave. Ferry to Marrero and follow La 30), one has the choice of many waterways and great expanses of swamp and marsh, where snipe, duck, and deer hunting are dependable. Beyond lie Little Lake, the lower Barataria Country, and Grand Isle, all excellent hunting and fishing grounds. A tarpon rodeo is held every summer at Grand Isle. There are not many public camps in this district, but the facilities of numerous clubs are available to visitors, who can secure common tackle and ammunition from stores at Barataria or Lafitte. Guides, boats, and bait are also obtainable. There are hotels at Grand Isle.

West of New Orleans on US 90 is Lockport, convenient base for hunting on lower Bayou Lafourche, including duck grounds about Larose, Cut-Off, Cher Ami, and Golden Meadow. A little farther west, out of Houma, waters and marshes affording some of the best hunting and fishing in Louisiana are accessible. At Wonder Lake the black bass fishing is exceptionally fine.

The Bonnet Carré Spillway area, 32 miles up the Mississippi River from New Orleans, is a fishing preserve, under control of a club that leases the area from the Government. The spillway tract extends from the Mississippi River to Lake Pontchartrain and includes good spots for bass, good rabbit country, and some snipe grounds near the lakeshore.

Between New Orleans and Hammond is a great deer-hunting district near Pass Manchac, Lake Maurepas, and the lower Amite River. There are also fine fishing grounds for bass and other species in this territory. Bears are encountered occasionally in the Lake Maurepas region and sometimes wild hogs furnish an exciting form of sport.

For some kinds of fresh-water fishing and for quail and turkey hunting it is necessary to go north and northwest of New Orleans. Bogalusa, Covington, Pontchatoula, Hammond, Baton Rouge, and New Roads are good bases for anyone interested in sport with inland types of game and fish. The quail shooting in the Feliciana Parishes is especially good, and some of the best woodcock and wild turkey shooting in the Florida Parishes is available in this area.

AMATEUR SPORTS EVENTS

Baseball is played every Sunday afternoon by a number of semi-professional and amateur teams at the following parks: *Hi-Way Park*, 3800 Jefferson Highway (out S. Claiborne Ave. and US 61); *Holy Cross Park*, 4900 Dauphine St. (St. Claude car from N. Rampart and Canal Sts.); *Lincoln Park*, S. Broad and Clio Sts. (West End or Cemeteries car, any place on Canal St. — transfer to southbound Gentilly-Broad bus at Broad St.); *Warren Easton Park*, Hagan Ave. and Bienville St. (West End or Cemeteries car, any place on Canal St. to Jefferson Davis Park way; walk two blocks downtown). College, high school, and other amateur teams of the city play on diamonds throughout New Orleans.

Basketball games are played, in season, by Dillard University (Negro), Dominican College (female), Loyola University, Tulane University, Ursuline College (female), Xavier University (Negro), and the high school and private preparatory schools. During the Mid-Winter Sports Carnival a basketball game is staged between two outstanding teams.

Boxing contests are staged under the auspices of the Southern Amateur Athletic Union at various times at the *New Orleans Athletic Club*, 222 N. Rampart St., the *Kingsley House*, 1600 Constance St. (Magazine car from Canal and Magazine to Felicity St.; one block toward river), and the *Knights of Columbus*, 836 Carondelet St. Annual (Southern Amateur Athletic Union) championships are held at the *Coliseum*, 401 N. Roman St. (West End or Cemeteries car from any place on Canal St.; walk four blocks downtown). Tulane University's team engages other teams of the Southeastern Conference at the gymnasium (Freret car from Canal and St. Charles Sts. to Tulane Campus). Negro matches are held irregularly at the St. Joan of Arc School, Cambronne and Freret Sts. (St. Charles car from Canal and Baronne Sts. to S. Carrollton and Freret; walk three blocks uptown), and the San Jacinto Club, 1422 Dumaine St. (City Park car from Canal and Bourbon Sts. to Marais St.). A boxing tournament between city teams is conducted under the auspices of the Mid-Winter Sports Association.

Football games of national importance are played by Tulane and Loyola Universities with Southern and intersectional teams. The *Tulane Stadium* is located at Willow and Calhoun Sts. (Freret car from Canal and St. Charles St. to Calhoun; walk four blocks north), and the *Loyola Stadium* at Freret and Calhoun Sts. (Freret car at Canal and St. Charles Sts.). The annual Sugar Bowl game is played at the former on New Year's Day. High schools and preparatory schools usually play at the above-mentioned stadia in addition to the old Tulane stadium and 'prep' field located in the intervening area, and at the new Municipal stadium built under the Works Progress Administration in City Park. Dillard and Xavier Universities (Negro schools) also play football at Dillard University, Gentilly Road (Gentilly car from Canal and Bourbon Sts.), and Xavier University, Washington and Pine Sts. (Tulane car from any place on Canal between the river and Loyola St. to Washington; walk three blocks right).

Golf tournaments, the Men's City Open and the Women's City Tournament (the latter for club members only) are held annually at various courses in the city (*see* under *Golf*, above, for location of links). Admission is free. Tulane University's golf team engages other universities in dual matches. An intercollegiate tournament is held during the Mid-Winter Sports Carnival.

Polo is played at Jackson Barracks, St. Claude Ave. and the St. Bernard Parish line (St. Claude car at N. Rampart and Canal Sts.), every Wednesday, Saturday, and Sunday afternoon between three local teams. Admission is free, except for charity games played with out-of-town teams, for which the charge is usually 50¢. Ample parking space is afforded along both sides of the playing field.

Tennis matches, the City Tournament (held at various courts) and the New Orleans Public Park Tournament (held at City Park) are staged annually. Admission to the former is free, but charges are usually made for the finals of the Public Park matches (see under Tennis, above, for location of courts). The tournament conducted at the close of every year under the auspices of the Mid-Winter Sports Association attracts many of the Nation's ranking stars. Tulane, Loyola, Dillard (Negro), Xavier

(Negro), and Dominican College (female) also play tennis.

Track and Field meets are held at Loyola and Tulane stadia. The most outstanding meet is held annually in conjunction with the Sugar Bowl game. World and national champions participate. Each year on the Saturday closest Jackson Day (January 8) leading cross-country men from the city and vicinity run over a course (Spanish Fort to the Cabildo) which in December, 1814, was the route taken by the garrison of Spanish Fort as it ran to join Jackson's forces leaving for the Chalmette front. Dillard (Negro), Xavier (Negro), and Dominican College (female) also engage in track and field meets.

Yacht races are held Saturday and Sunday mornings and afternoons, weather permitting, under the auspices of the *Southern Yacht Club.*

Schooners, 21-footers, star class, knockabouts, fish class, auxiliary knockabouts, Gulf one-designs, and yawls engage in races over a six-mile and a seven-and-a-half-mile triangular course. Long-distance races to Biloxi and the Chefuncte River are held every year.

PROFESSIONAL SPORTS EVENTS

Baseball

Heinemann Park, Carrollton and Tulane Ave. (Tulane car from any place on Canal St. between Loyola and the river), is the home of the 'Pelicans,' New Orleans' representative in the Southern Association. Both night and day games are held. The seating capacity is 9500, with 2000 additional temporary seats available for the Dixie Series. The Cleveland 'Indians,' who 'farm' players with the local team, train at the park each spring.

The Crescent Stars, the New Orleans Black Pelicans, and the Algiers Giants (Negro teams) play irregularly at *Crescent Star Park,* Dorgenois and St. Anthony Sts. (Frenchmen bus from Canal and Chartres Sts. to Dorgenois; walk three blocks uptown), *Lincoln Park,* S. Broad and Clio Sts. (West End or Cemeteries car, any place on Canal St., transfer to outhbound Gentilly-Broad bus at Broad St.), and *Heinemann Park.*

Boxing

Coliseum Arena, 401 N. Roman St. (West End or Cemeteries car, any place on Canal St. to Roman; walk three blocks downtown). Five preliminaries of four rounds each and a main bout of ten rounds usually make up the card. White and colored are admitted. Seating capacity is 7500.

Cockfighting

Cockfights are held on Sundays from October to July at one or the other of the following pits: *Bisso* and *Mills Pit,* South Kenner, located about 18 miles above the city on the west bank of the river (US 61 from Canal St. and S. Claiborne Ave.; cross Huey P. Long Bridge (toll-free) and turn right on US 90); *Four Horsemen Pit,* located in St. Bernard Parish below Menefee Airport (State Highway 1 from Canal and N. Rampart Sts.).

Shall's Pit, Shall's Dairy Farm, is situated two miles east of Kenner (State Highway 1 – Jefferson Highway – from Canal St., and S. Claiborne Ave.).

Racing

Fair Grounds, main gate, Sauvage and Fortin Sts. (Esplanade bus from Burgundy and Canal Sts. to Lopez; shuttle bus to entrance), offers approximately 100 days of racing beginning on Thanksgiving Day each year. Seven races are held daily starting at 2.30; Daily Double, second and third races, Quinella, last race. The certificate system of betting, much the same as pari-mutuel is in effect. The glass-enclosed, steamheated grandstand has a seating capacity of about 6000. Several $1000 handicaps are held each year, with the Louisiana Derby ($6000 purse) the feature race. White and colored are admitted.

South Kenner Park (see Cockfighting above for directions) offers racing on its half-mile track on Sundays and holidays, the season extending from April to November. A bus, leaving from Canal and Saratoga Streets at 1 P.M., makes a round trip (25¢) to the track; taxis, leaving from Canal and Rampart Sts., offer round trips for 50¢. The eight-race program starts at 2.15 P.M. Book-making, or oral betting, is in practice with a quinella offered in the last race.

St. Bernard Kennel Club, St. Bernard Parish, 5.3 *m.* from Canal and Rampart Sts. (St. Claude car from Canal and Rampart; transfer to St. Claude bus; taxi $1), stages ten dog races nightly on its quarter-mile track. The season extends from late spring to fall. Seating capacity is about 1200; the pari-mutuel system of betting is used.

Wrestling

Coliseum Arena (see Boxing) stages wrestling matches every Thursday evening at 8.30 P.M. Three bouts are usually held. The first event is a half hour, one-fall match, and the others are one and two hour bouts, best-two-out-of-three falls. White and colored are admitted.

RESTAURANTS

EATING and drinking rank as fine arts in New Orleans and the traveler finds the flavor of the past kept vitally alive in its restaurants. Year after year the older institutions go on, in the same buildings and the same atmosphere, serving the famous Creole dishes in undiminished excellence; and even the newer restaurants conform to the tradition of good food and service.

New Orleans Creole cuisine, evolved many years ago, had as its basis French delicacy piquantly modified by the Spaniard's love of pungent seasoning, the Indians use of native herbs, and the Negro's ability to mix and bake. Into its evolution, too, went a singularly abundant and diverse food supply, with not only a wide variety of fish, game, and vegetables at the very door and exotic products available from the near by tropics, but a steady flow of delicacies imported from the old country. A traveler to New Orleans in 1803 commented on the astonishing import of luxuries, 'out of keeping with so small and new a place: Malaga, Bordeaux, Madeira, olive oil (a most important article of consumption), brandied fruits, liqueurs, vinegars, sausages, anchovies, almonds, raisins, prunes, cheese, vermicelli.'

New Orleans restaurateurs still scour far countries for certain important ingredients of their dishes; and, although game, long the pièce de résistance of restaurant cuisine, has been made contraband by recent laws, and many of the flavorous old herbs have disappeared, much remains. The Gulf pompano, which Mark Twain called 'delicious as the less criminal forms of sin'; the sheepshead, a fish almost equally as popular; redfish, red snapper, oysters, shrimp, crabs, crawfish, and frog legs; chicken or poulet, cooked in a hundred different ways, each one better than the last; avocados, burr artichokes, fresh pineapple, fresh mushrooms, and fresh asparagus – these are only a few of the products available to local chefs today as in the past.

New Orleans, having taken the trouble to concoct its delicious, many tasting foods, may raise a quizzical eyebrow at the occasional spinach and lettuce-leaf devotee who happens along, but to the appreciative gourmet she extends a joyous welcome. This spirit of gracious catering, found alike in the noted restaurants and in many of the humblest, is a sort of noblesse oblige deriving from the fine tradition of the past; for the city boasts of a long line of distinguished old hostelries.

The first restaurateurs were largely Spaniards, who laid small emphasis on food and featured rather delectable drinks, Spanish music, and Spanish dancing. Fashionable Creole gentlemen, when they foregathered to sip their wines and discuss the price of indigo, the imminent duel, or the latest news from Europe, preferred, however, the quieter and more elegant cafés: Maspéro's, Hewlitt's, or John Davis's. If a man required good, solid food and was unfortunate enough not to be able to eat at home the prevailing practice there was only the Restaurant d'Orléans, the exclusive Le Veau Qui Tète, and the somewrhat rowdy Hôtel de la Marine, haunt of the Lafitte pirates and other colorful characters.

With the period of phenomenal wealth which began about 1830, the habit of dining out really began. Many brilliant banquets were given under the frescoed dome of the old St. Louis Hotel, or at the St. Charles, whose famous gold service was brought out on state occasions. Suppers and after-the-theater parties took place at those rival city restaurants, Moreau's and Victor's, who vied in the excellence of their dishes and the distinction of their guests. And the Gem sprang into fame with its fabulous free lunches.

But it was at the suburban inns that the most skillful chefs presided and memorable feasts occurred. At Carrollton Gardens, near the levee where today the St. Charles street-car turns into Carrollton Avenue, inviting meals were served on the broad verandas of the hotel overlooking the grounds, with their summer houses and pagodas, their jasmines and honeysuckle vines. The 'lake end' restaurants at Milneburg, Spanish Fort, and West End were popular. These were quaint wooden buildings with large rooms and many porches, set on piles over the lake, with welltended parks and flower gardens in front. It was at Milneburg, and under the supervision of the noted chef Boudro, that a dinner was tendered in 1856 to Thackeray. 'At that comfortable tavern on Pontchartrain,' Thackeray commented afterward, 'we had a bouillabaisse than which a better was never eaten at Marseilles and not the least headache in the morning, I give you my word.'

At a later date, came 'Léon's,' a resort of both high-class gamblers and fastidious epicures; the unique market restaurants, Begué's, Maylié's, Tujague's; and the innumerable little French restaurants, with names like Les Quatres Saisons (The Four Seasons), Le Pèlerin (The Pilgrim), etc., of which Lafcadio Hearn said, 'Each one, like those of Paris, has some particular specialty, and the chicken, shrimps, mushrooms, and wines are universally excellent.'

Today, the restaurants are largely French and Italian, but it is also possible to get good German and Mexican food.

French Restaurants

Antoine's, 713 St. Louis St., proprietor, Roy Alciatore, open 11 A.M. to 10.30 P.M. Make reservations in advance. Ala carte service only, with minimum charge of $1 per person. Private rooms for dining and for banquets. A representative meal can be had from $3 to $3.50 per person.

This old restaurant, with its tall, gabled roof, wrought-iron balconies, and mellow lighting, possesses an air of quiet distinction. Almost a hundred years old, it has become widely known both here and abroad for the perfection of its cuisine. Antoine Alciatore, founder of the restaurant, was born in Marseilles, France, and had already acquired skill as a chef before coming to New Orleans in 1840. By 1876, with his establishment in the present building, he was ranked as a leading restaurateur.

The interior of the restaurant is quaintly old-fashioned, and is both lighted and heated from antique gas chandeliers in the ceiling. No jazz music breaks on the diner's ears; as one of its proprietors was wont to insist: 'The aroma of good food and the tinkle of wine glasses is music enough.'

What to eat at Antoine's? There is so much that is excellent one becomes slightly confused, as did Will Rogers: 'Why, listen, they got a soup they herded around in front of me that was crawfish boiled in white wine and aromatic herbs. Why, they got tortoise-shell terrapin that is served in its own shell. Omelette souflee historiee! Say, they make all of them out of golden pheasants' eggs.' The two dishes invented by the restaurant which have won greatest fame are the *huitres en coquille à la Rockefeller* (oysters Rockefeller) and *pompano en papillote* (pompano cooked in a paper bag with a particularly luscious sauce); no other restaurant has been quite able to equal them on these dishes. Antoine's is also noted for its *bisque d'écrevisses à la cardinal* (crayfish bisque), *poulet chanteclair* (chicken marinated in red wine before cooking), and *omelette soufflée*, a superb dessert.

Antoine's 'mystery room' (so called because of a famous picture which originally hung there) is a most popular place for intimate dinners, and on its walls are testimonials from prominent guests. There one will find Calvin Coolidge's laconic 'With appreciation' and Taft's flourishing signature. But perhaps Irvin S. Cobb's comment is the most characteristic: 'Once upon a time, being seduced by certain poetic words of Thackeray, I made a special trip to a certain café in Paris to eat bouillabaisse. I found it distinctly worth while. Later I went to Marseilles, the home of this dish, and there ate it again and found it better. And then I came back to America and ate it at Antoine's in New Orleans and found it best of all.'

Arnaud's, 813 Bienville St.; proprietor, Arnaud Cazenave; open 9 A.M. to 12.30 A.M. Table d'hôte lunch, 10.30 A.M. to 3 P.M., 50¢ to 75¢, depending on entrée; there is also a lunch consisting of appetizer or soup, dessert or coffee, for 30j. Table d'hôte dinner, 4.30 to 11 P.M., 75¢ to $1.25, depending on entrée. French specialties à la carte.

Arnaud's was established as late as 1921, but has been a leading restaurant almost from the beginning. Arnaud himself is a very popular host.

The restaurant employs a large staff of cooks and waiters, ready to serve, on short notice, almost any French or Creole dish, with perhaps slightly more emphasis on French cooking than Creole. Among its specialties are shrimps Arnaud, *filet de truite* Amandine, breast of turkey *en papillote*, oyster Whitney, *langouste* Sarah Bernhardt, stuffed crab Réjane, and *crêpe suzette* Arnaud.

Begué's, 504 Madison St.; proprietor, Katie Laporte. Hours: breakfast, 11 A.M. to 3 P.M., $1 to $1.25. Begué's, a market restaurant located originally at 207 Decatur Street, lives today chiefly in its past. This restaurant, flourishing in the 'gay nineties' and the favorite haunt of Eugene Field on his New Orleans visits, was famous for its Bohemian breakfasts, six-course affairs lasting from 11 o'clock to 2 or 3 P.M. Its specialties were kidney stew with red wine and calf's liver *à la* bourgeoise. The present restaurant is situated upstairs over a corner garage in the rooms where Hypolite Begué had his latter-day restaurant.

Broussard's, 819 Conti St.; proprietor, Joseph Broussard; open 9 A.M. to 10.30 P.M. (later, if necessary). Creole breakfast, 9 to 11 A.M., 75¢; table d'hôte lunch, 11.30 A.M. to 2 P.M., 50¢ to 75¢, depending on entrée; table d'hôte dinner, 5.30 to 10 P.M.; seafood dinner, $1; chicken dinner, $1.25; steak dinner, $1.50. Banquet room and rooms for private dinners. Reservations should be made for a party.

Broussard's Restaurant is a small plain building, with no attempt at ornamentation beyond a few tavern lights in front. When the weather permits, guests usually prefer to dine in the courtyard, a large, narrow strip, part of a fine old garden, with shrubbery and bright flowers lining the walls. Roses, calla lilies, violets, chrysanthemums, and hibiscus bloom here as late as December.

The forte of this restaurant is preparing 'little dinners' for special parties. Some of the dishes from which the place has made its reputation are chicken *papillote,* oysters *à la* Broussard, and the Broussard Surprise, a dessert resembling *crêpe suzette.*

Commander's Palace, 1403 Washington Ave.; manager, Felix Tranchina. Hours: 10 A.M. to 12 midnight. Private dining-booths; reservations not necessary. One item that it claims as an exclusive dish is soft-shell turtle ragout, which is obtainable during the warm months.

Galatoire's, 209 Bourbon St.; proprietors, Gabriel, Léon, and Justin Galatoire. Hours: 8 A.M. to 10.30 P.M.; merchants lunch, 11 A.M. to 2 P.M., 60¢; table d'hôte dinner, 5 to 8 P.M., $1; with small bottle of wine, $1.25. Reservations should be made for dinner parties; private diningrooms available.

Galatoire's excels in its *Marguery* sauce, served usually with *filet de truite.* The crab meat here is all hand-picked, and all of the crab dishes are delicious, particularly crab meat *au gratin.* Dinkelspiel salad is a meal in itself, its base being crab meat, surrounded by many tempting hors d'œuvres.

Lucien Gaye's, 603 Royal St.; proprietor, Lucien Gaye. Hours: 7 A.M. to 10 P.M. Lucien Gaye's is a French restaurant of the bourgeois type, where good, plain French food is obtainable.

La Louisiane, 725 Iberville St. ; proprietor, Mrs. Omar Cheer. Hours: 8 A.M. to 10 P.M.; table d'hôte lunch, 11-2, 75¢; table d'hôte dinner, 5.30-8, $1. Private dining-rooms, ballrooms, banquet rooms; make reservations for dinner party, banquet, or ball.

La Restaurant de la Louisiane, established in 1881 by Louis Bézaudin, has been the scene of many brilliant social affairs. The restaurant occupies one of the most interesting and beautiful buildings of New Orleans, the former mansion of the merchant prince Zacharie. It is a three-story structure, with white façade and green shutters; balconies, edged with handsome ironwork, jut over the arched entrance and windows beneath. Inside, there is a succession of spacious rooms, with mirrored walls, crystal chandeliers, brocade draperies, and softly carpeted floors.

Under the management of Fernand Alciatore, the French cuisine was brought to a rare perfection that attracted guests from far and near. La Louisiane's guest-books are full of the names of people famous in the early years of the twentieth century.

Some of the dishes featured by the restaurant are *bisque écrevisse Louisiane,* canapé crab Louisiane, redfish courtbouillon, turkey Rochambeau, *filet de truite marguery,* and baked Alaska.

Maylié's, 1001 Poydras St.; proprietor, W. H. Maylié. Hours: 11 A.M. to 9 P.M.; table d'hôte lunch, 11-2, 50¢; table d'hôte dinner, 5.30-9, $1; open Sunday for dinner only, 5.30-9. Make reservations for party.

Maylié's Restaurant, in the neighborhood of the old Poydras Market, was established in 1878 as an informal market restaurant. Later, when it became noted for the excellent quality of its food, it was conducted on a strictly 'stag' basis. Its patrons are still mostly men, many of them prominent in business circles, who go out of their way to enjoy what Maylié's offers them in the way of both food and relaxation. The two dishes by which the house is best known are the *bouilli* (boiled beef) and hardshell crab stew. Wine is included with both lunch and dinner.

Rising out of a boxed space within a small central hallway of the restaurant, and extending through the roof, is a wistaria vine sixty-five years old. The stem of this vine is as large as an ordinary tree trunk, and the foliage grows both inside and outside of the building.

Tujague's, 823 Decatur St.; proprietor, John Castet. Hours: 6 A.M. to 9.30 P.M.; table d'hôte breakfast, 10-2.30, 50¢; table d'hôte dinner, 5-8.30, 60¢; make reservation for private parties.

This restaurant, established about 1880 and located near the French Market, retains some of the characteristics of the old-fashioned market restaurants. Marketmen are still served here in a special room in the back. The food, though usually plain French fare, is very appetizing.

Vieux Carré, 241 Bourbon St.; proprietor, P. Lacoste. Hours: 10 A.M. to 10 P.M.; table d'hôte luncheon, 10-3, 50¢; table d'hôte dinner, 3-10, 75¢. This is one of the best of the small restaurants of New Orleans. Though it has no noted specialties, it serves an excellent type of French cooking. The restaurant is quiet and conservative, both in its appearance and clientele.

German Restaurants

Kolb's, 125 St. Charles St.; proprietor, Conrad Kolb. Hours 7 A.M. to 1 A.M. for à la carte service; breakfast and luncheon à la carte; table d'hôte dinner, 5 to 9 P.M., grill 85¢ to $1.25; dining-room, $1 to $1.50. Private dining-rooms and banquet rooms; make reservations for parties.

Kolb's, though serving a great variety of dishes, is the only restaurant in New Orleans that makes a specialty of German food. The interior of the main dining-room at Kolb's is a very interesting reproduction of some of the features of a German tavern, while on one side is a Dutch Room with fireplaces and chimneys. The food in general is excellent and the surroundings are very pleasant. Among the German dishes the proprietor recommends the following: wiener schnitzel with vegetables, German pot roast with potato pancake, stewed goose with dumplings, pig knuckles with sauerkraut, and home made pork sausage with red cabbage.

At night a Tyrolean orchestra in costume plays wine and beer classics, and both orchestra and guests join in singing old folk songs.

Italian Restaurants

Masera's, 807 St. Louis St.; proprietor, Joseph Masera. Open 9 A.M. to 12 midnight, à la carte orders. Table d'hôte dinner, 5 to midnight, $1. Masera's was established toward the beginning of the present century, and is well known for its Italian specialties.

B. Montalbano, 724 St. Philip St.; proprietor, B. Montalbano. Open 10 A.M. to 10 P.M.; table d'hôte, 65¢ up to 6 P.M.; 75¢ from 6 to 10 P.M.; make reservations for a party, as seating capacity is very limited.

This establishment is a unique mixture of delicatessen shop, religious shrine, and restaurant.

The Roma Room, where meals are served, has been blessed by Pope Pius XI. Here has been constructed an improvised altar, with a copy of the Vatican at the top, and in the corners on either side small votary candles are kept burning continuously. Colored prints of religious pictures from Rome are inset into the wall by means of gay-colored strips of oilcloth. The ceiling is decorated with Christmas-tree trimmings of colored balls and tinsel. In these Italian peasant surroundings, there has been placed a long table with room for about a dozen guests. The usual dinner is chicken ravioli or spaghetti and chicken, with an elaborate dish of Italian antipasto.

Turci's Italian Gardens, 223 Bourbon St. ; proprietor, Ettore Turci. Open 11 A.M. to 11 P.M. for à la carte orders. Table d'hôte dinner, 5.30 to 9 P.M., 80¢.

Turci's is one of the leading Italian restaurants in New Orleans. It was established by Signor and Signora Turci, opera singers from Northern Italy, who toured the United States with various companies before settling down to the restaurant business. As a consequence, Turci's has always been the favorite haunt of visiting opera singers. The restaurant serves home-made ravioli, home-made noodles, and various kinds of Italian spaghetti.

The following Italian restaurants are also well known for their Italian food and seafood specialties: *Tortorich Restaurant*, 441 Royal St.; *Gentilich Caterers*, 900 Rampart St., situated across from the Municipal Auditorium and patronized by after-theater parties; and the uptown places: *S. Dominici*, 3633 Prytania St.; *Manale's Restaurant*, 1838 Napoleon Ave.; *Zibilich Restaurant*, 3750 S. Claiborne

Ave.; Tranchina's, 2505 Carondelet St.; and Delmonico's, 1300 St. Charles Ave.

In connection with the Italian restaurants, it is interesting to note that Ursuline St., between Royal and Chartres, is commonly called 'Spumone Block' from the number of little confectionery shops established there which serve Italian ices (spumone, cassata, alkeno, and sciallotti) and cakes (cannola, etc.).

Mexican Restaurants

La Lune, 800 Bourbon St. Open 9 P.M. to 6 A.M. The Mexican food at La Lune is excellent and reasonably priced.

Tea Rooms and Restaurants

Court of the Two Sisters, 615 Royal St.; proprietor, Jimmie Cooper. Open Sundays and weekdays. Lunch, 12 to 2.30, 50¢; dinner, 5 to 10.30, 60¢ to $1.

The Court of the Two Sisters possesses an interesting background. The courtyard, originally one of the finest in New Orleans, is quite large, and still attractive with its old willow and fig trees. It is a favorite spot for dining in the summer. Seafood dinners and chicken dinners are featured.

Courtyard Kitchen, 820 St. Louis St.; proprietor, Mrs. J. P. Burton. Open weekdays only. Lunch, 12 to 2.30, 85¢; tea, 2.30 to 5, 25¢ up. Breakfast à la carte may be obtained from 8 to 12. Special party breakfast by arrangement, particularly on Sundays. Make reservations for parties.

The Courtyard Kitchen is so called from the fact that it is in the out-of-door kitchen of a former home. The dining-room is furnished as an antebellum kitchen and during the winter months log fires are kept burning in its huge fireplace. On sunshiny days tables are set for luncheon and tea in the courtyard, one of the most beautiful in New Orleans.

This establishment is noted for gumbo, stuffed crabs, Southern style chicken, hot biscuit, home-made cakes, and desserts. Colored maids dressed as mammies serve the food.

Green Shutter Tea Room, 710 St. Peter St.; proprietor, Miss Céleste Eshleman. Open weekdays only, from October 1 to June 1, 9 A.M. to 5 P.M. Lunch, 12 to 2 P.M., 45¢ to 75¢; tea, 2 to 5 P.M., 25¢ up. Sunday breakfast served at 12 o'clock, by reservation. For minimum party of thirty, $1 each.

The Green Shutter is housed in a quaint old Spanish home, with low, sloping roof and heavy green shutters on windows and doors. The uneven brick floor, wooden beams, and plastered walls of the main diningroom remain exactly as when this house was built. Featured dishes are Creole gumbo, jambalaya, grillades with yellow grits, and waffles with sausage and bacon.

Patio Royal, 417 Royal St.; proprietor, Mrs. Jeanne Castellanos. Open weekdays; lunch, 11.30 A.M. to 3 P.M., 75¢ to $1; dinner, 5 to 9 P.M., $1; Sunday night supper dances, 8 P.M. to 12, $1.50. Bar open from 10 A.M. to 9 P.M.

Patio Royal, located in the old Paul Morphy Home, has many beautiful and striking features. The Spanish Room is furnished with treasures from abroad – rugs from Algeria, tapestry and brass from Morocco, torchères from Granada, lamps from Seville, and red straw-bottomed chairs from Paris. Two lovely wrought-iron gates swing under the arches separating the Spanish Room from the dining-room proper. The porte-cochère entrance leads from the dining-room into a passage way, embellished with large stone jars, to an attractive courtyard in the back.

The Patio is very popular for luncheon parties and dinner dances. Private rooms available for parties. Make reservations for parties only.

The Southern Marigold, 619 Royal St.; proprietor, Mrs. Mary B. Baldwin. Open weekdays only, December 1 to April 1. Luncheon, 12 to 2.30, $1; dinner, 6 to 8, $1.50.

This place is unique in New Orleans, in that absolutely no French or Creole dishes are served. Instead there is the best of Southern cooking. Mrs. Baldwin is also proprietor of a very successful restaurant at Niagara Falls.

Hotel Restaurants

Jung Hotel (Florentine Room), 1500 Canal St.; manager, Arthur Landstreet. Open 8 A.M. to 9 P.M.; à la carte service all day; table d hôte lunch, 12 to 1.30 P.M., 75¢; table d'hôte dinner, 6 to 9 P.M., $1.

Monteleone Hotel, 214 Royal St.; maître d'hôtel, René Cazaubon. Open 6 A.M. to 12 midnight for à la carte service; lunch, table d'hôte for business men, 11 to 2 P.M., 40¢ to 50¢ (lunch is not served table d'hôte on Sunday); dinner, table d'hôte, 5 to 9 P.M., 75¢ to $1.

Roosevelt Hotel (Fountain Room), 123 Baronne St.; manager, Lou Lemler. Open 6 A.M. to 12 midnight for à la carte service; table d'hôte lunch, 12 to 2 P.M., 45¢ to 90¢; table d'hôte dinner, 5 to 9.30 P.M., 85¢ to $1.50; club breakfast, 6 A.M. to 12 noon, 30¢ to 75¢.

Music for dinner dancing from 6 to 9.30 P.M. is furnished by ranking orchestras from large metropolitan cities. For the luncheon period there is a local orchestra.

St. Charles Hotel, 211 St. Charles St.; manager, H. O. Guion. Open 6 A.M. to 12 midnight; breakfast, 6 to 11 A.M., 35¢ to 90¢; table d'hôte lunch, 11 A.M. to 2 P.M., 45¢ to 80¢ table d'hôte dinner, 5 to 8.30 P.M., 85¢ to $1.50.

Store Restaurants (*not open on Sundays*)

D. H. Holmes, 819 Canal St.; manager, M. J. Briant. Open 7 A.M. to 9 P.M.; lunch, 11 A.M. to 2 P.M., 50¢, 60¢, and 75¢; dinner, 5 to 9 P.M., 50¢ to $1.

Maison Blanche (The Rendezvous), 901 Canal St.; manager, W. H. Renaker. Open 9 A.M. to 6 P.M., à la carte; club breakfast, 9 to 10.30 A.M., 15¢ to 35¢; lunch, 10.30 A.M. to 3 P.M., 25¢ to 65¢.

Solari's, 201 Royal St.; manager, Mrs. O. M. Harshman. Open 7.30 A.M. to 6.30 P.M.; breakfast, 7.30 to 11 A.M., 10¢ to 50¢; lunch, 11 A.M. to 3 P.M., 45¢ to 65¢; à la carte service all day.

Miscellaneous Restaurants

French Market Cofee Stands, Decatur and St. Ann, and Decatur and St. Philip Sts. Open day and night, except from 12 noon to 4 P.M. Delicious coffee and doughnuts, 10¢.

Gluck's, 124 Royal St.; manager, Henry A. Gluck. Open day and night. Special lunch, 45¢; special dinner, 65¢ and 75¢; special plates, 25¢ to 40¢.

Martin Brothers, 2004 St. Claude Ave.; proprietor, Benny Martin. Open day and night. Prices: poorboy sandwich, whole loaf, 25¢, half loaf, 15¢, one third loaf, 10¢, quarter loaf, 5¢; special plate lunch, 20¢ and 25¢; special supper (plate), 20¢; Sunday chicken dinner, 25¢.

St. Regis, 121 Royal St.; proprietor, Gaston Bertoniere. Open 6 A.M. to 12 midnight for à la carte orders; table d'hôte lunch, 11 A.M. to 5 P.M., 45¢; table d'hôte dinner, 5 P.M. to 12 midnight, 65¢.

Thompson's, 133 St. Charles St.; manager, W. H. Dodds. Open day and night; lunch starts at 10.30 A.M.; dinner at 4.30 P.M.

Cafeterias

(While some of the New Orleans cafeterias feature American food, most of them also serve Creole dishes.)

Holsum's, 718 Gravier St.; manager, W. G. Brown. Breakfast, 7 to 9.30 A.M.; lunch, 11 A.M. to 2.30 P.M.; dinner, 5 to 8 P.M.

Morrison's, Masonic Temple, 333 St. Charles St.; manager, G. H. Ptomy. Breakfast, 7 to 9.30 A.M.; lunch, 10.45 A.M. to 2.30 P.M.; dinner, 4.45 to 8 P.M.

Morrison's, 918 Gravier St.; manager, R. C. McClammy. Lunch, 11 A.M. to 2.30 P.M.; dinner, 5 to 8 P.M.

St. Regis, 121 Royal St.; manager, Gaston Bertonière. Lunch, 11 A.M. to 2 P.M.; dinner, 5 to 8 P.M.

Wise's, 233 Carondelet St.; manager, Herbert Wise. Breakfast, 7 to 10 A.M.; lunch, 10 A.M. to 2.30 P.M.; dinner, 5 to 8 P.M. Closed all day Sunday.

Negro Restaurants

Astoria, 235 S. Rampart St.; manager, Miss Vera Braden. Open day and night; à la carte service at all times; table d'hôte lunch, 12 to 1.30 P.M., 15¢ to 35¢; table d'hôte dinner, 2 to 6 P.M., 25¢ to 40¢.

Douglas, 1320 Iberville St.; manager, C. Douglas. Open day and night; à la carte service at all times; table d'hôte lunch, 12 to 2 P.M., 15¢ to 25¢; table d'hôte dinner, 2 to 7 P.M., l5¢ to 25¢.

National Lunch Room, 501 S. Rampart St.; manager, A. Harris. Open from 7 A.M. to 7 P.M.; à la carte service all day; table d'hôte lunch, 12 to 2 P.M., 10¢ to 25¢; table d'hôte dinner, 2 to 7 P.M., 15¢ to 25¢.

Pelican, 301 S. Rampart St.; manager, A. J. Fabacher. Open day and night; à la carte service at all times; table d'hôte lunch, 12 to 1.30 P.M., 15¢ to 35¢; table d'hôte dinner, 2 to 6 P.M., 20¢ to 30¢.

CALENDAR OF EVENTS

The abbreviation 'nfd' signifies that the event occurs during the month, but has no fixed date.

Dec.	27	Mid-Winter Sports Carnival. Sugar Bowl football classic
Jan.	9	(New Year's Day), tennis and golf tournaments, basketball game, yacht regatta, track and field meet, and inter-city boxing match.
Jan.	1	Emancipation Day.
Jan.	6	Twelfth Night (King's Day and the official beginning of Carnival). During short seasons balls are held before King's Day.
Jan.	8	Jackson Day (Battle of New Orleans).
Feb. or March	nfd	Mardi Gras (Shrove Tuesday). Parades start on previous Thursday with night parade of Momus; followed on Friday night with parade of Hermes; Saturday with Nor, children's parade; Proteus Parade on Monday night, and Rex and Comus parades on Mardi Gras. Zulu King and neighborhood organizations have parades in various parts of the city.
March	19	St. Joseph's Day (*mi-carême*).
March or April	nfd	Spring Fiesta, second or third week before Easter.
March or April	nfd	Flower Show.
March or April	Easter	Sunrise Services. Tulane Stadium, 7 A.M.
April	nfd	Opening of Southern League baseball season.
April	nfd	Lower Mississippi Valley Musical Festival. Dillard University.
April	nfd	Horse Show.
April	30	Louisiana Livestock Show.
May	1st Fri.	McDonogh Day. Statue in Lafayette Square decorated by school children.
May	nfd	Cooking School.
June	3	Confederate Memorial Day (Jefferson Davis' birthday).
June	nfd	Automobile Show.
Aug.	nfd	Southern Yacht Club Regatta.
Aug.	nfd	Governors' Yacht Race. New Orleans and Biloxi alternate as host.
Oct.	nfd	Opening of theater and concert season.
Nov.	1	All Saints' Day. Decoration of cemeteries.
Nov.	Thanksgiving	Beginning of racing season.
Dec.	24-25	Doll and Toy Fund Christmas Tree for poor children. Whites on Christmas Eve and Negroes on Christmas Day.

I. NEW ORLEANS: THE GENERAL BACKGROUND

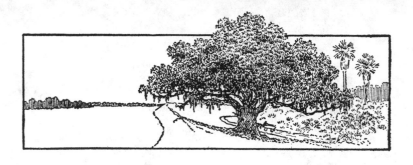

NATURAL SETTING

Geography. Surrounded by swamps and low-lying delta lands, New Orleans proper (29° 56' North Latitude; 90° 84' West Longitude) is an urban oasis lying in a dike-enclosed area between the Mississippi River and Lake Pontchartrain, 107 miles from the mouth of the river. The city and parish boundaries are coterminous, New Orleans being the fourth largest city in land area (365 square miles, of which 166 square miles are water) in the United States. The boundary is very irregular; its total length is 115 miles. On the north lie Lake Pontchartrain and Rigolets Pass; on the east, Lake Borgne and St. Bernard Parish; on the south, St. Bernard, Plaquemines, and Jefferson Parishes; and on the west, Jefferson Parish. The Mississippi forms part of the boundary on the east, south, and west. The greatest distance within the city limits is thirty-four and a half miles from northeast to southwest; the distance between the river and the lake varies between five and eight miles.

Although the built-up section occupies only a small proportion of this large area, the city has expanded to a considerable extent beyond its original limits (the present Vieux Carré). Extension has been made both upstream and downstream and northward to Lake Pontchartrain; a strip of territory (Algiers) on the west bank of the river has also been annexed.

The popular name, 'Crescent City' is derived from the fact that the site of the original town was on a sharp bend of the river.

Topography. The average elevation of the city, which is below the highwater levels of both the Mississippi River and Lake Pontchartrain, is but one foot above mean Gulf level. The highest natural formations in the city, about fifteen feet above mean Gulf level, are the strips of land adjacent to the river, the natural levees which confine the water to the channel during ordinary and all but the highest stages of the river.

The greater portion of the city would suffer from floods every year were it not for the surrounding artificial levee system. Levees constructed along the river and the Pontchartrain lake-front, across the swamps and along the waterways are all interconnected, thus enclosing completely the built-up section of the city, which is drained by means of canals and pumping stations. The levees along the river average about 23 feet and those along the lake-front and across the swamps and marshes about nine feet above mean Gulf level. Approximately thirty-nine per cent of the total land area of New Orleans is enclosed within levees. The unprotected sixty-one per cent is the peninsula and lands which lie along Lakes Pontchartrain and Borgne and extend northeastward from Micheaud to the Rigolets Pass. This area, for the most part subject to overflow by high tides from the Gulf, consists of delta fingers, coastal islands and ridges of low elevation, and intervening coastal marshes.

There are several navigable waterways within the municipal limits of the city, all connecting with Lake Pontchartrain. The New Orleans Navigation Canal begins at South Rampart Street at the edge of the business district and runs northward, entering the lake near the northwestern corner of the city. Farther east, the Inner Harbor Navigation Canal, commonly known as the 'Industrial Canal,' provides a channel five and one half miles long, with a depth of thirty feet and a width of three hundred feet, connecting the river and the lake. Bayou St. John, formerly a navigable stream, begins at Lafitte Avenue and Jefferson Davis Parkway and runs northward to the lake. Other navigable waters include Chef Menteur Pass, Lake St. Catherine, and a number of small passes and canals in the marsh area northeast of the built-up section of the city; the Mississippi River, Lakes Pontchartrain and Borgne, Rigolets Pass, and Bayou Bienvenue, all navigable, form part of the boundaries.

Lake Pontchartrain on the north, one of the largest lakes in the United States, is approximately forty-one miles long and twenty-five miles wide and comprises an area of 635 square miles. Of this area 146 square miles are included within the boundary of New Orleans.

Climate. Semi-tropical in nature, with an average yearly temperature of 69.5, the weather of New Orleans is remarkably equable, subnormal cold and excessive heat being rare. The winters and summers are generally moderate, Gulf breezes and the proximity of numerous bodies of water serving to modify extremes of temperature. Recordings of over 100° and below 20° very seldom occur. The mean annual precipitation is 59.45 inches, an annual rainfall that exceeds that of any other large city in the United States with the exception of Mobile and Miami. The highest annual rainfall in New Orleans, 85.73 inches, occurred in 1927; the lowest, 31.7, in 1899.

The prevailing winds are from the Gulf, generally from the southeast. Tropical hurricanes, which harass most points of the Gulf Coast, very seldom strike New Orleans. Occasional fogs occur in the spring and winter months, particularly along the river-front, but are, as a rule, of short duration.

Geology and Paleontology. The Parish of Orleans, located near the southeastern extremity of the Mississippi Alluvial Plain, lies wholly within the delta. With the exception of a few minor outcrops of sea-island sand and lake-shore deposits of sand and clam shell, all surface formations within the parish are alluvial. The major topographic features are the natural levees along the Mississippi and Gentilly ridges and along Bayou Sauvage, a former outlet of the river.

The higher parts of these ridges, or 'frontlands,' are composed of sandy loams. These dip and graduate into the backlands, where the soil is composed of a lighter loam and waxy clay. Deposits of stiff, blue clay fill the area between the ridges, except near the lake shores and passes, where the alluvial material has been reworked by tidal action. Here the soil consists of mucky masses of partly decomposed vegetation interspersed with a fine, drab-colored clay. Fine peat soil formed by marsh vegetation in a state of partial decay sometimes accumulates over extensive low areas to a depth of from one to three feet on the surface of the blue clay.

Fossils consist mainly of marine shells and oysters associated with sea shore deposits, and clam shell (*Rangia cuneata*) associated with the clay deposits. Indian relics are numerous on the shell ridges near the lakes, and broken bits of pottery can be found mixed with oyster and clam-shell fossils along the lake beaches. Iron concretions and fossil cypress wood are found in the blue clay.

Drainage. The low elevation of New Orleans makes drainage of the city a difficult problem. Water has to be removed by pumps from the metropolitan section of the city, which is protected from outside high water by encircling levees. Ten pumping stations and more than 870 miles of drainage canals and pipelines have been installed for that purpose. Underground tributary canals, fed by gutters and drainpipes, lead the water into the main system, from which it is pumped into Bayou Bienvenue and flows by gravity into Lake Borgne. An additional safety measure is provided for in the Bonnet Carré Spillway, which makes possible the diversion into Lake Pontchartrain of Mississippi flood waters at a point twenty miles above New Orleans.

HISTORY
SPANIARDS DISCOVER THE LAND

LEGENDARY accounts of early voyages by Spanish explorers are curiously substantiated by ancient maps which show that the mouth of the Mississippi River and the immediate vicinity of present-day New Orleans were known to Europeans only a short time after Columbus led the way to the New World.

On the *Tabula Terre Nove*, a map made by Waldseemüller before 1508 from an original, probably the Cantino map of 1502, and on other early charts, there appears the three-tongued mouth of a river, whose location, west of a well-defined Florida, suggests the delta of the Mississippi. Inasmuch as the discovery of Florida is attributed to no earlier an explorer than Ponce de Leon (1513), the only possible inference is a previous discovery, unrecorded in history except by cartographers.

Later knowledge of the river may have come from the half-legendary voyages of Alvarez de Pineda and Cabeza de Vaca, intrepid adventurers who explored the Gulf Coast from Florida to Mexico. According to a picturesque account, Pineda in 1519 discovered the great river, to which he gave the name Rio del Espiritu Santo. At its mouth he found a large town, and for a distance of six leagues upstream counted forty villages in habited by giants and pigmies wearing ornaments of gold in their noses and ears. All that was lacking in this beautiful and densely populated El Dorado, where the rivers ran to the sea heavily laden with gold, was the Fountain of Youth, for want of which, perhaps, the Spaniards thought the country not worth conquering.

Less fantastic is the voyage of De Vaca, leader of the survivors of the Narvaez expedition, which was commissioned by the Spanish Government in 1528 to explore and conquer the Gulf Coast from Florida to Mexico. Escaping from the hostile Indians at Apalachicola Bay, De Vaca and his men, making their way along the coast in makeshift boats, passed the mouth of a broad river, presumably the Mississippi, which poured so large a stream into the Gulf that his men were able to obtain fresh water far out at sea. One account of this journey relates that, with the exception of De Vaca and three men, the entire force capsized and was lost in the current, while another narrator states that a tropical storm destroyed all but the leader and a few men, who tarried six years among the Indians before reaching Mexico.

The first white men to view the site of New Orleans were Luis Moscoso and the survivors of De Soto's expedition, who sailed down the river in 1543 on their way back to civilization. More than a century later, during which time the lower Mississippi lay neglected by explorers, Sieur de la Salle, with a party of fifty men, descended from the Great Lakes, making a stop on March 31, 1682, at the Indian village of Maheoula, a Tangipahoa settlement, which, from Tonty's mention of it as being twenty leagues from the western channel of the mouth, must have been close to the present location of New Orleans. On April 9, 1682, at a point not far downstream (27° North Latitude), a cross was erected with a column bearing the arms of France and an inscription claiming the territory in the name of Louis XIV.

THE FRENCH FOUND THE CITY

Although the Mississippi was one of the first great rivers of North America to be discovered and explored by Europeans, and although every other important stream on the Atlantic seaboard had a fortified settlement erected at its mouth shortly after its discovery as a safeguard against inland exploration by rival European nations, it was not until almost a hundred and fifty years after the discovery of the Mississippi that an attempt was made to establish a settlement at the mouth of the river. For that purpose Louis XIV sent out an expedition under La Salle in 1684; but sailing too far westward, he landed at what is now Matagorda Bay, Texas, in the belief that he was entering the western channel of the Mississippi. Convinced of his error after landing, he sought the Mississippi in vain, and was finally forced to abandon the project and attempt an overland journey to Canada, during which he was treacherously killed by one of his men.

A more successful attempt to rediscover and secure the mouth of the Mississippi was made in 1698, when Pierre Le Moyne, Sieur d'Iberville, sailed from Brest with four ships and the wherewithal of colonization.

In February, 1699, the French arrived at Mobile Bay, where they learned from the Indians that the Mississippi was a short distance to the west. Proceeding to Ship Island, the fleet anchored and Iberville set out in small boats in search of the entrance to the river. The mouth of the Mississippi, lined with mud-coated tree trunks, which they mistook from afar for rocks, was found on March 2. Running their boats ashore, the party sang a *Te Deum* in honor of the occasion, and the next day, Shrove Tuesday, began the ascent of the river, the appropriate name of Mardi Gras being given to a bayou twelve miles upstream. Farther on, Indians of the Bayagoula and the Mongoulacha tribes were met, and on the following Friday the party arrived at the present site of New Orleans, where a buffalo was killed, a cross erected, and some trees marked. The expedition continued as far as the Red River and made its way back to the convoy by way of Bayou Manchac and Lakes Pontchartrain and Maurepas, which were named after the Minister of Marine of France and his son, respectively.

The following year Jean Baptiste Le Moyne, Sieur de Bienville, Iberville's brother, left the fort at Biloxi for further exploration of the river. He ascended as far as the Ouchas and on his way back met an English frigate of sixteen guns which had anchored twenty-eight leagues from the mouth of the river. Bienville adroitly dissuaded the English captain from proceeding up the river by informing him that his was but a small detachment of a large French force stationed upstream. The English, being taken in, weighed anchor and, turning about, sailed to the Gulf; thus giving rise to the name English Turn, a part of the river not very far from New Orleans, which has been particularly unlucky for the English, since at the Battle of New Orleans, a century later, they were turned back again a short distance from the same spot. By a slim margin – the differencebetween the personalities of two men – was the founding of New Orleans accomplished by the French rather than the English.

For twenty-four years (1699-1723) the capital of Louisiana remained on the Gulf Coast. Because of the belief that ships would find difficulty in gaining entrance to the shallow and débris-obstructed mouth of the river, no attempt was made to establish a settlement on the lower Mississippi. Adrien de Pauger urged that a narrowing of the channel through the construction of jetties would increase the current and make the river a self-dredging agent, but his advice was not heeded for more than a century. In the meantime, exploratory work in the vicinity was carried on by Jesuit priests, *voyageurs* from the Great Lakes, and *coureurs de bois*, traders who did business with the Indians.

It being ascertained that suitable passage could be made for vessels at the mouth of the river, Bienville decided upon the settlement of New Orleans. A spot thirty leagues from the mouth, where Bayou St. John ran from Lake Pontchartrain to within a short distance of the river, was selected as the location, the place having been used by the Indians, long before white men invaded the region, as a portage offering a short cut between the Mississippi and the coastal waters to the east. An additional advantage afforded by the site was the relatively high land found there, a consideration not to be overlooked in that annually flooded region where the land hugged the sea in an endless labyrinth of cypress swamps, sluggish bayous, and coastal bays.

The exact date of the founding of *La Nouvelle Orléans*, named in honor of the Regent of France, Philippe, Duc d'Orléans, has been disputed, though most historians agree upon the year 1718, at which time, in February, Bienville entrusted his engineers with the plotting of the town, the exact location of which corresponds to the French Quarter of today.

EARLY GROWTH

The new settlement superseded Biloxi in 1723 as the capital of the vast Colonial empire of Louisiana. Eighteen miles of levee were constructed above and below the town, government buildings erected, and efforts made to drain the land. As part of the 'Mississippi Bubble' John Law's grandiose real-estate project, New Orleans enjoyed an early increase in population, although the majority of immigrants coming to Louisiana in quest of the easy living advertised in Europe chose to settle along the river outside of the small town. Beside the civil and military officials, the population consisted of slaves, soldiers, trappers, and merchants. Classes of slaves included (1) Negroes imported directly from Africa or from the French possessions in the West Indies; (2) *esclaves naturels*, Indian prisoners of war; and (3) 'redemptioners,' impoverished Europeans, most of whom were Germans, who had bound themselves to serve for a period of three years in payment of their passage and were 'sold' to the planters by ship captains. Because of the rapid increase in slaves, the French practice of populating Louisiana with convict labor soon came to a stop, resulting in an improvement in the type of colonist settling in and about New Orleans.

Under the Company of the Indies, a John Law enterprise, the government of the Colony was vested in a Superior Council consisting of the directors of the trading company with a commandant-general, in place of a governor, at its head. Lower courts were established for the administration of justice, and a right of appeal to the Superior Council was granted. In 1724, the *Code Noir*, a compilation drawn up for the regulation of Negroes on the island of Santo Domingo, was promulgated in Louisiana by Governor Bienville. Among its additional provisions were those having to do with the expulsion of Jews from the province, under penalty of confiscation of property and imprisonment, and the establishment of the Catholic religion as the State faith. For more than a century it formed the basis of white treatment of enslaved Negroes.

The religious administration of the Colony was divided among three religious orders. The Jesuits were given charge of all territory north of the Ohio, the Capuchins were assigned to the territory west of the Mississippi River, and the Carmelite Fathers were placed in charge of the settlement east of the river with headquarters at Mobile. The Carmelites failed to fill their assignment and the Capuchins were given charge, while the Jesuits were allowed to do missionary work among the Indians in the Capuchin territory, with the understanding that there would be no interference with Capuchin activities. Both orders were under the supervision of the Bishop of Quebec.

Care for the sick and education for girls were provided for with the arrival in 1727 of six Ursuline nuns, who founded the Ursuline Convent. Equally important, however, was the importation during the following years of young French women (called *files á la cassette* because of the chests of clothes and linen given them as dowries by the French Government) to supply wives for the colonists.

In 1731 the Company of the Indies relinquished its charter and Louisiana once more became a province of the Crown. A governor, appointed by the King as his representative, regulated the simple affairs of the Colony, and in his executive capacity exercised military and administrative authority, enforced by the soldiery of which he was the head. His dictatorial power also embraced judicial and legislative activity, limited to a great extent, however, by the fact that all ordinances and royal edicts emanated from France. The Superior Council was reorganized to consist of the intendant, *procureur-général* (King's attorney), registrar of the province, and six prominent citizens. In conjunction with the Governor and a *commissaire ordonnateur* (agent of the King in charge of commce and Crown property) the Council discharged the executive, legislative, and judicial affairs of the Colony. Justice was administered, without trial by jury, by inferior courts subject to the appellate jurisdiction of the Superior Council. The Custom of Paris, a codification of ancient French law, formed the basis of Colonial law from the beginning.

Early in its history the town took on a gay and light-hearted appearance. Under the governorship of the Marquis de Vaudreuil (1743-53) the social life of the town was modeled after Versailles, and citizens sought to outdo each other in the splendor of their social affairs.

The capital of one third of the present area of the United States grew slowly. At first only that manufacturing which had to do with supplying the immediate needs of the Colony was undertaken. Sawmills were in operation soon after the town was founded, and by 1729 brick, pottery, and tiling were being sold in New Orleans. Shipbuilding, especially the construction of pirogues, brigantines, and other small craft, developed as an industry to meet the demands of growing commerce on the Mississippi.

Never fully realizing her importance as the port of the Mississippi Valley, New Orleans lay dormant during the first half of the eighteenth century. Trade restrictions prohibited commerce with any but the mother country, and illegal trade with England, Spain, Mexico, Florida, and the West Indies had to be resorted to. With merchants and officials conniving with smugglers and pirates, smuggling grew to such an extent that in 1763 the illicit traffic was estimated to represent one sixth of the official trade total. The bulk of cargoes, shipped in exchange for slaves and European merchandise, consisted of lumber, pitch, tar, wax from the wax myrtle, brick, rice, indigo, sugarcane, cotton, sassafras, and fur pelts. As settlers crossed the Allegheny Mountains and developed the Middle West, New Orleans began to grow as a commercial port. The extent to which the river traffic had grown by 1750 may be seen in the frequent requests of Colonial officials for sailors to man the boats used on the river. By 1763 exports totaled $304,000; indigo accounted for $100,000, skins and furs $80,000, and lumber $50,000.

UNDER SPANISH RULE

By the Treaty of Fontainebleau, 1762, and the Treaty of Paris, 1763, Louis XV ceded New Orleans, along with the portion of Louisiana lying west of the Mississippi River, to Spain. It was not until 1764 that the French officials were informed of the transaction amd instructed to relinquish the Colony. For two more years the city remained abandoned by France and unclaimed by Spain. Indignation on the part of the citizenry against the transfer ran high, and was expressed in open resentment toward the Spanish commissioner, Don Antonio de Ulloa, who took possession of the Colony in 1766.

On October 28, 1768, a mass meeting of citizens, at which Ulloa's expulsion was demanded, was held in New Orleans. The Superior Council, acting upon the demands of the assembled populace, issued an order expelling the Spanish commandant, who, with his household, had retired to a ship lying at anchor in the river. During the night a band of insurgents carrying torches and flares cut the vessel loose from its mooring, and morning found the head of the government well on the way toward the Gulf of Mexico. Serious consideration was given a proposal to found a republic with a 'Protector' at its head, but fear of foreign intervention acted against the scheme.

For two years the Colony, the first in America to revolt against a European power, enjoyed freedom from foreign rule, but on July 24, 1769, the whole town was thrown into a tumult by news of the arrival at the mouth of the river of twenty-four Spanish men-of-war and twenty-six hundred soldiers under the command of Spain's most illustrious general, Count Alexander O'Reilly. No opposition was made upon the arrival of the flotilla in August, and O'Reilly took formal possession on August 18, replacing the French flag in the Place d'Armes with the flag of Spain. Shortly afterward, twelve leaders of the October revolt were imprisoned, six being executed for their participation in the bloodless rebellion.

Changes in government were made, and the French law was abolished and supplanted by the law in force in other Spanish colonies. The Executive Department consisted of a governor assisted by an intendant, auditor of war, auditor of the intendancy, comptroller, and various minor officials. Both civil and military powers were vested in the Governor, who appointed commandants in the same capacity for each parish or district. The Superior Council of the French régime was replaced by a legislative and quasi-administrative council called the Cabildo, which was composed of six perpetual *regidors*, two *alcaldes*, an attorney-general *syndic*, and a clerk. Its judicial function was limited to the jurisdiction of appeals from the *alcaldes* courts set up in New Orleans and the chief towns of the provime. For lack of a legislative body, laws came either directly from Spain, the Captain-General of Cuba, the *Audencia Habana* (Cuban administra tive council), or from the Governor himself, who, at the outset of his term, promulgated a list of laws in an inaugural address, the *bando de buen gobierno*. Centralization of power in the hands of a few officials, lack of a legislative body, and bureaucracy continued under Spanish rule to characterize the government of the Colony.

O'Reilly, before his departure in 1770, relieved the commerce of the Colony to some extent. Its trade had been confined, since Ulloa's administration, to six ports of Spain. Trade had also been forbidden with any but Spanish vessels owned and commanded by the King's subjects. Don Luis de Unzaga, Governor in 1772, tolerantly ignored the forbidden trade with the British, which had grown considerably, and without which the commerce of the Province would have suffered greatly. In 1774 the estimated value of Louisiana commerce was $600,000, of which only $15,000 passed through legitimate Spanish channels.

With the outbreak of the American Revolution, Spanish officials became involved, conniving with the revolting colonists in the war against England. American agents were permitted to establish bases in the city, through which they supplied the Atlantic colonies with munitions and supplies. Most active in this work was Oliver Pollock, a merchant granted freedom of trade in New Orleans and Louisiana in return for the shipload of flour he had placed at O'Reilly's disposal in 1769, when the Spanish general was hard pressed in supplying his troops with provisions. By advancing supplies and credit totaling $300,000 to the revolting colonists during the Revolution, Pollock played an important part in the success of the American cause.

Large numbers of French settlers and free Indians, who had refused to take the oath of allegiance to England after West Florida had been ceded to that country in 1763, moved to New Orleans or elsewhere in the vicinity. Under Don Bernardo de Galvez, son of the Viceroy of Spain and Governor of Louisiana, an expedition was permitted to be fitted out in New Orleans and sent against Fort Bute, an English settlement in the Manchac country. The fort was captured, and British territory as far north as Natchez was terrorized by the expedition.

As a result of these and other acts, Great Britain declared war against Spain in 1779, whereupon Galvez, with an army of militia, Indians, Negroes, and volunteers of every character, took advantage of the opportunity to make a series of successful raids against the enemy at Baton Rouge, Natchez, Manchac, Mobile, and Pensacola.

In 1788 the city was almost completely destroyed by a great fire. Tapers lighted in observances of Good Friday of that year ignited the curtains of the Nunez house on Chartres Street. Swept by a strong south wind, the conflagration spread through the town, consuming 856 houses and laying waste four-fifths of the city. While New Orleans was being rebuilt, most of the inhabitants were forced to seek refuge among the planters along the river.

The year 1794 was notable. The first newspaper in Louisiana, *Le Moniteur de la Louisiane,* appeared on the streets of New Orleans; Étienne de Boré, a sugar-cane planter, successfully granulated sugar; Governor Carondelet authorized construction of a canal from Bayou St. John to the city ramparts, and the new St. Louis Church, not yet a cathedral, was dedicated. A most disastrous occurrence, however, was a fire that razed 212 of the buildings erected after the Great Fire of 1788.

UNDER THREE FLAGS

By the Treaty of San Ildefonso (1801) Louisiana was ceded to France. The colonists were not formally notified of the transfer until the arrival in March 1803 of Pierre Laussat, the Colonial Prefect sent by Napoleon to take over the Colony. He was coldly received, for although New Orleans was preponderantly French, the townspeople were not enthusiastic about the change. The substitution of French assignats of fluctuating value for Spanish silver, the possibility of new laws affecting commerce, and the revolutionary policy that had bred the revolt at Santo Domingo were cause for alarm to a populace grown accustomed to peace under the Spanish. Laussat was considered a dangerous *revolutionnaire* by the royalists and émigrés, and so frightened were the Ursuline nuns of the emissary of an anti-Catholic government that most of them left for Havana in June, despite the assurance and pleadings of Laussat.

News of the sale of Louisiana to the United States (April 30, 1803) arrived in August and placed Laussat in an embarrassing position. The great plans he had contemplated for the Colony during his régime were of no consequence, since his official capacity was now concerned merely with the taking over of Louisiana from Spain and the immediate cession of it to the United States.

The ceremony of transfer to France was fixed for November 3. By noon that day the principal part of the population of New Orleans had assembled in the Place d'Armes to wait in the rain while Salcedo, Governor of Louisiana, the Marquis of Casa Calvo, Spanish Commissioner, and Laussat met in the Hôtel de

Ville (Cabildo) to read the proclamation of transfer. Absolution from their oath of allegiance was granted to all Spaniards not wishing to retain their citizenship, and the keys to Fort St. Charles and Fort St. Louis were handed to Laussat on a silver plate. The official party then made its way to the square, where the Spanish flag was taken down and the French Tricolor raised in its stead.

Twenty days later transfer of the Colony to the United States took place. Claiborne, Wilkinson, and Laussat met at the Cabildo, and after conducting ceremonies similar to those of November 30 joined the crowd assembled in the Place d'Armes. After the American troops had arrived the ceremony of the interchange of flags was gone through. Although the Tricolor of France descended without a hitch, the American flag stuck and caused some difficulty in hoisting. A banquet of 450 places, started at three o'clock in the afternoon, was followed by a dance, which ended late the next morning.

New Orleans was as dissatisfied with the transfer to the United States as it had been with retrocession to France. The Creole element of the town, which outnumbered the American residents twelve to one, disliked Claiborne as governor because he knew little concerning their country, people, or language. He surrounded himself with Americans, and the number of them he put in office seemed to the Orleanians to be out of all proportion to their representation. The introduction of new customs, and particularly the use of English as the official language, outraged the town. Insurrectionary placards posted at night, and duels and clashes between Orleanians and Americans in the streets and in ballrooms, added to the bitter feeling, which culminated in a petition to Congress for admission to the Union and the right to elect a governor.

OLD NEW ORLEANS

At this period in its history, New Orleans was still a small town extending about a mile along the turn of the river, from Fort St. Charles to Fort St. Louis. Three suburbs skirted the fossé and the dilapidated palisades of the original city (now the French Quarter); the Faubourg Ste. Marie on the south in the region that is now the commercial section; the Faubourg Trémé on the west above Rampart to the cypress swamps of Bayou St. John; and the Faubourg Marigny on the east below Esplanade, on the lands of Bernard de Marigny. In this entire area there were twelve to fourteen hundred buildings, housing a population of approximately 10,000 – 4000 whites, 2500 free Negroes, and the remainder slaves.

The Place d'Armes (Jackson Square), slightly larger then, opened on the river. Facing the square and the Mississippi stood the most imposing building in town, the twin-towered St. Louis Cathedral. Quite as magnificent was the Principal or Hôtel de Ville (Cabildo) beside the church, back of which stood the Calaboose or prison. Other public buildings were the Ursuline Convent, the Custom House, two hospitals, a barracks, and a government house.

The buildings on Levee (Decatur), Chartres, and Royal Streets were constructed of brick, faced with lime or stucco, and had roofs of tile and slate. Those in the rear were made of cypress with shingle roofs, and were so combustible that an ordinance had to be passed forbidding the further erection of timber buildings. As a precaution against flooding during rainstorms the houses were set on pillars, leaving a kind of cellar on the surface of the ground. Flights of stairs, vestiges of which remain to this day in the Vieux Carré, encroached upon the *banquette*, a sidewalk four or five feet wide, constructed of bricks with a retaining wall of cypress planks.

Visitors to the city at this time were unanimous in their condemnation of the unpaved streets which, though well laid out, were little better than muddy canals. The city blocks were three hundred and twenty feet long; the streets were thirty-seven feet wide and were lined with ditches to carry off the seepage from the levee. Advantage was taken in the construction of the sewerage system of the curious phenomenon of water draining away from the river. Criss-cross ditches, when flooded by means of sluices in the levee, carried the refuse of the town to the swamps and Lake Pontchartrain. The system proved a failure, however, because of the indolence of the garbage men (four carts were detailed for removing filth from the streets), who permitted the conduits to become clogged. As a result, the slop and garbage thrown in the gutters created a stench that was only dispelled by flushing rains. The blocks after a hard rain were completely surrounded by water, and as a consequence came to be called *îlets*. The streets were lighted by means of lanterns hung from hooks attached to corner buildings. They swung in the wind, were put out by rain, and at best afforded poor light. What with the pitfalls, the uneven banquettes, and the detours occasioned by lakes of standing water, walking was an adventure. On more than one occasion high-born ladies went to balls with their skirts lifted high and their party shoes and stockings in their hands.

Fire-fighting must have been a thrilling and terrifying affair. The Dépôt des Pompes (engine house) was located at the Cabildo and housed four engines, twelve dozen buckets, twelve ladders, ten grappling irons and chains, ten gaffs, twelve shovels, twelve pickaxes, and ten sledgehammers. From twelve to twenty-two men served each machine, all volunteers, with an additional company of 'sappers' whose duty it was to tear down buildings if the fire threatened to spread. When a fire broke out it was announced to the town by the watchman who stood on the porch of the St. Louis Cathedral for that purpose. He rang the alarm bell of the church and waved a flag to indicate to the people the direction of the fire. All policemen who could be spared were obliged to aid in the fire-fighting, as were the townspeople met on the way. A reward of fifty dollars to the engine company first reaching the fire encouraged speed.

The police force, which was frequently reorganized in an effort to preserve law and order, continued inadequate, judging from the complaints made to the City Fathers about the numerous pigsties permitted within the city limits, the removal of ground from places reserved for the town, and the reckless driving of Negro cart drivers, who violated the ordinance against standing while driving. Censure was also brought on the City Guard when a murdered man found in the Faubourg Ste. Marie was buried by 'charitable persons' after the police had left him lying in the streets for three days. To improve the efficiency of the force in catching desperados stalking the streets at night a sentry box was placed every four blocks, around which watchmen, carrying swords and lances, were to patrol in the 'greatest silence,' since the noise that they had hitherto made enabled the prowlers to know of their whereabouts.

Two cotton mills and a crude sugar refinery were the main industries of the city. Seafaring craft anchored at the levee near the Place d'Armes, and barges and flatboats from the Mississippi Valley tied up at the Batture, ten steps from Tchoupitoulas Street. Three banks, the first of which opened in 1805 on Royal between Conti and St. Louis Streets (now the Patio Royal), administered to the business needs of New Orleans.

Described by travelers as a Babylon where Creoles, English, Spanish, French, Germans, Italians, and Americans did little else than dance, drink, and gamble, New Orleans soon gained notoriety as a 'wide-open' town. Every sort of entertainment was afforded the citizenry, from bear and bull-baiting to Voodoo rites conducted by the Negroes in Congo Square (now Beauregard Square). In fact, such was the gaiety of New Orleans on Sundays that horrified visitors were wont to think it a 'convenient religion' which, while it administered to the needs of the soul, took care that it did not 'interfere with the more important pleasure of the body.'

The mania for dancing kept a public ball going twice a week during the winter, adults attending one day and children the other. Dancing lasted from seven until 'cock-crowing the next morning.' Quadroon balls, at which ladies of slight color and of extraordinary beauty entertained the *jeunesse dorée* of the town, were gay affairs compared to the sedate balls held by the white women of society. Latin temperament ran high, and swords or pistols were often resorted to when a question of honor arose. Concubinage between whites and blacks was an established custom, but New Orleans 'society' with its roots imbedded in European culture and elegance, ran its course sedate and unperturbed.

In addition to these amusements the general public found entertainment at the French theaters on St. Philip and St. Peter Streets. They were open three times a week, drawing the greatest crowds on Sunday. Their presentations, as they were announced in the newspapers, competed for public favor with exhibitions of elephants and displays of fireworks.

AMERICANS DEVELOP THE CITY

After American annexation numerous Americans, aware of the fortunes to be made in a city so advantageously situated, began to settle in New Orleans. Because of the antipathy of the Creoles, who pictured all Americans as boorish rowdies, the newcomers settled in the Faubourg Ste. Marie on the upstream side of the town in what is now the business section of New Orleans. Here they developed a town quite distinct from the old New Orleans. As time passed and the city began to benefit from unrestricted trade with other States of the Mississippi Valley the two elements merged, and though the Creoles held themselves aloof socially, common civic interests and the leveling effect of commercial intercourse tended to unite the inhabitants.

New Orleans was incorporated February 17, 1805, and the city limits defined.

The municipal government consisted of a mayor, a recorder, a treasurer, and fourteen aldermen. The latter formed a council whose function it was 'to make and pass all by-laws and ordinances for the better government of the affairs of the city corporation.' Free white males, residents of New Orleans for a year, either owners of real estate of five hundred dollars' value or renters paying one hundred dollars a year, were qualified to vote. James Pitot, builder of one of the first cotton presses in New Orleans (corner of Toulouse and Burgundy Streets) succeeded Étienne de Boré as mayor, and on March 4, 1805, the townspeople first exercised their franchise in an election of aldermen.

In the same year the Legislature provided for the establishment of New Orleans' first higher institution of learning, the College of Orleans. Schools in the Colony had been scarce. The Ursuline nuns offered instructions to seventy or eighty young girls and maintained a schoolhouse near the convent where 'female children appeared at certain hours to be gratuitously instructed in writing, reading, and arithmetic.' No mention is made of similar schools for boys; they had to rely, possibly, upon private schools such as that conducted by the Reverend Philander Chase on Tchoupitoulas Street, or that opened at 29 Bienville Street by Francis Hacket, teacher of English, arithmetic, geography, and history. The College of Orleans, which was finally opened in 1811 through a government appropriation of $15,000, had a president and four professors and a curriculum which included Latin, Greek, English, French, Spanish, philosophy, literature, and the sciences. From 1822 to 1825 the college was under the direction of Joseph Lakanal, prominent for his work in reorganizing the French school system under the Directory and Napoleon.

The New Orleans Library Society was incorporated April 19, 1805, when an unlimited number of twenty-five-dollar shares were sold and the first library in New Orleans was established. During the same year, after a vote of the Protestants in the city favored an Episcopal clergyman, the first Protestant church was organized.

Many improvements were made in the town during the next few years. A waterworks carrying water from the Mississippi in wooden conduits laid a foot and a half below the banquettes was installed by Louis Gleise; a Negro chain gang was employed in filling in the streets; sidewalks were built and crossing bridges constructed; and meat markets, notoriously unclean, had their water closets torn down.

As the center of Aaron Burr's filibustering schemes, New Orleans was thrown into a panic in the winter of 1806 when a large flotilla with Burr as its leader was reported descending the Mississippi to use the city as a base in furthering his intention of separating the Western country from the United States or, failing in that, to wrest Mexico from Spain. The banks were to be plundered of $2,000,000 and Louisiana revolutionized.

Great efforts were made to fortify the city against what was said to be a formidable force. The Chamber of Commerce met to consider ways and means of defense, money was subscribed, orders given for organization of the Battalion of Orleans, and volunteers and the militia cavalry ordered out. In the meantime, Burr with sixty to eighty men kept ahead of orders for his arrest until he was stopped at Natchez and held for trial, at news of which the hysteria in New Orleans subsided as quickly as it had been aroused.

The first steamboat to descend the Mississippi River arrived in New Orleans amid great enthusiasm on January 10, 1812. Propulsion by steam solved the problem of upstream navigation, and was the greatest single factor in the rapid growth of New Orleans to a major North American port.

Louisiana was admitted to the Union April 30, 1812. New Orleans, then the capital of the State, had a population of 24,552 in 1810, having more than doubled its population in the first decade of the nineteenth century. This increase was caused largely by the immigration of refugees from Santo Domingo; almost six thousand arrived in two months in 1809. The city, hard pressed at first to find room for the immigrants, absorbed them in the course of time. Gay and luxury-loving, they infused a new spirit into the town and tended to offset the American influence then beginning to be felt.

REDCOATS STRIKE AT THE CITY

In the last year of the War of 1812 New Orleans became the objective of an attempted British invasion of the Mississippi Valley. Throughout the war an attack had been anticipated, but it was not until after the sack of Washington that the British turned their attention to the Gulf. The Spanish port of Pensacola was used as a base, from which a campaign was conducted against General Andrew Jackson. The Lafitte brothers, Pierre and Jean, who had built up a lucrative privateering business at Barataria, were invited to join forces with the British. Although the British offered him rank as captain and protection for his buccaneering enterprises, Jean Lafitte rejected the offer, but, feigning acceptance, sent the letters of the English official to Governor Claiborne, along with an offer of aid in the defense of New Orleans. The 'hellish banditti,' with whom Jackson was loath to associate, later acquitted themselves bravely during the Battle of New Orleans.

Jackson and his troops arrived in New Orleans on December 2, 1814, six days after General Sir Edward Pakenham had left Jamaica with his fleet and the pick of Wellington's Peninsular veterans. Immediate preparations were made for the defense of a town which looked to the future with 'distrust and gloomy apprehension,' in which banks because of lack of specie had suspended payment on notes for several months, and which hoped to be saved 'only by miracle.' The outlying forts at Chef Menteur, the Rigolets, and along the river were inspected and reconditioned; the coastal bayous were ordered to be blocked against the British ascent.

The enemy arrived at Chandeleur Island December 10, 1814. Since Lake Borgne was too shallow to permit the frigates to land troops, a transfer was made to small boats. An engagement for the control of the waterway occurred on December 14, in which the British with forty-five open boats manned by twelve hundred men defeated five American gun boats detailed for scouting purposes in Lake Borgne. During the following week, while two British officers succeeded with the help of some Spanish fishermen in reconnoitering Bayou Bienvenue as far as the Villeré Plantation, seven miles below New Orleans, seven thousand troops were transferred to the mainland.

News of the defeat on Lake Borgne excited feverish activity in the city. Jackson assumed dictatorial powers and declared martial law. Lafitte's men were enlisted and messengers were sent to hurry Carroll and Thomas with their detachments of Tennessee and Mississippi volunteers; Coffee and his men, who had been sent to Baton Rouge, were ordered to advance by forced marches. Great patriotic fervor swept the town; the *Marseillaise*, *Yankee Doodle*, and *Chant du Départ* rang through the streets, as men of many nationalities white, black, and Indian prepared to repulse the redcoats who were coming from no one knew what direction.

At noon, December 23, 1814, the vanguard of the British army succeeded in advancing unseen, via Bayou Bienvenue, as far as the Villeré Plantation, where Major Villeré and the militia under his command were captured. While the British set up camp and brought up troops from the fleet at anchor in Lake Borgne, General Andrew Jackson, having been notified of the strength and position of the invaders, mobilized his men and drew up plans for an immediate attack. The war-schooner 'Carolina' was to anchor off of the levee close to the enemy encampment and give the signal for a general attack by pouring a broadside of hot shot at the British. Coffee and his Tennesseans, who had previously marched 120 miles in two days, were to move through the cypress swamps and fall upon the British flank and rear, while Jackson and his regulars, Plauché's city volunteers, who ran all the way to New Orleans from Fort St. John (now commemorated in the Jackson Day Run), d'Aquin's colored battalion, McRea's marines, and eighteen Choctaw Indians were to strike along the river.

At 7:30 P.M. the 'Carolina' sidled up to the levee and opened fire upon the unsuspecting British as they were cooking supper and preparing their bivouacs. Confusion reigned as the redcoats put out their fires and ran for shelter behind a secondary levee. Simultaneously, Jackson and Coffee advanced to the attack. In the hand-to-hand combat in the dark, in which bayonets, tomahawks, hunting knives, and fists were used to advantage, the Tennesseans made murderous inroads on the British right flank, although Jackson's charge was met with stubborn resistance. After two hours' fighting a heavy fog terminated the battle, neither side having gained any decisive advantage.

The American forces retreated two miles toward New Orleans during the night and established a breastwork on an abandoned canal between Chalmette and Rodriguez Plantations. During the following week, while the intervening area was flooded by a break in the levee to impede an advance by the enemy, eight batteries were erected and preparations made for the British attack. The army under Jackson consisted of about five thousand men made up of volunteers, free Negroes, Choctaw Indians, Baratarians, and volunteers from Tennessee, Kentucky, and Mississippi. This motley crew, as strange a force as ever served under one flag, was expected to withstand the assault of between eight and nine thousand British veterans.

The British, with Pakenham now at their head, brought up more troops and artillery. On January 1, in an effort to open breaches in the American fortifications, twenty-four English guns began a steady fire upon the entire extent of Jackson's line. The Americans, with twelve or thirteen guns, replied with enthusiasm. Round after round rattled down the breastwork from the river to the swamp as the defenders of the city manned their batteries in the manner that had won for Americans the reputation of being the best artillerymen of their day. So steady were their rounds of fire and so deadly their aim that within an hour the fire of the enemy was broken. By three o'clock in the afternoon the British ceased firing and abandoned their guns, conceding victory to Jackson's men, among whom none handled their guns better than You and Béluche, battle-scarred members of the Barataria brigade.

Pakenham now elected to wait for reinforcements to come up from his fleet. Jackson benefited little by the delay, for although two thousand Kentuckians arrived, few could be put into service due to a shortage of guns and equipment. While rumors circulated to the effect that New Orleans was to be burned to the ground in the event of defeat, or was to be surrendered to the British by the city officials who were unduly alarmed by the reputed watchword of the enemy, 'Beauty and Booty,' preparations went ahead for a major encounter.

THE BATTLE OF NEW ORLEANS

Had there been faster means of communication in those days, news of the signing of peace at Ghent, December 24, 1814, would have been received to lift the siege and avert the battle of January 8. As it was, the morning broke with the roar of cannon and the orderly advance of the British main army. Preceded by showers of Congreve rockets, the British, carrying scaling ladders, advanced with precision and arrogant slowness. The main attack was directed to the American left near the cypress swamp, where Generals Carroll, Adair, and Coffee were stationed with their 'dirty shirts,' as the British called the riflemen from Kentucky and Tennessee. Grape and canister were poured into the ranks of the oncoming redcoats, while the backwoodsmen, unabashed by either the elegance or the reputation of the veterans who had harassed Napoleon, cut great swaths in the enemy line. Standing knee-deep in mud and water, these bedraggled, tobacco-chewing mountaineers handled their 'shootin' irons' with great precision and devastating efficiency. British reserves came up to keep the line intact, but the advance was checked short of the breastwork, the British retreating from the hail of fire that crackled across the plain. Pakenham, in an attempt to rally his men, was shot from his horse and carried to the rear, mortally wounded. A second rally was effected but was completely routed, only a few valiant British meeting death at the American breastwork. By 8:30 in the morning the enemy was entirely defeated, and retreated, leaving the field covered with dead and wounded. Thirteen of Jackson's men were killed, 30 wounded, and 19 missing, as compared to the British casualties of 700 killed, 1400 wounded, and 500 missing.

The Americans kept up a ceaseless artillery fire until January 17, when the British retired to their fleet, leaving the Americans in possession. The march of the victorious defenders into the town was a triumphant procession.

January 23 was declared a day of Thanksgiving, and an impressive ceremony was given in Jackson's honor in the square now bearing his name. A huge throng gathered to watch him pass under an arch, as girls tossed flowers in his path. A *Te Deum* was sung in the Cathedral, and in the evening the city and suburbs were 'splendidly illuminated.'

THE TOWN BECOMES A METROPOLIS

New Orleans entered upon an era of almost unbroken tranquillity, prosperity, and commercial expansion, which lasted until the Civil War. The value of exports reached nearly $10,000,000 in 1815. After the Fulton-Livingston monopoly of Mississippi steamboat traffic had been declared null and void by the United States Supreme Court, steamboats multiplied rapidly, and increased from 21 in 1814 to 989 in 1830. As the steamboat became an accepted fact, trade along the entire extent of the Mississippi increased, and New Orleans began to vie with New York as an important port for European commerce. The levees at New Orleans were piled high with merchandise, and thousands of dock-hands unloaded steamboats to transfer the cargo to ships which carried the produce of the valley to ports all over the world. Cotton, tobacco, grain, and meat came down the river in enormous quantities, as sugar, coffee, and European manufactures went back to the pioneer homes of the new settlements.

As commerce grew, the city rapidly expanded. The American Quarter came into its own and was recognized as a very definite factor in the city's growth. Tchoupitoulas Road, near Canal Street, was by now an important commercial center. Under Samuel J. Peters, James H. Caldwell, and William H. Sparks the suburbs beyond what is now Howard Avenue were developed, and rural homes, dairies, orchards, and farms grew closer together as the region took on an urban aspect. Below Esplanade Avenue the Marigny Plantation was being developed as a suburb, while beyond Rampart Street along the Bayou Road numerous homes were being erected.

Immigration of gamblers, criminals, and riffraff from all over the world, lured to New Orleans because of its reputation as a lawless river town, brought on an acute crime problem, and the city's first criminal court was established to cope with the situation in 1817. A custom of the time for the preservation of peace – one which lasted for many years – was the sounding of the curfew nightly. A cannon was fired at 8 and at 9 P.M. to warn those who were out without permission to return to their homes, and sailors to return to their ships. A special pass issued by a respected merchant or employer was required of those wishing to be on the streets after curfew. At nine o'clock most of the taverns and shops closed their doors, although some of the better hotels or taverns, by virtue of their position, were not restricted by the curfew.

In March, 1818, the first steam waterworks was completed. Located on the levee near the French Market, it supplied water for both drinking and general use. Prior to its being put into operation, most of the drinking water taken from the Mississippi had been peddled through the streets at a picayune (about 6$\frac{1}{4}$ ¢) for four bucketfuls.

In 1821 the city was excited by a rumor that an expedition was being fitted out under Dominique You with the intention of rescuing Napoleon Bonaparte from St. Helena. Ever since Napoleon's incarceration on the island, certain French citizens in the city had been interested in a plan to bring him to New Orleans. Nicholas Girod, mayor from 1812 to 1815, offered his house at the corner of Chartres and St. Louis Streets as a refuge for the former emperor, and legend has it that he had a boat built and provisioned for the rescue. Three days before sailing word was received that Napoleon had died, and the expedition was abandoned. Legend persists in investing at least two houses on Chartres Street with importance as being possible homes of Napoleon Bonaparte.

Because of the French-speaking population, theaters had limited their offerings to that language. An English actor by the name of James H. Caldwell presented, in 1820, the first English play to be staged in New Orleans. His success was so great that in 1822 he laid the cornerstone of the 'American Theater' on Camp Street between Gravier and Poydras, the first building of any pretension to be constructed in the American Quarter. With the opening of this theater in 1823 New Orleans was introduced to illuminating gas.

Within the next few years many civic improvements took place. Two hundred and fifty street lights were placed in the diagonals of the principal streets in 1821. Each intersection was hung with twelve lanterns, but although street lighting was greatly improved, the old custom of carrying a lantern when going abroad after dark was continued until 1840. A few streets were partly paved, Chartres Street having the distinction of being the only street paved its full length. The first paving in the American Quarter was done when two squares of St. Charles Street were laid with cobblestones and covered with fine gravel. Those streets which were not paved had wooden gutters and sidewalks, swept and kept clean by Negro chain gangs. Trees were planted in the Place d'Armes, along the levee, in Congo Square, and along many of the streets. Sycamores were the principal trees chosen.

Masked balls and street masking became features of the Mardi Gras celebration early in Colonial times. They were continued under the Spanish until the governors suppressed street masking because of rowdyism. Street masking again came into vogue about 1835 and the news papers described a Mardi Gras parade for the first time.

In 1831 the Pontchartrain Railroad was put into operation between New Orleans and Milneburg, a distance of four and a half miles. A financial success from the start, the railroad soon increased its facilities for freight and passengers, and a harbor and a town (Milneburg) were laid out at the lake end of the line.

The city was visited by a terrible epidemic of yellow fever and Asiatic cholera in 1832 and 1833. In the two-year period that the epidemic raged, approximately ten thousand people died.

The Medical College of Louisiana, the forerunner of Tulane University, was founded in 1834, and was opened the following year with sixteen students in attendance. The school grew slowly until it was made the University of Louisiana by legislative act in 1847, and became Tulane University in 1883, after a large bequest was left to it by Paul Tulane.

Ill feeling between the Americans and Creoles was manifested in many ways, more so because the Creoles outnumbered the Americans in the City Council, and as a result received the benefit of Council enactments. This animosity came to a climax in 1836 when a young American was killed in a duel by a Creole. In conformance with the law, the survivor was placed on trial, but was acquitted. The decision was taken by the Americans as an individual insult, and justice was demanded by a mob which surrounded the judge's home. The State, taking heed of the trouble in the city, withdrew the charter and issued another, with the provision that the city be divided into three separate municipalities, to be governed over by an autonomous board of elected aldermen, presided over by a recorder. A fourth board, which was to constitute the City Council, was drafted from the three boards and was presided over by the Mayor. Only those problems which were of common interest to all three municipalities were handled by the City Council. The first municipality embraced the Creole section, the second comprised the American or uptown section, and the third contained the remainder of what is now New Orleans. In 1852, after sixteen years of tripartite government, the city was reunited into a single municipality.

The nationwide panic of 1837 caused a serious disruption of business in New Orleans and threatened to disturb the financial structure of the city. Fourteen banks announced suspension of the payment of specie. In an attempt to improve financial conditions, more money was put into circulation, each municipality issuing its own money, which ranged in denomination from twenty-five cents to four dollars. In the mad scramble for money, which depreciated as rapidly as it was issued, corporations, and even individuals, issued their own money. Depreciation was so great that money had to be carried about in large sacks. Credit was stagnated until 1839, when prosperity returned, and the city again forged ahead.

By 1840 New Orleans, with 102,192 inhabitants, had grown to be the fourth largest city in the United States. Second only to New York as a port, it was contesting with that city for first place. Commerce of that year reached the total of approximately $200,000,000. Imports, which in 1815 had represented 50 per cent of the total commerce when New Orleans was the only port of entry for the upper valley, declined to $33\frac{1}{3}$ per cent by 1840, a diminution attributable to changing trade conditions following the construction of the Erie Canal and the building of railroads from the Atlantic Seaboard to the Middle West. Competition from Eastern seaports for the valley trade became noticeable after 1835, when thousands of tons of produce were moving out of the Ohio country to New York instead of to New Orleans. No impression was made upon the business interests of New Orleans, however, because the continued increase in the population of the Mississippi Valley caused an actual increase in river shipments, notwithstanding the divergence of trade to the East. From 1830 to 1850 railroads were regarded largely as local feeders to river and canal, but after 1850 connections were completed between Chicago and the Atlantic coast and the trade of the Valley began, slowly at first, but with increasing rapidity, to leave the river route. Warning came in 1846, when, for the first time, flour and wheat receipts at Buffalo exceeded those at New Orleans. Little concern was felt in New Orleans at this shift in trade routes, since cotton was becoming more and more the chief economic reliance of the city. By 1850 it accounted for forty-five per cent of the total commerce. Along with the shift to cotton as a commercial staple went the trade in slaves, New Orleans becoming the greatest slave market in the country.

Literature and the arts kept pace with economic and social development, as New Orleans became the cultural center of the South. Opera flourished, theaters attracted European stars, artists abounded, and *bon vivants* thrived in a city which had already become famous for its fast and loose manner of living. Gambling, horse-racing, dueling, steamboat racing, and cock- and dog-fighting, in addition to the magnificence of balls, receptions, and Mardi Gras, made New Orleans, which was even then becoming a winter haven for well-to-do Northerners, a gay metropolis.

A new public-school system was put in effect in 1847, the State providing funds on the basis of educable children ranging in age from 6 to 16 years. In 1848 approximately 7000 children attended the free schools, and by 1860 the number rose to 12,000. After 1850 the public-school system was enlarged to a great extent through the beneficence of John McDonogh.

Yellow fever broke out sporadically in 1852, to reach epidemic proportions in the following summer. At the height of this, the worst epidemic in the history of the city, barrels of tar were burned at the street corners and cannon were fired to purify the atmosphere, a practice which threw the sick into convulsions. Doctors and nurses toiled heroically, and many who might have fled from the city remained behind to volunteer their services. Money was contributed from all parts of the country. After 'Black Day,' August 31, 1853, on which 230 deaths from fever were reported, the plague began to abate. The number of deaths from all causes between June and October is estimated to have exceeded 11,000, yellow fever accounting for 7,189.

The frequency with which yellow fever and cholera epidemics occurred and the abnormally high death rate (said to have been 100 per cent higher in 1849 than that of Boston, New York, Philadelphia, or Charleston) gave New Orleans the reputation of being the graveyard of the Nation. Local pride, which persisted in regarding yellow fever as a 'strangers' disease,' a conception curiously borne out by the fact that very few natives were stricken by the malady (only 87 native-born Orleanians perished in 1853), caused the citizens to minimize the extent of the recurrent scourges, the attitude being taken that denial of its presence was the best cure for fever. Lack of underground sewers, the filthy condition of the streets, and pools of stagnant water, in which mosquitoes bred freely, were contributing factors which, though offset to some extent by quarantine regulations, continued to make yellow fever the greatest peril to the city. Only after the true origin of the disease was determined and efforts were made to control mosquito breeding, was New Orleans made a healthy city.

THE FEDERALS CAPTURE THE CITY

Because it, more than any other city of the South, depended upon slavery and the cotton crop for prosperity, New Orleans had little choice when it became necessary to make a decision on the question of secession – as the cotton States went the city had to follow. The small 'Union Party' was silenced by the tide of circumstances. The much larger 'Co-operationist' group likewise found its efforts futile after South Carolina forced the issue. Citizens of all opinions began preparing themselves for war after the State legislature adopted the ordinance of secession on January 26, 1861. A week later the Custom House and Mint in New Orleans were seized by the State militia.

For more than a year the city saw no fighting. Instead of war there was preparation – enlisting and equipping troops for action on distant fronts. Gold and silver disappeared, and Confederate money became the leading currency. The price of food and clothing rose as the value of money went down. The State had one paper issue, the city another. First there was a lack of currency and then a flood of 'shin-plasters'; merchants issued their own 'money,' in which enterprising liquor dealers took the lead. A joke was current that 'you could pass the label of an olive-oil bottle because it was greasy, smelt bad, and bore an autograph.'

As the port of the Mississippi Valley, and an important source of supplies for the Confederacy, the city became the objective of a Federal offensive in 1862. With the intention of cutting the Confederacy in two by gaining control of New Orleans, a fleet of twenty-five wooden ships and nineteen mortar schooners, under Admiral David G. Farragut, a former citizen of New Orleans, passed through the mouth of the river and opened fire on Forts Jackson and St. Philip below the city.

For five days and nights the unceasing bombardment continued from the mortar schooners situated at a bend in the river two miles below the forts. Although great damage was done to the forts, they continued firing, and Farragut, overruling his staff, decided to attempt a passage with his war vessels. At 2 A.M. on the morning of April 24, 1862, while the mortar schooners poured bombs into the fortifications, seventeen ships in three divisions began the hazardous ascent. Lack of fire-rafts, and the ease with which the great chain stretching across the river was broken, permitted the fleet to slip by. As the ships passed they poured broadside after broadside into the forts, which replied ineffectually. The Confederate boats in the river made a heroic effort to stay the advance, but the Federal armada was not to be stopped.

After passing the fortifications at Chalmette without much difficulty, Farragut arrived at New Orleans in a pouring rain on April 25. Since General Lovell and his 3000 men had been dispatched elsewhere, the Federal forces had only the half-armed citizenry to fear. The city authorities refused to surrender, and Farragut threatened to open a bombardment, an act he was reluctant to perform. Crowds gathered in the streets shouting that they had been betrayed, and milled about in futile rage, committing senseless acts of violence. Cotton was tumbled out on the levees and set on fire, and ships lying at anchor were cut loose to drift down the river in flames.

On May 1, General Butler's troops marched into the city and assumed command. The municipal authorities were removed from office and Federal officers appointed in their place. The hand of a stern ruler was felt throughout the city. In an attempt to restrain any manifestation of the people against the Federal occupation a woman was sentenced to two years on Ship Island under Negro guards for laughing during the funeral of a Federal officer, and a man was given the same punishment for displaying a skeleton as that of a Union soldier. William Mumford, who had removed the United States flag from the Mint before the city had been surrendered, was tried by court-martial and hanged. Under the 'Woman's Order' (No. 28), any woman who might 'by word, gesture, or movement show contempt for any officer or soldier' was to be treated as a 'woman of the town plying her vocation.' Special taxes were levied against those who had aided the Confederacy, and soldiers were sent to search the houses of citizens for arms; any slave offering information against his master in this respect was freed. All persons over eighteen years of age were required to take an oath of allegiance to the Federal Government or surrender their property and leave the city.

Such acts, whatever may have been their justification, aroused the resentment of the whole Confederacy and led President Davis to decree that General Butler, should he be captured, was to be treated as an outlaw and hanged. Popular opinion in France and England was also affected, and pressure brought to bear in Washington was influential in bringing about General Butler's removal. He was succeeded by General Banks, who was more moderate in attitude. Under his direction a Union Government was formed for the State.

THE CITY RECONSTRUCTED

The years between 1865 and 1877 were the blackest in the history of New Orleans. It was a period of violence, lawlessness, political agitation, and corruption. Politics, as the order of the day, colored and shaped every activity. Returning Confederate soldiers found Unionists in charge of all civic affairs. Negroes, bewildered by their new liberties and constituting a threatening problem to the whites, crowded the city under the protection of the Freedmen's Bureau. Northern fortune-hunters – derisively called 'Carpetbaggers' – were coming into the city daily and were fast taking possession of commercial as well as political vantage points. The Southerners, however, earnestly went to work to repair their shattered fortunes and regain their former place in the community. This they did successfully, in spite of poverty and dispossession. The Unionists fearing a return of the Southerners to power, and the Carpetbaggers fearing that they might be ousted, took action which resulted in the 'massacre' of July 30, 1866, at the Mechanics' Institute, in which four white men and forty-four Negroes were killed and over one hundred and sixty others wounded. The Reconstruction Acts and the Fifteenth Amendment soon followed, and New Orleans became a city occupied by Federal troops under the ruthless control of General Phil Sheridan.

City and State affairs were closely allied during the Reconstruction Period. During the War the City Hall had been the State Capitol, which was next moved to the Mechanics' Institute on Dryades Street, and then to the old St. Louis Hotel, in 1872. The Democrats managed to retain control of the city government, although the State became Republican with the election of Governor Warmoth in 1868. This control was soon taken from them by a new city charter establishing an administrative form of government and providing for the appointment by the

Governor of all officials.

The city was slow in recovering its former commercial advantages. Successive crop failures, as well as the increased advantage held by the Northern railroads, kept down the volume of commerce. River trade revived slowly but never again became what it was in ante-bellum days. Only one railroad – the Jackson Road, afterwards the Illinois Central – connected the city with the outside world. The extravagance of the city and State governments caused the bonded debt of the city to pile up rapidly. Tax collections were increasingly bad because of business conditions. Real-estate values declined steadily, and empty stores were to be seen in every block. Work and money were scarce, and floods of local paper money complicated the situation. White people were compelled to adjust themselves to the strange experience of living under Negro officials and Negro police, and were also required to associate with them on an equal footing in restaurants, railroad cars, and schools. It cannot be said that the white population adjusted itself very gracefully to these conditions; it practically abandoned the public schools to the Negroes, education receiving a setback that required years to remedy.

The political situation went steadily from bad to worse. The Republicans began fighting among themselves because Governor Warmoth proved too moderate to please their aims. Fights, often resulting in fatalities, occurred at every election. Administrations were installed and ousted at the City Hall by military edict regardless of election results, while crowds milled about in Lafayette Square. Voting was an adventure surrounded with menacing dangers; getting the vote counted was quite as bad. Gambling houses and low dives ran wide open on the main streets, and to walk through the streets at night was to invite trouble. Dan Byerly, manager of the *Bulletin*, met ex-Governor Warmoth on Canal Street one day and attacked him with a cane. Warmoth clinched, and in the resulting fight stabbed Byerly to death. Violence and robbery were daily occurrences, and the city seemed doomed and hopeless.

The Crescent White League, an organization military in character, was formed in June, 1874, for the defense of white rights against Negro aggression. A call was issued for a gathering of citizens at the Clay Statue on Canal Street on the morning of September 14, 1874, where plans were made to take possession of the city and State governments, thus once and for all breaking the power of the Metropolitan Police. The crowd dispersed to reassemble in the afternoon with arms and equipment at their headquarters at Camp and Poydras Streets. General Longstreet stationed his Metropolitan Police at vantage points in JacksonSquare and around the Custom House, the main body taking position under General Badger at the head of Canal Street. Governor Kellogg sought safety in the Custom House, where a company of United States soldiers was quartered.

The White League forces formed in Poydras Street, and a large body under General Behan advanced down the levee at four o'clock. General Badger saw them coming and opened artillery fire. Having no artillery of their own, the White Leaguers charged and in a few minutes cleared Canal Street of Metropolitan Police. The White Leaguers swept on around the Custom House and drove the police back to Jackson Square. Both sides remained armed during the night, and in the morning the police surrendered the State House, Arsenal, and Jackson Square. The White Leaguers suffered twenty-one killed and nineteen wounded; the Kellogg forces, eleven killed and sixty wounded. Liberty Monument, around which the street-cars turn at the foot of Canal Street, marksthe site of the battle and commemorates the valor of those who fought in it.

Victory was short-lived, and although Lieutenant-Governor Penn was installed in the State House by jubilant citizens on the afternoon of the fifteenth, President Grant immediately sent reinforcements and demanded the reinstatement of Kellogg without delay. Governor McEnery promptly complied upon his return to the city on September 17. The full fruits of victory were not enjoyed by the White Leaguers until two years later, when on April 24, 1877, Governor Francis T. Nicholls was given possession of the State House (the act is said to have been the result of Louisiana's casting of the deciding electoral votes in Hayes's favor), and the carpetbag politicians were deprived of power and removed to other fields of action. The White League was then disbanded.

GROWTH OF THE CITY

After the Civil War the city boundaries expanded rapidly. The city of Lafayette had been absorbed in 1852, and Algiers and Jefferson City were annexed in 1870 as the fifth and sixth districts; two years later Carrollton became the seventh district, rounding out the present boundaries of the city and parish.

The Faubourg Ste. Marie extended at first only to Delord Street (Howard Avenue), but soon reached Felicity Road. The city of Lafayette began at Felicity Road and extended to Toledano Street, from which line Jefferson City extended to Upperline Street. Several plantations, including the present Audubon Park, lay between Jefferson City and Carrollton, which began at Lowerline Street. These boundaries included many smaller communities such as Hurstville, Greenville, and Burthville.

The city developed much more slowly toward the lake because the swamp had to be cleared and drained. Bayou Road led to the old French settlements on Bayou St. John near the present head of Esplanade Avenue. Faubourg Trémé developed back of Congo Square in the 1830's, and the building of the Pontchartrain Railroad in 1831 developed Elysian Fields Avenue and Milneburg. There was also a road along Bayou St. John to Spanish Fort. In the 1840's Common Street was the chief road to the cemeteries and Metairie Race Track. A bridge crossed the New Basin Canal at this point and a shell road, a favorite 'speedway,' led to Lake End (now West End). Until about 1858 Canal Street still had an old plank-covered canal from Claiborne on, and was slow in developing.

The present thickly settled Dryades Market section was a swamp with a dirty shallow lake called Gormley's Basin until about 1870. All of the residential sections of the city beyond Claiborne Avenue, with the above exceptions, were swamp tracts and dairy farms until the drain age system was built and their development began – about 1900.

In 1878 the city was again visited by its ancient and devastating scourge – yellow fever. Panic ensued as thousands of inhabitants left the city for the Gulf Coast.

The mortality rate among children was pitiable – in one block there were 105 cases, with an average of five deaths per day. In all more than 3800 people died.

After five years of brilliant effort, in 1879 Captain James B. Eads succeeded in overcoming the greatest single obstacle in the commercial development of New Orleans – shallow water at the mouth of the Mississippi. A depth of from twenty-six to thirty feet was secured by a system of jetties which forced the current to deepen its channels and carry the silt out into the Gulf of Mexico. Incidentally, this was accomplished along lines similar to those proposed by Adrien de Pauger more than one hundred and fifty years before.

After the jetties proved successful, railroad expansion began. Legislative franchises for railroads being obtained, new lines were constructed. Rates favored the railroads, and the steamboat business, although active and important up to the Spanish-American War, steadily declined. Five large trunk lines entered New Orleans by 1880, and a new era in the commercial development of the city began. The volume of railroad business increased from 937,634 tons in 1880 to 5,500,000 tons in 1899.

In 1882 Canal Street was illuminated by electric lights. Royal Street came next in 1884, while the system was extended to include practically the entire city in 1886.

In 1884 and 1885 the Cotton Centennial Exposition, popularly called the 'World's Fair' was held in New Orleans on the present site of Audubon Park. Hundreds of thousands of visitors were drawn to the city. The Exposition did much to bring about a better understanding between the North and South, and gave an added impetus to the city's fast recovering commerce.

In 1892 the first electric street-car was operated along St. Charles Avenue. Within a year or so several electric lines were in service, supplanting the horse cars which had been used for years.

The legislature of 1868, which was made up almost entirely of carpet baggers, had granted a twenty-five-year charter to the Louisiana Lottery, in exchange for a yearly payment of $40,000 to the New Orleans Charity Hospital. Renewal of this charter became a major political issue. It was felt that the proposed fee of $1,000,000, to be paid to the State annually was not sufficient for the privileges of running what was generally conceded to be a 'gold mine,' to which the company replied that 93 percent of its revenue was drawn from sources outside of Louisiana. An article granting the company a three-year lease was put into the State Constitution in 1892, but the lottery was definitely outlawed by both the Federal and State Governments in 1895, after which it operated in Honduras as the Honduras Lottery Company.

Between 1890 and 1895 a semi-private organization called the Sewerage and Drainage Company undertook the construction and operation of the city's first extensive system of sewage disposal. The company went into receivership in 1895, however, and that important phase of public improvement lagged for several years.

DEVELOPMENT IN THE TWENTIETH CENTURY

The birth of the twentieth century marked the start of an era of prosperity and municipal development for New Orleans. The Federal census of 1900 disclosed a population of 287,104; one hundred years of growth had seen the number of the city's inhabitants increase by more than 2800 per cent. Total commerce in 1900 was valued at $430,724,621. Many changes were in evidence: the river passes had been brought under control; the steamboat had yielded first place to the railroad, the bulk of all freight now arriving in New Orleans by rail; export shipments were carried mainly in foreign ships; and a large proportion of freight was delivered directly to the steamship side and reshipped without the necessity of the old style of rehandling on the levee.

Along with commercial and industrial expansion came labor disputes and serious strikes. In 1902 there occurred a violent dispute between the various street-car companies operating in the city and their employees. The trouble was brought about through the introduction of a larger type of car and a change in schedule which enabled the companies to dispose of a large number of men. The street-car men, interpreting the action as a direct violation of a previous agreement, walked out on strike on September 27, demanding that the discharged men be returned to their jobs, the working day be reduced to eight hours, and an hourly wage of twenty-five cents be paid. In the fifteen-day strike that ensued, public sympathy was, for the most part, on the side of the strikers. Using buggies, wagons, automobiles, and improvised vehicles, the citizens boycotted the street-cars. No violence occurred until October 8, when the companies attempted to run four cars under police guard with strike-breakers imported from the Middle West. Strikers attacked the cars at Galvez and Canal Streets and quickly put them out of commission, several men being injured in the disturbance. Street-car service was finally resumed with the work day fixed at ten hours, the hourly wage at twenty cents, and only such men as were necessary to operate the larger cars taken back into the company.

Another serious strike occurred in 1907, when 8000 dockworkers walked out on a strike which began when 'screwmen' demanded that the stowage of 160 bales of cotton should constitute a day's work for which they should be paid six dollars instead of the old pay of five dollars for the stowage of 250 bales. Numbers of strike-breakers were imported from outside cities. However, a few concessions were won by the strikers.

The year 1907 saw the completion of the magnificent publicly owned water purification and pumping plant which still serves the city. In 1908 another important step in municipal ownership was taken when the New Orleans Public Belt Railroad was constructed. Efficient and economical operation soon effected material reductions in former excessive switching and handling charges. Two large girls' schools, the Sophie B. Wright and John McDonogh High Schools, were built in 1911, costing $195,777 and $188,037 respectively. Crowded conditions which had prevailed for some time were greatly relieved. Warren Easton High School for boys was completed in 1913, at a cost of $311,000.

Radical changes were made in the form of the city government in 1912. The aldermanic system was done away with and the commission form instituted.

A tropical hurricane of great intensity struck the city and vicinity on September 29, 1915. The wind attained a speed of from 80 to 110 miles per hour, while 8.36 inches of rain fell within 21 hours. The waters of Lake Pontchartrain overflowed into the city. During the succeeding fifteen days more than twenty-two inches of rain fell, seriously handicapping the drainage and sewerage systems. Property damage ran into the millions and scores were injured, but only one person was killed.

Shortly after the United States entered the World War several important military camps were established in New Orleans. The largest of these was located on the site of the old City Park racetrack, where thousands of soldiers were quartered and trained. Various civic organizations led the citizenry in a patriotic and full-hearted response to the Government's appeal for money and military supplies. The influenza epidemic of 1918 and 1919 was at its height when the Armistice was signed. Thousands were stricken – at times the death toll reached one hundred daily.

In 1921 the New Orleans Inner-Harbor Navigation Canal, connecting Lake Pontchartrain with the Mississippi River, was completed at a cost approximating $20,000,000. This waterway is now an important link in the intracoastal canal system.

HUEY P. LONG

As the center of many activities of the late Huey P. Long, former governor (1928-1932) and United States Senator (1932-1935), New Orleans witnessed the rise and tragic fall of perhaps its most colorful citizen since Bernardo de Galvez. Soon after being elected governor, he built up one of the most powerful political machines in the history of the United States, and in the face of almost incredible obstacles was enabled, by pure force of personality, to put over much of his somewhat radical program. His endorsement of a candidate for local or state posi tions was tantamount to election, and his power over the State legislature made it possible for him to secure passage of his entire legislative program.

His career as virtual dictator of Louisiana was marked by extremely bitter political strife. On one occasion (August, 1934) the militia had to be called out to prevent the seizure of the Orleans Parish registration office by a rival faction headed by Mayor T. Semmes Walmsley, who employed a hundred special policemen to hold his position. For weeks the public was treated to the sight of militia and police, both heavily armed with rifles and machine guns, swarming about the registration office and the City Hall opposite. To enliven the opéra bouffe, radical groups of the city staged a demonstration of unemployed in Lafayette Square, demanding that the thousands of dollars being expended daily in political buffoonery be used to relieve unemployment. Long was finally victorious, and the registration office was reopened under his supervision.

To Long, who was assassinated in Baton Rouge September 8, 1935, New Orleans is indebted in a large measure for its extremely modern Shushan Airport, extensive lake-front development, magnificent Huey P. Long Bridge, enlarged Charity Hospital, the Louisiana State University Medical Center, and free school books in the public schools.

THE OLD AND THE NEW DEAL

In common with other cities throughout the country, New Orleans suffered from the unprecedented economic depression following 1929. Until 1933 the city and State governments struggled to relieve the suffering incident to wholesale unemployment. Social and welfare agencies were overtaxed, and the problem facing the people was greater than the local government could meet. Upon President Franklin D. Roosevelt's inauguration, prompt and efficient measures were taken to relieve the situation and various 'New Deal 'agencies (C.W.A., E.R.A., F.E.R.A., W.P.A., and P.W.A.) were set up to carry on the work of relief. Among the improvements undertaken in the city were the preservation and restoration of some of the fine old buildings in the Vieux Carré, extension of the lake-front development, remodeling of the French Market, extensive street paving, and beautification of parkways and parks.

OUT OF THE PAST

FORT PIKE

WHITEWASHING THE TOMBS FOR ALL SAINTS' DAY

LAFITTE BLACKSMITH SHOP

'NAPOLEON HOUSE,' RESIDENCE OF MAYOR GIROD

THE OLD URSULINE CONVENT

TOMBS REFLECTED IN THE LAGOON, METAIRIE CEMETERY

'SIEUR DE BIENVILLE

THE BARONESS PONTALBA

ANTIQUE SHOPS, ROYAL STREET

THE FORSYTH HOUSE WHERE JEFFERSON DAVIS DIED

THE ORLÉANS CLUB

MARGARET'S STATUE

OLD ST. LOUIS CEMETERY

GOVERNMENT

THE city of New Orleans received its first charter under the American régime from the legislature of the Territory of Orleans, in 1805. Since then the charter has been revised many times. The last important revision was in 1912, when the system of government was changed from the 'aldermanic' to the 'commission' form. Since the boundaries of the city and Orleans Parish are identical there is some duplication of activity with the various city and parish agencies, though not so much as might be supposed. An analysis of the present city charter reveals a definite decentralization of authority – no official has complete freedom ofaction.

The city is divided into seven municipal districts and seventeen wards. Under the present 'commission' plan, a mayor and four commissioners are elected every four years, and constitute the Commission Council, the city's legislative body.

The five principal city departments, presided over by the Mayor and four commissioners, at the historic City Hall, 543 St. Charles Street, are as follows:

(1) Department of Public Affairs, presided over by the Mayor, has charge of the city's legal affairs, civil service, and publicity.

(2) Department of Public Finance, directed by the Commissioner of Finance, controls receipts, expenditures, assessments, and accounts.

(3) Department of Public Safety, presided over by the Commissioner of Public Safety, supervises the police, fire, and health departments and has charge of municipal charity and relief agencies.

(4) Department of Public Utilities, directed by the Commissioner of Public Utilities, supervises the franchising and control of utilities corporations.

(5) Department of Public Property, directed by the Commissioner of Public Property, has charge of all public property – streets, parks, playgrounds, buildings, etc.

In addition several major activities are handled by independent boards and commissions such as the Sewerage and Water Board, Public Belt Railroad Commission, Orleans Parish School Board, Board of Liquidation of the City Debt, and a number of smaller commissions such as the Parking, Playground, Public Library, City Park, etc.

The Orleans Levee Board and the Board of Commissioners of the Port of New Orleans (Dock Board) function almost wholly within the city, but are under complete control of the State.

The judicial department of the city is made up of:

Recorder's (Police) Courts (four judges, appointed).

City Courts (civil cases only, four judges, elective).

Juvenile Court (one judge, elective).

Civil District Courts (Orleans Parish constitutes an entire 'district,' five judges, elective).

Criminal District Courts (five judges, elective).

The city seal, in much its present design, dates from February 17, 1805, at which time the Legislative Council of the Territory of Orleans authorized the Mayor of New Orleans to procure and use a seal on all official acts and documents. After the city divided into three separate municipalities in 1836 each subdivision adopted a seal of its own. A common seal, probably that in use today, was adopted with the reunion in 1852 of the municipalities. A description of the seal and an explanation of its symbolism are lacking. Below and partly within the semicircular inscription 'City of New Orleans' an Indian brave and maiden stand on each side of a shield, upon which a recumbent nude figure is shown saluting the sun rising above mountains and sea. Above the shield are twentyfive circularly grouped stars, and below, an alligator.

The official flag of New Orleans, designed by Bernard Barry and Gus Couret and previously accepted by the Citizens' Flag Committee of the Bienville Bicentenary Celebration, was adopted by the Commission Council on February 8, 1918. It consists of a white field embellished with three golden fleur-de-lys; a crimson stripe at the top and a blue at the bottom, each one-seventh of the flag's width, form borders. The flag was dedicated at the City Hall, February 9, 1918, with appropriate ceremonies.

The oleander (*Nerium oleander*) was adopted by the Commission Council of New Orleans, June 6, 1923, as the city's flower. Cuttings of this plant, brought to the city from Havana at the time of the Spanish Domination, were planted in patio gardens after the fires of 1788 and 1794. Since that time oleanders have been prominent among the plants in the city, conspicuously so in the old gardens laid out at Carrollton in 1835, and at West End and Spanish Fort. At present, they are found in the city parks, in private gardens, and along the neutral grounds of many avenues.

RACIAL DISTRIBUTION

THE melting pot has been simmering in New Orleans for over two centuries, and the present-day Orleanian is a composite of many different racial elements. Intermarriage has broken down distinctions and destroyed the boundaries of racial sections. With a few minor exceptions, there are no longer any districts occupied exclusively by one group.

The United States Census of 1930 gives the population of New Orleans as 458,762, of which 327,729 are whites and 129,632 Negroes. The total white foreign-born population is placed at 19,681, and the native whites of foreign or mixed parentage at 65,766, or about one-fourth of the total white population. Of these the predominating racial groups, in the order of their numerical importance, are the Italian, German, Irish, English, Scotch and Scotch-Irish, and the Jewish groups from Russia, Poland, and Austria. Almost every nation of the earth is represented by a few people at least. A census estimate for July 1936 places the population at 482,466.

In the last century the city was divided into racial districts. The Creoles occupied the Vieux Carré and the sections adjoining Esplanade Avenue as far as Bayou St. John. The Americans developed Faubourg Ste. Marie and Lafayette, extending from Canal to Toledano Street. The Germans settled mostly in the Third District, below Esplanade Avenue. The Irish occupied the river-front sections immediately above and below Jackson Avenue, giving to that section the familiar name of 'Irish Channel,' and the district between the New Basin and Canal Street extending out Tulane Avenue as far as Broad Street.

Intermarriage and changes in circumstances resulted in the removal of many from these racial groups into other neighborhoods. Some still live in the old neighborhoods, but their new neighbors are of everyconceivable national mixture.

Some of the Creole families cling to their old quarter, but the Vieux Carré, especially around the French Market, is now an Italian district, and Esplanade Avenue has many non-Creole elements in its population.

The Irish Channel is no longer Irish, and the Germans of the Third District are pretty well scattered. A small Chinese center exists on Tulane Avenue, between Rampart Street and Elk's Place, but the members of the Chinese colony live where their places of business are located. Carondelet Street, from Jackson to Louisiana Avenue, is the street of the Orthodox Jews. A few Filipinos have a center on Dumaine Street near the French Market, and a small colony of Greeks center their activities in the Greek Church at 1222 North Dorgenois Street. The Spanish, French, and Latin-Americans have national clubs, but their homes are to be found in the various residential sections. There are also groups of Scandinavians and Czechs in small centers, but no special settlements.

The Negroes account for more than one-fourth of the entire urban population. While scattered all over the city, they are most numerous in the district between Rampart Street and Claiborne Avenue and Canal Street and Louisiana Avenue. South Rampart, just off Canal, is the largest Negro shopping district. Magnolia Street, between Howard and Jackson Avenues, and the Dryades Market district around Dryades and Felicity Streets, are lively Negro centers. Large settlements are also to be found along the levee above Lowerline Street, on Burgundy Street in the French Quarter, and in the neighborhood of Claiborne Avenue and 33Orleans Street.

CENSUS of 1930

	Foreign-Born Whites	Native Whites of Mixed Parentage
Austrian	314	865
Canadian	468	1,090
Czechoslovakian	85	156
English	1,428	5,498
French	1,838	9,648
German	2,159	15,953
Greek	341	311
Hungarian	53	107
Irish	647	6,115
Italian	6,821	17,190
Lithuanian	12	11
Polish	408	548
Russian	985	1,464
Scandinavian	821	1,181
Spanish	479	1,626
Yugoslavian	130	221
All others	3,171	5,408
Total	20,160	67,392

Total white population 327,729   Total Negro population 129,632

The total population of the city is 458,762. The difference between this figure and the total of whites and Negroes (1401) is apparently represented by other races.

II. ECONOMIC AND SOCIAL DEVELOPMENT

COMMERCE, INDUSTRY, AND LABOR
COMMERCE

FOR the first 150 years of its existence New Orleans was almost wholly a commercial city, and indeed is primarily so today. The first European dream of commercial greatness for Louisiana must have been inspired in 1705, by the arrival in France of daring Canadian voyageurs with fifteen thousand bear and deer skins obtained through barter with the Indians. But New Orleans made negligible progress commercially under France, owing in part to the fact that the colonists were permitted to do business only with that country; to France, New Orleans proved a liability rather than an asset. Although the city fared somewhat better under the Spanish, abortive restrictions confining trade to certain ports of Spain further retarded expansion for many years. During that period there sprang up an extensive illegal traffic with the British, and later with the Americans.

The Colonial Period saw lumber, pitch, tar, rice, indigo, cotton, tobacco, sassafras, fur pelts, and – toward its close – sugar exchanged for slaves and European merchandise; the pelts were obtained from Indians of the Illinois country in exchange for firearms, knives, and brandy; tobacco and lumber from Kentucky pioneers who floated their products down the Ohio and Mississippi Rivers to New Orleans, braving currents, river pirates, and unfriendly Indians.

New Orleans commerce began to make tremendous strides with the lifting of trade restrictions incident to the Louisiana Purchase (1803) and with the advent of the steamboat (1812), which solved the problem of upstream navigation. By 1840 New volume, with cotton, grain, sugar, and slaves forming the bulk of trade. Then, with the increase of east-west traffic via the Erie Canal and the Great Lakes, and the competition of the country's fast-expanding railroad system, the growth of river traffic was arrested. The economic, political, and social chaos of the Civil War and Reconstruction Periods not only hampered progress but resulted in much lost ground; it was not until after the turn of the twentieth century that New Orleans regained its former commercial importance. Today it is one of the leading ports of the nation.

Ships flying the flags of every maritime nation, and a dozen railroad systems play a part in New Orleans vast world commerce. Cotton and lumber are the principal foreign exports, just as they were a century ago; coffee, sugar, vegetable oils, and bananas head the imports.

Commercial Statistics for New Orleans, 1935

Imports	Value	Exports	Value
Coffee	$29,003,347	Cotton (raw)	$75,299,368
Sugar	25,648,466	Lumber and mill work	12,611,541
Vegetable oils	8,525,168	Machinery and parts	10,451,693
Bags and bagging	7,586,569	Tobacco	8,153,731
Bananas and plantains	7,247,950	Cotton manufactures	4,695,266
Sisal and other fiber	4,127,778		

Receipts		Shipments	
Foreign	$110,798,951	Foreign	$156,014,128
Coastwise	124,248,643	Coastwise	126,879,688
Internal	100,218,423	Internal	104,293,420
	$335,266,017		$387,187,236

INDUSTRY

New Orleans' first ventures into industrial fields were in connection with the manufacture of articles such as bricks, tile, boats, and mill work, which – because of their bulk, weight, or other reasons – commanded prohibitive prices when imported from Europe, and for which raw materials were available in Louisiana.

The contempt with which the Creoles viewed manual occupations and the consequent shortage of skilled labor were no small retarding factors in development along industrial lines. Eventually, despite these and other deterrents, an advantageous climate, abundance of raw materials, and the infusion of American enterprise as well as capital resulted in more efficient utilization of the vast natural resources upon which New Orleans could draw. The city may be said not to have entered fully upon its industrial phase until the beginning of the twentieth century.

New Orleans' industrial growth during the past three decades has been due in large part to almost perfect co-ordination of transportation agencies – railroads, coastwise and foreign steamship services, and inland waterways. The expansion has been reflected in diversification rather than specialization.

The city boasts, with perhaps pardonable pride, several industrial 'firsts' and 'seconds': what is said to be the world's largest twine mill and the second largest sugar refinery, as well as the South's largest furniture factory and syrup-canning plant. Eighty per cent of the country's men's washable suits and half its industrial alcohol are manufactured in New Orleans.

In the city are twelve hundred factories, large and small, turning out nine hundred different products with a total annual valuation of $325,000,000; sugar heads the list, pouring $60,000,000 into New Orleans pocketbooks annually, with Celotex, a sugarcane by-product used as a lumber substitute, bringing in an extra $12,000,000; the manufacture of bags, burlap, and cotton textiles, with a yearly value of $17,300,000, is second; next come cottonseed products, $17,000,000; the production of commercial alcohol in a multitude of manufacturing processes, $16,000,000; petroleum products, $12,000,000; baking, $11,000,000; clothing,

$10,000,000; coffee-roasting and packing, $9,000,000; mahogany, $6,000,000; rice milling, and the manufacture of roofing materials and fertilizer are all in the million-dollar class.

These various industries account for little more than half the total: countless lesser industries, individually small but important in the aggregate, bring to New Orleans the remaining $160,700,000.

LABOR

New Orleans was founded on a system of slave labor, and continued so for almost a century and a half. In addition to Negro slaves there were at the first 'redemptioners' – Germans who had voluntarily bound themselves to work for a period of years in payment for their passage to Louisiana and Indian prisoners of war. The lot of the individual slave varied with the character of his master, who though under some legal restraint, tended in practice to be sole ruler. The slaves were prohibited, of course, from open organization for the betterment of their condition.

The whites – predominantly of French and Spanish extraction – looked with disdain upon any mode of gaining a livelihood involving manual effort. And, indeed, in the semi-tropical climate manual labor was particularly arduous.

Following upon the heels of the Louisiana Purchase (1803) skilled workers were attracted to New Orleans from other parts of the United States, and soon set about organizing themselves into trade unions. The first to be formed was a typographical union, in 1810; in 1837 members of this group went on strike for a reduction of the working day from sixteen to twelve hours. Their success gave impetus to the union movement, for in 1838 a carpenters' union was formed and by 1852 nearly all the skilled trades had some form of organization.

Abolition of slavery and the aftermath of social and economic confusion served as temporary setbacks to the union movement. But from the chaos arose the Knights of Labor, the first mass labor movement in New Orleans. Upon its organization, the American Federation of Labor drew much support from the Knights of Labor ranks, eventually displacing it.

The racial problem has proven a difficult one to organized labor, the color line being carefully drawn in some instances, and in others not at all. As early as 1880, particularly among the dock-workers units, mixed unions were admitted to the 'Trades and Labor Assembly,' and today the building trades unions have dual membership, but in the present-day 'Trades and Labor Council' only white delegates are seated. In unions such as the bricklayers', cement finishers', and plasterers', Negro membership is in the majority. The dock-workers have separate divisions for Negro and white members under the same charter.

A number of strikes, both minor and serious, have marked the progress of the labor movement in New Orleans. Among the more serious have been those of the street-car men in 1902, 1920, and 1929; the longshore men in 1907, 1918, 1923, and 1935; and the taxicab drivers in 1927.

Organized labor in New Orleans has instituted and supported much legislation pertaining to factory inspection, safety devices, workingmen's compensation, and other occupational regulatory laws.

There are today 113 unions in New Orleans, embracing virtually every trade, from Trappers' and Fishermen's Local 18408 to Iron Workers Local 58.

TRANSPORTATION

PROBABLY no settlement in America faced fewer difficulties in transportation in Colonial days than New Orleans. Located near the Gulf of Mexico, in a section traversed by dozens of navigable lakes, rivers, and bayous, the pioneer settlers soon developed a network of waterways extending in every direction. On their penetration of the lower Mississippi Valley in 1699 the French found the Indians utilizing Louisiana's countless waterways as the principal means of transportation, and, instead of constructing roads throughout the region, the colonists followed the example set by the natives, thereby gaining a distinct commercial advantage over other settlements along the coast.

From the Indian tribes the French settlers borrowed the idea of the 'pirogue,' or dug-out canoe, building them on an increasingly larger scale until some are said to have had a displacement of 50 tons. To build the pirogues great cottonwood and cypress trees were felled, the logs hollowed by burning, and their exteriors shaped to conform with the basic lines of half a watermelon. While the giant pirogue admirably suited the needs of the French, the scarcity of sufficiently large trees led to the creation of other types of boats. As early as 1700 Iberville ordered the construction of light *bateaux plats*, or flat boats, on which large quantities of buffalo hides, wool, and furs were freighted from various points in the Mississippi Valley down the river to the Gulf of Mexico.

By 1742 the keel boat had come into use. This craft, from sixty to seventy feet long, and with a beam of fifteen to eighteen feet, drew only twenty to thirty inches of water. Near the close of the French Domination the *radeau*, a boat resembling the flatboat, made its appearance, and came to be used extensively for carrying freight on the Mississippi and its tributaries.

Until about the middle of the nineteenth century *radeaux* were used by the settlers of the upper Mississippi Valley as the principal means of transporting hides, corn, wheat, livestock, lumber, and whisky. The levees at New Orleans were lined with these picturesque craft, whose standard signal, indicating that the proprietor was ready to do business, was a bottle of whisky strung up on a pole. Brokers would then make bids for the entire outfit, including the flatboat itself, which was dismantled for its lumber. Everything disposed of, the up-country pioneer usually embarked upon two or three weeks of hard drinking and celebration before beginning the long trek afoot to his Missouri, Illinois, Kentucky, or Tennessee home.

Although there were several kinds of boats in use by the close of the eighteenth century, all were propelled in much the same manner, usually by poles, oars, or sails, both upstream and downstream. Sails exclusively were used whenever possible, but could not be depended upon for a river voyage. Numerous difficulties were encountered in coaxing a clumsy keel or flatboat up a winding river against both wind and current. The time required for a trip from New Orleans to the Illinois country varied from three to four months, but the return trip could be made downstream in twelve or fifteen days. Such voyages were for many years extremely dangerous, savage Indians and white river pirates lurking around every other bend.

As commerce increased the problem of upstream navigation became more and more acute. One attempt was made to propel a boat upstream by means of horses walking a treadmill, but between New Orleans and Natchez several horses were completely broken down, and the idea was abandoned.

The problem was finally solved in January 1812, when the first steam boat ever to be seen on the Mississippi River arrived, amid great excitement, in New Orleans. The boat, with a three-hundred-ton capacity and a low-pressure engine, was built in Pittsburgh for Fulton and Livingston of New York, at a cost of approximately $38,000, and was named the 'Orleans,' in honor of her destination. On her maiden voyage down the Ohio and Mississippi Rivers the banks were lined at times with startled spectators who stared in wonder at the rhythmical puffing of steam and the steady swish of paddles. The 'Orleans' never returned north but was put into regular service between New Orleans and Natchez. Averaging eight miles per hour downstream and three against the current, she continued in service until July 14, 1814. That night as she was lying at anchor in Baton Rouge the river began to fall suddenly and the boat settled upon a snag and sank. The engine was afterwards raised and transferred to another boat.

In 1819 the first mailboat on the Mississippi, the 'Post Boy,' began operating between New Orleans and Louisville. During the next few years improvements and refinements in river steamers steadily increased; the whistle, the gangway, multiple engines, and finally electricity – to illuminate landings, dark channels, and the boats themselves – were added. Large steamboats were in use before the Civil War. Paddlewheels grew to a diameter of forty-five feet, and speed climbed to twenty miles per hour. Packets became floating palaces, featuring a cuisine prepared by skilled chefs, and carrying a full orchestra for the pleasure of their passengers. Travel by steamboat became popular with all classes – planters, business men and their wives, adventurers, prostitutes, and professional gamblers. The golden day of the steamboat was the period from 1830 to 1860. Every year saw a tremendous increase in freight and passenger volume. The average life of a river boat was only four years, but profits were so large that the sinking or burning of a vessel was to the operators a mere incident, and such losses were casually set down to operating cost.

One by one the luxurious packets disappeared. In their wake came towboats with a cargo tonnage equivalent to several hundred carloads of freight. During the

World War the Government began operation of an extensive barge service on the Mississippi and Warrior Rivers. Rate protection against the railroads and completion of the final links in the 'Lakes-to-the-Gulf' inland waterway system have greatly stimulated barge traffic during recent years. It is now possible for a 'tow' of barges to go from New Orleans up the Mississippi River to any point on the Great Lakes, to New York City via the Erie Canal, and to Montreal, Canada, by way of the St. Lawrence River.

Railroads have played almost as important a part in the development of New Orleans as have its facilities for water transportation. One of the first railroads to be completed in America and the first built west of the Alleghenies was established in New Orleans. In 1825 plans for the construction of a four-and-one-half-mile railway extending from New Orleans to Milneburg were discussed in the city, and in 1829 the Pontchartrain Railroad Society was formed.

A number of obstacles lay in the path of the company's directors, few of whom had ever seen a railroad, and none of whom had more than a vague idea of railway construction or operation. To complicate matters there seemed to be no experienced railroad engineer available. Innumerable questions, such as whether the rails used should be of iron or cedar, and whether the newfangled steam engine was as reliable as the less picturesque horse, kept the directors in a quandary. In 1831, after a year of construction, the first train, drawn by horses, was run over the imperfect tracks.

Many other difficulties beset the State's first railway venture. The most serious, perhaps, lay in the tracks, which consisted of strips or bars of iron spiked to 'stringers' or crossties of wood. These rails became known as 'snake-heads,' and constituted a great peril to passengers and crew. The iron strips were wont to free themselves as the train passed over, and turn suddenly upward with sufficient force to pierce the floors of the cars, frightening seated passengers and sometimes throwing the train from the tracks. It is said that whenever the feeble locomotive broke down, the crew would hoist sails and bring the little train gliding into 'port,' its sails flapping in the breeze.

By 1852 additional lines were operating in and out of New Orleans, including the Carrollton Railroad, extending the six-mile stretch between New Orleans and Carrollton, a small community which later became a part of New Orleans. In this year, at a railroad convention held in New Orleans, the organization of large, country-wide lines was approved. By 1880 at least four such major lines were operating in and out of the city, connecting it with various points north and west.

Airplanes made their appearance in New Orleans in the spring of 1910, when an exhibition flight was made at the City Park Race Track by Louis Taulhan. From December 24, 1910, to January 2, 1911, the first international aviation tournament to be held south of New York was conducted in New Orleans at City Park. Eight 'world-famous airmen,' two of whom were killed in crashes, participated in the meet. A record for the mile was set at fifty-seven seconds, and a height of 7125 feet was attained. In each of a series of match races an automobilist driving a Packard defeated aviator John Moisant by a margin of several seconds.

The second official air-mail trip to be successfully completed in the United

States was made between New Orleans and Baton Rouge by George Mestach on April 10, 1912; time, one hour and thirty-two seconds.

The third airline in the country to carry foreign mail was established between New Orleans and Pilottown, at the mouth of the river, in 1923. This route, which provided a late dispatch of mails to connect with outgoing steamships and expedited delivery at New Orleans of mails from incoming ships, was discontinued in 1934.

New Orleans is at present served by two well-lighted airways, by which overnight mail and passenger service is provided to Northern and Eastern cities, and regular daytime service to points west; the lines have terminals at the new Shushan Airport on Lake Pontchartrain. Scheduled flights are also maintained between New Orleans and cities in Mexico, and Central and South America.

New Orleans, the junction of a new modern highway system, serves as the southern terminus of two national highways, US 51 and 61, and is served by east-west US 90. A number of paved State highways, with toll-free bridges, converge at New Orleans. The Pontchartrain Bridge (toll), a 4.78-mile highway bridge, furnishes a short cut across the lake. The Huey P. Long Bridge (toll-free for automobiles and pedestrians), nine miles above the city, is Louisiana's only span across the Mississippi and gives New Orleans an unbroken highway to the West. The city is served by ten trunk-line railroads, and a number of branch lines, which connect it with every important market in North America. Steamships from every quarter enter New Orleans, ninety lines with regular sailings connecting the port with all parts of the world. Five steamship companies maintain regular passenger schedules, and many of the freighters plying in and out the city have passenger accommodations of a sort – coastwise, tropical, and round-the-world. Harbor sightseeing excursions, with trained lecturers, are provided throughout the year out of New Orleans. Two companies operate air-cooled busses between New Orleans and all parts of the country. Street-cars and busses operate between all parts of the city, and ferries connect New Orleans with the west side of the river. Taxicabs are available at all large hotels and railroad and bus terminals, with numerous sub-stations scattered throughout the city.(*See General Information.*)

FOLKWAYS

'R-R-R-R-R-RAMONAY! R-r-r-ramonez la chiminée du haul en bas!' Sleepily you get up, and, pulling something around you, step out on the balcony of your Vieux Carré studio – of course if you live in the Vieux Carré you have a studio, even if your only art is drink-mixing. You rub your eyes and stare at the extraordinary creature who is emitting these blood-curdling noises. He is a tall, unbelievably black Negro with crooked toes peeping out of shuffling shoes, nondescript trousers, a venerable frockcoat carrying the dirt of ages on its frayed threads, and cocked over one eye a stupendous top hat with most of the crown bashed in. He carries an unwieldy bundle containing a rope, a sheaf of broom straw, and several bunches of palmetto. Look at him closely. He is the last of his guild, a chimney sweeper; and it may be a long time before you see him again, for he and his *compère*, the coal peddler, who calls 'Mah mule is white, mah face is black; Ah sells mah coal two bits a sack!' are rapidly being forced to retreat before the increasing popularity of gas heat. *Adieu, ramoneur!*

Across the little iron guard-rail that separates your gallery from the one next door, a pleasant-looking chap wearing a white linen suit puffs a pipe with a philosophic air and surveys the scene below as if it all belonged to him. You crane your neck over the balcony to get a good look at the overflowing bundle of wash which a Negro woman balances on her head as she strides down the street, unconcernedly swinging her arms at her sides. Your neighbor views the sight unmoved. Curiosity gets the best of you. 'Have you been living here long?' you ask.

The coated one turns slowly. 'I've lived here all my life. I'm a Creole.' Possibly you had an idea that a Creole was a man of color. You realize now that this is not true. A Creole ! Well, well, well. You always wondered what Creoles looked like. This one, who is typical, is courteous, but rather distant. He seems to have forgotten all about you.

'How do they do it?'

'What?'

'Those bundles. How do they balance them on their heads?'

'Oh, they ve always done that. They learn it when they are just able to walk.'

In a little while, down the street come the berry men and women. In season, the streets are overrun by them. Men always sell strawberries, women, blackberries, your all-knowing Creole friend says. 'Why?' you ask. Ah, it has always been that way. When you get to know Creoles better, you realize that the phrase 'It has always been that way' justifies everything.

Down the winding staircase you climb with your new friend, who has volunteered to show you around. You are in luck. It appears that besides French, your Creole is fluent in the Negro-French patois, called Gombo, which is so different from standard French as to be unintelligible to any but a native of the city.

A strange character, typical of a class of peddlers which has all but disappeared, rambles into view. You notice that he carries not only a bundle of clothespoles – 'Long, straight clothespole!' – but a bundle of palmetto root fibers – 'Latanier! Latanier! Palmetto root!' Your new friend, addressing him familiarly in Gombo, inquires where he has been, why he should be selling two articles. The old Negro answers, 'Me beezness, it so bad, I gotta eencriss ma stock.' Poor Alphonse! No recovery in sight for you, my friend! People don't scrub their floors with palmetto root any more; and as for clothespoles, the Laundry Syndicate has taken all the business from the black *blanchisseuses* who used to boil the family clothes in an old iron pot, and stir them with a well-worn piece of broomstick.

You get to the corner of Royal and St. Peter Streets just in time to see a 'spasm band' go into action. A 'spasm band' is a miscellaneous collection of a soap box, tin cans, pan tops, nails, drumsticks, and little Negro boys. When mixed in the proper proportions this results in the wildest shuffle dancing, accompanied by a bumping rhythm. You flip them a coin, and they run after you offering to do tricks for '*lagniappe*'; and without waiting your approval, one little boy begins to walk the length of the block on his hands, while another places the crown of his skull on a tin can and spins like a top. '*Lagniappe*,' your Creole explains, is a little gift the tradesmen present to their customers with each purchase. By extension, it means something extra, something for nothing.

'Look out!' suddenly cries your friend, pulling you out of the way just as a tin bucket on the end of a rope dives from a third-story balcony.

'Oop! Excuse me, mister,' cries the housewife on the balcony. 'I just wanted the grocery man to hear the bucket drop so's he'd come out.' The Creole explains that this clever little step-saving device is in common use among people living in third-floor apartments. 'Poun' a coffee,' she calls to the groceryman. You continue on your way resolved to keep your head out of the reach of Vieux Carré housewives tossing their homemade dumb-waiters over iron railings.

Soon there comes down the street a 'snowball wagon.' It is a two wheeled cart, with a canopy top, a bell, and a man who is both proprietor and motive power. In the bottom of the cart is a block of ice, and on each side gaudy syrup bottles. Flavors include strawberry, orange, lime, grape, pineapple, spearmint, and whatever ingenious 'special' the vendor may concoct. A 'snowball' is a lump of shaved ice drenched in one of the colored syrups, and served on a paper plate. Often the grimy-faced little customer requests variegation in his colors, and the effects achieved are startling to any but the trained Sicilian eye. The finished product has come to be regarded as a delicacy in New Orleans. The visitor must remember that real snowballs are seen in the city only once every forty or fifty years.

'Listen,' you tell your Creole friend, 'all that is well and good, and no doubt very interesting in its place; but how about Voodoo? I came all the way to New Orleans to hear about Voodoo, and you talk about the weather. Back to the point, man.'

'*Eh bien,*' says the Creole, heaving a sigh, and turning unwilling feet toward the Negro quarter near Claiborne Street. 'My friend, the Voodoo is a thing which has caused much trouble to us from earliest times. The Voodoo was brought here from Africa by the niggers our ancestors bought as slaves. And let me tell you, my friend, those early colonists, they had to keep a sharp eye out for trickery. Those Voodoo queens, they knew things no white man ever knew. They could make people die, have them buried, and raise them again two weeks or a month later. I know, because my grandfather told me a story that has always been told in our family.

'It seems that on the plantation of one of my ancestors – I forget if it was grandfather's grandfather or his great-grandfather – there was a mulatto woman, *une négresse de toute beauté*, a very beautiful woman, you understand.' Here your Creole's voice drops to a confidential whisper – he is going to take you into his confidence, let you hear one of the most jealously guarded of secrets. Obviously he likes you. 'Enemies of the family even said she was a half-sister of this ancestor who had inherited her from his father. In a duel, he had killed a man who had dared to hint the fact in a cabaret. But to get back to the *mulattresse*, she was a *Mamaloi*, a Voodoo queen, and her power was known up and down the river. One day she came to her master with the sad news that Ti Démon, the six-year-old son of one of the best laborers, had suddenly passed away. Slaves were always dying, it is true, but somehow this death was too sudden to please my ancestor. He asked to have the body brought to the big house, in order that he might see for himself. In the meantime, he sent for the family doctor in the city – the plantation was near where Audubon Park is now, and was quickly reached in a pirogue – who assured him that death, so far as he could see, was from natural causes. With appropriate ceremony, the slaves buried the child, while my ancestor went inside and erased his name from "Assets" and inscribed him under "Profit and Loss."'

'And where,' you interrupt, 'is all this leading?'

'Ah,' the Creole points out, 'that's just it. Two days later my ancestor, having nearly forgotten the incident, happened to think that St. John's Day was not far off. St. John's Eve, you know, is the great festival of the Voodoos. So the old fellow, being of an inquisitive turn of mind, went for a stroll in the most off-hand sort of way at about ten o clock on the festive night, with a sword-cane in his hand and two small double-barreled pistols in his pockets. After floundering about the cypress swamp for a while he noticed the glare of a small fire, and made for it. He heard muffled drums. Climbing a tree, he saw his mulattress in all her regal splendor, poising a cane-knife above a victim, who appeared drugged, but quite obviously alive. On closer inspection the victim proved to be the *négrillon* who had been buried a few days before.'

'That's not very much of a story,' you say. 'I knew how it would come out all the time. But tell me, how did the mulattress do it? And do they still sacrifice children?'

'Ah,' the Creole sighs, answering the last question first, 'if they do, the authorities had better never hear of it. And as for the resurrection, the old Voodoos distilled strange potions from herbs, the lore of which was handed down from their African forbears. They have forgotten most of that now, but they are still clever with hypnotism and allied arts. They really do conjure a person and make him waste away, but it isn't the charm that does it, and most of them know it. The resurrection trick was done with a poison that induced a coma so deep that it exhibited all signs of death, even to cooling of the body and rigor mortis. The 'resurrected' victims' reason is definitely impaired, and if they are allowed to live, have neither will nor intelligence. They are docile, and apparently healthy enough, however. In Haiti, they are the *zombies* you have heard about.'

'Well, now you become a little more interesting, my friend. I'd like to hear more about this.'

But he retires into his shell, a trick all Creoles have, even when speaking to people they like, and you fear you have heard all you will about Voodoo. By this time, you have reached the Negro quarter and have well penetrated it. Occasionally you pass an old crone, sitting on her wellscrubbed stoop, who thoughtfully puffs a corncob pipe and talks to her younger neighbors in Gombo-French. They, of course, answer her in English.

'Look out!' warns your Creole friend, pointing to a doorstep ahead of you. A group of Negroes, apparently helpless, stand around and stare at it. You elbow your way through the crowd. There on the lowest step a white candle burns in the center of a cross made of wet salt. At the end of each arm of the cross a five-cent piece has been placed.

'What is that?' you inquire.

'That's a gris-gris,' he answers in a hushed voice. 'Somebody put that there to bring harm on the people who live in the house. That same harm will befall anyone who touches the charm.'

'You believe in that?' You are amazed that a man, obviously cultured . . .

'No, no, not exactly,' he says reluctantly. Then, suddenly stooping, he picks up the candle, blows it out and throws it into the gutter, flicks the salt off the step, and puts the nickels in his pocket. Whistling off-key, he shoulders his way through the crowd. 'That will buy us a couple of good poor boys.'

'A couple of what?'

'Sandwiches. They're edible. Come along.' You turn a corner and go into a little shop having as a sign a crude picture of a small boy eating a sandwich nearly as large as himself. 'You like roast beef?'

'Yes.'

'Two roast beefs.' In a moment appear before you two large sandwiches made by cutting a twenty-eight-inch loaf of bread in two, then splitting it lengthwise, piling it with sliced roast beef, lettuce, and tomatoes, and drowning the whole in gravy. You are surprised to find them remarkably good, though a trifle unwieldy. Then you realize why they call them 'poor boys.' They cost a dime, and a half of one makes a meal.

RIVER, TOWN, AND SEAPORT

SHIPS OF ALL NATIONS AND ALL TYPES DOCK AT NEW ORLEANS

THE STEAMBOAT 'NATCHEZ' LOADED WITH COTTON BALES

NEW ORLEANS SKY LINE

SHUSHAN AIRPORT

HUEY P. LONG BRIDGE ACROSS THE MISSISSIPPI

THE CRESCENT CITY

PUBLIC GRAIN ELEVATOR ON THE WATER-FRONT

CANAL STREET, SEPARATING THE OLD FROM THE NEW CITY

FERRIES CROSS AND RECROSS THE MISSISSIPPI TO ALGIERS

THE NEW FRENCH MARKET

UNLOADING BANANAS

EVERYONE DRINKS CAFÉ AU LAIT AT THE FRENCH MARKET

COFFEE WHARF, SHOWING FLAGS USED TO ASSORT COFFEE

THE SEA WALL ALONG LAKE PONTCHARTRAIN TOWARD THE BEACH AND AMUSEMENT PARK

NETS HUNG UP TO DRY NEAR LAFITTE

On leaving the sandwich shop, you look at your Creole's face. He seems tobe thinking of things miles distant. You wish he would get started on Voodoo again, but you are afraid to ask. He seems to guess your thought. 'Suppose we go seean old Voodoo woman my colored nurse used to consult when I was a child.' The offer is obviously made from a sense of duty. You protest, butyour Creole must not disappoint you.

You pass many long, narrow little houses on the way. They are one room wide, and seem to stretch back into infinity. 'Shotgun cottages,' your Creole calls them. He says they are so called because all the doors open one behind the other in a straight line. With all doors open, you could fire a gun from front step to backyard wall without leaving a scratch.

The Voodoo woman lives away down on Pauger Street, near where Bagtelle, Great Men, Love, and Good Children Streets used to be. They were named by the gallant wastrel, Bernard de Marigny, when he divided his plantation into building lots in hopes of recouping the fortune lost at 'craps.' You start out on foot, as you always do if you want to see anything in New Orleans. Along the way, you are surprised by the number of freshly scrubbed doorsteps, sprinkled with powdered brick, which you see. Your Creole tells you that powdered brick not only keeps off evil spells, but witches and ghosts as well. Out of a cottage window you are just passing come the strains of an old Creole lullaby, sung in a husky Afro-American contralto. The Creole knows the song, remembers it from his childhood, hums a few bars, and breaks into the words, in the soft Gombo you have been hearing along the way. The song goes something like this:

'Pov piti Lolotte à mouin
Pov piti Lolotte à mouin
Li gagnin bobo, bobo,
Li gagnin doulè.
Pov piti Lolotte à mouin
Pov piti Lolotte à mouin
Li gagnin bobo, Li gagnin doulè.

Calalou poté madrasse, li poté jipon garni;
Calalou poté madrasse, li poté jipon garni.
D'amour quand poté la chaine, adieu courri tout bonheur;
D'amour quand poté la chaine, adieu courri tout bonheur.

> *Chorus:*
> Pov piti Lolotte à mouin,
> Pov piti Lolotte à mouin,
> Li gagnin bobo, bobo,
> Li gagnin doulè, doulè,
> Li gagnin doulè dans ker a li.'

The Voodoo woman, of course, is a disappointment. The Creole never honestly expected she would divulge any of her secrets, but she is very pleasant, and tells you with a flashing smile that '*Zaffaire Cabritt ça pas zaffaire Mouton*' (The goat's business is none of the sheep's concern). The Creole expected that too. But she is quite willing to talk of other things, tells you one of the thousand and one animal tales in Gombo, which your Creole later repeats and translates. He remembers that one, too, from his childhood. And she does tell you where there is a drugstore which does an extensive business in Voodoo paraphernalia, bearing witness to the fact that Voodoo is far from extinct even today. So you head for the Voodoo drugstore, which is in the uptown section, and the Creole gets a chance to repeat the animal tale:

COMPAIR BOUKI ET MACAQUES

Bouki mette di fé en bas so léquipage et fait bouilli dolo ladans pendanteine haire. Quand dolo là té bien chaud Bouki sorti déyors et li commencé batte tambour et hélé macaques yé. Li chanté, li chanté:
Sam-bombel! Sam-bombel tam!
Sam-bombel! Sam-bombel dam!
Macaques yé tendé et yé dit: – Qui ca?
Bouki gaignin quichoge qui bon pou manzé, anon couri, et yé tous parti pou couri chez Bouki. Tan yé té apé galpé, yé té chanté:
Molési, cherguinet, chourvan!
Chéguillé, chourvan!
Quand Bouki oua yé li té si content li frotté so vente. Bouki dit macaques: – Ma lé rentré dans chaudière là, et quan ma dit mo chuite, oté moin. Bouki sauté dans chaudière dans ein piti moment li hélé: – Mochuite, mo chuite, oté moin, et macaques halé li déyors. Quand Bouki té déyors li dit macaques:– Astère cé ouzotte tour rentré dans chaudière. Quand ouzotte va hélé mo chuite ma oté ouzottes. Macaques yé rentré. Dolo là té si chaud, si chaud, sitot yé touché li, ye hélé: Mo chuite, mo chuite. Mais Bouki prend so grand couverti et couvri so chaudière sérré, et tan li tapé ri li dit pove macaques yé: – Si ouzottes té chuite ouzottes té pas capabe dit ouzottes chuites. Quand macaques yé té chuites pou même, Bouki découvri so chaudière. Asteur ein tout piti macaque, qui té dans ein piti coin chapé sans Bouki oua li. Asteur, Bouki assite, et li mangé, mangé jouqua li té lasse. Mais ein jou li fini mangé dernier macaque et li di: Fo mo trappé lotte macaques. Li prend so gros tambour, li couri en haut la garli et li batte, li batte et li chanté:
Sam-bombel! Sam-bombel tam!
Sam-bombel! Sam-bombel dam!
Et macaques commencé vini et apé chanté:
Molési, chériguillé!
Molési, chériguillé, chourvan!
Quand tous macaques yé té là Bouki rentré dans dolo chaud qui té dans chaudière, et dit: – Quand ma dit: Mo chuite, oté moin. Dans ein ti moment Bouki hélé: Mo chuite, mo chuite. Ah oua, macaques yé prend gros couverti, et couvri pove Bouki et yé dit li: – Si so té chuite to sré pas héél.

COMPAIR BOUKI AND THE MONKEYS

Compair Bouki put fire under his kettle, and when the water was very hot he began to beat his drum and to cry out:
'Sam-bombel! Sam-bombel tarn!
Sam-bombel! Sam-bombel dam!'
The monkeys heard and said: 'What! Bouki has something good to eat; let us go'; and they ran up to Bouki and sang:
'Molési, cherguinet, chourvan!
Chéguillé, chourvan!'
Compair Bouki then said to the monkeys: 'I shall enter into the kettle, and when I say, "I am cooked," you must take me out.' He jumped into the kettle, and the monkeys pulled him out as soon as he said, 'I am cooked.'
The monkeys, in their turn, jumped into the kettle, and cried out, immediately on touching the water, 'We are cooked.' Bouki, however, took his big iron pot cover and covering the kettle said: 'If you were cooked you could not say so.' One little monkey alone escaped, and Bouki ate all the others.

Some time after this Compair Bouki was hungry again, and he called the monkeys:

'Sam-bombel! Sam-bombel tam!
Sam-bombel! Sam-bombel dam!'
When the monkeys came they sang:
'Molési, cheriguillé!
Molési, cheriguillé, chourvan!'
When the monkeys arrived, he jumped into the kettle again and said, 'I am cooked, I am cooked.' The monkeys, however, having been warned by the little monkey who had escaped the first time, did not pull Bouki out, but said, 'If you were cooked you could not say so.'

At Canal Street you board a street-car with your friend. Two blackrobed nuns enter, giving the conductor a polite nod instead of a fare. The instant the nuns appear in the car, all the gentlemen seated scramble to their feet, vying with one another for the privilege of relinquishing their seats.

The gentleman next to whom you are standing is reading the classified section of a local newspaper. You glance at the 'Personal' column and see:

$50 REWARD

Parrot, green, lost from 214 Calliope, answering to 'I love you,' 'Oh! Doctor,' and imitates children crying.

C. Smith

I am applying for a pardon.

Robert Barrot

Thanks to Saint Peter, Saint Margaret, and the Little Flower of Jesus for favors granted.

J.G.

Thanks to Saint Jude for hayfever.

Mary T.

I am not responsible for any debts contracted by my wife.

George J. Jones

Thanks to Saint Rita for bicycles found and preservation from drowning.

C. R. M. and his cousin

Thanks to Saint Expedite, my boy turned good.

Mrs. L. B. Day

You get off the street-car, and right there in front of you, on a wide straight avenue, with tall palm trees down the center, and houses occupied by the better class of Negroes, is the Voodoo drugstore. You go in, meet the proprietor, and attempt to get a catalogue of his charms. He is very reticent, since he is in an illicit business, but by dint of haggling you and your Creole friend leave, triumphantly carrying a vial of Love Oil and a list of all other charms to be purchased in the store. Here is your list:

Love Powder, White & Pink .25	Pink Wash .25
Drawing Powder . 50	Lode Stone .25
Cinnamon Powder .25	Steel Dust .25
War Powder . 50	Saltpeter .25
Controlling Powder . 50	Van Van .25
Anger Powder . 50	Gamblers' Luck .75
Peace Powder . 50	Dice Special 1.00
Courting Powder . 50	Oil Geranium . 25
Delight Powder . 50	Oil Verbena . 25
Yellow Wash . 25	Oil Rosemary . 25
Red Wash .25	Oil Lavender .25
Black Wash .25	Love Oil . 50

Mind Oil . 50
Devil Oil . 50
Incense (Vantines) .25
Love Drops .50
Drawing Drops .50
Luck around Business .50
Robert Vinegar .25
French Love Powder .75
Get Away Powder 1.00
Easy Life Powder 2.50
Goddess of Luck 1.50
Midnight Oil .75
Goddess of Love 2.00
Lucky Jazz 1.00
Come to Me Powder 1.00
Goddess of Evils 1.50
Love and Success Powder 1.00
Straight XX 1.00
XXX 3 Cross Powder 1.00
Lucky Floor Drops .75
3 King Oil .75
Controlling Oil 1.00
Sacred Sand, All Colors 1.00
Love Drawing Powder 1.50
St. Joseph Powder 1.00
Black Cat Oil 1.00
Mexican Luck .50
Angel's Delight .75
Black Devils .50

Snake Root .25
Dragon's Blood .50
Devil Shoe Strings .25
War Water .50
Peace Water .50
Mad Water .50
Moving Powder .50
Draw Across Powder .50
Flying Devil Powder .50
Separation Powder .50
Lucky Lucky Powder .50
Good Luck Drops for Hand .50
Mad Luck Water .50
Extra Good Luck Drops .50
Fast Luck Drops .50
John Conquer Root .25
Cinnamon Drops .25
Get Together Powder .50
Good Luck Powder .50
Hell's Devil Powder .50
Bend Over Oil .50
St. Joseph Oil .75
As You Please Powder .75
5 Century Grass .50
Goofer Dust .50
6th and 7th Book of Moses 1.00
Oil Bend Over .50
Get Together Drops 1.00

'What is goofer dust?' you inquire.

Your Creole smiles. 'Would you like to have some?'

'Certainly – if I knew what to do with it.' So the two of you go to the old St. Louis Cemetery. It is late afternoon and the sexton is unwilling to let strangers in. The Creole tells him something in French, bows, and enters the gate. You wander about among the old, crumbling whitewashed tombs, which look like little houses. The Creole stops before a tall tomb, and cautioning you to be quiet, climbs to the top and comes down with a handful of damp earth.

'This is Marie Laveau's grave. Marie was the most famous, most powerful of all the Voodoo Queens. On Saint John's Eve, petitioners come and deposit coins in the chinks of the grave to have her spirit answer their prayers. Goofer dust is the earth from a grave, any grave. But I thought I d get you earth from Marie Laveau's own grave, because that, of course, would make the charms doubly potent,' he says, smiling.

Then you leave the cemetery, talking of Marie Laveau, and how she used to charm policemen sent to imprison her so that they were unable to move; of how her *tignon*, or headdress, was tied in a way no other woman was permitted to tie hers; and how she was said to converse with and advise those who inherited her authority after her death; and of many other sinister things.

'That,' says your Creole, pointing to a house on the corner of Royal and St. Ann Streets, 'is one of the many haunted houses in the Vieux Carré.'

'Really?'

'Certainly. A man whose integrity I respect told me that he himself, on a wintry night, saw the naked figure of a woman walking up and down the edge of the roof, shivering and wringing her hands. Tradition says that a beautiful octoroon slave girl, over a century ago, fell in love with her white master. Jealously she guarded her secret as long as she could, and finally, no longer being able to stand the sight of him passing her by as unconcernedly as if she had been a piece of furniture, she blurted out her love for him. Taking the whole affair as a broad joke, the master agreed that if she would walk naked on the roof top all that night (one of the coldest of the year) he would become her lover. To prove her love and obedience, the girl climbed the roof shortly after nightfall, and taking off her clothes began to walk up and down the edge of the roof. By midnight, she was so frozen that she could no longer move and lying down in exhaustion, fell into a coma from which she never awoke.

'New Orleans is kind to ghosts,' your Creole adds, 'and almost all of our old houses are haunted. In your own studio ...'

SOCIAL LIFE AND SOCIAL WELFARE

NEW ORLEANS was a provincial French and Spanish city already a century old before it became a part of the United States. Set in a lush tropical wilderness near the mouth of the Mississippi, a city of contrasts, it was both elegant and brutal. Operas and lavish balls were given, and there was a fine choice of wines; but men were being tortured under Spanish law, and pirates and smugglers made neighboring waters unsafe for the traveler. Riots were frequent. Each residence was built like a fort.

In the century and a quarter since the Americans came flocking to New Orleans after the Louisiana Purchase in 1803, social life has developed and modified itself into the usual American pattern; but there remains a Latin culture – a culture not founded on books but on the art of life itself – which makes New Orleans different from other cities of the country. The celebration of Mardi Gras with masquerade balls and pageantry is perhaps the city's most typical gesture.

A new city has grown up around and beyond the limits of the old walled city of *La Nouvelle Orléans*. Some of the old remains; but New Orleans today is a melting pot of many nationalities. From the little French settlement of 1718 the present-day city has emerged.

The transition was the result of various contributing factors, but the Church, particularly during the first century of the city's existence, was a dominant influence. Jesuit missionaries brought over to administer to the spiritual needs of the settlers found time also to aid in the development of agriculture and industry, thereby helping to attract additional and higher type immigration. The Ursuline nuns, who came to the Colony in 1727, added a touch of civilization by establishing a school, tending to the sick, and carrying on other activities devoted to public welfare. Slavery was introduced almost from the beginning, and the Negro has always been a definite part (at times, a problem) of the city's social life.

During the French and Spanish régimes (1718-1803) New Orleans remained little more than a town, the population within the city wall never greatly exceeding five thousand. Except for officialdom and a small circle of aristocracy, which was augmented after the French Revolution by the coming of émigrés, the inhabitants consisted mainly of the bourgeoisie, soldiers, and the American frontiersmen, who came in increasing numbers after 1800. From the lowest to the highest social stratum in this community there was a very definite distinction assumed by the Creole element (descendants of the original French and Spanish settlers) of the population. Averse to all foreign intercourse but that with the mother countries, they maintained their social and cultural identity, regarding as unfortunate any increase in the foreign population of the city. So marked was this attitude that after American annexation resulted in an influx of Anglo-Saxons, the newcomers found it advisable to settle outside the confines of the Creole section. Ultimately surrounded by suburban foreigners, the Vieux Carré became a city within a city, in which Creole society maintained its own high social standards.

During the great plantation era, from the eighteenth century to the beginning of the Civil War, New Orleans became an unrivaled social center and the scene of many brilliant functions. The planters became immensely wealthy, erecting great plantation houses, many of which were classic in architecture and luxuriously furnished. The more affluent of these country gentlemen established separate 'town houses' in New Orleans, residing in them while on visits to the city.

Many plantation mansions were erected on the outskirts of the city along the Mississippi and Bayou St. John. The 'big house' of the planter usually faced the river or bayou, set back about a hundred yards and surrounded by spacious grounds. In architecture it ranged from a temporary log cabin to an elaborate mansion. In general the plantation home followed a pattern – simple two-story structures, the lower of brick and the upper of wood, with wide verandas (called 'galleries') supported on the lower floor by squat columns of brick and above by thin colonnettes of cypress. Set back from the house, usually at some distance, were the kitchens, smokehouses and storehouses, and the chapel. The slave quarters were situated further to the rear, their one- or two-room cottages, each with its large chimney, forming a long street in the manner of a miniature village. Between the slave quarters and the mansion the overseer, should the number of slaves or the size of the plantation demand the services of one, had his house.

Plantation life was feudal and patriarchal. Based upon serfdom, in which the slaves were attached to the owner's land and regarded as personal property, the system was in many respects similar to that in practice under the *ancien régime*, with the exception that the ownership implied in the term 'slavery' distinguished the lot of the Negro from that of the European peasant. The system was patriarchal in that the life of the community centered around the planter and his family. The members of such a feudal community were necessarily separated into three distinct classes, the planter and his family, the household servants, and the slaves employed in the fields. The bond uniting them was essentially economic in nature, all relying upon the land for subsistence.

The position of the planter's wife was an important one. While he attended to the business of the plantation she supervised its daily existence, exercising in her field as much power and undertaking as great a responsibility as did her husband in his, ruling as she did an enormous black family as well as her own. Invariably there were young cousins or orphan kin to be educated or cared for, or old aunts and uncles for whom a home had to be provided. Education of the young was taken care of by a tutor or governess, more often than not from the North, who was accepted and treated as one of the family. In short, the mistress was entirely responsible for the daily routine, welfare, and happiness of all.

A typical plantation usually had about a hundred slaves, over which the planter occupied a position similar to that of a petty feudal lord, with emphasis always upon the responsibility rather than the power of his station. Theoretically accountable to the law, in practice he tended to be sole ruler. The welfare of his family was directly dependent upon that of his slaves, for in order to prosper the planter had to see that they were properly clothed, fed, housed, and kept in good health. Discipline had to be maintained and work accomplished under the most trying conditions. Education had to be attended to – classical for his sons, cultural for his daughters, and practical for his slaves. Health was exceedingly important, and could be maintained only upon the closest supervision, a physician being kept in constant attendance for that purpose. The attitude of the planter toward his slaves in matters of religion differed with the individual. Some masters interfered as little as possible, while others considered it their duty to assume full responsibility.

As the city expanded, the nearby plantation holdings were subdivided and became part of the enlarging city. Where brilliant fêtes once marked a round of genteel social intercourse, where culture flourished under the guiding hand of a landed gentry, now only plantation homes, many still kept in excellent condition, others fallen into decay, stand surrounded by modern and less glamorous dwelling-places as symbols of a once impressive social order.

Private clubs have played an important part in the development of New Orleans' social life. In the early days men gathered in saloons and coffee houses, known as 'bourses' or 'exchanges,' after business hours for the enjoyment of friendly discussion, wine-drinking, games, and reading. The most popular of these places were La Sère's and Maspero's, located in the Vieux Carré. The good fellowship and congeniality which predominated at these gatherings laid the foundation for the promotion of later organizations. Several groups originated simultaneously with the carnival associations, and are today closely identified with them, although the extent of the relationship is a secret closely guarded by members. More prominent among the older organizations were the Elkin, the Pelican, Orleans, Chalmette, Boston, and Pickwick, of which only the last two now survive. The Elkin Club, named after the owner of a hotel building situated on Bayou St. John, was formed in 1832 by a small group of influential men who desired great privacy and exclusiveness in their pleasures. The members, who drove to their clubhouse every afternoon in their carriages, enjoyed a fine dinner and spent the remainder of the day in drinking and gambling. Chivalry being the order of the day, they offered sumptuous balls and entertainments, to which socially prominent ladies were invited. The Harmony Club, founded in 1862, was for years an important medium of the Jewish social life, and the Chess, Checkers, and Whist Club was the rendezvous of many players of those days, including Paul Morphy, world-famous chess expert.

In former days the lines of social caste were more sharply drawn, and in no phase of social life was this more apparent than in the membership roster of the exclusive clubs. The business of merchandising and ordinary trading was considered plebeian, and the members of this group were excluded from the aristocratic club life of New Orleans. Plantation owners, bankers, politicians, and cotton and sugar brokers were considered eligible, however. Today, with the expansion of democratic ideas, and because of the fact that members of many aristocratic families have gone into various types of business which were outlawed socially under the old régime, the modern clubs of New Orleans, although exclusive in the choice of their members, have broadened their membership standards.

Women's clubs, though of later origin, today play a major part in women's activities in the city. Among the more prominent of the women's organizations are the Colonial Dames, the Junior League, the *Petit Salon*, and the Orleans Club. Several country clubs for both men and women are also prominent.

The work of the Ursuline nuns in administering to the sick and indigent among the first settlers is today greatly magnified in the efficient and well-organized welfare agencies in the city. The Department of Public Welfare, organized in 1934, has charge of the city's many institutions for the sick, the poor, the aged, and orphaned or delinquent children. In addition to the Department of Public Welfare, there are a large number of social and philanthropic institutions devoted to the welfare of orphans, delinquents, and the aged and indigent. Among these are several casework agencies, such as the Family Service Society, dealing primarily with domestic or marital difficulties; the Associated Catholic Charities, also dealing with family problems; and the Children's Bureau, whose function is to care for and place neglected children in foster homes whenever possible. The Travelers' Aid Society and the American Red Cross are also active.

The Tulane School of Social Work, organized at Tulane University in 1927, has been an important factor in stimulating social consciousness in the community through education and specialized study of social conditions. Students preparing for this type of work are given practice cases (with supervision) at some of the above institutions in connection with their regular class work.

There are also twenty-three asylums for children located throughout the city, some of which are privately endowed while others are supported from Community Chest funds. Practically all of the large hospitals of the city conduct social service departments which co-operate with other case-work agencies in the treatment of charitable cases. For the aged and indigent there are a number of institutions which are maintained by the city and are non-sectarian.

The present system of curbing juvenile delinquency in New Orleans has been much improved since the establishment in 1933 of the new Milne Municipal Boys' Home, a corrective institution. The need for recreational facilities bv the youth of the city has been recognized in a number of neighborhoods in the establishment of community centers, which offer health supervision, swimming and other sports, supervised play, and instruction in crafts.

The Community Chest, organized in 1924, functions as a centralized disbursing agency for the various institutions and welfare groups of the city.

EDUCATION

EDUCATION was advocated in New Orleans almost from the beginning. Soon after the town was founded, Bienville importuned the French Government to establish a college under the patronage of the Crown. The request refused, he asked that the *Sœurs Crises* of his native Canada be sent to New Orleans to teach and to care for the sick colonists. Again disappointed, he was advised by Father Beaubois to secure the services of the Ursulines of Rouen. After several months of preparations, six Ursuline nuns and two Jesuit missionaries arrived in New Orleans in 1727, and began the instruction of a limited number of girls and the nursing of the sick. A few Indians and Negro slaves also were taught during evenings and Sundays. To this small group New Orleans owes its first educational institution, Ursuline Convent – a school which has operated continuously for more than two hundred years and is one of the oldest girls schools in the country.

There is a brief account of a school for boys having been opened in 1724 on the site of the present Presbytery, directed by Father Cecil, a Capuchin monk, but little information relating to it is available. Governor Unzaga also attempted to establish a public school in 1772, while Louisiana was under the rule of Spain, and for a short time students, varying in number from six to thirty, were taught reading and writing.

Despite these efforts education made little progress in the first century of New Orleans existence. Lack of funds, social and religious difficulties, and apparent apathy on the part of the governing powers retarded the development of schools. Free education was frowned upon by those who could provide private instruction for their children, and early Creole families who could afford to do so sent their sons to European universities. As elsewhere in the Nation, the need for free public schools was not recognized until early in the nineteenth century; even then, many considered it undesirable. Because they felt, undemocratically, that it would necessitate an indiscriminate mingling of all classes, and perhaps give their children undesirable associates.

It was not until after 1803, when Louisiana was transferred to the United States, that appreciable gains were made in education. William C. C. Claiborne, first American Governor, in his address to the Legislature in 1804, advocated the establishment of free schools, open to all classes, and as a result an act was passed in

1805 authorizing the founding of a college in New Orleans. Appropriations for the college, however, were not made until 1811, owing to lack of funds. In 1826, after the college had flourished and expired, two elementary schools and a central high school were established in the city, the former giving training in French, English grammar, reading, writing, and arithmetic, and the latter, courses in literature, mathematics, and the languages. To assist in the support of these institutions, taxes were levied on the city's two theaters, and these funds supplemented by revenue from the Louisiana lottery. While only a small percentage of the city's educable youth was enrolled in them, the schools were a factor in molding a more favorable opinion of public education.

Although the schools were supported with tax funds, small tuition fees were charged each student, a condition which prevented many children from attending. In 1833 Governor Roman sponsored additional legislation extending free school facilities to the indigent, and providing for State assistance in the support of city schools. As the number of students increased following this measure, additional taxes were assessed to meet the growing demands.

With the reorganization of the State educational system and the appointment of a State superintendent in 1847, a number of free schools were set up throughout New Orleans, and a more uniform system of taxation was planned to maintain them. The year following more than 6500 students were enrolled. In 1850 New Orleans received a large portion of the estate of John McDonogh, who at his death left a will requesting that his fortune be divided equally between the public schools of Baltimore, his birthplace, and New Orleans, his adopted home. From this source New Orleans realized approximately $750,000, which was used to erect more public school buildings. Twelve of the thirty-five schools built are still in use. By 1860, 12,000 students were enrolled in the public schools of the city.

During the middle of the nineteenth century a number of convents and parochial schools were established in New Orleans, including the schools of the Redemptorist Fathers and Immaculate Conception, St. Mary's German School, the New Orleans Female Dominican Academy, the First Convent of Mercy, and Notre Dame Seminary. These schools, semi-private in character, were affected in a lesser degree by the Civil War, and fared better during that period than the public schools of the city.

The Civil War and the Reconstruction policies in the era following were a serious blow to the education of whites in New Orleans. Schools were disorganized. Enrollment fell to twenty per cent of its normal figure. Negro education, which heretofore had been left almost entirely to slave owners, made rapid strides with carpetbag legislation, which made provision for joint Negro and white instruction. Negro school superintendents were appointed to direct the State educational system. As a result practically all of the white students withdrew from the schools.

It was not until the late 1870's, under the administration of Robert M. Lusher, that the city school system was restored to normal conditions. By the turn of the century there were more than seventy school buildings in New Orleans, and an enrollment of almost thirty-two thousand students. In 1906 the State Board of Education introduced a uniform curriculum into public schools and New Orleans, four years later, enforced the law making the attendance of children between the ages of seven and fifteen compulsory.

Advanced education in the city was a nineteenth-century development, the founding of the College of Orleans in 1811 having been the first attempt to establish an institution for higher learning. This school, privately endowed, was maintained for only fifteen years, owing to enmity between Americans and Creoles, and was abandoned in 1826. In 1834 a group of local physicians founded the Medical College of Louisiana, which, despite a lack of adequate funds, flourished for several years, and in 1847 was absorbed by the University of Louisiana, established by the State Legislature a few years earlier. Occasional appropriations kept the university barely alive until 1883, when the munificent bequests of Paul Tulane gave it a new name and made possible its expansion to its present proportions. Four years later Newcomb College, one of the most popular women's schools in the South, was opened, and in 1911 Loyola University, conducted by the Jesuit Order, was established.

As elsewhere in the South, the Negro institutions of New Orleans are of fairly recent origin. During the latter part of the nineteenth century a number of colored schools were founded; the first in 1869, under the auspices of the Freedmen's Bureau, was known as the New Orleans University. Later schools included Flint Medical College, which developed into the Flint-Goodridge Hospital, and Straight University, founded and maintained by the American Missionary Society of New York. The latter merged with New Orleans University to form Dillard University, which had its first formal session in 1935 and which promises to become one of the outstanding Negro institutions of the country. In 1915 Xavier College was opened – the only Catholic school of higher learning in the United States conducted solely for Negroes.

The Notre Dame Seminary, under the supervision of the Archbishop of New Orleans, provides training for secular priests. The Baptist Bible Institute, open to both men and women, is strictly a theological seminary, and was established in New Orleans in 1917.

New Orleans has had a number of private schools, only a few of which, however, survived the depression. The Louise S. McGehee School for Girls, an accredited elementary and high school founded in 1912, is one of the most popular in the city. Others continuing in operation include the Metairie Park Day School, the New Orleans Academy, the Isidore Newman School, Rugby Academy, the New Orleans Nursery School, and Miss Aiken's Primary School. The 'Home Institute,' founded by Sophie Wright, was formerly one of the outstanding girls' schools of the city, and a public high school today is named for the Institute's late founder. A French school for children of the grammar grades is maintained on a part-time basis by the French Union. A description of an early private school – one opened in 1847 by Madame Marie Louise Girard for the instruction of young children – is given in Grace King's *Madame Girard.*

New Orleans also has a number of commercial, technical, trade, and business schools located throughout the city, as well as schools of art, music, dancing, and dramatics.

The Isaac Delgado Central Trades School, offering training in printing, carpentry, metal work, architectural and mechanical drafting, mathematics, the trades, English, plumbing, cabinet-making, interior decorating, electricity, applied science, and stewardship, is recognized as one of the leading trade schools in this section of the country. The L. E. Rabouin Trade School for Girls offers a wide range of courses in manual arts, home-making, and crafts. The Joseph A. Maybin Commercial School for Graduates, said to be the only institution of its kind in the South, offers advanced work for graduates in commerce. The building was originally a Jewish private school founded in 1868 by the Hebrew Education Society.

During the last few years numerous methods and courses have been incorporated into the public-school system in an effort to facilitate the training of the mentally and physically handicapped. Sight-saving classes for the near blind, corrective classes for children with physical defects, and opportunity classes for students mentally inferior are being conducted. At the Robert C. Davey School night classes are offered three times a week to foreigners wishing to learn the English language. Illiteracy, still very high in the city, is declining as a result of the introduction of free textbooks, whereby indigent families are aided in their efforts to educate their children, and as a result of the educational work being done in that field by the Works Progress Administration.

At present there are sixty-one elementary public day schools and eleven high schools for white students, and twenty-three elementary and four high schools for Negroes. The figures for 1934-35 showed a total enrollment of 77,000 students in the city's public schools, approximately 25,000 of whom were colored. Catholic schools in the city include thirtynine elementary, eleven high schools, two colleges, and one normal school, for white students, and eleven schools, including both elementary and high schools, for Negroes. There are also two Hebrew and four Lutheran schools.

The present Orleans Parish school board, with offices at 701 Carondelet Street, consists of five members, elected by ballot every four years. The board selects its own officers and the operating officials of the school system. The City Commissioner of Public Finance automatically becomes treasurer of the board.

RELIGION

THE first religious services in New Orleans were conducted by the Jesuit missionaries who came to Louisiana with Iberville and Bienville for the purpose of establishing the Catholic Church and converting the Indians. The earliest direct reference to a house of worship in the city is in the account of Father Charlevoix, who, when visiting New Orleans in 1721, found only 'a hundred houses, and half a miserable warehouse, where Our Lord is worshipped.' A temporary church built during the priest's stay was later destroyed by the hurricane of 1722.

In 1722 the Company of the Indies issued an ordinance dividing the territory into three ecclesiastical sections. Under this division New Orleans came under the jurisdiction of the Capuchins, whose first task was the erection of a church to replace that one destroyed by the hurricane. The new building, a brick edifice, was dedicated to Saint Louis in honor of the patron saint of France. A later alteration in the ecclesiastical administration of the Province permitted the Jesuits to work in the original Capuchin territory, and in 1723 the New Orleans mission of the Jesuits was established. The following year Bienville promulgated the Black Code, a system of laws providing for the control of slaves, the expulsion of Jews from the territory, and the establishment of Catholicism as a State religion. In spite of the provisions of the Code, both Jews and Protestants came into the Colony at an early date, as is indicated by the reports of the Spanish governors and by O'Reilly's expulsion of a few Jews in 1769.

The Jesuits, who besides their spiritual activities did much toward the furtherance of industry in the Colony by introducing the cultivation of figs, oranges, indigo, and sugar cane, were expelled in 1763 as a result of European opposition.

An incident which might have profoundly affected both New Orleans and the entire territory was the attempt in 1789 of Padre Antonio de Sedella, later known and revered as Père Antoine, to establish the dreaded Spanish Inquisition in Louisiana. Governor Miro, quick to sense the danger of such an institution in the French Colony, cleverly arranged the seizure and deportation of the priest.

A new diocese was formed of Louisiana and the Floridas in 1793, and Bishop Penalver became the first permanent Bishop of New Orleans. The third church to occupy the original site of Saint Louis Cathedral was dedicated and consecrated as a cathedral by Bishop Penalver in 1794.

The transfer of Louisiana from one to another of three different nations within a month in 1803 disrupted the work of the Catholic Church for a dozen years. Many of the priests and nuns, unwilling to remain in the Colony under French rule, withdrew; the subsequent announcement of the sale of the territory to America completed the disorganization. Père Antoine, back in New Orleans after his exile, was the storm center of a controversy arising over the differences between Spanish and American laws regarding church property. He refused to recognize the authority of the Archbishop of Baltimore, and was supported in this by his congregation, who organized a Board of Trustees to whose care the Cathedral was entrusted. The contest between the Bishop and the Trustees was finally carried to the United States Supreme Court, where a decision was obtained in 1843 transferring the property to the Archbishop's jurisdiction.

In 1837 the Jesuits were recalled to Louisiana, where they again took up their work, establishing in New Orleans a number of institutions, largely educational, from which several fine high schools for boys, and Loyola University, a large and important institution of higher learning, have grown. These and other activities spurring recovery from the setback, the Catholic Church again grew steadily in the city; religious orders were called in, additional churches and parochial schools were established, and in 1850 New Orleans became an archdiocese, with Bishop Blanc its first Archbishop.

Protestantism, in the first one hundred years of New Orleans' existence, was very meagerly represented; but early in the nineteenth century the number of its adherents, gradually swelled by the influx of American colonists, was of sufficient size to justify organization. In 1805 a meeting was called by the several denominations of the Protestant faith for the purpose of establishing a common meeting-house. In the vote to decide which denomination should erect the building, the Episcopalians won; Christ's Church, the first Protestant house of worship in the city, was built in 1816 at the corner of Bourbon and Canal Streets. As the city grew additional Episcopalian congregations were organized, of which the best known is Trinity Church, on Jackson Avenue. Several of the pastors of this church became bishops, and one of them, the Reverend Leonidas Polk, rector from 1855 to 1861, resigned at the outbreak of the Civil War to become a general and the 'fighting bishop' of the Confederate Army.

The first attempt to introduce Methodism also began in 1805 when the Western Conference sent Elisha W. Bowman, a minister, to New Orleans for the purpose of founding a Methodist church, voting an appropriation of one hundred dollars for his expenses. Reaching the city, Bowman obtained permission from the authorities to preach at the 'Capitol' (presumably the Cabildo), but when he arrived at the building on the appointed day he found its doors locked. A protest to the Mayor brought a renewal of the permission, but probably owing to the interference of members of another denomination, Bowman was for the second time disappointed, whereupon he left the city, his mission a failure. Other assignments made to New Orleans by the Conference between 1811 and 1818 were similarly unsuccessful, although the Reverend Mark Moore had in the latter year actually procured a meeting-house and gathered a considerable congregation – only to have the deadly yellow fever claim a number of his flock and force the closing of his church. But in 1830 the perseverance of the Methodists was rewarded, when yet another attempt resulted in the erection of a substantial church building at Gravier and Baronne Streets, the site now occupied by the Union Indemnity Building. The foothold once gained, steady progress was made, the First Church congregation quickly outgrowing its building, and moving to larger quarters. Methodists meanwhile increased in number in the fast-growing city, and soon a number of additional churches were built, definitely establishing the Methodist faith.

From the year 1816, when the first Baptist missionary came to New Orleans, the Baptist Church had a hard struggle for existence in the city, outside aid having been necessary to maintain the separate church buildings until the early twentieth century. But from a total membership of only twelve hundred in six churches in 1918, it has grown in the intervening years to more than seven thousand members in twenty-six churches. These figures, however, include the entire New Orleans Association, which extends as far as Westwego in Jefferson Parish.

The foundation of the Baptist faith was laid here by James A. Reynoldson, who came to New Orleans in 1816 as a missionary from the Triennial Convention. His church, organized about 1820, with a congregation of sixteen white and thirty-two colored members, was later dissolved. For the ensuing several years Baptist affairs in the city were in a perturbed condition, the members worshiping at various places, and without a definite organization. But in 1860 the First Church, which had been founded seventeen years before and later disbanded, was reorganized, resumed its services, and began to grow steadily; the Coliseum Place Baptist Church, erected in 1854, also began to increase in membership, and other churches became necessary at intervals in the following years.

In 1918 the Baptist Bible Institute, a school devoted to religious education, was founded, and, maintained by the Southern Baptist Convention, is now well established with an enrollment of more than two hundred.

The first successful effort to implant Presbyterianism in New Orleans originated with the Congregationalists of New England. In 1817 the Connecticut Missionary Society sent the Reverend Elias Cornelius to New Orleans to 'examine its moral condition,' and 'to invite friends of the Congregational or Presbyterian Communion to establish a church.' On his way South Doctor Cornelius became acquainted with Mr. Sylvester Larned, a theological student, and invited him to come to New Orleans upon the completion of his studies. Following his ordination Larned did so, joining Doctor Cornelius and assisting him in the negotiation of a loan of $40,000, with which to build the church. Two years later, in 1820, the city's first Presbyterian church was dedicated, with the Reverend Mr. Larned as pastor. At his death in 1820 the church was for eighteen months without a regular minister, but eventually the Reverend Theodore Clapp, a native of Massachusetts, was chosen to fill the office. In 1830 a famous theological controversy developed in the church; Doctor Clapp was charged with heretical teachings and divested of his office and pulpit by the Presbytery. Exception was taken, and the case was carried to the General Assembly, which body sustained the exception. Meanwhile part of Doctor Clapp's congregation, siding with the opposition, seceded, and formed a separate group, which later was reabsorbed by the First Church. In 1833, after the congregation split, Judah Touro, noted Jewish philanthropist, bought the First Church and turned it over to Doctor Clapp and his remaining congregation rent-free, because of his admiration for the clergyman. In 1840 Presbyterianism began to grow rapidly, and in 1843 the Lafayette Church, an offshoot of the First Church, was founded; this was followed by the Second Church (1843), the Third Church (1844), and the Prytania Street Presbyterian Church (1846). Today the number of Presbyterian communicants in the city has grown to more than 5500.

The religious history of the Jewish people in New Orleans had its beginning early in the nineteenth century. Although there had been some Jews in the city previous to the Louisiana Purchase, there had been no organization among them; but by 1828 the number of Jews had increased considerably, and in that year Shaaray Chesed (Gates of Mercy), the first synagogue, was built. In 1846 the Portuguese Jews, of whom there was a small number in the city, founded a second congregation known as Nefutzoth (Dispersed of Judah), and this was followed by several other organizations. After an interrupted period of development during and following the Civil War, Jewish congregations in the city entered upon an era of rapid and prosperous growth. The arrival of Rabbi Max Heller as leader of Temple Sinai inaugurated a period of great religious activity, and drew other brilliant men of the Jewish faith here. There are to day three orthodox and three reformed Jewish congregations in the city.

The establishment of Lutheranism in New Orleans is, of course, closely connected with the settlement of Germans in and about the city. Although a large number of these early German settlers were of Roman Catholic faith, some were Protestants, and the majority of the latter were Lutherans. The first German Protestant church was organized in 1829, and occupied a site on Clio Street, between St. Charles Avenue and Carondelet Street; but although attended by Lutherans, it was not designated a Lutheran church. In 1840 the Reverend Christian Sans, who had held services for Germans in a Methodist church, was denied further use of that church when he refused to preach the Methodist doctrine. As a result, Sans transferred his services and congregation to the old engine house at Clouet and Louisa Streets, on August 2, 1840, and that date has since been regarded as the birthday of the Evangelical Lutheran Church in New Orleans. In the same year a parochial school, still in existence, was opened by John and Jacob Ueber.

In 1883 the Reverend G. C. Francke organized the English-speaking Lutherans of the city and introduced the delivery of sermons in English. Until 1901 the church had been chartered at various times under several different names, but in that year it was named 'The Evangelical Lutheran St. Paul's Congregation' and has remained that since. As the number of German immigrants to the city increased, other churches were built. The total membership is now about six thousand.

Mary Baker Eddy's *Science and Health with Key to the Scriptures* introduced Christian Science to New Orleans shortly after 1875. Persons interested in Mrs. Eddy's teachings formed a group known as the First Christian Science Association of New Orleans. On October 15, 1895, under the name 'Church of Christ, Scientist, of New Orleans,' they secured a charter from the State 'to practice Apostolic Healing.' Services were held at various places before a church on Melpomene Street, seating about three hundred, was taken over. Increase in membership necessitated larger meeting quarters, and the First Church of Christ, Scientist, was erected in 1913-14 at Nashville Avenue and Garfield Street. Since then, two other churches have been built and several free reading-rooms have been established in the city.

Other denominations in the city include Adventist, American Old Catholic, Assembly of God, Church of Christ, Church of God, Church of the Nazarene, Disciples of Christ, Greek, Latter Day Saints, Rosicrucian, Theosophical Society, Unitarian, and Unity.

Negroes in New Orleans belong chiefly to the Baptist and Methodist Churches, although there are many Catholic Negroes, and several substantial Negro Catholic church buildings. White Catholic churches in the city permit the attendance of Negroes, usually seating them in the rear pews, a custom not usually followed in the Protestant churches.

During the French and Spanish régimes the slaves, under the requirements of the Black Code, were baptized and instructed in the Catholic faith, but after 1803, when new settlers, mostly Protestant, began to build up great plantations, the slaves were taught the religion of their masters. A great many of them, however, clung to African religions and observed their rituals openly or clandestinely, as circumstances dictated. Congo Square (now Beauregard Square) was given over to slaves on Sunday afternoons for dancing, singing, and the performance of Voodoo rites. As long as Negroes were imported as slaves, the old religions were kept alive. With the end of slave traffic and as a result of constant proselytism, the Negro transferred his emotionalism to Christian creeds; but Voodooism and other primitive rituals have persisted in various forms down to the present.

The emotional character of the Baptist and Methodist revival meetings seem to have a special appeal for the Negroes. During Reconstruction when refugee slaves were cared for by the Freedmen's Bureau, many of them joined Northern church organizations, with the result that today the great majority of Negroes are members of the various Baptist and Methodist church bodies.

Several Negro churches have been organized in New Orleans by selfappointed leaders, usually women, who adhere to no set doctrine but claim communion with 'the spirits,' and profess to practice 'faith healing.' One or two of these churches have built up congregations of extraordinary size and have even won a considerable following among white people. Beside the major Negro churches, there are scores of smaller organizations.

Although a recent directory lists 492 churches in the city, it is estimated that there are 600 churches for Negroes alone.

SPORTS AND RECREATION

NEW ORLEANS has a history replete with strange and barbaric sports brought to Louisiana by the French and Spanish, diversified by the Creoles, and added to by the Americans. Early nineteenth-century newspapers carried notices of bull fights and cock fights. The latter were well attended, and interest ran high as heavy wagers were posted on the contestants, who were revived during the fray by having garlic and whisky blown into their beaks. One dollar admitted one to a dog and alligator fight, and gorier fare was afforded at the bear- and bull-baiting arena, where the spectator was privileged to hurl stones and brickbats at the animals to incite them to the proper fury. Today, cock fights and occasionally even dog fights are still to be witnessed. Street boxing and wrestling of the catch-as-catch-can, bar-nothing variety, was a popular form of entertainment in old New Orleans, as were the Voodoo dances held on Sunday afternoons in Congo Square.

A sport popular in the Colonial Period was the traditional game of rackets, once the tribal sport of the Choctaw Indians. It combined the more violent features of lacrosse, football, cross-country racing, and rioting. The young Creoles took it up and formed two clubs, the La Villes and the Bayous, and the game soon worked up as much enthusiasm as football does now.

Players, of whom there were any number from five to a hundred, were furnished with a pair of *kabucha*, or rackets, three feet long, made by bending the top of a sapling over and tying it to the base about eight inches from the end; the frame thus formed was then interlaced with rawhide thongs, in the manner of lacrosse rackets. The *bambila*, about the size of a golf ball, was made of rags stuffed into a white buckskin cover.

The goals, or *plats*, were placed two hundred yards apart and consisted of tall poles having a crossarm ten feet long and one foot wide, tied to the pole some distance above the ground. The center of the field was marked with a small peg, at which spot one of the captains tossed up the ball to put it in play. Two men scrambled for it as it came down, and began a mad dash for the opposing goal with the ball held between the rackets, the object being to toss the ball against the crossarm of the goal, thus scoring a *plat*. One hundred *plats* constituted a game. Anything was fair, and the man carrying the ball was stopped by being tripped, thrown, tackled, or simply clubbed from behind with a racket. The game often took several days to finish, and the resulting casualties, all in good clean fun, would pale our most stalwart football heroes.

The Negroes of the section known as *La Plaine Raquette* (Racket Plains), which is bounded roughly by present Galvez Street and St. Bernard, North Claiborne, and Elysian Fields Avenues, perpetuated the ancient game for some time after the Creoles gave it up, but even they have long since become too 'soft' for it.

Fencing was once the sport *de rigueur* in New Orleans in the days when Creole blood ran hot and 'men of honor' had to be well versed in the art, not only to hold their rank in the popular sport, but to preserve their lives and honor. Duels were fought either at St. Anthony's Garden behind St. Louis Cathedral, or under the 'Dueling Oaks' in what is now City Park. Perhaps the most famous duelist and fencing master of the city was José 'Pepe' Llulla, whose numerous successful encounters won him a formidable reputation. When New Orleans became the headquarters of Cuban filibustering expeditions in the 1850's and 1860's, Pepe, a loyal Spanish subject, offered to meet any or all insurrectionists brave enough to engage him. Legend claims that Pepe maintained a cemetery for the benefit of the countless persons he is reputed to have slain.

Fencing is still a popular sport in the city. The *Fencers' Federation of Louisiana*, located at the Salle d'Armes de la Nouvelle Orléans, 528 Royal Street, fosters numerous small organizations, among which are *Les Chevaliers de la Nouvelle Orléans*, *Le Bataillon d'Orléans*, and the fencing clubs of Louisiana State University, the New Orleans Athletic Club, and the Young Men's Christian Association. Several traditional exhibition tournaments are staged annually, among them being the *Mardi Gras Duello*, held at 2:30 P.M. Mardi Gras Day in the garden behind St. Louis Cathedral, and the *Dueling Oaks Encounter*, held under the Dueling Oaks on the formal opening day of City Park, usually the first or second Sunday in May. Much of the recent activity of the fencers has been directed toward the development and establishment of a dueling technique with that most American of all weapons, the bowie knife. Much progress has been made, and an encounter proves to be a most thrilling spectacle, with comparatively small danger to the combatants.

New Orleans at one time was the recognized boxing center of the world. In 1891 Louisiana became the first state in the Union to legalize prize fighting, and bouts were permitted to be staged openly, with little restrictions other than the use of gloves and the observance of the Marquis of Queensberry rules. The Olympic Athletic Club, organized shortly after legalization of boxing, conducted a three-day carnival in September, 1892, the highlight of which was the twenty-one-round knockout victory of Corbett over Sullivan for a $21,000 purse and a $10,000 side bet. The longest bout in the history of boxing was staged in the city on April 6, 1893, when the lightweight, Burke, and Bowen, a Negro, battled seven hours and nineteen minutes to a no-round draw. Peter Herman and Tony Canzoneri, native sons, have won world championships.

Baseball in New Orleans was first played on open lots by local amateur and semi-professional teams. By the 1870's, however, visiting teams from New York and other large cities were playing the famous Robert E. Lee Clubs at the old Fair Grounds, and the public became sufficiently inter ested by 1885 to support a two-team league (New Orleans and Mobile) organized by a patent medicine company. The Southern League, composed of six teams playing a full season of professional baseball, was organized in 1887, but lasted only one year; and it was not until 1901, after the formation of the Southern Association, that regular seasonal games were played in New Orleans. The Pelicans have won pennants in the league in 1905, 1910, 1911, 1915, 1918, 1923, 1926, 1927, 1933, and 1934. In 1933 and 1934 the team won the 'Dixie Series,' an annual play-off with the Texas League for the championship of the South. Prominent native sons who have gone to the big leagues include Mel Ott (Gretna), Zeke Bonura, Bill Perrin, and Johnny Oulliber; other stars who have 'gone up' from the Pelicans include Joe Sewell, Dazzy Vance, Buddy Myers, Eddie Morgan, Pinky Whitney, Al Milnar, and Denny Galehouse.

Football was first played in New Orleans at Tulane University in 1890. The Southern Athletic Club organized a team two years later and won the championship of the South in 1893; but interest in the game lagged, and it was not until 1924 that high-school and college games attracted large crowds. The peak in football was reached in 1932 when the 'Green Wave' of Tulane journeyed to California to engage the University of Southern California 'Trojans' in the Rose Bowl. Tulane lost (21-12) only after a valiant struggle.

Racing has long been a popular sport in the city. In ante-bellum days New Orleans had five of the finest tracks in the country and witnessed many outstanding races, the most famous of which was the contest on April 1, 1854, between Lexington and Le Compte, giants of the turf of that era. The old Metairie course, now a beautiful cemetery, was the most famous track in the United States at that time. At present racing is perhaps the leading sport in the city. Approximately one hundred days of racing, beginning on Thanksgiving Day, are held annually at the Fair Grounds under the auspices of the Louisiana Jockey Club.

In 1934 the Mid-Winter Sports Association was organized for the purpose of staging an annual sports carnival during the week preceding and following New Year's Day. The Sugar Bowl football game, vying with the Rose Bowl game for national interest, is played on New Year's Day between the outstanding team of the South and a team of championship caliber from some section of the Nation. The calendar of sports events includes an outdoor track and field meet participated in by outstanding national and world champions, a tennis tournament attracting ranking national stars, an intersectional basketball game, intercity boxing matches, a golf tournament, and yacht races on Lake Pontchartrain.

A variety of trips to nearby hunting and fishing grounds add to the popularity of New Orleans for tourists and seasonal visitors. Within quick reach by road, boat, or train there are at least a score of places tempting to the sportsman. In the late fall and early winter duck shooting is good, sometimes exceptionally so, in the waters and marshes surrounding the city. Black bass and smaller salt-water fish alternate in abundance with changing tides and weather conditions in the bayous and lagoons.

Chef Menteur and other nearby tide races afford the highest type of sport with large sheepshead, redfish, jackfish, and tarpon during the fishing season, which is at its best from April to October. For exclusively fresh-water fishing and quail and turkey hunting, it is necessary to go north of New Orleans.

RADIO

DURING the 1920's practically every newspaper in New Orleans owned and operated its own radio station in conjunction with its daily paper. In addition there were a number of privately owned stations, all vying for recognition. One of the first musical programs to be broadcasted in the Mississippi Valley was presented on the night of March 30, 1922, by Station WWL of Loyola University. In the summer of 1926, because of unfavorable weather conditions, all newspapers of the city discontinued operation of their stations, and the total number of stations in the city was reduced to six, which were recognized by the Federal Radio Commission when it came into existence. One of these stations, WJBO, has since moved to Baton Rouge, leaving five active stations in New Orleans. In addition to these there are a number of stations in the parish serving the police department, ships at sea, airplanes, etc., and several amateur stations operating under special license.

RADIO STATIONS

WBNO, studios on the mezzanine floor of the St. Charles Hotel, 211 St. Charles St. (*open during broadcasting hours; free*), broadcasts on a frequency of 1200 kilocycles with a power of 100 watts. The Coliseum Place Baptist Church, 1376 Camp Street, owns the transmitting equipment. Strictly commercial programs, with electrical transcriptions providing music, are put on the air from noon to 5 P.M., and from 8 to 11 P.M. Time is divided with station WJBW.

WDSU, studios at 1456 Monteleone Hotel, 214 Royal St. (*open daily* 8 A.M.-10 P.M.; *free*), broadcasts on an assigned frequency of 1220 kilocycles with a power of 1000 watts. Programs of the N.B.C.'s Blue Network and electrical transcriptions of the World Broadcasting System are presented from 7 A.M. to midnight. Broadcasting of 'Pelican' ball games and other local events are featured. The transmitting station is located at Gretna, Louisiana.

WJBW, studios at 619 Godchaux Bldg., 527 Canal St. (*open during broadcasting hours; free*), and transmitter at 947 Howard Ave., broadcasts on an assigned frequency of 1200 kilocycles with a power of 100 watts from 5 to 8 P.M., and from 11 P.M. throughout the night until noon. Commercial programs are given, recorded music being the usual form of entertainment.

WSMB, owned and operated by the Saenger Theater and the Maison Blanche Company, has studios on the thirteenth floor of the Maison Blanche Bldg., 921 Canal St. *(open during broadcasting hours; free)*. Local and chain programs of the National Broadcasting Company are presented from 7 A.M. to midnight on an assigned frequency of 1320 kilocycles with a power of 5000 watts. The transmitting station is located at the United States Naval Base in Algiers.

WWL, studios on the second floor of the Roosevelt Hotel, 123 Baronne St. *(admission only by special permission of the management)*, and transmitting station 2 *m.* east of Kenner, Louisiana, on State 1, is supervised by Loyola University. Local and chain programs of the Columbia Broadcasting System are presented from 6.30 A.M. to midnight on an assigned frequency of 850 kilocycles with a power of 10,000 watts.

NEWSPAPERS

THE development of the New Orleans press is closely linked to the development of native literature, and the newspapers, for many decades the chief cultural influence of the Colony, had many contributors whose names are now prominent in Louisiana literature. These included, among others, George W. Cable, Lafcadio Hearn, Henry Castellanos, Mollie Moore Davis, and Catherine Cole. For several months Walt Whitman was a New Orleans newspaperman, contributing light verse, essays, and short stories to the *Crescent*, a publication which flourished for a few years during the middle nineteenth century.

The first newspapers in the city were published in both French and English. Set in large, badly worn type and turned out on hand presses, the papers devoted very little space to local current events, since news happenings were usually common knowledge long before the sheets were off the press. The columns were a mélange of advertisements, clippings from European newspapers, fiction, poetry, and letters from readers. Illustrations were limited to woodcuts of houses, boats, and trees, which were used over and over.

Louis Duclot, a refugee printer from Santo Domingo, established the first newspaper in New Orleans in 1794. Known as *Le Moniteur de la Louisiane*, with 'Bombolio, Clangor, Stridor, Taratantara, Murmur' as its motto, it was published irregularly as a weekly, semi-weekly, and tri-weekly for a little more than twenty years, having been sanctioned by Governor Carondelet as the official news organ of the government. As the town became more cosmopolitan news sheets were published in other languages, but few of these survived for more than a year or so. The foreign-language presses were operated on Chartres Street, in the Vieux Carré, while most of the English publications were issued from offices along Camp Street, known in the early days as 'Newspaper Row.'

During the early part of the nineteenth century a number of newspapers made their appearance, the most important of which were the *Louisiana Gazette* (first English paper), *L' Ami des Lois*, *Le Courrier de la Louisiane*, and *L'Abeille*. The most successful and probably the best known of these was *L'Abeille*, a French newspaper established in 1827 by François Delaup. This publication was issued continuously in both French and English for almost fifty years. In 1872 the English editions were discontinued, and early in February 1921 the paper was purchased by the Times-Picayune Publishing

Company. Under the new management *L' Abeille* was issued weekly until 1925 when, after almost a century of publication, an editorial, 'La Fin de *l'Abeille*,' announced that the paper was going out of existence.

The history of the *Times-Picayune*, the oldest present-day newspaper in New Orleans, epitomizes a century of journalistic development in Louisiana during which only those papers which combined with others attained any degree of longevity. The *Picayune*, established in 1837 by Francis Asbury Lumsden and George Wilkins Kendall, began a new era in Southern journalism. Patterned after the 'Penny Press' of the North, it sold for a picayune, whence its name. The word 'picayune' is the Anglicized form of *picaillon*, a term then in use in New Orleans to designate the smallest current coin, a piece of silver worth about six and one-fourth cents.

G. W. Kendall, while reporting the Mexican War, gained national renown for the *Picayune* by using a pony express to relay his copy to New Orleans, where it was first published before being forwarded to the East. The *Picayune* is given credit for being the first to use this method of news transmission.

In 1874, at the death of E. J. Holbrook, editor, the management of the *Picayune* was taken over by his widow, better known as the poet, Pearl Rivers. Mrs. Holbrook is said to have been the first woman in the world to edit a metropolitan daily, and the first woman in the South to enter journalism as a profession.

Dorothy Dix (Mrs. Elizabeth M. Gilmer) came to New Orleans in 1896 and has maintained an 'advice to the lovelorn' column for the *Picayune* over a period of forty years – an unsurpassed record for newspaper features.

The present *Times-Picayune* is the result of numerous newspaper mergers since the Civil War; the *New Orleans Times* absorbed the *Crescent* in 1868 and in turn combined with the *Democrat* to form the *Times-Democrat* in 1881, which merged with the *Picayune* in 1914 to form the *Times-Picayune*. The *Democrat* had been established in 1875 with Richard Tyler, son of President Tyler, as its first editor. *Le Propagateur Catholique* and the *Deutsches Zeitung* were both founded before the Civil War and published for several years.

Before the outbreak of the War Between the States, Gallic journalism in New Orleans had increased in importance and prestige. At this period there began a definite decline in the use of the French language, the reason for which is readily apparent. Post-war poverty forced the oncewealthy Creole planters to forego their frequent visits abroad, and their sons were placed in the public schools of New Orleans instead of the universities of Europe. Here the students were taught the English language, a fact which resulted in a gradual break with French culture and tradition, and a waning of the influence of the French press. Subsequent writers have deplored the fate of the French newspapers, and the passing of the gay and witty Creole editors who were 'equally at home with pen, pistol and sword, and who lent such spice and color' to New Orleans journalism. Today there is only one French newspaper, *Le Courrier de la Nouvelle Orléans*.

The New Orleans *Item*, founded June 11, 1877, is said to be the oldest afternoon newspaper in the South. The paper was established by eleven journeymen printers, who, out of work, banded together to form a cooperative news publication. Mark Bigney was made managing editor with Edwin L. Jewel assistant. At the end of the first week, when the profits were distributed, each member of the staff received $2.65.

In June of the following year, Lafcadio Hearn, who had spent a miserable seven months in New Orleans, sick, hungry, and out of work, was introduced to the editor of the *Item* as a literary fellow 'after your own heart.' When Hearn's experience as a journalist in Cincinnati became known, he was given work as 'assistant,' with a salary of ten dollars a week. Hearn's literary ability was recognized almost immediately, and he was soon given a free hand in molding the policies of the *Item*. Within a few months the paper had changed from a dry colorless sheet of advertisements, letters, and excerpts from foreign papers to a flourishing publication filled with local and national events, literary criticisms, dramatic reviews, poems, and cartoons. Hearn was soon serving, not only as chief editorial writer, but cartoonist and critic as well.

In 1881 John W. Fairfax gained controlling interest of the paper, retaining Bigney as editor until the latter's death in 1886. During these years the *Item* employed a number of prominent writers on its staff, including, among others, J. B. Wilkinson, Henry Guy Carleton, Judge Alexander Walker, and Thomas G. Tracey.

When Fairfax sold the paper in 1894 it was purchased by Dominick O'Malley, a stormy Irishman who had come to New Orleans from Cincinnati shortly before. Scathing editorials began to appear in the columns of the *Item*, as O'Malley denounced the political scandals of what he contemptuously dubbed the 'boodle council.' Fist fights and cane lashings, as a result of these editorials, were frequent occurrences, with fatalities not uncommon.

The *Item*, now in its sixtieth year, was begun as an independent publication. Today, while perhaps more conservative than a great number of other Southern newspapers, it is strictly a Democratic paper.

The most important newspapers at present published in New Orleans, in addition to the *Times-Picayune* and the *Item*, are the *States*, an evening daily founded in 1880 and owned and published by the Times-Picayune Publishing Company, and the *Morning Tribune*, established in 1924 and now a tabloid, published by the *Item*. In addition to these there are more than forty other news publications issued regularly in the city, including weekly, monthly, and quarterly periodicals. Among these are several commercial, labor, trade, school, and religious publications.

Straight News Publications

American Progress, 822 Perdido St., published monthly by John D. Klorer, is a political organ established in 1933 by the late Senator Huey P. Long. It carries no advertising and is not published for profit.

Herald, 1124 Lafayette St. (Algiers), is a weekly newspaper published each Thursday by Dr. C. V. Kraft.

Louisiana Weekly, 632 S. Rampart St., is a Negro publication edited by Mayme Osby Brown.

Morning Tribune, 722-730 Union St., is a tabloid published daily except Sundays, when it is combined with the *New Orleans Item*. The paper is edited by Marshall Ballard.

New Orleans Item, 722-730 Union St., edited by Marshall Ballard, is a daily evening newspaper which combines with the *Morning Tribune* on Sundays.

New Orleans States, 615 North St., a daily evening newspaper edited by J. E. Crown, is under the same management as the *Times-Picayune*, having been purchased by the latter in 1933.

Times-Picayune, 615 North St., edited by L. K. Nicholson, is the oldest daily newspaper published in New Orleans, having been founded in 1837.

Weekly Crusader, 417 Canal Bank Building, is published by Sidney W. Keats.

Foreign Language Publications

Courrier de la Nouvelle Orléans (*New Orleans Courier*), 702 Camp St., printed in both English and French, is published twice a month by André Lafargue and Mrs. J. G. de Baroncelli.

Deutsche Zeitung (*The German Gazette*), 200 South Galvez St., edited by Walter Zachiedrich, is published weekly by the Deutsches Haus for members of the organization.

Il Messaggero (*The Messenger*), 941 Royal St., an Italian weekly, is edited by Paul Montelepre.

La Voce Coloniale (*The Colonial Voice*), 604 Iberville St., an Italian weekly, is edited by Joseph R. Colleta.

Vox Latina (*The Latin Voice*), 702 Canal St., a Spanish newspaper, is published twice a month by Joaquin Barcenas.

Labor, Trade, and Commercial Journals

American Cotton Grower, 535 Gravier St., is published monthly under the editorship of Stanley Andrews.

American Insurer, 217 Carondelet St., is published monthly by Louis Phillips.

Cotton Trade Journal, 810 Union St., is published weekly under the editorship of Will Branan.

Daily Journal of Commerce, 427 Camp St., is edited by A. L. France and E. Washofsky.

Federationist, 520 Conti St., is published each Friday by William L. Donnels.

Louisiana Grocer, 217 Pan-American Building, is published monthly by the Retail Grocers Association.

New Orleans Medical and Surgical Journal, 1430 Tulane Ave., edited by John H. Musser, is published by the Louisiana State Medical Society.

Proceedings of the Louisiana Engineering Society is published bi-monthly by the Louisiana Engineering Society, with James M. Robert as editor.

Rice, Sugar, and Coffee Journal, 201 Bienville St., the official organ of the respective industries in the South, is edited and published by R. J. Martinez.

Southern Plumber, 207 Board of Trade Annex, edited by Theodore A. Walters, is published monthly by the New Orleans Association of Master Plumbers.

Sugar Bulletin, 407 Carondelet St., is published bi-monthly by Reginald Dykers.

School and Religious Publications

Catholic Action of the South, 712 Louisiana Building, is published weekly by the Rev. Peter M. H. Wynhoven.

Christian Advocate of the Southwest, 631 Baronne St., is a colored publication issued monthly by L. H. King.

Jewish Ledger, 938 Lafayette St., is published weekly by Dr. Mendel Silber.

Lagniappe, Newcomb College, is published quarterly by Newcomb College students.

Maroon, Loyola University, is published weekly during the regular school session by Loyola students.

New Orleans Christian Advocate, 512 Camp St., is published each Thursday by W. L. Duren.

Tulane Hullabaloo, Bienville Hall, Tulane University, is published weekly by Tulane students.

Miscellaneous

Court Records, 430 Chartres St., is published daily by K. P. Montgomery.

Louisiana Conservation Review, Department of Conservation, New Orleans Courthouse Building, 400 Royal St., is published quarterly with James P. Guillot as editor. Free distribution.

Louisiana Digest, edited by E. R. Greenlaw, 6831 West End Boulevard, is the official journal of the Police Jury Association of Louisiana, and is published monthly.

Menagerie, 2640 Upperline St., is a small literary magazine published irregularly by Bennett Augustin.

New Orleans Directory, published annually by Soards, 502 Stern Building, 548 Baronne St.

Police Reporter, 623 Godchaux Building, John C. Roth, editor, is published weekly.

ARTS AND CRAFTS

THE story of art in New Orleans begins with the almost legendary figure of Ferdinand Salazar (or Latizar), the artist whose full-length portrait of Don Andres Almonester hangs in the Cathedral. Salazar also painted portraits of Trudeau, the Spanish surveyor, and of Madame Trudeau, about 1769, but beyond these few works nothing is known of him. There is a tradition that an even earlier artist, Miguel García, came to Louisiana with Bienville, but there are no facts to substantiate this.

During the French and Spanish régimes the inhabitants of New Orleans had little time for other than practical pursuits. Objects of art in the finer homes and in public buildings were almost without exception imported from Europe.

Building design, however, made notable progress, and presented the opportunity for a combination of the constructive and the artistic. The early New Orleans architects usually followed the styles then prevalent in European countries, as evidenced by many examples of French and Spanish influence in older buildings of the Vieux Carré; gradually, however, various originalities crept into their work, and ultimately a distinctive 'Creole' style was developed.

Possibly no single feature is more typical of this Creole architecture than the delicate ironwork which decorated the finer buildings. Of the two distinct kinds, wrought iron and cast iron, the wrought decorations are the older.

After the annexation of Louisiana to the United States, New Orleans began to grow rapidly in wealth and population, attracting both visitors and new residents in increasing numbers. Artists from other American cities began to come here, lured partly by the mild winters, but principally by the prospect of finding a lucrative field for their work. Perhaps the optimism of the earliest of these 'pioneer' painters was justified, for still others came – among them many prominent artists of that day.

Artists from France, Italy, Spain, and England were drawn to the city. Many of them established studios in old homes in the Vieux Carré, which were admirably suited to that purpose. Dominique Canova, Pomarede and Ciceri, members of that group, were instrumental in founding the Bohemian center which has long colorfully characterized the French Quarter, and to which at a later date Degas, Wikstrom, and others added their influence. At times the supply of painters exceeded the demand for portraits, and that the artists sometimes suffered privation – as recorded in letters and journals like those of Audubon – is not surprising. Many of the better portraits and pictures which came out of that interesting era – unfortunately most of them unsigned – are still in the possession of old families of the city; others have been scattered far and wide through auction sales, but a considerable number have been preserved in the Cabildo, the City Hall, the New Orleans Courthouse, and other public buildings.

Perhaps the painter most closely identified with New Orleans is John James Audubon, who first came to the city in 1821. The artist-naturalist was at that time working on his monumental 'Birds of America,' and made studies of game birds brought to the French Market, meanwhile earning his livelihood by painting portraits. Audubon's diary is filled with many vivid word-pictures of his experiences in New Orleans. He seems to have written the journal hurriedly, for there is carelessness in his spelling, punctuation, and grammar. This is especially true of some of the lines in which he made reference to his contemporaries – lines not always complimentary, and sometimes caustic. He also has left descriptions of the various residences he occupied while living in the city, one of which was 'in Barracks Street near the corner of that and Royal Street – between Two Shops of Grocers and divided from them and our Yellow Landlady by Mere Board Partitions. . . .' Another entry, dated October 21, 1821, is: 'Rented une Chambre garnie in Rue St. Anne No. 29 for $16 per Month....' A later inscription records the rental of a house on Dauphine Street.

Audubon seems to have disapproved, too, of the city's social life of that day, making mention elsewhere in the diary of 'french Gayety that really sicked me.' However, he must have found the New Orleans atmosphere at least conducive to work, for by the fall of 1821 he had completed '62 drawings of Birds & Plants, 3 Quadrupeds, 2 snakes, and 50 Portraits of all sorts.' In 1822 he left the city for Natchez, going from there to Louisville and Philadelphia. He returned to New Orleans in 1837, but spent most of his time in the Barataria section, painting and sketching.

A complete set of the elephantine edition of Audubon's 'Birds of America' can be seen at the Cabildo; the artist's drawing of his son, James Woodhouse Audubon, is displayed on the second floor of the Cabildo, Room B.

A contemporary of Audubon was John Wesley Jarvis, a native of England and the nephew of John Wesley, the founder of Methodism. Jarvis, who was an annual winter visitor to the city from 1816 to 1834, was considered by his contemporaries an artist of 'astonishing powers' and one of the best portrait painters of his day. He displayed remarkable speed in his work, often completing six portraits within a week. He, too, kept a diary, which shows that, unlike many painters, he did not lack financial reward for his art. One of his visits to New Orleans is described as follows: 'My purse and pocket were empty. I spent 3000 dollars in six months, and brought back 3000 to New York.'

In character Jarvis was erratic: his studio and living quarters were in a constant state of disorder, he was careless of his appearance, and his peculiarities plainly stamped him an eccentric. At one time he was accustomed to wear a long coat heavily trimmed with furs, and took two large dogs with him wherever he went.

Audubon once made an effort to collaborate with him, but their temperaments were entirely incompatible.

In the Cabildo are two oil portraits by Jarvis, that of Armand Beauvais, Governor of Louisiana 1829-30, and that of Louis Philippe de Roffignac, Mayor of New Orleans 1820-28. There is also a painting on wood said to represent the Lafitte brothers and Dominique You, and to have been painted by Jarvis, who was friendly with the pirates, at their rendezvous on Grand Isle.

John Vanderlyn, called by Audubon 'the historical painter,' was in New Orleans from 1820 to 1830. While best known for his portraits, he painted a number of splendid panoramas, of which his 'Versailles' is considered best. A copy of Vanderlyn's portrait of Andrew Jackson, for which Audubon posed for the body, is now in the Cabildo.

Among other well-remembered painters of this period were Matthew Harris Jouette, a pupil of Gilbert Stuart, who painted Lafayette on his American visit in 1824-25; Theodore S. Moise and Jacques Amans, who won the prize of a thousand dollars offered by the Municipal Council in 1844 for a painting of Andrew Jackson on horseback; Jean François Vallée, a Frenchman, who painted the portrait of Jackson best liked by the old warrior himself; Duval, another Frenchman, who did the best known portrait of Governor Claiborne; Enoch Wood Perry, who painted John Slidell, and an unusual portrait of Jefferson Davis – with a map of the United States for a background; and A. G. Powers, who executed a full-length painting of General Zachary Taylor. The French artist Lion also lived in New Orleans for many years (1830 to 1845) and painted many fine portraits.

In the meantime, as the city's population and wealth increased, skilled artisans established themselves in New Orleans. Many of their productions, built to suit the ideals of a class whose members were wealthy and cultured, were exquisite in both material and design. In most of their work the French influence was predominant.

Fine furniture and furnishings had been a feature of the wealthy homes of New Orleans since the city's earliest days. In Colonial times these were brought over from Europe; later American 'immigrants' also brought European importations, as well as Early American pieces.

The earliest locally made furniture now extant was fashioned by carpenters from native cypress. In style these chests and tables and chairs resembled French Provincial pieces. Beds, because of the necessity of mosquito *baires*, were always four-posted. By 1822, however, there were more than fifty cabinet-makers listed in the city directory. In the period that followed (1822-63), Mallard, Seignouret, and Seibrecht, all of whom had their shops on Rue Royale, were outstanding. Mallard was especially noted for his 'duchesse table,' an ornately carved dressing-table. Seignouret, whose work was less detailed than Mallard's, stamped his best creations – French chairs and four-posted beds – with the letter S.

There are still some shops in the Vieux Carré where excellent reproductions of old pieces are made. Antique shops on Royal and other streets in the Quarter are filled with articles both imported and collected from old New Orleans homes.

Other woodwork of note is to be found in the simple but beautifully proportioned mantels and paneling of the earlier homes. Marble mantels were imported at a later date, as were designs for plaster ornamentation of walls and ceilings in the general tradition of the Greek Revival.

In addition to the architectural ironwork already discussed, local smiths produced the usual household utensils such as the *chaudiére à trois* – a three-legged iron pot with a handle, used especially for cooking gravies – along with such objects as the slave collar, now to be seen at the Cabildo, fitted with bells that would ring whenever the wearer moved his head. The wrought-iron triangular strap hinges still to be seen on the storm blinds of many old houses were known as 'smith' or 'smithy' hinges and were frequently hammered out by slaves. Cast-iron benches in elaborate grape and flower designs were placed in front of family tombs, so that the bereaved might rest while they mourned. Only at a much later date were these employed as 'garden' furniture; and even today they are still called 'cemetery' benches.

In the cemeteries was to be found another interesting example of local craftsmanship: everlasting wreaths made of beads or shells. In some instances the same wreath was brought out year after year on All Saints Day to decorate the family tomb.

The tradition of fine French embroidery and needlework, brought to New Orleans by the Ursulines in the eighteenth century, has been continued by them and others, notably the nuns of the House of the Good Shepherd, to the present. Elaborate church vestments, 'in memoriam' embroideries with the face of the deceased in white against a black background, and the more usual samplers form interesting museum pieces. The Ursulines also made a highly valued point lace, petit point tapestries, a 'cork' lace, so called because it was made on a piece of cork into which pins had been stuck, and quilts. Early quilting designs included the palm, the oak, and the banana. There was also a log cabin appliqué pattern.

In the matter of dress the wealthier classes followed the French fashion books as closely as possible, the French Opera and the Carnival balls affording opportunity for elaborate costume designing. Atakapas cottonade, a locally made cotton cloth of indigo interwoven with white, was used extensively for men's suits in the nineteenth century; and until the present decade, when they became popular elsewhere, New Orleans was one of the few places in the United States where men habitually wore linens, seersuckers, and other 'wash' suits. Field Negroes were long distinguished by red madras handkerchiefs imported from the West Indies which they wore tied about their heads; house Negroes by blue. The latter were better educated and held themselves socially superior to the field workers. Even today Negro house servants frequently refuse to wear red dust caps.

Although as early as 1822 there were twenty-four silversmiths and goldsmiths in the city, no really local designs in jewelry or silverware seem to have originated here. Most Creole ladies wore brooches of black onyx or enamel outlined with gold scrollwork. Sometimes the black stone was left plain, sometimes ornamented with a gold or jeweled design inlaid or in relief. In silverware the French 'thread' pattern was the most popular. Several examples of the work of Hyde and

Goodrich are to be seen at the Delgado Museum.

It is said that Hyde and Goodrich were put out of business for manufacturing and supplying guns to the Confederate soldiers, but it is surprising how few guns, swords, and knives were made in New Orleans. Most of the examples that turn up in museums and antique shops were imported, even when they bore the stamp of a local dealer. The only knives manufactured to any great extent locally were knives for opening oysters.

From 1887 until 1889 the Hernandez Brothers manufactured china of exquisite craftsmanship in their shop on Carondelet Walk. They came from France, where they worked in the factory at Sevres, and the glaze and composition of their own productions were equal to Sèvres china. The china was unsigned, white with a blue border and a raised monogram. Examples of a white and gold china, said to date back to the forties, and an elaborate flowered china are also extant; but the names of their makers are not known.

As might be expected in a city as French as New Orleans, perfumes were highly prized; and the manufacture of certain local scents is still an interesting industry in the city. Jessamine, sweet olive, and magnolia are among the most popular. Vetiver, a root from the East Indies that grows with ease near New Orleans in the country around Covington and Hammond, has been used as a sachet in the linen closets of Creole ladies for generations. It is not known which if any of these were in the stock of the 'Benjamin Franklin, essence maker,' who in 1830 had his place of business on Tchoupitoulas near Julia. But it is certain that he was supplied with rice powder, rose essence, and a hair pomade made with oil of Bergamot – an oil of frequent use today in Voodoo potions.

Fans, hats, baskets, brooms, and chair seats were all made from the native palmetto, known locally as *latanier*. Strips of *lalanier* are still carried by Negro chimney sweeps, and the fronds are still to be seen used as thatching on the homes of occasional trappers, fishermen, and squatters. In hot weather it was long the custom for the lady of the house to supply her guests with palmetto fans. Frequently these were bound along the edges with cloth from the 'scrap' box and ornamented with a rosette or a bow. Ladies in mourning had their fans bound in black.

For many years Choctaw and Chitimacha Indians sold their reed cane baskets at the French Market. A display of these baskets, as well as several other examples of the craftsmanship of Louisiana Indians, may be seen at the Cabildo.

These Indians must have greatly interested George Catlin, the noted painter of Indian life, who paid several visits to New Orleans in the late forties. A portrait of a woman of color wearing a *tignon* and said to be Marie Laveau, the famous New Orleans Voodoo Queen, is attributed to Catlin. A copy by Frank Schneider now hangs in the Cabildo. The identity of the portrait is, however, not authenticated. The appearance greatly resembles a Choctaw woman of the time.

The *Bee* for February 21, 1844, speaks of West's picture, 'Christ Healing the Sick,' being on exhibition in the Cathedral. Forty thousand people are said to have viewed it at twenty-five cents' admission. The occasion for the notice was furnished by a heavy rainstorm which leaked into the church and wet the picture.

As the city developed, the era of large buildings began with the erection of the St. Louis and the St. Charles Hotels, the City Hall, and numerous churches, theaters, and splendid private homes. This opened a field for the work of decorators and mural painters.

Dominique Canova, a nephew of the famous Canova of Napoleon's day, was engaged to do the frescoes in the St. Louis Hotel, which were later purchased by the French Government when the hotel was demolished following the storm of 1915. Canova came directly from France to New Orleans, and remained a number of years teaching and painting. The fine mural decorations in the Robb Mansion, now the Baptist Bible Institute, are also his work.

Ciceri, another French painter, who came to New Orleans in 1859 to decorate the French Opera House, remained to paint and teach, becoming widely known for his pastels and *gouaches*. Érasme Humbrecht came from St. Louis to paint the walls of St. Louis Cathedral in 1872, and returned in 1892 to retouch them for the Cathedral Centennial.

The best known New Orleans work of Leon Pomarede, also a French painter, is the group of three large murals in Saint Patrick's Church on Camp Street, which are copies of famous works of Italian masters.

By 1844 New Orleans was sufficiently interested in art to support a gallery for the exhibition and sale of foreign, American, and local works of art. Known as the National Gallery of Paintings, it was located at 13 St. Charles Street (old number). Sully and Stewart were said to have held exhibits of their paintings here. The last notable sale was that of the collection of Colonel James Robb, February 26, 1859, which included paintings by Rubens, Salvator Rosa, David, and Horace Vernet.

An added impetus was given to art in New Orleans in 1847 when a collection of three hundred and fifty paintings, assembled in Italy and sent to America in an unsuccessful attempt to establish a national gallery, was auctioned in the rotunda of the St. Louis Hotel. The pictures found a ready sale among the planters and the wealthy leisure class.

The Civil War, however, caused a break in artistic activities, and several years elapsed before pre-war interest in art revived. Alexander Alaux, one of Ernest Ciceri's most brilliant pupils, became noted for his portraits, historical pictures, and exquisite miniatures. A number of his miniatures formed part of the Cusachs Collection in the Cabildo. One of his last paintings, the panoramic 'Discovery of the Mississippi River by De Soto,' is in the State Capitol at Jackson, Mississippi.

Edgar Degas visited relatives here in 1873, and painted them at work in his 'Cotton Factor's Office.' Of this picture, which recently hung in the Degas Exhibition at Philadelphia, *Time* (November 23, 1936) said:

> In 1873 Painter Degas went to N. O. to visit his uncle Michel and his two younger brothers, René and Achille, who were working there in the cotton house. Brother Edgar painted an excellent view of his relatives during office hours, which hung last week in Philadelphia's Exhibition. Uncle Michel in his silk hat and frock coat sits in the foreground peering at a sample of cotton. Behind him brother René is sprawled in a chair, reading

a newspaper, while customers finger samples and clerks tot up books. When the picture was painted, Louisiana had a Negro Acting Governor, P. B. S. Pinchback. The director of the little provincial museum at Pau in Southern France snapped up the cotton market picture for $200 when it was exhibited in 1876. It is valued today at about $75,000. The picture last attracted attention in Paris at the colonial Exposition of 1931 where it was shown as a memento of France's lost colony, Louisiana.

In the 1880's a revival set in, and art flourished as never before. The Southern Art Union was organized in 1883, and held at least one formal exhibition in a gallery which was opened at 203 Canal Street (old number) near Dauphine Street. The membership of the Union rose steadily to five hundred, when the feminine influence became too strong, and an attempt to add 'art embroidery' to the list of interests resulted in the withdrawal of the professional painters.

The revival in the eighties brought many good painters to New Orleans and developed some excellent local talent. Among the most famous visitors may be mentioned George Innes and William Keith, who married a New Orleans woman. A characteristic story is told of Innes while in New Orleans. A local artist called at his room in the St. Charles Hotel on Mardi Gras just as the Rex parade was passing and, to his amazement, found Innes quietly painting, utterly unmoved by the riotous carnival in the street below. Keith is best known for his California landscapes, but many of his paintings done here were highly regarded and commanded a good price.

B. A. Wikstrom, a Norwegian who came to New Orleans in 1883, was widely known as a painter of marines and the designer of numerous Mardi Gras pageants. He promoted a new organization in 1885, known as the Artists' Association of New Orleans, which held exhibitions annually on Camp Street until 1899. In 1901 William and Ellsworth Woodward, in charge of the Newcomb Art School, promoted a new group called the Arts and Exhibitions Club, which merged with the Artists' Association in 1904. The resulting organization, the Art Association of New Orleans, since its inception, has been the artistic mainstay of Delgado Museum.

Joseph Pennell, who made sketches for George Cable's Creoles of Louisiana, had a studio on Royal Street in 1883; and William Hamilton Gibson spent some time here in 1886 making sketches of New Orleans scenes for Charles Dudley Warner's articles in *Harper's Magazine.*

Richard Clague is noted for his French Market scenes, one of which hangs in the Cabildo, and for his Louisiana landscapes. Paul Poincy, born in New Orleans and educated in Paris, did many splendid portraits, pictures of children, and religious subjects. A number of his pictures now hang in various churches and institutions of the city; perhaps the best known of these are the portrait of Archbishop Perche and the large painting (done in collaboration with Moise) of a Volunteer Fire Department Parade, now in the City Hall. Andres Molinary, a native of Gibraltar, in the years he spent here painted many of the portraits which line the walls of the New Orleans Courthouse and the Charity Hospital. Molinary also conducted an art school.

Achille Parelli, a French sculptor and painter, some of whose work is in the Delgado Museum, spent a number of years in New Orleans, and died here in 1899; Achille Peretti, often confused with him, was an Italian who came to New Orleans in 1885. His paintings in the Church of Saint John the Baptist on Dryades Street, and his copy of Raphael's 'Saint Stephen' in Saint Stephen's Church on Napoleon Avenue are well known.

Other artists who should be mentioned include William H. Buck, who painted Louisiana landscapes; August Nogieri, whose paintings of the 'Lee' and the 'Natchez' are now in the Cabildo; Edward Livingston, a pleasing landscape artist; E. D. B. Fabrino Julio, born in St. Helena, painter of the 'Last Meeting of Generals Lee and Jackson,' and Miss Jenny Wilde, granddaughter of Richard Henry Wilde, the poet, who is remembered both as an artist and for her work as a designer of carnival pageants.

Joe Jefferson, the actor, who maintained a home in Louisiana, followed painting as a hobby all through his life. Francis Wilson, his biographer, writes:

> On an occasion ... I had called upon him at New Orleans. After greeting me he said: 'I don't give you my hand,' presenting his elbow to be shaken, 'because it is so dirty.' Then I observed how besmeared he was. His face had a streak of green and yellow, and his fingers were shining with all the colors of the painter's palette .... I asked him if it were true that he would rather paint than act. He replied it most emphatically was.

Oscar Wilde on his visit to New Orleans expressed the feeling that the Negro, with his picturesqueness of manner and dress, had been largely overlooked as an interesting art subject. But the Negro at that time occupied virtually no position in the city's art – either as subject or producer. Julian Hudson, the one exception, was an octoroon, whose portraits were highly praised.

Among the artists of a later date, A. J. Drysdale, painter of misty Louisiana bayous and live oaks in an impressionistic style distinctively his own, was perhaps the most prolific. P. M. Westfeldt was an excellent water colorist. Robert B. Mayfield, an artist who also devoted part of his time to newspaper work, is remembered for his fine New Orleans sketches. The late Charles Woodward Hutson, who began to paint when past middle age, won the Blanche Benjamin prize for Louisiana landscape when he was more than eighty. Later, when the picture was exhibited in New York, critics stated that it was obviously the work of a young man of surprising talent who should be encouraged.

The late Ronald Hargrave spent several years in New Orleans. Aside from his portraits remaining in the city a series of his colored etchings hang in the Roosevelt Hotel and in Arnaud's Restaurant.

Ellsworth Woodward, Dean of the Newcomb Art School, and painter of both portraits and landscapes, has long been identified with art in New Orleans. His most recent work of importance is a mural decoration in the new Criminal Courts Building at Broad Street and Tulane Avenue. He is also known for his etchings and water colors. His brother, William, is likewise well known for portraits and landscapes. There is an interesting collection of ten portraits of former faculty members by William Woodward in the Faculty Room at Tulane University.

A magazine, called *Arts and Letters*, issued bi-monthly, and sponsored by Wikstrom and the Woodwards, existed for one year – 1887. It contained fine etchings and literary material by the artists and writers of that day, and deserved a better fate.

Today a long line of artists, many of whom are in the midst of their careers, either live in New Orleans or make frequent visits. Charles Bien, Laura Bodebender, Douglas Brown, George Castleden, Josephine Crawford, Boyd Cruise, Caroline Durieux, Xavier Gonzalez, Weeks Hall, Knute Heldner, Rita Hovey-King, Catherine Howell, George Izvolsky, Alberta Kinsey, Jeannette LeBoeuf, Myron Lechay, Olive Leonhart, John McCrady, Clarence Millet, Paul and Jane Ninas, Nell Pomeroy O'Brien, Clay Parker, Gardner Reed, Charles Reinike, Margaret Robinson, Helen Samuels, Claire Silber, Gideon Stanton, Will Stevens, Jacques De Tarnowsky, Helen Turner, Dan Whitney, and Ella Wood are only a few of those who have won recognition. Gertrude Roberts Smith, now retired, is well known for her work at Newcomb with textiles and design; Inez Lugano for miniatures; Sadie Irvine and Martha Westfeldt for pottery; Anita Muras and Mary Butler for jewelry and silver. Sculptors include Albert Rieker, a native of Germany, who has done outstanding work both here and abroad; Enrique Alferez, a young Mexican sculptor, who is also winning rapid recognition; Angela Gregory, and Rai Graner Murray. Miss Kinsey's studio at 823 Royal, and Mr. Rieker's at 628 Toulouse, are usually open to visitors.

In 1928 a group of young Negro men, encouraged by Fannie Williams, Negro teacher, formed the Little Arts and Crafts Club and obtained instruction in art by mail. They gave three exhibitions of their work, one at the Dryades Street Public Library and two at the Negro Y.M.C.A. The work was crude, but showed promise, and deserves mention as an indication of the Negro's capacity for and interest in art.

Richmond Barthé, young Negro sculptor, passed his youth in New Orleans, where his modeling of small clay animals attracted the attention of a local critic. He studied at the Art Institute in Chicago, and has within he last few years gained national recognition. Several of his bronzes are in the Whitney Museum in New York, and he has exhibited elsewhere in New York and in Paris. His bust of Roland Hayes is well known. Recently he designed an eighty-foot frieze for a Negro auditorium in Harlem.

New Orleans has two well-recognized schools of art. The *School of Art*, Newcomb College, Tulane University, 1229 Broadway, offers, for girls only, a regular four-year course in art with special classes in pottery, ceramics, interior decoration, bookbinding, jewelry designing, and modeling. A gallery is maintained in which oil paintings, water colors, and pastels are always on display. An outstanding department in the arts chool is the pottery division. Its product has gained international recognition, mainly through the work of Joseph F. Meyer, prominent figure in the development of Gulf Coast pottery, who was engaged as a thrower at Newcomb for some thirty years, and the late Juanita Gonzales, Instructor in Pottery from 1931 to 1935. A talented sculptress, Miss Gonzales was noted in ceramics for her research work in the development of glazes and enamels. The fine collection of pottery on display has won one international and several national awards.

The *Arts and Crafts School*, 712 Royal St., was organized by the Arts and Crafts Club in 1922 to furnish an opportunity for training to those interested in art. At the beginning, the subjects offered were limited to painting, but the school now furnishes a complete art course, including oils, charcoal, still-life, landscapes, perspective, water color, sculpture, design, and criticism. Children's classes are conducted in drawing, posterpainting, and clay. The school operates from October 1 to May 30, with classes from 9.30 to 4.30. Night classes are also offered from 8 to 10. Exhibits by nationally known artists are held every two or three weeks, and there is a general student show at the end of the term. The school is under the direction of a committee, of which Xavier Gonzalez is chairman.

Dillard University, 2300 Gentilly Road, in addition to art instruction, holds six exhibits each year, an annual feature being the exhibit, through the co-operation of the Harmon Foundation, of the work of nationally distinguished Negro artists. A permanent collection of paintings, prints, and photographs by Negro artists is steadily being enlarged. An *Arts Quarterly*, stressing creative efforts among Negroes, and including general information on art development, is published by the University.

Private classes are also held by individual artists throughout the city. The *Reinike Academy of Art*, 632 Royal St., has a small gallery where students' work is placed on exhibit.

The *Art Association of New Orleans*, organized in 1900, promotes the appreciation of all branches of esthetics. The association, which meets at the Delgado Museum of Art, has a permanent collection of paintings, drawings, and prints, some of which are loaned to the museum at intervals during which special exhibits are arranged in monthly series. Annual scholarships are awarded at the exhibits.

The Fine Arts Club was chartered in 1916 by a group of New Orleans women interested in the study and advancement of the fine arts. Activities center at Newcomb College, where semi-monthly lectures are given and social meetings are held three times a year. The club co-operates with museums and art organizations of the city in promoting public appreciation of cultural studies, and awards occasional prizes to art students showing unusual ability in some field.

The New Orleans Art League, 632 Toulouse St., organized in 1927 by a group of professional artists, meets monthly and holds annual exhibits at Delgado Museum. Prizes are occasionally awarded for compositions of exceptional merit.

The Southern States Art League has for its object the union of local art groups and individual artists and patrons, and the promotion of art in the South. It was organized in Charleston, S.C., in 1921, and since then annual exhibitions have been held in various Southern cities. Mr. Ellsworth Woodward has been President.

ARTS AND CRAFTS

THE CABILDO DOOR

THE CABILDO

THE GEORGE W. CABLE HOUSE

THE GRACE KING HOUSE

LE PETIT THÉÂTRE DU VIEUX CARRÉ

ANNUAL OPEN-AIR ART EXHIBIT IN THE FRENCH QUARTER

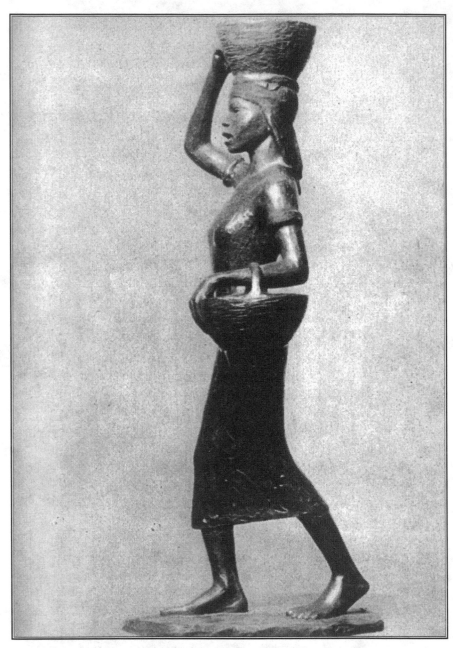

THE BLACKBERRY WOMAN
(BRONZE BY RICHMOND BARTHÉ)

THE CITY HALL, DESIGNED BY GALLIER

DELGADO ART MUSEUM

ST. JOSEPH'S ALTAR

of the League since its inception, except for one year, and Miss Ethel Hutson has served as Secretary-Treasurer since 1924.

The Federal Art Project of Louisiana, under the direction of Gideon Stanton, has produced much interesting creative work as well as drawings and research for the Index of American Design.

The most important art collections in the city available to the general public are at the *Isaac Delgado Museum of Art* at City Park and the *Louisiana State Museum* in the Cabildo. The *Linton-Surget Collection* at Tulane University is also noteworthy. Commercial galleries include the *Reed Art Gallery*, 520 Royal St., *Lieutaud's*, 529 Royal St., and the *Art Shop*, conducted by Dr. I. M. Cline at 622 St. Peter St. In the French Quarter, numerous antique shops contain valuable objects of artistic worth.

On the mezzanine floor of the St. Charles Hotel there is a permanent exhibit of paintings by both American and European artists. The collection includes two Wikstroms and a series of New Orleans scenes by Robert W. Grafton and R. O. Griffith. Grafton also painted portraits of a number of prominent New Orleanians as did Luis Graner, who likewise was in the city for some time. Other permanent exhibits of both contemporary and earlier artists may be seen in the mezzanines of the Roosevelt Hotel and the Saenger Theater, and in the D. H. Holmes Company's restaurant.

Public murals are to be seen at the *Shushan Airport* (by Xavier Gonzalez), the *Roosevelt Hotel* (by Paul Ninas), the *Criminal Court Building* (by Ellsworth Woodward), the *United Fruit Company*, 321 St. Charles St. (by William Woodward), and the *Army Supply Base*, 4400 Dauphine St. (by Ella Miriam Wood).

For several years a picturesque feature of New Orleans art life was the open-air picture fair held in the early spring in the alleys adjoining the Saint Louis Cathedral. Discontinued in 1935 and 1936 it was revived in 1937, and is to be held annually as part of the Spring Fiesta.

LITERATURE

IN THE cultural life developed in New Orleans between 1820 and 1860, literature was well represented – a literature written almost entirely in French and inspired by the French Romantic writers. Indeed, Chateaubriand, the great French exponent of Romanticism, in his brilliant novels of the Louisiana Territory, *Atala* (1801) and *René* (1802), had first made Louisiana writers aware of the literary possibilities of their State.

The excellent French newspapers and revues published in New Orleans had a large share in the creation of this native literature, opening theirpages generously to poems, short stories, and novels. By 1850 there were fifty-two writers of sufficient importance in the city to be included in Charles Testut's *Portraits Littéraires de la Nouvelle Orléans*. Much of the writing borrowed merely the weaknesses of the Romantic style without its compensating beauty; but when it is remembered that there existed no local literary background and that, as citizens of the United States using the language of another country, these writers were isolated both from America and France, the literary accomplishment appears creditable.

The two best-known writers of this early period were the gifted Rouquette brothers, Dominique and Adrien. The sons of a wealthy New Orleans merchant, whose home with its monogrammed balcony can still be seen at 413 Royal Street, Dominique and Adrien were educated in France. Each wrote his first book, a collection of poems, in Paris, and was acclaimed by leading French writers – Victor Hugo, Béranger, Barthélemy, Deschamps, Sainte-Beuve. Dominique published only two collections of poems, *Meschacebéennes* (1839) and *Fleurs d'Amériguc* (1856), though he continued as a sort of unofficial bard of New Orleans until his death many years afterward. Adrien, who shortly after his *Les Savanes* appeared in Paris (1841) had become a missionary among the Choctaw Indians near New Orleans, continued writing throughout his life. His most noteworthy effort besides *Les Savanes* was the pantheistic novel of Indian life, *La Nouvelle Atala* (1879), pronounced by Lafcadio Hearn 'the most idyllic work in the literature of Louisiana.' The prevailing theme of both Rouquettes was the beauty of Louisiana scenery and love for their native State.

While lyric poets predominated among these early writers, there were many who were fascinated with history. The Battle of New Orleans was celebrated in such works as Tullius St. Céran's poems, *Mil huit cent quatorze et mil huit cent quinze*, and Urbain David's ten-canto epic, *Les Anglais à la Louisiane en 1814 et 1815*. The rebellion of 1768 against Spanish domination in Louisiana inspired the historical novel *Louisiana* by Armand Garreau, and the dramas, *Les Martyrs de la Louisiane*, by Auguste Lussan and *France et Espagne* by Placide Canonge, a talented dramatist whose plays were very popular in New Orleans and whose *Le Comte de Carmagnola* achieved a hundred-night run in Paris.

In 1843, a group of free men of color published a magazine called *L'Album Littéraire* containing poems, short stories, and editorials. Poems by this same group appeared in an anthology, *Les Cenelles*, edited by Arnold Lanusse, the first anthology by American Negroes. Three contributors, P. Dalcour, Victor Séjour, and Camille Thierry, gained literary distinction in France.

With the Civil War, the importance of French literature in Louisiana diminished rapidly. Alfred Mercier, one of its most brilliant representatives, belongs, however, to the post-war period. Educated in France, he had begun his literary career there, but after the Civil War he returned to New Orleans, dividing his time between medicine and writing. A widely cultured and versatile writer, he produced noteworthy fiction, poetry, literary criticism, essays on scientific questions, and even a grammar of the Negro-French patois in Louisiana. His novel, *L'Habitation Saint-Ybars* was praised by both Lafcadio Hearn and Edward Larocque Tinker as a permanent contribution to Louisiana literature. In 1876, Doctor Mercier founded in New Orleans the French literary society, *L'Athenée Louisianais*, still existent, in whose official publication, *Comptes rendus*, practically all the French literature produced in Louisiana since 1876 has first appeared.

There is no complete collection of the French literature of Louisiana, nor has any of it been translated; but two valuable bibliographies of the writings have recently appeared, Caulfield's *The French Literature of Louisiana* (1929), and Tinker's *Les Écrits de la Langue française en Louisiane* (1932). In recognition of his work, Tinker was awarded a doctorate in literature by the University of Paris and made a member of the French Academy.

There were only a few isolated writers in English connected with New Orleans before 1860.

John J. Audubon resided in Louisiana from 1821 to 1830, making most of his drawings and accumulating voluminous notes for his *Birds of America*. Audubon's *Journal*, kept day by day during the winters of 1821 and 1822, which he spent in New Orleans, is an intensely human and interesting document, valuable for its side-lights on the life of the time. Two houses in which he lived while in the city are still standing, at 706 Barracks Street and 505 Dauphine Street. Audubon Park was named after the great ornithologist, and a bronze statue of him has been erected there.

François Xavier Martin published in 1827 his *History of Louisiana*, the basis for all future histories of the State. This book and Charles Étienne Gayarré's *History of Louisiana*, written both in French and English, furnished much material for later literary works.

B. M. Morman's *New Orleans and Environs* (1845) is not only interesting as the first local guide-book, but valuable for its historical background.

In 1848, the New Orleans *Crescent* gave young Walt Whitman a part-time job for a few months. While Whitman's newspaper work in New Orleans is comparatively unimportant, and the one bit of literature directly resulting was the poem 'I Saw in Louisiana a Live Oak Growing,' the experience had much bearing on his psychological development. The cosmopolitan old city exerted a broadening influence; but of still greater significance was a passionate love for a New Orleans woman whose identity, however, was never revealed.

Vincent Nolte, the international financier who lived intermittently in New Orleans from 1808 to 1838, related in his book of reminiscences, *Fifty Years in Both Hemispheres* (1854), many anecdotes and adventures connected with his life here. Nolte carried on his cotton commission business from 1819 to 1827 in the building known as 'The Court of the Two Lions,' 641 Royal Street, and lived for a time in the house still standing at 621 Toulouse Street. Nolte's book also served as source material for the recent novel, *Anthony Adverse*, by Hervey Allen, of which several scenes are laid in New Orleans.

The most unusual book to appear in this period was *Bliss of Marriage, or How to Get a Rich Wife* (1858), by S. S. Hall, a New Orleans attorney. The book contained interesting views on love, courtship, and marriage, and an appendix in which the author listed all wealthy marriageable prospects in and around New Orleans, both men and women, with the amount of their fortunes explicitly stated. The book created a sensation in New Orleans, causing no less than six duels. Mr. Hall himself was forced to leave town.

Between the years 1857 and 1861 Samuel Clemens, as a Mississippi River steamboat pilot, traveled regularly between St. Louis and New Orleans, but beyond a few broadly humorous articles contributed by him to the New Orleans newspapers, and the fact that he acquired his famous pen name here, there was little significance in the contact. In 1882, as Mark Twain the writer, he revisited the city, and in *Life on the Mississippi* he devoted ten delightful chapters to the incidents of this visit and his impressions of New Orleans.

During the dormant period immediately after the Civil War, *De Bow's Review*, published in New Orleans between 1847 and 1870, was almost the sole representative of literary effort in New Orleans, sandwiching in between its statistics an occasional poem, essay, or well-written editorial, as well as interesting bits of information on contemporary life. Only a few books, of purely local significance, were published – John Augustin's collection of war poems, *War Flowers* (1865), M. F. Bigney's *Forest Pilgrims and Other Poems* (1867), and Charles Patton Dimitry's novel, *House in Balfour Street* (1868).

But following came the most vigorous period of literary activity in the city's history. Edward King, a representative of *Scribner's*, made a lengthy visit to New Orleans in 1873 while collecting material for his 'Great South' series. The Cotton Centennial Exposition in 1884 brought many more such visitors. Writers like Joaquin Miller, who for six months covered the Exposition for a New York daily, and Julia Ward Howe, in charge of the Woman's Department, became for a time part of the city's cultural life. Richard Watson Gilder, editor of *Century*, and Charles Dudley Warner, an editor of *Harper's*, were also in New Orleans during the

Exposition, Warner subsequently returning for several winters. These publishers and writers, who were alert for literary material, entered into the life of the city and assisted obscure but promising young writers such as Lafcadio Hearn, George W. Cable, Grace King, and Ruth McEnery Stuart to secure recognition.

Following publication of "Sieur George," in *Scribner's Magazine* (1873), George W. Cable found himself hailed as a genius; he had opened a rich and unexplored vein in his stories of New Orleans Creole life. So exclusively did he use the New Orleans locale, and so factual were his charming descriptions of the old homes, gardens, and streets of the city, that he has been accredited along with Bret Harte as being the cause of the 'local color episode' in American fiction. His short stories, reprinted in the collection *Old Creole Days* (1879), and *The Grandissimes* (1879), a novel, are the most enduring of his works. Other important books dealing with New Orleans are the novel *Dr. Sevier* (1887), and the historical writings *The Creoles of Louisiana* (1884) and *Kincaid's Battery* (1908). Three of Cable's fictional houses remain today almost exactly as he described them: 'Sieur George's House, 640 Royal Street, Madame John's Legacy, 632 Dumaine Street, and 'Tite Poulette's Dwelling, 710 Dumaine Street. His own home which he built in the Garden District, 1313 Eighth Street, is occupied today by the New Orleans writer, Flo Field.

In 1877 there arrived in New Orleans Lafcadio Hearn, who was to bring Romanticism to a brilliant fruition. In the ten years he spent here, for one so little anchored, so eternally distracted by 'the pathos of distance,' Hearn identified himself curiously with New Orleans, finding fulfillment for himself as artist, and making his own splendid contribution to the city's literature and cultural life. Perhaps his most notable work during these years were his translations and 'reconstructions' from other literatures, but of more local interest are *Chita*, *Gombo Zhèbes*, and his newspaper writings in the *Item* and *Times-Democrat*, later collected and published by Albert Mordell in *An American Miscellany*, and by Charles Woodward Hutson in *Editorials* and *Fantastics and Other Fancies*. *Chita* (1889), a story of the destructive tidal wave which swept over Last Island near New Orleans in 1856, contains some of Hearn's most brilliant word-painting; *Gombo Zhèbes* (1885) is a little book of Creole proverbs which he collected with infinite pains; the newspaper writings constitute a day by day record of his moods, experiences, and reactions to New Orleans, his explorations into strange literatures, and gleanings from his wide reading of foreign newspapers. Hearn is also supposed to have written *La Cuisine Créole* (1885), and to have collaborated with Coleman in his *Historical Sketchbook and Guide to New Orleans* (1884); two articles previously published by Hearn appeared in the latter, 'The Scenes of Cable's Romances' and 'Père Antoine's Date-Palm.'

Among houses in which Hearn lived while in New Orleans are his first boarding-house, now a tire shop, at 813 Baronne Street, and Mrs. Courtney's boarding house at 1565 Cleveland Street, still standing.

Grace King, who was drawn into writing by the challenge of Richard Watson Gilder, 'If Cable is so false to you, why do not some of you write better?' and who won immediate recognition through her first short story 'Monsieur Motte' (1886), remains one of the more important writers of New Orleans. Among her best-known works are *New Orleans: the Place and the People* (1907); *The Pleasant Ways of St.*

Médard (1916), a novel based on her own girlhood; and the short stories contained in *Balcony Stories* (1892). The home in which Miss King lived for the last twenty-eight years of her life, at 1749 Coliseum Street, is still occupied by the King family.

Cable, Hearn, and Grace King enriched their writing through the use of Louisiana folk literature, which, because of the wide variety of the sources from which it is drawn, has distinctive color and great literary value. There are animal tales, resembling those of Uncle Remus, although showing a less marked interest in nature and a somewhat greater faculty for endowing the animal heroes with human characteristics, together with a keen sense of the laughable in human nature. Tales of witchcraft and conjuration were strongly influenced by the insidious power of Voodoo worship. Fairy tales adapted by the Louisiana Negroes from the French provincial tales, some of which show a marked Celtic flavor, and tales of the supernatural, contributed by the Acadians of the Bayou Country, as well as by their German neighbors, all help to make the wealth of background from which Louisiana writers have drawn from time to time.

In addition, there are the legends, such as those surrounding Père Antoine, the Lafitte brothers, and the royal runaway lovers, Princess Charlotte and Chevalier d'Aubant. Indian legends have also occasionally been used.

Ruth McEnery Stuart, a native of the State, began her literary work in New Orleans and even after she moved to New York, in 1888, continued to draw on her early environment for her stories. She was one of the popular writers of her day, especially skillful in stories of the plantation Negro. Her books with a New Orleans locale are *The Story of Babette* (1902), a Creole story for children, and *Solomon Crow's Christmas Pockets* (1896), a collection of quaint Negro tales.

Cecilia Viets Jamison, who had married a New Orleans man, lived in the city from 1887 to 1902. She wrote charming children's stories of New Orleans – *Lady Jane* (1891), *Toinette's Philip* (1894), and *Thistledown* (1903) – which attracted a wide audience at the time and are still dear to the hearts of New Orleans children. Mrs. Jamison pictured the everyday, homely details of Creole life, and her books are important by reason of their fine local color and interesting character types.

Mrs. M. E. M. Davis moved to New Orleans in 1879 when her husband became editor of the *Daily Picayune*. She wrote novels, short stories, poems, and plays, being perhaps most successful in her delineation of Creole types. Her writings having a New Orleans setting are the novels *The Queen's Garden* (1900), *The Little Chevalier* (1904), *The Price of Silence* (1907), and the poems contained in *Christmas Boxes* (1896). She is best remembered today, however, as one of the famous hostesses of New Orleans who, in a historic old home on Royal Street, brought together in charming and informal fashion all local persons of any note as well as visiting celebrities. In a little book, *Keren-Happuch and I* (1907), Mrs. Davis has told of the famous people who were her guests.

Mary Ashley Townsend ('Xariffa'), the local poet laureate of her day, is represented in two volumes of poems, *Xarijfa's Poems* (1870) and *Down the Bayou* (1882). Mrs. Townsend achieved mention in Clarence Stedman's *Poets of America*, and her sonnet 'Down the Bayou' has been included in a recent anthology, Alfred Kreymborg's *Lyric America* (1935).

The newspapers of the city were also flourishing during this period, and attracted to their staff whatever was promising in the way of local literary talent. Noteworthy was a little group of women writers, pioneers in the newspaper field. Mrs. E. J. Holbrook, as owner and editor of the *New Orleans Picayune*, was the first woman publisher of a daily city newspaper in the United States. Mrs. Holbrook, who later became Mrs. Nicholson, was also a poet, and published a small volume of verses entitled *Lyrics* under the name of Pearl Rivers. Julia K. Wetheril (Mrs. Marion A. Baker) wrote verses and articles for the local papers, and contributed literary criticism to *Lippincott's Magazine* and the *New York Critic*. Elizabeth Bisland, a native of Louisiana, was a friend of Lafcadio Hearn and his contemporary on the *Times-Democrat*, who, according to Hearn, occasionally contributed 'superb poetry' to the paper. She later moved to New York, and as Elizabeth Bisland Wetmore became well known for her novels and her *Life and Letters of Lafcadio Hearn*. Mrs. Martha R. Field (Catherine Cole) did noteworthy work for the *Times* and *Daily Picayune*, attracting attention with her travel articles on European countries and her 'Outings in Louisiana' series. In 1896, Mrs. Elizabeth M. Gilmer ('Dorothy Dix') arrived in New Orleans to begin her brilliant career as a journalist.

Henry C. Castellanos, a veteran journalist, published, in 1896, *New Orleans As It Was*. Described by him as the unwritten history of the city, it contained much interesting and valuable information on nineteenth century New Orleans.

In the summer of 1896, William Sidney Porter ('O. Henry'), charged with embezzlement of bank funds in Texas, fled to New Orleans. Very little is known about his stay here, but in the brief time he remained he stored up enough fictional background for four stories of the city: 'Blind Man's Holiday,' 'Cherchez la Femme,' 'Renaissance at Charleroi,' and 'Whistling Dick's Christmas Stocking.' It was in New Orleans, O. Henry always insisted, that his pen name was acquired.

The literary activity of the seventies and eighties had died out almost completely by 1900. The first two decades of the century brought forth only a few books, with the city apparently unaware that important new movements and 'freedoms' were being expressed abroad. In 1904, Helen Pitkin Schertz published *An Angel by Brevet*, a novel dealing with Voodoo in New Orleans. Eliza Ripley's *Social Life in Old New Orleans*, a delightful book of reminiscences covering her girlhood here from 1835 to 1852, appeared in 1912. The *Jack Lafaience Book*, a collection of the news paper letters in Creole patois written by James J. McLoughlin under the pen name of 'Jack Lafaience' during the preceding thirty years, was published in 1922.

In January, 1921, a group of young intellectuals, deciding it was time that the city break with the old literary traditions and become acquainted with the new, established the *Double Dealer*, a cosmopolitan, anti-puritanical, and liberal magazine with decided modern tendencies. The first issue declared: 'To myopics we desire to indicate the hills; to visionaries, the unwashed dishes .... We mean to deal double, to show the other side, to throw open the back windows stuck in their sills from misuse, smutted over long since against even a dim beam's penetration.' These were strange words in New Orleans, whose literature was conceived in the Romantic tradition and had continued so through a hundred years. The publication held out for five years, becoming known nationally as an excellent literary journal. It was devoted almost exclusively to fiction, poetry, and literary criticism, radical and conservative literary movements of the 1920's being represented. The importance of the magazine as a medium for the expression of all literary trends and the extent to which it discovered and encouraged notable talent may be seen in the number of contributors who have since attained literary recognition – Sherwood Anderson, William Faulkner, Ernest Hemingway, Jean Toomer, Thornton Wilder, and others.

Sherwood Anderson, who had bought an old home at 715 Governor Nicholls Street, in the Vieux Carré, and who lived in the city from 1922 to 1925, contributed various articles, among them a series of impressionistic studies called variously 'New Testament' and 'More Testament.' *Sherwood Anderson's Notebook* (1926), written largely while he lived in New Orleans, contains articles first printed in the *Double Dealer* and his short story of the city, 'A Meeting South,' published originally in the *Dial*.

William Faulkner, who resided in New Orleans during 1924 and 1925, for a time sharing an apartment with Sherwood Anderson, published both poems and articles in the magazine, and during his stay here wrote most of his first novel, *Soldier's Pay*.

Associated with the *Double Dealer* were the local writers John McClure, literary critic and poet; Flo Field, author of the play *À La Creole*, produced in Philadelphia (1929) as *Mardi Gras;* Richard Kirk, author of several volumes of epigrammatic verse, *A Tallow Dip, Penny Wise*, etc. ; Louis Gilmore, Basil Thompson, Julius Friend, James Feibleman, Lillian Marcus, Paul Godchaux, Jr., Albert Goldstein, etc.

Among writers living in New Orleans today are Lyle Saxon and Roark Bradford.

Lyle Saxon, a native of the State and a resident of the city for twenty years, is the author of *Father Mississippi* (1927), *Fabulous New Orleans* (1928), *Old Louisiana* (1929), *Lafitte the Pirate* (1930) and *Children of Strangers* (1937). He served an apprenticeship in newspaper work with the *Times-Picayune*.

Roark Bradford, who has lived off and on in the city for the past fourteen years, first came to New Orleans to do newspaper work, but abandoned it for fiction. An early short story, 'Child of God,' won the O. Henry Memorial award for 1927. He soon became widely known, also, for *Ol' Man Adam an' His Chillun*, which furnished the material for Marc Connelly's play *The Green Pastures*. In his treatment of the oldtime Southern Negro, Roark Bradford, who 'knows his blacks of the deep South better than perhaps anybody else writing today,' continues to use the Louisiana and Mississippi plantation for his background. His novels *John Henry* (1931), and *Kingdom Coming* (1933), touch slightly on New Orleans; the latter contains a fine picture of the Voodoo organization in New Orleans during the Civil War.

Leona Queyrouse Barel, a friend and contemporary of Lafcadio Hearn, whose early poems were written in French and printed in *L'Abeille* and *Comptes rendus*, published in 1933 *The Idyll, My Personal Reminiscences of Lafcadio Hearn*, containing reproductions of letters written to her by Hearn during his stay in New Orleans.

Hermann B. Deutsch, well-known New Orleans journalist, has written numerous articles and stories, the most recent of which have appeared in *Esquire* and in the *Saturday Evening Post*. His first book, *The Incredible Yanqui* (1931), a biography of General Lee Christmas, is laid partly in New Orleans. His novel, *The Wedge* (1935), is a story of revolution in Mexico.

E. P. O'Donnell's first novel, *Green Margins*, published in 1936, is a story of the lower Mississippi delta; the novel won a Houghton Mififlin scholarship prize and was also chosen by the Book of the Month Club.

Elma Godchaux has recently published *Stubborn Roots* (1936), a story of-the-soil novel with a Louisiana cane plantation setting, whose strongly drawn heroine invites comparison with Becky Sharp.

Innis Patterson is the author of two detective novels, *The Eppworth Case* (1930) and *The Standish Gaunt Case* (1931).

Gwen Bristow and her husband, Bruce Manning, have written a number of detective stories with scenes in New Orleans. One of these, *The Ninth Guest*, was produced on Broadway and later made into a movie. Mrs. Manning's first serious novel, *Deep Summer*, was published early in 1937.

Mary Barrow Linfield's novel, *Day of Victory* (1936), depicts an eventful day in the life of a New Orleans business man.

Sallie Lee Bell of Algiers is the author of *Marcel Armand* (1936).

Non-resident writers who use New Orleans locale almost exclusively in their books include Edward Larocque Tinker, Robert Emmet Kennedy, and Hamilton Basso.

Edward Larocque Tinker, a native of New York, has made New Orleans practically a second home. In 1916 he married Frances McKee Dodge of this city, and for years spent his winters here. He has delved extensively into the folklore and history of New Orleans, and has contributed vitally to the city's literature. Much of his writing has been in the form of magazine articles, but he has also published the following books: Lafcadio Hearn's *American Days* (1924), concerned largely with Hearn's New Orleans life; *Toucoutou* (1928), the story of a New Orleans octoroon; *Old New Orleans* (1931), four novelettes written in collaboration with his wife and depicting life in New Orleans from 1860 to 1900; and *Les Écrits de la Langue française en Louisiane* (1932), a study of French literature in Louisiana.

Robert Emmet Kennedy, a native of Gretna, Louisiana, immediately across the Mississippi River from New Orleans, in his short stories *Black Cameos* (1924) and *Gritny People* (1927) and his novel *Red Bean Row* (1929), has made himself known as one of the more gifted writers dealing with Negro life. Although he now lives in New York, all his stories are centered around East Green, a Negro settlement in Gretna, and the True Vine Baptist Church, near the Carrollton Levee in New Orleans.

Hamilton Basso, born in the city but now residing in North Carolina, continues to write about his early environment. *Relics and Angels* (1929) is a novel depicting the reaction of a student recently returned from Europe to New Orleans toward the changing manners of the city. *Beauregard the Great Creole* (1933) is an interesting, authoritative biography of the New Orleans Civil War general.

Another non-resident writer, claimed originally by New Orleans but of late years belonging almost exclusively to New York, is Fannie Heaslip Lea, whose *Chloe Malone* (1916) and *Jaconetta Stories* (1912) are based on her life in New Orleans.

Interesting contributions to New Orleans literature have also been made by visiting writers and those who have remained only a short time in the city. Only a few of the better known of these writers are included here.

Thomas Bailey Aldrich lived in New Orleans as a boy from 1849 to 1852, as he recounts briefly but delightfully in his *Story of a Bad Boy* (1877). One of his most famous short stories, 'Père Antoine's Date-Palm,' in *Marjorie Daw and Other People* (1871), is about a legendary date-palm which stood, until recent years, at 837 Orleans St.

Eugene Field, one of the most beloved of New Orleans' visitors, spent three months here in the spring of 1894. He haunted the antique shops, particularly Waldhorn's, and the old Begué Restaurant, and was a frequent guest at the home of Mrs. M. E. M. Davis on Royal Street. Among his poems written about New Orleans are 'Good Children Street' and 'Dr. Sam' (a Voodoo doctor).

John Galsworthy, who visited New Orleans toward the close of the past century, was so impressed with the melancholy grandeur of the St. Louis Hotel, then tottering on the brink of dissolution, that he wrote one of his haunting 'prose poems' about it, 'That Old-Time Place,' in *The Inn of Tranquillity* (1924).

Frank Stockton, author of *The Lady or the Tiger?* was a friend and frequent guest of Mrs. M. E. M. Davis during his visits here. He has written a delightful love story of New Orleans, 'The Romance of a Mule-Car,' in *Afield or Afloat* (1900).

Winston Churchill's novel *The Crossing*, involving the acquisition from France of the Louisiana Territory, is laid partly in New Orleans. The Court of the Two Lions was the home of his heroine.

Rex Beach, an enthusiastic sportsman who came often to New Orleans in the early years of the century for duck hunting, used New Orleans locale in *The Net* (1912), a novel dealing with the Mafia, and 'The Crimson Gardenia,' a short story in *The Crimson Gardenia* (1916).

Charles Tenney Jackson married Carlotta Weir of New Orleans and spent a great deal of time in and around the city from 1911 to 1919. In *Captain Sazerac* (1922), a novel dealing with the Lafitte pirates, he has made skillful use of the historical background of New Orleans.

William McFee, the English writer of sea stories, has been in the city at various times. A chapter in his *Harbours of Memory* (1921), entitled 'The City of Enchantment,' is devoted to New Orleans, and he also makes use of New Orleans locale in *Captain Macedoine's Daughter* (1920).

Two of Joseph Hergesheimer's stories, Quiet Cities (1928) and Swords and Roses (1929), are laid partly in New Orleans, the latter containing an interesting study of the Creole Civil War leader, General Beauregard.

Oliver LaFarge, whose *Laughing Boy* was awarded the Pulitzer Prize for 1929, spent two years, from 1926 to 1928, in New Orleans as assistant in ethnology at Tulane University, where he was associated with Frans Blom in the Department of Middle American Research. He wrote *Tribes and Temples* (1927) in collaboration with Mr. Blom, author of *Conquest of Yucatan* (1936).

Carl Carmer, best known for his novel *Stars Fell on Alabama*, lived for two years in the city, serving for a while as columnist on the New Orleans *Morning Tribune*. While here, he published *French Town* (1928), a collection of short poems about the French Quarter.

Harris Dickson, the Mississippi author, who has written extensively of New Orleans in newspapers and magazines, has also published three historical novels with a New Orleans setting: *She That Hesitates* (1903), *Gabrielle, Transgressor* (1906), and *Children of the River* (1928).

LIBRARIES

Public Libraries

Howard Memorial Library, 601 Howard Ave. (*See Tour 3.*)

Italian Library, Italian Hall, 1020 Esplanade Ave. (*open Tuesday, Thursday, and Saturday*, 5-7), is a very small reference library consisting of Italian classics, fiction, and current periodicals. A comfortable reading-room is provided.

Louisiana State Library, Room 415, New Orleans Court Bldg. (*open weekdays* 9-5; *Sat.*, 9-12), possesses the most complete collection of reference law books in New Orleans, numbering approximately 60,000, available to the general public as well as to the law profession. The library and reading-room are in charge of Miss Alice M. Magee, Librarian.

Louisiana State Museum Library, 545 St. Ann St., lower Pontalba Bldg. (*See Tour French Quarter.*)

New Orleans Public Library, 1031 St. Charles Ave. (*See Tour 3.*)

Archives

City Hall Archives, City Hall (*open Mon.-Fri.*, 9-1; *Sat.*, 9-12), contain a complete file of New Orleans newspapers from 1804 to date (with the exception of the year 1868), which includes the first American news paper published in New Orleans, the *Louisiana Gazette*, and all newspapers published in New Orleans during the Civil War, both Confederate and Federal. City Hall Archives are also the repository for the mayors' messages, minutes of the City Council, and digests of city ordinances.

St. Louis Cathedral Archives, St. Louis Cathedral, 615 Père Antoine Alley (*open weekdays* 2-5). The archives of the St. Louis Cathedral, for more than a century the only Catholic church in New Orleans, cover baptismal, marriage, and burial records from 1720 to date, contained in 123 registers.

The first period covers the years from 1720 to 1777, written in French, with no division between white and colored. Baptismal records are available from 1731 to 1733 and from 1744 to 1777; marriage records from 1720 to 1733, 1759 to 1762, and 1764 to 1768; burial records from 1731 to 1733. Loss of the missing records was due to conflagrations, or the use of inferior ink or paper, causing deterioration.

The second period covers records from 1777 to date, written first in either French or Spanish, but by the beginning of the present century almost entirely in English. For whites, the baptismal and marriage records are complete; burial records are available from 1777 to 1843. For colored, baptismal records are available from 1777 to 1873; marriage records from 1777 to 1866; burial records from 1777 to 1843.

These records are of much importance. Requests for genealogical research in the Cathedral's archives are received constantly from every State of the Union and from almost every country of Europe. In addition, various marginal notes have been made by the priests, particularly in the early years, which form a running commentary on interesting and important historical events. The Battle of New Orleans is recorded thus:

> On the 8th of January 1815 great battle between Americans and British in which the latter lost four thousand men between killed, wounded and prisoners, and they were compelled to withdraw.

Presbytère Archives, Jackson Sq. (*See French Quarter Tour.*)

University and College Libraries
Baptist Bible Institute Library, 2828 Camp St. (*See Tour 4.*)

Loyola University Library, Loyola University, 6363 St. Charles Ave., opposite Audubon Park. (*See Tour 3.*)

Newcomb College Library, Newcomb College, 1229 Broadway. (*See Tour 3.*)

Tulane University Library, Tulane University, in 6300 block of St. Charles Ave., opposite Audubon Park. (*See Tour 3.*)

Private Libraries
Walter S. Lewis Collection, 806 Carondelet Bldg. This collection includes the Robert Lawson Correspondence, consisting of military correspondence to Lawson from such men as Lafayette, Jefferson, Von Steuben, Hardy, General Nelson, Muhlenberg, and Richard Henry Lee. One unsigned letter is thought to be from General Washington.

Dr. Rudolph Matas Collection, 2251 St. Charles Ave. Dr. Matas' Medical Library, one of the most complete in the country, covers every phase of medical history. Dr. Matas contributes internationally to medical and surgical journals and is now writing a history of medicine in Louisiana.

E. A. Parsons Private Library, 5 Rosa Park, known as the Bibliotheca Parsoniana, was founded about 1900. It consists of a collection of historical documents, autographs, manuscripts, incunabula, bindings, medals, and ancient and modern private presses. About 50,000 items have been collected, including what is probably the finest Louisiana Americana in the world, and 500 incunabula, among them one of the two *Canon Missae*. Mr. Parsons will permit qualified students to use the library, if appointment is made previously with him.

T. P. Thompson Private Library, 1912 Calhoun St., is one of the most complete private collections to be found in New Orleans. The library comprises interesting historical documents, many connected with the early history of Louisiana, including the valuable B. F. French Historical Collection, the works of Lafcadio Hearn, Grace King, George W. Cable, Charles Étienne Gayarré,

Alcée Fortier, and the unpublished letters and correspondence of John James Audubon; many English and early American writers of note, as well as the older classics; and a comprehensive set of books on European art. There is also an admirable collection of oil paintings, many by early American artists.

Other important private libraries in New Orleans are the *Charles H. Behre Collection*, 2800 Jefferson Ave.; *Crawford Ellis Collection*, 5411 St. Charles Ave.; *Hunt Henderson Collection*, 1410 Second St.; *André Lafargue Collection*, 1116 Carondelet Bldg.; *Walter Parker Collection*, 924 Moss St.; *Robert Polack, Jr. Collection*, 1424 Whitney Bldg.; *Henry Soulé Collection*, 836 Pine St.; *John Wisdom Collection*, 1415 Cadiz St.

Libraries for Negroes

Dillard University Library, Dillard University, Gentilly Rd. (*See Tour 1.*)

New Orleans Public Library, Dryades and Philip Sts. (*open weekdays* 9-9; *Sun.* 1-8; take Jackson car at Canal and Baronne Sts., or Freret car at Canal and St. Charles Sts., and walk one block), contains approximately 14,500 volumes, including books on Negro history written by nationally famous Negro writers.

Xavier University Library, 3912 Pine St. (*See Tour 3.*)

THEATER

FOR the half-century preceding the Civil War New Orleans was an important center in the theatrical world. The population of the city, made up in large part of pleasure-loving Latins, was quick to support the first efforts at establishing a theater. As a result several theaters sprang up during the early part of the nineteenth century, and the drama in New Orleans for a time achieved a standard of excellence rivaling, or perhaps surpassing, that of any city in the country.

While New Orleans was yet under the rule of Spain, there arrived in 1791 a home-less refugee band of actors and actresses who had fled the terrors of a murderous Negro uprising in the French West Indies. This troupe, which was headed by a Monsieur Louis Tabary, for a time gave performances in improvised quarters such as tents or vacant shops, and received such enthusiastic acclaim that before long it obtained a more permanent and commodious location. This first theater was known under various names through the years, but is best remembered as Le Spectacle de la Rue St. Pierre. The building was located at 732 St. Peter Street; it is not known whether any part of the original structure remains.

A noisy and boisterous element, as well as the élite, must have frequented the playhouse, because on November 28, 1804, the following police orders were pub-lished and posted in the theater:

Article I
No person shall present himself to the several entrances of the theater without hav-ing a ticket of admittance, and if any be proven to have gained admission by cun-ning or otherwise or by having used violence, he will be brought before a compe-tent magistrate to be punished by imprisonment or fine in accordance with the varying degree of trouble he may have occasioned.

Article II
If good order is to be maintained, the orchestra of the hall cannot be subject to fanci-ful demands to play this or that tune; the management binds itself to satisfy the pub-lic's demand by the rendition of national airs; no person by bringing up any request in this regard shall disturb either the orchestra or the audience without running the risk of being brought before the magistrate as is provided in the first part of the ordinance.

Article III
Neither shall anyone have the right of taking possession of a box or any place which shall have been rented to someone else.

Article IV

No one shall express his approval or his disapproval in such a way as to disturb the calm of the theater, either by noisy clapping if pleased or hissing – if displeased.

Article V

No one will be allowed to throw or to pretend to throw oranges or anything else, be it in the theater or in any part of the hall, nor in a word, shall anyone be allowed to start quarrels with his neighbor or with any one; nor shall anyone insult anybody or come to blows or speak ill of anyone in order to stir up trouble under penalty of being punished with all the severity allowed by the present ordinance, as a disturber of public peace.

The department desires greatly that the order of the theater and the pieces played will contribute to the keeping of harmony, good-will and good manners, for alone on these rests the permanence and success of this institution.

The second theater to be founded in New Orleans was the St. Philip, erected in 1808 on St. Philip Street between Royal and Bourbon at a cost of approximately $100,000. It had a seating capacity of seven hundred and included a large parquet with two tiers of boxes. One of the early programs here included the first *corps de ballet* to be presented in New Orleans; for several years the best dramatic talent available was offered. The theater continued to be a successful enterprise until 1832.

The Orleans Theater, the third to be established in the city, was located at 721 Orleans Street, just off Royal. The first building, erected in 1809, was destroyed four years later by fire, but rebuilt soon after in a more pretentious style, the exterior being adorned with Doric colonnades. Besides a spacious parquet, the building contained several galleries, two tiers of boxes, and loge seats set off by lattice or iron grillwork. Performances began at six in the evening and frequently lasted until two or three o'clock the next morning. One night's program might include an opera or vaudeville, a comedy, and finally a heavy drama to complete the bill. It was here that Lafayette was entertained in 1825, a special performance having been arranged in his honor. In the building next door, and operated in connection with the theater, was the Orleans Ballroom, scene of many of the most noted entertainments of the period; for a time the famous quadroon balls were held here.

These first theaters were given over to programs in the French language. It was not until an American troupe known as the Commonwealth Company, with Noah Ludlow as one of its members, came to New Orleans in 1817 and obtained temporary use of the St. Philip Theater that plays were produced in English. These first performances were so well received by the English-speaking element of the city that James Caldwell, an English actor who came to the city in 1820, was encouraged to build a theater in which only English plays would be produced. This was accomplished with the erection of the American Theater in 1822-23, the first building in New Orleans to be illuminated with gas. Located on the lake side of Camp Street, between Gravier and Poydras, and seating 1100 people, the building was put up at a cost of $120,000. The theater, formally opened on January 1, 1824, became noted throughout the country for its excellent entertainment. Almost every prominent actor or actress of the day appeared there.

Caldwell erected another theater, the St. Charles, at 432 St. Charles Street, in 1835 and in 1842 took over the New American, the second theater of that name erected on Poydras near Camp Street. The St. Charles, then perhaps the most magnificent in America, is said to have compared favorably with the opera houses of Naples, Milan, and Vienna. Construction of the building alone cost $350,000. The huge central dome and mammoth chandelier attracted hundreds of people from all over the country; the chandelier, weighing more than two tons, had 250 gas lights and 23,300 cut-glass drops. Playing to a full house containing four thousand seats and forty-seven boxes, the theater opened with the 'School for Scandal' and the 'Spoiled Child.' Seven years later it was destroyed by fire, and a second theater by the same name was built on the site by Noah Ludlow and Sol Smith, competitors of Caldwell.

This theater was operated with success until it was destroyed by fire in 1899. A new theater, built on the site in 1902, was used by the Orpheum Company before the present Orpheum Theater on University Place was constructed in the early 1920's. After remaining closed for several years, the St. Charles was used from time to time for legitimate stage productions; at present it is a motion-picture house.

Many famous players appeared at the three theaters, among them Edwin Booth, James Brutus Booth, Jenny Lind, and Fanny Ellsler. Joe Jefferson, who made his home at Jefferson Island, Louisiana, after 1869, appeared often at the St. Charles. Returning from a tour of Texas during the Mexican War, he mentions seeing Mr. and Mrs. James W. Wallack, Jr., in 'Richard III,' a play 'finely acted but indifferently mounted.' What impressed him most, however, was the after-piece, 'A Kiss in the Dark,' a farce featuring the rising young comedian, James E. Owens, whose 'effec- tive style and great flow of animal spirits' aroused the professional jealousy of Jefferson, who 'had hoped to see something not quite so good.'

Another popular theater of the nineteenth century was Placide's Varieties, opened in 1849, on Gravier Street between Baronne and Carondelet. The establishment was under the management of Tom Placide, the actor. After five successful seasons the theater was partially destroyed by fire, but reopened the next year under a new name, the Gaiety. In 1870 the building burned down completely, and the owners built a new theater, afterwards called the Grand Opera House, on the present site of the Maison Blanche, a Canal Street department store.

The old Varieties experienced its greatest period of prosperity during the three-month stay in 1853 of Lola Montez, the famous dancer who was created Countess of Lansfield by the King of Bavaria. Upon arrival in New Orleans she was met by two large groups – one representing the more puritanical element in the city, which bitterly opposed her appearance; the other hailed her coming with glee and boister- ous celebration. A near-riot occurred at the St. Charles Hotel a few hours later, when the music of a band employed by the welcoming young blades was drowned out by boos and catcalls of the opposing faction.

Perhaps the most amusing series of many hilarious incidents surrounding Lola's stay in New Orleans ensued when she, replying with a kick to amorous advances made by the theater prompter, was very much astonished to be soundly kicked in return; the stage manager and others intervened, and the luckless Lothario suffered a severe beating. He then very ungallantly proceeded to file charges of assault and battery against the dancer. A great crowd scrambled madly to her trial, cheering when Lola exhibited as evidence a swollen, angry bruise high upon her thigh. Thereafter the prompter cherished his one rather dubious bid to fame as the 'Man who kicked the Countess.'

On December 1, 1859, the initial performance was given at the French Opera, which housed plays as well as operas until it was destroyed by fire in 1919.

The National Theater, established about the middle of the nineteenth century, was located on Baronne Street, at the present site of the De Soto Hotel. The theater was founded for the production of German plays, and for a time was known as the German National. The playhouse had a varied but successful existence until it burned in 1885.

Other places of amusement in existence before 1880, but which played comparatively minor rôles in the development of dramatic art in the city, include the Club Theater, the Bijou, Atlantic Gardens, and Wenger's Garden.

The showboats were in their heyday from 1870 to 1890. These 'floating palaces' bore such picturesque names as 'Cotton Blossom,' 'Daisy Belle,' and 'River Maid.' Up and down the Mississippi and its tributaries they plied, playing the old favorite melodramas over and over, to a thousan miles of audience. 'East Lynne' and 'Tempest and Sunshine' were enjoyed time and again by young and old, white and Negro, often so many times that the audiences knew the lines as well as the actors did; but when the showboat came round the bend, calliope screaming, band blaring, and flags flying, excitement spread along the levee and back into the fields like wildfire, as if an entirely new and wonderful thing wereabout to happen.

The Greenwald Theater, 201 Dauphine Street, opened in 1904 with a stage presentation of 'The Wife.' But the following season it opened with a burlesque show, which type of entertainment continued for some years. Then, for a time, the building was used by a stock company, the 'Emma Bunting Players,' and the name was changed to the Emma Bunting Theater. From 1915 to 1930 the building was operated – when it was operated at all – as a motion-picture and vaudeville house, under the name of the Palace. In 1935 it was made a Negro theater, offering motion pictures and vaudeville.

The Tulane Theater, Baronne between Canal and Common, built in 1898, and demolished in 1937, had a seating capacity of 1500, with a parquet, balcony, and gallery including four boxes on each floor. Special attention was given to the acoustics, the design imitating the drumlike formation of the old French Opera. A great number of famous actors and actresses appeared at the Tulane, including Julia Marlowe, George Arliss, Richard Mansfield, Maude Adams, De Wolf Hopper, Robert Mantell, Katharine Cornell, and Anna Held. For the last five years New Orleans has had no regular theatrical season, only occasional plays having been presented at the Tulane before it was razed. The Municipal Auditorium, in which concerts, operas, and dance programs have been given since its dedication in May, 1930, has recently housed its first dramatic production.

New Orleans has produced a host of lesser theatrical lights and about a half-dozen who attained world-wide recognition and fame. At the head of the list is Adah Isaacs Menken, born in Milneburg, a suburb of New Orleans, about 1835. Her parentage and early life are shrouded in mystery; her own accounts, conflicting statements apparently given out for publicity purposes, add to the confusion. She began her career as a dancer, graduated to drama in her early twenties, and in the short space of her life – thirty odd years – became remarkably versatile, adding poetry, painting, sculpturing, singing, and a knowledge of French, Hebrew, German, and Spanish to her accomplishments. In 1856, at Livingston, Texas, she married Alexander Isaacs Menken, the first of a series of four or more husbands, and the following year made her stage debut at Shreveport, Louisiana, as Pauline in 'The Lady of Lyons.' A few months later she appeared in New Orleans as Bianca in 'Fazio,' and thereafter, using her first husband's name, began a theatrical career that made her the toast of Europe and America.

Her remarkable beauty, her extravagant and uninhibited manner of acting, and the aura of rumored immorality attached to her name caused her every performance to be a sell-out. Adept in the modern Hollywood technique of acquiring box-office value through publicity stunts, she committed one sensational act after another. She was involved in bigamy with her second husband, John Heenan, famous prize-fighter of the day, was arrested as a Secessionist, and at Astley's Theater in London in 1864 created a sensation as a scantily clad Mazeppa, the first woman to essay the rôle and the first performer to ride a horse in the scene in which a dummy had always been strapped to a horse.

Celebrities of two continents – Mark Twain, Bret Harte, Artemus Ward, Walt Whitman, Georges Sand, Alexandre Dumas, Théophile Gautier, Charles Dickens, Algernon Swinburne – paid homage to her, and she went from triumph to triumph, amusing herself and the world. She died in Paris in 1868 while rehearsing for a new version of 'Les Pirates,' and was buried in Montparnasse. The simple inscription on her tomb, 'Thou Knowest,' epitomizes her brilliant career, as does Swinburne's remark written on a copy of her volume of poems, *Infelicia;* 'Lo, this is she that was the world's delight.'

Cora Urquhart Potter, another native star, made her first professional appearance in London, in a play called 'Man and Wife,' produced in 1877. She later played at the Fifth Avenue Theater in New York and toured the United States in Shakespearian and other rôles.

Minnie Maddern Fiske was born in New Orleans in 1865. She made her first appearance at the age of five as the little Duke of York in 'Richard the Third.' In 1897 she attained her greatest success in 'Tess of the D'Urbervilles,' one of the greatest pieces of emotional work done by any actress of her time.

Edward Hugh Sothern was born in a boarding-house on Bienville Street, New Orleans, in 1859, while his parents were on tour. During the first years of his career he was known as a comedian, later as a romantic and Shakespearian actor. Between 1904 and 1914 he and Julia Marlowe were considered the leading Shakespearian exponents in the United States.

In Sothern's entertaining reminiscences, *Melancholy Tale of Me,* he tells of how, on a visit to New Orleans, an old lady gave him 'a small fawn-colored coat, very old-fashioned, with high collar, bell-shaped cuffs, pearl buttons as large as a half dollar, much moth-eaten,' which Dion Boucicault had lent to Sothern's father to wear on the stage. In a pocket of the coat he was pleasantly surprised to find some memoranda written in his father's hand.

Sidney Shields, who for many years was Walker Whiteside's leading lady, was born and reared in New Orleans. She came of a family long active in theatrical circles of this city.

Robert Edeson, born in New Orleans in 1868, spent his childhood in Brooklyn, and began his successful stage career in New York. He was one of the first actors of the legitimate stage to enter motion pictures.

Marguerite Clark (Mrs. Harry P. Williams), famous star of the silent films, has lived in New Orleans many years.

Many plays have been written in, about, and for New Orleans, ranging from French printings on the intrigues of the nineteenth century to a very modern play, 'Stevedore,' based on Negro life of the city's wharves.

One of the earlier plays, titled 'Mis' Nelly of N'Orleans,' was written by Lawrence Eyre; Minnie Maddern Fiske toured in it for several years. 'Danse Calinda,' by Ridgely Torrence, is a pantomime of nineteenth-century Mardi Gras in New Orleans. 'À La Creole,' a three-act play by Flo Field produced in 1927, is of authentic New Orleans atmosphere, and has genuine Creole and Cajun characters; as presented in New Orleans, the play was considered one of the best ever written about the city. 'Stevedore,' by George Sklar and Paul Peters, is the latest play with a New Orleans setting. This three-act race tragedy, performed by a cast of Negroes and whites, is a dynamic portrayal of a wharf strike. The play has been highly successful in the East.

A history of the amateur theatrical groups about which theatrical activity in the city now centers would begin with what is believed to have been one of the earliest 'little theaters' in the country. On the spacious grounds of her mansion 'Roselawn' (now 3512 St. Charles Avenue) Madame Rosa Salomon da Ponte, a noted beauty, built and equipped a miniature theater. She engaged a director in 1891, and presented the first play, 'Called Back, a Romance Drama,' a thriller with subtitles such as 'The Blind Witness,' 'Recognition,' 'The Vanished Past,' 'A Black Lie,' and 'Tracked to Siberia.'

Madame da Ponte carried stage illusion into her drawing-room; her friends remember teas in caverns of ice, and balls in Egyptian marble palaces. After a few years the Roselawn's patroness left for Europe in search of new triumphs; she succeeded in her quest, gaining international fame as a beauty and belle. But the hitherto promising little theater, no longer blessed with Madame da Ponte's extraordinary personality and generous purse, went into a decline and died an almost unnoticed death.

Today Le Petit Théâtre du Vieux Carré, 616 St. Peter Street, the outgrowth of 'The Drawing Room Players,' headed by Mrs. Oscar J. Nixon and organized in 1916, has become one of the best-known little theaters in the country. The Group Theater, 2211 Magazine Street, organized in 1934, has given a number of noteworthy modern productions. Le Petit Théâtre du Reveil Français, 939 North Rampart Street, was started in 1930 with the purpose of preserving the French language in New Orleans. The Civic Theater, the Algiers Little Theater, and the dramatic clubs of the schools and colleges throughout the city are also active. A limited number of tickets for non-members are usually on sale for the various productions.

MUSIC

THE music of New Orleans has been as varied and colorful as the nationalities which have made up its population. From the operas of Paris, Milan, and Vienna came the classics which gained such popularity in the city during the middle of the nineteenth century; from the West Indies came barbaric, rhythmic chants that evolved through a period of years into work songs, dance melodies, blues, and jazz; from Canada and the outlying French settlements came the Cajun songs. The Creoles, descendants of pioneer French and Spanish families, absorbed it all, and contributed, in their turn, light airs and whimsical melodies.

New Orleans was the first Southern city to establish an opera company, and for more than half a century the city was recognized as one of the leading music centers of the country. As early as 1810 light operas, romances, musical comedy, and drama were presented at the Spectacle, St. Philip, and Orleans Theaters, all of which were located in the French Quarter. It was not until 1837, however, that serious attention was given to opera. In that year Mlle. Julia Calvé made her début at the Orleans Theater, scoring a great success. Three years later Charles Boudousquié, who afterwards became the husband of Mlle. Calvé, brought from France the first important company of singers to visit New Orleans. Their first appearance in the city was made at the Orleans Theater, in 'Le Chalet.'

Ole Bull, famous violinist of his day, gave many concerts in New Orleans over a ten-year period, 1844-54. On his first visit the old rivalry between Creoles and Americans was reawakened; the Frenchman Vieuxtemps, an arch-rival of Bull's, being in the city at the same time, competition between the two performers evoked warm discussion as to their comparative artistry. In 1845, at the conclusion of his concert series, a practical joke was played upon Bull at a banquet held at the St. Charles Hotel. The violinist, upon being asked to show his silver medal and famous Cremona violin, was horrified to find that the medal had turned to lead and the violin had been crushed and broken. Tension was relieved when a magician, the perpetrator of the trick, produced the real articles. In the concert series of 1853, Maurice Strakosch, appearing with Bull, introduced his protégée, little Adelina Patti. It is interesting to note with what perspicacity the *Picayune*, on February 27, 1853, predicted that if proper attention were paid the prodigy she might 'certainly become a vocalist of remarkable power.' Seven years later at the French Opera House Orleanians thunderously applauded a mature Patti, who soon after won international fame in London.

Jenny Lind, while under the management of P. T. Barnum, created a furore among opera-loving Orleanians during her month's stay in the city in 1851. Crowds lined the levee at her arrival, and it was only through a ruse employed by Barnum, who, with an associate, escorted two veiled ladies down the gangplank, that the famous singer was able to reach her quarters in the lower Pontalba Building without discomfort. Seats for her first concert, held on February 10 at the St. Charles Theater, were sold at auction, the first being purchased for $240. The theater was sold out for each performance, and so great was public acclaim that Barnum was induced to extend the 'Nightingale's' engagement.

Eliza Ripley's *Social Life in Old New Orleans* contains an interesting account of the opera of the forties:

It was on Orleans Street, near Royal – I don't have to 'shut my eyes and think very hard,' as the Marchioness said to Dick Swiveller, to see the old Opera House and all the dear people in it, and hear its entrancing music. We had 'Norma' and 'Lucia di Lammermoor' and 'Robert le Diable' and 'La Dame Blanche,' 'Huguenots,' and 'Le Prophète,' just those dear old melodious operas, the music so thrillingly catchy that half the young men hummed or whistled snatches of it on their way home.

There were no single seats for ladies, only four-seated boxes. The pit, to all appearances, was for elderly, bald gentlemen only, for the beaux, the fashionable eligibles, wandered around in the intermissions or 'stood at attention' in the narrow lobbies behind the boxes during the performances. Except the two stage boxes, which were more ample, and also afforded sly glimpses towards the wings and flies, all were planned for four occupants. Also, all were subscribed for by the season. There was also a row of latticed boxes in the rear of the dress circle, usually occupied by persons in mourning, or the dear old *messieurs et mesdames*, who were not chaperoning a *mademoiselle*. One stage box belonged, by right of long- continued possession, to Mr. and Mrs. Cuthbert Bullitt. The opposite box was *la loge des lions*, and no less than a dozen lions wandered in and out of it during an evening. Some were blasé and looked dreadfully bored, a few were young and frisky, but every mortal one of them possessed a pompous and self-important mien.

If weather permitted (we had to consider the weather, as everybody walked) and the opera a favorite, every seat would be occupied at 8 o'clock, and everybody quiet to enjoy the very first notes of the overture. All the fashionable young folks, even if they could not play or whistle 'Yankee Doodle,' felt the opera was absolutely necessary to their social success and happiness. The box was only five dollars a night, and pater-familias certainly could afford that.

Think of five dollars for four seats at the most fashionable Opera House in the land then, and compare it with five dollars for one seat in the top most gallery of the most fashionable house in the land today. Can one wonder we old people who sit by our fire and pay the bills wag our heads and talk of the degenerate times?

Toilets in our day were simple, too. French muslins trimmed with real lace, pink and blue *barèges* with ribbons. Who sees a *barège* now? No need of jeweled stomachers, ropes of priceless pearls or diamond tiaras to embellish those Creole ladies, many of whom were direct descendants of French nobles; not a few could claim a drop of even royal blood.

Who were the beaux? And where are they now? If any are living they are too old to hobble into the pit and sit beside the old, bald men.

It was quite the vogue to saunter into Vincent's, at the corner on the way home. Vincent's was a great place, and he treated his customers with so much 'confidence.' One could browse about the glass cases of patés, *brioches*, éclairs, meringues, and all such toothsome delicacies, peck at this and peck at that, lay a dime on the counter and walk out. A large Broadway firm in New York attempted that way of conducting a lunch counter and had such a tremendous patronage that it promptly failed. Men went for breakfast and shopping parties for lunch, instead of dropping in *en passant* for an éclair.

As I said, we walked. There were no street cars, no buses, and precious few people had carriages to ride in. So we gaily walked from Vincent's to our respective homes, where a cup of hot coffee put us in condition for bed and slumber.

Monday morning, Mme. Casimir or Mam'selle Victorine comes to sew all day like wild for seventy-five cents, and tells us how splendidly Rosa de Vries (the prima donna) sang '*Robert, toi que j'aime*' last night. She always goes, '*Oui, madame, toujours,*' to the opera Sunday. Later, dusky Henriette Blondeau comes, with her *tignon* stuck full of pins and the deep pockets of her apron bulging with sticks of bandoline, pots of pomade, hairpins and a bandeau comb, to dress the hair of mademoiselle. She also had to tell how fine was 'Robert,' but she prefers De Vries in 'Norma, *moi.*' The Casimirs lived in a kind of cubby-hole way down Ste. Anne Street. M. Casimir was assistant in a barber shop near the French Market, but such were the gallery gods Sunday nights, and no mean critics were they. Our nights were Tuesday and Saturday.

Society loves a bit of gossip, and we had a delightful dish of it about this time, furnished us by a denizen of Canal Street. He was 'horribly English, you know.' As French was the fashion then, it was an impertinence to swagger with English airs. The John Bull in question, with his wife all decked out in her Sunday war paint and feathers, found a woman calmly seated in his pew at Christ Church, a plainly dressed, common-appearing woman, who didn't even have a flower in her bonnet. The pew door was opened wide and a gesture accompanied it, which the common looking somebody did not fail to comprehend. She promptly rose and retired into the aisle; a seat was offered her nearer the door of the church, which she graciously accepted. Lady Mary Wortley Montague had asked for a seat in that pew, as she bore a letter of introduction to its occupant. This incident gave us great merriment, for the inhospitable Englishman had been boasting of the coming of Lady Mary. I introduce it here, for it has a moral which gives a Sunday school flavor to my opera reminiscences. Now they have all gone where they are happily singing, I hope, even better than Rosa de Vries, and where there are no doors to the pews.

The French Opera Company, which came into existence near the middle of the nineteenth century, had a long and successful career, during which many of the old classics were presented. The French Opera was one of the South's greatest contributions to music. The building was erected in 1859 in the Vieux Carré, five blocks from Canal Street, on the uptown lake corner of Bourbon and Toulouse Streets. The house was opened in December with the presentation of 'Guillaume Tell,' conducted by Professor Eugene Prévost, a New Orleans musician.

The opera became the focus of social life in New Orleans – 'a scene of costly jewels, elaborate costumes, lovely women, gallant gentlemen, and magnificent music.' European artists coming to New Orleans for engagements lived in the city throughout the opera season. People of all walks in life attended the opera, even those who wished solitude. For these persons the *loges grillés*, or boxes enclosed with lattice work, were intended, being occupied chiefly by those in mourning and *femmes enceintes*. A favorite New Orleans anecdote is that of the Creole belle who was almost born in the opera house. For it was not until the middle of 'Faust' that her mother, Mme. Blanque, turned to M. Blanque and said, 'Pierre, I do not think I can wait for the ballet!'

Among the outstanding stars who appeared at the French Opera were Adelina Patti, Mme. Urban, Mlle. Hitchcock, and Julia Calvé. Among works given here for the first time in America were Gounod's 'La Reine de Saba' and 'Le Tribut de Zamora,' Bizet's 'L'Arlésienne,' Massenet's 'Hérodiade,' 'Werther,' and 'Don Quichotte,' Saint-Saën's 'Samson and Delilah,' and Lalo's 'Le Roi d'Ys.' The opera house was destroyed by fire in November 1919 and has not been rebuilt.

Since the early period of its history New Orleans has developed a definite type of music in its Creole and Negro songs. The former originated among the slaves of French and Spanish refugees who came from the West Indies to New Orleans during the first decade of the nineteenth century. The Negro songs are heard in a patois with local variations wherever the French language and Negro dialects are found along the Gulf Coast and throughout the West Indies. A mixture of humor and pathos runs through the apparently nonsensical lyrics, and with their original theme based on some French or Spanish melody, well disguised by a novel interpretation, the songs express the passions of the Louisiana Negro. 'Po' Pitié Mamzé ZiZi,' one of the best of their love songs, was used by Gottschalk in a piano composition; his 'La Bamboula' was based upon what he heard and saw in Congo Square as a boy. A favorite of the more modern songs is 'Mary Blane,' composed almost entirely of eighth and sixteenth notes.

The plantation songs of the Southern Negro have constituted one of the most interesting developments in American folk music – the quaint melodies and fascinating rhythms of the 'befo'-de-war' Negro offering, in addition to their own beauty, a rich field for future composers. Both Chadwick and Dvořák made use of these melodies in their symphonies.

The following (taken from Emmet Kennedy's *Mellows*) is an excellent example of the Negro song:

Tell yuh 'bout a man wot live be-fo Chris'–
His name was Adam, Eve was his wife.
Tell yuh how dat man he lead a rugged life,
All be-cause he tak-en de 'ooman's ad-vice.
She made his trou-ble so hard – She made his trou-ble so hard –
Lawd, Lawd, she made his trou-ble so hard.
Yas, indeed – his trou-ble was hard.

In the Creole songs ran a lighter, more whimsical vein. Death is treated in a matter-of-fact fashion, as in the song 'Grenadié, ca-ca-yié,' the words of which give a feeling of fatalism: 'What matter, the death of one soldier, simply one ration less, so much the worse for him, indeed.' Love in these songs was treated lightly, and gossip ran from an account of some minor incident to the hushed whisper of scandal. The gay life of old Creole days, when casket girls were wooed by soldiers, is musically related in Victor Herbert's 'Naughty Marietta.'

Street cries among vendors have always been a characteristic of New Orleans. Crude rhymes are composed by peddlers who saunter along the streets crying their wares to housewives, servant girls, or any who will listen.

The blackberry woman, having walked miles from the woods and bayou banks, with skirts tucked gypsy-fashion around her waist and bare legs showing traces of dusty travel, calls in a melancholy tone:

'Black-ber-ries – fresh and fine, I got black-berries, lady,
Fresh from de vine, I got black-berries, lady, three glass fo' a dime,
I got black-berries, I got black-berries, black-berries.'

New Orleans has often been said to be the birthplace of jazz (originally called 'jass'), the outgrowth of cacophony turned out by 'spasm' bands, which made their appearance in the last decade of the nineteenth century. Playing in front of the theaters, saloons, and brothels of the city, these bands regaled the public with their informal 'ear' music.

One of the earliest of these organizations, the 'Razzy Dazzy Spasm Band,'was composed of such colorful individuals as Stalebread Charley, Family Haircut, Warm Gravy, Cajun, Whisky, Monk, and Seven Colors. Instruments consisted of a cigarbox fiddle, old kettle, cowbell, pebblefilled gourd, bull fiddle constructed of half a barrel, harmonica, and numerous whistles and horns. However abhorrent the clamor produced by this assortment of instruments might have seemed to music-loving Orleanians, the band attained sufficient popularity by 1911 to warrant an engagement in New York, where its name was changed to 'Jazz Band.'

Other early bands – New Orleans Rhythm Kings, Crescent City Jazzers, Creole Jazz Band, Original Dixie Land Jass Band – popularized the new type of 'hot' music and introduced it to the North, where its acceptance in the form of a national craze was instantaneous. The famous Dixie Land Jass Band, composed of five players, none of whom could read or write music, reached the height of its popularity in 1915, when it is said to have serenaded Sarah Bernhardt. In the same year the band started on a tour of the country, aiding in glorifying jazz as the national dance music.

A diversity of influences – white and Negro folk music, brass band and military numbers, and French tunes – are reflected in jazz. 'Tiger Rag,' for example, is said to be based upon a French quadrille; musicians of the old school can still break it down into the tempi and movements of the original dance form. The clarinet chorus of 'High Society Blues,' practically a definitive form for 'swing' players, derives, supposedly, from the flute passage of a march by John Philip Sousa. The influence of Negro folk music is apparent in the numerous blues that have appeared. 'Canal Street Blues,' 'Basin Street Blues,' 'Milneburg Joys,' and other songs celebrate the city and show its influence.

The originality and creativeness of New Orleans composers contributed much to the development of jazz. In its formative stage; 'bucking' and 'cutting' contests, friendly and informal competitions in improvisation constantly vitalized the new music form, adding originality and variety to a field already rich in unconvention- alities. In these contests, which usually were held on the streets of the city or at Milneburg resorts, cornetists of rival bands would 'cut' choruses of tunes until one or the other would throw away his instrument in a gesture of defeat.

Negro jazz, made popular by Louis Armstrong, a New Orleans Negro now cred- ited with being one of the world's greatest trumpeters, deserves mention. Armstrong's success in this field was probably due to his practice of leading or 'cry- ing up' to a note instead of striking it immediately and decisively. His long-drawn- out high notes on the trumpet also added to the weird, bizarre appeal of his music. Armstrong, one of the first exponents of the 'scat' style of singing – the substitution of such syllables as 'da-de-da-da' for words – is noted principally for his individual technique with the trumpet, one of his most popular recordings being 'Basin Street Blues.' Clarence Williams, remembered for his swing technique on the piano, and now a music publisher in New York, published 'I Wish I Could Shimmy Like My Sister Kate,' composed by A. J. Piron, who conducts an orchestra aboard the steamer 'Capitol,' a pleasure craft and one of the few remaining Mississippi paddle-wheelers.

Other New Orleans Negro composers and exponents of jazz are Henry Allen, Jr., Buster Bailey, Sidney Bechet, Barney Bigard, Johnny Dodds, Jelly-Roll Morton, Joe Oliver, Kid Ory, and Spencer Williams.

Among the prominent white jazz artists are George Brunies, Eddie Edwards, Nick LaRocca, Wingy Mannone, Henry Rogas, Leon Rappolo, Larry Shields, and Tony Sparbaro. Louis Prima, another native son, has won wide acclaim on Broadway, over the radio, and in moving pictures.

A peculiar form of jazz, which has been called the 'polyphonic,' a type concen- trating on rhythm and time, also developed in New Orleans. Although never pop- ular, and now almost extinct, it portrays an interesting style of harmony. Very little orchestration is used; three or four melody instruments improvise at once, each playing a solo, and contributing to the whole with an almost perfect sense of bal- ance in relation to the other instruments. The success in such a presentation lies in the strict adherence to rhythm and time on the part of each player. This school of jazz is not basically different from original jazz music, the chief difference lying in the method in which the melody is handled.

A novel attraction of New Orleans today is the 'soap-box' orchestras frequently stationed on street corners of the French Quarter. The instruments, which include perforated tin cups, pie pans, bucket lids, and bottles, are attached to a wooden box and played by a Negro boy, usually between the ages of ten and fifteen. With him are other Negro children, who, in ragged, unkempt garments, dance to the music. New Orleans visitors are attracted by the surprising amount of rhythm and harmo- ny pounded from these crude 'one-man' orchestras.

During the nineteenth century New Orleans produced a number of recognized musicians. Louis Moreau Gottschalk, the State's most eminent pianist and compos- er, was born in New Orleans May 18, 1829. At the height of his career he was well known both in America and abroad for his compositions, among which were 'The

Last Hope' and 'Tarantelle.' It is said that his own interpretations of his compositions held an undeniable sensual charm that few, if any, pianists could approach. Gottschalk, who gave his first European concert at the age of sixteen, gained wide acclaim in Paris, both for his virtuosity and his compositions. 'Bamboula,' built around a dance of the Louisiana Negro, written while Gottschalk was convalescing from a severe attack of typhoid fever, took the French capital by storm. 'La France Musicale,' a Parisian paper, bestowed great praise upon the young American pianist.

An amusing incident connected with one of Gottschalk's tours occurred in San Francisco, where he had arranged Wagner's march from 'Tannhäuser' for fourteen pianos. On the eve of the concert one of his pianists fell sick and Gottschalk was at a loss to find a capable substitute. He searched in vain for an accomplished musician, but in all San Francisco he could find none. The proprietor of the hall finally offered to speak to his son, an amateur pianist, whom he claimed could easily perform the part. Gottschalk was skeptical, but decided to test the son's ability. The amateur derided the suggestion of a rehearsal, but Gottschalk insisted. After the young man had played two bars the great musician realized the impossibility of accepting his services, but he could not easily refuse the enthusiastic son nor the beaming father. Gottschalk's tuner suggested that the hammers of the piano be removed so that the instrument would produce no sound. Gottschalk acceded to this plan and arrangements were completed for the performance. The auditorium was filled to capacity, and the young amateur, in full evening clothes, paraded back and forth before his friends. He had even succeeded in having his piano placed in the center of the stage.

The concert began with a flourish, and continued to an almost flawless finish. The young man had behaved superbly, employing all the elaborate gestures at his command, and perspiring freely. An encore was demanded. The youth, greatly pleased with himself, could not resist playing a short prelude before the others began, so he ran a chromatic scale, but the piano was mute. Gottschalk, seeing the danger, ignored the youth's frantic gestures and gave the signal for the others to begin. To save appearances the young man pantomimed the passages, striking the instrument furiously. Gottschalk said later, 'God protect you, O artists, from the fathers of amateurs, from the sons themselves, and the fathers of female singers.'

Gottschalk died in Rio de Janeiro when, tired of his wanderings, he was planning a quiet retreat in Paris. For some time he had been weakened by fever and fatigue. During one of his concerts he seems to have been seized by a presentiment of death, and was unable to finish his last composition, 'La Morte.'

Ernest Guiraud, also a native of New Orleans, another of the city's prominent nineteenth-century composers, is best known for 'Sylvia,' the 'Kobold,' and 'Piccolino.' His first opera was produced in New Orleans when Guiraud was only fifteen years of age. Seven years later he won the Prix de Rome in Paris, giving him the privilege of four years' travel and study at the expense of the French Government. In 1864 his 'Sylvia' was presented at the Opéra Comique in Paris, scoring an immediate success.

Emile Johns won considerable recognition through his *Album Louisianais*, a collection of original compositions. Johns, also one of the city's pioneer publishers, was a great admirer of beautiful Creole women, dedicating many of his works to them. Florian Schaffter, although not a native of the city, came to New Orleans while still a youth, and in addition to composing music served as organist and choirmaster at the Christ Church Cathedral for forty years. He was also one of the best-known instructors of the city, giving lessons in theory, piano, organ, and voice. Theodore von La Hache, a native of Germany, spent the greater part of his life in New Orleans composing and acting as organist at various churches of the city. In his *Yearly Musical Album* were many compositions portraying life in New Orleans, 'By the Banks of the River' being one of his most popular melodies.

'I Wish I Was In Dixie,' written in 1859 by Daniel D. Emmet as a 'walk-around' for Bryant's Minstrel Troupe of New York, attained its widespread popularity, according to one authority, after its appearance in New Orleans in the fall of 1860, when Mrs. John Wood sang it at a performance of John Brougham's burlesque, 'Pocahontas.' It became popular overnight, and within a short time the entire city was humming the tune. A New Orleans publisher, P.P. Werlein, aware of the possibilities of the hit, had the air harmonized and rewritten. Various versions of the song appeared in different parts of the country and 'Dixie' became almost as popular in the North and East as in the South. After the Civil War started it became the war song of the Confederacy. Werlein's version, expressive of the strong Southern feeling on the eve of the war, differs slightly from the modern song, as shown in the first and third verses of the original:

I wish I was in de land of cotton, Cinnamon seed and sandy bottom look a-way
    a-way in Dix-ey.
Dix-ey's land where I was born in early on one frosty morning look a-way
    a-way in Dix-ey.

.   .   .   .

Buckwheat cakes and good strong butter makes my mouf go flit-ter flut-ter
    look a-way a-way a-way in Dix-ey.
Here's a health to the good ole Mis-sis or to all the gals dat want to kiss us look
    a-way a-way a-way in Dix-ey.

All music lovers are familiar with the meteoric rise of Adelina Patti, who had her first extended engagement at the New Orleans French Opera House in 1860. Her initial performance was in 'Lucia,' a rôle which won her instant recognition in the musical world. While in New Orleans Patti resided in the Vieux Carré at 629-631 Royal Street, two blocks from the Opera House. From New Orleans she went to Havana and to London, to one of the most remarkable careers in the history of modern music.

Catarina Marco, who shared honors with Patti in Moscow in 1875, was born in New Orleans in 1853, the daughter of an actor named Mark Smith. Most of her life was spent in Europe. She made her American début in New York in 1872, and sang again in America in 1878 and 1879. In 1927, when over seventy, she gave a 'come-back' concert in New York and was acclaimed 'the oldest soprano in the United States.'

One of the most popular bands ever to appear in New Orleans was that under the direction of Patrick Sarsfield Gilmore, commonly called Bandmaster Gilmore. An excellent example of his showmanship was demonstrated in 1864 when Louisiana, under the carpetbag legislature, elected Michael Hahn as Governor. Gilmore sought out, in public schools, saloons, and alleys, all available tenors and basses and finally assembled a grand chorus of five thousand voices. All the military bands, about five hundred strong, and a huge drum and trumpet corps were merged into this assembly. The concert was given at Lafayette Square amidst a thunderous roar of cannon and the continuous pealing of bells. It was a tremendous triumph for Gilmore. Just before the close of the Civil War he brought out 'When Johnny Comes Marching Home.' It is unknown whether the pseudonym Louis Lambert belongs to him or another, but he claims the air as his own.

The years of depression following the Civil War brought about a noticeable decline in music in New Orleans. Several theaters closed their doors, and numerous music groups and societies were disbanded.

The renewal of interest in music in New Orleans during the late nineteenth and early twentieth century may be attributed in large part to a number of able instructors, some of whom were born in the city, and others of whom came to New Orleans from European countries. Giuseppe Ferrata, a pupil of Liszt, taught at the Sophie Newcomb College of New Orleans for many years and also produced original compositions. Gregorio Curto, a native of Spain, was responsible, according to contemporary critics, for 'a generation of singers' in New Orleans. Like Ferrata, he produced compositions of his own, many of them being published as church music. Mme. Marguerite Samuels was well known for her work as teacher of piano. Mark Kaiser, who was sent to Paris for instruction by his New Orleans admirers, was a noted violinist and teacher. Mme. Jane Féodor, who sang in the French Opera in 1902, and the late Ernesto Gargano were both well-known teachers of voice.

There were numerous choral organizations in New Orleans during this period; and in 1890 the city was chosen for the national *Saengerfest* of German singing societies. Among the old choral societies which are now no longer active were the *Orphéon Français*, of male voices, with George O'Connell as leader; the Polyhymnia Circle, for many years the only mixed chorus in the city; a women's chorus directed by Victor Despommier which gave large choral works with the assistance of soloists from the East; the Quartet Club, an organization sponsored by German singers; and the Choral Symphony Society, which was directed by Ferdinand Dunkley and consisted of orchestra and chorus.

Today the New Orleans Philharmonic Society, which succeeded the Choral Symphony Society in 1906, is one of the city's leading musical organizations. The society was formed by Miss Corinne Meyer and held its first concert in the spring of 1907. The main object of this organization is to bring to New Orleans outstanding artists and concert groups, whose programs are presented at the Municipal Auditorium. In April 1936, in celebration of the thirtieth anniversary of the founding of the society, the directors secured the Philadelphia Orchestra under the direction of Leopold Stokowski.

The Philharmonic Society also sponsors concerts of chamber music groups such as the Dixon Hall Series, which gives performances at Newcomb College for the benefit of a scholarship fund, and the Junior Philharmonic, which offers competitive auditions to amateur artists.

The New Orleans Civic Symphony Orchestra, a newly organized group under the direction of Arthur Zack, opened its initial season October 12 to March 25, 1936-37, presenting six concerts in all. The orchestra included sixty professional artists who presented selections from Bach, Handel, Mozart, Beethoven, Schubert, Mendelssohn, Brahms, Wagner, Franck, Debussy, Ravel, Elgar, and Strauss. The last concert in the series presented a symphonic prelude, 'Orleans Alley,' an impression of New Orleans and its early-morning street cries composed by John Beach, who taught and composed in the city from 1904 to 1907. Included on the same program was 'New Orleans,' an overture based on Mardi Gras, which won for its composer, Mortimer Wilson, a five-hundred-dollar prize offered by Hugo Riesenfeld of New York in 1920 for the best original American overture. Youth concerts, showing the relation to the orchestra of various groups, such as percussion, wind, brass, and string, are also presented.

The Newcomb College of Music, in existence since 1909, is well recognized throughout the country. Doctor Leon Ryder Maxwell, who has been director since 1910, has a national reputation as a music educator. Recitals are held at Newcomb every Thursday afternoon throughout the school year at Dixon Hall, local, faculty, and outside artists participating. The music department of Loyola University is under the direction of Doctor Ernest Schuyten, founder of the New Orleans Conservatory of Music and Dramatic Art, which was absorbed by Loyola. The Loyola orchestra is one of the best college orchestras in the State. Dillard University sponsors the Lower Mississippi Valley Musical Festival, an annual event. At the inaugural festival in 1937 more than three hundred Negro choristers from some twenty communities sang at the school. Part of a twenty-five-thousand-dollar fund is devoted to the development of the Music Department which has a fine collection of more than eight hundred records.

There are several orchestras in the city, only a few of which, however, are permanent organizations. Albert Kirst's Orchestra, which plays daily at the Fountain Room of the Roosevelt Hotel and broadcasts over WWL, is one of the best known. There are also numerous 'spot' orchestras which have no permanent location but play intermittently as dance, wedding, or banquet engagements are booked. Among them are Johnny De Droit's Orchestra and Gordon Kirst's Orchestra. The Filiberto Mandolin Orchestra, composed of thirty Orleanians under the direction of Roger G. Filiberto, won first place in the Music Guild contests in 1934, 1935, and 1936.

Among the fifty or more Negro bands in the city, Célestin's Tuxedo Orchestra stands out as one of the foremost in the South. Many outstanding musicians obtained their start with Oscar Célestin. There are a variety of Negro choral groups in New Orleans which specialize in spirituals, hymns, and classic and semi-classic melodies; performances are given at churches, radio stations, clubs, and schools. The James A. Gayle Music Company, Pythian Temple Building, is the only Negro publishing company in New Orleans. Phonograph records of local music may be purchased at stores along North Rampart Street.

There are a number of concert band groups in New Orleans which present complimentary programs at various charitable institutions and parks. Harry Mendelson's Band, composed of students from the Mendelson School of Music, gives free concerts at City Park twice a week (Sunday and Wednesday afternoons). The State Band and Orchestra School (for children) and the Stephenson Boys and Girls Band both give free concerts at Audubon and City Parks, and frequently at school programs, asylums, and hospitals. The Federal Music Projects of Louisiana, under the able direction of René Salomon, conducts several music groups, including a small symphony orchestra.

Choral societies now active include the Treble Clef, a women's chorus: the Cercle Lyrique, a mixed chorus of French singers under the direction of Mrs. Dupuy Harrison; the Deutsches Haus male chorus, a merger of the Harugari and Turnverein choral clubs of former years, which continues the traditions of German Maünerchor singing under Professor Drueding; and the Apollo Club, a male chorus under Louis Panzeri. The usual church and school organizations are also active.

Among the other contemporary musicians of New Orleans who have won recognition for their achievements are Ferdinand Luis Dunkley, composer, organist, and conductor now affiliated with Loyola University; Henri Wehrmann, violinist and composer of Creole melodies; Mme. Eugenie Wehrmann-Schaffner, now head of the piano department of Louisiana State University; Walter Goldstein of Newcomb School of Music, and well-known piano teacher and lecturer on musical subjects; Mme. Eda Flotte-Ricau, René Salomon, and Maynard Klein, also of Newcomb; Mrs. Anita Socola Specht, who won the first prize as the best amateur pianist in the United States at the Columbian Exposition in Chicago, in 1893; and Miss Ruth Harrison, formerly connected with the French Opera and now a teacher of voice. Claire Coci is a well-known organist.

Among the present singers of note are Edna Thomas, mezzo-soprano, who has gained a reputation both in America and Europe for her Negro spirituals, folk songs, and New Orleans street cries; Sidney Raynor, now with the Metropolitan; Kitty Carlisle, who has appeared both in movies and on Broadway; Rose Dirmann, Bernadine Wolf, Julian Lafaye, and the Boswell Sisters.

Those interested in musical collections will find at the Howard Memorial and New Orleans Public Libraries several shelves devoted to sheet music, old scores, and historical data relating to composers and their productions. At the former will be found a fine collection of Creole and Negro songs portraying life among the slaves and early residents of New Orleans. Both libraries are open to the public.

ARCHITECTURE

THE United States has but few cities wherein the architecture of their original inhabitants has left a permanent stamp of distinctiveness and individuality. New Orleans is one of them. As a city within a city, its Vieux Carré, or French Quarter, is unique; for this original portion of New Orleans still retains the same architectural dress and flavor that characterized it more than a hundred years ago. Perfectly conceived and admirably suited to the needs of its early citizens, the straight, narrow streets and brick houses of this old town remain as a monument to the people who first settled Louisiana.

But the architecture of New Orleans is more than that. It is a living chapter in the changing panorama of the city's historical and social development. The original city plan, as designed by Bienville and his engineers, was similar to that employed in the erection of most outposts in Louisiana. The town was rectangular in shape and was surrounded by a palisade and foss fortified by five forts. The streets, of even length and width, ran at right angles, and a *place d'armes*, or public square, occupied the central portion of town facing the levee in front of a small church. As the old quarters became too cramped, the city sprawled out gradually in several directions; while from its distant outskirts an inward movement took place. The curvature of the river, and the annexation of suburbs before the development of low-lying, swampy central areas was completed, made uniform street-plotting a difficult matter.

All the environmental changes brought about by the growth of the city coincided with other changes – in wealth, social consciousness, desires, ambitions. These influences crept in as the city grew in size and importance; so that instead of retaining their original aspect, the houses and public buildings of New Orleans acquired a motley appearance, which owes its existence to the fusion of many tastes and temperaments. Thus the individuality of New Orleans, which is at variance with the character of other cities, likewise varies within itself. Certain localities stand out by virtue of their own peculiar architectural make-up, to which they cling tenaciously in the face of changing modes and modern standardization. Besides the old French Quarter, the two other sections of the city that most amply repay the architecturally minded visitor for his trip are the Garden District and the headwaters of the Bayou St. John.

Two centuries of expansion and change have not robbed the Vieux Carré of its identity. Few of its present buildings, to be sure, were erected by the founders of the city; yet most of those that stand today are reminiscent of the eighteenth century, having absorbed its charm, it would seem, through heredity. The earliest structures, hurriedly built of split cypress slabs, were of no architectural importance. They merely served as makeshift residences until the advent of the Ursuline nuns and the *files à la cassette*, whereupon more substantial and comfortable buildings became necessary. The half-timber method of construction was borrowed from Europe. Durable structures built of brick laid in between timbers (*briqueté entre poteaux*, in which the soft porous quality of the domestic bricks was reinforced by stout cypress timbers) gradually replaced the wooden dwellings, although not until after the great fires of 1788 and 1794 did this type of construction gain widespread acceptance. These early buildings were of a type frequently found in European towns; that is, they usually combined shop and residence in one, the proprietor and his family dwelling above his place of business, in the gabled rooms under the roof. The houses were all low-roofed, seldom over a story and a half in height, with a wide, projecting overhang protecting the sidewalk, the roof sloping invariably toward the front and rear, and generally having gable-ends at the sides. Occasional dormer windows and centrally located chimneys relieved the monotonous pitch of the roofs. This style of building persisted long after brick, stucco, and slate roofs were introduced; so that today the visitor may wander along street after street in the Vieux Carré and see many small shops of brick plastered over, the falling off here and there of the plaster revealing the soft-toned orange brick.

The finest example of the original French construction remains standing today in an excellent state of preservation. It is the Couvent des Ursulines, later known as the 'Old Archbishopric.' The exterior of this two-storied brick edifice, with its plain stucco-finished façade, its highpitched roof and well-spaced dormer windows, and its tall slender chimneys, strongly suggests the contemporary French Renaissance architecture. The interior, however, is quite plain and unpretentious. Its great bare beams remain today just as they were left by the axe that fashioned them. Completed in 1734, this building is said to be the oldest now standing in the Mississippi Valley, although recent research shows that Madame John's Legacy, 623 Dumaine Street, has a claim to the distinction.

Half a century after the city was founded it was under Spanish domination. And despite their unpopularity, the Spaniards gradually superimposed their own architectural ideas upon those already established. The eventual result was a native style, part French, part Spanish, but not quite either or even both, which has no duplicate on the American continent. This new type of architecture flowered during the third epoch of the city's growth; that is, in the years following the two conflagrations that ravaged the town of virtually all its original residences and public buildings. At first the changes in design were relatively slight. One-and-ahalf-story buildings, which served as residence and shop, continued in vogue; but tile and slate roofs replaced shingled ones, and brick houses superseded frame ones, in a concerted city-wide effort to prevent future disasters. Now, however, a more dignified class of establishments began to appear, two full stories in height, or two stories and an attic.

This was the era of the patio or courtyard dwelling. Wealthy citizens began building large houses along Royal, Bourbon, Conti, St. Louis, and Toulouse Streets, the chief function of which was to provide comfort and spaciousness in a neighborhood which, with its sloppy, poorly drained streets and narrow lots, gave evidence of neither. Originally created for the sake of expedience, these houses form the most architecturally interesting group of buildings in the Vieux Carré. They are in a real sense, as one authority says, 'architecture, inasmuch as their style and arrangement are founded upon the fundamental conditions of a contemporary society. Social customs, climate, local materials, and cultured taste have each contributed toward making these delightful dwellings almost personal witnesses of their environment.' Latter-day architects have found it difficult to devise anything more suitable for year-round habitation in New Orleans than these elegant courtyard dwellings.

They were built flush with the street line, and instead of affording a broad, flowered front-lawn vista from a wide veranda, such as was common to their contemporaries, the plantation dwellings on Bayou St. John, they hid their interior beauties from the outside world. Casual passersby saw nothing but a plain, two-story façade fronting the banquette, above which hung a lacy, web-like pattern of ironwork galleries adorning the second stories. These delicate traceries, which offset the austerity of the smooth-stuccoed brick walls and delighted the eyes of generations of visitors, have been pronounced by critics the chief distinction of New Orleans' architecture.

Of the two distinct kinds of ironwork, wrought and cast iron, the wrought decorations are the older. For grace and balance of mass, and painstaking craftsmanship, this is the finer work; but the intricate detail of the cast iron is more varied.

Charming but preposterous tales have been circulated concerning the making of these grilles and balconies. They are supposed to be the handiwork of unskilled slave labor, sweating before open hearths; other legends have them made by the brothers Lafitte, Jean and Pierre, whose black smith shop was a blind for the lucrative trade of slave-smuggling. The Lafittes were even said to number among their 'black ivory' customers such respectable citizens as the church wardens of the cathedral, and the Governor himself, all entering the shop ostensibly to contract for ironmongery.

These tales, though interesting, are highly improbable; although records show that the Lafittes did own a blacksmith shop there is nothing to show that the shop was ever anything other than a blind. The earliest ironwork was imported, there being then no known deposits of iron ore near New Orleans. According to Stanley Arthur's *Old New Orleans*, the wrought-iron decorations were probably made in the vicinity of Seville. Mr. Moise Goldstein and other authorities, however, dispute the Seville origin. Later, local artisans began to produce wrought iron comparable to the imported article.

The more pretentious houses used monograms, the initials woven repeatedly through the design. This fashion extended well into the cast-iron era, which dawned in New Orleans in the late 1820's. By 1840 cast iron had superseded the finer, but more costly, hand-wrought decorations. It was clear that there were great possibilities for freedom of design in a material that could be easily worked into intricate and delicate lines, and the early architects immediately put aside the tendency to appropriate the architectural forms and ornaments of other nations and sought their motifs of design in the infinite variety of plant growth luxuriant in their own southern climate. The tulip pattern, the rose vine, the morning glory, the maize, and the live oak predominate in the work produced at this time. Among the other designs one of the most interesting is the bow-and-arrow, in which the bow is a bow of ribbon tying two crossed arrows.

To enter the courtyard house one passed through massive portals into a high-arched flagstoned alleyway which, wide enough to admit a carriage, led from the banquette to an inner courtyard garden, surrounded by high walls that provided an abundance of shade throughout the day. Life in such habitations as these possessed a distinctly European flavor; for the inhabitants, seated in their cool patios or on the verandas that surrounded them, enjoyed absolute freedom from the hot, dusty streets. Most of the houses of this type were built during and immediately after the first quarter of the nineteenth century. The exquisite details of fan windows, spiral staircases, handrails, door panels, and cornices are still revealed today.

After 1840, a new era, born of ante-bellum opulence and expansion, had begun. Along with the demand for more cotton and more slaves, flush times on the Mississippi created a corresponding demand for newer, finer, costlier mansions. During the quarter-century between 1835 and the Civil War probably more elegant homes were built in Louisiana than during any other period before or since. It was the era of the 'Greek Revival.' Archaeological discoveries in and around Athens set a new mode in American architecture: residences, public buildings, hotels, churches, theaters, tombs – all were designed in what was thought to be the best tradition of ancient Greece. The effect was extremely imposing.

Many of the finer residences built during this period are still in use. Most of them are concentrated in the neighborhood above Jackson Avenue, now known as the Garden District because of the spacious and beautifully flowered grounds that surround the houses. As a class, the houses themselves are large, and 'represent the highest expression in domestic architecture that the wealth and talent of the day were capable of producing.' Usually designed with an L-shaped plan, these massive brick houses rise to a height of two or three stories, their side-wall surfaces of plain, smooth stucco or plaster, adorned with richly designed cast-iron galleries, ending in a parapet unbroken by conspicuous horizontal band or cornice. Two tall chimneys, which serve the fireplaces in their double drawing-rooms, break the raked lines of the side wall that mark the gable end of the roof; while tall windows and doors relieve the classic plainness of their colonnaded façades – the arrangement being one of perfect symmetry.

The interiors of these mansions are stately and elegant in effect, and often monumental in proportions. High ceilings, often sixteen to eighteen feet on the ground floors, blend harmoniously with tall French windows and double doors; the mahogany handrails of the gracefully curving staircases are most delicately turned. Smooth, white plastered walls, surmounted with cornices of ornate plaster scroll-work and the fine marble mantels and full-length mirrors, standing in adjoining drawing-rooms, complete a background of classic beauty.

Coincidental with the development of the two types of residential architecture mentioned above, a third style of dwelling arose. It may be called the plantation house, for want of a more specific name, since that was its original purpose. This style of architecture probably owes its origin to the Spaniards, though the dictates of climate and environment were primarily the cause of its widespread adoption. Basically, this type of dwelling differs from the courtyard and Greek Revival residences in that it generally has all its main rooms on one floor, through the center of which runs a wide hall that gives independent access to each room. The house is raised some eight or nine feet above ground level and is completely surrounded by a broad veranda that rests on massive, round brick columns, which are in turn surmounted by slender wooden posts that support the overhanging eaves. The piazza or corridor beneath the veranda is usually paved with flagstones, and the basement beneath the house may be used for service quarters, laundry, and the like. A straight, wide staircase in the center front leads to the veranda, which is accessible from virtually all rooms because of their tall French windows. There were, of course, numerous variations in this basic type, particularly in exterior columnar treatment.

Many simple plantation homes as well as a number of extremely elaborate ones are still scattered throughout Louisiana, but in New Orleans only a few remain. They are most concentrated in the neighborhood of the Bayou St. John headwaters, where they stand today, long after the plantations that surrounded them have been subdivided into city blocks. The Schertz residence, formerly the old custom house, typifies this style of architecture, though variations of the plantation house can be seen in the Westfeldt residence at 2340 Prytania Street, the Delord Sarpy home at 534 Howard Avenue, the Olivier Plantation house at 4111 Chartres Street, the Stauffer home, No. 3 Garden Lane, which was formerly the Hurst Plantation, and Madame John's Legacy in the Vieux Carré.

New Orleans' best-known monument to the age of the Spanish domination is the Cabildo. The solid repose of this edifice, originally known as the 'Casa Curial,' or courthouse, emanates from the graceful repetition of massive arches that make up its façade. Yet an air of delicacy is also manifest: the French wrought-iron balconies and the proportioning of the cornices, pilasters, and pediment are delightful to an eye trained in the appreciation of architectural details. The one incongruous note in the whole conception is the mansard roof, which, with its dormer windows and cupola, was added half a century after the Cabildo's erection in 1795. As originally conceived, both the Cabildo and its neighboring counterpart, the old Presbytère, which was built in 1813, were flat-topped structures, their pediments rising several feet above the roofs; while the Cathedral, originally designed in the Spanish mission style, with short bell-shaped towers on each side of a central pediment, was considerably different from its present appearance.

Nevertheless, Jackson Square today possesses an individual charm of its own. Together with its entourage of stately buildings, it is a monument to Don Andres Almonester y Roxas, the altruistic Spanish grandee whose funds built the cathedral where he lies buried; and to his daughter, Micaela, Baroness Pontalba, who in 1848 built the long row of handsome red-brick apartments that still bear her name, and bestowed the name of her friend General Jackson upon the *place d'armes*.

Among other public buildings of the city's early period, the French Market deserves mention. Built in 1813, it is an arcaded structure of stuccoed brick, with a flagstoned floor. The plan is that of a central corridor or promenade from end to end, with stalls between the arches or columns.

Another fine old building, designed in 1822 by Latrobe, one of the architects who designed the Capitol at Washington, stands at the corner of Conti and Royal Streets. Heavily constructed of brick, and as nearly fireproof as was then possible, this building originally housed the Louisiana State Bank. Diagonally across from it stands another brick building, massive and colonnaded, which was erected in 1826 for the Bank of Louisiana. The list of public buildings in the Vieux Carré runs on, too extensive to permit individual treatment here; yet each building deserves more than the visitor's merely casual attention.

Paul Morphy's house, another former bank building, the old United States mint, the old arsenal behind the Cabildo – these can still be appreciated because they can be seen. But the splendor that belonged to such buildings as De Pouilly's master-pieces, the St. Louis Hotel, and the Citizens' Bank adjoining it, and to Gallier's French Opera House, and to the old St. Charles and Orleans Theaters, has perished forever. The loss of the St. Louis Hotel, with its dome constructed of hollow cylindrical earthenware pots, has been termed an architectural calamity. A still greater calamity is in store, however, for unless the famous old buildings of New Orleans are carefully and properly preserved against the corrosive effects of time and modern standardization, the city will eventually lose its most distinctive claim to fame – a native architecture that flourished a century ago and has never been equaled since.

But perhaps New Orleans is fortunate in that even a few of its most impressive old edifices still stand, gallantly serving their original purpose. The men who built them built well: the Dakins, the De Pouillys, and the Galliers, *père et fils*. The elder Gallier was perhaps the ablest exponent of the Greek mode; at least he preferred it to the exclusion of all other styles. Besides the numerous fine residences he built, he was commissioned to design several public buildings, churches, banks, and the original St. Charles Hotel. The City Hall is probably the finest example of Gallier's art. Completed in 1853, this building is hardly surpassed in dignity and beauty of proportion by any other building of the Greek Revival in the United States.

Some of the most interesting architectural forms in New Orleans are to be found in the churches and cemeteries. Generally speaking, the earlier churches, like their contemporary dwellings and mansions, deserve the greater recognition; for they were designed and built by men whose sole idea was to create simple, straightforward edifices for the purpose of worship. One is immediately struck with the dignity of conception and precise workmanship evident in such fine old buildings as these: Saint Louis Cathedral; Saint Alphonsus, on Constance and Josephine Streets; Our Lady of Guadalupe, on Rampart and Conti Streets; The Holy Trinity, on St. Ferdinand and Dauphine Streets; Saint Augustin, at Bayou Road and St. Claude Avenue; Rayne Memorial, on St. Charles Avenue and General Taylor Street; and Saint John the Baptist, 1139 Dryades Street.

Nathaniel C. Curtis writes: '1850-1860 was a period when brick masons of rare skill flourished in New Orleans.... In these old churches built entirely of brick, architectural forms and details appropriate to brick have been devised and employed with an intelligence superior to that shown in later work. It may be said with probable truth that as

CITY OF MANY BUILDERS

ST. LOUIS CATHEDRAL, SEEN FROM THF PONTALBA APARTMENTS

THE CABILDO, ST. LOUIS CATHEDRAL, THE PRESSYTÈRE AND THE LOWER
PONTALBA BUILDING IN JACKSON SQUARE

THE OLD BANK OF LOUISIANA, DESIGNED BY LATROBE

DETAIL OF THE CATHEDRAL

THE BRITTEN HOUSE FAMED FOR ITS CORNSTALK FENCE

A BAYOU ST. JOHN PLANTATION HOUSE

OUR LADY OF GUADALUPE, OLD MORTUARY CHAPEL

THE PONTALBA APARTMENTS

STAIRWAY IN THE PONTALBA APARTMENTS

TRINITY CHURCH (EPISCOPAL)

examples of the organic expression of brick architecture, these edifices are hardly equalled by any elsewhere in the United States, and are fairly comparable to the latter fifteenth century brick churches of Rome.' The exteriors of these early churches are, on the whole, in better taste than their interiors. The splendid little Holy Trinity Church on St. Ferdinand Street, however, proves an exception to that statement, for there are combined grace, harmony, and simplicity of design and execution, both inside and out.

On the other hand, what New Orleans' more recent churches lack in grace and simplicity they make up for in ornateness and 'gingerbread': lavish accessories imported from foreign lands that often do not blend harmoniously with their surroundings, but stand out rather too boldly in exaggerated relief. An infinity of combinations is manifest. But the Roman Catholic churches, in the main, have retained not only a certain homogeneity of design but also a great deal of beauty, despite the vagaries of their divers builders. Modified Gothic motifs prevail in many of them, so that one grows accustomed to finding certain minor variations in spires and rose windows and lofty, pointed arches – all of which reflect the same general idea. The interiors of many of these churches are highly ornate; their focal point is an elaborate display of towering altar at the intersection of nave and transept. Among the city's most interesting churches in this category are the Church of the Immaculate Conception, an adaptation of Hispano-Moorish architecture; Saint Stephen's Church, on Napoleon Avenue; Holy Name of Jesus, on St. Charles Avenue; Saint Joseph's, on Tulane Avenue; Our Lady of Lourdes, on Napoleon Avenue; and Saint Anthony of Padua, on Canal Street.

The other denominations have on the whole less lavish churches, though hardly less varied architectural styles. At least three Jewish synagogues in New Orleans are outstanding. Foremost among these is Temple Sinai on St. Charles Avenue and Calhoun Street, a modern interpretation of Byzantine architecture built of light-colored brick and limestone. Another, Touro Synagogue, at St. Charles Avenue and General Pershing Street, is notable for its perfectly spherical tiled domes and for the variegated color effects which the tiles produce. The third, Beth Israel, 1622 Carondelet Street, shows an Arabic influence.

Many of the Protestant churches are designed in modified Gothic styles, some in simpler classic styles, and some in styles that defy precise identification. Among the most impressive Protestant churches are: Christ Church Cathedral (Episcopal) at St. Charles Avenue and Sixth Street; the Napoleon Avenue Presbyterian Church, at St. Charles and Napoleon Avenues; the St. Charles Avenue Presbyterian Church, at St. Charles Avenue and State Street; the Saint Mark's Methodist Episcopal Church, at Rampart and Governor Nicholls Streets; and the Prytania Street Presbyterian Church, at Josephine and Prytania Streets.

The fame of New Orleans' many cemeteries has become so widespread that little need be said about them here. They resemble miniature towns. Ever since the early days, when earth burial was found to be impracticable in New Orleans, custom has decreed that the tombs of the dead be as magnificent as money can buy. As a result, nearly every burial place in the city presents row upon row of tombs built of marble, granite, sandstone, and limestone, and designed in countless variations and adaptations of architectural patterns – Egyptian, Greek, Gothic, and modern.

Post-bellum architecture in New Orleans, owing to an ill-digested eclecticism, as well as to an impoverished 'reconstructed' South, was an unfortunate synthesis of bad taste. After the Civil War, foreign architects were no longer attracted to New Orleans, and native talent was virtually nonexistent. The city, however, was not alone in its poverty; throughout the Nation as a whole the art of building had fallen upon evil days. Out of a welter of incongruous styles prevalent during the Victorian era, only one arose which seemed destined to revive American architecture and stabilize it. That was the Romanesque style adopted by Henry Hobson Richardson. Richardson was a native of Louisiana, who had studied abroad in the École des Beaux Arts, but who spent the most fruitful years of his life in New England. New Orleans has but one building actually designed by Richardson, the Howard Memorial Library, and only a few others, notably on the Tulane University campus, that are done in his manner.

Splendidly executed in massive brown sandstone, the Howard Library resembles nothing so much as a medieval fortress. The exterior clearly shows Richardson's deep feeling for solid masonry; but the interior, despite its high-vaulted ceiling, has a dim, somber aspect. Nevertheless, it is one of the most substantial pieces of architecture in the city, and may outlast many a more recent structure.

Some extraordinary examples of bad carpenter architecture are to be found among the more pretentious residences erected during the last decades of the nineteenth and the first of the twentieth centuries. These are interesting by virtue of their extreme confusion in mass and their elaborate and wholly incongruous ornamentation. Innumerable wings, bay windows, turrets, dormers, and galleries were put together without rhyme or reason; wooden fretwork, in tortured design, was attached to almost every available surface; stained-glass windows and cut-glass front doors heightened the effect. Topped by mansard roofs, in turn surmounted by weather vanes and lightning rods, these houses today present amusing and at times almost terrifying examples of 'Steamboat Gothic.'

The smaller houses of this period offer several interesting types: the double cottage or, as the English say, 'the semi-detached villa'; the 'camel-back house,' of which the front is one story, the rear two; and the 'shotgun cottage,' so called because the rooms are built one behind another with the doors in line, so that a charge of shot fired in the front door could pass through the entire house and out the back door.

Of strictly modern architecture New Orleans has but few examples. The most recent of its skyscrapers are the Hibernia, American, and Canal Banks, and the Père Marquette Building. Possibly the closest approximation to what is now considered modern architecture is the Shushan Airport's administrative building.

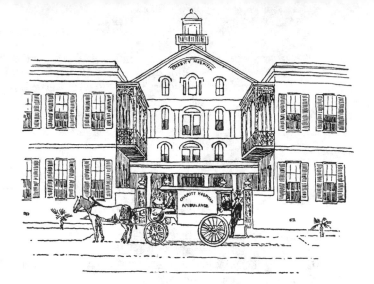

SCIENCE

NEW ORLEANS has long served as a proving-ground for applied science. In overcoming the problems arising from the soggy nature of the subsoil, the low elevation of the city, climatic conditions favorable to malignant diseases, and the danger of Mississippi flood waters, New Orleans has made many contributions to scientific advancement.

Noteworthy work has been done in medicine, especially in the control of yellow fever, malaria, cholera, smallpox, hookworm, and dysentery diseases which once, because of climatic conditions, lack of adequate sewage disposal, and poor drainage, proved a scourge to the city. They are now under control, and the danger of epidemics has been minimized.

Although the discovery of the causative agent of yellow fever was made elsewhere, many of the problems of practical control in large cities were solved in New Orleans by local physicians. Samuel Chopin, C. B. White, A. W. Perry, and others introduced quarantine and disinfecting methods which, though the carrier of the disease was unknown at the time, were instrumental in checking the fearful toll of yellow-fever epidemics. Doctor Charles Faget contributed an indispensable diagnostic sign of yellow fever – a fall in the pulse rate during the first days of the disease.

In other fields of medicine New Orleans physicians and surgeons have done much pioneer work and have made many important contributions: C. C. Bass and F. M. Johns, cultivation of the plasmodium of malarial fever; A. W. De Roaldes, establishment of the first eye, ear, nose, and throat hospital in the South; Ernest S. Lewis, pioneer work in gynecology; C. A. Luzenburg, removal of a gangrenous bowel in hernia; J. L. Riddell, invention of the binocular microscope; H. D. Schmidt, demonstration of the origin of bile ducts in intercellular spaces; A. W. Smyth, ligation of the innominate artery; Warren Stone, work on aneurysm, and resection of a rib to secure permanent drainage in empyema. Doctor Edmond Souchon developed two methods of retaining the color of muscles and organs in the preservation of anatomic dissections; the curing method using arsenic, calcium chloride, and formol; and the physical or paint method by which colorless muscles in a dissection are given permanent color. In addition to founding the Souchon Museum of Anatomy at Tulane University, he did much original work on aneurysm of the subclavian artery and aorta. Doctor Rudolph Matas, world-famous surgeon, has made many contributions to surgery, especially to vascular surgery, as well as a method of reducing and securing fixation of zygomatic fractures, an original method of blocking nerves in regional anesthesia, and the application of spinal subarachnoid anesthesia for surgical purposes. Valuable contributions to the medical profession have also been made by Caine, Bruno, Jamison, Couret, Parham, Martin, Compton, and Lynch.

In dentistry, Doctor Edmund C. Kells, about thirty-five years ago, was the first to employ the X-ray in his profession. A recent noteworthy accomplishment in dentistry was the method devised by Doctor S. C. Fournet and his assistant, C. S. Tuller, for stabilizing and retaining lower dentures. The Loyola Dental School, established in 1914, is rated as a class A dental school, and is one of the best-equipped institutions of its kind in the South.

In Charity Hospital New Orleans has one of the finest medical institutions in the country. Almost every physician in the city and a number practising in the neighboring parishes do part-time work at the hospital. The Medical Schools of Tulane and Louisiana State Universities train their students at the hospital and carry on much valuable research. Both medical schools rank with the best in America. The Tulane Medical School began in 1834 as the Medical College of Louisiana and merged in 1845 with the University of Louisiana, forerunner of Tulane University. In the Department of Tropical Medicine much important research is carried on in tropical diseases. The Medical Center of Louisiana State University, established in 1932, is domiciled on Charity Hospital grounds and has all the facilities of the hospital at its command. It is one of the few medical schools in the country requiring a fifth year of interneship. The Flint-Goodridge Hospital is one of the South's leading hospitals for Negroes.

A constant menace to New Orleans ever since its founding has been the danger of overflow of the Mississippi River. Levees were built soon after 1718 as a protective measure, and the two centuries of maintenance and improvement that followed have added much to man's knowledge of the river and the means of controlling it. Various flood-control measures have been tried, but the most important, and one which gives the city the greatest assurance, is the recently constructed Bonnet Carré Spillway, a dike-enclosed runway used during high-flood stage to divert a great portion of water (maximum capacity 250,000 cubic feet of water per second) from the Mississippi to Lake Pontchartrain. The spillway was first used in 1937, when it was estimated that the stage at New Orleans was lowered approximately three and one-half feet through its use.

Flood-control work is carried on by the War Department, which maintains a district office (United States Engineers, Second New Orleans District) at New Orleans.

A floating asphalt plant and a fleet of dredge boats, cranes, launches, etc., are in constant use in dredging, revetment work, and levee construction.

In making the Mississippi navigable for large ocean-going ships great difficulties were encountered by engineers in maintaining a channel at the mouth of the river, where deposits of silt are built up in the form of banks and bars. Adrien De Pauger, Colonial engineer, as early as 1721 advocated the construction of jetties as the best means of obtaining a channel of suitable depth. Various other methods were tried, and much money was spent before De Pauger's plan was carried out by James B. Eads, whose 'no cure, no pay' proposition was endorsed by Congress in 1874. Eads proposed to create and maintain, by means of jetties, a twentyeight-foot channel for $10,000,000, payments to begin when a depth of twenty feet was secured and continue as certain other depths were reached. Final payment was to be made upon permanence of the channel for ten years. A wall of willow mattresses, stone, and debris was constructed on each side of the proposed channel, confining the current of the river and forcing it to cut and maintain a deeper channel. By 1880 a depth of thirty-two feet was reached. Today a thirty-five-foot channel of an average width of one thousand feet is maintained at the mouth of the river.

Because of the low elevation of the city and the fact that it is entirely surrounded by levees, the drainage and sewerage systems of New Orleans differ radically from those of other American cities. Drainage has to be pumped out of the city from a network of canals, and the pumping apparatus, to take care of torrential rains, must necessarily be of the best type obtainable. Screw pumps developed by a local engineer, Albert B. Wood, are employed, and are said to be the largest of their kind in the world. Since 1900 a modern sewer system has been developed, in which underground mains have been substituted for the former unsanitary open conduits.

Furnishing the rapidly expanding city of New Orleans with pure water was another problem which taxed the ingenuity of its inhabitants. For more than one hundred years after the founding of the city the townspeople were dependent mainly on water taken manually from the river and from cisterns. Drinking water was peddled through the streets, usually at exorbitant prices. Early waterworks piped a limited amount of water to residences near the river, but the water was usually muddy and unfit for domestic purposes. Between 1892 and 1900 much valuable information concerning methods of purification was gathered by George G. Earl, General Superintendent of the New Orleans Sewerage and Water Board, and an experimental purification plant was established in Audubon Park. The modern and highly efficient system in use today is a result of these long years of experimentation. Water is pumped from the river into a thirty-six-acre tract of open reservoirs, where it is permitted to settle before passing through a battery of twenty-eight filters to be purified with a chlorine treatment. Four steam-driven and two electrically driven pumps, with a total capacity of 160,000,000 gallons per day, force the water through more than five hundred miles of city mains.

Scientific advancement was also made as other public utilities were developed. The present street-car system is a result of a century of experimentation in which horsecars, steam engines, 'walking cars,' 'fireless engines,' and electric trolleys were employed. Gas was introduced in 1823 by James H. Caldwell, who imported a 'gas machine' from England to illuminate his American Theater. Electric lighting was one of the wonders of the Cotton Centennial Exposition of 1884, and came into general usage some years later. The growth of these services has kept pace with city expansion, but development has been made possible only by local scientists who through engineering skill and inventive genius overcame problems of construction and improvement.

In the industrial development of New Orleans applied science has played an important part, as exemplified by the sugar industry. Early sugar-cane planters tried various methods of refining the cane, but were successful only in producing a milk sugar or 'marmalade' of poor quality. Étienne de Boré finally succeeded in granulating cane on a commercial scale on his plantation (now part of Audubon Park) in 1795. His success immediately encouraged other planters to build sugar factories and employ his refining method. Since then the industry has developed as improvements were made by pioneer refiners. John J. Coiron, in 1822, introduced steam power in the manufacture of sugar, and, about 1840, burners for the utilization of cane pulp, or bagasse, as a fuel were perfected. Norbert Rillieux, a native of New Orleans, revolutionized sugar-boiling through his invention of the 'multiple effect' apparatus in 1830. The invention of the centrifugal machine in 1844, the use of bisulphate of lime for bleaching in 1840, and the invention of the filter press in 1853 aided in developing the sugar industry by speeding production and decreasing manufacturing costs. Along with these mechanical improvements went agricultural experiments, resulting in the development of superior types of cane. The Sugar Experiment Station was established in 1885, and in conjunction with the Audubon Sugar School, founded in 1891, conducted research in the agricultural and technological fields of the sugar industry and trained experts for sugar-mill operation. The Audubon Sugar School was taken over by Louisiana State University in 1899, and the Sugar Experiment Station functioned until 1923. In 1922 a plant at Marrero, across the river from New Orleans, began the production of Celotex, a building material made of bagasse, sugar-cane refuse formerly discarded or used as fuel.

Various scientific societies, along with the educational institutions of the city, serve to popularize theoretical science and stimulate research and experimentation. The New Orleans Academy of Sciences, founded in 1853, has done much in this respect, and has co-operated with various civic bodies in scientific work of benefit to the city. The cotton cushion scale, camphor tree scale, and Argentine ant were eradicated as a result of the academy's work. The Junior Academy of Sciences, composed of members having interest in sciences of the type taught in high schools, is affiliated with the older institution through Tulane University. The Louisiana branch of the American Chemical Society, established in January, 1906, by Professors B. J. Caldwell and W. R. Betts, is concerned with all phases of chemistry, its object being to promote interest in that science among its members. The Louisiana Engineering Society, a branch of the National Engineering Society, is composed for the most part of engineers and professors of the local colleges of engineering, who are encouraged to do individual experimentation and report upon their findings.

In the realm of pure science much important work is being done in the Department of Middle American Research of Tulane University. Under the direction of Frans Blom, research in archeology, ethnology, anthropology, and allied sciences is conducted in Mexico, Central America, and the West Indies. Since its establishment in 1924 the department has developed the foremost library in its field in the world. Material collected on more than a dozen expeditions is housed in a museum and in various places on the campus.

In the collection and publication of meteorological data, the work of Doctor Isaac M. Cline, forecaster and director of the local station of the United States Weather Bureau from 1900 to 1935, is particularly noteworthy. Doctor Cline has written extensively on climate in New Orleans and in Louisiana and on general meteorology; his treatise, *Tropical Cyclones*, has been acclaimed as an outstanding contribution to the science.

Seismological and meteorological data are recorded at the Nicholas D. Burk Seismological Observatory of Loyola University, where vertical and horizontal instruments of the Wiechert astatic type are under observation.

In airplane designing and research in aeronautics much valuable work has been done in New Orleans. James Wedell, in his famous '44,' a plane of his own design, broke the land-plane speed record in 1933. He made many improvements in plane designing and was known internationally for the fast ships he built. The 'Delgado Maid,' designed by Byron Armstrong, head of the aeronautics department of the Isaac Delgado Trades School, and built by students of the school, was one of the fastest planes ever constructed in the United States. It attained a speed of 420 miles per hour in trial flights before it crashed at the air meet held in New Orleans in 1936.

Because of its semitropical climate, long growing season, and geographical position New Orleans is the logical site for an arboretum, plans for which are now under consideration. A general botanical garden, with an assemblage of trees, shrubs, and woody vines, including sample forest types of the South, and a collection of woody plants used in agriculture, industry, and medicine is to be established in City Park. The facilities for plant research thus created will enable scientists of local universities and private and public organizations to improve economic and horticultural plants and devise new methods of combating insect pests and fungus diseases. The arboretum, in addition to its educational work, will also render valuable service to the community through the importation and cultivation of flora from foreign countries, especially from Central and South America.

CREOLE CUISINE

CREOLE cuisine is a combination of the French and Spanish influence – the Spanish taste for strong seasoning of food combined with the French love for delicacies – and it originated in Louisiana. The slaves of Louisiana had their share in refining the product, and likewise the Indians, who gathered roots and pungent herbs in the woods.

Although several of the customs in regard to the serving of food passed with other customs as the city became more cosmopolitan, still today no Creole kitchen is complete without its iron pots, bay leaf, thyme, garlic, and cayenne pepper. Some of the restaurants of New Orleans are known the world over for their Creole cooking; yet you will be served just as fine a meal in a Creole home.

If you have no faith in the potency of herbs and seasonings, don't try Creole cooking. Remember there is a difference between one bay leaf and two bay leaves; and the difference between one clove of garlic and two cloves of garlic is enough to disorganize a happy home.

Some of the Creole dishes can be procured in the larger restaurants of other cities; others are still typical of New Orleans and can seldom be found elsewhere. Among these are wine or baba cake, a large porous cake dipped in claret or rum – many of the older caterers would dip it in anisette; pie Saint-Honoré, made with a puff paste and a vanilla, or striped vanilla and chocolate cream filling with little balls of puff paste on top; and daube glacé, a highly seasoned, jellied meat.

Louisiana has valuable natural resources which are a great asset in the preparation of food: partridge, snipe, quail, ducks, and rabbits; fresh and salt-water fish of every description; numerous fruits, the most outstanding being oranges and figs; many nuts, the most delicate being the pecan.

The Creole *déjeuner* or breakfast was quite a feast. Black coffee would be taken the first thing in the morning. Then at nine o'clock the *déjeuner* was served, consisting of several different meats and always *grillades*, grits, biscuits, and *pain perdu* (lost bread), more commonly known as French toast.

The French Market was the scene of social gatherings on Sunday morning. Some of the Creole ladies (followed by their servant carrying the basket) and gentlemen would attend early mass at the St. Louis Cathedral and later buy the food for the day at the market. Others would attend later mass and afterwards take breakfast at the restaurant of Monsieur and Madame Begué on Decatur Street.

This breakfast was served from eleven in the morning until three o'clock in the afternoon, and consisted of several dishes, including Begué's famous preparation of liver and all the wine one could drink. In the afternoon practically everyone would attend the matinee at the French Opera House; at six o'clock there was dinner, another huge meal.

The Choctaw Indians were very friendly with the white men, and to them New Orleans is indebted for the filé, which is used in one of the best-known Creole dishes – 'gumbo.' The filé is made from dried sassafras leaves pounded to a powder. The Indians would come to the city from their settlements in Lacombe, Louisiana, three times a week. On weekdays they would sell their wares at the French Market and on Sunday the tribe would gather in front of the St. Louis Cathedral with an array of baskets, beads, pottery, and filé; Negro women would likewise be there selling their *calas tout chaud* (hot rice cakes).

Although the Creoles are lavish entertainers and can prepare a sumptuous meal which is a source of never-ending pleasure to the gourmet, they also follow the French trait of economy and were taught early in life the secret of a perfect blending of a quantity of well-cooked simple foods which are nourishing, but not a strain on the budget. An example of one of these simple meals consists of *soup-en-famille*, or vegetable soup as it is most commonly known. *Boulli*, a beef brisket, is cooked with the soup and served either hot or cold with a sauce made from oil, vinegar, horse-radish and Creole mustard; catsup may be added if desired. Some of the vegetables from the soup are placed around the dish in which the *boulli* is served, as a garnish; a salad of lettuce or lettuce and tomatoes, French bread, and a bottle of claret are added. This is a very good, economical, and nourishing meal.

Native Orleanians are fond of sea food, and will drive miles to partake of any well-seasoned dish of this delicacy. At West End, a park situated on Lake Pontchartrain, there are numerous stands which specialize in the serving of boiled crabs and shrimp. In warm weather tables are placed along the sea wall, and nothing is more enjoyable on a warm night, or after a swim in the lake, than to ride to one of these places for a feast. On certain nights (usually Thursday, Friday, and Saturday) many bars serve free crabs, shrimp, and crayfish with the purchase of a glass of beer or any other drink.

The following is a list of New Orleans Cook Books:
Cooking in the Old Days. Célestine Eustis.
La Cuisine Créole. Believed to have been compiled by Lafcadio Hearn.
The Old and New Cook Book. Mrs. Martha Pritchard Stanford.
200 Years of New Orleans Cooking. Natalie V. Scott.
Mirations and Miracles of Mandy. Natalie V. Scott.
Gourmets' Guide to New Orleans. Natalie V. Scott and Caroline Merrick Jones.
The Creole Cook Book. The Times-Picayune, New Orleans, La.
Below are some Creole recipes written down exactly as given by local chefs and bartenders.

FAMOUS DISHES
Bouillabaisse
(Antoine's Recipe)

A great variety of firm fish should be served, such as red snapper, red fish, sheepshead, green trout, black fish, and the like.

The heads should be used for a thorough boiling, in order to extract the essence. After straining the bouillon, same should be somewhat reduced by boiling.

The fish should be cut in pieces, and properly smeared with virgin olive oil, then laid to pickle for some time with a seasoning of salt and pepper, fresh peppers, thyme, and bay leaves.

After the bouillon of the heads has been reduced, pour in a large fish dish and boil therein hard shell crabs, crayfish, and lake shrimps, together with the pieces of fish aforementioned, taking care to add sufficient first class French dry wine, such as 'Château de Cursan.'

Let the whole simmer down.

Prepare, in a separate dish, on a slow fire, some shallots, a dash of garlic, and fresh peeled tomatoes cooked in virgin oil, and nicely reduced, in order to pour over the fish, as aforementioned (when same is cooked) to impart color and flavor.

When almost ready to serve, pour over the whole a small quantity of saffron, which has been dissolved in a small amount of white wine (non-alcoholic).

A last simmer, and the bouillabaisse is ready to serve.

Cut squares of stale bread and toast lightly – cover same with a very light mixture of chopped chevril and pounded garlic.

The toast should be served separately, to be placed in each individual plate.

Calas Tout Chaud
(Hot Rice Cakes)

1 cup boiled rice	½ teaspoon nutmeg
3 eggs	1 cup flour
½ cup sugar	3 teaspoons baking powder
½ teaspoon salt	

Beat the eggs until thick; add sugar and other ingredients. Beat vigorously until thoroughly blended. Drop by teaspoon in deep hot fat. Fry until golden brown. Drain on heavy paper and sprinkle with powdered sugar and serve hot.

These cakes are delicious, and when properly made they puff up and are extremely light.

Courtbouillon

6 slices red fish	1 lemon sliced
1 coffee spoon allspice	½ cup chopped celery
1 pint can tomatoes	1 chopped green pepper
2 tablespoons olive oil	1 onion
3 sprigs each of parsley,	2 tablespoons flour
thyme, and bay leaf	1 large glass claret
3 pods garlic	

Salt and pepper to taste.

Make a *roux* by browning flour and olive oil. Brown onion. Add tomatoes, seasonings, salt, pepper, and lemon. Let all simmer about half an hour in a large iron pot. Salt and pepper fish, add to sauce, being careful not to let the slices overlap. Cook until fish is done, about fifteen minutes. Before serving add claret. Serve on toast.

Red snapper, which is smaller and tenderer than the red fish, is also delicious stuffed with an oyster dressing and baked with a tomato gravy. All Creoles have their fish set, which consists of a large platter and twelve plates, each having a different fish painted in the center.

The most frequently served Creole entrée is the red snapper, which is boiled or poached in a highly seasoned water, containing lemon, onion, celery, parsley, thyme, bay leaf, salt and pepper. The fish is served cold in large pieces with mayonnaise to which capers have been added. The fish plates are garnished with lettuce, sliced tomatoes and celery curls.

Crabs
(Boiled)

Crabs can be found at all seasons in the markets. They must be purchased alive, and washed thoroughly.

Into a pot of water put several stalks of celery, thyme, bay leaf, parsley, an onion, sliced lemon, salt, and cayenne pepper. If desired, allspice and a few blades of mace may be added. The water should be salted to a brine, as crabs require much salt and it cannot be added after cooking. When the water boils, add the live crabs and boil about twenty minutes, or until the shell turns a bright red. Let cool awhile in the seasoned water. Serve either hot or cold.

Shrimp and crayfish are cooked in the same manner. In New Orleans there are two kinds of shrimp – river and lake. The river shrimp is seasonable and more delicate in flavor, and is usually boiled and served on a bed of ice as an entrée or as a salad. The lake shrimp is abundant all the year. It is larger and is used for cooking purposes, being served in various ways.

Crabs
(Soft Shell)

This is considered one of the greatest delicacies. Unlike the hard crab, the shell and all is eaten. The soft-shell crabs can be found in the markets all year round. They are more plentiful in the summer months.

Great care must be taken in cleaning the crab; it should be carefully washed in cold water, as boiling water ruins its fine flavor. The feathery substance under the side points must be taken off, also the eyes and the sand bag under the shell between the eyes. Dry in a towel after washing. The crabs may be dipped in flour or flour meal to which salt and pepper have been added. To obtain the best results in frying the crabs, dip them first in cracker meal, then in beaten egg, and again in the cracker meal. Fry in deep fat, drain on brown paper, and serve hot with tartar sauce.

Crayfish Bisque
(Madame Begué's Recipe)

Choose about forty nice crayfish and let them have a good boiling. Remove from fire and drain. Clean the heads, keep thirty of the shells and also the remains which you will set to boil in a quart of water. Peel the tails and chop fine. Make a paste with the meat to which add a cupful of soaked bread, a large spoonful of chopped onions, two pods of garlic, chopped parsley, and salt and pepper to taste. With this fill the thirty shells and set them aside. Start your soup by frying in butter an onion, some flour for thickening, and a cupful each of green onions and parsley chopped fine, a sprig of thyme, and two bay leaves. When brown pour in the bouillon made with the remains of the heads, and season with salt and strong pepper; let boil slowly for half an hour. Add more water if needed. When ready to serve take each head, roll it in flour, and fry all in butter until crisp all around and throw in the soup. Let boil three or four minutes. Serve with boiled rice.

Daube Glacé

3 pounds beef or veal round (have the butcher lard the meat with pieces of fat)	Parsley, thyme, bay leaf, cloves, green pepper, red pepper, onion, celery,
4 pig feet	garlic and salt
2 veal knuckles	

Soak the meat in vinegar over night. Next morning salt, pepper, and flour the meat. Put a kitchenspoonful of lard in a deep iron kettle. Put in meat, cover, and let cook on slow fire until it makes its own gravy. In another pan boil the pig feet and veal knuckles with two onions cut in quarters, celery, and parsley. Boil until meat comes from the bone. When daube is tender take it out of the pot and make the gravy. Slice an onion and cook until light brown, add a tablespoon of flour, and cook until flour is brown. Put daube back in the pot with the gravy and water in which the knuckles and pig feet were boiled, add the green pepper, thyme and bay leaf chopped fine, a handful of cloves, salt, and red pepper. Cook about two hours on a slow fire. If gravy becomes too thick, add a little warm water. When the small center bone is detached from the meat it is done. Chop the meat from the veal knuckles and pig feet fine and add to jelly. Put daube in a round bowl, pour the gravy over it. When cool put in refrigerator to jell. Next day unmold daube on a dish and garnish as desired. This is a delicious dish, and when sliced the meat is in the center of the jelly. If desired, some of the gravy may be strained, put into fancy molds, and served as a garnish. Chicken or turkey may be used in place of the veal.

Grillades

Veal rounds	Flour
1 can tomatoes (or 6 fresh ones)	Lard
1 onion, green pepper	Parsley
1 clove garlic	
Salt and pepper to taste.	

A deep iron pot or skillet with a tight cover is necessary for making this dish. Cut the rounds in size appropriate for individual serving. Two rounds will make four ample servings. Make a *roux* by browning a tablespoonful of flour in a tablespoonful of lard. Add the finely cut onion, pepper and garlic, and the meat, which has been seasoned with salt and pepper. Let this cook on a slow fire until the meat is brown, and enough juice extracted from the meat to make a little gravy. Add the tomatoes and simmer on a slow fire until done (about two hours). After this has cooked an hour add a teacupful of hot water.

Gumbo

½ dozen hard-shell crabs	2 stalks celery
1 pound shrimp	1 onion
2 dozen oysters	2 pods garlic
1 green pepper	Thyme, bay leaf, and parsley

Salt, black pepper, and cayenne to taste.

Scald the crabs, clean, and cut in quarters. Make a *roux* by browning a kitchenspoonful of flour in the same amount of hot lard. Add the sliced onion and brown. Put in the crabs and shrimp, cover, and cook about fifteen minutes. Add the other seasonings, chopped, and two quarts of warm water. Cover and cook on a slow fire about two hours. Fifteen minutes before serving add the oysters and their liquor. Just before serving turn off the fire and add a tablespoon of filé. Pour into a tureen and serve with boiled rice. Never cook the file, as it will become very stringy. Okra may be used in place of the file, but it is cooked with the gumbo. The basic recipe is the same, but chicken, veal, and ham or a combination of veal and a hambone can be substituted for the crabs and shrimp. After Thanksgiving and Christmas the left-over turkey may be made into a gumbo with oysters. A deep iron pot is preferable for making gumbo.

Gombo Zhèbes
(Gumbo of Herbs)

There is a legend that this gumbo should be cooked on Holy Thursday for good luck. Upon passing the French Market on this day, you will hear the vendors crying, 'Buy your seven greens for good luck!'

2 tablespoons lard
2 tablespoons flour
1 bunch spinach, mustard greens, beet tops, turnip tops, outside leaves of Creole lettuce, green cabbage, green celery leaves, green onion tops or almost any combination of greens.
Bacon strips, salt meat or a hambone. The hambone is preferable as it gives the best flavor.
Chopped onion, parsley, thyme, bay leaf, green pepper, salt, pepper, red pepper pod.

Wash the greens thoroughly and boil all together with sufficient water to cover. When tender take from fire, drain off water and save it. Make a *roux* by browning the flour in a deep pot with the lard. Add the onion and let brown. Fry the meat. While this is cooking chop the greens and other seasonings thoroughly. Add the greens, and fry for a few minutes, stirring constantly to prevent burning. Add the water in which the greens were boiled. Simmer in a covered pot about two hours. If it should get too thick add a little boiling water. Serve with boiled rice.

Hollandaise Sauce Supreme
(For fish)

Take the yolks of two eggs and beat. Drip one half pound of melted butter (like mayonnaise) in a double boiler or on a slow fire until thick. Add the juice of one lemon, twelve shrimp, one half can of mushrooms, two truffles cut in slices, and a little water from the fish. Take off the fire and serve over the fish.

Jambalaya au Congri

This is a very popular dish and is more generally called 'Congri.'

1 cup rice	1 pint cowpeas
1 large onion	1 square inch ham
½ pound salt meat	

Wash the salt meat and chop; cut ham into small pieces. Boil the cowpeas, salt meat and ham together. Boil the rice. After the peas and rice are cooked pour the rice into the pot of peas, which must not be dry but very moist. Mix well, let all simmer for five minutes, and serve hot.

Jambalaya à la Créole

1 pound chorices (pork sausage)	2 pods garlic
1 slice ham	1 onion (chopped)
1½ cups rice	2 sprigs parsley, thyme,
1 can tomatoes (small)	and bay leaf (finely chopped)
Salt, pepper, and cayenne to taste.	

Wash rice thoroughly. Brown the ham, cut in small pieces, and fry the chorices in a little lard. Drain off the lard which accumulates from frying the meat, leaving only a tablespoonful. Brown onion and other seasonings; add tomatoes. Let cook a few minutes. Pour over the rice and mix thoroughly. Place in a heavy pot, cover, and cook until gravy is absorbed and rice is soft and dry.

The meat may be omitted, and the Jambalaya made with shrimp or oysters, the basic recipe being the same.

Oyster Rockefeller
(Galatoire's Recipe)

For serving six people, one-half dozen oysters each. One bunch of parsley and one bunch of green lettuce. Chop all together with one pound of butter and one handful of fine bread crumbs. To thicken add to mixture three tablespoons of Worcestershire sauce, one spoonful anchovy sauce, season to taste with salt and pepper, also a few drops of tabasco sauce. To this add two ounces of absinthe. Mix all together. Pour this sauce over oysters that are on the half shell and are set on a bed of rock salt in a pie pan (this is to keep the oysters hot) . Sprinkle with grated Parmesan cheese and fine bread crumbs. Bake until brown. Serve hot.

Pecan Pralines

2 cups sugar   2 cups milk or cream
1 cup molasses   1 tablespoon butter
2 cups pecans

Combine above ingredients, except nuts, and cook, stirring constantly until a soft ball forms when dropped in cold water. Remove from fire, beat until creamy, add pecans, and drop by spoonful on a greased marble slab or greased porcelain-top table.

Pralines can also be made of equal portions of brown sugar, pecans, and a lump of butter. Moisten the sugar with a little water; cook until sugar melts to a thick syrup, add pecans; remove from fire and beat until creamy. Proceed as above.

Pompano En Papillotes
(La Louisiane Recipe)

Pompano is considered one of the best fish, since it is peculiar to the waters of the Gulf of Mexico, Mississippi Sound, and the Louisiana Grand Isle. The flounder is another fine fish. It is sometimes called sole.

Cut the pompano in filet five ounces each, parboil or sauté about five minutes. Sauce; sauté in one spoonful of butter, four chopped green onions, chopped mushrooms, two truffles, two ounces of white wine, add one spoon of flour, and one pint of fish stock, and boil ten minutes. Season to taste. Add to the above sauce three ounces of crabmeat, sauté with a dash of white wine and a yolk of an egg. Pour the crabmeat in the fold of the filet and pour sauce over it. Fold it in a heart-shaped paper bag and bake in a hot oven ten minutes. Serve in the bag.

Red Beans

Red beans are to New Orleans what the white bean is to Boston and the cow-pea is to South Carolina.

This is a very nutritious and economical dish and is one of the most popular of all Creole cuisine. Red beans are always served with a dish of boiled rice. Until a few years ago, when New Orleans was not so commercialized, you could purchase a 'quartee beans, quartee rice and a little lagniappe to make it nice.' Quartee means a half a nickel and lagniappe was a gift given with a purchase, seasoning of some sort, for instance.

The red beans are soaked in water until the skins shrivel. Pour off the water and put in a deep pot. Cover with water, add chopped parsley, an onion and green onions, a tablespoon of lard, salt and pepper, a slice of meat, ham or several strips of bacon. Cook for several hours on a slow fire until thick and creamy.

Rice

When wood stoves were in use the old Creole method for cooking rice was to use an iron pot and a very low fire, adding just enough salted water to cover the rice. This was cooked for several hours, untfl the rice was done and every grain separate.

The modern way is as follows: Wash rice thoroughly and cook in rapidly boiling salted water until tender. Do not stir. Drain in colander, letting cold water run through it thoroughly. Place the colander with the rice over boiling water, cover, and steam until every grain flakes or stands apart.

Shrimp Salad with Arnaud's Shrimp Salad Dressing

The ingredients, mixed well, chilled and served on cold boiled shrimp; about twelve to a portion, enthroned on crisp chopped lettuce, will satisfy four persons who know how to begin a luncheon or supper.

6 tablespoons oil	½ teaspoon salt
2 tablespoons vinegar	4 tablespoons Creole mustard
1 tablespoon paprika	½ heart of celery, chopped fine
½ teaspoon white pepper	½ white onion chopped fine
A little chopped parsley	

Trout Marguery
(Galatoire's Recipe)

Clean the trout of skin and bone. Cut into filets tenderloin and roll them. Put three tablespoons of butter in the pan with the fish and season with salt and pepper. Add one-half glass of water and bake in a hot oven. When cooked dress on platter. Serve Hollandaise sauce suprême over the fish. (See above.)

FAMOUS DRINKS

Absinthe
(Dripped)

Chill a tumbler, then fill one-third with finely cracked (not crushed) ice. Drip one ounce of absinthe from absinthe dripper or from a spoon, stirring rapidly. When the absinthe and melting ice have produced a heavily clouded mixture, remove spoon and serve; or the absinthe may be strained off into a chilled cocktail glass.

Café Brûlot

1 cup French brandy (cognac)	2 handfuls cloves
2 lumps sugar per cup of coffee	2 sticks cinnamon
½ orange rind sliced thin	broken to bits
½ lemon rind sliced thin	1 quart coffee
alcohol	

Into the brûlot bowl (which is a metal bowl with a tray) put the spices, peel, brandy, and sugar. Pour some alcohol in the tray under the bowl and ignite it. Stir the contents of the bowl and it will ignite. Let it burn a few minutes, so it will not destroy the alcohol. Pour in the coffee. Serve in coffee cup.

This is very effective if the lights are turned out and the shadows allowed to play on the faces of the guests.

Creole Coffee

Creole coffee is a mixture of pure coffee and about twenty per cent chicory.

Use a heaping tablespoon of coffee to every cup. The water should be boiling, as the Negroes say, at a 'rollin' jumpin' boil.' Drip a very little at a time, about an after-dinner coffee cup, over the coffee. Creoles do not like cream in their coffee, preferring hot milk; café au lait is about half coffee and half hot milk.

Petit Brulé

Take an ordinary size thick-skinned orange; cut through the peel entirely around the orange like the line of the equator, then force off the peel by passing the handle of the spoon between it and the pulp. Into the cup thus formed put two lumps of sugar and some cinnamon, and fill with fine French brandy (cognac) and ignite for a few minutes. The brulé will be found to have a pleasant flavor given it by the orange. This recipe is from 'La Cuisine Créole,' compiled by Lafcadio Hearn.

Planters Punch

Juice ½ lemon	Equal parts Jamaica rum
A dash grenadine syrup	and rye whisky
Cracked ice	Sugar

The finest granulated sugar (almost powdered) must be used for this drink. Mix the above ingredients and stir thoroughly – do not shake. Garnish with a slice of orange and a cherry. Put a float of red wine on top and serve.

Ramos Gin Fizz

1 teaspoon powdered sugar	1 egg white
1 jigger gin	5 or 6 dashes orange
Juice ½ lemon and ½ lime	flower water
1 ounce sweet cream	

Shake vigorously with cracked ice until mixture is foamy and ice cold. Strain and serve in eight-ounce glass. Fill up with soda water.

Sazerac Cocktail

The formula for this drink is privately owned. It is bottled in New Orleans, and sold throughout the country. The ingredients are as follows:

1 jigger Bourbon whisky	1 lump sugar
½ jigger vermouth	1 dash bitters
1 dash orange bitters	absinthe

Put a small amount of absinthe in a cocktail glass used for old-fashioned cocktail, stir until it touches all parts of the glass, then throw the absinthe out. In another glass mix the other ingredients with cracked ice. Pour into first glass, stir well, rub rim of glass with lemon peel, and serve.

THE CARNIVAL

Social Calendar

BEGINNING late in December and interspersed with the customary breakfast-dances, luncheon-dances, supper-dances, cocktail parties, and receptions, the following 'special' events of the Carnival season exclusive of operas, ballets, concerts, etc., ended with Mardi Gras Day, February 9, 1937. The calendar is typical of all carnival seasons. For the current year see the daily papers.

December
    29, Tuesday. Ball of Harlequins.
    30, Wednesday. Ball of Les Pierrettes.
January
    2, Saturday. Ball of Olympians.
    6, Wednesday. Ball of Twelfth Night Revelers.
    8, Friday. Ball of Caliph of Cairo.
    9, Saturday. Ball of Bards of Bohemia.
    13, Wednesday. Ball of the Krewe of Hypathians.
    14, Thursday. Ball of the Krewe of Nereus.
    15, Friday. Ball of the Krewe of Eros.
    16, Saturday. Ball of Osiris.
    22, Friday. Ball of the Krewe of Aparomest.
    23, Saturday. Ball of Athenians.
    27, Wednesday. Ball of the Krewe of Iridis.
    28, Thursday. Ball of Mithras.
    29, Friday. Ball of Marionettes.
    30, Saturday. Ball of Prophets of Persia.
February
    1, Monday. Ball of Oberon.
    2, Tuesday. Ball of Atlanteans.
    3, Wednesday. Ball of the Krewe of Mystery.
    4, Thursday. Parade and Ball of the Krewe of Momus.
    5, Friday. Parade and Ball of the Krewe of Hermes; Ball of the Krewe
       of Apollo; Ball of the New Orleans Country Club.
    6, Saturday. Children's Parade (Krewe of Nor); Ball of the Mystic Club.
    7, Sunday. Parade and Ball of the Mid-City Carnival Club.
    8, Monday. Algiers Water Pageant (Krewe of Alla); Parade and Ball of the
       Krewe of Proteus.

9, Tuesday. Mardi Gras – street masking; parades of Zulu King,Rex, and Krewe of Orleans; neighborhood parades – largest in Carrollton Section; night parade of the Mystic Krewe of Comus; balls of Comus, Rex, Druids, and Zulu.

The Carnival

Derived from Latin and medieval Latin forms meaning 'the putting away of flesh (meat),' Carnival is an offspring of the Lupercalian, Saturnalian, and Bacchanalian festivals of Rome in pre-Christian times. To determine the day of Mardi Gras (French for Fat Tuesday) one must first know the date of Easter Sunday for the year; then count back forty days, omitting Sundays, to the day before the beginning of Lent.

Mardi Gras has been known to Louisiana since the year 1699, when Iberville took possession of the country. He remembered, as he made his way up the Mississippi on Shrove Tuesday of that year, that Mardi Gras was being celebrated in France, and he appropriately bestowed the name to a spot twelve miles from the river's mouth. The first Carnival demonstrations in the South were held in Mobile. The 'Cowbellian de Rakin Society,' who paraded on New Year's Eve, developed the method of a parade of floats depicting some given theme.

Masked balls and street masking of a sort became features of the Mardi Gras celebration early in Colonial times. They were continued under the Spanish until the governors felt called upon to suppress street masking because of the rowdy- ism which the flatboatmen and the free people of color began to inject into it. Masked balls continued until 1805-06, when the City Council suppressed them because of the Burr plot and the resulting general unrest. As times improved mas- querade balls were resumed in 1823 and authorized by law in 1827. Street mask- ing again came into vogue about 1835, and the newspapers describe a Mardi Gras parade for the first time in 1838. There may have been parades earlier, but after that date the celebrations became regular events. In 1866 Mobile gave her first demonstration on Mardi Gras day, thus adopting the New Orleans date of cele- bration, as New Orleans had adopted her style of parades.

Features of the various Carnivals of Europe may be seen in the season in New Orleans. In Paris there are six gay weeks of masked and fancy balls. In Rome, for eleven days, from two o'clock in the afternoon until dark of each day, happy maskers throng the streets, and throw bouquets and sugar plums to the watchers on the balconies. The balconies are decorated in brilliantly colored cotton cloth, and if a house has no balcony, one is built for the Carnival season. In Venice, the poor save all winter that they may wear fine costumes, mask, and appropriately welcome their monarch, who arrives in a gondola, and remains for a merry Carnival rule of several days. In Spain, people mask and do all sorts of foolish things; there are great dignified parades, and large and small balls. In New Orleans, Carnival is the voice of a people determined to be gay always.

Southern art, music, and literature have been enriched by a century of Carnival. Pageantry, costuming, dancing, stage effects, and lighting have likewise been influenced.

Carnival is sponsored by social and secret organizations. Each club has a Captain, a prominent person, and one with innumerable Carnival responsibilities. He receives no financial remuneration; his one reward is a job well done, and the renewal of his captaincy.

Next to the Captain in importance is the designing artist. He plans the floats, the costumes of the maskers on the floats, the tableaux or setting for the balls, the invitations, the dance programs, and the souvenirs at the balls. Themes for the parades or balls have an historical, legendary, or mythological basis. Approval of a theme depends upon its adaptability to color, romance, and illusion. The artist designs plates for each float, drawing them to scale and indicating the placement of the maskers.

When the artist's plates are finished they are submitted to the builders. Often an artist's designs cannot be transferred to canvas, papier-mâché, satin, and gauze with complete effectiveness. The result may be entirely different from the one intended, despite the worker's sincere attempt to reproduce the fantasy in lumber, cloth, paint, paste, and gilt. In designing floats, proportion and perspective are distorted. The floats are built on wheeled flat carts about twenty feet long and eight feet wide. The floats can measure no more than twenty-four feet in length and nine feet in width, in order that corners may be turned with ease; and only eighteen feet in height, because of telegraph and telephone wires. Space for the men on the floats must be taken into consideration, and so, with these limitations, the figures are made grotesque in order to achieve an illusion of hugeness.

The platforms are of heavy timber, and are metal-braced where the maskers stand. Iron rods are also placed at the maskers' stations for their support. Models of the floats are made of clay, from which plaster molds are cast. The papier-mâché covering is made by pressing a paper pulp and glue mixture into the molds. When dried hard these molds are lifted out and set aside for the carpenter. A wooden framework of columns, animals, or figures is put on the platforms, and foundations forming the mass of the float are stuffed into shape with excelsior and covered with light canvas. The papier-mâché and the fragile, quivering, lovely devices that shake and give the floats their living appearance are then fitted into place.

In setting off the brilliant coloring of the floats an ingenious device is employed. In the day parades the gold and silver leaf used in trimming the floats is applied in such a manner that the rays of the sun are caught and deflected upon the ornamental platform, while at night the leaf is pointed downward to take advantage of the glare of the torches. The coloring used in the daytime is more subdued; at night, more intense, in keeping with coloring used with artificial light.

Soulié and Crassons and John H. Deutschmann and Sons build all the floats. Their work is done in secluded 'dens,' old cotton warehouses on Calliope Street near South Claiborne Avenue. It is a location which few people know, and even fewer ever see. A special permit from the manager of the organization is necessary for a visit. Work on the floats begins in April, and thirty to fifty men are employed. Dates of progress must be set and adhered to without exception. If work is not on schedule, more men are employed. An organization giving both a parade and a ball spends between $20,000 and $35,000, all expense being absorbed by the dues of the members. The night parades, which are more expensive, employ about 885 people – 525 Negroes to carry the lights, an average of 40 men to carry the signs for the floats, 40 men to lead the mules, 200 to 250 musicians, and mounted and motorcycle police. Parades usually cost about $15,000 now that the organizations have many accumulated properties. The same pageantry given for the first time would cost nearly $60,000.

The parade program opens on Thursday night preceding Mardi Gras with the procession of the Krewe of the Knights of Momus, organized in 1872. The Krewe of Hermes, an organization which held its first parade and ball in 1937, parades on Friday night.

The night parades begin at seven o'clock. All parades, except that of Hermes, which forms at Washington and St. Charles Avenues, start at St. Charles Avenue and Calliope Street. Generally, the processions march up the lakeside of St. Charles Avenue to Washington Avenue, down the riverside of St. Charles, past Lee Circle to Canal Street, where they parade on both sides of the neutral ground, some going down North Rampart Street, and others down Royal and Orleans Street to the Auditorium (consult daily newspapers for parade routes). Here the ranks are broken, the maskers disembark to attend the ball, and the floats are returned to the dens.

Parades may be viewed from the street, balconies, windows of homes and business houses, or from specially constructed tiers a story or so high. Each view has its advantage, but to mingle with the joyous crowd of the street is to feel the real spirit of the Carnival. Many await the parade on St. Charles and Canal Streets, for it is on these streets that the kings meet their queens: Momus and Comus at the Louisiana Club, 636 Gravier Street; Hermes at the City Hall, 543 St. Charles Street; Proteus at the Boston Club, 824 Canal Street. Although the varicolored lights of Canal Street give the parade a certain splendor, St. Charles Avenue is the better place to see a night parade. The avenue, with its beautiful homes and wide neutral ground, is not so highly lighted as Canal, and stars overhead wink back to the twinkling lights. Red-robed Negroes carry gasoline torches, calcium burners, and star-sparkling flares.

Soon after noon, when there is a night parade, 'pop' stands, hot dog counters, peanut wagons, cotton candy sheds, and souvenir boards sprout up along the streets like mushrooms after a spring rain. Cars, whose tops will be used as reviewing stands, are parked on the side streets near St. Charles Avenue. At five o'clock spectators begin to appear, and the crowd thickens so fast that one must walk in the streets. On the night of the parade all traffic along the way is rerouted to prevent interference. Children form human chains to whip through the crowd, and there is much laughter and noise.

Suddenly a glow spreads in the sky, and there is a rumbling sound as a squad of motorcycle policemen approaches. You back out of the street to the sidewalk. You press closer and closer to the people already there. The thundering motorcycles pass, only to give place to mounted policemen four abreast, who are determined to clear a passageway. The horses' hoofs terrify and succeed in their purpose; you are well out of the street by now.

Following the mounted policemen come the public utility truck, organization repair truck, the Marshal of the parade, and the Captain with his eight aides. The Captain is masked and costumed as a knight. His glowing velvet cape is draped over the back of his horse; and while the horse prances, the plumes in the knight's helmet nod and flutter as he attends to the task of keeping all in order.

Most parades consist of twenty floats: one title car, the King's float, and eighteen floats interpreting the theme. Two Negroes carry mounted title cards announcing the subject of each float. Beside the floats dancing Negroes carry torches. Between floats march the bands, usually fourteen in all, and more Negroes with flares and torches.

The King's float moves slowly as he waves his scepter and bows to his gathered subjects. The title float passes; everyone reads aloud and wonders if the designs will be recognizable. Then – the first float of maskers. Hands wave and clap; people jump up and down, and everyone cries for the trinkets that the maskers carry in little bags or in their hands, shouting 'Mister, throw me something!' The trinkets are small; they are cheap; you can buy a dozen for a penny or so, but – a string of beads flies into the crowd, and the people go mad as they snatch for it. It is a belief in New Orleans that it is lucky to catch favors from passing floats. The maskers hold tight with one hand to the supporting iron pole; with the other hand they throw gaudy necklaces and toss kisses from the mouths of their grotesque masks. They pivot on their toes; they kick their heels high; but don't be bewitched by the 'women' on the floats; all maskers are men, without exception.

At the municipal auditorium the maskers descend, and go inside to begin their ball.

On the Saturday before Mardi Gras, since 1934, the school children's parade has begun at noon. The idea of a children's parade originated with the Association of Commerce, and local business and professional men became interested. Each of these men, numbering about 150, contributes ten dollars a year toward the expense of the project. The various public and parochial schools of the city apply for admission into the Krewe of Nor (New Orleans Romance), and membership is limited to approximately fifty. Business organizations furnish the rolling equipment for the floats; but the floats themselves are built in the school basements by the manual-training departments, assisted by the history, geography, and sewing classes. The cost of each float is not in excess of twenty-five dollars, the money being supplied by the Mothers' Club of every school. Each school is represented by one float, and a king and queen are alternately chosen, one from a public school and one from a parochial school. Early in January the names of the children who have won honors for scholarship, conduct, popularity, and personality are listed by the school heads. These names are put in a wheel at the City Hall, and the two names drawn. The same secrecy prevails in the children's Carnival as in the large organizations; the identity of the King and Queen of Nor is not known until the day of the parade.

The children's floats, though not as fanciful as those in the regular parades, are clever in their realism.

The first parade of Nor, in 1934, had as its theme 'The History of New Orleans,' the second parade, in 1935, 'Streets of New Orleans,' the third parade, in 1936, 'Le Vieux Carré,' and the fourth, in 1937, 'What New Orleans Makes.' Some two hundred children take part in the parade, and about twenty school bands furnish music. The children are directed in the rôles they play by Charles H. Hamilton, representative of Rex.

Costumed boys draw the floats, and princes in white and yellow satin precede the floats on Shetland ponies. None of the children wear masks. First-aid stations are set up along the route, and doctors, nurses, and Boy Scout messengers are waiting to ensure protection against mishap.

The King goes to the City Hall, where he receives a bouquet of flowers, and the Mayor and Nor drink to each other (on cold days hot chocolate; on mild, raspberry lemonade). Nor meets his Queen and her court on Canal Street. As Nor approaches, the Queen arises and waves her scepter. Nor stands, bows, and they drink to each other's health. The Queen greets her King: 'Sire, the Royal Household of Nor is assembled to greet you on your visit to the city. Never have I witnessed such an outpouring of the masses.' And the King solemnly answers: 'I feel deeply the homage given by the grown-ups.' The Queen has the royal jewels of the Kingdom of Nor, and she wears an expensive mantle. Her maids are dressed in taffeta with bouffant skirts, and carry flowers. The ball of the Krewe of Nor is held that evening.

On the Monday afternoon before Mardi Gras, Algiers, that part of New Orleans directly across the river from Canal Street, gives its Carnival parade. The parade is an unusual procession of water floats ascending the Mississippi River. Countless small craft ply the water carrying the King's loyal subjects. The river is filled with shrill and guttural boat whistles proclaiming the royal presence.

The Krewe of Proteus, a god of the sea and close friend of Neptune, was organized in 1882, and parades on Monday night preceding Mardi Gras.

As you awake the morning after the Proteus parade you are conscious of something different in the air. It is Mardi Gras, and already the streets are swarming with people, but with people who have undergone a great change and have cast aside their everyday, prosaic selves. For on Mardi Gras every man may be a king for a day or, if he prefers, a tramp or a clown or an Indian chief. In ever-changing groups the maskers make their way through the throngs of spectators who line the streets on the route of the parades. Dutch boys, Gypsy girls, Spanish caballeros, huladancers, country bumpkins, artists, pirates, sailors, devils, French maids, old-fashioned ladies, Russian peasants, and Chinese coolies eat, drink, and are merry. The shrill cries of delighted children are almost drowned by the cries of their equally delighted elders. Maskers in the earlier carnivals generally wore animal costumes with tremendous heads that wobbled and grinned at everything in the manner of maskers costumes in Chinese celebrations. But these have almost entirely disappeared, and their places have been taken by comic-strip characters, movie stars, and men and women whose clothes are completely covered with buttons or playing cards or peanuts or vegetables. In commercial sections throughout the city there are reviewing stands at which the best dancers and the wearers of the most original or most beautiful costumes are awarded prizes.

Beginning early Mardi Gras morning, various clubs of the city, of which the Jefferson City Buzzards is the oldest and perhaps the best known, hold small costumed 'walking' parades all over town. The streets are lined with trucks that have been decorated, with all maskers aboard in appropriate costumes. Almost all the trucks carry a good jazz band and a keg of something or other. With special permits from the Mayor, these trucks fall in line after the Rex parade. Some reviewing stands also give prizes for the best ornamented trucks.

At ten o'clock Mardi Gras morning, with the coming of Zulu, King of the Africans, a burlesque of Rex, one enjoys the heartiest laugh of the day. King Zulu arrives, presumably from the sweltering black land, on a decorated yacht steaming through the New Basin Canal. (For place and time of arrival see daily papers.) In early days the King wore a grass skirt, with tufts of dried grass at his throat, wrists, and ankles. His body was incased in black tights, on which were painted stripes of red and green. His face was further blackened, and was decorated with green and red circles and lines. His throne was a Morris chair, his headdress a tin crown, and his scepter was a broomstick with a stuffed white rooster atop. The throne was shaded by a sacking canopy, and the float was decorated with bedraggled palm and palmetto leaves, paper flowers, and red and purple flags. Painted warriors stood in attendance.

When Zulu first began his annual one-day reign, only two floats awaited him on shore. The floats were quite bare; there was not even a throne. The matter was settled simply by transferring the Morris chair and the other decorations of the barge, including the warriors, to the float.

The float second in the parade was occupied by a cook, a basket of fish, and a cooking stove. The fish-fry float was for the feeding of subjects along the route. The King's henchmen, and high Negro officials in full dress with red and purple scarves draped from shoulder to waist, made up the remainder of the parade.

The King of the Zulus still wears a grass skirt, but a rabbit skin vest and a gold crown have been added. His henchmen are dressed in bright blue police uniforms with huge badges. His parade has several floats, all parts of the home-town jungle. King Zulu now has a Queen, always a beauty, who awaits her monarch on the balcony of a sumptuous undertaking parlor on Jackson Avenue near Dryades Street (Jackson streetcar, Canal and Baronne). The King drinks to his Queen in champagne, and beer and sandwiches are served. The parade is routed down South Rampart Street to Tulane Avenue; along Saratoga Street, and up Jackson Avenue. Zulu and his jungle beasts gaily toss autographed coconuts to a chosen few along the line of march. The climax of the day is a large ball at which the city's best Negro bands play 'as long as anybody has rhythm.'

At eleven o'clock, at the corner of Calliope Street and St. Charles Avenue, the parade of Rex, King of Carnival and Lord of Misrule, starts. His father was old King Cole, his mother Terpsichore, his home on Mount Olympus over the Vale of Tempe in the classic realm of Greece. Rex made his first appearance in 1872 for the entertainment of Duke Alexis Romanoff Alexandrovitch. The royal anthem of Rex, 'If Ever I Cease to Love,' was first used because it was a favorite of Duke

Alexis. In former years, Rex arrived on the Monday preceding Mardi Gras in a river pageant.

Rex is supported by two co-operative associations working under the charter designation of the School of Design. One of these associations, secret in character, is known as the Royal Host, all of whose members have close relations with the King and bear the honorable title of Duke. The other association, also secret, is known as the Carnival Court, and consists of young men who mask and man the floats. The organization is supported by membership dues, and a few subscriptions from various business men who benefit by the tourist trade. Rex chose as his motto 'Pro Bono Publico,' and in 1872 he first used the accepted Carnival colors: green, gold, and purple.

Rex rides out at the head of his parade, unmasked, gracious, and grand. His make-up is so theatrical as to make him unrecognizable. However, his identity is revealed in that day's newspapers. The King's mantle cascades down the back of the float, and two golden-curled page boys stand at the foot of the throne. The floats follow one after the other like giant frosted cakes, the sunlight reflecting in the tinsel.

Usually the parade goes to Louisiana Avenue before turning. Within this limit, Rex stops on St. Charles Avenue at the homes of his former queens, and drinks a toast. On St. Charles Street near Canal, Rex stops at the City Hall to receive the keys of the city. At the Boston Club on Canal Street, the Queen of Carnival and her court wait in afternoon dress. Rex pauses to greet his Queen, give her flowers, and drink champagne. Casting his glass to the pavement below, he then proceeds.

Like the tail of a blazing kite follow the decorated trucks and colorful maskers after the floats of Rex. During the afternoon many parades are given by the business concerns of various neighborhoods. The largest among these is routed in the Carrollton section. The parade, which consists of several floats, as well as walking clubs and maskers, starts about two o'clock, and marches only in the vicinity of Carrollton Avenue.

The maskers continue in their revelry until sunset. At six o'clock all masks must be removed.The parade of Comus, founded in 1857, and the oldest Carnival organization in the city, begins at seven o'clock. Comus, god of festive joy and mirth, is reputed the richest king of Carnival; his parade is always a highlight of the season, and a beautiful closing of Mardi Gras.

The designers of Comus seem always to use some new art in the decoration of floats. Comus parades seem to have more of the 'fluttering, moving things.' Flowers and the like are not flattened, but are able to nod their heads and wave as the wagons roll. In the 1936 parade a sort of shimmering cellophane was used to great advantage.

The King of Comus carries a golden goblet from which he drinks a toast to his Queen, who awaits him at the Louisiana Club on St. Charles Street near Canal. In former years the Queen waited at the Pickwick Club, when its home was on Canal Street. Comus leads his parade into Canal Street, pausing to greet the King and Queen of Rex, who are at the Boston Club in royal costume. Originally the parades

AT THE MARDI GRAS

READY FOR THE CARNIVAL

REX, LORD OF MISRULE

MASKS FOR THE REVELLERS

KING ZULU

DEATH AND MEDUSA AT THE CARNIVAL

AN OLD-FASHIONED GROUP IN A CARRIAGE

THE KING OF COMUS GREETS THE ROYAL FAMILY OF REX

THE MASKERS ON THE FLOATS TOSS FAVORS INTO THE STREETS

THE KNIGHTS COME RIDING

MASKERS DANCE IN THE STREET

CLOWNS WAITING FOR REX

STREET MASKERS

marched in the Vieux Carré, but for many years the section was not included in the routes. In 1937, however, Comus and several other parades passed down Royal and Orleans Streets to the municipal auditorium on North Rampart.

The majestic procession of a Carnival parade through the old French Quarter is a charming scene. Narrow balconies are arrayed in balloons and lanterns, and confetti and serpentine flow from high casement windows. The narrow streets and dim lights of the old section seem to recall all the glamour and witchery of the first carnivals.

The Comus ball starts immediately after the parade, and together with Rex brings the wonderful weeks of Carnival to a close. The Carnival balls of New Orleans are the culmination of the city's social life, especially to the short whirl of a débutante's season.

The balls originated as a private homage to the fair; the season's débutantes usually comprise the court. Because the balls were so beautiful, so different, and so complete, visitors began to come from far and wide to see the Carnival balls of New Orleans. But they have met with disappointment, since they cannot always see the very things for which they come. Invitations are issued for all balls, but are hard to secure from the larger and older societies unless one has a particular friend or relative in the organization.

One reason for creating Rex and Hermes was to help relieve this disappointment. It is possible to receive invitations to these balls through the Association of Commerce. However, the number issued to strangers is limited, because of inadequate ballroom space. The 'call-out' section is a prepared seating arrangement for those who partake in the dancing of the regular Carnival balls. At a few of the balls women mask and call out the men, selecting the King and his court of dukes.

The original Carnival balls were more elaborate than now. As much time was given to preparing stage sets and tableaux for the balls as for the street parades. During the first carnivals the papier-mâché of the floats, costumes, royal garments, jewels, and invitations were made in Europe. Gradually this has been changed, and now only the royal jewels are made in France. Although these jewels are only imitations, American workmen have been unable to secure the same perfection as the French artisans. Invitations, once gorgeously designed, carried a separate card of admittance, but now invitation and card of admission are usually combined and taken up at the door. A simple invitation entitles one only to a spectator's post in the balcony. Those selected for the call-out section receive separate invitations by mail.

The Carnival balls present a glittering spectacle of beautiful women beautifully gowned. Most of the court gowns are made in New Orleans. One of the most magnificent queens' costumes made in this city was worn by the Queen of Comus in the Golden Jubilee of 1924. The Queen wore gloves dipped in fourteen-karat gold. Her mantle, measuring six and one-half yards in length, was topped by a winged collar of gold net entirely embroidered in Strassburg rhinestones. The center of the mantle, running lengthwise, was of gold net embroidered in tiny tubes and rhinestones to represent a trellis. The border was woven of gold metallic cloth with huge grapes of pearls, relieved by leaves of silver cloth, embroidered in rhinestones. The mantle was later used as an altar cloth at the wedding of the Comus Queen, and is now on display at the Cabildo museum.

The Twelfth Night Revelers, organized in 1870, were the first to have a queen and maids, and their manner of selecting the court has continuedthrough the years in its pleasing originality. A large cake of papier-mâché is brought on to the floor during the first call-out dance, and the débutantes file by the cake to receive the small white boxes taken from its filling. One of these boxes, which are distributed by masked 'cooks,' contains a gold bean, the others a silver one. The maiden receiving the golden bean becomes Queen, and the young ladies receiving silver beans become her maids. The selection is supposedly left to chance, and it is true that the débutantes do not know before hand whether they will be lucky or not. All débutantes in the call-out section are requested to wear white, preferably their début dresses, and in this way are prepared for any honor they may or may not be given. The Twelfth Night Revelers is the only organization to employ this method of selecting a Carnival court. In other organizations the regal courts are requested, many months previous, to accept the various appointments.

As the accompanying social calendar reveals, there are innumerable and beautiful balls given during the season. All have their king and queen, their maskers, their call-outs, and their feature tableaux, or a setting on some definite theme. All such balls require invitations, of which a limited number are allowed each member, and those attending must wear full dress.

As has already been stated, there is less difficulty in securing an invitation to the Rex ball, but it is not the best example of a Carnival ball. Only Rex, his Queen, and her maids are in regal costume. There is no call-out section, and after the third dance by the 'nobility' everyone is privileged to go on the floor. At eleven o'clock Rex and his court go to join Comus. As they enter, the Comus band strikes up 'If Ever I Cease to Love'; Comus escorts the Queen of Rex, Rex accompanies the Comus Queen, and the two courts fall in line. It is for the distinction between these two assemblies that the court of Rex wears formal dress. The combined courts are a glowing, glittering spectacle as they promenade; but after midnight there are no ball, no costumes, no music – only stillness. It is Ash Wednesday, first of the forty subdued days of Lent.

And if you wake up at all on Ash Wednesday you will know what Ring Lardner meant by feeling 'like Rex in a state of Comus.'

CEMETERIES

THE cemeteries of New Orleans are truly cities of the dead. In place of marble and granite slabs set in green lawns or hillsides under trees, one finds closely built-up, walled enclosures filled with oblong house-like tombs, blinding white under the hot southern sun. The deceased reside in the midst of the great living city of their descendants.

Very little is known concerning burial of the dead in Colonial times. Interment was beneath the surface of the ground, and there are no remains of tombs or monuments, or even slabs, bearing a date earlier than 1800, the older graves having disappeared. After 1803 the rapid increase in population, together with the inroads made by yellow fever and cholera, created a real municipal problem. New cemeteries were established and old ones enlarged to meet the situation. Rigid regulations regarding methods of burial were issued. Interment in the ground was forbidden, and brick tombs were required in all cemeteries, which were enclosed within high brick walls. The recurring epidemics of yellow fever, however, sent so many dead bodies to the cemeteries that these regulations could not always be carried out. At times the burial grounds were so overtaxed that the only possible way of disposing of the dead was to bury them *en masse* in shallow trenches as on the field of battle. It is estimated that more than 100,000 are buried in the old St. Louis cemeteries on Basin and Claiborne Streets alone.

A graphic picture of the condition of the epidemic in 1853, drawn by Cable in *Creoles of Louisiana*, describes a lack of gravediggers:

> Five dollars an hour failed to hire enough of them. Some of the dead went to the tomb still with martial pomp and honors; but the city scavengers, too, with their carts went knocking from house to house asking if there were any to be buried. Long rows of coffins were laid in furrows scarce two feet deep, and hurriedly covered with a few shovels full of earth, which the daily rains washed away, and the whole mass was left, 'filling the air far and near with the most intolerable pestilential odors.' Around the graveyards funeral trains jostled and quarreled for places, in an air reeking with the effluvia of the earlier dead. Many 'fell to work and buried their own dead.' Many sick died in carriages and carts. Many were found dead in their beds, in the stores, in the streets.....

The death rate per thousand from 1800 to 1880 in some decades was appalling. The lowest figure was 40.22 from 1860 to 1870, while the highest was 63.55 from 1830 to 1840.

The manner in which rain and water seepage hampered burials is vividly described in *DeBow's Review* of September 1852:

> A grave in any of the cemeteries is lower than the adjacent swamps, and from ten to fifteen feet lower than the river, so that it fills speedily with water, requiring to be bailed out before it is fit to receive the coffin, while during heavy rains it is subject to complete inundation. The great Bayou Cemetery (afterwards St. Louis Cemetery No. 3 on Esplanade Avenue) is sometimes so completely inundated that inhumation becomes impossible until after the subsidence of the water; the dead bodies accumulating in the meanwhile. I have watched the bailing out of the grave, the floating of the coffin, and have heard the friends of the deceased deplore this mode of interment.

The method of tomb burial in New Orleans is unusual. The tombs, which usually consist of two vaults, with a crypt below in which the bones are kept, are carefully sealed to prevent the escape of gases from the decaying bodies. Sometimes they are built in tiers, resembling great, thick walls, and are called 'ovens.' After a period of time prescribed by law, the tombs may be opened, the coffins broken and burned, and the remains deposited in the crypts. By this method a single tomb may serve the same family for generations.

The oven vaults line the walls of the cemetery. In some of the graveyards single vaults can be rented for a certain period, after which, if no disposition is made of the remains by relatives when the period expires, the body is removed and buried in some out-of-the-way corner of the graveyard, the coffin destroyed, and the vault rented to some other tenant. This seemingly heartless procedure was the only possible manner of interment in the restricted areas of the old burial grounds. The system is giving way to burial in the ground in the more modern cemeteries where family tombs do not already exist, but although it is quite safe nowadays to bury the dead beneath the ground, many tombs are still built.

There have always been certain exceptions to the practice of tomb burial. In the Hebrew cemeteries burial has always been in the ground, and only marble and granite slabs and monuments are seen. The Potter's Field and Charity Hospital Cemetery, where the unclaimed or destitute poor are buried, present another and quite different appearance. The Charity Hospital Cemetery on Canal Street, for instance, has the appearance of a well-kept green lawn. Close examination, however, discloses the existence of small square stones in rows, flush with the ground and marked with numbers. These stones mark the graves of white persons at the Canal Street entrance and of Negroes at the Banks Street end. Only a few rows of stone markers are visible, since the entire cemetery has recently been raised about three feet. Underneath the present surface are the forgotten graves of many thousands buried there since the cemetery was established in the 1830's.

The absence of trees in the older graveyards is due to the fact that in so constricted a space the roots would cause an unsettling of the walls and tombs. Flowers, except cut flowers in vases, and lawns are also lacking, since there is no place for them to grow. However, on All Saints' Day, November 1, Orleanians make up for the lack of flowers, every tomb displaying a remembrance in floral form. The observance of All Saints' Day is a distinctive Creole custom of European origin. Other sections of the country decorate graves on May 30, Memorial Day, or, in Catholic cemeteries, on All Souls' Day, the day following All Saints', but in New Orleans neither of these days is observed in that way. The Confederate dead are remembered on June 3, while Protestants and Catholics alike fill the cemeteries with flowers on All Saints' Day.

In former times the Creole ladies made the day an occasion for the display of winter fashions, and iron benches can still be seen before some tombs where it was the custom for members of the family to sit and receive friends during the day.

During the week preceding November 1, Negroes can be seen hard at work cleaning and whitewashing the tombs. Gilt paint is sometimes used to make more legible the inscriptions on the tombs and on the blocks of marble used as bases for flower containers. New Orleans is flooded with flowers, chiefly chrysanthemums, which have become definitely associated with the occasion. The plants are grown in the city and surrounding countryside, and are sold at hundreds of shops, along with cut flowers imported from California and elsewhere. The floral decorations make the cemeteries gay with spots of white, yellow, and bronze. Here and there painted palm fronds, paper flowers, and ornate wreaths made of beads are to be seen. The same wreath is sometimes brought out year after year. Although a solemn occasion, the city takes on a holiday air. Crowds of people swarm through the burial places. From dawn until dusk the long procession continues, while hundreds of vendors supply refreshments and toys to pacify the children.

New Orleans has more than thirty cemeteries at the present time (1937). The first Colonial cemeteries and some later graveyards such as Locust Grove Cemetery, now the site of the Thomy Lafon Negro school and playground, are no longer in existence. Many of these cemeteries are controlled by church congregations, and several are city property. Almost every one now has a section for Negroes; and there are no exclusively Negro cemeteries.

An Old Spanish document in the Cabildo, dated 1800, and dealing with an auction sale of lots in the old cemetery on Rampart Street 'in front of the Charity Hospital,' mentions that shortly after the founding of the city 'the dead were buried on the grounds where later the capitular houses were erected and now stand, and that due to the increase in the population of the city, the said cemetery was transferred to the city block that corners with Bienville and Chartres Streets, being located on the second block coming down from the levee of the river toward the cathedral,' on a plot now bounded by Bienville, Chartres, Conti, and Royal Streets. The cemetery was maintained here until 1743, when it was moved to the ramparts opposite the Charity Hospital of that day, on the square between Toulouse, Burgundy, and St. Peters Streets. In 1788 it was moved beyond the ramparts and a little further south. Basin Street was cut through afterwards and the ground from Rampart to Basin Street detached from the cemetery. Human bones dug up as late as 1900 in this area indicate that it once formed a part of the burial ground. Trémé Street (Marais) was cut through in 1838 and the graveyard confined to the river side of the street. The present St. Louis Cemetery No. 1, with the strip on Marais Street, formerly called the American Cemetery, is all that now remains of the original Basin Street burial ground. Soon after 1803 a strip in the rear of the Basin Street cemetery was set aside to serve as a burial place for the Protestants.

As the nature of yellow fever was not understood, every conceivable method of protection was tried. It was felt, for one thing, that contagion spread from the cemeteries, and the City Council carried on a prolonged controversy with the wardens of the Cathedral in an effort to remove St. Louis Cemetery to some other location. In those early days all the ground between Rampart Street and Lake Pontchartrain was a swamp laced with bayous and foul with stagnant water and refuse from the city. Bayou Ridge Road and Bayou Metairie were the highest places. It was decided to leave the old cemetery as it was and establish a new cemetery on Claiborne Avenue reaching from Canal to St. Louis Streets. The square at Canal and Claiborne was afterwards reclaimed. A new Protestant cemetery was also established at the head of Girod Street. The ground now occupied by the City Yard and the Illinois Central Hospital was subsequently detached. Girod Cemetery was in use before 1820, and St. Louis Cemetery No. 2 on Claiborne Avenue dates from 1822. The city found it necessary to establish a pauper burial ground in 1833, and a location on 'Leprous Road' was selected. 'Leper's Land' was the name given to the neighborhood on Galvez Street, between Carondelet Canal and Bayou Road Ridge, because Galvez (1777-1785) banished the lepers, of whom there was a dangerous number in his day, to that neighborhood, and Miro, his successor (1785-1792), built a house for them there. The new cemetery was situated on the bayou on the present site of St. Louis Cemetery No. 3, and is referred to in old city directories as the Bayou Cemetery.

As the city grew and the yearly epidemics continued, more and more burial grounds were needed. The present group at the head of Canal Street began about 1840, the Fireman's, Cypress Grove, and St. Patrick's being among the first.

The suburban towns of the period above New Orleans, which were afterwards absorbed into the city, also had their cemeteries. Lafayette Cemetery No. 1, at Washington Avenue and Prytania Street, was the first planned cemetery in New Orleans, the lanes being laid out in symmetrical order and provision made for driveways for funeral processions. The first Jewish cemetery, at Jackson Avenue and Benton (Liberty) Streets, dates from the 1820's. It was closed in 1866, but still exists intact and is well cared for. St. Joseph's, on Washington Avenue and Loyola, was established in 1850. In Bouligny, or Jefferson City, the Soniat Street Cemetery began to be used about 1850, while the Hebrew cemetery of the Congregation Gates of Prayer, farther out in Hurstville (on Joseph Street), was established in 1852. Carrollton Cemetery goes back to the 1830's.

After the Civil War the Metairie race track was turned into a cemetery and has become the finest in the city. The Hebrew cemeteries on Frenchmen Street and Elysian Fields, and St. Roch's also date from this period.

Mark Twain once said that New Orleans had no architecture except that found in its cemeteries. He had the public buildings of the city in mind, and his statement was truer when made in 1875 than it is today. There are many beautiful tombs in the modern cemeteries, especially in Metairie. The material used ranges from the soft, cement-covered brick of early days, found chiefly in the St. Louis Cemeteries, to the finest of marble and granite carved and shaped into many striking and effective designs, and representing outlays of thousands of dollars. All styles and combinations of styles of architecture are to be found – Egyptian, Greek, and Gothic. The prevailing color is dazzling white, but striking effects are also secured with gray and red granite. A feature of some of the old tombs in St. Louis Cemetery No. 1 is the use of small wrought-iron fences topped with a cross of the same material enclosing a little space in front of the tomb. Every large tomb has a place for flower vases, and most of the 'oven' vaults have a small shelf for the same purpose, some of which are never without floral offerings. The prevailing design in tombs is a rectangle with a rounded top, but diminutive temples, Gothic cathedrals, and irregular designs of various kinds are to be found in all cemeteries. Many mausoleums erected by societies are scattered through all the burial grounds. Sometimes these are plain square beehives, but often they are unusual in design, like the mound tomb of the Army of Tennessee in Metairie, and the Elks' tomb in Greenwood.

Fewer epitaphs are to be found in the New Orleans cemeteries than elsewhere. The large number of people usually buried in a family tomb and the consequent lack of space on the slab make anything more than the name and dates impracticable. Wordings in many different languages are found; French and English, however, are most frequent. Perhaps the outstanding epitaph, at least from the old-fashioned Southern point of view, is the rhetorical tribute to Albert Sidney Johnston by John Dimitry, carved on the rear wall of the vault of the tomb of the Army of Tennessee in Metairie.

In Girod Cemetery there is a forgotten tomb in which Jane Placide, the once-famous actress of the American Theater, rests. James H. Caldwell, manager of the theater and notable for many activities in early New Orleans history, had her tomb built and selected the epitaph. They were lovers, and Caldwell's tribute, in the verses of Barry Cornwall, were often on the lips of romanticists:

> There's not an hour
> Of day or dreaming night but I am with thee;
> There's not a breeze but whispers of thy name,
> And not a flower that sleeps beneath the moon
> But in its hues or fragrance tells a tale
> Of thee.

There is one that sounds like the language of the Jabberwock:

> Alas that one whose dornthly joy had often to trust in heaven should canty thus sudden to from all its hopes benivens and though thy love form off remore that dealt the dog pest thou left to prove thy sufferings while below.

Sacred to the memory of Robert John, a native of this city, son of and Jane Creswell died June 4, 1845 age 26 years, 7 months (Girod Cemetery).

Here also may be found what is probably the briefest epitaph in the city – 'D. J. C. 1839.'

Perhaps the most arresting epitaphs in the old St. Louis Cemeteries are those on the tombs of the men who fell in duels:

Mort sur le champ d'honneur' (Died on the field of honor)
'Victime de son honneur' (Victim of his honor)
'Pour garder intact le nom de famille' (To keep unsullied the name ofthe family)

St. Louis Cemetery No. 1, Basin St. between St. Louis and Toulouse, along with St. Louis Nos. 2 and 3, contains practically all of the tombs of the old Creole families. Many of the early Americans – Daniel Clark, his daughter, Myra Clark Gaines, the two wives of Governor Claiborne – and many others of similar prominence are buried in what used to be called the American Cemetery, the rear part of St. Louis No. 1 reserved for Protestants. Governor Claiborne himself was buried here until 1906, when his remains were taken to a tomb in Metairie, where they now rest. The oldest decipherable epitaph is that of 'Nannette F. de Bailly. Died the 24th of September, 1800. Aged 45 years.' The low brick tomb of Étienne de Boré, the man who developed sugar-refining in Louisiana and the first mayor of New Orleans, is in this cemetery; his grandson Charles Gayarré, the historian, is buried in the same tomb. Paul Morphy, the famous chess expert, is also buried here. In the De Lino family tomb lies Chalmette, the marble slab bearing his own name having been stolen long ago by vandals and used as a portion of a walk in another part of the cemetery until broken beyond repair. The well-known Voodoo leader, Marie Laveau, is thought by some to lie in a well-kept grave inscribed as follows:

FAMILLE VVE. PARIS
née LAVEAU
Ci-Git
MARIE PHILOME GLAPION
décédée le 11 Juin 1897
agée de soixante-deux ans
Elle fut bonne mère, bonne amie et
regrettée par tous ceux qui l'ont connue
Passants priez pour elle.

FAMILY WID. PARIS
born LAVEAU
Here Lies
MARIE PHILOME GLAPION
deceased June 11, 1897
aged sixty-two years.
She was a good mother, a good friend and
regretted by all who knew her.
Passers-by, please pray for her.

The little church of Our Lady of Guadalupe, at Rampart and Conti Sts., was originally the mortuary chapel where all Catholic funerals were held from 1827 to 1860. Convinced that the dead bodies which were taken into the Saint Louis Cathedral during funerals were a means of spreading disease, the City Council forbade the holding of funerals in the Cathedral after 1827. The mortuary chapel was erected near the cemetery by the wardens of the Cathedral to fill this need. After the Civil War the ban on cathedral funerals was removed and the little chapel became a parish church.

St. Louis Cemetery No. 2, N. Claiborne Ave. and Bienville St., contains several curious tombs. Most interesting is that of Dominique You, pirate-captain under Jean Lafitte, veteran of the Battle of New Orleans, and afterwards a ward politician, whose funeral was the event of the year. Here also is the unmarked 'Voodoo' grave, another supposed resting place of Marie Laveau. The uninscribed concrete is covered with crosses made by the faithful with bits of red brick; and devotees still bring contributions of food and money, especially on St. John's Eve (June 23). 'Hoodoo money,' in two-cent and eleven-cent combinations, left at the base of the tomb will bring good luck to the depositor or bad luck to his enemy. Marie is said to converse with her followers through the walls of her oven, imparting such information as they desire. Other interesting tombs include those of Alexander Milne, the Scotch philanthropist, in whose honor Milneburg is named; Francois-Xavier Martin, historian; Pierre Soulé, United States Senator, Ambassador to Spain, and Confederate statesman; Claude Trémé, who founded Faubourg Trémé; and Oscar J. Dunn, the mulatto Lieutenant-Governor under Henry Clay Warmoth.

St. Louis No. 3, 3421 Esplanade Ave. (*Esplanade bus from Canal and Burgundy Sts.*) occupies the site of the old Bayou Cemetery established by the city in 1835. It became the property of the cathedral in 1856 and is now the finest of the three St. Louis Cemeteries. Its location on very low ground has always been a detriment, but the grounds are well kept and many fine tombs are to be seen. The priests of the diocese are buried here, and many of the religious orders, both priests and nuns, have their mausoleums in this cemetery. Bishops and archbishops are always buried beneath the altar of the cathedral. There is an impressive monument to the memory of James Gallier, Sr., the famous architect who was lost with his wife at sea, erected by his son. Thomy Lafon, the mulatto philanthropist, also has a tomb in this cemetery.

Girod Cemetery, S. Liberty St. between Cypress and Perilliat Sts. (*S. Claiborne car from Canal and St. Charles St. to Girod; walk four blocks right*), the oldest Protestant cemetery in the city, is hidden away in the railroad yards at the head of Girod Street. Christ Church came into control of it through a purchase from the city in 1825. It has not been used much in recent years, and the luxuriant vines and shrubs with which it is overgrown give it a haunted appearance. Gnarled fig trees push their way through the bulging sides of some of the old tombs, and the wall ovens are damp and green with maidenhair fern. Many famous people of former days are buried here, including Glendy Burke, prominent citizen and financier of ante-bellum days, and Col. W. W. S. Bliss, survivor of many battles in the

Mexican War. Another tomb is that of John David Fink, founder of Fink Asylum for Protestant Widows and Orphans, who, according to tradition, excluded maiden ladies from his charitable enterprises because of having once been refused by a girl who preferred working out her own destiny as an old maid.

Metairie Cemetery, intersection of Pontchartrain Blvd. and Metairie Rd. (*West End car from any place on Canal St.*), is the finest of all New Orleans cemeteries and one of the show places of the city. The site of a famous antebellum race track, it occupies a beautiful location among groves of green trees and quiet waterways. In 1873 the racing was discontinued and the Metairie Cemetery Association formed. In 1895 the grounds were beautified and landscaped, with a series of drives, paved walks, lagoons, and many fine trees. Marble and granite in beautiful and costly designs line every roadway. Here cemetery architecture is to be found at its best.

In the center of a large green mound surrounded by palm trees is the handsome granite shaft, the Army of Northern Virginia Monument, commemorating the Confederate general, Stonewall Jackson, and the men of the Louisiana Division of the Army of Northern Virginia who fought under him. The monument was dedicated May 10, 1881, the eighteenth anniversary of the death of Jackson, in the presence of a great throng of spectators. Above the mausoleum, in which 2,500 men are buried, rises the granite monument, 32 feet in height. Atop this is the statue of Jackson, 'neither calmer nor grander than Jackson stood in flesh.' On the pedestal are carved two crossed flags with the inscription 'From Manassas to Appomattox, 1861 to 1865.' The statue was the work of Achille Perelli of New Orleans.

The monument erected to the memory of the Louisiana Division of the Army of Tennessee is one of the finest Confederate monuments in New Orleans.

It was dedicated April 5, 1887, the twenty-fifth anniversary of the Battle of Shiloh. The handsome bronze equestrian statue represents General Johnston as he led the charge at that battle in which he received his mortal wound. On the right of the entrance to the mausoleum stands a lifelike marble statue of an orderly sergeant calling the roll of the soldiers. The Gothic arch at the entrance of the tomb is surmounted with a bronze medallion with flags and arms, and at the sides are the names of the battles in which the division fought. The remains of General Beauregard repose inside, and the vault contains a memorial tablet to Johnston. The work was executed by Alexander Doyle and Achille Perelli.

At the intersection of Aves. D and I, a short distance from the entrance of the cemetery, stands the white granite monument erected in memory of Louisiana's Washington Artillery, one of the best-known military organizations of the South. The company was organized in 1840 and saw its first service in the war with Mexico. During the Civil War the company, which had by then expanded into a battalion of five companies, saw service in more than sixty great battles from Bull Run to Appomattox. The monument is 32 feet in height, and is topped with the figure of an artillery soldier leaning on a gun swab. Granite posts, shaped like upright cannon and connected with iron chains, surround the mound. The base of the pedestal consists of a graduated pyramid of three steps, with sculptured cannonballs at the bottom. On the face of the pedestal appears the emblem of the company, a tiger's head, with the motto 'Try us,' and also the badge of the artillery, the State seal, and a basrelief bust of Washington. The dates '1846' and '1861-1865' are engraved on one side, together with the names of the battles in which the company fought and the members who lost their lives in service. George Doyle was the sculptor.

Elsewhere in the cemetery are the tombs of Generals John B. Hood, Richard Taylor, and Fred N. Ogden, all prominent Confederates. Jefferson Davis was first buried here, but his remains have since been removed. The remains of Governor Claiborne, the first American Governor of Louisiana, were brought to Metairie from St. Louis No. 1. Other famous names are those of the Reverend Thomas Riley Markham, Chaplain General of the Confederacy; Dr. B. F. Palmer, pastor of the First Presbyterian Church; Bishop Sessums, of the Episcopal Church; Governor Henry Clay Warmoth, and John Dimitry.

Many of the prominent families of the city have tombs in Metairie, and the remains of many others have been brought there from their original resting-places in other cemeteries. Magnificent family tombs rise on all sides, and certain oddities are to be seen as well. The tall shaft of the Moriarity Monument stands just to the left of the entrance. Amusing stories are told about the four female figures at the base of the shaft, but all are without foundation in fact. The four statues are simply stock figures placed on the monument for effect by the builder. Mr. Dooley, upon observing the statues, is said to have remarked: 'Faith, Hope, Charity – and Mrs. Moriarity.' Somewhat to the rear on the right, near Pontchartrain Blvd., stands the red granite tomb of José Morales, with torches of flaming stone and a bronze female figure in the act of knocking at the door of the tomb. It was built originally for Josie Arlington Duebler, of Storeyville fame, and many stories have been told of it.

Greenwood and Cypress Grove Cemeteries, City Park Ave. and West End Blvd. (*Cemeteries or West End car from any place on Canal St.*). The Firemen's Benevolent Association controls these two cemeteries, which are situated across the street from one another and just across the Basin from Metairie Cemetery. They contain the tombs of many prominent people of earlier days, including that of Warren Easton, the New Orleans educator. Here are also the mausoleums of the Swiss Society, the Association of Alsace Lorraine, the Typographical Union, and the Elks.

In the front left-hand corner of Greenwood Cemetery, plainly visible from City Park Ave., stands the monument erected in honor of the Confederate dead. The mausoleum, in which more than 600 soldiers are buried, consists of a large mound in the shape of a pyramid, buttressed with granite on the edges. Steps in front lead up to a granite slab, about 8 feet square, and in the center rises a marble shaft 9 feet in height. On the shaft is a life-size statue of a Confederate outpost guard, body bent and bayonet pointed, an expression of dogged watchfulness on the face. Life-size busts of Stonewall Jackson, Robert E. Lee, Leonidas Polk, and

Albert Sidney Johnston adorn the four faces of the shaft. On the south side is the engraved inscription, 'Erected in Memory of the Heroic Virtues of the Confederate Soldier, by the Ladies' Benevolent Association.' B. M. Harrod of New Orleans selected the design for the monument, and its erection was under the management of George Stroud. The material used in the structure is Carrara marble, and the approximate cost was $12,000.

At the entrance, standing beneath a group of Gothic arches, is the 6-foot statue of a fireman, erected in 1887 in honor of the members of the Volunteer Fire Department who lost their lives in service. The statue of the fireman is of marble and was designed by Alexander Doyle. The pedestal and arches are of white Maine granite.

Cypress Grove Cemetery has a gateway in Egyptian style. Here one finds the monuments and tombs of Dr. Warren Stone, outstanding physician; Maunsel White, veteran of 1815; James H. Caldwell, actor, banker, and impresario; and Mayors John P. Conway, Charles J. Leeds, and John T. Monroe. Among the 'ovens' along the Canal St. wall is one with a slab marked 'Grave of Mumford,' in which rests the young Confederate sympathizer who was court-martialed and hanged for pulling down the American flag from the United States Mint in April 1862. A fine monument of Irad Ferry, the first volunteer fireman to meet death while on duty, at afire in Camp Street in 1837, stands just to the right of the entrance. The mausoleum contains the bodies of other members of Ferry's company who lost their lives in combatting fires.

One of the most interesting tombs in this cemetery is the Chinese Mausoleum, a plain square concrete structure with vaults opening on an inside covered court. The slabs all have Arabic numerals, and some have Chinese symbols. In one corner there is an open grate in which incense is burned during burial services. The custom of leaving food as an offering to the dead is no longer observed. The mausoleum belongs to the Chinese tongs and affords a temporary resting-place to its members, since all Chinese are taken to China for burial, regardless of the length of time they have been absent from their native land. At intervals of about ten years the vaults are opened, the bones removed, cleaned and packed in steel boxes, about 30 inches high and 20 inches square, for shipment to China for permanent burial.

St. Roch Cemetery, St. Roch and Derbigny Sts. (*Frenchmen bus from Canal and Chartres Sts. to Derbigny; walk four blocks downtown*). St. Roch is one of the quaintest of New Orleans cemeteries. Modeled after the famous Campo Santo dei Tedeschi (Holy Field of the Germans) near St. Peter's in Rome, it was called the Campo Santo by its founder, Father Thevis, a young German priest, who had come to New Orleans at the request of the Bishop of New Orleans because of the scarcity of native priests. As assistant pastor of the Holy Trinity Church, he was confronted in 1868 with the loss of his pastor and many of the parishioners, victims of a yellow fever epidemic. In this extremity Father Thevis invoked the intercession of Saint Roch, famous for his wonderful work among the plague sufferers of the Middle Ages, promising to erect with his own hands the chapel of St. Roch, which has been a favorite shrine ever since. The cemetery soon grew up around it; its walls, with their chapel-like niches containing the Stations of the Cross within and tombs beneath, and Saint Michael's Mausoleum in the second section of the cemetery, were added soon afterwards. A steady stream of devout Catholics have made their journey to St. Roch for many years. Mass is said there every Monday morning, and on any day candles can be found burning before the altar, either in thanksgiving or in petition for some favor received or desired.

The chapel is a diminutive chancel of a Gothic church, and is constructed of brick covered with cement. Tall, narrow windows pierce the upper walls, while the lower reaches are covered with metal in imitation of wood paneling. The little altar is made of carved wood and has a small statue of Saint Roch and his faithful dog just above the tabernacle. The painted folding panels of the altarpiece are so badly faded that only the gold halos on the heads of the saints remain. Along the walls on each side of the altar are marble emblems and plaques, together with artificial limbs and crutches testifying to the cures that have been wrought through the intercession of the patron saint. In the floor of the chapel in front of the altar is the marble slab covering the grave of Father Thevis. Each Good Friday for many years young girls of New Orleans have made a pilgrimage to St. Roch's Chapel because of a local legend which promised a husband before the year was out to the maiden who said a prayer and left a small sum at each of nine churches. It was considered doubly lucky to end this pilgrimage at St. Roch's and to pick a four-leaf clover in the old cemetery. The red spots which appear on the clover there are said to result from the blood spattered by a bride-to-be who committed suicide on the grave of her lover.

OTHER CEMETERIES

The cemetery of St. Vincent de Paul, 1322 Louisa St. (*take St. Claude car at Canal and N. Rampart Sts.; get of at Louisa St. and walk two blocks left*), is notable because of its connection with Pepe Llulla, who is credited with having established it, although it appears that he merely developed it after he became connected with the family who started it. A native of Mahon, Spain, heavily bearded and of striking appearance, he was noted for his swordsmanship, and was said to have been a veteran of more than thirty duels. His prowess in this respect was so great that popular tradition states that he started the cemetery in order to have a convenient place to bury his victims. St. Vincent de Paul's also contains the tombs of Mother Catherine Seals, Negro spiritualist leader, and of Queen Marie of the Gypsies, who died March 19, 1916. The large marble tomb of the latter bears the name 'Boacho' and the legend 'Tomb of the Tinka-Gypsy.' Gypsies are said to make regular visits to the resting-place of their Queen.

There are many Hebrew cemeteries in different sections of the city, while the Masons and Odd Fellows have well-kept burial grounds at the head of Canal St. The three St. Patrick Cemeteries, in which many of the old Irish pioneers are buried, are also on Canal St. The Lafayette Cemeteries No. 1, 1427 Sixth St. (*take*

Magazine car at Canal and Magazine Sts.; get off at Sixth St. and walk two blocks right), and No. 2, Washington Ave. between Loyola and Saratoga Sts. *(take St. Charles car at Canal and Baronne Sts.; get off at Washington Ave. and walk four blocks right)*, contain tombs of many well-known residents of the old Garden District; St. Joseph's, Washington Ave. and Loyola St., contains the original frame church of St. Mary's Assumption, which was moved there from its original site, when the present brick church was erected. The National Cemetery at Chalmette was laid out in 1865 and contains the graves of more than 12,000 soldiers, almost half of them unknown.

SOME NEGRO CULTS
MOTHER CATHERINE'S MANGER

The Church of the Innocent Blood, later the Church of the True Light, 2420 Charbonnet St. Drive down N. Rampart St. and St. Claude Ave.; left from St. Claude on Flood St.; park at the 2400 block and walk three blocks right. It is not advisable to attempt the trip in wet weather. Services at 8.30 P.M. Sundays.

MOTHER CATHERINE SEALS, the High Priestess of New Orleans Negro cults, was born in Huntsville, Kentucky, and came to New Orleans at the age of sixteen. In 1922, Catherine left the kitchen of a Mrs. Nettles to organize her 'Church of the Innocent Blood,' which was the forerunner of the many 'spiritualist' churches among the Negroes in New Orleans.

Brother Isaiah, the white prophet who astounded New Orleans in 1921-22 by curing sick and lame persons with a magic touch and prayers on the levee of the Mississippi River, may be indirectly responsible for the Church of the Innocent Blood. It is said that because of her color he refused to cure Catherine of a paralytic stroke resulting from a fight with her third husband. This inspired her to pray more intensely for religion and better health. 'De Lawd heahed me,' she later contended. 'He healed me; Ah heals all colors.' A spirit told her that her prayers would be answered and suggested that she hold a religious meeting of sinners as soon as she became well. She cured by 'layin' on ob hands and anointin' dere innards' with a full tumbler of warm castor oil, followed by a quarter of a lemon to kill the taste. 'Ya gotta do as Ah says ef ya wants to be healed an' blessed,' she told those who objected.

Without any money or followers, on a large lot beyond the Industrial Canal, Mother Catherine started her Manger and the Church of the Innocent Blood. Mother Catherine declared, 'De Lawd tol' me to have a twelve beaded fence round ma Manger but de contractors give me only ten. Ah's been gypped.' Each 'boad' represented a nation. The extraordinary height of the church fence was intended to keep curious persons off the grounds. The Manger is sixty feet long, fifty feet wide, and can accommodate 300 people. It was started November 4, 1929, and completed January 4, 1930. It was planned in minute detail by Mother Catherine herself. She even made most of its statues, and painted the pictures that adorned its walls. The room was dominated by an altar as centerpiece, surrounded by the fourteen stations of the Cross and banners of the Sacred Heart, Jehovah (whom Mother Catherine called 'Jehovia') and the Innocent Blood. Flanking this were several feast tables from which blessed lemonade in summer and blessed coffee in winter were served. Twenty feet from the altar a large choir balcony hung, containing a single piano and enough chairs to accommodate the Manger's numerous singers. Small clay figures of Mother Catherine were scattered about the Manger, and in the rear stood a five-foot statue of the priestess. To the congregation this statue represented a messenger of fear and fate, and they prayed to it for forgiveness.

The High Priestess slept in the Manger in an ornate brass bed, from which, late at night, she conversed with spirits. An array of weaponless bodyguards watched over Mother Catherine while she slept. At midnight, as in the blaze of day, persons came to her to be prayed over and blessed.

The Church of the Innocent Blood was approximately forty feet from the Manger. Flags of the Sacred Heart, Jehovah, and the Innocent Blood flew from atop the building. Rituals borrowed in part from the Roman Catholic Church were used, and the building was crowded with holy pictures, statues, and altars; five hundred oil lamps burned constantly. 'Wish Lamps' were interspersed among them. The petitioner put water in the lamp instead of oil; if the water turned dark – as it usually did – the wish would come true. In the center of the church, a small manger, surrounded by miniature animals, hung seven feet from the floor.

Mother Catherine had no particular uniform. The Lord told her what to wear, and it was usually spectacular. One of her favorite costumes was a voluminous white dress and white cap. A large key dangled from a blue cord tied around her waist. The members were permitted to kneel at her feet and make wishes as they kissed this key. Mother Catherine did not wear any shoes on her grotesquely large feet during the church services; she reminded her people that 'de Lawd went widout shoes.'

Mother Catherine always entered the church through a hole in the roof of a side room, intimating that she was sent down from Heaven to preach the gospel. The men of the congregation helped her to the top of the church by means of a ladder, and she made a very solemn entrance; all remained quiet until she had blessed everyone. Then a rhythmic out burst of chanting voices and stamping feet began as she started preaching. The High Priestess stood in the center of the altar and raised her hand in blessing. 'Chillen, Ah's come heah to do good, not evil.' The response was unanimously favorable. Such statements as 'She sho did'; 'Look a heah, she done cured me'; and 'Ah believes in ya, Mother,' came from whites as well as blacks. Mother Catherine did not bother with the Bible: she could remember everything in it. 'Ah's read de Bible all de time. Ah's gonna gib ya facts.' She began her talks with a short history of the church. For every 'Amen' from Mother Catherine came a chorus of, 'Yas,' and 'Preach it.' When the congregation started singing much improvising was done, chiefly by Mother Catherine and her co-workers, who were clad in long white robes and sat in the front pews. A favorite hymn was:

Hurry Angel, Hurry
Hurry Angel hurry! hurry down to the pool.
I want you to trouble the water this mornin'
To bathe my weary soul.

Angel got two wings to veil my face.

Two wings to fly away
Early in the mornin', bout the break of day
Two angels came from heaven and rolled the stone away.
Angel got two wings to veil my face
Angel got two wings to fly away.

I would not be a hypocrite
I tell you the reason why
'Cause death might overtake me
And I wouldn't be ready to die.
Angel got two wings to veil my face
Angel got two wings to fly away.

When a brother or sister wanted to be healed, he was escorted to the altar by a co-worker. Mother Catherine surveyed the candidate closely and asked, 'Has de Lawd got His rod (curse) on ya? Ah can't cure anyone what's got de rod on dem.' The candidate first took his castor oil or black draught, then Mother Catherine prayed over him, making various motions and calling, 'Heah me, Sperrits,' while he stood silently before her. If he were not healed, someone would say, 'Sumpins wrong wid him. Boy, clean yo soul 'fo de debbil gits ya too much.' Paralytics were rubbed and prayed over with the assistance of unseen spirits; the lame were; often whipped with a wet towel and told to run out of the church. The most spectacular cures were those of the blind. Easy cases were treated with blessed rainwater; in stubborn cases, Mother Catherine 'called lightnin' right down from hebben' to clear the clouded visions of her patients. To the statue of Jehovah women prayed that their men would 'do whut's right'; but the men told their troubles directly to Mother Catherine. The High Priestess did not charge a fee for her services or remedies but with a finger pointed towards the voluntary contribution box said, 'Ah's gotta pay ma expenses an eat, ya know.'

Mother Catherine often invited prominent people to dine at the Manger, saying that she liked to have 'letter red' people around her. At dinner, she would sit at a table apart from the guests, remarking, 'In de nex' worl', Ah will be high up in things, but in things of dis worl', Ah knows ma place.'

Mother Catherine died in 1930 believing she would rise from the dead as did Jesus Christ. She contended, 'Ah's gonna sleep awile, not die. De great Gawd Jehovia, he's callin' me to come an rest awile. But on de thud day Ah's comin' back; Ah's gonna rise agin. Ah's gonna continue ma good wuk.' Thousands attended the funeral, at which many feeble and timorous guests fainted. The congregation of the Church of the Innocent Blood intended that the High Priestess should be buried in the middle of the Manger next to the statue of Jehovah, but the city health officials objected and Mother Catherine was buried in the St. Vincent de Paul Cemetery, vault number 144, 4th tier.

Many of the persons Mother Catherine cared for still inhabit three dilapidated houses on the grounds. Eliza Johnson, better known as Mother Rita, and actually the mother of fourteen children, is Mother Catherine's successor. Eliza came to New Orleans from Baton Rouge. She states that she suffered with lumbago prior to her visit here, but 'Mother Catherine looked me in de face an de lumbago it disappeared.' Mother Rita left a career as cook for a wealthy family to become the favorite co-worker of the High Priestess. She is past seventy and stands ready to bless or ban anyone who visits the old Manger and church, nowcalled 'the Church of the True Light.' The old 'mammy mother' says that Mother Catherine prays and sings with her every night but never talks about the church, for 'Mother Catherine's wuk is done. She's restin'.'

THE CHURCH OF GOD AND CHRIST OF
FAITH TABERNACLE

(Bishop L. H. Treadwell) 1619 South Rampart St. Jackson street-car at Canal St. to Euterpe. Walk right one block. Services daily 4.30- 6.00 P.M. and 7.30-10.30 P.M.

This church was founded in 1932 by Bishop L. H. Treadwell, who was born in Wilmington, North Carolina, and started preaching at the age of fifteen. Father Treadwell was given the title of bishop because of his healing powers and biblical knowledge; he now controls more than 150 churches throughout the country.

One of the sisters opens the service; singing and praying follow, continuing for an hour. Songs improvised from unrelated bits of Scripture and imagery, such as the following, are popular here.

> Tell me what harm has my Jesus done,
> Tell me what harm has my Jesus done,
> Tell me what harm has my Jesus done,
>> That the sinners all hate him so?

> Old man Josua had seven sons,
> Little David being the youngest one.
> David was the shepherd boy,
> He knew all about the shepherd's voice.
> It kept on rainin' an' the lightnin' flashed.
> He said, Don't call the roll 'til I get there.

> Tell me what harm has my Jesus done,
> Tell me what harm has my Jesus done,
> Tell me what harm has my Jesus done,
>> That the sinners all hate him so?

> Lookin' over in the empty sky
> I saw King Jesus come riding by.
> I said, Ride on, Jesus, I know you're the king;
> You got the power under your wings.

> Tell me what harm has my Jesus done,
> Tell me what harm has my Jesus done,
> Tell me what harm has my Jesus done,
>> That the sinners all hate him so?

In between the songs the members testify as to the healing powers of the Bishop and the church. 'Ah been suff'ren wid a pain in ma right side sumpin' awful all week,' says a tall mulatto, 'but since Ah been settin' heah Ah's had relief.' A large black woman in the rear of the church gets to her feet with difficulty. 'Ah been feelin' so dizzy an' faint Ah cuddin' do no inin' all day long,' she declares, 'but since Ah come into dis heah House ob Gawd de dizziness done passed away.'

When the Bishop finally begins the sermon, cries of joy, hymns, and shouts burst from the congregation. The emotional pitch rises; the younger sisters and brothers perform peculiar dances, and the more elderly bite their fingers, shake their skirts, and parade around the church crying, 'Preach it, Father. Lay it to me, Father.' Some of the more overwrought members are visited by the 'sperrits' and shout exhortations in 'strange tongues.' Guests are urged to become members in a seemingly endless hypnotic chant:

> OH! come on, come on, come on,
> OH! come on, come on, come on,
> OH! come on, come on, come on,
> Ple-e-e-e-ease do too.

When the noise lessens, the sermon continues. Later the lame, diseased, and blind are led forward to be healed amid the noisy rejoicing of the brethren. Bishop Treadwel's most remarkable recent cure, he claims, was that of a person whom the doctors of a well-known hospital had given up as hopeless.

THE CHURCH OF HELPING HAND AND SPIRITUAL FAITH

(Mother L. Crosier) 2925 Audubon St. Claiborne street-car at Canal to Broadway and S. Claiborne Ave. Transfer to Broadway bus to Pritchard and Pine Sts. Walk right one block. Daily services at 8.30 P.M.

This two-story, red-brick church has a membership of five hundred, led by Mother L. Crosier, fortune-teller and healer. Easily approached and very sympathetic, Mother Crosier relates how the Blessed Virgin Mary appeared one day while she was washing and commanded her to go out and preach the gospel. Opening a small church on South Claiborne Avenue, her success was instantaneous, and in less than a month she was forced to move into larger quarters. In 1923, with the financial assistance of some white people, she constructed the present church, which cost more than $20,000.

Mother Crosier's services are similar to those held in other spiritualist churches; there is singing, dancing, and fainting. Those to be cured are brought to the altar during the service and healed by means of prayer and holy water. During the service Mother Crosier shakes hands with those members who are in good standing, 'financially and spiritually.'

THE JERUSALEM TEMPLE BAPTIST CHURCH

(Father James Joseph) Corner Fourth and S. Johnson Sts. S. Claiborne street-car from Canal and St. Charles Sts.; transfer (right) to Louisiana bus at Washington Ave.; walk one block right at S. Johnson St. Services: 12 noon Monday, Wednesday, Friday, and Saturday; 7.30 P.M. Monday, Wednesday, Friday, and Sunday. Noon services on Saturdays for men only.

The building housing this church was formerly a neighborhood grocery. It is a small, one-room, clapboarded building furnished with benches, chairs, and a central altar. Flowers, pictures of saints, and religious paraphernalia give an added churchly touch. In one of its three small windows a sign identifies the little place as the Jerusalem Temple Baptist Church.

Father James Joseph, the pastor, is tall, very black, and burly. His speech is precise and fluent, accented with frequent bows and smiles. Brother Brushback, his chief deacon, is his antithesis – short and blatant. Before the businesslike pastor can be approached, his bodyguard, a tiny, frail, lemon-colored, sharp-tongued Negro, must be interviewed. Private consultation with Father Joseph costs two dollars and a half.

The services here are so well attended that the crowds fill the building and spread out into the streets. Blind, lame, and diseased persons are accompanied by hopeful relatives expecting miraculous cures. Many white people are numbered among the congregation.

After a preliminary service, in which the congregation sings and prays, and the deacons exhort and 'pass the basket,' Father Joseph enters the church. His entry calms the fervor momentarily, but when he begins to speak hysteria sweeps like a flame throughout the room. Groans, shouts, the tapping of feet, and the swaying of bodies punctuate his sermon. In Negro parlance, the church gets 'hot.'

While collectors pass through the congregation with embarrassing frequency, insisting on sums that diminish in size as the services progress, Father Joseph rambles on bombastically:

'Ah guarantee y'all everlastin' happiness if ya stick wid me. Ah'll run ya outta dis church if ya mess aroun'. Don' say Ah cain't run ya. Ah got power! To tell de truth Ah can tell anybody whar to git off at. Take de day when Ah went down to de cou't. Ah tol' de judge to let a man go what had done stoled. Ah said let him go an' dey let him go. An' Ah didn't use no hoodoo, neither. Ah ain't no hoodoo man, me. But ya jest let dem hoodoo people mess wid me. Ah know dere is hoodoos right heah in dis church. Ya cain't fool me. Dey come ta see what Ah can do. Ah'm gonna show dem, too. Ah am a healer. Ah kin heal people right fo' ya eyes, Ah don' go behin' ya back.

'Now, Ah dare anybody to tell me dat Ah cain't tell dey fortune. But ya better watch out, cause if ya is messin' wid another woman's man or another man's woman Ah's gonna tell it! If ya men is back-biting, Ah am gonna tell on ya.

'Now is de time for dem whut wants ta be healed to come to de front.'

Murmurs of awe and the shuffling of feet are heard, then a hush of expectancy falls on the crowd. Father Joseph places his hand on the Bible and declares, 'Now, Ah am gonna kill all dem hoodoo sperrits.' He wraps a white cloth around the head and eyes of a blind girl and intones solemnly, 'In de name of de Father, de Son, and de Holy Ghost, Ah comman's ya to see.' After this is said the girl exclaims, 'Ah see light.' Father Joseph asks her to point to the light and the young girl points to the door and windows. All of this does not seem to startle anyone. 'Father does dat all de time.'

Other persons step forward to be cured. One woman is told, 'Ya husband put hoodoo on ya. He put dried snake dust in yo eyes and sent ya blind, but da's all right. Use dat water Ah gave ya.' The pastor talks to the white folks, explaining, 'Ya be hoodooed, too. Dat one was hoodooed, wasn't ya, child? I cure ev'rybody, white and black alike. Makes no difference to me.'

When the healing is over, the money collector returns with blessed candles, asking five cents for each. They are sold without any difficulty and the congregation is then dismissed.

ST. JAMES TEMPLE OF CHRISTIAN FAITH

(Mother C. J. Hyde) 2802 Second St. at the corner of Clara St. S. Claiborne street-car at Canal to Second St. Walk left two blocks. Services: Sunday, Wednesday, and Friday at 8.30 P.M.

The St. James Temple, founded by Mother Hyde in February 1923 in accordance with her paraphrase of Christ's words, 'Great things I am doing, but greater things you shall do,' attracts a large number of persons through reputed cures by prayer. To derive the full benefit of the prayers one must believe in the teachings of Mother Hyde; this belief is made known in an open confessional called 'testifying.' She then reads the Bible, calls on departed ancestors (now angels), begs assistance from the spirits, and shakes herself into a frenzy, tossing her head and crying, 'Chile, ya is free from sin an' will get what ya so desire.' The fortunate one then makes a donation. As he prepares to leave, an assistant impresses upon him the obligations which he owes to Mother Hyde, warning him that to disobey her is to disobey God. He nods assent, smiles, and departs confidently.

Mother Hyde, a house servant before she heard the call, has a charter, of which she is very proud, from the State Government. Any of her coworkers may receive a sub-charter from her upon acquiring the knowledge of how to cure sickness through prayer, and upon the payment of fifteen dollars. Upon receipt of her charter the co-worker, with Mother Hyde's co-operation and blessing, usually organizes a church of her own.

Services at Mother Hyde's church are impressive. The staccato rhythm of clapping hands, the chanting and yelling of voices, and the swaying and writhing of bodies are most exciting to the visitor. The ghostlike figure of Mother Hyde moves in and out of the crowd, preaching affectionately but solemnly. Her favorite brothers and sisters sit nearest her, and as the leader searches for a text the congregation reverently inquires, 'Yas, Mother. Yas, Mother. Git right. What ya gonna say? Amen.' She finally speaks. 'Sisters and Brothers, Ah am talking to ya.' Then she begins to preach and prophesy. The peopcle back away and shout 'Amen' above the voice of Mother Hyde, who moves up and down the aisle. Some of the sisters work themselves into a frenzy and have to be quieted. The story of a member who gave money and received a special blessing is woven into the sermon as a reminder to the congregation that financial help is necessary.

At the close of the service, the faithful ask their leader for her blessing as a protection against evil. Dramatically, she lifts her arms and intones the words of benediction; then, with a gesture of finality, dismisses the congregation.

ST. JAMES TEMPLE OF CHRISTIAN FAITH NO. 2

(Mother E. Keller) 2312 Felicity St. Jackson Ave. street-car at Canal to Jackson and LaSalle. Walk right three blocks. Services: Sunday, Tuesday, Thursday, and Friday at 8.30 P.M.

The St. James Temple No. 2 was organized and founded by Mother E. Keller. The interior of this tabernacle, which seats three hundred persons comfortably, is decorated with numerous statues, pictures of saints, candles, and an altar.

Mother Keller claims she received training in Voodooism from a Mohammedan prince in New York, met some of the greatest Voodoo doctors in the country, and became well versed in this mysterious art. When,however, she cured her sister, after doctors had said the sick girl would not live, Mother Keller renounced Voodooism, as a means of showing her appreciation to the Lord. Turning to the spiritualist church, she became a protégé of Mother Hyde and soon had a large following for her reputed ability to read minds and to heal. Members of the church feel that no thing is more dangerous than to disobey Mother Keller; she explains the necessity of belief in her, and no one is allowed on the platform unless he has accepted her teachings.

An atmosphere of nervous tension is maintained by Mother Keller's frequent spasmodic announcements that she reads the hearts of various members of the congregation. Often she singles out an individual and foretells his future. Her people throw themselves into their hymn-singing and dancing with a passion rarely seen even in spiritualist churches. Members writhe, quiver, and shout; often they dance themselves into a state of complete insensibility.

ST. MICHAEL'S CHURCH NO. 1

(Mother Kate Francis) Corner Jackson Ave. and Willow St. Jackson Ave. street-car to Willow St. Services: Sunday, Monday, Wednesday, and Friday at 8.30 P.M.

Mother Kate Francis burst into sudden prominence in 1931 when, with the sense of drama typical of 'spiritualist' leaders, she led, through the streets of New Orleans, a barefoot procession to end the depression.' Robed in long white gowns belted with baby-blue sashes, the group paraded through the streets singing and praying loudly 'fo' de Lawd to rain jobs down on ev'ybody.' Prior to that time, she had been just another of the numerous Negro cult healers of the city.

The Temple is a small tent in Mother Kate's side yard. Sacred pictures decorate the walls of the tent, and on the altar is a large statue of the Mother of Perpetual Help. On entering the tent, each co-worker kneels and prays before two large crucifixes that flank the altar. While the congregation awaits the entrance of Mother Kate, a testimonial meeting is held. The co-workers stand and lead the congregation in singing. After each hymn, co-workers testify. Each testimony or 'determination' is begun with this prayer:

'Mah fust obed'ence is to Gawd de Father; mah secon' to Mother Kate, mothers, co-wukkers, visitin frien's – an' sinnahs likewise, ef theah be any.'

The co-worker then asks the people to pray that Mother Kate may be 'strenkened' where she is weak, and 'built up' where she is 'tore down.'

Other hymns are sung, and the congregation sways to the insistent rhythm of clapping hands and patting feet. At the moment excitement has reached its highest intensity, Mother Kate makes a dramatic entrance, striding majestically to the holy-water font before the altar. Here she pauses, and a hush falls on the congregation as she dips her finger symbolically into the water, and genuflects with outstretched arms and bowed head before the altar. She remains in this attitude of devotion a moment, then rises and faces the people, who immediately burst into song once more. Neither Mother Kate nor her co-workers wear shoes, and the patting of their bare feet on the hardpacked clay floor can be heard distinctly, even above the music of the tambourines, piano, and drums which forms a background for the singing.

The basket is passed for collection during the song. When it is brought back to Mother Kate, she eyes its contents critically, and if not satisfied takes it from the co-worker and personally makes a second collection, exclaiming, 'Dat's not 'nuf fo one little po'k chop, an' Ah sho can eat po'k chops.'

In addition to her preaching, Mother Kate Francis tells fortunes; but this she does at her residence, the temple being reserved for the 'servus ob de Lawd.'

ST. MICHAEL'S CHURCH NO. 9

(Father Daniel Dupont) 2810 Melpomene St. S. Claiborne street- car at Canal St. to Melpomene. Walk right two blocks. Services: Sunday, Monday, Wednesday, and Friday at 8.30 P.M.

Father Dupont, brother of Mother Kate Francis, founded St. Michael's No. 9 in 1932, after he had acquired the ability to cure diseases and mental ailments. He joined the faith when Mother Kate began making 'big money' in her spiritual work. A spirit came to him promising unlimited success, and although he can give no description of the spirit, he maintains that the good spirits come in the guise of people and saints, while the bad appear as animals.

While conducting services Father Dupont wears a dark robe and a black cap, with a cross fastened to his waist. Sometimes, during the middle of the sermon, spirits arrive and are given by him to members of the congregation, who begin singing, shouting, and dancing to the beat of a piano and the stamping of feet. Postures and movements of the dance, which appear indecent, are said to be caused by the spirits who enter and sway the bodies of both young and old. The climax of the dancing is reached when Father Dupont springs into action, his leaps and gyrations exceeding those of the others both in speed and intensity. After this outburst there are prayers, confessions, and invocations.

The four days of services held at St. Michael's No. 9 are not devoted exclusively to preaching, as the following statement by one of the 'assistant fathers' proves:

'Y'all know Friday is our hoodoo night. Amen! Sunday is prayer night, when y'all comes jes to pray. Ya also come heah on Wednesday night to pray, but Monday and Friday is the hoodoo days.'

On the 'hoodoo' nights, after the usual preliminaries, the lights are turned out while Father Dupont preaches some such sermon as the following :

'Ah'm tellin' all of ya, if ya never git on yo knees to pray, ya had better learn how now an' pray some. Ah mean, stay on yo knees on Monday an' Friday an' do yo'sef some prayin'. Cause if ya ain't on yo knees prayin' fo' yo enemies, dey's on dere knees prayin' fo' ya – an' Ah'm tellin' ya, good sisters an' brothers, yo enemies ain't prayin' fo nuthin' good 'bout ya. So Ah says fo' ya to pray! Do ya heah? PRAY!'

The people respond, 'Amen! O Lawd, hab mussy, Jesus!' and begin to sing:

> 'Pray, pray, oh, help me pray
> That my Savior will help me on dis day.
> O, say pray, oh pray, help me pray.
> Father, sisters and brothers, help me pray.
> I don't want to get religion
> But I just want to pray.
> So pray, pray, pray.'

Father then proceeds with the sermon: 'Now, ya kin say dat ya don' belieb in hoodoo – dat nobody kin be hoodooed. Ah kin hoodoo ya, an' anybody else kin dat knows how to do hoodoo. If ya don' belieb me, jes lemme know an' Ah'll show ya!

'Ya know some people say dat man's lyin'; he cain't do nobody no harm. Well, Ah'm tellin' ya, sisters and brothers, Ah kin do ya harm – where anybody says a good word fo' ya, Ah'll say two bad ones agin ya. So don' say nobody cain't harm ya!

'Ya knows Ah kin do hoodoo, but Ah does it private, an' git paid fo' ma wuk. Now if anybody heah want me to do any hoodoo fo' dem, jes see me private.

'Dere's somebody by dat winder over dere dat's got religion, but dey's 'fraid to git up an' say so. Le's he'p dis sister out. Come on, le's sing an' shout. *God Called Adam* is whut she needs.'

> 'Adam was in the garden
> He didn't hab nothin' to worry 'bout.
> Eve made Adam sin an' dat's when de trubble begun to start.
> God called Adam, Adam refused to answer.
> God called Adam, Adam refused to answer.
> The second time God called Adam
> Adam said, "Here am I, Lawd,
> I'm most done packin' mah crosses."'

Then, with songs and ejaculations from the congregation, and admonitions from the father to 'be sho to come bac' Monday,' the curtain falls on another of the amazing services of the New Orleans Negro 'spiritualists.'

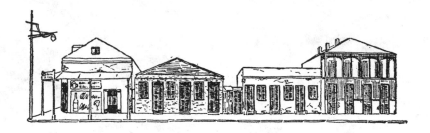

GAY TIMES IN OLD NEW ORLEANS

ALL early travelers to New Orleans who recorded their impressions found it a gay town. Some welcomed this gaiety; others looked upon it with marked disapproval. New Orleans was a French and Spanish city for almost a century before it became part of the United States. From its founders it inherited a Latin *joie de vire*, as well as a freedom from certain types of race prejudice; and its position as a seaport added to its cosmopolitan sophistication. Deservedly or not New Orleans early acquired a reputation as a wicked city.

The freedom from race prejudice gave rise to many unusual customs. By Governor Miro's time (1785-92), New Orleans, then a city of less than eight thousand, had fifteen hundred free, unmarried women of color. Free men of color had grown numerous enough by 1815 to form a regiment and to play a creditable part in the defense of the city.

During the entire first half of the nineteenth century, the quadroons consorted for merrymaking and display in the balls, which took place first in the Salle St. Philippe on St. Philip Street, and at a later date in a large brick building situated on Orleans Street, between Royal and Bourbon. In those days the ballroom was connected with the old Orleans Theatre and Opera House. The building still stands, but today, by a twist of irony, its atmosphere is sanctified. It is the Convent of the Sisters of the Holy Family, a school for mulatto children conducted by mulatto nuns.

No social stigma was attached to the quadroon balls in their heyday. They were conducted with great propriety and distinct elegance. Supremely exclusive, like many a Parisian salon of the same or earlier periods, but on a slightly altered scale, they were simply gatherings of the town's wealthy white young men and their present or prospective mistresses. From all accounts, the balls seem to have been gay, lavish, even fabulous, but highly decorous affairs. And well may they have been so, for the quadroon mistresses were often creatures of rare beauty and distinction, meriting even the glance of royalty. The Duke of Saxe-Weimar describes them as follows:

> A quadroon is the child of a mestize mother and a white father, as a mestize is the child of a mulatto mother and a white father. The quadroons are almost entirely white; from their skin no one could detect their origin; nay, many of them have as fair a complexion as many of the haughty Creole

NEW ORLEANS FOLKS

CHIMNEY SWEEPS

'LITTLE' COMMUNION

A SPASM BAND

TOURISTS

CEMETERIES

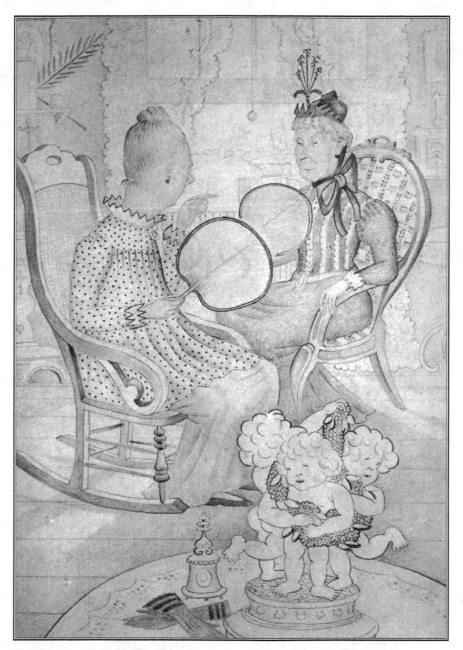

TANTE EULALIE ET MADEMOISELLE MIMI

SHUTTER GIRL

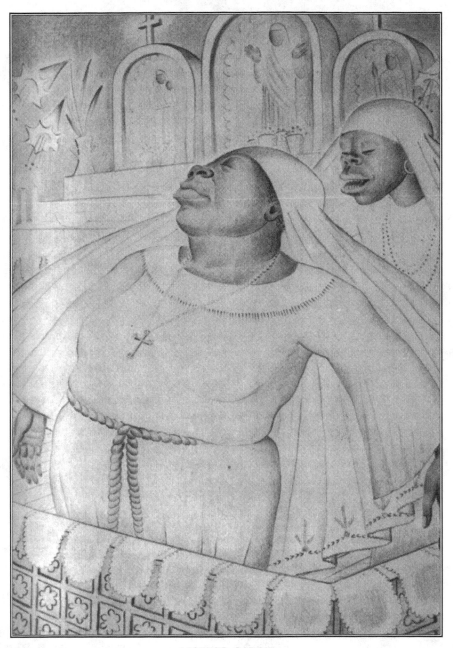

MOTHER CARRIE

ZELINE AND JOE

females. Such of them as frequent these balls are free. Formerly they were known by their black hair and eyes, but at present there are completely fair quadroons male and female. Still, however, the strongest prejudice reigns against them because of their black blood, and the white ladies maintain, or affect to maintain, the most violent aversion toward them.

When a young white man took a fancy to one of these girls, he approached her mother, and having given satisfactory proof of his ability to keep the girl in becoming style, struck a bargain with the old woman. Money changed hands, and the quadroon regarded this arrangement in the same light as a marriage. The young man established a home for his mistress in the quadroon quarter, which was in that section of the Vieux Carré below Orleans Street and near the Ramparts, and enjoyed all the comforts and amenities thereof without actually residing there himself. This arrangement lasted as long as he wished it so. The *placée*, as she was called, took her 'friend's' name, which was also given to their children, many of whom were reared in an atmosphere of culture, and were often sent to Paris to be educated. The young girls were particularly well schooled in the arts of courtesanship so that they could follow in their mothers' footsteps.

Quadroon mistresses had their quadroon friends and amusements, and, of course, the quadroon balls; but they could not mix with the white ladies, could not sit down in their presence, nor ride through the streets in carriages. A white woman could have a quadroon whipped like a slave upon accusation borne out by two witnesses. Quadroon men were never allowed to attend the balls. Scorned by women of their own class as well as by whites, they either followed some trade in the city or went into the country on plantations. They usually married mulatto women.

When the young white man decided it was time to marry, he simply broke off his arrangement and was free to make another alliance. Some men continued the arrangement even after marriage by maintaining two homes, one in each section of the city. Some really loved their quadroon mates and never married at all.

According to Harriet Martineau, writing in 1837, 'the quadroon connection was all but universal; every young man early selects one and establishes her in one of those pretty and peculiar houses, whole rows of which may be seen in the ramparts.'

Twenty years later, Frederick Law Olmsted describes this Creole institution in virtually the same words, but adds a characteristic Yankee touch. He tells of meeting a northern 'drummer' who claimed that he always made an arrangement of this character while in New Orleans because 'it was cheaper than living in hotels and boarding-houses.'

These women were not prostitutes. White enough to refuse to mix with the Negroes, since the law forbade their marriage with white men they apparently had no alternative but to become the mistresses of white men who were willing to support them. They regarded such arrangements in the same light as marriage and are said to have been generally faithful to their bargain. When their lovers broke off the relationship they sometimes took another 'friend,' but usually they drifted into the rooming-house business, in which they were very successful. Even as late as the Cotton Exposition of 1884, they were favorably known for their success in this line.

After the Civil War the quadroon balls lost their former character. Tinker describes a visit to one of them which Lafcadio Hearn made in 1880. It was conducted by a noted procuress named Hermina in an old mansion on Bienville Street, between Burgundy and Dauphine Streets. A new era – that of the 'honky-tonk' – had long since gained the ascendancy. The Reconstruction Era worked such devastating havoc upon the fortunes of Southern white aristocracy that they were hard put to shift for themselves, let alone maintain luxurious institutions in antebellum style. Besides, the decades following the War brought a steadily increasing influx of Northern ideas and customs to the South, so that by 1880 the quadroon balls had lost all their old-time glamour.

The first tenderloin section of New Orleans was in Gallatin Street, a short alley that runs from the French Market to the Mint, between North Peters and Decatur Streets. Its proximity to the river front long ago helped to earn for Gallatin Street a most unsavory reputation, which clung to it until about 1900. Prostitutes from every nation gathered there, living a life of boisterous lawlessness and open vice. In recent years it became a street of empty houses, the lower floors of which were sometimes used for the storage of produce. In 1936 the houses on the river side of Gallatin Street were torn down to make way for new market buildings.

As the city grew in size disorderly houses gained footholds in other sections. About 1850, some of them were driven off Canal Street. A newspaper account of the great fire of 1851, when the St. Charles Hotel and many other buildings were burned, mentions the destruction of two houses of ill fame on Poydras Street next to the Methodist Church. Commercialized vice often followed in the wake of disappearing respectability. Fine old homes, once occupied by the city's élite, later became boarding houses as the neighborhoods changed, and still later, scattered havens of prostitution. Annunciation Square, residential sections of Camp, St. Charles, and Carondelet Streets, the famous '13 Buildings' on Julia Street, on the uptown side between Camp and St. Charles where many of the prominent families of the forties and fifties made their homes, and many a fine home in the French section, all passed through this checkered experience.

The first action against immoral establishments was taken in 1817 by the city council, which imposed a fine on both woman and house-owner for disturbing the peace or occasioning scandal. In 1845 lewd women were forbidden to frequent or drink in coffee houses. In 1857 a detailed ordinance was passed, defining the limits beyond which prostitution would not be tolerated, imposing taxes on the inmates and house-owners, and requiring that each woman should take out a yearly license, to be issued to her by the Mayor upon proof that her taxes had been paid. White women and free women of color were forbidden to live in the same house. Standing or sitting on the sidewalk in indecent posture, and the accosting of passersby, were prohibited under penalty of a fine or jail sentence.

The territorial limits prescribed at that time are interesting. They were: Felicity Road, Hercules (South Rampart), New Canal (New Basin), Claiborne, and Canal

Streets in the First District; Canal, Basin, Toulouse, and Bayou St. John (Carondelet Canal), Esplanade and Toulouse in the Second District; Esplanade, Broad, and Elysian Fields Streets in the Third District. These boundaries indicate that the establishments in Basin Street were of an early origin.

Following the emancipation of Negro slaves and the legalization of gambling in Louisiana in 1869, social life in the New Orleans underworld assumed a new status. Centralization began anew, and the restricted 'district' was but a step ahead. An eyewitness gives us a graphic picture of Royal Street during the Cotton Exposition of 1884:

> Brilliantly lighted by a new electric flare system, the street is thronged with men of all classes, who enter or emerge from its many saloons and gambling houses, which throb with the raucous sounds of pleasure-bent men and women. Timid crowds of men stand upon the curbstone to catch a glimpse of female limbs draped in gauze of pink and blue . . . Arrayed in scant garments, but gorgeous in combinations of color, are young and middle-aged; youthful and fresh, together with wearied and worn, whited sepulchers; watching among the throng which enters, those whom their judgment dictates have money to spend or throw away upon them in remuneration for a display of their utter unconsciousness of virtue.

During the reform agitation of the eighties and nineties a school of thought developed which advocated a restricted district for the better control of prostitution. This plan finally found expression in an ordinance, sponsored by Alderman Story, and passed by the city council on January 26th, 1897, at the first session under Mayor Flower. Definite limits were set down for the district, but even so, residence there was not legalized, so that the city held complete control of the situation. The theory was that all prostitutes could be confined within these limits, policed, and controlled, and that thus the evil could be kept in hand. This theory was not entirely successful in practice, for houses of assignation were to be found elsewhere, sometimes on the finest residential streets. Nevertheless the restricted district soon became one of the most amazing spectacles of legalized vice that had ever been seen.

The limits of the district, as defined by the ordinance, were: the south side of Custom House (Iberville) Street, from Basin to Robertson Streets, east side of Robertson Street from Customhouse to St. Louis Streets, south side of St. Louis from Robertson to Basin. At first the Negroes and mulattoes were allowed in certain sections of the restricted district, but on March 1, 1917, a restricted Negro district was established. The boundaries were: Perdido Street to the lower side of Gravier, and from the river side of Franklin to the wood side of Locust (Liberty).

The restricted district enjoyed a legal existence from 1897 to 1917. During those two decades it attained the zenith of its fame; it was the show place and scandal of the city. Visitors from near and far, lured by the tales of wantonness and tinseled gaiety, almost invariably included the district in their itinerary. Depending upon their temperaments and viewpoints, they left elated or appalled by the scenes they had witnessed, scenes that usually far surpassed even their most fantastic expectations. To the average well-bred native

Orleanian, however, the district was no 'thing of beauty'; it was merely a rather bad civic sore, which one was aware of but avoided. It was a world of 'honky-tonks' and 'dives,' 'palaces,' and 'cribs,' sordid indeed, but militantly gay and carefree. Jazz and swing music are said to have originated in the dance halls and saloons of New Orleans' red light district.

At Carnival time, and especially on Mardi Gras Day, the district opened its arms to welcome everyone. King Zulu, leader of the Negro carnival celebration, had his headquarters in the black section of the district, back toward Robertson and St. Louis Streets. Maskers thronged its streets and peals of celebrations rang from every house. In other seasons, the district flourished only at night, for it was drab and deserted by day. As it adjoined the tracks leading into the Terminal Station on Canal Street, visitors arriving in the city were treated to a broadside view of its 'palaces' and glimpses up side streets of the 'crib' sections, before they saw much else; and respectable citizens who otherwise never went near the place furtively surveyed the scene when departing on, or returning from, a trip.

The restricted district was ironically dubbed 'Storyville' in honor of the alderman whose ordinance created it. Storyville's central spot was the 'Arlington Annex,' Tom Anderson's main saloon, at the corner of Customhouse and Basin Streets, adjoining the Arlington palace. The Annex was figuratively the 'city hall' of Storyville, and Tom Anderson was its 'mayor.' He bossed the restricted district and in addition was a member of the State Legislature, the owner of a chain of saloons, and the head of an oil company.

In Arlington Annex one could obtain for twenty-five cents a copy of the *Blue Book*, official directory and guide to Storyville. The *Blue Book* listed in alphabetical order and in separate sections respectively the names and addresses of all the prostitutes in the place. It also contained many advertisements from local and national distillers and cigarmakers, as well as a few from neighboring drugstores and taxi companies. Most enticing of all *Blue Book* contents, however, were the puffs and occasional photographs, which extolled the graces and qualifications of Storyville's most prominent sirens.

'Why visit the playhouse to see the famous Parisian models,' urged one of these, 'when one can see the French damsels, Norma and Diana? Their names have been known on both continents, because everything goes as it will, and those that cannot be satisfied with these must surely be of a queer nature.' Another assures the reader that he 'can travel from one end of this continent to the other, but to find another good fellow as game as Gipsy (Shaffer), who is always ready to receive and entertain, will be almost an impossibility.' A third proclaims that Miss May Spencer has the distinction of conducting one of the best establishments in the Tenderloin District, 'where swell men can be socially entertained by an array of swell ladies.' 'If you have the blues,' says a fourth, 'the Countess (Willie Piazza) and her girls can cure them.' And so they went on and on, each mistress attempting to outdo her rivals in luring the wealthy 'sport' to her palace of joy.

Two other publications in the flush times of the district contained, together with much more reporting of the *Police Gazette* kind, notices of the doings of the prostitutes, prominent and obscure. In 1894, the *Mascot*, the more important of the two, inaugurated a Society column in which the gay whirl of life 'on the turf' was reported. The *Sunday Sun,* the other of these weeklies, soon followed suit with a Chat column.

Having purchased a copy of the *Blue Book* from the 'Annex,' one could go 'down the line' on Basin Street, where the exclusive mansions stood, or along Custom House (Iberville) Street, where rows and rows of 'cribs' stretched out before him. The Basin Street 'palaces' were lavishly furnished in the barbaric taste of the inhabitants. Heavily carved plush-covered furniture, and gaudy tapestries and drapes, provided a rococo atmosphere that was further accentuated by massive gilt statuary, ivory curios, leopard-skin rugs, potted palms, and cut-glass candelabra. Everything was in the worst possible taste. But to the various Spanish, French, Italian, Egyptian, and Octoroon damsels as well as their sundry mistresses, their environs rivaled the courts of kings.

This entertainment offered a direct contrast to that provided in the 'cribs' which were bare one-room affairs that abutted on the sidewalk, and contained nothing more than a bed, a table, and a chair. There were from twenty to thirty cribs in a single block – ancient structures with a common roof and low-hanging eaves. The barest of them, however, brought a rental of at least seventy-five dollars a month.

But whatever the crib sections lacked in quality and distinctiveness, they more than made up for in volume, boisterousness, and *joie de vivre.* The women were not permitted to leave the house, so they solicited vocally from behind doorways and window blinds. Those who went to see caught glimpses of beckoning hands and chalk-white faces in the poorly illumined rooms along the row. Some cribs outshone others by the variety and arrangement of red light bulbs that glowed in their interiors, but for the most part they presented a striking uniformity in every respect. Eventually in some sections restrictions as to color disappeared, and whites and blacks and all the possible variations were to be found in the same block.

From dance halls and saloons came the jangling of pianos and the shuffling sounds of dancers. Dice games were always in progress. Gruff voices of men and high-pitched tones of women intermingled in argument or laughter. Drunks who had spent or lost all their money were shoved away from one place after another until a policeman took them into custody. Finally, in the small hours of the morning, the last visitor made his rounds of the houses – the rent collector who would listen to no excuse and whose business methods were ruthless.

Storyville today is not as we have here depicted it. In the last twenty years, its inhabitants have undergone many vicissitudes; its palaces and cribs have become decaying hulks. Many have disappeared altogether to make way for the increasing spread of automobile parking grounds.

On the heels of much persistent vice-crusading by Miss Jean Gordon and other civic leaders for the suppression of the restricted district, came a request from Josephus Daniels, Secretary of the Navy under President Wilson, urging, as a war measure, the large cities of the nation to curb all forms of vice. A local ordinance therefore closed the district officially on October 10, 1917. The red-light district never regained its pre-war legal status.

That this is so can easily be demonstrated; for where can one find the equals of former celebrated procuresses? Countess Willie Piazza, under whose roof a Central-American revolution was hatched, is dead. She is dead and her gilded mirrors and green plush chairs and white piano sold at auction; the piano, badly in need of tuning, going for $1.25. Josie Arlington was buried in and later removed from Metairie Cemetery, but a bronze maiden, representative of the virgins whom Josie never allowed inher house, still knocks in vain on the door of her tomb; and a legend which tells of a red light mysteriously issuing from the grave is current. Tom Anderson's name is in tile on the corner of Iberville and Saratoga Streets, and Lulu White's name may still be seen cut in the glass transom of her palace at 235 Basin Street; but the palace is now a warehouse. When Beth Brown wrote *For Men Only* in 1930, her heroine, Lily Love, flourished in the whalebone period, as did Mae West in her cinematic portrayal of another 'sporting house – Lulu,' in 'Belle of the Nineties,' which at first was to be called 'Belle of New Orleans.' The Basin Street Blues' hark back with a nostalgic wail to an era dead and gone.

> Won't-cha come a-long with me,
> To the Mis-sis-sip-pi?
> We'll take the boat – to the lan' of dreams,
> Steam down the river down to New Orleans;
> The bands there to meet us,
> Old friends to greet us,
> Where all the light and the dark folks meet –
> This is Ba-sin Street.
> 'Basin Street Blues'

GARDENS

THERE is not a day in the year when flowers are not to be seen in some New Orleans garden. The warm, humid climate of the city and the fertile alluvial soil have combined to produce a luxuriance and variety of plant growth that astonishes visitors. New Orleans, originally a cypress swamp, is now noted for the extreme diversity of its plant life. As one garden authority has said, 'Almost everything from tropical palms to Himalayan deodars and Arctic cedars thrives here.'

Seasonal changes are comparatively inconspicuous. Many of the trees, shrubs, and vines are evergreen. Flowering seasons overlap each other; poinsettias are sometimes still blooming in the summer, dahlias in the spring; and common annuals frequently become biennials.

Wild trees, shrubs, grasses, herbs, and vines, primarily subtropical bog and water types, flourish in the outlying undrained areas. Live oaks, heavy with Spanish moss, stand in palmetto thickets; tall cypress trees raise their knees above the waters of the swamps on which the lavender water hyacinth floats; white and pink mallows, blue and copper-colored irises, yellow pond lilies, and orange-flowered trumpet vines are of frequent occurrence on the outskirts of the city proper.

Extraordinarily well favored by nature, New Orleans, as a garden city, has in recent times been greatly aided by engineering science. Its modern drainage program, particularly, has borne interesting horticultural results. A few native trees, principally cypress and tupelo gum, and numerous wild flowering herbs and marsh grasses tend to disappear as sub-surface water is withdrawn. This reclamation, essential to the growth of certain introduced varieties, does not, however, interfere with the luxuriant growth of most of the native plants. Today in the parks and residential sections, transplanted Louisiana wild flowers and traditional garden plants grow side by side with strange exotic flora.

Live oaks and Spanish moss are everywhere. Streets and neutral grounds are planted with camphor trees, magnolias, crepe myrtles, and oleanders. The latter, with its leathery green leaves and its flowers varying from white to a deep rose, was introduced by the Spanish in the eighteenth century, and has been made the city's official flower. There are nineteen varieties of palms, ranging from the towering *Cocos australis* to the scrubby 'sago' palm, the fronds of which all good Catholics carry to church on Palm Sunday.

New Orleans gardens, aside from those of the Vieux Carré, are of two kinds: the old-fashioned Southern type, fragrant with jasmine, camellias, magnolias, and sweet olive; and the newer landscaped type, almost continuously vivid with roses, lilies, irises, cannas, azaleas, poinsettia, wistaria, and a variety of showy annuals. Tropical and subtropical growths that enhance the brilliance of many New Orleans gardens include rosa montana (Antigonon), yellow bignonia (cat's claw), purple bignonia (clytostoma), mimosa, and Parkinsonia.

When the Garden District was planned in the early 1820's, homes were laid out in spacious grounds so rilled with flowers as to resemble an immense park. This gave the section the name it still bears. Much of the original beauty of this District has faded with time, but many handsome old gardens are still to be seen. The more pretentious gardens are now centralized in the newer residential sections, particularly along the upper part of St. Charles Avenue and some of the streets crossing it. The hidden gardens in the courtyards of the Vieux Carré, green throughout the year with ivy, palms, oleanders, banana plants (the fruit of which never ripens in New Orleans), Japanese plums, and yucca; and the 'hanging gardens' on the iron balconies of some of the French Quarter homes are of particular interest.

The New Orleans Garden Society conducts a tour every year on the Sunday before Mardi Gras, and another one in connection with a flower show early in April. Visits to some of the best private gardens of the city are included. Tickets are a dollar for those having their own cars, and two dollars for those using buses.

The gardens in these tours differ from year to year. The listing that follows is merely representative of the types of gardens that have been included in tours of the past. Individual tourists may visit most of these gardens at other times as specified.

Garden District

Jackson Ave. to Louisiana Ave., St. Charles Ave. to Magazine St. This general neighborhood may be. reached by Jackson or St. Charles Ave. street-cars from Canal and Baronne Sts. (*see Motor Tour* 4.)

David B. Fischer's Garden, 1122 Jackson Ave. (*visitors admitted free*). The visitor will find the garden of Mr. Fischer one of the highlights of his tour of the city regardless of the season. Here one finds a riot of flowers blooming all the year round, and some of the most beautiful azaleas to be found in the city. Near the entrance are a large fountain and pool, and at the back is another rock-bordered pool surrounded by flowering shrubs. A walk lined with flowers on either side leads through the garden.

Mrs. David W. Pipes, 1238 Philip St. (*one block above Jackson Ave.; visitors admitted free*). One of the oldest and most beautiful gardens of this neighborhood is that at the home of Mrs. Pipes, who has made a specialty of camellias. For more than twenty years she has been collecting those varieties most popular in ante-bellum days, and now has one of the largest collections of camellias in New Orleans. Many of the bushes in this garden are seventy to one hundred years old, several being descendants of the first plants brought over from France in Colonial times. One variety, in which the owner takes especial pride, was transplanted from an ancestral home in West Feliciana Parish. These older, sturdier varieties present a marked contrast to the more developed types.

Mrs. Thomas Terry, 1417 Third St. (*three blocks up Prytania St. from Philip St., half block to the right; visitors admitted free*). The diversified garden of Mrs. Thomas Terry is a typical semi-tropical garden which has twice won awards from the Garden Society of New Orleans for its arrangement and beauty. At the rear of a plant-bordered swimming pool are a number of flower beds, irregularly grouped, containing a great variety of blossoming shrubs.

Audubon Park District

Audubon Park (*Formal garden and live oak avenue section reached by Magazine car from Canal and Magazine Sts. Landscaped section, planted with large variety of trees and shrubs, reached by St. Charles Ave. car from Canal and Baronne Sts.*). For flower-lovers two important points of interest are Odenheimer Court and the Aquarium presented to the city by Sigmund Odenheimer. Popp Gardens, situated near the center of the Magazine St. section, attract many visitors because of the typical Southern garden flowers. Around Hygeia Fountain is a profusion of dwarf orange and banana trees, arbor vitae, magnolias, mimosas, and crepe myrtles. An iris study field is located behind Popp Gardens east of the aquarium. Audubon Park is also noted for its magnificent live oaks. The oldest of these, 'George Washington,' measures 28 feet and 6 inches in circumference, and is considered the second largest in Louisiana.

Audubon Place (*residential subdivision, St. Charles Ave. entrance op posite Audubon Park*). Many gardens flank the parkway and double drive of Audubon Place. Handsome palms, water oaks, and exotic evergreens fill the parkway. Smooth lawns and fine trees and shrubbery are continuous between the homes. The Spanish patio and rockery of *Mr. and Mrs. Henry C. Flonacher*, at No. 27 Audubon Place, is noteworthy. Beyond the Moorish façade of the home lies a landscaped rock garden with a sunken pool below. Behind the stone fountain there is a weeping willow tree, while the entire garden is shadowed by fan palms, banana clumps, and East Indian bamboo. A small camphor tree, against a rocky intervening slope, provides foliage contrast. Cedars, Chinese paper plants, oleanders, and crotons are included in this shrubbery group. Bushy kumquat, Japanese plum, yellow jasmine, and flowering almond blend admirably with the Moorish architectural effect.

Mrs. C. S. Williams, 1912 State St. (*four blocks downtown from lower boundary of Audubon Park at St. Charles Ave. to State St. and turn left; only visitors with Garden Society cards admitted*). One of the best examples of New Orleans' winter gardens will be found at the home of Mrs. Williams, who has taken great pride in semi-tropical plants and flowers. Early in January azaleas and camellias are in full bloom, and border plantings of narcissus and violets make the garden one of the loveliest in this neighborhood.

Mrs. G. C. Atkins, 3008 Calhoun St. (*continue on State St. to S. Claiborne Ave.; left from State on Claiborne to Calhoun St.; visitors admitted free*). This garden, now under the care of Mrs. Atkins, was the private experimental garden of the late George Thomas, who developed and cultivated plants rarely found in Louisiana. Among his collection were summer blooming bulbs, and Texas and Mexican shrubs infrequently grown in this State. Mrs. Atkins now has one of the finest collections of azaleas to be found in New Orleans.

VIEUX CARRÉ

All points within walking distance from Canal and Royal Sts.

Perhaps the loveliest gardens in New Orleans are those found in the courtyards of the French Quarter. Flowers, vines, and shrubs of every description grow in profusion in patios hidden from the street. Pools, fountains, trellises, and Spanish ollas, or oil jars, add beauty to the floral settings. Among the finest gardens of this section are those found at the *Reed Galleries*, 520 Royal St., the *Court of the Two Sisters*, 615 Royal St., the *Courtyard of the Twisted Vine*, 614 Chartres St., *Le Petit Théâtre Du Vieux Carré*, 616 St. Peter St., *Madame John's Legacy*, 632 Dumaine St., 823 Royal St., 731 Royal St., and the *Grima House*, 820 St. Louis St. (*See French Quarter Tour.*)

A tour of gardens in the Vieux Carré might well end on the other side of Canal St. in the heart of the business district, where the tourist will find a number of fine office patios, particularly at the *Association of Commerce*, 315 Camp St., the *Guardian Homestead Association*, 624 Poydras St., and behind the office at 822 *Perdido St.* Visitors are always welcome, and there is no admission charge.

CITY PARK AND GENTILLY SECTIONS

City Park (*Esplanade bus from Canal and Burgundy Sts., or City Park street-car from Canal and Bourbon Sts.*). Here one finds a lovely formal rose garden with a recently constructed pool and fountain enclosing a symbolic statue by Enrique Alferez, local sculptor, and the City Park Conservatories, where a large variety of tropical, semi-tropical and exotic plants are grown. In March a vanilla plant and a beautiful flame vine (Mexican bignonia) bloom, and some years a large *Monstera deliciosa* may be seen laden with its rare, heavy fruit. At the rear of the Delgado Museum thousands of mixed native and imported irises, which have been dedicated to a former New Orleans poet and newspaper woman, 'Pearl Rivers,' bloom each April. The celebrated 'Dueling Oaks' giant live oaks, are also to be seen in the park.

New Orleans Parkway Commission Nurseries, Gentilly Road between Mt. Olivet Cemetery and Dillard University (*Cemeteries or West End car from any place on Canal St.; transfer to northbound bus at Broad St.; free admission*). The 50-acre tract comprising the Parkway Commission Nurseries contains an unusual assortment of ornamental and decorative shrubs which has for many years supplied parks and neutral grounds of the city. Within the grounds are acres of young cedars, Japanese plums, willows, palms, pines, sycamores, chinaberries, and azaleas. Here also are a number of greenhouses sheltering cacti and other delicate plants and shrubs. In May a lotus pool facing Gentilly Road is a mass of white blossoms, attracting scores of tourists who pause to admire the spectacle. An azalea trail designed to extend straight through the entire tract of land comprising the nurseries has been almost completed.

Charles Mauthe's private cactus farm and greenhouse, 2934 De Soto St. (*Esplanade bus from Canal and Burgundy Sts. to N. Dupre St.; walk left half a block and right half a block on De Soto St.; visitors admitted free)*. There are many rare species in Mr. Mauthe's collection, which is one of the more notable floral exhibits of New Orleans.

E. A. Farley, 4300 Mandeville St. (*Cemeteries or West End car from any place on Canal St.; transfer to northbound bus at Broad St.; admission and guide service free)*. Mr. Farley specializes in orchid culture. Here may be seen an admirable collection of rare specimens of orchids in varying stages of maturity. A visit to the nursery during the Christmas holidays will amply repay one for his time and trouble. At this time the orchid plants may be studied in all their stages, and while they have no natural blooming period, a long and expensive process of artificial culture will induce the plants to blossom at the most profitable season.

Percy Viosca, Jr., 2940 Dreux Ave., Gentilly (*Gentilly street-car from Canal and Bourbon Sts.)*. Here Mr. Viosca, author of *Delta Irises and their Culture* and *The Irises of Southeastern Louisiana*, maintains a large experimental iris garden. The owner is glad to show iris students over his garden and explain phases of iris culture.

Frank Carroll, R.F.D. No. 4. Old Gentilly Road (*Cemeteries or West End car from any place on Canal St.; transfer to northbound Gentilly-Broad bus at Broad St.; admission free)*. Mr. Carroll maintains a private farm of native wild iris and has some exceedingly rare colors.

METAIRIE SECTION

Mrs. Edgar B. Stern, 11 Metairie Lane (*Cemeteries or West End car from any place on Canal St.; transfer to Metairie bus at Canal St. and City Park Ave.; open only during Carnival season)*. This place is noted for its plantings of azaleas and camellias, its old-fashioned Creole garden, and its orchid greenhouses. Much of the garden can be seen from the street at any season.

Mrs. Harold Newman, 600 Iona St. (*walk out Metairie Road to Duplessis St.; left on Duplessis St. three blocks to Iona St.; admission secured through the owner)*. Here one finds an unusual collection of beautiful Creole camellias of varying size and colors, as well as many other shrubs and flowers. The garden may be seen, from the street, directly in front of the home.

III. SECTIONAL DESCRIPTIONS AND TOURS

FRENCH QUARTER TOUR: 4 m.

NOTE: The French Quarter can best be seen on foot, but the complete tour given below can hardly be covered with ease in one morning or afternoon. If the tourist has a limited time, the best plan is to walk down Royal from Canal to St. Peter, out St. Peter to Chartres and Jackson Square, and then up Chartres to Canal. Even if the visitor has only an hour or so between trains, something of the Vieux Carré can be seen by taking a cab to Jackson Square and walking about in the immediate vicinity.

THAT portion of New Orleans lying north of Canal St. is called, paradoxically, the 'downtown section' of the city. In this area lies the French Quarter, or Vieux Carré (pronounced Vee-yuh Car-ray). The literal meaning of the term is 'Old Square,' but since this section was originally the nucleus or principal part of New Orleans, and was occupied for the greater part by French-speaking people, it has become known as the French Quarter.

Since the date of the founding of New Orleans has been disputed, Mr. Robert Usher, Librarian of the Howard Memorial Library, who is an authority on Louisiana history, has contributed the following paragraph:

When was New Orleans founded? Most reference books give the date 1718. It is only in recent years that there is found, here and there, some-one who maintains that New Orleans was founded in 1717. These pro-testers apparently rely chiefly on statements which appear in the work of Baron Marc Villiers du Terrage on the founding of New Orleans. This author says (Dawson's translation, *Louisiana Historical Society Quarterly*, vol. 3, 1920), 'So the date for the foundation of New Orleans may be fixed at pleasure anywhere between the spring of 1717 and the month of June, 1722...' The date 1717 is suggested because on October ist of that year the Marine Board, in co-operation with the Company of the West, appointed in Paris a cashier for the counter which was to be established at New Orleans, on the St. Louis (Mississippi) River. It is to be noted that even as late as April 14, 1718, no site had been selected for the contemplated town which was to be known as New Orleans (*Louisiana Historical Quarterly*, vol. 15, 1932, pp. 37-43, Sally Dart, 'French Incertitude in 1718 as to a Site for New Orleans'). Some preferred that it should be at Manchac, others favored Biloxi. It is quite certain that no work had been done on the site of New Orleans until 1718. De Villiers concludes that the first construction work was carried out between March 15 and April 15, 1718. It seems wise to accept De Villiers' statement, which is, 'the surest date would appear to be 1718.' If an official act providing for a town yet to be established and located may be considered as constituting a founding date, then, as De Villiers suggests, New Orleans might be said to date from the winter of 1715-16, when Crozat demanded that a post be founded where the city now stands; or even from 1702, in which year M. de Remonville proposed the creation of an establishment 'at the Mississippi Portage.'

When the plan of the Vieux Carré was imposed on the site, settlers had already established themselves, and there were disputes concerning the division of their land into city blocks. Credit for the plan, it is now generally agreed, should be given to Adrien de Pauger, an assistant engineer, and not to Le Blond de la Tour, Bienville's chief engineer, who opposed the establishment of New Orleans at this site.

The Old Square is bounded on the south by Canal St., the dividing line between the French and American sections of the city. The northern boundary is Esplanade Ave., a magnificent tree-lined thoroughfare which was, half a century ago, the most aristocratic neighborhood of the French city. The western boundary is North Rampart St., and on the east lies the Mississippi River.

At the four corners of the Vieux Carré forts were later erected to protect the city at its most strategic points. On the northern corner, at North Rampart and Barracks Sts., was *Fort St. Jean*; on the eastern corner, at Esplanade Ave. and Decatur St., *Fort St. Charles*; on the southern corner, at Canal and Decatur Sts., *Fort St. Louis*; and on the western corner, at Iberville and North Rampart Sts., *Fort Bourgogne*. On North Rampart St., halfway between Forts Bourgogne and *St. Jean*, *Fort St. Ferdinand* was later built, on what now is Beauregard Sq.

To those who have paid a visit to the Crescent City, it is unnecessary to say that this section is the most picturesque and colorful part of New Orleans. This is the city of Gayarré, of Hearn, and of Cable – men whose genius have made the French Quarter famous wherever the name New Orleans is known.

The traditions and characteristics of the Spanish and French dominations have been jealously preserved by the Creole element of New Orleans. Down through the generations have come stories of 'high-bred dames and gallant knights who laughed and sang and danced and loved, while the Fleur-de-lis of France floated from the flagstaff in the old *Place d' Armes.*' The quaint old Franco-Spanish town, despite much American remodeling, still retains a singular charm and an Old-World flavor peculiarly its own.

Some of the tall brick buildings with their balconies of wrought-iron work have been standing a century and a half. Many are decrepit and dingy, with doors sagging and ironwork rust-eaten; many have been turned into night clubs, apartments, and rooming-houses; others have been invaded by petty tradesmen and shopkeepers; and still others are standing vacant and in ruins, gaunt specters of a charm and culture that are gone. A few are in the possession of the descendants of the original owners, or of others who appreciate their worth, and have been kept in good repair.

The visitor will find in the French Quarter a strange and fascinating jumble of antique shops, flop houses, tearooms, wealthy homes, bars, art studios, night clubs, grocery stores, beautifully furnished apartments, and dilapidated flats. And he will meet débutantes, artists, gamblers, drunks, streetwalkers, icemen, sailors, bank presidents, and beggars. The Vieux Carré is definitely the place in New Orleans where people go to live their own lives.

The architecture found in the Old Square is at variance with that of other sections of the country. But this is not surprising, since the architects of New Orleans, foreign-born and trained, had little in common with American traditions of the Atlantic seaboard. The architecture of the section is a subject that has appealed to numerous writers and has attracted scores of artists who have made the Vieux Carré their home. And the dungeon-like entrances, the narrow, winding stairways, and the flag-paved courtyards attract thousands of tourists yearly.

Before 1800 there were few architects of note in New Orleans, but during the first half of the 19th century the city boasted men widely recognized in this field. Among these were Latrobe, the De Pouillys, the Galliers, and the Dakins, all of whom were born in Europe and received their architectural training abroad. Most of the buildings erected under the direction of these men were of European styles, or fusions of two or more styles. The Spanish and French influences were, of course, predominant.

The wrought-iron and cast-iron lacework decorating the galleries of these old buildings gives the architecture of New Orleans its great distinction. Vines, flowers, fruits, or Cupid's bow and arrow are favorite designs. In many of them may be seen the initials of the original owner hammered into the ironwork. Most of the structures are built of cement covered brick, painted in light tones with the shutters and woodwork a rich green. Practically all of the older buildings include cool, shaded courtyards which are approached from the street through tunnel-like entrances paved with flags or brick. Palms, banana trees, and other semi-tropical shrubs are found growing in most of the patios.

Downtown from Canal St. on Royal St.

Royal Street. In the early Creole days *Rue Royale* was the main street of the French city. Under its overhanging balconies fashionable New Orleans strolled a century ago. Today, it is a street of curio dealers, perfume shops, and antique shops, where one can find beautiful specimens of old furniture, jewelry, chinaware, and firearms. It was in these shops that Eugene Field is said to have found his 'greatest solace and delight.'

1. *Old Sazerac House, 116 Royal Street.* Before turning down Royal St. from Canal, the visitor passes 'Monkey Wrench Corner' (downtown river corner), known to seamen all over the world as a meeting-place. Every major port has a corner so named. There yarns are swapped, and 'monkeys' (unemployed sailors) put the

'wrench' (borrow) to their more affluent fellow workers. Then one may pause for a glance at the birthplace of the drink New Orleans made famous – the Sazerac Cocktail. In 1859, when John B. Schiller opened his place at 13 Exchange Alley, the rear of 116 Royal St., he called his establishment the 'Sazerac Coffee House' after the brand of cognac he used, which was manufactured by Messrs. Sazerac-de-Forge et fils of Limoges, France. The old bar is now occupied by a barber shop, but the word 'Sazerac' may still be seen on the sidewalk.

2. *Old Cosmopolitan Hotel, 121 Royal Street.* A few steps farther, on the opposite side of the street, stands a building now occupied by the St. Regis Restaurant, but which once housed the old Cosmopolitan Hotel. Half a century ago this was a favorite meeting-place for Latin-Americans. In a building on this site, Dr. Francisco Antommarchi, the physician of Napoleon, had his home and office during the 1830's. Here the famous death mask of 'The Little Corporal' was exhibited, a bronze copy of which may be seen in the Cabildo. In the front of the present structure are three memorial windows commemorating the champion chessplayer, Paul Morphy; the musician, Louis Moreau Gottschalk; and the famous ornithologist, John James Audubon.

3. *Merchants' Exchange, 126 Royal Street.* On the right-hand side of the street stands a marble-faced building erected a century ago by the well-known architects, Dakin and Gallier. This was known as the Merchants' Exchange, and in its halls traders, auctioneers, gamblers, and merchants met for business transactions. In 1842 the ground floor was used as the U.S. Post Office, and later the exchange room on the second floor, which was topped by a beautifully proportioned dome, was occupied by the U.S. District Court. It was here that William Walker was tried in 1856 for his filibustering expeditions in Nicaragua. After his acquittal, Walker returned to Central America where he was captured and shot by Hondurans in 1860.

Following the Civil War the old Merchants' Exchange was turned into an elaborate gambling-house, known the country over as 'Number 18 Royal Street.' Today, the old Exchange is a quiet, inexpensive lodginghouse, with little left to tell of the drama that once took place within its walls.

4. *The Gem, 127 Royal Street.* Directly across the street from the Merchants' Exchange stands a building which won early fame for its bar. The establishment was built and opened for business by John Daniels and Alfred Arnold Pray in 1851, and soon became one of the most popular saloons of the city. Here, on January 10, 1857, was organized the Mistick Krewe of Comus, the first organization to give New Orleans a street parade at night during Carnival. It is claimed that a restaurant located here was the first in the city to serve midday meals, the old Spanish custom of closing business houses for the two-hour siesta having been adhered to previously.

5. *Department of Conservation Exhibit Rooms, 237 Royal Street.* The exhibits of natural resources housed here are under the control of the Bureau of Education, Louisiana Department of Conservation. Visitors are admitted free between 9 and

4.30 on weekdays; Saturdays, 9-12.

The exhibits of the Conservation Department are housed on two floors, and include a rather comprehensive and well-prepared display of fish, birds, animals, sea foods, minerals, forest products, and other natural resources of Louisiana. On the first floor are the fish, bird, and mammal collections, while on the second floor are the exhibits representing the oyster and shrimp industries, and such products as petroleum, salt, sulphur, sand, and shell.

At the entrance to the building is a handsome window display of pelts and mounted fur-bearing animals, such as muskrats, skunks, raccoons, minks, and opossums. These are attractively arranged in settings and poses characteristic of the various animals. In the large exhibit room are nearly 350 species of birds indigenous to the State, most of which are excellent examples of taxidermy. Prominent among these are specimens of the great ivory-billed woodpecker, burrowing owl, heron, and duck.

Models of the better-known game and food fishes of Louisiana waters form a frieze above the cases of birds and animals. Specimens showing the color variation of the Louisiana timber wolf may also be seen on this floor.

Mineral and forestry exhibits occupy most of the space on the second floor, with several specimens of fauna, including a collection of fish in preservatives. There are numerous commercial exhibits, such as canned shrimp, oysters, and examples of crushed oyster shells. Several specimens of sands, clays, and gravels used in building and paving may be seen, as well as exhibits of petroleum, sulphur, and many grades of salt.

An interesting part of the exhibit shows examples of the various kinds of woods found in Louisiana. Among these are the long-leafed pine, short-leafed pine, oak, hickory, hackberry, maple, sycamore, magnolia, pecan, cypress, tupelo gum, cherry, and beech. These are illustrated with their various uses in construction and in the arts and trades. The by-products of the pine industry form an interesting display, with the oils, resins, and other products deposited by the sap stream. There are also examples of Spanish moss, which is used extensively as an upholstering material.

L. from Royal St. on Bienville St.

6. *The Absinthe House, 238 Bourbon Street.* Few buildings in the French Quarter have become better known than this structure to which, for sixty years, adventurers, traders, and Creole gentlemen flocked to sip absinthe.

The building was erected by Pedro Font and Francisco Juncadella, early in the 19th century, as a combination residence and business establishment, and despite numerous offers to purchase it, the property is still in the possession of the descendants of the original owners. Cayetano Ferrer, a native of Barcelona, who had won recognition while at the basement bar of the old French Opera House, was chief bartender here. Later he took a lease on the establishment, and it became known as the 'Absinthe Room.' There is a legend that General

Andrew Jackson and Jean Lafitte, the Baratarian smuggler, planned the defense of New Orleans here in a secret chamber on the second floor. The original stair case, erected with wooden pegs instead of nails, is still in use. The marbletopped bar, the old water dripper, the cash register, and the paintings that once adorned the walls are to be found at 400 Bourbon St.

Return and continue on Royal St.

7. *Mallard's Furniture Store*, 301-05-07 *Royal Street*. At the downtown lake corner of Bienville St. stands a red-brick structure where almost a century ago Prudent Mallard, a native of Sèvres, France, carved and sold the furniture which is today so rare and expensive among the antiques of the city.

Mallard was for many years one of the best-known furniture dealers of New Orleans, ranking with François Seignouret. Among his specialties was an elaborate dressing-table known as the 'Duchesse,' which he carved from Central-American rosewood, or palissandre. As the name of Mallard gained wider recognition, wealthy planters purchased his mahogany chairs and settees, his great four-poster beds, and his exquisitely carved armoires of rosewood. Today the building is occupied by the Bienville meat market.

8. 312 *Royal Street*. The brick structure standing here was, in 1839, owned and occupied by John Slidell, of 'Trent Affair' fame. The building is one of a group built by the Earl of Balcanes, soon after 1828.

Slidell, a native of New York, came to New Orleans in 1819, and after a series of political contests finally succeeded in making himself virtually the political boss of Louisiana. He was captured with Mason aboard the British steamer 'Trent,' while en route to England, and after his release he landed in France, where he formed a friendship with Napoleon III. Slidell was never allowed to return to America after the war.

9. *First U.S. Post Office*, 333 *Royal Street*. Near the end of the third block of Royal, on the left-hand side of the street, is the site of the city's first U.S. Post Office. It was established in 1804 and was at that time '23 Rue Royale.' Mail was brought in from the north by riders and sailing vessels.

10. 339 *Royal Street*. On the corner of Royal and Conti Sts. stands a building which dates back to 1800. The building in 1811 housed the Planters' Bank, and in 1820 became a branch of the United States Bank of Philadelphia. In 1836 the property came into the possession of the New Orleans Gas Light and Banking Company, and it was from this concern that the bank acquired the name Gaz Bank by which it has since been known.

The wrought-iron balcony railings constitute one of the best examples of the craft to be seen in New Orleans. There was originally a vaulted corridor which led into a large court, but this has recently been closed up with brick walls. Today the building houses the antique shop of Waldhorn and Company.

11. *Mortgage Office* (*American Legion Home*), 344 *Royal Street*. The stately building standing at the right-hand corner of Royal and Conti Sts. was erected in 1826.

It was the second institution to be known as the Bank of Louisiana and for many years was the city's financial center. With the crisis brought on by the Civil War, the bank was forced to close its doors. In 1871 the building became the 'Royal Street Auction Exchange,' and later the Mortgage and Conveyance Office, the name by which it is best known to the older residents of the city.

Following the World War, the building became the home of the local American Legion, and the interior underwent a number of changes and repairs to accommodate that organization.

Architecturally, this building is one of the best on Royal St. In general it follows the lines of Graeco-Roman classicism, but it also reflects the architectural trend of the Old Square. Along the front of the stuccocovered brick edifice is a series of six lofty Ionic pilasters adorning the walls between the windows. It is said that the iron gates at the entrance are a facsimile of a pair at the garden entrance to Lansdowne House, Berkeley Square, London, which were designed for the Marquis of Lansdowne in 1765.

R.from Royal St. on Conti St. to Exchange Alley.

Exchange Alley, originally extending to the St. Louis Cathedral, is now only three blocks in length, running from Canal to Conti St. It was in this alley that a number of noted fencing masters resided in the early days of New Orleans existence. The only remaining part of the alley in the vicinity of the Cathedral is a narrow passageway leading from the 600 block of St. Peter St. directly through to the Cathedral.

Return on Conti St. to Bourbon St.

12. *Judah P. Benjamin's Home, 327 Bourbon Street.* This three-story building was at one time the home of the eminent Jewish lawyer and statesman, Judah P. Benjamin. For many years Benjamin was an outstanding figure in the South, serving as U.S. Senator from Louisiana, and during the last two years of the Civil War, as Secretary of State in the Confederacy. He has frequently been called 'the brains of the Confederacy,' but when the Southern States were defeated he fled to England, an exile. At the British bar he attained wide recognition and was considered for elevation to the bench.

The old mansion on Bourbon Street was built in 1835 by Auguste St. Martin, the father of Benjamin's wife. The most attractive feature of the building is the bow and arrow design which decorates the cast iron of the balcony.

Return and continue on Royal St.

13. *The Old Bank of Louisiana, 401 Royal Street.* On the downtown lake corner of Royal and Conti Streets stands an impressive structure which was erected in 1821 to serve as quarters for *La Banque de l'État de la Louisiane.* This is the building known as the Antique Dome, so named by a furniture dealer because of the domed ceiling.

The building was constructed from a design submitted by Benjamin Henry

Bonneval Latrobe, who had assisted in designing the Capitol at Washington. Like the majority of other buildings in the Old Square, the Antique Dome is built of cement-covered brick. The wrought-iron balcony railing with the monogram 'LSB' is one of the most distinctive examples of the Creole style of decoration. At one time there was a spacious driveway admitting carriages into the courtyard, but this has since been walled up and the patio roofed over.

14. *The Rouquette Home*, 413 *Royal Street*. This structure, a century and a quarter ago, was the home of one of New Orleans' most prominent families – the Rouquettes. Here in 1813 was born Adrien Rouquette, who became widely known and respected, both for his writings and for his missionary work among the Indians of St. Tammany Parish. Legend says that as a young man he loved an Indian maid of this tribe, and that after her death he decided to enter the priesthood. Tiring of his parish in New Orleans, he obtained permission to open a mission among the Indians, living like one of them, and adopting the name 'Chata-Ima' (Choctaw-like) by which he is now better known. He remained a missionary until his death in 1887.

On the balcony railing may be seen the original owner's monogram: 'DR.' The building is now occupied by the Diamond Antique Shop.

15. *The Patio Royal*, 417 *Royal Street*. Few buildings in the French Quarter are more interesting than the Patio Royal.

The history of this building has been the subject of much conjecture and discussion, but Stanley Arthur has recently placed the date of its erection around 1801. The original owner was Don José Faurie, but four years later it was purchased by the president of the *Banque de la Louisiane* to house this organization, and the monogram 'LB' enclosed in an octagon may still be seen on each end and in the center of the balcony railing.

The building was next occupied by the socially and politically prominent Gordon family. When General Jackson revisited New Orleans in 1828, he was a guest of Martin Gordon, and the two became such intimate friends that after the general became President of the United States he made Gordon Collector of the Port of New Orleans.

Later when Gordon met with financial reverses, the property came into the possession of Judge Morphy, father of the celebrated chess king. It was here that the child attained the skill that enabled him to defeat the world's foremost champions of the intricate game.

The property is now owned by Tulane University. Recently a French restaurant was opened, and the old mansion was given the name 'Patio Royal.' The courtyard is open to visitors.

16. *Peychaud's Drugstore*, 437 *Royal Street*. Near the uptown lake corner of Royal and St. Louis Sts. stands an old building where in the early days a native of Santo Domingo served what is said to have been the first American cocktail. Stanley Arthur in his recent book, *Old New Orleans*, says that Peychaud,

the apothecary, brought with him from Santo Domingo a secret formula for compounding his bitters with cognac. The potion was mixed in an egg-shaped cup, the French name for which was *coquetier*. It is said that the incorrect pronunciation frequently given this term by the English resulted in the name 'cocktail' being applied to the highly flavored drink. The old Peychaud pharmacy is now occupied by Feldman's Antique Shop.

17. *New Orleans Court Building*, 400 *Royal Street*. The imposing white structure between Conti and St. Louis Sts., designed by Brown, Brown, and Marye of Atlanta, was built in 1908-09 with funds totaling $1,090,000 appropriated by the city and State and property owners of the Third District. Many buildings dating back to the Spanish régime were torn down to make way for the courthouse, and the striking contrast the new building creates with the century-old houses that surround it makes it stand out as an unwelcome intruder in the French Quarter. A Renaissance adaptation characterizes the architecture. The ground plan is that of a decorative 'T.' The four-story building is set on a concrete foundation with a superstructure of reinforced concrete. The first and second stories are faced with Georgia marble and the upper stories with terra-cotta of the same color. An ornate terra-cotta balustrade surrounds the flat roof. The Royal Street entrance opens from a wide stone platform into a high corridor lined with Doric marble columns set on large bases. A bronze statue of Chief Justice White of the United States Supreme Court, a native of Lafourche Parish, stands in the center of the platform at the Royal Street entrance. P. Bryant Baker, sculptor of the 'Pioneer Woman,' designed the statue, which was unveiled on April 8, 1926.

The building houses the State Supreme Court, Court of Appeals, Civil District Court of the Parish of Orleans, State Library, Attorney-General's office, and various State departments.

18. *Mollie Moore Davis House*, 505 *Royal Street*. This building has been the home of many prominent families since its erection more than a hundred years ago. Here, not so long ago, lived the well-known writer of Vieux Carré stories, Mollie Moore Davis.

19. *St. Louis Hotel Site*. On the downtown river corner of Royal and St. Louis Sts. is a vacant lot where the St. Louis Hotel, for many decades the scene of important social and civic functions, once stood.

Construction of the building was begun in 1836, but it was not completed and opened to the public until the summer of 1838. It was originally intended that the building should occupy the entire block enclosed by Royal, St. Louis, Chartres, and Toulouse Sts., but the financial crisis of 1837 made it necessary to erect a more modest structure. The hotel, given the name 'Saint Louis,' in honor of the patron saint of the city, cost approximately $1,500,000.

In 1841 the building was destroyed by fire, but another was erected almost immediately on the same site and along the lines of the original structure. In 1874 the Louisiana Legislature purchased the building and the hotel became the State capitol. Eight years later, when the capital was moved to Baton Rouge, the hotel was reopened under the name 'Hotel Royal,' but this venture was not successful. In 1915 the building was so badly damaged by a hurricane that the owners allowed it to be torn down.

For several years before the building was demolished it stood unfurnished and abandoned, a gaunt specter of its former elegance. For 'two bits' one was permitted to wander through the apartments, otherwise there was no admittance. In 'That Old Time Place,' John Galsworthy tells of meeting a white horse in the hall.

The first hotel was designed and constructed by the famous De Pouilly brothers, J. N. B. and Joseph Isadore. The structure was simple and dignified, yet of such magnificent proportions that it was regarded as one of the most spectacular buildings in the State. The lower story was composed of granite and the upper portions of stuccoed brick.

Perhaps the most magnificent feature of the building was the great copper-plated dome, which is said to have weighed 100 tons. It was constructed of earthen pots or cylinders, showing the influence of early European church architecture. Another interesting feature of the hotel was the rotunda, which had a diameter of 66 feet and was paved with varicolored marble laid in geometric pattern. To the right of the entrance was a raised dais or platform from which slaves were auctioned. Across the front of this was a small railing, which was gradually whittled away by visitors for souvenirs. On the walls were beautiful mural paintings by Dominique Canova, nephew and pupil of the famous Italian sculptor, Antonio Canova. When the building was torn down these were preserved and later purchased by the French Government.

The hotel had accommodations for 600 guests, and was conducted on an American and European style combined, there being a restaurant in which American meals were served to those preferring them to Creole cooking.

L. from Royal St. on St. Louis St.

20. *Antoine's, 713 St. Louis Street.* Few restaurants in America have served a greater number of celebrities or been more highly praised for delectable dishes than this establishment. The building was originally a residence, but was purchased by Antoine Alciatore in 1868.

21. *Warmoth-Soulé Home, 716 St. Louis Street.* Facing Antoine's is a building which was erected just a hundred years ago by John A. Merle, a New Orleans commission merchant. Soon after its completion the structure was purchased by the well-known Louisiana diplomat and attorney, Pierre Soulé, who occupied it for several years. It was also the home of Henry Clay Warmoth, Republican Governor of Louisiana in the carpet bag days following the War between the States.

22. *The Grima House, 820 St. Louis Street.* The Grima House possesses one of the most beautiful courtyards of the Old Square. Refreshments may be secured from the courtyard kitchen within. Little is known about the early history of the building, but it is believed to have been erected in the 1820's by Samuel Hermann, a

wealthy commission merchant. In 1844 the property passed into the possession of Félix Grima. In 1921 it became the Christian Women's Exchange.

R. from St. Louis St. on Dauphine St.

23. *Audubon's Home*, 505 *Dauphine Street*. Here in the small wooden cottage, now occupied by a colored family, the famous ornithologist, John James Audubon, lived in 1821-22 and worked on his well-known book, *Birds of America*. The dingy old structure with its low sloping roof and green shutters is in a bad state of repair, but despite its age it appears to be still a sturdy building. Stanley Clisby Arthur's recently published biography of Audubon gives detailed information concerning his residence in New Orleans and elsewhere in Louisiana.

Return and continue on St. Louis to Royal St.

24. *The Spanish Commandancia*, 519 *Royal Street*. On the left-hand side of the street facing the Reed Art Gallery is an old plastered-brick building which tradition claims housed the Spanish mounted police during the régime of Don Estevan Miro. Records show that the structure was in existence and occupied as early as 1774, but recent historians discredit the claim that the Spanish police were ever quartered here. Notarial acts show that the above building was the business establishment of one Don Jacob Cowperthwait in December 1774. Later it became the market for 'fish oil,' the fuel then used in street lanterns.

25. *Brulatour Residence*, 520 Royal Street. This building, one of the finest structures to be seen in the Old Quarter today, was erected in 1816 by François Seignouret, a native of Bordeaux, who came to New Orleans to import wines from his native province.

Seignouret was a wine merchant and also a furniture-maker who produced some uf the best designed chairs, lounges, and armoires to be found in the South. On each piece of furniture the letter S was carved into the design by his workmen. In 1870 the building was rented by Pierre Brulatour, who continued the wine-importing business, and after whom the building has since been most frequently called.

For several years it housed the New Orleans Arts and Crafts Club, and is at present the location of the Reed Art Gallery, located just off the patio.

An interesting feature of the building is the *entresol*, or mezzanine, a half-story just above the ground floor where Seignouret stored his wines. The visitor should observe the ironwork enclosing the balcony of the third floor. Here also is a quaint, fan-shaped *garde de frise* (guard screen) with the letter S hammered into the design.

The courtyard is one of the loveliest in New Orleans.

26. 534 *Royal Street*. Near the uptown river corner of Royal and Toulouse Sts. stands a typical old Spanish-Creole building which was for many years the home of the Soniat du Fossat family. The building represents a later and more pretentious adaptation of the early business-home dwelling, in which the proprietor and his family lived above the shop in the gabled rooms under the low roof. As build-

ings in the Vieux Carré increased in size and became more elegant, the living quarters of the shopkeeper were enlarged to a full story above the ground-floor shop, a gallery was affixed, and certain other embellishments typical of French Quarter architecture were added.

Today the ground floor houses an interior decoration and antique shop.

27. *Miro House, 529 Royal Street.* This Spanish structure is believed by many to have been the one-time home of Don Estevan Miro, Spanish Governor of Louisiana from 1785 to 1791. Whether the ruler actually occupied the building is not known, but notarial acts show that it was standing in 1792.

On the second-floor balcony is an excellent example of the iron railing so popular during the early days. The detail of the courtyard is also notable.

L. from Royal St. on Toulouse St.

28. *Court of the Two Lions, 708 Toulouse Street.* At the uptown lake corner of Royal and Toulouse Sts. stands the Court of the Two Lions, known first as *El Patio de Los Leones*, and later by the French term *La Cour des Lions*.

This structure was built in 1798 by Don Juan Francisco Mericult and was retained by the family until it was purchased twenty years later by Vincent Nolte, a German merchant. Nolte, whose *Fifty Years in Both Hemispheres* proved so helpful to the author of *Anthony Adverse*, built up a commission business which he carried on until the property was taken over a few years later by a banking establishment. During the last half of the 19th century there followed a long succession of owners. Today it is a rooming-house with an antique shop on the ground floor.

The small courtyard with the two crouching lions facing each other from atop the gate posts has long been a delight to photographers, painters, and writers interested in the French Quarter. The building has the added distinction of having been the birthplace of the American actor, Robert Edeson, and the residence of Winston Churchill's heroine in *The Crossing.*

29. *French Opera House Site.* On the uptown lake corner of Toulouse and Bourbon Sts. is the site of the old French Opera House. Probably no building in the South housed more celebrities or witnessed more musical triumphs than this one.

The building, erected in 1859 at an approximate cost of $118,000, was opened to the public for the first time on December 1, 1859 with a presentation of 'Guillaume Tell.' In 1860 the immortal Patti appeared here, but the following season saw the close of the Opera House because of financial difficulties resulting from the Civil War. Again in 1914 the building was closed because of war, but reopened in 1919, in which year the structure was destroyed by fire, leaving only a mass of charred brick and twisted iron.

The Opera House was one of the famous Gallier masterpieces. The interior was beautifully arranged, with a color scheme of red and white. The great elliptical auditorium had a seating capacity of 1800, with four tiers of seats.

Today the site is boarded up and used by a wrecking company as a storage lot for lumber. The property is owned by Tulane University.

30. *Lafcadio Hearn's Rooms*, 516 *Bourbon Street*. The building facing the site of the old French Opera is of particular interest to those who know of 'Chita' and 'Youma.' Here in a small rented room Lafcadio Hearn struggled tirelessly over the stories which have made his name immortal in Louisiana literature. The building, now well over a century old, was occupied by Hearn soon after he came to New Orleans in 1878, and during the period in which he was employed on the *City Item*, located then at 39 Natchez Alley.

31. *Charles Gayarré's Home*, 601 *Bourbon Street*. This is the old home of the famed Louisiana historian, Charles Gayarré. Located on the down town lake corner of Bourbon and Toulouse Sts., it was occupied by the Gayarrés during the early part of the 19th century, having been erected some time before the year 1777.

Gayarré, the grandson of Étienne de Boré, the first successful sugar refiner, was of Spanish and French ancestry. Before delving into the history of Louisiana, Gayarré had been one of the State's most successful lawyers and legislators. His principal work, originally written in French, comprises a history of Louisiana in four volumes.

Return and continue on Royal St.

32. *Governor Roman's Residence*, 611 *Royal Street*. The sixth block of Royal St. is lined on either side with century-old structures where the élite of Creole society resided during the early years of the 19th century.

The old brick building at 611 was the one-time home of André Bienvenu Roman, twice Governor of Louisiana. The upstairs apartment kept by Roman became a popular rendezvous for the Creoles, and many brilliant dinners were given here for visiting celebrities.

33. *Court of the Two Sisters*, 613 *Royal Street*. Standing here on the site of the former residence of Governor Périer, ruler of the French Colony in the early part of the 18th century, is an old building whose spacious courtyard is one of the largest and best-known in New Orleans. The earlier building was also, according to one tradition, occupied by Governor Vaudreuil, the 'Great Marquis' and arbiter of fashion of his day, under whose régime New Orleans patterned its social life after that of Versailles under the Marquise de Pompadour. The present three-story brick edifice was built in 1832, but did not receive its popular name until more than fifty years later, when it was occupied by two sisters, Emma and Bertha Camors, who for twenty years carried on a 'fancy and variety store.'

The ground floor of the building is now decorated so as to give one the impression of being in a sidewalk café. At one time in the rear of the court there stood a fountain – a charming Cupid who blew sprays of water from the horn of a ram. A few years ago the fountain was uprooted and sold, and is now installed in the patio at 731 Royal Street.

The large gates at the entrance with their quaint ironwork designs are open to visitors. The building now houses a restaurant and bar.

34. *Crawford House, 612 Royal Street.* Directly across the street is a building which was erected in the early part of the 19th century by Dr. Devèze, who purchased the property from the Pontalba family. The history of the site dates back to the last decade of the 18th century, and the property has been in the possession of a number of distinguished families. In 1826 John R. Grymes, the Lafitte Brothers' attorney, who had married Governor Claiborne's widow, bought the residence. In 1839 François Bienvenu acquired the property, and it is still in the possession of his descendants, the Crawford family.

35. *Spanish Courtyard, 616 and 624 Royal Street.* These 'twin homes,' built by Dr. Isadore Labatut in 1831, were in the early part of the 19th century the scene of many brilliant social affairs, having been occupied by some of the most prominent families of the Creole aristocracy.

Both buildings are constructed of cement-covered brick and consist of three stories with winding stairways connecting the ground floors with the upper apartments. No. 616 has an especially interesting courtyard; No. 624, occupied by Dr. Labatut himself, housed during his occupancy a law office on the ground floor in which Edward Douglas White received much of his training.

36. *628 Royal Street.* On the right-hand side of the street almost facing Patti's Court stands an ancient two-story structure which for some unknown reason now bears the name 'Royal Castilian Arms.' This structure was the home of many prominent Creole families during the last days of Spanish rule. The date of its erection is indefinite, but it seems probable that it was built soon after the second great fire (1794). It was originally the town house of Charles Loubies, a wealthy planter from St. Charles Parish, and adjoined the home of James Pitot, the city's second American mayor. Like numbers of other old Creole homes, it served a double purpose, the ground floor housing a business and the upper apartments being used as living quarters for the family.

37. *Patti's Court, 631 Royal Street.* The modest, unimposing building standing here, which was the home of the celebrated prima donna, 'la petite Patti,' is said to be the second oldest structure now standing on Rue Royale.

The early history of this building has been a matter of conjecture, but notarial acts indicate that one Antoine Cavelier set up a mercantile establishment here more than 150 years ago, which was still being carried on by his sons in 1809.

The account of Adelina Patti's sojourn in the Crescent City, and her appearance at the French Opera, constitutes a delightful chapter in the history of Old New Orleans. Her début here was made December 19, 1860, in the title role of 'Lucia di Lammermoor,' under the direction of Maurice Strakosch, the husband of the star's sister. The season had been a failure and the newly opened opera house was on the verge of closing when Patti was induced to cancel her concert engagements and appear before the music-loving audience. The sensation which followed her success, and the royal reception given the young star is now common knowledge.

The picturesque court in the rear is open to visitors. Here one finds a great profusion of semi-tropical shrubs, vines, and flowers, with here and there seats arranged for visitors. The patio may be reached through Chapman's Novelty Shop.

38. *The 'First Skyscraper,' 640 Royal Street.* The four-storied old building standing on the uptown river corner of Royal and St. Peter Sts. is one whose history is of peculiar interest. It is known by three names, the 'First Skyscraper,' 'Dr. Le Monnier's Residence,' and "Sieur George's House."

It is commonly believed that this was the first structure in the Old Square to be built more than two stories high. A plaque on the front of the building reading 'First "Skyscraper" in the Colony 1774' is erroneous. The present building was erected in 1811 by Dr. Yves Le Monnier, well-known physician, and François Grandchamps, the Royal St. druggist. The architects were Latour and Laclotte, of 'Major Latour's School.' Upon completion of the building it was occupied by Le Monnier, who some years after purchased Grandchamps' interest in the property. When its three stories were completed it was predicted that the soft soil of its foundations would not support such a building, and that adjoining homes would be endangered. The heavy brick edifice became a curiosity, a phenomenon which tradition claims was shunned on stormy, windy days. The fourth floor was not added until 1876.

The oval-shaped corner room on the third floor is declared by architects to be the most artistically conceived in the city. It has a domed, plastered ceiling, and French doors open into a curved corner balcony.

George W. Cable, noted writer of Creole stories, was responsible for the building's being called "Sieur George's House," for it was here that his fictional hero lived and romanced, 'loved the wrong woman and grew poor from lottery and liquor.' It was here, too, that Kookoo, the landlord, finally pried into 'Sieur George's mysterious trunk while the owner lay in a drunken stupor, only to find lottery tickets instead of the gold which he would have given 'ten sweet dollars to see.'

The building has been in the possession of a number of families since its erection. Today it is an apartment house, with antique shops and a bar occupying the ground floor. The exterior, however, remains the same. In the wrought-iron railings enclosing the balconies are circular designs containing the monogram 'Y L M' of the original owner.

39. *Labranche House, 700 Royal Street.* At the downtown river corner of Royal and St. Peter Sts. stands an old edifice whose handsome cast-iron decorations make it one of the greatest attractions of Royal St. The quaint design, of entwined oak leaves and acorns, is regarded as one of the finest examples of ironwork in New Orleans. The building was erected a hundred years ago by Jean Baptiste Labranche of St. Charles District.

40. *Arts and Crafts Club, 712 Royal Street.* The mansion now housing the Arts and Crafts Club was the original home of Dr. Pierre Thomas, and was erected in 1823. During the remainder of the century it passed through the hands of many owners, the property being greatly prized because of the delightful views of the cathedral garden and Royal St. from the upstairs galleries.

In 1932, the New Orleans Arts and Crafts Club, which had previously been quartered in the old Seignouret home, moved into this building. This club is a local organization whose purpose is the training of those interested in the arts.

Return on Royal St. to St. Peter St.; L. from Royal St. on St. Peter St.

41. *Green Shutter Shop, 712 St. Peter Street.* The house with the green shutters, a low one-story structure, was built in the last decade of the 18th century and was once the residence of J. H. Holland, keeper of the Cabildo prison. The building is now the 'Green Shutter Shop,' a small restaurant.

42. Site of *Le Spectacle*, 732 *St. Peter Street.* The actual site on which the first theater of New Orleans stood has been a subject for much dispute. Guides in the Old Quarter have frequently pointed out to visitors the old building standing at 716 *St. Peter St.*, but Stanley Arthur's recent examination of notarial records shows that Le Spectacle was located at 732 St. Peter St.

R. from St. Peter St. on Dauphine St.

43. *The Le Prète Home, 716 Dauphine Street.* The tall structure on the corner of Dauphine and Orleans Sts. is the home designated as the Le Prète Mansion.

The century-old building with its high basement and exquisite cast-iron balconies is one of the most admired houses in the old section. Jean Baptiste Le Prète's family occupied the house almost half a century before it was taken over by the Citizen's Bank.

Helen Pitkin Schertz, in *Legends of Louisiana*, tells an interesting story concerning this house. A Turk, known as the 'Brother of the Sultan' is said to have migrated to New Orleans with a bevy of beautiful young girls purloined from his brother's harem and to have lived in great secrecy at this address. The curiosity of the townspeople was satisfied only after the mysterious stranger and his entourage were found murdered the morning after a gay reception. Officers of the ship which had brought the Turkish household, fearing the wrath of the sultan, were said to have done the deed, absconding with the dead man's jewelry to live as pirates.

R. from Dauphine St. on Orleans St.

44. *Pere Antoine's Date Palm, 827 Orleans Street.* Just opposite the old Le Prète home, on a site now occupied by a small wooden cottage, stood not so many years ago a tall palm tree known today as 'Père Antoine's Date Palm.' There is a legend which claims that Père Antoine and Émile Jardain, close friends, were preparing for priesthood when both fell in love with the same girl. It is said that Émile and the girl eloped, and that sev-

eral years after, when the mother lay dying, their small child was sent to Père Antoine. The child died soon after and was buried in his garden. From her grave the famous palm which the priest tended with such care is said to have sprouted. (See Thomas Bailey Aldrich's *Marjorie Daw.*)

45. *St. John Berchman's Orphanage for Girls (Negro), 733 Orleans Street.* The building occupies the site of the old Orleans Theater, where the Creole élite were entertained with French drama. The Sisters of the Holy Family, still in charge of its management, erected this building in 1881, shortly after Abbé Roufillon established the order in New Orleans. A colored high school is likewise housed in the building.

46. *Orleans Ballroom, 717 Orleans Street.* On the left-hand side of the street (just before coming into Royal) stands an old three-story building, long designated as the scene of the 'quadroon balls.'

According to Gayarré, Cable, Grace King, George Kernion, and other writers this building housed, before the Civil War, the celebrated quadroon balls, where 'the gallants of the city were wont to flock – duels frequently followed the dancing, and many a party of gentlemen, after having quarreled in the ballroom over some fair partner, adjourned in the early morning to the "Oaks" where "coffee and pistols for two" were served.' Here the beautiful quadroon women, 'whose slight Negro taint was betrayed only by the soft olive of their skin and the deeply increased brilliancy of their eyes,' appeared in all their glory to dance with the aristocratic white gentlemen of the city.

Stanley Arthur, however, states that this structure was for several years the scene of many brilliant affairs, but was never used for quadroon balls. In 1828 when the Government House was destroyed by fire, the State Legislature moved into the building. The popularity of the place waned with the completion of the St. Louis Hotel, and in 1881 the property was purchased by Thomy Lafon, a Negro philanthropist, to be used for the colored Catholic nuns.

47. *The Orleans Restaurant, 718 Orleans Street.* Just across the street from the Orleans Ballroom is an old, yellow, two-story structure, erected in 1809 by Antoine Angué. Here a century ago was housed the Restaurant d'Orléans, so famous during this period for its delectable Creole meals.

L. from Orleans St. on Royal St.

48. *823 Royal Street.* In the early part of the 19th century this building was the home of Daniel Clark, a 'gritty Irishman,' who was one of Lafitte's merchants and secret agents and was the father of Myra Clark Gaines, central figure in a sensational lawsuit. Clark held the distinction of having shot Governor Claiborne in the leg when the Chief Executive challenged him on the field of honor. He was the Territory of Orleans' first representative in Congress, serving from 1803 to 1812. When Philippe de Comines (later Louis Philippe, King of France) was visiting New Orleans in 1798, Clark became his intimate friend.

It is not known whether or not this house was standing on the site when Clark purchased the property in 1803. The façade has been remodeled on the lower floor. The principal attraction is the large patio in the back with its profusion of flowers and vines. Here grows one of the largest oleander trees in the downtown section.

The building is now occupied by the artist Alberta Kinsey.

R. from Royal St. on Dumaine St.

49. *Madame John's Legacy, 623 Dumaine Street.* Before crossing Dumaine St. the visitor may walk a few yards to the right and see 'Madame John's Legacy.' This building, according to recent research by Laura E. Porteous, is the oldest in the Mississippi Valley, an honor usually given to the Ursuline Convent at 1114 Chartres St. This old structure, immortalized by Cable's Creole stories, has a long, colorful history dating back to 1726 when the first owner, Jean Pascal, a sea captain from Provence, France, came to New Orleans and was given this site by *La Compagnie des Indes*, which then controlled the Louisiana colony. Here Captain Pascal lived with his wife and daughter until he was slain by the Natchez Indians in the massacre of 1729.

In the 1770's the house was occupied by René Beluche, captain of the 'Spy,' a smuggler in the days of Lafitte.

In the years following, 'Madame John's Legacy' was owned and occupied by a number of families who, happily, preserved the old edifice. In 1925 Mrs. I. I. Lemann purchased the property, and the home has remained in her possession since.

The building is of the raised cottage plantation type – lower floor of brick, upper of wood – and at variance with the 'town' houses which make up most of the Quarter. The first floor is a great shadowy place with thick brick walls, an uneven brick floor, and holes in the walls covered with heavy iron bars. From the gallery of the second floor slender wooden colonnettes support the hipped and dormered roof.

It was George W. Cable who gave the old house its odd name. Here it was that his hero John lived with his parents until their death. When John himself lay dying he bequeathed the house to Zalli, 'the handsome quadroon,' and her infant, 'Tite Poulette. But 'Madame John,' as she was called, sold the legacy and placed the money in a bank, 'which made haste to fail.'

Return and continue on Royal St.

50. *The Miltenberger Homes, 902-910 Royal Street.* The three large, red brick buildings standing on the downtown river corner of Royal and Dumaine Streets were occupied almost a hundred years ago by the distinguished Miltenberger brothers, Gustave, Aristide, and Alphonse. The structures were erected in 1838 by Madame Miltenberger.

It was in the building at 910 Royal St. that Alice Heiné, granddaughter of Alphonse Miltenberger, was born. After the death of her first husband, the Duc de Richelieu, Alice married Prince Louis of Monaco and reigned over Monte Carlo royalty until she divorced him in 1902.

Despite their hundred years, these old buildings are still in an excellent state of preservation. The ironwork on the balconies of the second and third floors is one of the finest examples of this style of decoration to be found on Royal St. In the back are spacious courtyards enclosed by high brick walls. The ground floors are occupied by small shops, and the upper apartments are rented as living quarters.

51. *The Cornstalk Fence, 915 Royal Street.* Of interest to visitors of the French Quarter is the cast-iron fence enclosing the garden at the above address. The date of its construction is indefinite, but it seems probable that the fence was built around the year 1850.

The design represents growing cornstalks entwined with the vines of morning-glories. The fence has been kept painted in the natural colors – the cornstalks green, the ears yellow, and the morning-glory blossoms a sky blue. A butterfly with spreading wings has been added to the design on the gate, and at the bottom a spray of holly leaves.

The only other fence in New Orleans built in this style is the Garden District at Prytania and Fourth Sts.

52. *The Old Courthouse, 919 Royal Street.* This is the site of the old courthouse in which General Andrew Jackson was fined $1000 for contempt of court, shortly after he had defeated the British army at the Battle of New Orleans. The original building was a small one-story structure with a red Spanish tile roof. The second story was added many years later.

When Jackson persisted in maintaining martial law in the city, despite rumors of a declaration of peace, prominent Creole citizens became indignant and criticized the general bitterly. Following the publication of an article in which 'Old Hickory' was denounced, Jackson ordered the writer arrested, and when Judge Hall issued a writ of habeas corpus the general banished the judge from the city. After martial law ended, Judge Hall returned, opened court again, and fined Jackson $1000 for contempt of court.

The court's action aroused the citizens of New Orleans, and a mob repaired to Pierre Maspero's Coffee Shop, at Chartres and St. Louis Sts. Here a speech was demanded, and Jackson, standing on a marble-topped table which had been dragged into the street, 'spoke briefly and without rancor.' The enthusiastic crowd quickly made up the $1000 to return to their hero, but Jackson refused the money, requesting that it be given to the widows and orphans of those men who had lost their lives in the Battle of New Orleans.

53. *934 Royal Street.* The residence standing here was the home of 'the Great Creole,' Gen. P. G. T. Beauregard, from 1867 until 1875.

The two-story brick building has a plain façade with batten shutters and dormer windows. The arched entrance is set in an alcove off the street. The entrance gate to the courtyard has a cast-iron design of love birds, a pair of doves facing each other across a bowl of fruit.

L. from Royal St. on St. Philip St.

54. *Lafitte's Blacksmith Shop*, 941 *Bourbon Street*. On the uptown lake corner of St. Philip and Bourbon Sts. stands a building known as the 'Lafitte Smithy.' For years this small one-story brick structure has been pointed out as the location where the famous smugglers posed as blacksmiths instead of dealers in 'black ivory.'

Notarial records in existence give a history of this building dating back to 1772, but the question of the Lafittes' occupancy has been disputed, despite the plaque on the Bourbon St. wall. The broken plaster of the walls discloses the *briqueté entre poteaux* method of construction (soft bricks reinforced with timbers) in vogue among the early settlers.

Return and continue on Royal St.

55. *Gallier's Residence*, 1132 *Royal Street*. More than three-quarters of a century ago the famous James Gallier, Jr., architect of some of the city's finest structures, bought this lot and designed his own home.

In the history of New Orleans architecture the name Gallier stands high. Both James Gallier and his son of the same name were designers of the first rank. They were the architects of the old French Opera House, the original St. Charles Hotel, the Pontalba Buildings, and the present city hall.

The Gallier residence is a two-story building of cement-covered brick in block shape, fronting which is a splendid portico with slender columns. Granite steps lead up to a landing of black and white marble squares. The doorway is flanked by two columns of the ornate Corinthian style.

The courtyard at the rear of the building was once one of the loveliest in the French Quarter with its fountains, flagged walks, and trailing vines. Today the patio is barren and deserted.

The ground floor of the building now houses a barber shop, and two of the trim wrought-iron poles supporting the portico have been striped in red and white. The second floor has been converted into apartments.

56. *The Haunted House*, 1140 *Royal Street*. On the uptown river corner of Royal and Governor Nicholls Sts. stands a typical old French mansion whose grim and weird history has given it the eerie title the 'Haunted House.' Probably no building in the Old Square has been the subject of more fantastic tales than the home of Madame Lalaurie.

The legends are full of interest. Madame Lalaurie, twice widowed by the deaths of Don Ramon de Lopez and Jean Blanque, married Dr. Louis Lalaurie in 1825. In 1832 when the Lalaurie mansion was completed, the family moved into the home, and it soon became the scene of many brilliant social gatherings.

There is the story of a fire which gained such headway in the Lalaurie home that neighbors rushed in to assist in extinguishing the flames. Here, in varying degrees of starvation and torment, seven slaves were discovered. An enraged mob attacked the home and carried the miserable and wasted slaves to the Cabildo. During the confusion Madame Lalaurie and her husband escaped in their carriage, made their way to Mandeville, from there to Mobile, and finally to Paris.

During the years of the Civil War the house was used as Union headquarters, and in the 1870's the building became a gambling-house. Stories were told and retold of the strange lights and shadowy objects that were seen flitting about in different apartments, their forms draped with sheets, skeleton heads protruding. 'Hoarse voices like unto those supposed to come only from the charnel house floated out on to the fogladen air on dismal and rainy nights, with the ominous sound of clanking chains coming from the servants' quarters where foul crimes are said to have been committed.' One of the most frequently repeated of the ghost stories was that of the little Negro girl who, trying to escape the cruel lashings of her mistress, sprang from the roof of the building to her death in the paved courtyard below.

The 'Haunted House' is a three-story structure of cement-covered brick, and was built at an approximate cost of $100,000. The architectural detail is designed in the French Empire style with classic scroll work, arabesque figures, appliqué, etc. It is now a social welfare institution known as the Warrington House, conducted by William J. Warrington, a kindly, gray-bearded man, who has spent his entire life assisting hungry and destitute men and women. During 1935 more than 104,000 people received aid. Hunger and want are the only prerequisites necessary to admit an individual to the Warrington House.

The Warrington Movement is non-sectarian and does not employ a large staff of salaried workers. Warrington's welfare work is no longer confined to the Warrington House, but embraces five houses, all partly self-sustaining. At 820 Esplanade Ave. is the Warrington House for Boys, where youths are cared for and clothed; at 1133 Chartres St. (a former home of General Beauregard and the birthplace of Paul Morphy) is a small trade school where youths are taught a variety of trades; at 1133 Royal St. is a salesroom and furniture repair shop where a number of young people are employed; at 623 Ursuline St. is a home where destitute women and children are fed and sheltered and given different kinds of employment. Visitors are cordially received at the Warrington House at any time.

L. from Royal St. on Gov. Nicholls St.

57. *Préval's Livery Stable, 724 Governor Nicholls Street.* The old structure known a hundred years ago as Préval's Livery Stable was erected by Judge Gallien Préval in 1834. It became the subject for a ludicrous Creole song in which the judge was described as a comical figure joining in a dance given for Negroes in the stables, and ending with his arrest for failing to secure a permit to hold the dance:

1. Miché Préval, li donnin gran bal;
Li fait negue payé pou sauté in pé.
Chorus:　Dansé Calinda, boudoum, boudoum.
　　　　　Dansé Calinda, boudoum, boudoum.

2. Miché Préval, li té capitaine bal;
So cocher Louis té maite cérémonie.

3. Dans léquirie là yavé gran gala,
Mo cré choual làyé té bien étonné.

4. Yavé des négresses belle passé maitresse;
Ye volé bébelle dans l'ormoire Momzelle.

1. Mr. Préval, he gave a big ball,
And made niggers pay to dance a little.
Chorus:　Dance the Calinda, boudoum, boudoum.
　　　　　Dance the Calinda, boudoum, boudoum.

2. Mr. Preval, he was the captain of the ball;
His coachman, Louis, was master of ceremonies.

3. In that barn there was a really fine spread;
I'm sure the horses were mighty surprised.

4. There were negresses there dressed finer than the mistresses;
They stole fineries from Young Missis' armoire.

Return and continue on Royal St.; L. from Royal on Barracks St.

58. *Audubon's First Studio*, 706 *Barracks Street*. In this low brick building, just off Royal St., John James Audubon rented a small, inexpensive room in 1821 and established his first studio in the city. He lived here only four months, leaving to go to West Feliciana Parish.

59. *Maison Hospitalière*, 822 *Barracks Street*. This home was founded in 1879 and is one of the most interesting institutions of its kind in the city. As a home for old Creole ladies, it takes care of those unfortunate gentlewomen who, reared in refinement and luxury, are now old and without means of support.

The institution is housed in a large two-story building that stands flush with the pavement. The courtyard is one of the most spacious in the entire downtown section. It is paved throughout and additions to the main building encircle it on three sides. On the unenclosed end is a driveway which opens into Bourbon Street and is flanked on one side by a chapel, in which service is held twice a day, and on the other side by an infirmary, with two nurses in attendance. There are about 70 inmates, who are clothed, fed, and given medical attention on funds allotted to the hospital by the Community Chest.

60. *Morro Castle*, 1003 *Barracks Street*. The building standing at the downtown lake corner of Barracks and Burgundy Sts. has been for many years shrouded in mystery. Like many more of the structures of the old French city, numerous sto-

ries have been related about this so-called rendezvous of ghosts. Many believe that the marble-faced structure was erected during the Spanish régime and that it was used to quarter troops.

Stanley Arthur writes that the structure was begun in 1836 by Paul Pandelly, but before the building was completed he was forced to surrender to creditors because of financial difficulties. In 1838 Pierre Soulé purchased the property, completed the structure, and leased it to tenants. The building is now a modern apartment house.

R. from Barracks St. on N. Rampart St.; R. from N. Rampart on Esplanade Ave.

Esplanade Avenue. In the boom days of the 1830's this avenue was called 'Promenade Publique.' Here a half century ago the socially prominent of the French city resided in palatial homes surrounded by palms, elms, live oaks, and magnolias.

61, 62. At 1016 *Esplanade* stands a brick structure resembling a feudal castle, built in 1838 by Sampson Blossman. In the next block on the same side of the street, at 908, is the century-old residence of Céleste Destrehan, daughter-in-law of the famed Bernard de Mandeville de Marigny. This was one of the finest houses on the avenue, and has recently been restored to its former splendor.

63, 64, 65. In the adjoining block at 820 is the old mansion of J. B. Guérin, now occupied by the Warrington House for Boys. The buildings at 730-740 *Esplanade* are sometimes referred to as the homes of the Fisk brothers, prominent philanthropists of the city and founders of the New Orleans Public Library system. The buildings were never occupied by the brothers, but the corner building was erected by Edward Fisk in 1870, and the fine residence at 730 was once occupied by the widow of Alvarez Fisk. At 704 *Esplanade* (corner of Royal Street) is the old home of John Gauche. The stately proportions of the mansion, the beautiful courtyard, and the cast-iron balcony make it one of the most interesting buildings in the French Quarter. The structure was erected in 1856.

66. The large brick house at 604 *Esplanade* was, during the 1830's, the home of Judge Alonzo Morphy, father of the celebrated chess king, Paul Morphy.

67. At 524 *Esplanade* (corner of Chartres St.) stands what is probably the oldest building on the avenue. This was the home of Ggeneralneighaspar Cusachs, president of the Louisiana Historical Society for many years. The building is believed to have been erected in 1810 by Laurent Buzard.

68. *Old U.S. Mint, Esplanade and Decatur Streets.* The history of the old mint building standing at the corner of Esplanade Ave. and Decatur St. is one of drama and color. The three-story structure, erected in 1836 at a cost of $182,000, is constructed of river mud brick, stuccoed and trimmed with granite. Designed in the Classical Revival style it has an Ionic portico facing Esplanade Ave. The main vaulting is supported on piers without being tied into the walls, thus eliminating the danger of settlement to the exterior. The walls, offset both inside and outside, range in thickness from 3 feet on the

ground floor to 18 inches on the upper story. The 20-gauge galvanized iron roofing, laid in 1856, is still in good condition. Changes were made in 1931 in converting the building into a prison; large dormitories and two cell blocks were added to the rear end of the wings; the picturesque old smoke-stack was removed; and the two rear courts were enclosed by high walls.

It was on this site that Andrew Jackson reviewed his troops before the Battle of New Orleans. Soon after the appointment of officers in 1837, the mint began to turn out its first coined money. Gold or silver was purchased from any persons bringing the precious metal to the mint, and the customer received in American coins the full amount without deduction or expense – the United States Government bearing the expense of coinage.

Two outstanding events connected with the old mint should receive mention; the fancy dress ball of 1850 and the hanging of William Mumford in 1862.

The fancy dress ball, the first and only social event to take place within a United States mint building, was given by the superintendent, whose name was Kennedy, to celebrate the début of his daughter Rose. The ball was a brilliant affair with most of the socially prominent people of the city in attendance.

The hanging of William Mumford was one of the high lights of the Civil War in New Orleans. When the city had surrendered before Admiral Farragut's fleet, and the United States flag had been hoisted over the mint building, Mumford in company with three companions seized the flag and dragged it through the mud of the streets. Two months afterwards, despite the interces-sion of influential people, Mumford was hanged from a gibbet projecting from the peristyle of the mint, erected just below the flagstaff.

The mint operated continuously from 1838 to 1862, when New Orleans was captured during the Civil War. For the next few years it remained inactive, beginning operations again in 1879 and continuing until 1910, when coinage was concentrated in Philadelphia by Government orders. Again the mint building, except for the assayer's offices, was unoccupied for several years. From 1927 to 1930 the building was used by the Veterans' Bureau, and the following year the work of converting the building into a Federal prison was begun with Diboll and Owen as architects.

R. from Esplanade Ave. on N. Peters St.; R. from N. Peters on Barracks St.; L. from Barracks on Gallatin St.

Gallatin Street. This narrow street is only two blocks in length, beginning at Barracks and ending at the Ursuline St. intersection. A century ago it was 'the most noted cesspool of immorality, assassination, and crime ever known in New Orleans in ante-bellum times' and was frequently called 'Louisiana's Barbary Coast.'

The street was quiet and almost deserted by day, but the first shadows of night and the first flickering lights from the dance halls and barrooms brought the 'seductive chuckles of women, and the boisterous laughter of sailors.' It is believed that Gallatin St. was the favorite haunt of the Black Hand Gang, which once preyed upon the Italian population of the city.

The buildings along the river side of Gallatin St. have recently been razed to make room for the new, modernized French Market.

R. from Gallatin St. on Ursuline St.; R. from Ursuline on Chartres St.

69. *Beauregard House*, 1113 *Chartres Street*. The birthplace of the world's champion chess-player, Paul Morphy, is located near the corner of Ursuline and Chartres Sts. Here in 1837 was born the child who before reaching twenty became the country's master chess-player. The old mansion is, however, more generally known as the home of General Beauregard, who lived here for a time.

The building was erected in 1826 by Joseph Lecarpentier on a site purchased from the Ursuline Nuns. It is a single-story structure with a raised basement presenting a contrast to the usual homes of the French Quarter. The building is approached by two flanking, curved, granite stairways with wrought-iron rails of a Greek pattern. The house is open to visitors.

70. *Ursuline Convent*, 1114 *Chartres Street*. Just across the street facing the Beauregard House is the historic Ursuline Convent, which is perhaps the oldest building in the Mississippi Valley and the first nunnery to be established in Louisiana. The Ursuline Nuns, the first of their order to establish themselves in the United States, reached New Orleans in 1727, but their new quarters were not completed and opened until 1734. The nuns were first domiciled in the home of Bienville when they arrived in the city. The opening of the new convent in 1734 was a day of great celebration in New Orleans with Bienville and all the officials of the city in attendance.

The building was occupied by the Ursulines for ninety years. In 1824, because of the value of the real estate surrounding their quarters, the nuns sold their property and established a new home two miles below the city, on North Peters St. The building was then used for a short time by a young French priest, Father Martial, who conducted a Catholic school for boys. In 1831 the State Legislature, which had been meeting in the old Orleans Ballroom since the destruction of the State House, held their sessions in the nunnery. The Chartres St. convent then became the home of the archbishop of New Orleans. In 1899, when a new archbishopric was purchased, the old nunnery became a presbytère, being joined to a new structure which was called *St. Mary's Italian Church*. In the rear of the courtyard, on what is believed to be the site of the original chapel, is a parochial school. The courtyard is entered through a brick and plaster 'conciergerie,' one of the few remaining gateways of this type in the United States.

The archbishopric is still pointed out as the old Ursuline convent – a building whose two hundred years have been crowded with many events of historic interest.

71. St. Mary's Italian Church, joining the archbishopric on the downtown side, is one of the oldest Catholic churches in New Orleans. The building was erect-

ed around 1846, one end of the old convent being torn away in order to join the two buildings. The small church, built of stuccoed brick, has a pointed gable surmounted by a small cross. The surface of the façade is ornamented with raised cement work. Four imitation pilasters divide the surface into four equal sections. Two angels in flight carry a chalice between them on the frieze surmounting the door frame. Above the doorway, with its heavy wooden doors, each of which is carved with a cross and stained in imitation of bronze, is a small but elaborately designed rose window. The Papal coat of arms stands out in relief on the wall surface under the cross on the gable.

The interior is an oblong room with a flat roof. Two marble columns supporting an entablature frame the Sanctuary. The main altar is of marble carved in elaborate design, as are also the railing and altar steps. Eleven stained-glass windows depict scenes from the life of Christ and the Virgin Mary.

To the members of this church and other Catholic Italians throughout the city, March 19, St. Joseph's Day, is one of the outstanding holidays of the year. Usually falling near the middle of Lent, it is for this reason called Mi-Carême. The feast originated centuries ago among a small group of Italians exiled because of a religious dispute. Set adrift by their persecutors, the frightened voyagers placed themselves under the protection and guidance of St. Joseph, their favorite saint, promising that if land were safely reached they would honor his feast day every year by erecting an altar. On March 19, refuge was found on an island in the Mediterranean Sea. Here an altar was built of branches and palmetto leaves and decorated with red lilies, wistaria, and other flowers. This custom of consecrating an altar to St. Joseph has persisted until today.

In Italian homes, many of which are in the Vieux Carré, elaborate altars are erected and statues of saints or holy pictures are placed here amidst a profusion of flowers, shrubs, and lighted candles. The larger shrines are built in tiers, but large or small, they are always decked with all manner of foodstuffs. In the background of each are small disks of bread and toasted beans which are distributed to visitors, it being said that preservation of these will ward off poverty. Tables covered with food stand about the room. Visitors stroll from house to house making wishes and leaving silver coins to hasten their fulfillment.

Return to Ursuline and Decatur Sts.

72. *French Market, Decatur and N. Peters Streets.* The Old French Market, one of the oldest institutions of New Orleans, has for almost a century and a half been one of the chief attractions of the Old Quarter. Its sheds and stalls, remodeled under the P.W.A., extend along Decatur and N. Peters Sts. from Barracks to St. Ann St. The market consists of five separate buildings, huddled together and divided into stalls where fruits, vegetables, meats, and fish are sold.

Tradition claims that this was once the location used by the Choctaw Indians as a trading-post, and that here in the early days the redskins squatted about with their baskets of wild herbs and sassafras leaves, waiting to strike a favorable bargain.

The first market building was erected in 1791 by the Spanish, but this was replaced in 1813 by the present remodeled meat market. The other buildings were added at later dates, providing space for the handling of fresh fruits and vegetables. The coffee stands at opposite ends of the market are the traditional refreshment places of the Vieux Carré, celebrated in song and story for their fragrant cups of 'café noir' or 'café au lait.'

To see the market at its best, the visitor should stroll by the stalls near the end of the week – Thursday night for Friday's fish and Friday night or Saturday morning for produce of near-by farms. The busy rush of trucks and wagons, the ceaseless babble of foreign tongues, the strange mixture of humanity ebbing and flowing, and the confusion of odors give a setting and atmosphere truly characteristic of the old French city. Many farmers, in order to be on hand early in the morning, arrive late at night and sleep until dawn in their wagons. Others remain up all night grading and arranging fruits and vegetables for the early buyers.

73. *Madame Begué's, 823 Decatur Street.* Continuing up Decatur St. the visitor finds, at the corner of Madison, what was fifty years ago one of the most popular restaurants of the city's downtown section – Madame Begué's. In the spacious upstairs dining-room, Hippolyte Begué prepared and served his famous Sunday morning breakfasts – delightful, leisurely meals beginning at 11 A.M. and usually continuing until 2.30 or 3.00 in the afternoon. Here, many visiting notables dined, spending luxurious hours partaking of delicacies. The Begue's Visitors' Book holds the following inscription by Eugene Field: 'I'm very proud to testify the happiest of my days is March 11, '95 – breakfast at Begue's.'

74. *Jackson Square.* The next right-hand block of Decatur St. comprises Jackson Square. The best view is from the river side of the block, with the handsome bronze statue of General Jackson silhouetted against the façade of the old St. Louis Cathedral. Since the settlement of the original city, more than two hundred years ago, many flags have floated from the flagstaff in the old Place d'Armes, as the square was originally known.

While the Louisiana province was under the rule of Spain this open space was called *Plaza de Armas*, and the red and yellow flag of España waved in the square. But with the Treaty of San Ildefonso, in 1801, came the transfer to France (1803), and the flag of Spain was replaced with the tricolor of the French Republic. Twenty days later the Creoles were dismayed to see the Stars and Stripes of the United States hoisted in the square.

With the Civil War came another change in the emblems floating from the flagstaff of Jackson Square. For a year the State's 'Lone Star' flag flew side by side with the Confederate banner; then came Admiral Farragut's capture of the city and the Stars and Stripes were raised again in the Place d'Armes.

In 1856 the Baroness de Pontalba succeeded in having the Place d'Armes transformed from a parade ground into a garden with walks laid out and flowers and shrubs planted. She also made the largest contribution to the statue of Chalmette's hero, which was placed in the center of the square and unveiled from the gallery of one of her apartments by the Baroness.

Jackson's monument has been called 'the centerpiece of one of the finest architectural settings in the world.' It was constructed in 1856 by Clark Mills at a cost of $30,000. The manner in which the sculptor succeeded in effecting a perfect balance in the posture of the horse with out props was an achievement which won him wide praise. The bronze horse and rider weigh more than 10 tons. The inscription 'The Union Must and Shall be Preserved' was cut on the base of the statue by order of Gen. Benjamin F. Butler, when he occupied the city.

Each year on January 8, Jackson Square is the scene of ceremonies commemorating the gallant defense of the city under Gen. Jackson at the Battle of New Orleans. Speeches are made at the Square (scene of the jubilant thanksgiving celebration held following the battle); a wreath is placed on Jackson's statue, and a reception is held at the Cabildo. The New Orleans chapter of the Reserve Officers' Association and the Chalmette Chapter of the Daughters of 1812 usually conduct ceremonies at both Jackson Square and at Chalmette Field. One of the most interesting rites observed on this day is the pilgrimage of the sodalists to the Ursuline College Chapel, 2635 State St., where solemn benediction of the Most Blessed Sacrament is held before the shrine of Our Lady of Prompt Succor to whom Mother Marie de Vegien, Superioress of the Ursuline Nuns, prayed for the salvation of the city in 1815, promising an annual novena in perpetuity.

Jackson Square has been well preserved and is under excellent care. Seats have been placed among the shrubs and along the fence enclosing the square. Visitors are welcome on the grounds until 11 o'clock at night.

75. *The Pontalba Buildings.* The two huge red-brick buildings flanking Jackson Square on St. Peter and St. Ann Sts. were built by the Baroness de Pontalba in 1849. Few buildings in the French Quarter are better known, and few have had a more colorful history.

Micaela Leonarda Antonia was an only child of the wealthy Spanish philanthropist, Don Andres Almonester y Roxas, and Louise de la Ronde. At the age of 16 she was married to her cousin, Joseph Xavier Célestin Delfau de Pontalba, who was only twenty. The marriage, uniting two of Louisiana's wealthiest families, was one of the most brilliant in the social history of the city, but the union was not successful, and divorce proceedings followed.

In 1848 the Baroness, who had for several years made her home in France, returned to her native city. It was at this time that she began plans for the improvements of Jackson Sq., and the building of the two apartment houses. Both buildings were completed in less than two years, designs for which were prepared by James Gallier, Sr. The Baroness had hoped that these structures would check the gradual movement of business to the uptown section of the city; but such was not the case. The splendid buildings attracted much attention for a time, but gradually they fell into neglect. Today, they have won back their popularity, and the Pontalba Apartments are much in demand.

The houses are now publicly owned, the upper building having been purchased by the city, and the lower donated to the State.

Designed in the Renaissance tradition, they have a harmony of proportion restful to the eye. Both are four stories high with a ground floor arrangement for stores. The wide galleries, which run the entire length of the second and third floors, have fine cast-iron work and an entwined 'AP', the Almonester and Pontalba initials. The oblong windows of the fourth or attic story are all covered with heavy cast-iron grillwork. Each building is ornamented with three gables, one at each end and one in the center with an octagonal blind window covered with a monogrammed iron grill in the center of each gable. Heavy, red-brick chimneys rise above the slate roof at regular intervals. The windows of the second and third floors are very high and the rooms which they light, judged by present-day standards, are immense. The red brickwork and black ironwork of the façade give a touch of mid-Victorian, or more properly for New Orleans, Third Empire elegance.

76. *The Louisiana State Museum Library*, 545 St. Ann Street (*open from Tues. through Sat.*, 9-4), is located in the lower Pontalba Building. It was founded in 1910 by the curators of the Louisiana State Museum for the purpose of collecting and preserving historical, biographical, and genealogical data pertaining to Louisiana. Its collections include: archives of miscellaneous State documents in French and Spanish from 1718 to 1803; old maps of New Orleans and Louisiana; newspaper files dating back to 1807; historical and genealogical publications of various States; bibliography of Louisiana authors and their works; and the Louisiana Historical Society's collection of books and documents, including a full file of the society's quarterlies and other publications. The library is maintained on a strictly reference basis.

77. *The Presbytère.* Just below the St. Louis Cathedral stands a two story brick structure originally known by the Spanish ecclesiastical term, *Casa Curial.* This is the building now called the Presbytère. It is constructed along the same lines as the Cabildo, which adjoins the Cathedral on the upper side.

Erection of the building was begun in 1794, but when the great fire of that year destroyed the buildings on the other side of the Cathedral the construction of the Curial was discontinued until the other buildings could be replaced. In the meantime Don Almonester, who was financing the venture, died, and his widow brought suit to be absolved from obligations to complete the structure. It is believed that the building was completed by the American Government in 1813, for at this time a part of the State courts moved their quarters here. In 1853, after the building had been used to house the lower courts for forty years, the mayor of the city paid the wardens of the St. Louis Cathedral $55,000 for the Presbytère.

The building, which is now owned by the State, is two stories high and constructed of stuccoed brick. The architecture is typically Spanish, with a French mansard roof. The lower story is of the Hispano-Moresque order with a wide portico along the façade. Four of the nine semicircular arches are supported by columns, and those at the angles by pilasters.

Located in the Presbytère is the *Louisiana State Museum, Natural Science Division* (*open daily except Mon. 9-5; admission free*).

The museum began with a collection of products, resources, and specimens of Louisiana fauna and flora that constituted the State's display at the Louisiana Purchase Exposition held at St. Louis in 1904. When the exhibits were returned they formed the nucleus of a permanent exhibit, and an annual appropriation of $5000 was made for its maintenance. This first collection included agricultural products, such as rice, cotton, and sugar cane; a collection of native fauna; products relating to the State's mineral resources; and specimens from the fields of geology and zoology.

Numerous large panoramic groups of birds and mammals native to Louisiana are among the best exhibits in the museum, but do not occupy a prominent place, being in one of the wings. These groups are ranged along passageways and may be electrically lighted. They show pelicans, wild geese, sea birds, bald eagle, deer, black bear, and swamp and reptile life. As a display of characteristic Louisiana life and scenery they are without counterpart.

Just inside the entrance of the building may be seen some of the larger birds and mammals common to Louisiana, a bust and portrait of John James Audubon, the ornithologist, and under glass, a volume of Audubon's original edition of *Birds of America*. On the right of the lobby is a room used for lectures on scientific subjects, its walls lined with portraits of former sugar planters. In other rooms on the first floor are various agricultural exhibits of Louisiana, with their by-products. In this section are miniatures of a cotton field at picking time, a rice field during the threshing season, and a small model of a cottonseed oil factory. On the second floor one may see a model sugar-cane field and a perfect miniature of a modern sugar factory.

The hallway of the second floor and the rooms to the east contain a series of zoological exhibits, including a striking display of more than one hundred species of humming birds from Peru and Ecuador. An interesting collection of fishes presents a vivid view of fish life off the Louisiana Gulf Coast. The specimens are modeled with unusual accuracy from casts of actual fish, and are colored accordingly. The collection includes tarpon, jewfish, triple-tail, or blackfish, shovel-nosed shark, sawfish, flying fish, puffer, and numerous other species common to Louisiana waters. In this group are several specimens of turtles and terrapins, as well as a number of skeletons of rare types.

There is also an excellent display of various types of frogs occurring in Louisiana. They are very well modeled and colored from life.

The snake collection is one of the best in the museum, containing specimens of the banded rattler, diamond-back rattler, water moccasin, harlequin snake, horned or mud snake, blue racer, king snake, and several specimens of the numerous kinds of water snakes found in the State.

The general collection of birds attracts much attention because of the rare and striking species of native birds found in the group. The sandbill cranes, shown in a

VIEUX CARRÉ

A COURTYARD, 529 ROYAL STEET

MADAME JOHN'S LEGACY

THE COURT OF THE LIONS

LA PRÈTE HOUSE, ONE OF THE STRANGEST IN THE VIEUX CARRÉ

'SIEUR GEORGE'S HOUSE, MADE FAMOUS BY CABLE'S ROMANCE

ORLEANS STREET WITH A REAR VIEW OF ST. LOUIS CATHEDRAL
CONVENT OF THE HOLY FAMILY AT THE LEFT

THE BEAUREGARD HOUSE

OLD ABSINTHE HOUSE

LOOKING TOWARD THE CABILDO AND THE CATHEDRAL

A COURTYARD RESTAURANT, THE GRIMA HOUSE

setting of typical Louisiana lowland, include specimens of the young as well as the adult birds. There are examples of the large wood ibis, or wood stork, the scarlet ibis (a native of tropical America), the flamingo, spoonbill, and numerous small waders, such as the oyster-catcher, the long-billed curlew, and the black-necked stilt. In characteristic settings a variety of wild ducks are displayed, the adults and young in typical poses. Excellent examples of brown and white pelicans are shown, with several specimens of wild geese common to the State.

One finds, likewise, an unusual assortment of exotic fowls, especially the fire-back pheasant, hazel-hen, blackcock, Hungarian partridge, and red grouse. In a separate case may be seen an attractive exhibit of bright-colored pheasants collected from different parts of the world. There are also examples of the Laysan albatross, African hornbill, Australian bower-bird, and the king-bird of paradise, a brilliant red species.

In other sections displaying birds commonly found in Louisiana there are specimens of the snipe, woodcock, bald eagle, blue goose, and a variety of gulls, terns, and other seabirds, shown in typical settings, such as swamps or low marshlands.

The collection of mammals is confined chiefly to species common in Louisiana, including gray fox, raccoon, opossum, mink, and muskrat.

The precious old French and Spanish Colonial documents of the State archives, which are disintegrating with age, are being carefully repaired and deposited in fireproof vaults in the Presbytère. Copies in the original and translations in English are being made and will soon be available to research workers. Another valuable item is a card index to all inscriptions still decipherable on the headstones and tombs of the various cemeteries of the city.

78. *St. Louis Cathedral.* Facing the old Place d'Armes is the stately St. Louis Cathedral. The present structure, like its two predecessors, was named for the patron saint of Bourbon France, who was likewise made the patron saint of Nouvelle Orléans.

The first church to occupy the site was a small structure of adobe and wood, erected by Bienville soon after he founded the city and called the Parish Church. This primitive building was destroyed by the hurricane that swept the city in 1723. For four years the colonists held their services in a rented building, but plans were made immediately for the erection of a new church. This second structure, of brick and wood with adobe plaster, was completed and dedicated in 1727 and served as a place of worship until the memorable Good Friday of March 21, 1788, when the first great fire of New Orleans destroyed nearly the entire city.

So great was the financial loss resulting from the fire that the citizens were unable to rebuild immediately. At this time Don Andres Almonester y Roxas, the wealthy Spanish nobleman mentioned above, offered to erect at his own expense a new church for the city 'on condition that a mass would be said every Sunday in perpetuity after his death for the repose of his soul.' The offer was accepted, and in return, honors in the ruling body (the Cabildo) were bestowed upon him.

When Don Almonester died in 1798, his remains were at first interred in the parish cemetery. More than a year later they were removed to the Cathedral and placed under a marble slab beneath the altar of the Sacred Heart. On the slab are inscribed his name, coat of arms, and a brief account of his life and work.

The structure, completed in 1794 at a cost of approximately $50,000, was of the usual Spanish style with two round towers in front, resembling the church buildings erected by the Spaniards in Mexico and South America. In 1793, when Louisiana was detached from Havana and made into a separate diocese, the New Orleans church was raised to the dignity of a cathedral and called the *Catedral de San Luis*.

In 1851 the structure was remodeled and enlarged by J. N. B. De Pouilly, architect of the old St. Louis Hotel. Steeples were raised on the towers, and the present portico, with its columns and pilasters, was added, changing the appearance of the façade considerably. Thirty years later the interior was repaired, Humbrecht being employed to restore the paintings. In 1916 the building was again reconditioned, the money for this having been furnished by an anonymous donor.

On either side of the cathedral, running back the length of the block to Royal St., are Orleans and St. Anthony's Alleys. The former has of recent years come to be known as 'Pirates' Alley,' though there is no basis for this name. Facing Royal Street, behind the church, is St. Anthony's Garden, already mentioned.

Facing the Royal St. entrance to the garden stands a marble monument erected in honor of thirty marines, part of the crew of the French battleship *Tonnère*, who died at the Quarantine Station in August 1857 while serving (according to one account) as volunteer nurses during a yellow-fever epidemic. The monument was erected at the station by order of His Excellency, Admiral Hamelin, Minister of the Navy under Napoleon III. In 1914 the monument, along with the remains of the sailors, was removed from the station to its present location by the Souvenir Français en Louisiane, a French society.

Set in the midst of a small, square plot, planted with shrubbery and enclosed by a marble coping, the monument, in the form of a shaft, with a burial urn sculptured at the top, rises 15 feet from a pyramidal base. Inscribed on it are the names of the sailors buried there.

79. *The Cabildo.* On the uptown side adjoining the St. Louis Cathedral stands the Cabildo, the ancient seat of Spanish rule. The history of this building, dating back to the year 1795, is if exceptional interest. This was the scene of the formal transfer of Louisiana from France to the United States.

As early as 1770 the Spaniards had erected their government building on this site, but the fire of 1788 destroyed it. Another erected soon after likewise fell a prey to flames in 1794, when the second great fire swept the town. The new capital house was erected the following year, and the 'Very Illustrious Cabildo,' the Spanish administrative body for which it was built, moved into the new quarters. During the brief rule of the French in 1803, the building was called *Maison de Ville*, or Town Hall.

After the erection of the Cabildo, the rule of Spain continued only eight years before the Colony was returned to France. Then after twenty days Governor Claiborne, displaying the American flag from the balcony of the Cabildo, announced the transfer of the province to the young republic of the United States. The official transactions took place in a large room on the second floor. When Lafayette visited New Orleans in 1825, he was received and welcomed at the Cabildo. Among other notables who were received here in the early days were Henry Clay, Sarah Bernhardt, the Grand Duke Alexis of Russia, Mark Twain, Roosevelt, McKinley, and Taft.

The building, constructed of stuccoed brick, is one of the best examples of Hispano-Moresque architecture to be found in the city. The wide arches and the original flat tile roof showed definitely the Spanish influence. The French mansard roof, which was added in 1847, altered the appearance of the building to some extent.

The Cabildo now houses the *Louisiana State Museum* (*open daily except Mon.*, 9-5; *admission is free*), opened in 1911. Here is found a remarkable display of historical documents, relics, portraits, costumes, furniture, and mementos of every description. The art collection began with the portraits of General Beauregard and General Thomas and the painting of the Battle of New Orleans. Through gifts and purchases, additions were made to the collection until today scores of portraits adorn the walls.

An interesting exhibit of Indian trophies is on display here, as well as a number of personal mementos of famous characters. Louisiana's wild life is well represented with birds, snakes, and a large variety of animals. Specimens of agricultural products of the State, and old implements of various trades may be seen on the second floor.

On the first floor is an interesting collection including the outmoded cigar-store Indian, scale models of old ships and river boats, and implements of all the trades practiced in Louisiana – physicians' equipment, optical instruments, early typewriters, cameras, cash boxes, etc.

In the courtyard are one or two cannon. In the several prison rooms facing the court, displays have been arranged. In the first, a slave block, slave bell, and paintings of Negro characters such as Marie Laveau are found. The second room holds an old soda-water machine and an early American wood carving of a Negro figure (life-size) in the act of pounding a druggist's mortar. The other rooms contain Colonial locks and keys, a Colonial kitchen, and various articles of this period. The relics of the Baratarian pirates Jean and Pierre Lafitte comprise an interesting collection in the group. The most noteworthy among these are the box compass, spy glass, ship's lantern, water jug, candlestick, powder horn, folding knives, whisky bottle, drinking glasses, and playing cards. There are also specimens of the Spanish silver coin called by the pirates 'pieces of eight.'

The Louisiana Transfer Room on the second floor has been arranged as an art gallery, containing portraits of Louisianians who have become famous in the various fields of adventure, discovery, statesmanship, war, commerce, education, literature, and music. The collection of Louis Moreau Gottschalk, Louisiana's most eminent composer and musician, is of particular interest. This includes a jeweled silver wreath and several silk streamers from floral offerings given Gottschalk at various performances in North and South America. There is also a bust of the composer in plaster and several old manuscripts of his compositions, signed letters, concert programs, and tickets.

Probably the most interesting exhibit in this room is the famous death mask of Napoleon Bonaparte, made and donated to the city by the Emperor's personal physician, Dr. François Antommarchi. The bronze cast of the exiled general reposes on imperial red cloth of damask, enclosed in a glass case mounted on a base of ebony and gold finish. The mask rests on the very spot where it was presented to the city in 1834, and where thirty-one years before the Louisiana Transfer ceremonies were held. The mold of Napoleon's head was made by his physician just forty hours after his death on May 5, 1821. It is said that the bronze mask at the Cabildo is the first of the three replicas made of the original.

The archeological collection of the State Museum contains almost every form of prehistoric relic found in Louisiana. Typical specimens are shown in the various cases. Pottery presents great variation in details. There are specimens of the Greek, Roman, Oriental, and modern types of clay products. Several teapots, pitchers, and other objects of the well-known Bennington Rockingham ware are found in the collection.

The exhibition cases on the third floor contain the story of the Carnival, costumes, jewels, the story of the rise and fall in the fashions of men and women's clothes, early furniture, and a life mask of Enrico Caruso, a plaster cast made in the museum studio from an original bronze loaned by Col. R. E. E. de Montluzin.

80. The *Battle Abbey*, behind the Cabildo, contains relics and trophies of all the wars, from Indian days to the World War. A collection of personal mementos of famous characters and objects of their personal use are included. Relics of the Battle of New Orleans and those of the Civil War compose most of the exhibit. One particularly interesting object in the display is the catafalque used for the transfer on May 31, 1893, of Jefferson Davis from Metairie Cemetery to the railroad station for burial at Richmond, Va.

The Arsenal was formerly the site of the Spanish prison. The two buildings known as the *Jackson House* and *Calabozo*, which adjoin the Arsenal, were gifts of the late William Ratcliffe Irby, banker and philanthropist. Jackson House has recently been reconstructed on the original plans by the W.P.A. and is now a meeting-place of the Daughters of 1812.

81. *Le Petit Salon*, 620 *St. Peter Street*. Here stands another typical Creole home widely admired for the ironwork of its balconies. This residence, built in 1838 by Victor David, is now owned by an exclusive organization of New Orleans women known as 'Le Petit Salon.' Grace King, author and historian of old New Orleans, served as its first president. The group is now headed by Elizabeth Meriwether Gilmer, better known to readers as 'Dorothy Dix.'

82. The *Little Theater*, 616 St. Peter Street, is the outgrowth of an organization known as the 'Drawing-Room Players,' formed in 1916 by a small group of men and women interested in dramatic art and in the cultural traditions of the Vieux Carré. As the original name implies, performances were at first given in the drawing-rooms of members. While the initial productions were mostly one-act plays, they were modeled after the best examples of professional stagecraft.

Within three years the organization boasted a membership of 500 and it became necessary to lease special quarters. An apartment in the lower Pontalba Building was procured, and the members busied themselves transforming a dingy hall into a small theater which, when ready for occupancy, had a seating capacity of 184 persons, and a small but attractive stage. There were no paid employees, all work such as costume designing and stage decoration being done by members. In a short time membership increased to 600, and a few years later to 1000 with a waiting-list of several hundred.

In 1922 the present site on St. Peter St. was purchased and a building erected housing an auditorium seating approximately 500. The membership limit was extended to 2000 and plays were given six nights a week, once a month from October until May. Membership continued to increase until a maximum was reached for seven nights of performances.

Along with growth in membership the Little Theater progressed in artistic achievement. With adequate stage quarters full-length plays were billed, an art director, secretary and stage mechanic being employed. Among the first major productions were Eugene O'Neill's 'Beyond the Horizon,' Oscar Wilde's 'Lady Windermere's Fan,' and Flo Field's 'À La Creole.'

The building housing the organization is of characteristic Creole architecture, its façade being modeled along the lines of the old Absinthe House on Bourbon Street. Its broad doors, large fan windows, solid shutters, and projecting iron balconies make it one of the chief attractions of downtown New Orleans. The well-landscaped courtyard is usually open to visitors.

The original membership fee, placed at $10 a year, has never been changed. A few tickets for individual performances are set aside for sale to tourists.

Continue on Chartres St.

83. *Courtyard of the Vine*, 614 *Chartres Street*. Turning back into Chartres Street, one finds, near the corner of Wilkinson, an old building once owned by John McDonogh. It is not the house, however, that attracts the visitor, but the great, twisted wistaria vine growing in the courtyard at the rear of the building. The court is entered through a narrow passageway, the gates being open at all times.

The wistaria vine is said to be more than a hundred years old. The trunk of the vine has grown to enormous size, and the roots have spread so far that other sprouts have grown up, making a network. Wires have been strung across the court to support the heavy branches.

To see it at its best, the courtyard should be visited around the middle of March. At this time the great vine is full of purple blossoms, and the yard is fragrant with the heavy odor of the wistaria.

R. from Chartres St. on Toulouse St.

84. 628 *Toulouse Street*. Near the middle of the block, just off Chartres Street, stands a large Spanish Creole home which is the old residence of Jean François Jacob. Tradition, however, has designated this as the home of William Charles

Cole Claiborne, the first American Governor of Louisiana, but early directories show that the Governor resided on Old Levee St.

The building, erected in 1813, is a gray, three-story structure constructed of cement-covered brick with a paved, tunnel-like entrance and a flagged courtyard in the rear. Opening onto the courtyard is one of the largest fan windows to be found in the Quarter. Winding stairways, leading to the upper floors, are on either side of the court.

Return and continue on Chartres St.

85. *Site of the First Fire*, 538 *Chartres Street*. Almost 150 years ago Don José Vincente Nuñez, paymaster of the Army, had his home on the downtown river corner of Chartres and Toulouse Sts. It was in this home that the great fire which destroyed four-fifths of the French city began.

On the evening of Good Friday, March 21, 1788, a fire broke out in the Nuñez residence, a drapery having caught fire from a candle lighted before a shrine. Most of the citizens were at their devotions and the flames were not discovered immediately. When the alarm was raised, efforts to arrest the spread of fire were thwarted by a strong south wind, and before the evening was gone 856 buildings had been burned to the ground, including the old parochial church, the city jail, the barracks, the armory, and the greater part of the city archives. Only those buildings along the levee of the Mississippi River escaped destruction.

It is interesting to note that the second great fire of the city likewise happened when the citizens were at their devotions. The Feast of the Immaculate Conception was being observed December 8, 1794, when a fire broke out on Royal St. and consumed more than 200 buildings in the heart of the city. Following this second disaster, Governor Carondelet issued an order that all future buildings of two or more stories erected in the center of the city should be of brick.

86. 514 *Chartres Street*. The visitor will be somewhat confused when walking along the fifth block of Chartres St. to find two old buildings both displaying signs claiming the distinction of being the 'Napoleon House.' Probably no two buildings in the Vieux Carré have had occasion for more speculation than these. However, the old Girod home at 500 Chartres St. seems to have more claim to this name than the residence at 514, since Mayor Girod, who occupied the building, is said to have offered his home to the exile of St. Helena should he come to New Orleans.

But the legends are interesting. Guidebooks which have long subscribed to the claim that the building at 514 Chartres was erected and furnished for Napoleon with funds supplied by Nicholas Girod, the city's mayor. Plans were made to rescue the prisoner, and 'the expedition was actually planned and only fell through by the unexpected announcement of the death of the martyr-emperor.' Dominique You, lieutenant of the well-known Lafitte, was to have commanded a crew of Baratarians on this bold venture.

Examination of old records has disclosed what is probably an authentic account of the building. Six months after funeral services and mass were held at the St. Louis Cathedral for Napoleon, and almost a year after his death apothecary Dufilho purchased the site and erected his pharmacy there. The druggist opened his business on the ground floor and used the upper apartments for living quarters.

It was formerly one of the handsomest buildings in this section, but at present it is in ruins. Mayor Maestri has recently purchased the building, however, and it will be restored.

87. *Napoleon House*, 500 *Chartres Street*. The old Girod home, better known as the 'Napoleon House' carries with it a fascinating story of legend and romance. The 'Napoleon Refuge' tradition evidently grew out of an incident in which Mayor Girod of New Orleans offered his home to the exiled emperor, should he arrive in the city. An admiring and enthusiastic public perpetuated the tradition, and for almost 115 years a variety of stories relating to Napoleon's home have been handed down as factual.

Henry C. Castellanos, commenting upon the tradition, states that 'the only basis for this legend which has been discovered is the fact that when Napoleon escaped from Elba, the news reached New Orleans while the leading citizens were assembled at the St. Philip Theater, later the Washington Ballroom, at a dramatic performance there. The wildest enthusiasm prevailed; the entertainment broke up and the excited populace, among whom Napoleon was extremely popular, collected at the Cabildo. The impression was current that the Emperor would make for America; nowhere could he count on so warm a welcome and feel himself so entirely at home as in New Orleans. Mayor Girod made a speech in which he dwelt on those ideas and announced that he would place his residence at the disposition of the illustrious exile upon arrival.'

Early accounts claim that Mayor Girod, a wealthy philanthropist, was chiefly responsible for the organization of a plot to rescue the hero of Austerlitz from his St. Helena prison, and furnished the funds to build a yacht, the 'Seraphine,' which was to be used in the expedition. The boat was to be commanded by a certain Captain Bossier, and was to carry a daredevil crew of Baratarians under the leadership of the expirate Dominique You. 'His [Dominique You's] intention was to effect a landing on St. Helena by night, abduct the imperial prisoner, and rely upon the fleetness of his vessel to outstrip pursuit.' It was claimed further that the plot had the knowledge and approval of Napoleon and his bodyguards, and that they had entered into the scheme.

A frenzy of excitement gripped New Orleans as the citizens pictured a 'lonely prisoner, watching from the heights of a rocky island,' waiting to be rescued and brought to the new land. But the death of the famous exile before the expedition could be gotten under way 'deprived the world of a news sensation.'

A very recently publicized legend has it that Napoleon managed to effect an escape from St. Helena, and a dummy was buried instead of the one-time emperor's corpse. Napoleon then started to Louisiana, but died en route and his body was buried in Lafitte, Louisiana, along with John Paul Jones and the pirate Jean Lafitte.

It was in this same building in 1834, thirteen years after the death of Napoleon, that his physician at St. Helena, Dr. Antommarchi, located one of his offices, at which the poor of the city were given medical attention without charge.

The old Girod home, now more than 140 years old, is still in good condition. It is an excellent example of the French style of building during this period. The structure is of stuccoed brick, three stories high with a cupola at the top. There is a two-story ell along the St. Louis Street side, formerly used as slave quarters. A winding stairway connects the ground floor with the upper apartments.

The first floor now houses a grocery store, restaurant, and bar. The second and third floors have been made into living quarters. The building was recently selected by the advisory committee of the Historic Buildings Survey as one of the houses worthy of preservation because of its historical interest.

L. from Chartres St. on St. Louis St.

88. 533 *St. Louis Street.* The old Chesneau residence, frequently called the 'Lafitte Bank,' is a typical relic of the days of the Spanish builders. Few buildings in the downtown section have attracted more attention from architects or served as models for more homes than this building. Simple and unobtrusive, it is a two-story structure of stuccoed brick, with massive walls and large openings. The design of the wrought-iron balcony, of the brackets supporting it, and of the grills before the large windows is striking in its graceful simplicity. The ceiling of the first floor of the main body of the house is much higher than that of the second. The apartments to the rear of the house are so arranged as to make exactly two floors corresponding to the tall first floor of the house; the third floor is on the same level as the second floor of the main house. In the slave quarters, which are arranged along the rear wall of the courtyard, the ceilings are again of irregular height, each floor being taller than the corresponding floor of the wing, with the result that the slave quarters are taller than the house itself. An arched carriageway runs along one side of the house, opening on a flagged court in the rear. A glass-enclosed porch on the second floor, supported by three arches and having fine fan windows, overlooks the courtyard. A graceful spiral stairway, lacking a supporting center post, gives access to the rear apartments.

The structure was erected by Jean Louis Chesneau in 1800 as a residence. At the beginning of the Civil War the building (then 19 St. Louis Street) became the house of Lafitte and Dufilho, real-estate merchants, a fact which probably accounts for the general belief that this building housed a bank operated by the Lafitte brothers. There is nothing to show that the Lafitte member of the firm was related to the celebrated Baratarians.

Return and continue on Chartres St.

89. *Maspero's Exchange, 440 Chartres Street.* Of all the spots of historic interest in the French city, probably none has witnessed more actual drama than the old Exchange Coffee House, better known today as Maspero's Exchange. For many years during the early part of the 19th century this was the gathering place for the most picturesque characters of the Creole city. Here judges, generals, soldiers, merchants, and planters met to carry on commercial transactions, and the gay buccaneers of Barataria gathered in secret meetings. News and gossip of the day were

exchanged over cups of coffee, and public announcements of sensational events were read aloud by the town crier.

The Exchange building is one of the oldest in this part of the city, having been erected in 1788 by Don Juan Paillet. The property remained in the possession of his descendants almost a century. The establishment was probably the best-known auction mart of the city in the early days, and one of the most popular places for public entertainment.

The first two decades of the 19th century were filled with exciting events in New Orleans, and in these the Coffee House played an interesting role. It was here on the second floor, behind locked doors, that Jean and Pierre Lafitte and their followers met and planned many of their activities, and 'here it was that they received those so-called "respectable citizens" who came to see them in private.'

It is claimed that the defense of New Orleans was planned here by Lafitte and Jackson. When the general was arraigned before Judge Hall and fined $1000 for contempt of court, it was to the Coffee House that the mob repaired to hear Jackson make his speech and refuse the $1000 purse made up by citizens.

L. from Chartres St. on Iberville St.; R. from Iberville on Decatur St.

90. *Custom House.* The Custom House, occupying the block bounded by Decatur, Iberville, North Peters, and Canal Sts., stands on what in earlier days was the levee of the river. Fort St. Louis once occupied the site, but was torn down by the Americans for the erection of a court house, which in 1848 was razed, along with a bethel standing near-by, for the construction of the present custom house. It is interesting to note that in the space of two centuries the Mississippi has receded approximately four city blocks to the east and has built up an extensive batture of alluvial soil now the foundation for numerous large buildings.

Henry Clay was present at the laying of the cornerstone in 1849. A. T. Wood was the architect and General P. G. T. Beauregard the technical supervisor. The War between the States intervened, and it was years before the structure was even approximately finished, the upper floor never being completed. General Butler, after taking possession of New Orleans in 1862, used the Decatur Street side as an office suite. The unfinished upper portion of the building was used as a military prison for Confederate soldiers. In the room under the Sub-Treasury office, Mumford, Confederate martyr, who had torn down the United States flag, was confined before his execution at the Old Mint.

The preparation of the foundation of the present building affords an interesting contrast to modern construction methods in which deepdriven piles, steel, and reinforced concrete are used. Heavy cypress planking, 7 feet in depth, was surmounted by a grillage of 12-inch logs and topped with a 1-foot layer of concrete. This apparently flimsy footing has well supported the four-story structure, a subsidence of only a foot or two – one end more than the other – being noticeable.

It was built of Quincy (Mass.) granite on a brick base at a cost of $5,000,000. Its classic simplicity is reflected in the Egyptian exterior and Grecian interior. Four center columns are rather highly decorative, while four columns at each end of the building are severely flat, with only half of their surfaces in bas-relief. In order to decrease the weight of the building, the Egyptian cornice was redesigned and recast in iron; the cupola has never been added, for the same reason.

The 'Marble Hall,' the large business room of the Customs Department in the center of the building on the second floor, is considered one of the handsomest rooms to be found anywhere. Although not as large as the famous St. George's Hall of Liverpool, England, it is more remarkable in that only marble and iron have been used in its construction. Measuring 128 by 84 feet with a height of 58 feet, it has panels of life-size bas-reliefs of Bienville and Jackson. The ceiling consists of a white and gold iron frame set with enormous ground glass plates supported by fourteen columns of pure white marble. The floor, of white and black marble, is set with heavy glass to afford light to the rooms below. As one enters from the comparatively dark and narrow corridors, the sunlight-suffused hall appears to be the glorified counting-room of a king.

Grace B. Dunn

WATER-FRONT TOUR

ONE of the most interesting outings for the tourist in New Orleans is a trip along the docks and water-front. It is here that an entirely different phase of the city's varied life is to be found, and sweeping panoramic views of city streets and winding river shore may be enjoyed.

Early, on a clear morning, the tourist will be treated to a view of the sun rising in the 'western' sky, an illusion explained by the fact that although New Orleans is, geographically speaking, on the east bank of the river, and Algiers, behind which the sun rises, is on the west bank, the Mississippi runs due north at Canal St. One also has the unique experience of going 'up' to the river. The difference between the street level and the summit of the levee is noticeable at first glance. During periods of high water the level of the river is ten to twenty feet higher than the street level, but this condition is only seasonal, and at normal stages, or during low water, the river is slightly above the level of most of the city.

Standing on *Eads Plaza* at the foot of Canal St. and facing toward the city one has a magnificent view of Canal St., a crowded artery of traffic penetrating the heart of the city in a straight line that finally blurs in the distance. On each side, the crowded buildings of the business section pile up against the sky, while on the right is the Vieux Carré in venerable age, a striking and charming contrast to the new city built on the left by the Americans through decades of enterprise.

The river in front of New Orleans is about half a mile wide. The expanse of muddy water writhes between the yellow clay banks of the levees carrying driftwood, small boats, and oceangoing vessels on its surface. Sea gulls from the Gulf sweep and soar above it searching for fish. Cloud shadows darken its surface, and the wind writes mysterious script in swiftly changing ripples that swirl above eddies and whirlpools. Often, in the winter, fogs cover its surface, and the constant sound of fog horns echoes between its hidden shores. It is a dim place of mystery in the blanketing darkness of night, with only the stars and the diffused lights of the city reflected in its turbulent current. In late spring, swollen with the icy water of its tributaries, it rushes past the city, gnawing at the imprisoning banks it once had the privilege of overflowing each year. Yet, in spite of its hostility to man, it has a fascination, a calming influence, and an eloquent silence that tells of the distant and strange places from whence its waters come and go and of the history unfolded on its banks. A trip along the New Orleans waterfront is indeed an experience to be remembered.

The levee at the foot of Canal St. has been made into a riverside plaza with balustrade and steps and concrete platform. The attractive office building of the Board of Port Commissioners, familiarly known as the Dock Board, stands on the left of Canal St., while the high viaduct, which carries the Algiers traffic, cuts off the view on the right-hand side. The wharf-ends are finished in the same design as the office building, but the evident attempt at group architecture is impaired by the viaduct, which divides the plaza into uneven sections and hides the lower wharf-end from view.

A colorful pageant of many changes has been unfolded here for four hundred years. The followers of De Soto passed down the river, after he died in 1543, on their way to Mexico. La Salle and Tonti passed in 1682. Indians and French voyageurs followed in pirogue and canoe; sailing ships from far countries struggled up from the sea; flatboats and keel boats from the upper reaches of the Ohio descended in ever-growing numbers. Then, in 1812, a strange craft, belching smoke and traveling without the aid of oar or sail, arrived from Pittsburgh, after having passed through the terrors of the New Madrid earthquake, to inaugurate steamboat navigation of the Mississippi. By 1820, flatboats and oceangoing ships were piling the levee high with merchandise of every variety, and pouring out streams of passengers and workmen into the narrow lanes between the piles of goods. Sometimes the swollen river, laden with uprooted trees and wreckage, splashed over the levee top into the streets below, chilling the hearts of the citizens with fear of flood. It was here, in 1862, that Federal warships under Farragut covered the city with their guns while wharves and shipping went up in smoke and flame. King Rex used to land here on the day preceding Mardi Gras, arriving from his mythical kingdom to take possession of the city and rule over its gay and noisy crowds.

A walk on the levee was a favorite outing with Orleanians in the early days. After the levee became crowded with wharves and merchandise it was still a favorite Sunday promenade for the poorer classes, and even today it is not an unpopular walking place, especially on open stretches such as the one between Audubon Park and Southport.

A word picture of the old levee by Père Rouquette, one of the most gifted of the Creole poets, describes it as it was in 1837:

> *Promenade du Soir sur La Levée*
> Me voilà cheminant, le soir sur la Levée,
> L'oeil à terre baissé, l'âme au ciel élevée!
> Plus de hâve Irlandais, de rouge matelot,
> Qui roule le baril, ou pousse le ballot;
> Plus de ces *drays* pesants, à la chaîne bruyante,
> Qui voilent le soleil de poussière étouffante;
> Mais la foule, au bruit sourd, ce flot calme et mouvant,
> Qui cause et qui regarde un navire arrivant;
> La gros négotiant, l'âme tout inquiète,
> Qui cherche à lire au loin; *Salem*, ou *Lafayette*;
> La mère, qui vient voir s'il arrive un enfant;
> L'ami, s'il vient à bord un ami qu'il pressent;

Le marchand qui, cupide, attend ses modes neuves,
Modes de jeune fille et d'oublieuses veuves;
Et tandis que groupés, et dans l'anxiété,
Ceux-ci pleins de tristesse, et ceux-là de gaité,
Ils causent, moi, je passe; et, poursuivant mon rêve,
Je m'en vais, parcourant la longue et blanche grève;
Contemplant, tour à tour, les bois et le ciel bleu;
Jetant mes vers au fleuve, et ma prière a Dieu!

An Evening's Promenade on the Levee
Here, tonight, I wander on the levee;
My eye to earth cast down, my soul to Heaven lifted!
No more pale Irishmen, no more ruddy sailors,
To roll the barrel or wheel the bale;
No ponderous drays with clanking chains,
To veil the sun with stifling dust;
Only the rumbling crowd, a slow, surging wave,
Glibly prating and watching a distant packet;
The portly executive, anxiously
Squinting to discover what cargo she brings;
The anxious mother, ever hoping, half despairing,
Hoping to greet a son; the friend a friend expecting;
The greedy merchant, nervously awaiting
Latest styles for young maidens and forgetful gay widows.
Whereas, in anxious small groups they huddle,
Some filled with sorrow, some with joy;
While they chatter, I pass, pursuing my revery,
And wander along the endless white strand;
Distracted anon by the woods and the heavens,
I fling my verses to the River and my prayer to God!

Although differing slightly in outline and minor structural features, the wharves are, for the most part, all built on the same plan. The floor is usually of concrete on the levee top, and of heavy timber construction on the riverside extension. A high steel shed covers the entire area, with the exception of the loading platforms on each side. Railroad tracks parallel the platform on the city side so that merchandise can be handled directly from ship to car or vice versa. Occasionally, as at the banana wharves, the Stuyvesant Docks, and the Cotton Warehouse, the railroad tracks are built out on the shipside or riverside platform for greater convenience. It may also be noticed that none of these large wharves is built on solid foundations. The superstructure rests upon a series of posts, usually wood, but sometimes concrete, which in turn are based on piling driven deep into the levee side. A foundation of heavy material would slide into the river.

The Port of New Orleans, administered by the Board of Commissioners of the Port of New Orleans, a State agency, has a total water frontage, including river and lakes, of 133 miles. Of this, 50 miles is on the Mississippi and 11 miles on the Inner Harbor Navigation Canal. The wharf system of New Orleans proper extends about 10 miles along the river-front from the Public Coal and Bulk Commodity Handling Plant to the

Chalmette Slip. Approximately 6 miles of steel transit sheds, one stretch of which is more than 2 miles in length, are served by wharves, which, being parallel to the river, enable ships to dock without the assistance of tugboats. The wharves, concrete for the most part, rest on wooden piles; the sheds are constructed of steel framework with galvanized corrugated steel walls. Numerous fire walls make the quay system exceptionally fireproof. The standard width of the wharf-apron is 20 to 30 feet; of the sheds 200 feet; and of the concrete roadway in the rear 30 feet. The Public Belt Railroad services the sheds, while shipside tracks have been provided where needed.

Administration of the port is invested in the Board of Commissioners, consisting of five citizens appointed by the Governor and serving without pay for six-year terms. A general manager, who has active charge of all administration, is selected by the Board. Self-sustaining and without taxing power, the duties and privileges of the Board are: to regulate commerce and traffic of the port and harbor, and to take charge of and administer the wharves and public landings; to construct new wharves and sheds, and place and keep same in good condition; to maintain sufficient depth of water and to provide for lighting and policing; to collect fees from vessels using harbor and facilities, and to purchase and appropriate wharves and landings where necessary. All facilities are open on equal conditions to all shippers, and charges made against ships are based on gross cargo tonnage discharged or received.

Ninety steamship lines, two barge lines, and nine trunk railroad lines make use of the harbor. Warehouse facilities consist of 24 public warehouses for general use, 2 public cold-storage plants, 9 private cotton warehouses, and 5 railroad cotton warehouses. Wharves of various kinds and sizes are maintained by 28 industrial plants on the west bank and 18 on the east bank of the river.

The State controls 43 docks, the value of which, including equipment, amounts to $53,000,000. Chief among the port facilities are the 6 drydocks, the largest of which can accommodate ships up to 15,000 tons. Ten fuel oil companies operate in the harbor, each with private wharves. Bulk vegetable oil equipment, grain elevators, and a bulk loading plant are other major facilities. Sugar, bananas, and coffee are taken care of by special equipment.

The Erato, Desire, and Pauline Street Wharves are equipped with a total of 14 automatic pocket unloaders for the handling of bananas, each with an unloading capacity of 2500 bunches per hour. The normal movement of bananas through the port is 23,000,000 stems per year.

The river-front can be seen best in two separate trips, an uptown and a downtown tour, both of which start at the foot of Canal St. at Eads Plaza, and can be made either in an automobile or on foot. The levee, from Jefferson Ave. to Southport, however, can be seen only on foot. By automo-bile the road lies partly under the transit sheds, partly on paved outside roads on the city side of the docks, and at the cotton warehouse on the wide riverside platform of the wharf. The wharves are open from 7 A.M. to 4 P.M. The dock superintendents and foremen are courteous and pleasant. In making the tour on foot the best plan to follow is to walk along the riverside platform, looking into the open transit shed doors as one passes. When some point of interest on the inside of the levee is reached a crossing can be made through the transit shed to view it from the carloading platform. If an automobile is used, it will be necessary to park at times in the transit shed and seek out a better vantage point on foot. A tour of the harbor, taking in all the points of interest on both sides of the river, may be made on one of the excursion boats that dock at the foot of Canal St. (*See local newspapers for hours and rates.*)

UPTOWN RIVER-FRONT FROM; EADS PLAZA – 8 *m.*
(*For Points of Interest 1 to 159 see pages 302 to 380.*)

The following street-cars roughly parallel the tour route: Magazine car from Canal and Magazine Sts.; St. Charles car from Canal and Baronne Sts.

160. Coffee, to the extent of thousands of bags yearly, is unloaded at the *Poydras St. Wharf*, first stop on the uptown tour.

Concrete ramps lead to the second story on the city side for the convenience of trucks. Information can be readily obtained from the Dock Superintendent as to when the next coffee ship is to be unloaded.

An interesting feature of former days, still surviving in the handling of coffee, is the flag system of unloading freight, a method devised to take care of the many illiterate dock hands to whom written signs, used to sort materials, were meaningless. Flags, about 12 by 18 inches in length and of various colors with designs of stars, moons, birds, or alligators, are placed wherever different shipments or lots of merchandise are to be piled. The longshoremen, as they pass with their loads, are tapped on the shoulder by a foreman, who indicates the pile to which the carrier is to go by shouting the color or design of its flag. The system is very efficient, and provides employment to unskilled workers, with the exception of the color-blind illiterate.

A dredge boat can usually be seen at this section of the levee, especially during low water, dredging silt away from the dockside to maintain the required 30-foot depth. The current of the river shoots toward the west bank, and unless removed, silt will accumulate on the east bank in front of the wharves.

The freight sheds and railroad yards of the Louisville and Nashville Railroad, always a busy place, are at the foot of Julia St., just beyond the Julia St. Wharf.

161. Bananas are unloaded at the *Thalia St. Wharf*, which is used by the United Fruit Company. The wharf has two sheds, one for bananas and another for passengers. The greatest activity on the water-front will be found where the larger steamship companies make their landings, and here is always a lively scene when a passenger boat docks.

Half a dozen railroad spurs run into the banana shed at right angles and extend out to the riverside platform. Here are located the banana conveyors, constructed so that they can be lowered into the hatchways. Workmen in the hold of the ship place the bunches of bananas in the conveyor pockets which lift them to the wharf, where they are taken by carriers who tote them on their shoulders to railroad cars after being sorted, at sight, by men skilled in the profession. There is an element of danger in the work as tarantula spiders and large, green snakes (tree snakes and small boa constrictors) often hide in the bunches. The over ripe and broken bunches are sold to peddlers, who resell them in trucks and wagons in the city streets. The banana ships dock almost every other day. Exact information concerning their unloading can be obtained easily.

162. The *Railroad Ferry Landings* of the Trans-Mississippi Railroad Co. break the line of wharves between the Erato and Robin St. Wharves. Here the Texas and Pacific passenger and freight trains are transferred from the Annunciation Street Depot to the west bank. One of the ferries, the 'Gouldsboro,' saw service during the Civil War as the monitor 'Chickasaw.' All transcontinental railroad traffic had to be ferried across the river at New Orleans until the Huey P. Long Bridge was completed in 1935 at Nine-Mile Point. The landing of a railroad ferry, an interesting sight, is always attended with an element of risk; yet for more than fifty years many trains have been handled in this manner daily without a single serious accident.

163. The *Robin Street Wharf* begins at the foot of Terpsichore St. Here one sees a surprising variety of merchandise – hogsheads of tobacco, farm machinery, automobiles, cartons of carbon black, stacks of raw food products, and canned goods of every description. Lumber and millwork and bales of cotton are encountered in every transit shed.

At the foot of Market St., opposite the Market St. Wharf, stands the massive power plant of the New Orleans Public Service Corporation. Submarine cables from this plant carry power across the river bottom to the west bank. Near-by is the site of the old city water-works which supplied unfiltered water to the business section of the city for many years.

164. The *Jackson Avenue Ferry*, connecting the city with Gretna, makes another break in the wharf line. Here at the ferry landing, as well as at other points along the docks, boys may be seen diving and swimming in the river in warm weather. It is a dangerous sport and is discouraged by the port authorities. Until recently the river was the only swimmingplace available to the poor, many of the elders of the city having learned their first strokes under the wharves.

Just above Jackson Ave. and across the railroad tracks there is an open playground on Soraparu St., for many years the heart of the 'Irish Channel,' a district noted for its lawlessness in the decades following the Civil War. In the early part of the 19th century this section was the civic center of the City of Lafayette, which was annexed to New Orleans in 1852. It was a center of shipping and a favorite haunt of Lafitte, pirate and smuggler, who came up from Barataria into the river through what afterwards became Harvey Canal.

A driveway extends all the way from Jackson to Louisiana Ave. through the transit sheds. Many foreign ships dock in this section and on any day German, Norwegian, Japanese, Italian, or Russian ships may be seen. At the Louisiana end of the wharves a few fishermen may usually be found either fishing with lines from the docks, or with a dip net at the water level. The docks have long been a favorite fishing-place, especially with the Negroes, who find river catfish particularly to their liking.

165. The *Seventh Street Wharf* recalls an incident typical of the New Orleans levee. The old wharf which preceded the present one began to settle one day and,

despite attempts to hold it, gradually sank out of sight into the soft mud of the levee. A quicksand deposit had developed underneath. The same thing has happened to other wharves. In 1908 when the Dock Board was expropriating property along the river-front, an old open wharf which stood at the foot of Washington Ave. in those days and to which the Dock Board had just taken title suddenly disappeared into the river, carrying a train of freight cars with it. This sort of thing rarely happens now, but constant vigilance is required since weak spots may develop at any time in the levee. To ward off the danger every wharf is anchored by wire cables to buried dutchmen on the inside of the levee.

166. The *Stuyvesant Docks* of the Illinois Central Railroad Co. occupy the river-front from Louisiana to Napoleon Ave. These docks are the oldest on the river-front, having been built about 1907 to replace the docks destroyed by fire. Much of their area is empty now because of the recent slump in business, but during the World War many carloads of freight were handled here daily. The Illinois Central Railroad yards, repair shops, round houses, etc., lie behind the docks. One is impressed by the distance between the docks and the streets of the city in this section. Elsewhere, the city begins at the very foot of the levee, but here large unoccupied spaces and wide railroad yards intervene.

167. The *Public Cotton Warehouses* are situated just above Napoleon Ave. The group consists of three parallel rows of two-story concrete warehouses equipped with compressing machinery and affording 33 acres of warehouse space. The riverside loading platform and adjoining dock are over 2000 feet in length. Accommodations exist for the simultaneous loading or unloading of 258 cars. Electric traveling cranes, gasoline tractors, and trailers, and a complete machine shop make up the equipment. Three Webb standard high-density cotton presses have a capacity of 100 bales per hour. There are 33 acres of covered warehouse space with a storage capacity of 461,856 high-density bales. The daily unloading capacity is 7500 bales from cars, or 2000 bales from boats, with a wharf space accommodating four ships at a time. Visiting hours are from 7 to 4.

Built during the business peak of the World War, its capacity has never been taxed, owing mainly to changes in world agricultural and market conditions. But there is always plenty of activity. Tractors pulling trailers loaded with bales of cotton are constantly traveling about the warehouses and platforms. Workmen, both white and colored, shouting at one another, singing and laughing, move the heavy bales. Large shipments of sisal are also handled at the Cotton Warehouses.

168. The *Lane Cotton Mills* can be seen across the railroad yards, the buildings covering several city squares on Tchoupitoulas St. A modern pumping plant for handling oils in bulk from ship to railroad car is located on the upper end of the Cotton Warehouse riverside loading platform. Olive, palm, cocoanut, and linseed oils are among the items taken care of by this unit.

169. The *New Orleans Public Grain Elevators*, situated at the foot of Bellecastle St., were completed in 1917 and are built on an unusual kind of foundation. In preparing the levee for the heavy structure the baffle type of construction was used. Three lines

of piling, each some distance higher up the levee behind the other, were driven down and backed with a lining of concrete. Sand was filled in behind the concrete, providing a solid three-section foundation.

These elevators have a storage capacity of 2,622,000 bushels and are constructed of fireproof concrete. All machinery is electrically operated by a special type of dust-proof, ball-bearing motor. Weighing-scales of latest design, a modern laboratory for testing the grain, and a sacking plant with a capacity of 7700 bushels per hour are among the additional equipment. The unloading capacity from cars is 200,000 bushels daily; from boats, 80,000 bushels daily. The wharf is 2090 feet long, with five berths for loading and unloading vessels. Visitors may obtain a general view of the working of the elevators between 7 and 4.

170. The *Public Coal and Bulk Commodity Handling Plant*, situated at the foot of Nashville Ave., handles coal, coke, ore, and other bulk items. It has a storage capacity of 25,000 tons and an hourly loading rate, between vessels and freight cars, of 400 tons. The wharf can accommodate three vessels at one time. Loading and unloading is done by belt conveyors equipped with grab buckets; all machinery is electrically operated. Visiting hours are from 8 to 4.

From this point it is necessary to proceed on foot, as there is no roadway near the levee. The batture is very wide from Jefferson Ave. to Walnut St., and there is considerable space between the levee and the streets of the city. During low water the batture is covered with willows, and the young people of the neighborhood have swimming-places in their friendly shelter along the river's edge.

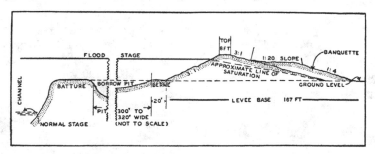

Levees are something more than ridges of grass-covered land shoveled up in a haphazard manner along the river bank. The diagram shows the grades of their various slopes and where the dirt is obtained to build them. It is taken from the riverside after a strip of land, or berme, twenty feet wide is skipped over. The excavation of land for the levee forms the borrow pit which lies between the levee and the batture. When the river is low, the berme, the borrow pit, and the batture are high out of water. At high water all are submerged and only the levees hold back the flood from pouring onto the land.

Houseboats and riverside shacks can be seen scattered here and there among the willows, but beyond Walnut St. they form an almost unbroken line as far as Protection Levee.

171. Across the railroad tracks on the right, beginning at State Street, are the beautiful grounds and new buildings of the *United States Marine Hospital* (*visiting hours 1-4 Tues., Thurs., Sun., and holidays*), the dome of the central building rising high into the sky. Sailors of both the naval and mercantile services are cared for in this hospital, which is owned by the Federal Government and operated by the United States Public Health Service. The reservation occupies four square blocks, bounded by the levee, Henry Clay Ave., and State and Tchoupitoulas Sts.

The first Marine Hospital was established in New Orleans in 1830. It was located on the west bank of the Mississippi and was not completed until after 1844. This hospital was used by the Confederates as a powder storehouse and was destroyed by an explosion in December, 1861. The second Marine Hospital was built after the Civil War, at Broad St. and Tulane Ave., where the new Criminal Court Buildings now stand. Removal to the present site was made in the 1880's. The first recorded ownership of this land dates to 1770, when Jean Baptiste le Moyne, nephew of Governor Bienville, sold the plantation two leagues above New Orleans to Jean Lafitte and François Langlois. The property changed hands a number of times, and while under the ownership of Étienne de Boré produced cane from which he successfully refined sugar. At the time the land was purchased by the Government there were two buildings, used as residences by the plantation owner and caretaker, and eight small, pegged, log cabins that had been used as slave quarters. The small buildings were razed, and four frame structures were erected to form the hospital. The two remaining buildings were repaired, and are still used as quarters by the commanding and executive officers of the institution. In 1929 the four frame buildings were replaced with fourteen modern brick structures, which serve as the present institution. The main building, of classic design with large columns, topped with an imposing dome, is five stories high, every room having an outer exposure. Grouped behind this structure, on spacious and well-landscaped grounds, are the smaller buildings which serve as quarters for attendants, laundry, etc.

An average of 430 patients are taken care of in the Marine Hospital, at tended by a staff of n medical and dental officers, 17 medical and dental internes, 55 nurses, and 7 laboratory technicians. Thirteen outside specialists in various fields of medicine and surgery are available for consultation.

A large mahogany lumber plant occupies the space between the Marine Hospital and Audubon Park. A stock of cut lumber is piled out in the yards, and a great raft of mahogany logs may be seen anchored in the river along the batture.

Audubon Park extends from Exposition Blvd. almost to Walnut St. (*See Motor Tour* 3.) This rear section, formerly neglected, has recently been landscaped with walks, driveways, and a lagoon. From the summit of the levee one can see the new zoo, the riding club buildings, and, in the distance, the large swimming pool. This part of the levee is a favorite camping spot for Boy Scouts and Camp Fire Girls, the latter having a cabin within the precincts of the park. A reclamation of the batture for a park addition is in progress. A levee, constructed with the aid of W.P.A. labor, extends out to the river from the main levee in the form of a wide U. It is planned to fill the enclosed space level with the levee top, land-scape it, and provide the city with a riverside park from which the river can be seen. As it is, the river is hidden by the levee from the view of persons at street level; the same obstruction makes it possible to see only housetops from the river.

172-173. After passing Walnut St. and the ferry, which was the main artery of auto-mobile traffic crossing the river before the new bridge, plainly visible from the levee, was constructed, the plants of the *North American Distillers, Inc.*, and the *United States Industrial Alcohol Company* can be seen on the right below the levee at the foot of Broadway. On the left, beyond the batture, a number of ships are tied up. The group includes ships belonging to several different steamship companies. Lack of business has put them out of commission, and as they are beyond the dock zone there is no charge for anchorage. Occasionally one is taken back into service; many of them may never be used again. Here also may be seen Negro batture dwellers, picturesque char-acters sunning and gossiping on the levee, seemingly without a care in the world.

174. The *Reservation of the United States Engineers, Second New Orleans District*, is one of the beauty spots of the levee. Here are situated the equipment yards and shops, together with several office buildings and beautifully kept grounds, all built above flood level on the batture. The Government unit stationed here is in charge of dredging, revetment work, levee construction, etc., for the southern half of Louisiana and Mississippi, and along the Mississippi River from Warrenton, Miss., to the head of the passes. The buildings occupy a tract of land on the levee one hundred yards wide and about a mile in length. A ranking United States Army offi-cer, usually a colonel, is in complete charge of the district office. The fleet, con-sisting of launches, dredge boats, cranes, steamboats, a tug, a floating asphalt plant, etc., is tied up at the foot of Burdette Street when not in use.

175. *Batture Dwellers*, who build their houses of driftwood salvaged from the Mississippi, inhabit a ramshackle shanty town sometimes called 'Depression Colony,' located between Carrollton Ave. and the protection levee at the Jefferson Parish line. It is composed of a wide variety of shacks, neat little cottages, and houseboats. The houses are built on stilts and are safe from all but the highest flood stages. During low water the batture is laid out in little gardens with chicken coops and pig pens. When the water rises, the livestock is taken up on the little galleries that run at least part way around each house and the occupants remain at home until 'Ole Man River' becomes too dangerous. Driftwood in the river supplies ample fuel; the river, plenty of fish; and the near-by willows, material out of which wicker furniture can be made and sold from house to house in the city. There is no rent to pay, as the batture is part of the river and the property of the United States, and consequently beyond the reach of local ownership or taxation. The varied occupations of the dwellers include fishing, wood-gathering, and automobile repair work; many work on Federal relief projects. Drinking water is procured from the neighborhood merchants.

176. The *Reserve Fleet* of the United States Shipping Board's Merchant Fleet Corporation, consisting (Nov., 1937) of 46 ships, is to be found on the west bank of the river opposite 'Depression Colony.' Most of these ships were built

in 1919 and 1920 and are all steel cargo boats ranging in size from 7500 to 10,000 tons. A Fleet Manager, with 5 assistants and a crew of thirty-five laborers and 6 watchmen, is in charge. While the boats are not kept painted, they are treated regularly with an oil preservative which prevents rust and decay. Most of these ships can be made ready for sea within a few weeks.

177-178-179. At the *Protection Levee*, which runs from the river to Lake Pontchartrain, protecting the city from a possible break in the upper levee, one can see the *Low-Water Intake Station* of the Sewerage and Water Board. On the other side of the protection levee in Jefferson Parish the several *Gambling Houses of Southport* present a well-kept and prosperous appearance. Although prohibited by law, these places will be found open or closed according to changes in local political conditions; usually they are open from 6 P.M. to 6 A.M.

180. Looming up against the sky, seeming all the higher because of the flatness of the surrounding country, the new *Huey P. Long Bridge* can be seen spanning the river at Nine-Mile Point. This is the only bridge spanning the Mississipppi below Vicksburg and is well worth crossing. A beautiful view of the city in the distance, as well as of the surrounding country, can be had from its summit. Bus connections may be made by walking in Oak St. four blocks to Leonidas St.

DOWNTOWN RIVER-FRONT FROM EADS PLAZA 6.3 *m.*

The following street-cars roughly parallel the tour route: Desire car from Canal and Bourbon Sts. to Desire St.; St. Claude car from Canal and N. Rampart Sts. to the American Sugar Refinery.

181. The second part of the river-front tour begins with the *Bienville Street Wharf* just below the viaduct leading to the Canal Street Ferry. Remodeled in 1931, it is used exclusively by the Morgan Line for both freight and passenger traffic and is always a busy place, as it is the connecting link between the eastern and western divisions of the Southern Pacific Railway System. Charles Morgan, for whom the line is named, was a prominent steamship and railroad promotor of the last century. Beginning his activities in the 1830's, he organized, in 1877, the Morgan's Louisiana and Texas Railroad on the bankrupt remains of the old Opelousas Railroad.

Before 1906, when the steel shed wharves began to replace the old open ones, this section of the levee was known as the sugar landing. The tall derelict of a building, without roof, floor, or window panes, just across the railroad tracks is all that remains of the first American Sugar Refining plant. The levee behind the wharf was covered with sugar sheds, and the neighborhood teemed with life. Here steamers may often be seen taking on passengers for a trip to New York, always a favorite sea voyage with Orleanians. Some of the old employees tell about the 'Louisiana,' a former Morgan Line boat, which has lain since 1905 at the bottom of the river just beyond the wharf. On account of improper loading, the boat broke her moorings at the wharf and turned over in the river. No lives were lost. Attempts were made to raise the ship, the mast of which still protruded from the water, but after lifting her almost to the surface the hoisting apparatus broke, and the boat, sliding toward the deep channel, completely disappeared from view. The river bottom at this point recedes rapidly, attaining a depth of well over 100 feet a short distance from shore.

An interesting difference in the handling of freight is to be noted in connection with the Morgan Line steamers. Elsewhere along the docks one sees freight being handled by derricks which lower the hoisting apparatus through hatches on the ship's deck, but the Morgan Line freighters have no hatches on deck; everything is handled through cargo doors in the side of the hull. The floor of the Bienville St. Wharf is cut with slanting ramps leading to the water's edge so that freight can be handled in this manner.

182. *Jackson Square* can be seen through the open doorways of the Toulouse Street Wharf. This is one of the few city squares in the United States where the architectural design is harmonious throughout. (*See French Quarter Tour.*) Here was the first ship landing and the front door of old New Orleans. All travelers coming to the city by river enjoyed this same view until it became obstructed by freight sheds and wharves. The sheds, which stood between the docks and the square, were razed recently, restoring the old view from the docks.

183. The *Dumaine Street Wharf* in front of the French Market occupies the site of the old Picayune Tier of the last century, where all the luggers docked. It was one of the most interesting sights of the old town – a gathering place for Greek, Italian, French, Negro, and Indian traders who brought their wares from the bayous and lakes of the lower Louisiana coast. While the huge square sails of their luggers flapped idly in the breeze these picturesque merchants would either be busily engaged in unloading and selling their oranges, oysters, fish, vegetables, etc., or cooking their meals over peculiar little charcoal stoves.

184. The *French Market* is still there, but the foodstuffs arrive by truck now. Part of the old market buildings, destroyed in the storm of 1915, have been replaced, and the entire market has been remodeled by the W.P.A. (*See French Quarter Tour.*)

185. The line of docks is again broken at the foot of Esplanade Ave. to provide landings for the *Third District Ferry* and the freight boats of the Southern Pacific Railroad Co. This was the first of the river railroad ferries and was established by Morgan about 1878. At first mules were used in place of locomotives to pull the cars on and off the ferry. Passengers crossed on the passenger ferry to Algiers, where the railroad train began its western journey.

186. The square fronting the river between Elysian Fields and Marigny St., occupied for years by the old Claiborne Power House, was originally the site of the famous *Marigny Mansion*, which stood at that point for almost a century. From the pillared galleries the city could be seen on the right; across the river lay the King's Plantation – afterwards Algiers; and far down on the right stretched the endless Marigny acres. Philip and Bernard de Marigny lived like kings, entertaining Louis Philippe, among other celebrities. Imitating his Yankee contemporaries, Bernard de Marigny converted his plantation into a city suburb. All of that part of the city from Elysian Fields Ave. to the Industrial Canal is built on his plantation.

187. The large brick building at the foot of Esplanade Ave. is at present the *Federal Jail*, but from 1838 until about 1900 it was used as a mint. (*See French Quarter Tour.*)

Several large buildings, of which the Alden Hosiery Mills and two industrial alcohol distilleries are the most important, stand out across the railroad tracks as one passes on through the wharves at this point.

188. The *Desire* and *Piety Street Wharves* are used chiefly by the Standard Fruit and Steamship Company, and one may see large quantities of coffee and bananas unloaded two or three times a week. The Central American passenger boats of this line also land here.

Cross railroad tracks and continue on Chartres Street, first street running parallel to the river.

189. At 3933 Chartres St., corner of Bartholomew St., is an *Old Cottage*, supposed to have belonged to the Macarty family. An incongruous later addition to this plaster-covered brick structure is the colored glass lattice-work framing four pillars on the front of the house.

190. The *Olivier Plantation Home* (formerly *St. Mary's Orphan Asylum*), 4111 Chartres St., once the palatial dwelling of David Olivier, was built about two hundred years ago. Its plantation life ended with the Civil War, at which time the occupant, Albert Piernas, was forced to sell. It was purchased by the Sisters of the Order of the Holy Cross to be used as a boys' orphan asylum.

The building, which is now occupied by an old lady and two children who migrated to the refuge from Pointe Coupee, is surrounded by new but deserted brick buildings, and can hardly be seen from the street. A wide gallery circles the house giving access to each room. The large rooms with old-fashioned fireplaces and very wide floor boards have beautiful fan-shaped transoms. On windows and doors can still be seen the motto, 'Silence is Golden,' testifying to the sisters' occupancy. The cisterns of the former plantation are interesting relics.

191. The U.S. *Army Supply Base*, just off Poland St. behind the Poland St. Wharf, dominates the surrounding neighborhood. These three large concrete buildings were constructed in 1918-19 at a cost of $15,000,000, and were intended to serve as a warehouse for Army supplies. The warehouses, identical in design, are each 600 feet long, 140 feet wide, and six stories high, with a floor area of over 500,000 square feet and a combined storage space of thirty-six acres. The first three floors of each unit are connected by ramps with the Poland St. Wharf, which stands directly behind on the river-front. At present only Unit 3 is used by the Government, partly as a warehouse for army supplies and partly for the offices of the W.P.A. The remaining storage space of the three units is under lease by the Dock Board. Unit 1 is occupied by the binder twine mill and bag factory of the International Harvester Company, and Unit 2 has been subleased as a commodity warehouse for shipside storage. The International Trade Exposition, backed by New Orleans manufacturers, was housed in Unit 2 from 1925 to 1929.

L. on Poland St. to St. Claude Ave.; R. from Poland St. on St. Claude Ave.

192. From the St. Claude Ave. Bridge an excellent view of the *Inner Harbor Navigation Canal* may be had. The locks to the left of the bridge were completed in 1921, and the canal was finally opened for general use in 1923. It is 5½ miles

long, with an average depth of 30 feet, has 11 miles of frontage, and an average width of 300 feet. The great entrance locks are built of reinforced concrete, and are 640 feet long and 75 feet wide, with a water depth of 31.5 feet. The Dock Board has constructed a public concrete wharf at Galvez St., 2400 feet long and 265 feet wide, with a steel transit shed 2000 feet long and 200 feet wide.

This inner harbor canal has fulfilled an ambitious scheme – a waterway connection between the river and the lake – advocated from the time Carondelet built his canal to Bayou St. John in the last decade of the 18th century. The canal as originally planned was to have been much smaller, but it was wisely decided to make it large enough to meet all requirements. It was hoped that private interests would build factories and wharf facilities along its banks, but as this idea failed to take root, the Dock Board constructed the Galvez St. public wharf and released the canal frontage for public service in the same manner and under the same terms as the other parts of the harbor are used. Shippers complained because of its distance from the heart of the city, but as soon as the freedom from traffic congestion which the location afforded was realized it gradually became one of the busiest sections of the port of New Orleans.

R. from St. Claude Ave. on Reynes St. to the levee.

193-194-195-196. The grounds and buildings of *Holy Cross College*, a boys' preparatory school; *Charbonnet Wharf*, the last of the public docks; the low buildings of the *New Orleans Compress Company*, a cotton warehouse behind the wharf; and the *Todd Dry Dock Company* are to be seen along the river in that order.

197. *Jackson Barracks*, facing Delery St. and the river and extending to the St. Bernard Parish line, were constructed during the administration of Andrew Jackson to be used as a garrisoned military post for the defense of New Orleans and as a depot for interchanging troops garrisoning the river forts during the months when yellow fever was prevalent. The construction of the post was unique, since it was designed much in the manner of an Indian fort, with a high surrounding wall and four towers provided with rifle slots and embrasures for small cannon. Large cisterns at each building supplied ample drinking water. It is said that Jackson, remembering his unpleasant relations with the Creoles in 1814-15, advised the War Department to construct the barracks not only for the defense of New Orleans but as a self-sustaining fort capable of resisting an attack by the townspeople.

Federal troops were quartered at the barracks until about 1920, at which time the place was abandoned by the War Department as a garrisoned post and leased to the State of Louisiana for the housing of National Guard units. Troops have embarked from the Barracks to participate in every major conflict engaged in by the United States. When Louisiana seceded in 1861 the post was taken over by the Confederate authorities but was later captured and garrisoned by Federal troops. Today Jackson Barracks maintains 14 units of National Guardsmen (about 700 men), provides warehouses for Federal and State property, and houses about forty families of Guardsmen.

The reservation consists of approximately 84 acres, extending from the river to St. Claude Ave. Eighty buildings, ranging from large, brick structures with 18- and 22-inch walls a century old, to small, temporary, sheet-iron buildings, are capable of garrisoning about 1500 soldiers. Temporary barracks and canvas shelter could accommodate from 2000 to 3000 additional troops. The buildings have been remodeled and cleaned up under a Works Progress Administration project at the present time (1937), and several new buildings constructed.

198-199-200-201-202. Adjoining Jackson Barracks, just across the St. Bernard Parish line, is one of the old plantation buildings of Spanish times, originally the *Home of the de Lesseps*. Dr. L. A. Mereaux, sheriff of St. Bernard Parish, is the present owner and occupant. Several blocks more bring one to the *Stock Yards* and *Abattoir*. On Friscoville Ave. stands the former *Jai Alai Building*, painted in dabs of color and now used as a gambling house. The large assembly plant of the *Ford Motor Company* follows, and adjoining it is the immense refinery building of the *American Sugar Refining Company* with wharves and conveyors along the levee and over the road. Visitors are admitted to the plant at 10 A.M. daily, except on Saturdays and Sundays; there is no charge for admission.

203. Just beyond the refinery buildings another fine old plantation home is to be seen with its pillared galleries and fine old oak trees. Known as *Three Oaks Plantation* and the former home of the Cenas family, it is now the property of the American Sugar Refining Company. During the bombardment of the Chalmette Batteries in April, 1862, by Admiral Farragut and his fleet the right end column was demolished and has since been replaced. Similar plantation homes, within spacious grounds, lined both sides of the river below New Orleans in ante-bellum days.

204. About a quarter of a mile farther on one comes to the *Chalmette Slip*, the property of the Southern Railway Co. Started about 1907 but not completed until 1915, it is the only slip of its kind on the Mississippi. With a length of 1800 feet, a width of 300 feet, and a depth of 30 feet, the slip has two concrete docks, one on each side. Dock 1 is a single-story structure 1300 feet long and 120 feet wide, with a floor area of 156,000 square feet. Dock 2 is two stories in height, 1780 feet long, and 130 feet wide, with a floor area of 418,000 square feet. Six vessels can be accommodated at one time. A specially constructed double-unit conveyor, electrically driven, is used for unloading copra from shiphold to freight car. The Macarty home, used by Jackson as his headquarters during the Battle of New Orleans, was razed in the construction of the slip.

205-206. Below the slip, *Chalmette Monument* and the *National Cemetery* occupy the old battlefield where Jackson and his gallant crew repulsed the British invasion of 1814-15, and where feeble batteries attempted to stop Farragut in 1862. (*See St. Bernard-Plaquemines Tour.*)

Return to American Sugar Refinery to obtain street-car.

MOTOR TOUR 1

From CANAL STREET *to* LAKE-FRONT, 30 *m*.

The following street-car and bus services roughly parallel the tour route: West End car from any place on Canal St.; transfer to Robert E. Lee bus (for Spanish Fort and Lake-Front) at West End; transfer to Gentilly-Broad bus (for Gentilly section of tour) at Canal and Broad Sts.

CANAL STREET, one of the widest streets in the United States and reputed to be one of the best lighted streets in the world, is the center from which all activities in New Orleans radiate and the goal to which all return. All street-cars, except the Napoleon Ave., and many bus lines begin and end here, and when a New Orleanian goes to town, be it for business or pleasure, he goes to Canal St. All side streets are num bered uptown and downtown (north and south) from Canal St. beginning with 100; and most of the streets between the river and Rampart change their names in crossing. Traffic at peak hours over-flows both roadway and sidewalk, and on occasions like Mardi Gras and New Year's Eve the street becomes a seething mass of pleasure-bent humanity.

A breadth of 171 feet is distributed between two spacious roadways, wide side-walks, and a wider neutral ground; both the sidewalks (called *banquettes* in New Orleans) and the neutral ground are paved in modernistic style with red and white terrazzo marble, reflecting the brilliant sunlight by day and the flood of electric lights by night. Lamp posts are ornamented with plaques illustrative of the French, Spanish, Confederate, and American dominations. Beyond Claiborne Ave. the street is residential and the neutral ground becomes a beautiful green lawn planted with clumps of palms at regular intervals. Canal Street extends in an unbroken line from the river to the cemeteries, a distance of 3½ miles.

Originally, a ditch or shallow canal, from which the street takes its name, ran here along the ramparts of the Vieux Carré. When the canal was filled up the place became the town commons, dividing the old city on the right or downtown side from the newer uptown section. At first, wash hung flying in the wind, and ped-dlers did business in the weed-grown center. Soon carriages were rattling over cobblestones before galleried residences. Then business broke in and took posses-sion. Today, although the chief retail stores of the city line its sides, few of the buildings along Canal Street are new and many of them, their façades remodeled, go back to ante-bellum days.

The tendency of certain business activities to concentrate in one section of the city, although not quite so pronounced as it once was, is to be noted in the side streets in the vicinity of Canal. Most of the fur dealers are still to be found along North Peters and Decatur Sts. Royal St. has become one of antique shops which, resembling the bazaars of the Orient, line the street on both sides for blocks and pour out their strange and beautiful wares on the sidewalk. Coffee roasters and packers are to be found, for the most part, along Magazine and Tchoupitoulas Streets from Canal to Howard Ave. Farther uptown, Poydras St. from Camp to the river is the wholesale fruit, produce, and poultry center, while the principal meat packers are found near Magazine and Julia Sts. The section between Camp St. and the river, and Canal St. and Jackson Ave., contains most of the wholesale jobbing houses and many of the manufacturing plants. Carondelet St. has always been the street of the cotton brokers and bankers.

1. The *Canal Street Ferry*, crossing between New Orleans and Algiers, is an excellent place from which to view the city, especially at night.

2. *Eads Plaza*, at the foot of Canal St., named in honor of James Buchanan Eads, who planned and constructed the jetties at the mouth of the river below New Orleans, affords an excellent view of both Canal Street and the Mississippi. Interesting foot and motor tours may be taken along the river-front from Eads Plaza (*see River-Front Tour*).

3. The *Louisville and Nashville Terminal* stands to the right beyond the viaduct by which traffic reaches the ferry.

4. *Liberty Monument*, Canal St. near N. Front St., is a simple granite shaft standing in the center of the neutral ground and commemorating the declaration that the citizens 'of right ought to be and meant to be free' of the obnoxious carpetbag rule. It was here, on September 14, 1874, that shots were fired by citizens of the city, challenging further invasion of their right to rule themselves. Seventeen years later the cornerstone of a monument to commemorate the event was laid, and a few months later the monument, designed by Charles R. Orleans, was erected. The granite shaft is thirty-five feet in height and cost a total of $8000. Each year, on September 14, a large crowd gathers about the monument for ceremonies.

5. The *Custom House*, 423 Canal St., is especially interesting for its Marble Hall. (*See French Quarter Tour.*)

6. The *Boston Club*, 824 Canal St., reputedly the second oldest club in the United States, was founded in 1841 by a group of mercantile and professional men for the purpose of enjoying more privacy in playing Boston, a card game much in favor at that time. The members first met on Royal St.; the present location, a handsome structure erected as a home before the Civil War by a Dr. W. N. Mercer, has been occupied since 1887.

Membership is limited to 400. Non-resident members are admitted, and temporary memberships are extended to Army and Navy officers, the clergy, and members of the diplomatic service. Out-of-town visitors invited by club members are extended the courtesies of the club.

The club's facilities include reading-rooms, a dining-room, and many other modern accommodations. An excellent French cuisine is served table d'hôte or à la carte from a large, well-equipped kitchen. Old Negro servants, in the employ of the club for many years, administer to the needs of the members. Dominoes and bridge are the games in vogue, Boston having become merely a tradition.

Women are entertained at a dance on New Year's Eve. On Mardi Gras day the club is host to the Queen of Carnival. It is here, while the socially élite view the scene from a balcony constructed across the façade of the club, that Rex toasts his queen with a goblet of champagne. A buffet supper is usually served after the evening parade of Comus. Election of officers is held annually on the first Saturday in December, an occasion for a lavish dinner and celebration.

Cross Canal St. neutral ground at Dauphine St.; return to Baronne St.; R. from Canal St. on Baronne St.

7. The *Immaculate Conception (Jesuit) Church,* 132 Baronne St., opened in 1857, is said to be the first in the world officially dedicated to the Immaculate Conception. Through purchases extending over a period of forty years and concluded in 1875, the Catholic Society for the Diffusion of Religious and Literary Education acquired land for the erection of a church and college proposed by the Jesuit Father Jean Baptiste Maisonnabe. When Father Maisonnabe died of yellow fever in 1848, Father Cambiaso, who became head of the New Orleans mission, purchased additional ground, enlarged the college, and drew plans for a new church. The original three-story church, which, despite its strong, compact foundations, had begun to sink into the soft alluvial underlying soil, was rebuilt in 1927-28. Intensive reconstruction followed as closely as possible the plan of the original structure

The new building is entirely fireproof. It is built on piling with reinforced concrete floor and roof slabs. The exterior, carrying out the Hispano-Moresque theme, is of tapestry brick with limestone and terracotta trim; the base is of granite. During the process of restoration, each tower of the Baronne St. façade was heightened and crowned with domes. The former front portico was eliminated and the structure built out to the street line in order to increase seating capacity. During renovation the strong Hispano-Moresque motif of the interior was preserved. The interlacing cast-iron arches of the triforium, the cast-iron columns and semi-columns of the nave and aisles, the cast-iron pews, the three altars and the communion rail, and all of the stained glass were retained. The entire first floor, with the exception of the sacristy and the space occupied by the pews, is of white and green marble. The stations of the cross are of stained glass, painted like glowing medallions in the side naves above large windows that portray, in vivid coloring, incidents in the lives of the saints of the Society of Jesus. These stations, genuine works of art, were prepared and painted under the direction of two French Jesuits, the Rev. Arthur Martin and the Rev. Charles Cahier.

Another artistic triumph is the great gilt bronze altar flashing back in dazzling splendor all the light thrown upon it. Its Moorish domes and miter-shaped arches harmonize architecturally. This altar, designed in New Orleans by Mr. James Freret, was made in Lyons, France. Displayed at the Paris Exposition of 1867-68, where it won first prize, the altar reached the city in November, 1873.

Above the high altar, in a niche ablaze with golden stars and snowy lilies, stands a statue of the Immaculate Virgin Mother of God, carved of stainless marble by Denis Foyatier, French sculptor. Designed originally for the private chapel of Queen Marie Amélie, wife of Louis Philippe, this statue was, upon the re-establishment of the French Republic, shipped to New York and sold.

The shrine, a gift of Mrs. James Denis Denègre, reproduces that of Our Blessed Lady in the church of the Jesuit Fathers at Pau, France. Three great silver candlesticks, the rare handiwork of old-time silversmiths, are decorated in motifs of live-oak branches, squirrels, and acorns. They were confiscated by Federal officers during the Civil War, but were later restored by order of General Benjamin Butler.

At the main entrance is a striking bronze figure of St. Peter seated on a marble throne. It is assigned to the sixteenth century and is a copy of a statue standing beneath the mighty dome of St. Peter's Cathedral in Rome.

L. from Baronne St. on Cramer St.

8. The *Hibernia Tower*, Hibernia Bank Building, 812 Gravier St. (*open weekdays* 9.30-4.30; *Sat.* 9-4; *admission* 25¢), the highest point in New Orleans, is twenty-three stories high, and is the only observation tower in the city. The lantern in the top of the tower is 355 feet above the street and can be seen at night for several miles. A walkway circles the bottom of the tower, and the directions north, south, east, and west are indicated so that one may know his exact position. Favrot and Livaudais were the architects.

Looking north from the tower on a clear day one can see the buildings of the Shushan Airport on Lake Pontchartrain 10 miles away. Looking toward the west along the New Basin Canal can be seen patches of the Illinois Central Railroad, the Jahncke drydocks, and a number of schooners lying in wait for freight. Still further in the distance is the Huey P. Long Railroad and Vehicular Bridge. Looking south from the tower one gets an excellent view of the largest crescent of the river, beginning near Governor Nicholls St., widening at Canal St., and swinging out to curve back in near the water purification plant on Jefferson Highway above Carrollton Ave. On the eastern side of the tower one looks directly down into the business section of New Orleans. From here there is an excellent view of the downtown docks, huge freighters coming and going, and the Canal St. ferries plying back and forth between New Orleans and Algiers just across the river.

The *Pickwick Club*, one of the older and more exclusive clubs of the city, has its quarters in the Hibernia Building. The club was founded in 1857 by a group of prominent young men from the Garden District of New Orleans. It was this group which planned one of the first of the Carnival organizations, the 'Mystic Krewe of Comus,' and shortly after started the Pickwick Club, named for Dickens' famous character. For some time the two organizations were identical, but in 1884 it was decided that each should become an independent club. In 1899 the Pickwick Club commissioned Stanford White, the noted New York architect, to design the handsome edifice at 1028 Canal St., which the club occupied until 1934, when the present quarters were obtained.

The quarters are spacious and well arranged, and include card rooms, reading-rooms, a library, and a large dining-room, all of which are decorated with paintings and statues. The carved figure of Mr. Pickwick in 'black frock coat, gaiters, red vest and breeches' stands as a silent host to those who enter the Pickwick Club.

Membership in the Pickwick Club is limited to 150. There are junior memberships for men between the ages of 21 and 25. Non-resident members are admitted, and there are special memberships for commissioned officers of the Army and Navy, the clergy, and members of the diplomatic corps.

Each Thursday evening the members enjoy their regular club dinner. During the carnival and football seasons women guests are frequently entertained. No resident non-members are admitted, but visitors to New Orleans may be given guest cards by members.

9. The *New Orleans Cotton Exchange*, Cotton Exchange Building, 801 Gravier St., founded in 1871 as successor to the Merchants Exchange, is said to be the second largest cotton exchange in the United States today. The chief purpose of the organization is to promote and regulate the buying and selling of cotton and to furnish information relative to this commodity. The exchange handles every variety of cotton from every section of the country. The present membership (1937) is approximately 400. The Board of Directors meets on the first Wednesday of each month, and election of officers is held annually. Membership fees are fixed each year by the board.

L. from Gravier St. on Carondelet St.; L. from Carondelet St. on Canal St.

10. From the *Southern Railway Terminal* at Canal and N. Saratoga Sts. a small, well-planted parkway may be seen to the right at Elk Place. The large building facing the parkway on the lake side was formerly the Elks Home.

11. The *John T. Gibbons House*, 2006 Canal St., lake corner S. Prieur and Canal Sts., was the headquarters of Cardinal Gibbons, brother of the former occupant, on his yearly visits to New Orleans.

12. The former *Straight University*, between S. Tonti and S. Rocheblave Sts., now houses a Negro school and the Negro Y.W.C.A. Straight University, established in 1869 by the northern Congregational Church for the education of Negroes, was first located at Esplanade and Bourbon. The present buildings were erected in 1877 after a fire had destroyed the original school. Straight University has become

part of Dillard University, which had its first formal session in 1935.

13. *Bolivar Place*, downtown side of Canal St. at Broad St., a memorial square, contains a granite block marked with a bronze plaque and dedicated by the city in 1930 to Simón Bolivar, the great South American warrior and statesman. The dedicatory exercises took place on December 17, the one hundredth anniversary of the death of Bolivar. Mayor Walmsley presented the memorial for the city, and it was accepted by Diego Matute Ruiz, consul general of Venezuela, the first country liberated by Bolivar. The plaque bears the following inscription: 'Bolivar Place, Dedicated by the City of New Orleans to Simón Bolivar, 1783-1830, the liberator of Colombia, Venezuela, Ecuador, Peru, Bolivia, and Panama.'

14. *Sacred Heart of Jesus Church*, uptown lake corner of S. Lopez and Canal Sts., is built of pressed brick with stone trimming in the Romanesque style; Gothic features – the pointed arch of the main entrance and the pointed gable of the roof – have been incorporated in the design. A tall, square campanile, one of the few to be seen in the city, rises from the right-hand side of the building. In the interior attention is centered on the high altar of varicolored marble, elaborately carved and inlaid with rich mosaic work. The two side altars harmonize in design and composition with the main altar, and the stations of the Cross are mosaics, with colored figures set against a gold background.

15. *Dreux Monument*, downtown side of Canal St. at Jefferson Davis Pkwy., honors Charles Didier Dreux, the first officer from New Orleans to volunteer his services in the Civil War. Colonel Dreux, who had organized the Orleans Cadets at the beginning of the war, was also the first Confederate officer from Louisiana to lose his life in the conflict. The bust, slightly more than life-size, rests on a six-foot pedestal, both being composed of Stone Mountain granite. It was designed by Victor Holm and greeted in 1922.

16. *Jefferson Davis Monument*, facing Dreux Monument, stands in the midst of a well-kept parkway, surrounded by palms and cactus. The champion of States' rights and the President of the Confederate States is represented in the attitude of addressing his people in behalf of the beliefs he cherished.

Davis was a citizen of Mississippi and a frequent visitor to New Orleans, where he had scores of close friends. In 1889 he died at the home of Charles E. Fenner, 1134 First St. (*See Motor Tour* 4.)

For some time his body lay in state in the City Hall, and for two years afterwards it reposed in the mausoleum of the Army of Northern Virginia, at Metairie Cemetery. In 1898 the Jefferson Davis Monumental Association was organized, and after a period of thirteen years, $35,000 was raised and Edward Valentine was employed to design the statue. On February 22, 1911, the fiftieth anniversary of the inauguration of Davis as President of the Confederacy, the statue was unveiled with an impressive ceremony.

The statue rests on a pedestal of South Carolina granite. The front side is ornamented with the seal of the Confederacy, surrounded by a laurel wreath in bronze. At the upper end of the dado is a row of thirteen stars, and on the back of the pedestal is engraved: 'His name is enshrined in the hearts of the people for whom he suffered, and his deeds are forever wedded to immortality.' The monument is 25 feet in height.

17-18-19. *Cypress Grove, Greenwood,* and *Metairie Cemeteries* are at the intersection of Canal St., City Park Ave., and Pontchartrain Blvd. (*See Cemeteries.*)

R. from Canal St. on City Park Ave.; L. from City Park Ave. on Canal Blvd.

20. *Wedell (James) Monument,* Canal Blvd., at intersection of City Park Ave., is a memorial to 'Jimmy' Wedell, popular young aviator of New Orleans, who lost his life in 1934 while engaged in routine instruction work at the Wedell-Williams Airport near Patterson, Louisiana. At the time of his death Wedell held the world speed record for land planes, and was making plans to compete in the London-to-Melbourne race which was to take place shortly. On the pedestal is an eagle with wings spread for flight, and at the base of the monument is the single word 'Wedell.'

Cross neutral ground at Rosedale and return R. from Canal Blvd., on City Park Ave.; cross New Orleans Navigation Canal; L. from City Park Ave. on Pontchartrain Blvd.

21. The *New Orleans Country Club,* 6440 Pontchartrain Blvd., has golf, tennis, and swimming facilities restricted to members and their guests. (*See Recreational Facilities.*)

Return and continue on Pontchartrain Blvd.

22. The *Lakewood Country Club,* Pontchartrain Blvd. beyond Metairie Cemetery, formerly known as the West End Country Club, has golf and tennis facilities restricted to members and their guests. The membership is largely Jewish. (See *Recreational Facilities.*)

Lake Pontchartrain Shore, one of the most popular spots in New Orleans for summer amusements, offers a variety of sports, such as swimming, boating, and fishing. Along the shore are found the settlements of West End and Milneburg, an amusement park and bathing beach, a State-owned airport accommodating both airplanes and seaplanes, and a number of lighthouses maintained by the United States Government. A few miles from West End are the ruins of Spanish Fort, erected by the Spaniards during their domination of Louisiana. A stepped concrete sea wall extends eastward from West End for about six miles; the steps lead directly into the water, which is usually quite shallow near the wall.

Besides the Rigolets, which is an outlet from Lake Pontchartrain into Lakes St. Catherine and Borgne, and Chef Menteur Pass, which connects Lakes Pontchartrain and Borgne, there are several canals intersecting the shore. The Inner-Harbor Navigation Canal, connecting the lake with the Mississippi River and popularly known as the Industrial Canal, and the New Orleans Navigation Canal are navigable waterways. Bayou St. John (*see Tour* 2) and two emergency drainage canals running along Orleans and London Aves. also extend to Lake Pontchartrain.

23. *West End*, Pontchartrain Blvd. at Lake Pontchartrain, is a small suburban area in the extreme northwest corner of New Orleans at the western border of Orleans Parish. The chief attractions are West End Park, 'Bucktown,' and the Southern Yacht Club. Several night clubs are also located here.

Formerly a favorite spot for outings, when gay young blades used the 'Shell Road' (now Pontchartrain Boulevard) as a speedway to test the mettle of their horses, West End is still a charming place for picnics. The park, which is protected from the lake by a concrete sea wall, has an abundance of shade trees, and a large number of refreshment stands where crabs and shrimps are served in season. A special attraction of the park is the large fountain in operation during the summer months. Here people sit for hours on warm nights watching the play of the waters in various colors, each spray an individual representation. One of the loveliest of these is known as the 'Prairie Fire,' a fountain of water illuminated by gold, red, yellow, and blue lights.

Just across the bridge in the western section of West End, in the 'Free State of Jefferson,' is a small settlement known as 'Bucktown.' At one time a wide-open spot, it is today a comparatively quiet place. A few of the raised camps extending out into the water, similar to the ones that once lined the entire lakefront, are still to be seen.

The home of the Southern Yacht Club is located in West End, its two-story frame structure extending over the lake from the left bank of the New Basin Canal. The building houses an office, clubrooms, dormitories, and a café. The facilities of the club are restricted to members and guests of members. Numerous boats and racing sloops are kept in the yacht pen. An annual spring regatta is held in April, and in the early fall the club acts as host to the Gulf Yacht Association, which comprises yacht clubs along the coast of Louisiana, Mississippi, Alabama, and Florida. On Saturdays and Sundays races may be watched from the sea wall.

Return to Lake Ave. Bridge; cross New Orleans Navigation Canal; L. on Lakeshore Drive.

24. *New Canal (Pontchartrain) Lighthouse*, opposite the Southern Yacht Club Pier, was built in 1890 on the site of a former station constructed in 1838. Mrs. Fannie Norvell, retired in 1932, was the last but one woman lighthouse-keeper serving in the United States.

Lake Shore Park, a five-and-one-half-mile parkway extending from West End to Shushan Airport, is being developed by the W.P.A. Picnic grounds, tennis courts, baseball diamonds, refreshment stands, and parking space are to be constructed within an area extending back 300 to 500 feet from the sea wall. The land now forming the park was created by an extension of the shoreline 3500 feet into the lake, where a concrete sea wall was constructed and the enclosed area filled in with sand pumped from the lake, thus transforming mosquito-breeding swamps into a valuable highland, which serves also as a dike protecting the city from backwaters of the lake. Along the sea wall, from West End to the Industrial Canal, the people of New Orleans swim throughout the summer months.

25. *Pontchartrain Beach* (*no adm. charge; suits rented at a nominal charge*), near the mouth of Bayou St. John, is a popular amusement resort. The sandy beach extends for several hundred feet along the shore. A small park, with bathhouses, numerous concessions, refreshment stands, lunch rooms, and mechanical rides such as the roller coaster, Ferris wheel, and whip, adjoins the board walk. A wooden pier extends out over the lake from the concrete sea wall along the lakefront. A powerful amplifying system broadcasts music from the bandstand. Throughout the season, which usually lasts from May until September, the management also offers free vaudeville acts.

26. *Spanish Fort*, .3 m. right from Pontchartrain Beach along Bayou St. John, was the first fortification erected in the immediate vicinity of New Orleans. Dating back to the early 18th century, it was at first nothing more than a redoubt called Fort St. John. During the Spanish régime the fort was enlarged and rebuilt of brick and popularly known thereafter as 'Spanish Fort.' The fort was garrisoned during the invasion of the British in 1814-15. As a fortification it lost its importance after the construction of Forts Pike and Macomb and fell into its present state of dilapidation. The building of the railroad to Milneburg made that place the entrance for passengers from the lake routes, and Spanish Fort became a resort. A large hotel was built and famous visitors, among whom were the Duke of Saxe-Weimar, William Makepeace Thackeray, General Grant, and Oscar Wilde, were entertained there. A casino and various amusement concessions, including a theater, were added about 1900, and several seasons of opera were given. Fire and changing conditions have brought about the complete disappearance of all these buildings. Today nothing is left but the foundations of the old fort and the unknown grave within its iron railing under the oak.

Several legends have been woven into the history of the fort. The unmarked grave is said to contain the remains of a Captain Pablo, a Spanish officer, who was slain by Wah-he-wawa, an Indian chief, at a near-by trysting place of the officer and the chief's daughter, Owaissee. The four large trees to the west of the ruins are supposed to mark the graves of four Spanish officers. Another legend has it that Princess Charlotte of Brunswick and her lover, the Chevalier d'Aubant, used to while away many happy hours under two live oak trees near the fort.

Grace King gives the following account in *Old Families of New Orleans*:

> Other settlers besides those of flesh and blood have given their name to the pleasant country-side of the Bayou St. Jean. Gayarré relates a romance, which the historians make a place for in their narratives, and which is still repeated by all guides. It deals with Charlotte, the beautiful daughter of the Duke of Brunswick, a paragon of virtue, beauty and talent, who was married to Alexis, the son of Peter the Great, after she had given her heart to the Chevalier d'Aubant, an officer of her father's household. On,the day of her marriage he received a passport and permission to leave the country.

To continue, in Gayarré's words:

> Whither he went no one knew, but in 1718 he arrived in Louisiana with the grade of Captain in the colonial troops. Shortly after this,

he was stationed at New Orleans, where, beyond what was necessary in the discharge of his duties, he shunned the contact of his brother officers and lived in the utmost solitude.

On the banks of the Bayou St. Jean, on the land known in our day as the Allard plantation, there was a small village of friendly Indians. With the consent of the Indians, d'Aubant formed there a rural retreat where he spent most of the time he could spare from his military avocations. Plain and rude was the soldier's dwelling, but it contained, as ornament, a full length and admirable portrait of a female, surpassingly beautiful, in the contemplation of which d'Aubant would frequently remain absorbed as in a trance. Near the figure represented stood a table on which lay a crown, resting, not on a cushion as usual, but on a heart which it crushed with its weight, and at which the lady gazed with intense melancholy. This painting attracted, of course, a good deal of observation, but no one dared to allude to it. By intuition, every one felt that it was sacred ground, on which enquiry ought not to tread.

Where was all the while the Princess Charlotte, the gilded victim of Imperial misery? One day, entering his wife's apartments, her husband requested her to receive a female scullion of her kitchen on whom he had bestowed his affections. She refused; he, heated by the fumes of his deep potations, worked himself into a paroxysm of frantic rage, and with wild gestures and terrific shrieks of a maniac, rushed upon her, and with repeated blows, laid her prostrate on the floor, senseless and cold in apparent death.

The Princess recovered from her swoon, and found herself alone with her friend and bosom companion, the Countess of Koeningsmark. Long did they discourse together in subdued tones. That night the Countess of Koeningsmark entered secretly the Princess' room, and there was re-enacted that scene where Friar Lawrence counsels Juliet to feign death. The imperial funeral took place according to the plan which had been laid; the whole of Europe was deceived.

With the two hundred emigrants who had arrived in March, 1721, there had come a woman who, by her beauty and by that nameless thing which marks a superior being or extraordinary destinies had, on her arrival at New Orleans, attracted public attention. She immediately enquired for the Chevalier d'Aubant, to whom she pretended to be recommended. She was informed that he was at his retreat on the Bayou St. Jean, and that he would be sent for. But she eagerly opposed it, and begged that a guide should conduct her to d'Aubant's rural dwelling.

It was a vernal evening, and the last rays of the sun were lingering in the West. Seated in front of the portrait, which we know, d'Aubant, with his eyes rooted to the ground, seemed to be plunged in deep revery. Suddenly he looked up – the dead was alive again, and confronting him with eyes so sweet and sad, with eyes so moist with rapturous tears, and with such an expression of concentrated love as can only be borrowed from the abode of bliss above! What pen could do justice to the scene? Suffice it to say that on the next day the Chevalier d'Aubant was married to the mysterious stranger, who gave no other name to the enquiring priest than that of Charlotte. In commemoration of this event, they planted two oaks which, looking like twins and interlocking their leafy arms, are to this day to be seen standing side by side, on the bank of the St. Jean, and bathing their feet in the stream, a little to the right of the bridge in front of the Allard plantation.

Certain it is, that although d'Aubant and his wife kept their own secret, and lived in almost monastic retirement, rumors about their wonderful history were so rife in the colony, and the attention of which they became the objects subjected them to so much uneasiness, that d'Aubant contrived to leave the country soon after, and went to Paris, where his wife, having met the Marshal of Saxe in the garden of the Tuileries, and being recognized by him, escaped detection with the greatest difficulty. D'Aubant departed for the Island of Bourbon, where he resided for a considerable time. In 1754, on his death, his widow returned to Paris with a daughter, the only offspring of her union with d'Aubant, and in 1781 she died in a state bordering on destitution.

The painstaking, conscientious historian, Hanno Deiler, after quoting Gayarre's account, ends by saying of it: 'It is a pity to destroy such a pretty legend.' Nevertheless he does so pitilessly. His cold-blooded investigations prove beyond a doubt that no such name as d'Aubant is to be met with in colonial documents. The marriage records of the St. Louis Cathedral between 1720-1730 register no such marriage.

'The legend, therefore,' says Deiler, 'may be pronounced a myth, although Allard's plantation is still pointed out as the dwelling-place of the lovers, and the two leaf-locked trees by the bridge still bear witness to their happiness.'

Picket, in his *History of Alabama*, claims the couple as residents of Mobile. Tschokke, the German novelist, places them on the Red River. But no fact in her history is so firmly believed by the romantic people of New Orleans as this lovers tale, and their dwelling-place has been assigned to various other localities favorable to the seclusion of true love.

Return and continue on Lakeshore Drive.

27. *Milneburg*, sometimes referred to as 'Old Lake' to distinguish it from newer settlements, was the first summer resort to be established on the lake-front. The old town, founded by Alexander Milne, New Orleans philanthropist, lies about a half mile inland from the lighthouse, which now stands high and dry on land where the lake has been filled in. A thriving lake port in the early 19th century, it

was the terminus of the Pontchartrain Railroad, the first railroad (1831) west of the Alleghenies.

Milneburg was the birthplace of Adah Isaacs Menken, actress and adventuress, who became the toast of Europe. She achieved fame as the first woman to play Mazeppa, and the first Mazeppa to ride a horse in the scene in which a dummy had been strapped to a horse.

Thackeray immortalized the bouillabaisse he ate here in a ballad of that name.

28. The *Industrial Canal*, completed in 1923, connects Lake Pontchartrain with the Mississippi. The section of the sea wall in this vicinity is reserved for Negroes.

29. *Shushan Airport*, Lakeshore Drive and Downman Road, is modern in design and artistically notable. Designed by Weiss, Dreyfous, and Seiferth and built on filled-in land, it was completed in the summer of 1935 at an approximate cost of $3,000,000. The two large hangars, which flank the Administration Building, possess ultra-modern equipment and provide space for offices and instruction rooms. The luxurious main building contains rooms with private baths for air-line passengers, in addition to a commodious pilots' suite. There are also a restaurant, radio room, post office, telegraph office, and information desk. On the mezzanine floor eight murals depicting early New Orleans history, including its founding by Bienville, which critics rate with the best of decorative murals to be found in the South, were executed by Xavier Gonzalez, a New Orleans artist and an instructor at the Newcomb Art School. Branch offices of various Federal agencies – Customs, Commerce, Immigration, and Weather Bureau – are located in this building. Octagonal in shape and rising to a height of 60 feet, the control tower surmounts the Administration Building and commands an unobstructed view of the lakefront and the city in the distance. A platform having a ramp which projects out into the water at the southeast corner of the landing field serves as a seaplane base. Shushan Airport is used by United States Army and Navy planes, and by both private and commerical aircraft.

S. from Lakeshore Drive on Downman Rd.; R. from Downman Rd. on Gentilly Rd.

30. *Gentilly Terrace Nursery*, 4300 Mandeville St. (*open daily; free guide service*), has about 500 registered varieties of orchids under cultivation.

31. *New Orleans Parking Commission Nursery*, 2829 Gentilly Rd., is a 5o-acre tract devoted to the raising of trees, shrubbery, and flowers for city beautification. The azalea trail in the nursery is particularly beautiful.

32. *St. John Berchman's Asylum*, 2709 Gentilly Rd., with a capacity for 70 inmates, is an orphanage for Negro boys from infancy to the age of 12 years. It is maintained by the Community Chest and supervised by the Associated Catholic Charities Social Agency.

33. *Dillard University*, 2300 Gentilly Rd., which formally opened its new campus buildings in 1935, is a co-operative enterprise. The American Missionary Association, the Board of Education of the Methodist Episcopal Church, the General Education Board, the Julius Rosenwald Fund, and the citizens of New

Orleans have all participated in its development. The new university occupies a 70-acre tract on Gentilly Rd. within the city limits. Five of the nine projected campus buildings are now in use. They are built of stone and brick, in a modified Georgian architectural style, with simple Doric columns and pilasters. The campus shows promise of becoming one of the city's show places.

Dillard University now offers four-year academic courses in arts and sciences, home economics, pre-medical training, music, and dramatics, which not only lead to the baccalaureate degree, but also prepare the student for entrance into professional schools and other institutions devoted to specialized graduate training. The university is likewise affiliated with the Flint-Goodridge Hospital.

34. *Orleans Tuberculosis Hospital,* 1931 Gentilly Rd., cares for indigent persons with funds provided by the Orleans Community Chest (*visiting hours* 8-8). It has a capacity of 100 beds; admittance to the institution must come through the clinic of the Orleans Anti-Tuberculosis League, which is located at the same address.

35. *Milne Asylum for Destitute Girls,* 1913 Gentilly Rd., the first institution of this type to be founded in Louisiana, was established in 1919 as a home for feeble-minded white girls and women. Prior to that time feeble minded persons had been committed to the State Insane Asylum. The original purpose of the Milne institution was to furnish a home for feeble minded girls of child-bearing age. The asylum has a capacity for 86 inmates.

The Milne Home occupies a 12-acre plot of land, which is used for recreation, gardening, and dairying. The New Orleans School Board furnishes teachers for the institution; the inmates having sufficient mental ability are given training through the grammar-school grades. Home economics, including basket weaving, quilting, and sewing, are also taught, some of the products being sold for the benefit of the home.

R. from circle on St. Bernard Ave.; R. from St. Bernard Ave. on N. Dorgenois St.; L. from N. Dorgenois St. on Aubry St.

36. *Louisiana Reptile Farm,* 2433 Aubry St. (*open daily; no charge*) supplies amphibians, reptiles, and tropical fish to pet shops, private collectors, and exhibitors. The farm specializes in baby alligators, green lizards, and the more ornamental baby turtles found in the vicinity of New Orleans. Among the oddities are various species of salamanders, newts, and treefrogs.

Continue on Aubry St. to St. Bernard Ave.; L. from St. Bernard Ave. on N. Claiborne Ave.; L. from N. Claiborne Ave. on Mandeville St.

37. The *Crescent Fish Farm,* 1624 Mandeville St. (*open only by special arrangement with the owner*), is one of the largest fresh-water aquariums in the South. The farm raises and ships about 750,000 fish annually, including about 45 different species. Some of the more important kinds handled are the blue, gold, and red moonfishes, Mexican and other swordtails, barbs, guppies, and several varieties of 'platys,' gouramis, and fighting fish.

Most of these tropical fish come under three groups: Those depositing eggs promiscuously, those forming nests on the surface of the water, and those bringing forth young alive. Very few importations of stock after the original are made, as the proprietor raises his own stock, specializing in a few species that have proved most profitable and easiest to breed; new species are added occasionally for experimental purposes. Most of the patronage of the farm comes from distant parts of the United States.

At different points in New Orleans, the Crescent Fish Farm owns and operates 800 concrete ponds, or basins, measuring 8½ by 7 feet and having a depth of 18 inches. About 500 of these are in the open, while the others are screened and in steam-heated buildings. The main plant on Mandeville Street covers about 2 acres. Here there are 400 glass aquaria for feeding some of the species in their earlier stages.

R. from Mandeville St. on N. Roman St.; R. from N. Roman on St. Roch Ave.

38. *St. Roch Cemetery*, 1725 St. Roch Ave., contains the Chapel of St. Roch, one of the most interesting shrines in the city. (*See Cemeteries.*)

L. from St. Roch Ave. on St. Claude Ave.; L.from St. Claude Ave. on Louisa St.

39. *St. Vincent de Paul's Cemetery*, 1322 Louisa St., is the burial place of Queen Marie of the Gypsies. (*See Cemeteries.*)

Return to St. Claude Ave.; R. from Louisa St. on St. Claude Ave.; L. from St. Claude Ave. on Port St.

40. *St. Paul's Evangelical Lutheran Church*, uptown river corner Port and Burgundy Sts., is built on the site of the oldest Lutheran church (1843) in New Orleans. The present church was built in 1889 and remodeled in 1915. Originally the services were conducted in German. It is a raised frame building with a square tower and belfry, and a tall spire above the portico. The façade and spire are reminiscent in design of New England Congregational Church buildings. A wide stairway leads up from each side meeting on a central landing. The interior is simple. A series of round arched memorial windows in stained-glass designs line the side walls.

R. from Port St. on Burgundy St.; R. from Burgundy St. on Elysian Fields Ave.; L. from Elysian Fields Ave. on St. Claude Ave.

Elysian Fields Avenue marks the site of the old Marigny Canal and the Pontchartrain Railroad, the first railroad west of the Alleghenies.

41. At 2004 St. Claude Ave. is the largest of the establishments selling *Poor Boy Sandwiches*, foot-long, French bread sandwiches (10¢) crammed with a choice of cheese, meats, or seafood and garnished with lettuce, tomatoes, and dressing, which constitute New Orleans' own answer to the depression.

Continue on N. Rampart St. in sweeping L. curve.

42. The *Étoile Polaire Lodge* 1, 1433 N. Rampart St., was erected shortly after Masonry was introduced in New Orleans in 1794. Because of Spanish suppression of the society, the meeting-place was located outside the city ramparts.

43. The *Carmelite Convent*, 1236 N. Rampart St., uptown river corner N. Rampart and Barracks Sts., one of the few convents maintained by the Carmelites in the United States, was founded in 1827 by two Creole ladies, Thérèse Roman and Marguerite Trémoulet, members of prominent and wealthy Louisiana families.

The rules of the order are extremely rigid. From the moment the Carmelite nun repeats her vows she passes within the high walls, never again to see the city streets or go on visits to relatives or friends. The barefooted nuns subscribe to the most rigorous ascetic life known to feminine religious orders. Their life is spent wholly in meditation and prayer. Visitors are admitted only to the small chapel, or to the reception room.

The building, a simple structure built along Gothic lines, is spacious and well designed. It is surrounded by a high cement wall.

44. *Fort St. Jean* stood at the intersection of N. Rampart and Barracks Sts. until after 1803, and the ramparts, from which Rampart Street takes its name, extended to Fort Bourgogne at Iberville and N. Rampart Sts. Old Bayou Road (now Governor Nicholls St.) led out of the city through a gate. Along the ramparts of the old town between Bayou Road and Dumaine St. were the establishments once maintained by the young men of New Orleans for their quadroon mistresses

45. *St. Mark's Community Center*, 1130 N. Rampart St., was erected in 1924 at a cost of $150,000. The church and community center comprise one of the most modern groups of its kind in the Southern Methodist Conference, and is the outgrowth of the efforts of a Methodist Episcopal missionary society established in 1908, at 615 Esplanade Ave.

Built around a central courtyard, with St. Mark's Church forming one side of the quadrangle, the architectural grouping has been patterned after that of the old Spanish missions. The church units are constructed of cement-covered brick; red tile is used for roofing.

In addition to the church auditorium there are clubrooms for children and adults, and apartments for the pastor and staff workers. A domestic science department, gymnasium, swimming pool, library, and free medical clinics have also been provided.

46. *Beauregard Square*, between St. Ann and St. Peter Sts., has a colorful history as the site of Fort St. Ferdinand and Congo Square. Fort St. Ferdinand, erected during the Spanish régime, was destroyed during the administration of Governor Claiborne, about 1803, in an attempt on the part of the Americans to stamp out yellow fever, which was thought to be caused by the stagnant water of the moats and the general filthy condition of the old forts then standing in ruins at the corners of the city ramparts. First used as a circus ground, the park was later enclosed with an iron fence and used by the townspeople as a Sunday afternoon gathering-place. The Negro slaves took advantage of the half holiday given them every Sunday to gather in Congo Sq., where they played games, sang to the accompaniment of tom-toms, and, it is said, performed their Voodoo dances and rites.

The first and second Charity Hospitals faced the Square on the river side of Rampart St. The open space on the uptown side across St. Peter St. was, until about ten years ago, the terminus of the Old Basin and Carondelet Canal. The canal, constructed under Governor Carondelet in the last decade of the 18th century, formed a waterway from the ramparts of the old city to Lake Pontchartrain.

47. The *Municipal Auditorium*, 727 St. Claude St., facing Beauregard Square (*open to inspection* 9-5 P.M.; Sat. 9-12; *free*), was dedicated May 30, 1930, as a memorial to the dead heroes of the World War. The auditorium, one of the largest buildings in the city, shows off to advantage across the lawns of Beauregard Square. Modern in every aspect, it forms a striking contrast to its environs of old buildings and historic sites. Behind the building on N. Liberty St., where the pumping station of the Sewerage and Water Board now stands, the first Parish Prison stood between 1830 and 1895. The riot and lynchings of March 4, 1891, took place there.

The building, of Italian Renaissance architecture, has foundations and walls of rusticated limestone. The three principal entrances on St. Claude Ave., St. Peter and St. Ann Sts. have large stone porches with roofs and vaulted ceilings supported by square columns. The façade on St. Claude Ave. has high, wide, churchlike windows. A large stage, 130 feet by 50 feet, can be raised or lowered by means of electrically operated screw jacks to afford area for balls or sports events. Two sets of proscenium walls, each set in three sections, can likewise be raised or lowered to provide stages for two halls. The total seating capacity, including balconies, is approximately 12,000. Eight double stairways and four ramps lead to the second-floor hallways. The adjoining exhibition building on N.Liberty St. is serviced with railroad tracks and has a completely equipped kitchen in addition to two concert halls. About 35,000 square feet of floor space is available to exhibitors in this building. The dividing walls of the concert rooms can be thrown open to form a complete unit of the entire second floor. Favrot and Livaudais were the architects.

48. The *Isolation Hospital*, 513 N. Rampart St., was originally one of the old McDonogh school buildings. The structure housing the Isolation Hospital was purchased by the city from the New Orleans Terminal Railroad Company in 1914 to be converted into a hospital for individuals with diseases of such a nature as to require isolation. Shortly after the beginning of the World War the city was alarmed to discover among the inmates of the Volunteers of America Home several cases of bubonic plague. Immediate action was taken, and the old school building was quickly remodeled into a hospital where those infected might be isolated. The building was soon well equipped, and during the World War whenhouses ot ill repute were closed, many prostitutes were detained here for treatment for venereal diseases.

In 1918 the railroad company repurchased the property, but the city still continued to lease it for emergency cases. Occasional smallpox cases are treated here, and it has frequently been used as a detention home for runaway lepers from Carville. Nurses and attendants are kept on hand to take care of emergencies.

Through the J. W. Sickle Fund indigent persons may obtain free medicine.

49. The *Church of Our Lady of Guadalupe*, downtown lake corner of N. Rampart and Conti Sts., was erected after a terrible yellow fever epdemic, raging in New Orleans during the early 1800's, induced the Board of Trustees of the St. Louis Cathedral to erect a mortuary chapel adjoining the then recently removed St. Louis Cemetery, in order to avoid 'those funeral processions which are but too apt to scatter throughout the city the fatal miasma of fever.' On December 27, 1827, Père Antoine de Sedella blessed the new sanctuary, where all funeral rites of the Vieux Carré were performed until 1860. Upon the completion of the mortuary chapel the City Council declared anyone who exposed a corpse in St. Louis Cathedral subject to a fine of $50. Known at first as St. Anthony's Chapel, it is now commonly referred to as the 'Mortuary Chapel.'

As cholera and yellow fever ran riot in the city, so many funerals were held that it became necessary to appoint Father Romero resident chaplain. By 1853, however, although the chapel continued its usefulness, the establishment of numerous churches throughout the city obviated the need for a single mortuary, and the sanitary ruling of 1827, becoming obsolete, was revoked. After the Civil War, Father Turgis, soldier-priest of the Confederacy, was given charge of this church, and there the faithful priest said mass daily for his old companions-at-arms, surviving veterans of the struggle. According to parish tradition, these old soldiers whom he had led through the war knelt with Father Turgis about the quaint confessional every Saturday night. In January, 1875, the Most Reverend Archbishop Napoleon Joseph Perché converted the former mortuary chapel into a parish church for the growing Italian population of the original city. Since 1921, under the patronage of Our Lady of Guadalupe, this church has ministered to parishioners of Spanish descent and to the city Fire and Police Departments.

The Shrine of St. Jude, 'Helper in Desperate and Hopeless Cases,' is designated by a statue and relic of the saint and is situated in the interior of the church, at the right side of the high altar near the communion rail. To the right of the church entrance is the Shrine of Our Lady of Lourdes, a miniature copy of the grotto of Our Lady of Lourdes, at Lourdes, France. To the left is the War Memorial erected by Father Bornes in memory of soldiers from the parish killed during the World War.

Cross neutral ground and return on N. Rampart St. to St. Louis St.; L. from N. Rampart St. on St. Louis St.

50. *St. Louis Cemetery 1*, St. Louis, N. Saratoga, Conti, and N. Liberty Sts., contains the tombs of many of the oldest New Orleans families. (*See Cemeteries.*)

L. from St. Louis St. on N. Robertson St.

51. *St. Louis Cemetery 2*, bounded by N. Robertson, St. Louis, N. Claiborne, and Iberville Sts., contains many interesting tombs, including that of Dominique You and the unmarked 'Voodoo grave.' (*See Cemeteries.*)

L. from N. Robertson on Bienville St.; R. from Bienwlle on N. Saratoga St.

52. This vicinity was once notorious '*Storyville*,' the wide-open red-light district where brothels flourished and jazz was born. Many of the 'cribs' little one- and two-room cottages, are still to be seen. The bagnios on Basin St. (N. Saratoga St.), where the Countess Willie Piazza, Josie Arlington, Kate Townsend, and other vice queens pandered flesh in luxurious establishments, are no longer standing, although part of Lulu White's palace at 235 N. Saratoga St. can still be seen with her name cut into the glass transom. (See *Gay Times in Old New Orleans.*)

MOTOR TOUR 2

From BAYOU ROAD *to* CITY PARK, 12 *m*.

The Esplanade bus (Canal and Dauphine Sts.) roughly parallels the tour route.

Downtown from Canal St. on Chartres St.; L. from Chartres St. on Gov. Nicholls St.

THE route here follows the old Bayou Road, an Indian trail connecting Bayou St. John and the Mississippi River, pointed out to Bienville by the Indians years before New Orleans was founded. Serving the city as a highway joining the Spanish Trail (Gentilly Rd.), the highroad to the Floridas and points east, the trail left the city through a gate next to Fort St. John at Rampart and Gov. Nicholls Sts.

53. *St. Augustine's Church*, 1210 Gov. Nicholls St., uptown lake corner St. Claude and Gov. Nicholls Sts., the third oldest Catholic parish church in the city, stands on the site of the College of Orleans, erected in 1811 as the first institution of higher learning in Louisiana. In the course of construction of the church in 1841 a troublesome problem arose. The Negroes attending Mount Carmel Convent, close by the ground donated to the diocese by the Ursuline Nuns for the erection of a church in honor of their patron saint, St. Augustine, were of the opinion that, since the school had been established for their benefit, the proposed church was likewise to be for the use of their race. To prevent this appropriation subscriptions were solicited all over the city. Free Negroes purchased many of the pews, with the result that Negroes and whites sat rather close to each other in the new church; traditional separation of races was restored by the abolition of the pew-renting system. In 1925, in remodeling the interior, the old Orleans College was demolished to make way for an extension of the sanctuary. The convent is still standing.

54. *The Goldthwaite House*, 1418 Gov. Nicholls St., designed by De Pouilly and built in 1834, has been occupied by the same family since 1840. A typical Creole house of the period, it is a one-story cement-covered brick building with plastered round pillars and high roof. The cypress woodwork is held in place with pegs.

Continue on Bayou Rd., the extension of Gov. Nicholls St., after crossing N. Claiborne Ave.

55. The Gayarré Place Monument, a stock figure, presumably of Liberty, on a red sandstone base, is a relic of the Cotton Centennial Exposition held in New Orleans in 1884-85. Gayarré Place is named for Charles Étienne Gayarré, the New Orleans historian.

56. The *Benachi Mansion*, 2257 Bayou Rd., is a two-story frame building erected about 1849 by Nicholas M. Benachi, a native of Greece, who made a fortune in this country operating a line of steamers. It is said that the house was first used as a sort of country club by a group of wealthy French and Creole residents of New Orleans and was known as the 'Rendezvous des Chasseurs.' Many prominent Frenchmen were entertained here. A wide gallery projects from the first and second floors of the façade. The ivy vine design in the ironwork and the pairs of square, wooden pillars of the galleries are distinctive.

57. *Le Breton Market*, corner Bayou Rd. and N. Dorgenois St., used to be an Indian trading-center, where the Choctaws brought their blankets, baskets, medicinal herbs, and *gumbo filé* (powdered sassafras root) to barter for guns, knives, or trinkets.

L. from Bayou Rd. on Grand Route St. John; R. from Grand Route St. John on Sauvage St.

58. *Fair Grounds* (*Louisiana Jockey Club*), main gate, Sauvage and Fortin Sts., is the last of New Orleans famous race courses. Shrubbery, flowers, fountains, and artificial lakes make it one of the most beautiful courses in the country. The glass-enclosed, steam-heated grandstand has a seating capacity of about 6000. Approximately 100 days of racing, beginning on Thanksgiving Day each year, are offered. Seven races are held daily starting at 2.30; Daily Double, second and third races; Quinella, last race. The certificate system of betting, much the same as pari-mutuel, is in effect. Several $1000 handicaps are held each year, with the Louisiana Derby the feature race. White and colored are admitted.

Return and continue on Grand Route St. John; L. from Grand Route St. John on Moss St.

59. *Bayou St. John*, which extends from Lafitte Ave. to Lake Pontchartrain, was at one time an important waterway. Its proximity to the Mississippi and the ease with which merchandise could be transported from the river to Lake Pontchartrain made it a deciding factor in Bienville's selection of the surrounding area as the site of New Orleans. The bayou became an important water route over which the Indians and early settlers transported their wares to and from the city. A canal, built by Governor Carondelet in the last decade of the 18th century, made it possible for boats to penetrate as far as the ramparts of the town opposite Toulouse St.

During the 19th century, the bayou district between Esplanade Ave. and Dumaine St. was regarded as a fine suburban area, and many beautiful homes were erected. Six of these plantation houses, two-story buildings with surrounding galleries and large high-ceilinged rooms, are still standing.

The bayou has always been a favorite place for outings. A number of famous resort hotels flourished in the vicinity of Spanish Fort during the last century. An amusement park, gambling palace, and theater, built in the 1880's, attracted many visitors. On St. John's Eve, strange Voodoo rites were performed along the banks of the bayou, in which Negroes, led by Marie Laveau, their priestess, indulged in weird orgies.

After the city filled in Carondelet Canal in 1927, Bayou St. John lost its commercial value. The channel in the lake end of the bayou filled in, all drainage came to a stop, and the whole section fell into a state of neglect. Under the W.P.A. the bayou has been cleared, and extensive beautification is under way.

Fire and the lapse of time have destroyed all trace of the former resort establishments. Only the crumbling ruins of Spanish Fort (*see Motor Tour* 1), the fine plantation homes along Moss St., and the houseboat colony between the railroad bridge and the lake remain of the commercial bustle and the holiday spirit of the old bayou.

The plantation homes still standing, all of which face Moss St. and the bayou, are typical of their period. They consist of two stories, with dormers projecting from the roofs. The high-ceilinged rooms, the doors and windows of which extend from ceiling to floor, open on broad galleries that surround the homes. Verandah railings are of ornamental iron with wooden handrails.

60. The *Walter Parker House*, 924 Moss St. (*open daily* 12-4; *adm.* 25¢, *benefit Anti-Tuberculosis League of Louisiana*) was built in 1798 on land purchased from Don Andres Almonester y Roxas. The columned porticoes, broad loggias, embrasured French windows, slave quarters, and spacious garden are typical of the period. The mantels throughout the house and the beautiful stairway which ascends to the third floor are of hand-carved Santo Domingan mahogany. The floor of the second story is constructed of boards riven from the central portion of cypress logs. The Moorish arches have *jalousies* in keeping with the tradition that a Spaniard peeps before entering his house.

Turn and return on Moss St.

61. The *Helen Pitkin Schertz House*, 1300 Moss St., often referred to as the Spanish Custom House because it was supposed to have been a storage place for contraband goods confiscated from the pirates who ran their boats up the bayou, is one of the best preserved and most attractive of the city's old plantation homes. Built about 1784, it is one of the West Indian type of plantation dwellings, broad galleries permitting free circulation of air through the original two rooms on each floor. The first floor is of plastered brick, with Pompeian brick columns supporting the gallery; the second story with its wooden gallery and slanting roof is constructed of wood. The two dormer windows in the American Colonial style were probably added later. A narrow outer stairway leads to the second floor at one end of the gallery. A floor of slate flagging overlays the original brick flooring, and an additional room has been added along the rear of the house.

Other plantation homes on the east bank of the bayou, built about the same time and similar in design, are *Our Lady of Holy Rosary School*, 1342 Moss St., and the *Louis Cucullu House*, 1370 Moss St.

62. The *Aristée Tissot House*, 1400 Moss St., built by the Ducayet family in the early part of the 19th century, presents a different design. There is a wide center hall with a double parlor on the right and a dining-room, also a double apartment, on the left. The front gallery is supported by circular brick columns; the upper columns are square and of wood; the roof is gabled with dormer windows. The house came into

the possession of Judge A. L. Tissot through his father.

Cross Bayou St. John at Harding Drive Bridge.

63. The *Elizabeth Wisner House*, 1347 Moss St., facing the bayou and bridge, was occupied in 1882 by the first fencing club to be formed in New Orleans. The place also housed a famous rowing club during the days when that fashionable sport centered on the bayou.

Return across bridge and continue on Moss St.

64. *Camp Nicholls*, 1700 Moss St., is a Confederate soldiers' home established in 1883 during the administration of Gov. Nicholls. Only a few veterans remain in the institution. On the grounds may be seen several old cannon taken from Spanish Fort and a submarine torpedo boat, said to be the first of its kind, constructed by a Captain Hunley during the Civil War. The boat sank in the bayou on its first trial, and lay submerged many years before being salvaged.

Turn and return on Moss St.; R. from Moss St. on Esplanade Ave.

City Park, extending along City Park Ave., from Bayou St. John to Orleans Ave. and running back to Robert E. Lee Blvd., is the sixth largest park in the United States, and will probably rank higher after extension work under the Works Progress Administration is completed. The tract of land, formerly the Allard Plantation, became city property in 1850 through John McDonogh's will and was reserved for park purposes, although actual improvements to that end did not start until 1896.

Since then, the park has been continually enlarged and beautified. Magnificent groves of live oaks, flower gardens, and lagoons and drive ways, flanked by oak, magnolia, palm, crêpe myrtle, camphor, and banana trees, form a setting for two 18-hole golf courses, a fine swimming pool, 33 tennis courts, a large football stadium, baseball diamonds, a concert platform, extensive picnic grounds, and an art museum.

On a raised mound at the Esplanade Avenue entrance to the park stands *Beauregard Monument*, the equestrian statue of the 'Great Creole,' Gen. P. G. T. Beauregard, who fought courageously in behalf of the Confederate cause at Fort Sumter, Bull Run, Shiloh, and on many other Civil War battlefields.

The Beauregard Monument Association was organized the day of the general's death, February 21, 1893, but it was not until twenty years later that the $22,000 required for the monument was finally raised. In 1913 the cornerstone was laid, and two years later the statue, the work of Alexander Doyle, the sculptor of Lee Monument, was unveiled by the general's granddaughter, Hilda Beauregard.

The handsome statue, showing in bronze the same 'perfect self-possessed soldier that he (Beauregard) was in life,' is set on an oblong block of granite. All the restraint and quiet dignity which characterized Beauregard are portrayed in the features.

At the end of Lelong Ave., a continuation of Esplanade Ave. into the park, is the *Isaac Delgado Museum of Art (open daily except Mon. 10-5; Sun. 11-5; closed on holidays; adm. free)*. It was built in 1911 through a $150,000 bequest of Isaac Delgado, prominent New Orleans philanthropist. Upon the death of its founder, the museum came into possession of Mr. Delgado's own extensive and rather valuable collection of *objets d'art*. This collection, consisting mainly of decorative work, ceramics, furniture, and enamelwork, formed the nucleus about which the museum was built. Numerous families in the city have made contributions of art and money.

The Isaac Delgado Museum of Art, referred to locally as the 'Delgado,' is under the control of a board of administrators composed jointly of members of the Art Association of New Orleans and the City Park Improvement Association. The former has been the principal support of the museum, although the municipality, according to the donor's stipulation, maintains the building. In the words of the architects, the design was 'inspired by the Greek, sufficiently modified to give a subtropical appearance.' There are six Ionic columns across the portico, and the limestone walls are bare, save where terra-cotta panels have been set in. On either side of the portico there are sculptural decorations set in panels below the entablature. The sculpture is formal Greek, in terra-cotta, designed to match as nearly as possible the limestone walls. On the outer walls of the building are engraved the names of many noted artists. The galleries, which overlook three sides of the spacious entrance hall, are supported by Ionic columns. They and the rooms above are hung with paintings, etchings, etc. The plan of each side, above and below, is identical : a long rectangular room in the middle, with a smaller square at each end, making a total of twelve rooms in addition to the large square entrance hall.

Since the most considerable portion of the museum's exhibits is from the homes of New Orleans families, the dominant influence is French.

The entire main floor, the entrance hall of which is two stories in height, is devoted to statuary, bronzes, and collections of jades and other *objets d'art*. The Morgan Whitney collection of more than 90 pieces of jade and other hard stones, the Alvin P. Howard collection of 60 pieces of Greek pottery, the Joseph Holt collection of some 40 examples of Oriental porcelain and cloisonné enamel, and the Isaac Cline collection of 130 pieces of Oriental bronzes are most outstanding. Among the statuary, most of which are reproductions of classic sculpture, Houdon's bronze 'Diana' and Rude's 'Hebe and the Eagle of Jupiter' are perhaps the most striking.

The galleries above are hung with paintings and etchings, the best group being the Hyams collection of 19th-century paintings, which includes Bouguereau's 'Whisperings of Love,' Kronberger's 'Head of Old Woman,' a Corot, and two pieces by Gérome. Particularly fine are Arkhipov's 'Russian Peasant Woman,' Reynolds's 'Portrait of Eliza Hartley,' and the 'Madonna and Child' attributed to Giovanni del Biondo. The canvases of many local artists, among them Clague, Perelli, Poincy, Wlkstrom, Molinary, the Woodwards, Smith, and Hall, are included.

Lectures on the arts and allied subjects are occasionally given, semi-annual shows in the interest of local artists are held, and loan exhibitions with other museums and art organizations throughout the country are arranged.

The '*Dueling Oaks*' and '*Suicide Oak*' are famous trees standing near the art museum. The former derived their name from the fact that they served as a favorite spot at which affairs of honor were settled by sword or pistol in the days when satisfaction for an insult was obtained by spilling blood; the latter is so called because of the fact that many disconsolate lovers and bankrupts committed suicide there. Of the Hueston-La Branche duel, one of the most dramatic and blood-stirring ever to take place under the Dueling Oaks, Henry Castellanos gives the following account in *New Orleans as It Was*:

> The principals were Alcée La Branche and Hueston, editor of the *Baton Rouge Gazette*. Hueston insulted La Branche through the pages of his paper; La Branche retaliated by giving Hueston a public beating. The affair aroused great interest, for both men were public figures numbering thousands among their friends. Many newspapers took up the matter, hastening the inevitable climax of the duel. Within twenty-four hours notes were exchanged, seconds selected, and the time set. The weapons chosen were double-barreled shotguns, loaded with ball; the distance 40 yards; the word of command was to be 'Fire – one – two – three – four – five,' each combatant to discharge his barrels after the word 'Fire' and before the word 'Five.'

> At the word of command both participants discharged their guns, but neither was hit. A second ordeal duplicated the first, but on the third trial Hueston received a scalp wound, indicating to the witnesses that La Branche's intent was to kill, rather than to maim or cripple, his opponent. Although members of the crowd tried to stop the affair at this point, believing that enough had been done to vindicate the honor and attest the courage of the antagonists, Hueston insisted upon a fourth round. The end came when his lifeless body fell at the feet of the man whom he had insulted, pierced by the eighth ball discharged from La Branche's weapon.

Louis Allard, who, as a destitute old man, was permitted to live on the land after it had been sold, is buried in a cement-covered brick tomb beneath a great moss-hung oak near a bridge about 1000 feet southwest of the art museum.

At the right of the main entrance on City Park Ave., surrounded by shrubbery, and with poppies growing at its base, is a 12-foot Corinthian column, a World War Memorial erected in honor of the soldiers of Louisiana who lost their lives in the war. The monument was erected by the American Legion of New Orleans and unveiled on May 29, 1921. The shaft represents a torch, and inscribed on the pedestal is the first stanza of 'In Flanders Fields.' On the capital are carved the emblems of the army, navy, air, and marine service.

The *Greek Peristyle*, near the Dumaine St. entrance to the park, the W. H. *McFadden House*, a private residence built on land purchased before the surrounding area became city property, which may be seen from the museum, and the formal garden across the lagoon to the rear of the museum are other points of interest.

W. on City Park Ave.

65. *Isaac Delgado Central Trades School* 615 City Park Ave., functions under the supervision of a board of managers consisting of ten members, five of whom, including the mayor of New Orleans and other public officials of the city and State, are ex-officio members.

The school, which is now operated by means of local, State, and Federal grants, owes its origin to Isaac Delgado, who conceived the idea of a trade school and bequeathed in 1912 about $750,000 for its erection. The Board of Managers took no immediate action, but allowed the funds to accumulate until they totaled roughly $1,250,000. The school was completed and opened to students in 1921. The cost of construction and equipment totaled nearly $1,000,000

Built of brick upon a limestone base, the school building follows no particular period of architectural style. It was designed primarily to utilize all available exterior space so as to give a maximum of daylight to the interior and is really four buildings in one, forming a complete square with a large courtyard in the center. The building is three stories high and has 166,723 square feet of floor space.

Workshops, with sliding partitions and adjoining classrooms, are located on every floor. By throwing open the sliding partitions, several adjoining workshops can be transformed into one, thus enabling the students to work on full-size construction rather than scale models. A large auditorium and exhibition hall and a modern cafeteria run by the students of commercial cooking are on the third floor.

The Isaac Delgado School is open for 44 weeks each year to all white boys over 16 years of age who are residents of the State and who have completed the grammar-school grades. Instruction is free, all equipment, except overalls, being furnished. So great is the popularity of the school that it cannot accommodate all those who wish to enter; the average enrollment in the day school is 550, but more than 900 attend the same courses which are offered at night six months during the year.

Training is outlined to cover a 3-year course, the first of which is given to preparatory work, the second to trade skill, and the third to advanced theory and extension teaching. Courses are offered in printing, carpentry, plumbing, commercial cooking, metal-working, cabinet-making, interior decorating, sign-painting, electricity, architectural and mechanical drafting, applied science, and trades English. Special attention is given to students who are handicapped by loss of sight or limb. Visitors are welcomed.

Cross neutral ground and return on City Park Ave.; R. from City Park Ave. on Esplanade Ave.

66. *St. Louis Cemetery* 3, 3421 Esplanade Ave., occupies the site of the old Bayou Cemetery established in 1835. (*See Cemeteries.*)

L. from Esplanade Ave. on Leda St.

67. The *Luling Mansion*, 1438 Leda St., now known as the Louisiana Jockey Club, was built by the elder Gallier from a rather crude design by its owner, an exile from Germany during the Revolution of 1848. The original estate totaled 80 acres, the building and the surrounding park-like grounds covering more than 10 acres. In 1880 the property passed to the Louisiana Jockey Club. The four-story building is of cement-covered brick, with a balcony projecting from each story and circling the entire building. The house was modeled after a French château. The cost of the structure, exclusive of appointments, amounted to a sum between $125,000 and $140,000. It was completed in 1865.

Return and continue on Esplanade Ave.; R. from Esplanade Ave. on N. Dorgenois St.

68. The *Hellenic Orthodox Church of the Holy Trinity*, 1222 N. Dorgenois St., erected in 1866, claims the honor of being the first Hellenic Orthodox Church in America.

Return and continue on Esplanade Ave.

A number of interesting houses, ranging in style from simple Creole cottages to elaborate Greek Revival mansions, are to be seen along Esplanade Ave. and vicinity from here on. (*See French Quarter Tour.*)

69. The *Baldwin House*, 1707 Esplanade Ave., was built in 1859-60 by Cyprian Dufour and was purchased in 1869 by Albert Baldwin, Sr., who made extensive repairs. It is a two-story, cement-covered brick structure with massive Corinthian columns supporting the spacious upper balcony and the roof. Immense rooms with high ceilings, carved Italian marble mantels, stained-glass windows, beveled mirrors, and a carved, mahogany winding staircase made it a show place of its day.

70. *St. Anna's Church*, 1313 Esplanade Ave., which started as a seaman's mission in 1846, is one of the oldest Episcopal churches in the city. The present church was erected in 1876, and contains memorial tablets dedicated to prominent Episcopalian clergymen of early days.

71. The *Col. Cuthbert Slocomb House*, 1205 Esplanade Ave., downtown lake corner Esplanade and St. Claude Aves., now occupied by the Sisters, Servants of Mary, was built ten years before the Civil War and served for a time, years after its construction, as the residence of the Archbishop of New Orleans. For many years it was the property of Col. Cuthbert Slocomb, a hardware merchant.

The two-story, cement-covered brick building has a highly ornamental exterior. The brick is made to imitate dressed stone. A paved marble walk leads ten feet from the street to the stone steps of the entrance and the tiled portico with roof supported by four Corinthian columns. The house has a side balcony of massive proportions and a beautiful mosaic pavement. The interior is exceptional because of a mahogany stairway surmounted with a dome of stained glass.

R. from Esplanade Ave. on N. Rampart St. to Canal St. (*See Tour 1.*)

MOTOR TOUR 3

AUDUBON PARK and UNIVERSITIES, 17 m.

The St. Charles street-car (Canal and Baronne Sts.) roughly parallels the tour route.

Uptown from Canal St. on St. Charles St.

72. *St. Charles Hotel*, between Common and Gravier Sts., stands on the site of two former hotels of the same name which vied for fame with the St. Louis Hotel on St. Louis and Royal Sts. during the 19th century. The original hotel, one of the finest in the United States at the time of its opening in 1837, was designed by Gallier and Dakin and erected at a cost of $800,000. It had columns across the façade and was topped with a magnificent dome, the first landmark seen by travelers entering the city. (A fine model of it may be seen in the Cabildo, Chartres and St. Peter Sts.)

Planters coming into the city to do business with their factors and engage in a bit of revelry usually selected the St. Charles. It was here that slaves were brought from the pens of the 'nigger traders' on Gravier, Common, and Carondelet Sts. to be auctioned off at the hotel's exchange. A new hotel was built after the original was destroyed by fire in 1851. General Butler, after he took over the city in 1862, being refused Parlor P, usually reserved for notables, assumed control of the entire establishment. A long list of famous persons, including John Wilkes Booth, McKinley, Cleveland, Theodore Roosevelt, Bryan, and Jefferson Davis, have stopped here.

The present hotel was constructed in 1896 after a second fire had destroyed its predecessor, and has since been remodeled.

73. *St. Charles Theater*, 432 St. Charles St., stands on the site of a former and more famous playhouse known by the same name erected in 1835 by James Caldwell, father of American drama in New Orleans. No other theater in this country, and only three auditoriums in all Europe – Naples, Milan, and Vienna – compared with it in size and splendor.

Fires in 1842 and 1899 destroyed the first two theaters on the site; the present structure dates from 1902. Now a movie palace, it once offered entertainment by such celebrities as James Brutus Booth, Edwin Booth, Joe Jefferson, Jenny Lind, J. H. McVicker, Tom Placide, and Charlotte Cushman.

74. *Lafayette Square*, bounded by St. Charles, South, Camp, and North Sts., an

attractively landscaped public square, was the American counter part of the Creole Place d'Armes. Formerly called 'Place Publique' and 'Mr. Gravier's Square,' it has been the site of many historic events.

Facing St. Charles St., on a white granite pedestal, is the *McDonogh Monument.* The figures of a small boy and girl are shown offering floral tributes to the man who left his fortune to the public schools of Baltimore and New Orleans. John McDonogh came from Baltimore to New Orleans when 22 years of age, and established himself in the social and business life of the city. Within a few years

he had accumulated a fortune, much of which he spent lavishly in the usual manner of popular young bachelors. It is said that two tragic love affairs changed his life completely and that by the time he had reached middle age he was a lonely, friendless old miser, 'from whom children shrank, and at whom dogs barked.' At his death in 1850 his entire fortune was left to the free schools of this city and those of his native home, Baltimore, with the simple request that 'the children of the free schools be permitted to plant and water a few flowers around my grave.'

New Orleans and Baltimore each received approximately $750,000. New Orleans built thirty-six public-school buildings, in each of which was placed a bust of McDonogh. In 1892 a movement to acknowledge the debt of New Orleans to McDonogh was begun, and by 1898 $7,000 – mostly five-cent contributions from school children – had been raised, and Atallio Picoirilli, a young New York sculptor, designed the statue of bronze and granite.

On December 29, 1898, McDonogh's birthday, the bust was unveiled. Each year on the first Friday in May, the school children of New Orleans make a pilgrimage to the statue and lay their floral offerings on or around the monument; the white children pay their homage in the morning, the Negro children in the afternoon. The body of McDonogh, first buried on his own plantation near Algiers, was removed to Baltimore, his native city, but the annual pilgrimage in New Orleans has been kept up, and is now one of the most impressive of civil observances.

In the center of the square stands the *Clay Monument,* a bronze statue of the 'Great Pacificator.' Clay, whose daughter had married a native of Louisiana, was a frequent visitor to New Orleans. Immediately after his death in 1852 a Clay Monumental Association was organized, and on April 12, 1856, the cornerstone of the monument was laid by his fellow Masons. Four years later the statue was completed and unveiled in view of one of the greatest gatherings ever to witness such a ceremony in New Orleans. Business houses closed, and hundreds of flags floated from buildings. The statue stood for forty-one years at the corner of Canal and Royal Sts., but in 1901, because of the heavy traffic, it was moved to Lafayette Sq., replacing the monument of Benjamin Franklin which had previously stood in the center of the square.

The bronze statue stands on a polished granite pedestal, with concrete steps on four sides. Clay is represented as he so often appeared in debate, with his sincere, intent look and outstretched hand. The monument was designed by Joel T. Hart of Kentucky, and executed in Munich. Lorado Taft, in commenting on the work, declared that the 'admirably ugly head' was well carved and 'full of life.'

Behind the Clay Monument on the Camp St. side of the square stands the *Franklin Monument.* The statue, which is slightly larger than life size, is an exact copy of the Franklin statue in Lincoln Park, Chicago. It is cast of bronze and bears the inscription on the base : 'Dedicated to all the People of New Orleans by Henry Wadsworth Gustine of Chicago, 1926.'

When the statue of Benjamin Franklin, designed by Hiram Powers, was removed from Lafayette Sq. to the New Orleans Library, Henry Wadsworth Gustine, a retired business man of Chicago, who spent his winters in New Orleans, donated to the city a second statue of Franklin to fill the vacant spot left by the first. A pedestal for the statue was donated by the various printers' organizations of the city. The statue was unveiled October 20, 1926, on the eighty-ninth birthday of the donor.

75. The *City Hall*, 543 St. Charles St., facing Lafayette Sq., is the finest example of Greek Revival architecture in the city. James Gallier, Sr., drew the plans and superintended the construction. After much delay, caused principally by the lack of funds, the building was finally dedicated on May 10, 1853. There is no corner-stone, only a tablet reading 'Erected 1850, James Gallier, Architect.'

In his autobiography Gallier wrote: 'The portico and ashlar of the front of the City Hall are of white marble procured from quarries near New York; the basement and steps are of granite. The style of architecture is Grecian Ionic, and the porti-co is considered a very chaste and highly finished example of that style.'

The building has a 90-foot front on St. Charles St. and extends 215 feet on Lafayette St. Counting the basement, it is three stories high. A hallway 12 feet wide runs from front to rear of the two upper floors, and is intercepted at right angles by a 14-foot hall at the Lafayette St. entrance. The latter hall contains a flight of very worn marble steps.

The entrance on St. Charles St. is reached by a flight of Quincy granite steps leading up between the pillars of the portico. There is a double row of these pil-lars, six in front and four in the rear. The pediment is decorated with bas-relief figures of Justice attended by Commerce and Manufactures.

The platform of the portico is 14 feet above the street level and runs entirely across the front. During Carnival time, and on other special occasions, a wood-en platform is built out over the sidewalk along the entire front, providing a reviewing stand with seats for invited guests. The roof is of peculiar design, being partly of wood and partly of iron, confined to a very flat pitch, and span-ning a width of 86 feet. The walls of the mayor's parlor, corridors, and Council Chamber are hung with many fine old paintings, some acquired in recent years, but many of them taken from the Cabildo and other former municipal buildings.

Many destructive changes have been made in the City Hall, and it is planned that sometime in the near future a new city hall will be built to accommodate the city's expanding governmental departments. At present the City Hall's auxiliary buildings total four: the City Hall Annex and the Sewerage & Water Board Building on

Carondelet St., and the Soulé Building and the *Howard Annex* on St. Charles St. The *Howard Annex*, the white building immediately adjoining the City Hall, was built before the Civil War by the Slocomb family, and in the seventies was the home of Cora Urquhart Potter, the well-known beauty and actress.

Many political demonstrations, especially during the Reconstruction Period and in 1934 between the forces of Mayor Walmsley and Senator Long, have taken place at the City Hall. After the capture of the city by the Federal forces in 1862, the lowering of the State flag at the hall caused a demonstration in which Mayor Monroe played an heroic part. Famous citizens, including Governor Isaac Johnson, Charles Breaux, Jefferson Davis, General Beauregard, Chief of Police Hennessy, Bertie Sneed, and Mayor Behrman, lay in state here before being carried to their resting-places. Harding addressed a vast gathering here in the winter of 1921 before taking office as President. William McKinley, Theodore Roosevelt, and Herbert Hoover were also received here.

76. The *First Presbyterian Church*, 630 South St., facing Lafayette Sq., occupies the site of a former church destroyed by fire in 1854. Dedicated in 1857, the architecture of the stucco-covered brick church is modified English Gothic. Dr. B. M. Palmer, noted civic leader and one of the most active secessionists in 1861, ably served the church as its pastor from 1856 to 1902.

At the time of writing, the Government is closing a transaction taking over the church, along with the adjoining property between Camp and Church Sts., for the erection of a Federal building.

77. The *Row of Buildings* on the uptown side of Julia St. between St. Charles and Camp Sts., was known in its heyday (about 1840) as 'the Thirteen Buildings.' These houses were, at that time, the homes of socially prominent 'Americans.' Eliza Ripley in *Social Life in Old New Orleans* tells of the elaborate ball given in one of them for Henry Clay. Oddly enough, this once fashionable street was named for Julia, 'a free woman of color,' said to have been the favorite of an early Louisiana planter.

78. The *George W. Campbell House*, 805 St. Charles St., uptown lake corner of St. Charles and Julia Sts., one of the finest mansions in its day, was built about 1857 by Dr. George W. Campbell, a physician and sugar planter. General Butler ejected the owners, permitting them to take only the clothes they wore, and made the place his residence for the final weeks of his stay in New Orleans.

The two-story brick house has 18-foot ceilings, doors with solid rosewood panels, and a beautiful circular staircase with balustrade of hand-carved rosewood. Each room has a magnificently carved marble mantel. The basement of the house has been converted into space for six shops, and the upper floors are now apartments.

79. *Lee Monument*, Lee Circle, intersection of St. Charles and Howard Aves., is the focal point of vistas converging at the circle. On a high pedestal placed in the center of a green, circular mound rises the magnificent bronze statue of General Robert E. Lee, one of the finest erected in the United States in honor of the popular Confederate hero.

IN AND ABOUT THE CITY

THE SEAL POOL, AUDUBON PARK

OAK TREES ON THE BEACH OF LAKE PONTCHARTRAIN

PACKENHAM OAKS

BRIDLE PATH, AUDUBON PARK

PERISTYLE, CITY PARK

NEWCOMB COLLEGE

THE BAPTIST BIBLE INSTITUTE

GIBSON HALL, TULANE UNIVERSITY

LOYOLA UNIVERSITY

AT THE RACE TRACK

ADMINISTRATION BUILDING, DILLARD UNIVERSITY

THE OLD CARROLLTON COURT HOUSE, NOW McDONOGH SCHOOL NO. 23

ALTAR OF THE CHURCH OF THE IMMACULATE CONCEPTION (JESUIT)

The Robert E. Lee Monumental Association was formed in 1870, the year of Lee's death, for the purpose of erecting a monument in memory of the Confederate general; but the difficult days during Reconstruction delayed the plans for several years. In 1876 sufficient funds were raised to begin work, and Alexander Doyle, a young New York sculptor, who also created the Beauregard and Army of Tennessee monuments, was employed to design the statue. Because the treasury in those days 'was more often empty than replenished,' the work did not progress rapidly, and seven years elapsed before the bronze figure on the tall, white marble shaft stood ready for the unveiling ceremonies. On Washington's Birthday, 1884, the memorial was dedicated in the presence of a vast throng of witnesses and many distinguished visitors. Among these were Jefferson Davis, General Beauregard, and dozens of other officials and friends of Robert E. Lee.

The marble shaft holding the statue rests on a 12-foot base consisting of pyramidal steps of Georgia granite. The fluted column, rising 60 feet in the air, is made of white Tennessee marble. Atop this, with arms folded and eyes gazing off, as if over a field of battle, is the bronze figure of Lee, $16\frac{1}{2}$ feet tall and weighing nearly 7000 pounds. The statue is illuminated by lights concealed in four bronze urns placed at its base in 1930.

Make three-fourths turn at Lee Circle.

80. The *Howard Memorial Library*, 601 Howard Ave., corner Lee Circle and Howard Ave. (*open weekdays* 9-6), was established through the efforts of Miss Annie T. Howard, who wished to perpetuate the memory of her father, the late Charles T. Howard. She donated $115,000 for the erection of the building, and in addition 8000 books and $200,000 for maintenance. The Library was formally opened March 4, 1889.

The structure was planned by Henry H. Richardson, a native of Louisiana and one of the best-known architects of his day. The design submitted by Richardson was Romanesque in treatment – the heavy style of frequent occurrence in Southern France. Sandstone from Massachusetts was used in the construction of the building. Surrounded now by modern American structures, the building reminds one of a medieval fortress.

The Howard Library does not circulate books but is used only as a reference library. The chief object has been to collect and preserve for the use of the public a wide variety of books and documents on all subjects, particularly Louisiana. It offers a complete set of documents bearing on the early Colonial history of the State and a special collection on genealogy used extensively by students of this subject. Many of the letters and manuscripts of John McDonogh, General Beauregard, Adrien Rouquette, and Lakanal are available here. The books of General and Mrs. W. J. Behan relating to the Confederate States were donated in 1929. The collection of the late Swiss consul, Émile Hoehn, has been loaned to the library for a period of time and is said to be one of the finest collections on Switzerland in the United States. The Ruth McEnery Stuart collection consists of a series of autographed books sent her by various authors previous to 1927, including many by Louisiana writers.

The library has a rather complete supply of newspapers, magazines, and periodicals, among which is a complete set of *De Bow's Review,* one of the few files available in a public institution. Although the library has no exhibits, there are many fine old books laid away on the shelves. One of the most interesting collections is that containing three books by John James Audubon, beautifully bound in 'elephant size' (about a yard and a half in length) and published in England in 1827-30.

At present the Howard Library has approximately 86,000 books catalogued and stacked for the use of readers. An interlibrary loan system is carried on throughout Louisiana and the United States in order to offer a still greater variety of reference material to New Orleans readers. Recently the W.P.A. has made it possible to enlarge the building to make space for large collections formerly stored in basement and attic.

81. The *Confederate Memorial Hall,* 929 Camp St., adjoining the Howard Library *(adm. free; open weekdays* 9-3), was built in 1891 to serve as a meeting place for the Louisiana Historical Association and as a repository of Confederate records and relics. Construction was made possible through a $40,000 gift of Frank T. Howard.

The building was designed by Thomas O. Sully, a New Orleans architect. Care was taken that the general style should harmonize with that of the adjoining Howard Library. The principal feature of the interior is a hall-like exhibition and meeting-room with a vaulted ceiling whose structural oak woodwork remains exposed.

Collections and exhibits, filling 89 exhibition cases, include tattered and blood-stained flags from the battlefields; the celebrated Jefferson Davis Collection of 6000 pieces, from cradle to war boots; paintings of famous generals and other noted Civil War figures; and countless souvenirs characteristic of the war zone. There are also interesting and important manuscripts, many of which have never been published.

Continue around Lee Circle to St. Charles Ave.

(For an alternate tour from this point see Motor Tour 4.)

82. The *Young Men's Christian Association,* 936 St. Charles Ave., has the usual recreational and other facilities. *(See Recreational Facilities.)*

83. The *New Orleans Public Library,* 1031 St. Charles Ave. at Lee Circle *(open weekdays* 9-9; *Sun.* 9-1), is an outgrowth of the various library societies formed in New Orleans early in the nineteenth century. The 'Commercial Library,' purchased by B. F. French and made available to the public, and later purchased by Alvarez Fisk and presented to the city for a free public library, formed the nucleus of the present library. Successive library consolidations and donations from Andrew Carnegie and the heirs of Simon Hernsheim have contributed to the growth of the institution.

The main building of the New Orleans Public Library, marking the site of the car barns of the New Orleans and Carrollton Steam Railroad, was erected in 1908 by Diboll and Owen, New Orleans architects. The structure is steel and concrete throughout and of fire-proof construction. The architecture is of the Renaissance order, with certain features copied from the Roman Temple, *Mars Ultor.* The material used is gray Bedfordstone. At the entrance portico are four Corinthian columns 32 feet in height. The upper end of the building is more irregular, terminating in an Ionic apse which harmonizes with the irregular shape of the site. The roof of the building is composed of slate with a central dome of bronze.

The Public Library and its six branches combined contain about 275,000 volumes, several thousand of which are in foreign languages. Among the outstanding collections is that of W. O. Hart, considered one of the most valuable on Dickens in the city or State, and the Le Monnier collection of Civil War material, including his personal scrapbook compiled during the war. A large number of the older classics and numerous volumes on early Louisiana history are also available. The section of the United States Library for the Blind which serves Louisiana, Mississippi, Alabama, Arkansas, and part of Texas is located in the main building of the Public Library. An unusually complete file of magazines and periodicals may be found in the reading rooms. The circulation for home reading runs well over a million books annually.

The statue of *Benjamin Franklin*, which stands just to the right of the entrance to the reading room of the New Orleans Public Library, has been declared by many to be the handsomest and finest piece of marble statuary in New Orleans. The famous printer-statesman is well portrayed in his three-cornered hat, pensively stroking his chin.

The statue has an interesting history. Richard Henry Wilde, afterwards the first Professor of Law in the University of Louisiana (1847), met Hiram Powers, a struggling young sculptor, in Florence in 1835. After Wilde settled in New Orleans Powers wrote him that he was making a statue of Franklin which he hoped some day to place in the National Capitol. Wilde interested a number of leading citizens, and the statue was bought for New Orleans, part payment being made to Powers in 1844. The remaining amount was to be paid upon delivery of the statue. In the meantime Wilde died, the Civil War came on, and Powers was forgotten; Powers, engrossed in his rapid climb to fame, likewise forgot New Orleans. In 1869 the contract was dug up, and the young sculptor was reminded forcefully of his obligations. Powers offered to finish the statue of Franklin and to ship it to New Orleans. The offer was accepted, and two years later the statue was duly shipped to the city. The statue arrived, and after much difficulty in raising freight charges, during which it was once advertised for sale, the amount was paid, and efforts were begun to secure the granite base which Powers had requested that it be placed upon. Two shipments of granite from Boston failed to reach New Orleans, and it was not until 1873 that the monument was set up and unveiled in Lafayette Square.

Some years later it was noticed that the soft Italian marble was being damaged by exposure, and in 1909 the statue was moved to the New Orleans Public Library.

Continue on St. Charles Ave.

84. The *First Methodist Church*, 1108 St. Charles Ave., was constructed in 1906 by the oldest Methodist congregation in the city. The Romanesque building, constructed of pressed brick on a stone face foundation, is designed to meet all congregational needs.

85. The *Jerusalem (Shriners') Temple*, 1137 St. Charles Ave., erected in 1916, has a large auditorium in which many of the city's plays and concerts are presented.

86. The *Athenaeum*, uptown lake corner of St. Charles Ave. and Clio St., the home of the Young Men's Hebrew Association, was erected in 1907, and served until recently

as the ballroom for Mardi Gras balls.

87. The *Standard Oil Company of Louisiana*, 2134 St. Charles Ave., occupies the building that was once the home of the Harmony Club, a private club no longer in existence.

88. The *Whitney House*, 2200 St. Charles Ave., stands on the site of a small brick house erected before the Civil War and occupied by Randall Hunt, brother to William Hunt, Secretary of the Navy under President Garfield. About 1850 the property was purchased by Mrs. Charles A. Whitney, one of the wealthiest women of the country, who spent large sums of money converting the building into one of the most palatial homes in New Orleans. Large collections of Oriental and European art were bought, and rare exhibits of mosaics, candelabra, and bronzes were installed. The structure, which is of English and Spanish design, painted a dark green, was the scene of much lavish entertaining.

89. *Christ Church Cathedral*, 2919 St. Charles Ave., the fourth Episcopal cathedral of New Orleans, was built in 1887. The Christ Church congregation, organized in January, 1805, comprised the first Protestant association of the Southwest. At this date the Protestant population of New Orleans was so small and belonged to so many denominations that it was found impossible to build separate churches. A general Protestant meeting was therefore called to decide by vote the denomination of the common church. The Episcopalians won by a considerable majority.

The first edifice was built at the corner of Canal and Bourbon Sts., and was demolished in 1835. The following year another church was erected on the opposite corner upon ground donated for the purpose by the city of New Orleans. In 1845 this site was sold, and a larger church erected on the corner of Canal and Dauphine, at a cost of $50,000. It was sold in 1886, the congregation moving to its present home on St. Charles Ave. In 1891, the present Christ Church was made the procathedral, the rector then becoming titular dean.

Christ Church Cathedral, of English Gothic style, is of brick and stucco construction. In 1890 Mrs. J. L. Harris presented to the church, in memory of her husband, the bishop's house on St. Charles Ave. and the rectory immediately behind the church on Sixth St. These parish dwellings communicate with the church building through a vine-covered cloister. The church bell now in use was purchased in 1855. The large window on the west side was obtained from the old Canal St. church, as was the stone baptismal font in use today.

L. from St. Charles Ave. on Delachaise St.; L. from Delachaise on Prytania.

90. *Touro Infirmary*, 3516 Prytania St. (*visiting hours* 2-4 *and* 6-8), is a private institution under Jewish management, but non-sectarian in its work. This hospital has 350 beds and operates a general clinic for both white and colored. Founded in the 1840's on the corner of Press and Gaiennie Sts., Touro Infirmary was the recipient of a large donation from the Jewish philanthropist, Judah Touro. In 1882 the institution moved to its present site, where many additions have been made to its facilities.

L. from Prytania St. on Louisiana Ave.

91. The *Freret House*, 1525 Louisiana Ave., was erected in the early fifties by James P. Freret, and was one of the first houses to be built upon the then suburban Louisiana Ave. The building is an example of one type of Louisiana plantation structure. The lower portion is of brick and square brick columns support the gallery. The upper columns are likewise square but are made of wood.

Retrace Louisiana Ave., Prytania St., and Delachaise St. to St. Charles Ave.; R. on St. Charles Ave.

92. The *Rayne Memorial Methodist Episcopal Church*, 3000 St. Charles Ave., uptown river corner St. Charles Ave. and General Taylor St., was established in 1875 as the St. Charles Avenue Methodist Episcopal Church. A merger, begun in 1858 with a sister church at Cadiz and Coliseum Sts., was finally effected, and later the present church was built, largely through the generosity of Mr. R. W. Rayne, a member of the congregation. This structure, costing $50,000, was opened for the first church service of January 3, 1876. A fine new Educational Building was erected in 1925 at a cost of $70,000. A Women's Foreign Missionary

Society, one of the earliest Protestant organizations of its kind in the city, was organized here in 1877. The church building is of red-brick construction in Gothic perpendicular style. In the belfry of its tall central spire a beacon light burns during evening services. Eight stained-glass windows add distinction to the interior.

93. *Touro Synagogue*, 4338 St. Charles Ave., corner General Pershing St. and St. Charles Ave., was named in honor of Judah Touro, wealthy and prominent local Jewish philanthropist of the 19th century. In 1909 the new synagogue of this amalgamated Reformed Jewish congregation was formally dedicated. In 1925 a new Sabbath School and Social Hall were built adjoining the main structure.

The origin of Touro Synagogue dates back to 1828, when the Congregation Shaarai Chesed was incorporated. One of the founders of this congregation was Jacob da Silva Solis, who, while on a business trip to New Orleans, was unable to buy Matzoth or unleavened bread for Passover and was therefore forced to grind his own meal and bake his own bread.

Built of grayish-yellow face-brick, Touro Synagogue follows the Byzantine style of architecture. Presenting an elaborate structural mass, Touro Synagogue is distinguished by the number of variously proportioned domes which form its roof. Vari-colored tiles, inlaid in the brick-work, ornament the entrances of the façade. Emil Weil of New Orleans designed the building.

94. The *Academy of the Sacred Heart*, 4521 St. Charles Ave., has primary and preparatory departments for girls; boys are admitted to the kindergarten only. The main portion of the academy was erected in 1899, though wings have since been added. It is under the jurisdiction of the Sacred Heart nuns, who established their first school in New Orleans in 1887.

95. *Orléans Club*, 5005 St. Charles Ave., founded in 1925, is a social and cultural club for women, affiliated with the American Women's Club of Paris, the American Women's Association of Clubs of New York, and the San Francisco and Chicago

Women's Clubs. The organization is housed in a handsome building constructed in 1868 by Col. William Lewis. It is well-equipped with card, reading, committee, dining, library, and lecture rooms. A limited number of bedrooms are kept to accommodate out-of-town members. Meetings held each Tuesday are devoted chiefly to discussions pertaining to literature, music, art, and current events. In addition regular Friday meetings, dances, and other social events are held at intervals.

Membership is limited to 750, including regular, associate, and non-resident members. There are first- and second-class junior memberships, and special memberships extended to the wives of Army and Navy officers. Three honorary memberships are granted annually to women who have been outstanding in some field of activity in New Orleans. The club building is occasionally rented out for weddings, receptions, dances, etc.

96. *Gilbert Academy*, 5318 St. Charles Ave., a Negro preparatory school, occupies the building in which New Orleans University was located until 1935, at which time it merged with Straight University to form Dillard University.

97. The *Jewish Children's Home*, 5342 St. Charles Ave., was created by the Hebrew Benevolent Society of New Orleans in 1855. Children from seven Southern States between the ages of 3 and 18 are admitted, and no person is released until he has found a means of earning a living.

The home is arranged in every detail to meet the convenience and comfort of the children. Their living quarters are attractively furnished with desks, comfortable chairs, books, and numerous articles of furniture, which add a homelike touch. To avoid the effects of uniformity, each room in the sleeping quarters has a different color scheme. Each child is given an allowance in cash, the amount varying with the age of the child. Special attention is given to the health of the children, and only the best of food is served. Doctors and nurses are in daily attendance. Each child is given special duties with ample time for recreation. Children are educated through high school at the Isidore Newman Manual Training School. Further education is provided those desiring it in the colleges and vocational schools of the State. Financial support is derived from the city, the Community Chest, private contributions, and the B'nai B'rith.

98. The *St. Charles Avenue Presbyterian Church*, corner St. Charles Ave. and State St., dedicated February 2, 1930, is the outgrowth of the Palmer Memorial Sunday School established by the First Presbyterian Church at this site in 1906 and of 'The Little Church' built here in 1912. French Gothic in design, with the feudal motif expressed in watchtowers and battlements, the edifice is constructed of variegated Indiana limestone. In the interior, the straight nave, flanked by wide side aisles roofed below clerestory windows, narrows at the sanctuary end into a rectangular chancel. A vestibule with a balcony above extends across the St. Charles Ave. front. A pitched, false ceiling, well below the main roof, roofs the nave and chancel. A choir room on the right and an organist's alcove on the left, with organ lofts above, flank the chancel, which has a raised choir loft at the rear. The walls are of imitation travertine, old bone in color, and the half-timbered ceilings have been stenciled with touches of vivid colors. All woodwork is quartered white oak in dark Flemish finish. The stained-glass

windows, made by the Oidtmann Studio of Linnich, Germany, are without picture or medallion and have a grisaillé field surrounded by deep reds, rubies, blues, and greens.

99. *Temple Sinai*, 6221 St. Charles Ave. at Calhoun St., was founded in 1872, when the first reform congregation in New Orleans dedicated the first temple.

Of imposing structure, with a domed roof surmounting the main auditorium, Temple Sinai is a modern interpretation of the Byzantine architecture of the mosques of Constantinople. Erected in 1927, the temple, its principal mass octagonal in shape, is constructed of grayish-yellow face-brick with limestone trim. According to the Jewish precept, this synagogue, like the temples of Jerusalem, is so oriented that the congregation faces east to worship.

Ornamentation throughout the temple is traditional and symbolic. Approached by a pentagonal arrangement of cement steps, the central entrance on St. Charles Ave. is distinguished by a triple grouping of bronze doors decorated with raised medallions, and surmounted by a plaster tablet representing the Ten Commandments. The façade is further ornamented by a stucco moulding utilizing traditional motifs of maize and wheat.

Constructed on the group plan, the new Temple Sinai includes a Sunday School Building, and a small auditorium or chapel equipped with a theater type stage. A suite, set apart for the rabbi's study, classrooms, service rooms, a kitchen, library, and parlors have also been provided. The entire group of handsome and spacious buildings is beautifully landscaped and set off by well-spaced plantings of semi-tropical shrubbery and evergreens.

The large auditorium, fronting on St. Charles Ave., seats 1000 people. Interest here is centered on the high gilt and marble altar, behind which are located the choir loft and massive pipe organ screened by an ornamental grill. Handsome Tiffany lighting fixtures and seven ornamental stained-glass windows illuminate the interior. These windows, three of them large and arched, and four of smaller dimensions, were made in Munich and assembled in America.

100. *Round Table Club*, 6330 St. Charles Ave., was organized in 1898 by a group of men interested in literature, science, and art. The club occupies a modern residence which contains rooms for reading, pool, billiards, a library, and lectures. There is also a limited number of bedrooms, used by a few of the members as living quarters.

The privileges of the club are not often extended to residents of New Orleans who are non-members, although distinguished visitors to the city are frequently entertained. Men of national and international fame are invited to lecture on subjects pertinent to the interests of the club, and on these occasions guests of members may be invited. The membership list of the club is 300. There are also honorary memberships, which are conferred on men of unusual or outstanding attainments.

101. *Loyola University*, 6363 St. Charles Ave., is a Catholic institution conducted by the Jesuit order. The university was established in 1911, after having evolved from Loyola Academy, a preparatory school that had been organized and located on the present site in 1904. The 14-acre campus, extending from St. Charles Ave. to Freret

St., adjoins that of Tulane University to form a compact mass of variegated university buildings. Those of Loyola University are all styled in the Tudor-Gothic pattern, constructed of red brick and terra-cotta trim, and grouped around three sides of a square which opens on St. Charles Ave.

To the visitor's right, upon entering the campus, stands the Louise C. Thomas Hall, used chiefly as a residence for the faculty.

Directly across from Thomas Hall, but facing St. Charles Ave., is the *McDermott Memorial (Holy Name of Jesus) Church*, which, with its lofty spires, is one of the most imposing edifices of its kind in the city. It was dedicated on December 9, 1918, and first used by soldiers domiciled on the campus. Endowed in 1913 by Miss Kate McDermott in honor of her brother, Thomas McDermott, it was one of the buildings designed by DeBuys, Churchill, and Labouisse for the Loyola University group fronting St. Charles Ave. Inspired by Canterbury Cathedral, this modern church retains throughout the simplicity and dignity characteristic of the Tudor-Gothic style. Constructed on a steel frame, and built of brick with limestone detail, the church has a seating capacity of 900. To the old bell, removed from the first church and placed on the end-roof of the new, were added in 1919 the chimes given by Mrs. E. J. Bobet.

The church is richly furnished and equipped. Fonts of holy water are upheld by sculptured angels. Notable interior details are the marble altar railing, the Altar of our Blessed Mother, and those of St. Joseph and St. Ignatius. The magnificent high altar has a great marble crucifix as the central figure. Impressive shrines of St. Anthony and St. Ann, a statue of Our Lady of Prompt Succor, and artistic representations in marble of St. Francis Xavier and St. Aloysius contribute to a decorative scheme of great religious reverence.

Marquette Hall, extending across the rear side of the square and facing the avenue, binds both the church and Thomas Hall into a unit by means of a cloister. This structure, the largest of the group, houses the administrative offices, the College of Arts and Sciences, and the General Library of about 60,000 volumes. Included are several very fine collections on Louisiana and Ireland, a complete set of the Greek and Latin Fathers, both in the original and in translation, and a very full collection of Jesuit items.

Bobet Hall, erected in 1924, stands directly behind Marquette Hall. In it are located the Scientific Department, the College of Pharmacy, the Dental School, and the Law School.

Of outstanding interest among the university's buildings is the *Nicholas D. Burk Seismological Observatory (admission by appointment)*. The seismological equipment consists of vertical and horizontal instruments of the Wiechert astatic type. This observatory, the only one of its kind in the city, is one of many controlled by Jesuit colleges and universities in all parts of the world in the interest of seismological and meteorological science.

On the rear end of the campus, with entrances on Freret St., are the Loyola Gymnasium and the stadium, a double-decked, steel and wood structure with a seating capacity of 20,000 people.

Loyola University maintains the only dental college and clinic in New Orleans, those of Tulane University having been discontinued in 1930.

A nominal charge is made for clinic work except in special charity cases. Another of the university's outstanding schools is the Loyola College of Music, which is situated in an old residence on the corner of St. Charles Ave. and Calhoun St. The College of Music was established in 1932, when the New Orleans Conservatory of Music, formerly located on the site, became affiliated with Loyola University.

Enrolment at Loyola for the 1936-37 session was 850 day students and 350 night students.

102. *Tulane University*, 6400 St. Charles Ave., offspring of the Medical College of Louisiana (1834) and the University of Louisiana (1847), adopted its present name in 1883 when a bequest by Paul Tulane made real expansion possible. The buildings occupying the 93-acre campus range in architecture from Romanesque to modern adaptations.

Gibson Hall, the first built unit on the campus, directly faces St. Charles Ave. and Audubon Park. Patterned according to Romanesque architecture and built of Bedford stone in 1894, the structure houses the College of Arts and Sciences, the main administrative offices, the printing office, a small auditorium, and the *Tulane Natural History Museum*.

The museum (*open Tues.* 2-5, *research workers permitted at other times*), which occupies the entire third floor of Gibson Hall, is, from the standpoints of representative material and scientific arrangement, one of the best museums in the South.

The first exhibits were housed in a building on University Pl. when the old University of Louisiana, predecessor to Tulane University, was located there. In 1894, when the university moved some of its departments to the present quarters on St. Charles Ave., the museum was established in Gibson Hall.

One of the exhibits attracting particular attention consists of two Egyptian mummies, wrapped in heavy linen cloth and preserved in wooden coffins. One of the bodies is that of a youth of nobility who died about 950 B.C., and the other is that of a young woman believed to have been of the same rank as the youth. The coffins are decorated in colors with scenes from the *Book of the Dead*, portraying the soul in the various tests on the way to the 'Underworld.' Another example of embalming is that of a shrunken head of an Indian girl belonging to one of the savage tribes of head-hunters still found in Ecuador.

Some extremely interesting exhibits of archeological material gathered from mounds in Louisiana may be seen at the Tulane Museum. Probably the most important display came from the Larto Mounds in Catahoula Parish. This included skulls and fragments of thighs and other bones of the mound builders. There are also fragments of pottery, shells, arrowheads, 'plummets,' axes, and bowl handles representing faces and heads. From the Riddle Mounds of West Feliciana Parish and the Harris Mounds of Franklin Parish has been brought an excellent display of implements and a number of unbroken skulls. Exhibits pertaining to the life of modern Indians include a

Choctaw crop basket made from strips of wild cane, notable for the uniformity of the material and design. One of the most interesting exhibits is the antelope hide suit, together with the bow and arrow used by Sitting Bull, the Sioux chief. There are also suits and sandals worn by the Blackfoot Indians of Montana.

In the biological division there are numerous illustrations in the comparative anatomy of man and other animals; also skull models of the various races of man showing fully the extremes of contour in the frontal bone, the jaw, and the various sinuses of the head. There is a series of brain casts showing examples of the more important races of man and a variety of mammals. The skeletons of a variety of vertebrates form another important collection.

In the general zoological collections are mounted heads as well as complete specimens of the larger species. Of the smaller mammals the most interesting perhaps are the two- and three-toed sloths, the armadillo, the porcupine, and the vampire bats.

In the case of both mammals and birds there are a number of specimens not on display but available for research specialists. These constitute what is known as the Gustave Kohn collection, acquired by Tulane from Mr. Kohn, a New Orleans naturalist, and his estate. The majority of the specimens were collected in Louisiana, and all are North American. In the collection are more than 2000 bird skins, representing approximately 250 species. There is also an interesting series of skins of muskrats, field mice, minks, and skunks.

The principal reptile specimens are in preservatives, although a small number of rattlers and water snakes, turtles, terrapins, and tortoises, principally from Louisiana, are mounted.

There are striking collections of invertebrates, including crustaceans, mollusks, starfish, crinoids, corals, and sponges collected from the seven seas. Among the oddities one finds the giant Japanese crab and other crabs from Australia, the Nicobar Islands, and the Indian and Pacific Oceans. There are shells of mollusks in attractive shapes and colors from the South Pacific, Singapore, the Red Sea, and off the coast of Louisiana. There is a small collection of marine creatures, such as sea urchins, starfish, sea cucumbers, and sea lilies. The coral collection from the tropical waters forms an interesting exhibit. Among the sponges is an unusually large example of Neptune's beaker, about 3 feet in height and 18 inches in diameter.

In the field of paleontology the Tulane collection includes specimens of teeth, vertebrae, and ribs of dinosaurs said to have been more than forty feet in length. There are also numerous fossil remains and imprints in ancient earth formations, and specimens of the various large prehistoric reptiles and mammals common in the shallow waters of the Mesozoic era. Other interesting exhibits include fossil remains of the prehistoric bison, the Irish elk of Europe, the mastodon (migrant from Asia), and the two types of sloths from South America. The specimens from Averq Island, Louisiana, attract much attention.

The geological exhibits are all in the east end room. The general arrangement is according to the origin and formations of rocks, and the secondary arrangement is based on gem and commercial values. There is also a separate exhibit of ores containing the chemical elements.

An interesting series of sandstone and limestone deposits with associated fossil shells is a unit of the geological exhibit. Models of famous gold nuggets make another interesting display.

There is an exhibit of the operations of a salt-mining company on one of the salt domes peculiar to the Gulf coastal area of Louisiana. Models of several of the 'Five Islands' near the Louisiana coast are in this display. There is also a generalized model showing the horizons of salt, sulphur, and oil, and the associated geological formations under a typical dome in this area.

On the west side of Gibson Hall stands the *F. W. Tilton Memorial*, built in 1902 and expanded in 1906. This building, architecturally similar to Gibson Hall, contains the main Tulane Library (*open* 8.15 A.M.-10 P.M. *during school session*: 9-4 *in the summer*). Its main collection, some 85,000 volumes, consists chiefly of works dealing with the humanities and the mathematical sciences. Elizabethan and 18th-century English literature are particularly well represented. The library also contains a complete card catalogue of the Library of Congress. On the second floor of the building is the special collection of books supervised by the School of Social Work. Although comparatively small, this collection is growing rapidly.

The *Linton-Surget Collection* of paintings distributed in various rooms in Gibson Hall and in the Tilton Memorial is now in process of being reassembled. A series of portraits including George Washington, Henry Clay, John Adams, James Madison, and Henry Wadsworth Longfellow, as well as a portrait by Benjamin West, should be noted. There are a number of excellent copies of well-known masterpieces and some interesting originals including 'Ruth and Naomi' by Chapman, 'Shooting the Rapids' by William Hopkins, and 'Société des Arts' by Boggs.

To the east of Gibson Hall, and directly facing Tilton Memorial, stands Dinwiddie Hall, newest of Tulane's academic buildings on the campus proper. Dinwiddie Hall was built in 1923, but received no name other than New Science Building until 1936, when it was dedicated in honor of Tulane's late president, Albert B. Dinwiddie. Built of stone in a pattern resembling that of Gibson Hall, the structure houses the College of Law, together with its library of 25,000 volumes, the biology and journalism departments, and the *Department of Middle-American Research*, with its library and museum.

The Department of Middle-American Research (*open weekdays* 9-5, *Sept.* 15-*June* 15, 9-3, *June* 15-*Sept.* 15; *adm. free*) was organized in 1924 to conduct research in every field of Middle America (Mexico, Central America, and the West Indies): in history, ethnology, archeology, botany, photography, architecture, linguistics, anthropology, natural resources and products, and other subjects. The department has gathered and disseminated much information about Middle America, and through friendly contacts with and a deeper knowledge of these peoples has aided in promoting closer relationship between the United States and its nearest Latin-American neighbors.

In 1924 a valuable collection of manuscripts and books pertaining to Middle America, the William E. Gates collection, was offered for sale. Realizing its worth to New Orleans, the logical center of contact with Middle-American countries, the editor of a local daily newspaper presented the facts to the public. An interested man of wealth, who preferred to remain anonymous, purchased the entire collection and presented it, together with an endowment of $350,000, to Tulane University. In that manner the Department of Middle-American Research was born.

During its brief period of existence the Department has developed one of the foremost libraries in its field in the world. It has conducted more than a dozen research expeditions, each of which produced invaluable results. The Department's staff numbers some of the most celebrated men in the field, among them Frans Blom, director, and Hermann Beyer, associate in ethnology.

Future plans of the Department include a building of its own, an authentic full-color reproduction of an early Mayan building. The university has allotted space on the campus, and there is a favorable prospect for early commencement of construction operations.

Important exhibits include relics of ancient Mayan civilization in gold, jade, shell, bone, clay, alabaster, obsidian, and flint. Owing to inadequate display space, more emphasis had been given the library than the museum. Masses of valuable material are stored everywhere about the university campus. One of these hidden objects of interest is an authentic reproduction of the Sanctuary in the Temple of the Sun, found in the great Mayan ruins at Palenque, Mexico, and presented to the Department by the Mexican Government, which had it made at tremendous expense for exhibition at the Century of Progress (Chicago, 1934). Countless visitors recall its magnificent bas-relief carvings, and the mute and mysterious hieroglyphs which have baffled scientists and scholars. Since the Department's field is limited to Mexico, Central America, and the West Indies, the exhibits are principally confined to those areas. They include precious stones, native objects artistically wrought, carved-shell gorgets and ear discs, pottery, figurines, and ornaments of clay, thousand-year-old dolls, a Maya chieftain's skull with filled and inlaid teeth, lip-plugs, pendants, monster spearheads, and chipped flint objects such as a finely balanced sacrificial knife used by priests to cut out the hearts of living human victims.

The library has become so widely known that scholars travel many thousands of miles to consult its treasures. The *Index of Maya Ruins* and the *Index of Maya Hieroglyphs* are invaluable sources in the study of Mayan archeology. Among many priceless collections is archive material dating from the days of the Spanish Conquistadores. A quantity of 16th-century manuscripts written in the Mayan language makes this section of the library the richest in the world, giving it probably as many manuscripts as all other similar collections combined.

Expeditions are an important function of the Department. The first, in 1925, was archeological, with Frans Blom in charge. Some 1200 miles of practically unexplored country from Vera Cruz to Guatemala City were covered. At Comalcalco (in Tabasco), a Maya tomb containing some of the finest stucco bas-reliefs known in the New World was discovered; one hitherto unknown Indian dialect was recorded, and vitally needed corrections to existing maps were made.

Ethnological and archeological expeditions were conducted in 1927 and in 1928. In 1930 an architectural and archeological Century of Progress expedition to Uxmal, Yucatan, was made. Its purpose was to reconstruct in full detail and size one of the finest and purest examples of pre-Columbian architecture, the famed Nunnery Quadrangle.

Directly behind Dinwiddie Hall is the *Richardson Memorial*, a large structure of stone and brick which was built in 1908. The building is used exclusively by the School of Medicine. The *Museum of Microscopic Anatomy* (*adm. by arrangement*), one of the finest collections of embryological specimens (approximately 1000) to be found in this section of the United States, is situated on the first floor. The exhibits, representing the life work of Dr. Harold Cummins, head of the museum, which are used in teaching and research, include a large number of normal embryos ranging from three weeks to term, among which are specially dissected specimens, cleared preparations, and casts. There is also a series of dissected pregnant uteri from about six weeks to term, illustrated variations of afterbirth, and a large number of malformations.

The *Souchon Museum of Anatomy* (*open weekdays* 8.30-5) occupies part of the third floor, and is regarded as one of the finest exhibits of anatomic dissections in the South. An important feature of the museum is the method perfected by Dr. Souchon of retaining the color of muscles, vessels, nerves, and organs in the preservation of anatomic dissections, for which achievement he was awarded the gold medal of the American Medical Association. The exhibits, representing dissections of all parts of the body, include surgical anatomy as well as an interesting bone collection.

To the right of Richardson Memorial stands the Richardson Chemistry Building, erected of brick in 1894. The architectural style of this structure marks a signal departure from that of the other buildings mentioned. Stanley Thomas Hall and the Engineering Building stand side by side to the rear of the Richardson Chemistry Building. They too are built chiefly of brick in rather nondescript patterns, but the vines that partially adorn their walls lend an appearance of old age.

The Physics Building is situated directly across the campus from the identically styled Chemistry Building, and faces in like manner the rear of Gibson Hall. Behind the Physics Building stands the Refectory, a brick structure built in 1902. The Social Science Building and a dormitory, erected in much the same pattern, are situated to the rear of the Refectory.

Crossing Freret St. the visitor comes upon the university's most recent building, the new Gymnasium, which was completed in 1932. It is a large metal-trimmed, red-brick building of a distinctly modern pattern. Beside it stands its smaller outmoded predecessor which, however, is still in use. The additional land that lies between Freret and Willow Sts. is devoted to athletics. The old stadium and football practice fields, together with tennis courts, adjoin the two gymnasiums. .

The new football stadium is situated beyond Willow St. in the third portion of the Tulane campus. Built in 1925 and enlarged in 1937, it has a total seating capacity of

50,000 people. The stadium is the site of the annual Sugar Bowl Game and the Mid-Winter Sports Carnival.

Tulane University, together with Newcomb College, possesses adequate facilities for the training of men and women in virtually all branches of advanced learning. Credits obtained in its various colleges are exchange able with those of most of the better universities in the United States. Particularly noteworthy are the Tulane Medical, Law, Engineering, and Social Service Schools, and the Newcomb Art School – all of which rank highly throughout the South. The Graduate School of Medicine, one of whose specialties is the study of tropical medicine, enjoys a nationwide fame. Its laboratories, lecture rooms, clinics, and offices are housed in the new Josephine Hutchinson Memorial Building, which was completed and occupied in 1930. The new building, erected in the modern sky scraper pattern, is situated on Tulane Ave. just across LaSalle St. from the Charity Hospital, thus forming an important unit in New Orleans' medical center. It is in every respect modern, even to the extent of providing the equivalent of private consultation offices for senior students (*see below*).

Enrolment for Tulane in 1936-37, exclusive of Newcomb, was 2343 day students and 543 night students. The Newcomb enrolment in the same period was 665.

Audubon Park, situated on St. Charles Ave. directly across from Tulane and Loyola Universities, comprises a 247-acre plot which extends back to the Mississippi River. The park is made up of the old Foucher Plantation and a part of the De Boré estate, upon which sugar was first successfully granulated in 1794. The plot was purchased by the city in 1871 and was first called the 'New City Park'; later it was renamed in honor of John James Audubon, famous artist and ornithologist. It was here that the World's Industrial and Cotton Exposition was held in 1884-85, commemorating the one hundredth anniversary of the first shipment of cotton from Louisiana to a foreign port. A striking feature for that day was the illumination of the building and grounds by electricity.

In the St. Charles Ave. section of the park between the lagoon and Magazine St. stands a *World War Memorial* honoring the soldiers of Louisiana who lost their lives in the war. The tall flag pole, with its base of granite, was unveiled December 8, 1921, with Marshal Foch officiating at the ceremonies. The motif of a torch is used, and effectively carried out by the bronze container which upholds the huge pole itself. The flag, floating from the top, represents the flame. On the four sides are bronze tablets, one for each of the four divisions of service, the army, navy, marine, and aviation. The circle of six live oaks surrounding the monument was planted by great leaders of the Allied forces. Gen. John J. Pershing and Gen. R. Nivelle of France planted trees in 1920; Marshal Ferdinand Foch, Commander of the Allied Armies, and Gen. Armando Diaz of Italy, in 1921; Field Marshall Allenby of England in 1928; and Gen. Takeshita and Lieut. Gen. Niomiya of Japan in 1935.

The *Zoological Gardens* are located in the rectangular area toward the western border of the park between Magazine St. and the river. A separate exhibit of lions, tigers, and leopards is located near Magazine St. on the downtown side of the park. To the west, or right, of these cages is the elephant house. Near-by is the *Odenheimer Aquarium*, located in the beautiful Popp gardens. In the center of the building there is a tiled pool, surrounded by a railing and containing a fountain. In the pool are loggerhead snapping turtles, mobilianers, and a number of small alligators. The principal exhibits of the aquarium are in the central building. There is a good collection of salt-water fish, including sheepshead, redfish or channel bass, speckled trout, striped bass, salt-water drum, and croaker.

The fresh-water collection contains specimens of the blue-gilled sunfish, white perch, blue or Mississippi catfish, alligator gar pike, the common eel, and the several varieties of bass.

Between the aquarium and the tennis courts stands the bronze Statue of *John James Audubon* on a granite pedestal surrounded with flowers and shrubs. The famed ornithologist is given an appropriate setting, standing half-isolated among trees and birds, with an intent look of watchfulness on his face, and holding a notebook and pencil in his hands.

Mrs. James L. Bradford, a great admirer of Audubon, was chiefly responsible for the erection of the memorial. In her grandfather's home, in East Feliciana Parish, the bird-lover had done much of his work. From a wealth of personal recollections of this family, Mrs. Bradford prepared a sketch of the life and work of John James Audubon which was published in 1900. For this work the author received $1000, which she used as the beginning of a fund to be employed in the erection of a monument to Audubon. Mrs. Bradford then organized the Audubon Monument Association, and for the next ten years devoted much of her time toward raising funds in various ways to erect the monument. The sum of $10,000 was finally raised, and Edward Valentine was employed as sculptor. The statue was unveiled November 26, 1910. South of the aquarium is the seal pool, also presented by Sigmund Odenheimer, donor of the aquarium.

At the north end of the principal zoo section there is a flight cage, about no by 55 feet, with a maximum height of about 35 feet. The birds in this enclosure are principally wildfowl and other water birds, including white and brown pelicans, cormorants, night herons, European stork, and various American species of geese, ducks, and gulls. Well to the right is a yard for Galapagos tortoises, and beyond that is an alligator pool, containing a number of specimens about 10 feet long.

Other features of the zoo rectangle include the monkey island and monkey house, the tropical bird house, a large central lily pond surrounded by flower beds, and enclosures for deer, zebras, camels, bison, Indian water buffaloes, and sacred cows. The cages for bear and some of the small animals are near the northwest corner, while an enclosure for flamingoes, storks, and cranes is at the southwest. Four large cages with eagles, condors, hawks, and other birds of prey are at the corners of the central area including the pool and flower beds.

Recreational facilities consist of tennis courts, baseball diamonds, football gridirons, picnic grounds, playgrounds (including merry-go-round, etc.), bridle path, swimming pool, bandstand, 18-hole golf course, boating, and fishing. (*See Recreational Facilities.*)

R. from St. Charles Ave. on Broadway.

103. *Newcomb College*, 1229 Broadway, on the uptown side of Tulane campus, an institution of higher learning for women, is an integral part of Tulane University. The college owes its existence almost solely to the munificence and the genuine interest of Mrs. Josephine Louise LeMonnier Newcomb, who donated more than $3,500,000 to this memorial of her only child, Harriet Sophie. The first home of the college (1886) was in an old residence at the corner of Camp and Delord (now Howard Ave.). Later, when these quarters proved inadequate, Mrs. Newcomb provided the group of buildings on Washington Ave., which is now used by the Baptist Bible Institute (*see Motor Tour* 4). Newcomb College remained in that location for almost thirty years, finally moving in 1918 to its present campus.

The college buildings, although not identical, are patterned much more consistently than those of Tulane. They are all built of red brick and white stone and in a classical style. Newcomb Hall, the administration building, faces Broadway, and set back some fifty yards from that avenue, is the cynosure of the group. It houses not only the main offices but also classrooms, laboratories, and an assembly hall. Flanking Newcomb Hall is the Josephine Louise House, a modern dormitory with accommodations for 190 students. Behind the dormitory stand the Newcomb Gymnasium and a separate building containing the swimming pool. These buildings face at right angles to the rear of Newcomb Hall; they border on a semi-elliptical paved drive that encloses a spacious lawn.

Alongside the gymnasium and swimming pool building, but fronting Audubon Blvd., stands the Art School Building. This building is a complete unit in itself, equipped with studios, kilns, workshops for pottery, metalwork, and bookbinding, a small library of technical books, and two toplighted galleries for exhibition purposes. The *Art Gallery* (*open weekdays* 8-5; *adm. free*) has an excellent display of oil paintings, water colors, and pastels by local artists, and has probably one of the best collections of pottery to be found on exhibit in the South. One international and several national prizes have been awarded the work of the Newcomb Art School. There is also an interesting display of jewelry made by students of the school and artists of the city. Another feature attracting much attention is a series of photographs of hand-wrought iron grillwork, an art peculiar to New Orleans almost a century ago. Several engravings in the Newcomb collections are also worthy of attention.

Across the wide lawn, where May Day pageants and commencement exercises take place, stands Dixon Hall, newest academic building on the Newcomb campus. Completed in 1929 and dedicated in honor of the college's first president, Dr. B. V. Dixon, this structure houses the major portion of the School of Music, an auditorium, and the Newcomb Library, containing about 36,000 volumes, including the McKoen collection of books and manuscripts.

Two more dormitories, Doris Hall and the Warren Newcomb House, situated on Audubon Blvd. across from the Art School Building, complete the number of brick edifices on the campus. These buildings accommodate about 80 students. The college has two additional frame buildings, also situated on Audubon Blvd., which were formerly residences but now serve the School of Music.

Retrace Broadway; R. on St. Charles Ave.

104. *St. Mary's Dominican College*, 7214 St. Charles Ave., is a secondary and normal school for girls, administered by the Dominican nuns. It dates back to 1860, when the Dominican Sisters of Cabra, Dublin, Ireland, came to New Orleans to teach in the parochial school of St. John the Baptist on Dryades St. After being in the city but a short time, the Dominican Sisters purchased an excellent site in what was then known as the village of Greenville. They transferred their boarding students to the new location in 1865, where they have remained to this day. Their old academy continued as a day school until 1914.

The original buildings of the Dominican Convent were adequate until 1872, when remodeling began. The present main building was erected in 1882, and others followed in 1892, 1906, and 1922. New plans, however, are now under way to replace all the old buildings with modern fireproof stone structures of Tudor-Gothic design. The first of these completed units serves as the faculty residence.

St. Mary's Dominican College became in 1908 the first Catholic institution in the State to establish a normal training-school. By an act of 1910, St. Mary's became the first Catholic women's college in Louisiana.

105. The *Levee* at Carrollton, which may be seen to the left at the junction of St. Charles and Carrollton Aves., is the highest and widest on the Mississippi River, and the gage there is a criterion of levels in all the lower river district. The United States Engineers and the Mississippi River Commission have made Carrollton a base for many studies, and much of the experimentation in river control.

R. from St. Charles Ave. on S. Carrollton Ave.

106. The *Carrollton Courthouse*, 719 S. Carrollton Ave., was erected in 1855 while Carrollton was the parish seat of Jefferson Parish. After Carrollton became part of New Orleans in 1874 it was used as a school and is now known as McDonogh 23. An imposing structure of brick trimmed with stone, with large columns across the front, the building is typical of the Southern courthouse of ante-bellum days.

The Carrollton section extends from the Mississippi River to Washington Ave. between the Protection Levee and Lowerline St. In its early days several miles of plantations, gardens, and swamplands separated the town from New Orleans. During the War of 1812, while en route to New Orleans to aid in its defense against the British, Gen. William Carroll and several hundred volunteers used the McCarthy plantation as a temporary camping-ground. A village sprang up some years later and was named in honor of the soldier. Samuel Short is said to have built the first house in 1834. The town's development was quickened by the coming of the Carrollton Railroad, which was planned to go along the river as far as Baton Rouge. Begun at the New Orleans end in 1833, the road reached Carrollton September 28, 1835. A depot was built a square beyond the present junction of St. Charles and Carrollton Aves., and still further toward the river, where the levee now stands, the railroad company built the hotel and grounds known for years as the Carrollton Gardens. The railroad never went beyond Carrollton, and the town gradually grew up beyond the depot. The old market square can still be seen at the head of Dante St. near the levee. The Carrollton Gardens became famous as a resort, and some prominent visitors were entertained there, including Thackeray in 1855 and Gen. Boulanger in 1889. Cable uses Carrollton Gardens as a setting for the opening chapters of *Kincaid's Battery*.

The Carrollton Railroad abandoned the use of steam in 1867 and for five years operated with horse-drawn cars. After that it used small steam locomotives, or dummy engines, which carried no fire. The secret lay in the use of boilers at each end of the line, a steam storage tank being employed on the locomotive. The equipment continued to be used until the railroad was absorbed by the public utilities interests of New Orleans in 1890.

Carrollton was incorporated by the legislature in 1845, and became the seat of Jefferson Parish ten years later upon the annexation to New Orleans of Lafayette, the former parish seat. In 1874 it became part of New Orleans.

The Carrollton section has retained much of its former beauty and quiet, reposeful atmosphere. Flower gardens, crowded shrubbery, old-fashioned walks, and a wealth of stately live oaks, elms, sycamore, camphor, walnut, cherry, and palm trees are to be seen on every hand. The surviving differences in neighborhoods formerly distinct as business, residential, and official centers are sufficient to identify the original arrangement of the town. Oak St. between Carrollton Ave. and the Jefferson Parish line, was, and still is, the principal business street; retail stores now occupy former public buildings.

L. from S. Carrollton Ave. on Spruce St.; R. from Spruce on Eagle St.

107. The *Water Purification Plant*, 2142 Eagle St. (*free daily inspection tours 9-6*), is one of two nitration plants supplying water to the city. The plant occupies a 74-acre tract and is situated about a half mile from the river, from which water is pumped through three large intake pipes operated by steam-driven pumps capable of a combined supply of 120,000,000 gallons a day. A low-lift station located near the levee, used during low water, has three electrically driven pumps with a capacity of 150,000,000 gallons per day.

The river water is first pumped into open reservoirs, which occupy an area of 36 acres, to settle, after which it is passed through a battery of 28 filters. The water is purified with a chlorine treatment and sent into the city mains by four steam-driven and two electrically driven pumps, which have a total capacity of 160,000,000 gallons per day. The clay slurry, or residue, which accumulates in the settling basins, is pumped back into the river. In a year's time this waste matter amounts to about 76,000 tons. Among the auxiliary buildings at the main plant is a large electric power station with five boilers which supply a maximum of 14,000 boiler horsepower, and motivate three turbogenerators having a total capacity output of 27,000 kilowatts. The meter repair plant is located near-by, and more than 9000 meters are manufactured or repaired here annually.

R. from Eagle St. on S. Claiborne Ave.; L. from S. Claiborne on S. Carrollton Ave.

108. *Notre Dame Seminary*, 2901 S. Carrollton Ave., under the supervision of the Archbishop of New Orleans, provides instruction for secular priests. Instruction and general management are in charge of the Fathers of the Society of Mary. Established by the late Archbishop John W. Shaw of the Catholic Archdiocese of New Orleans for the purpose of providing a permanent major seminary within his ancient see, Notre Dame draws students from the five subordinate dioceses of Mobile, Lafayette, Alexandria, Natchez, and Little Rock. Completed May 7, 1922, this seminary was dedicated November 7, 1923.

Notre Dame Seminary, a Gothic adaptation of locally used French and Spanish Renaissance styles, is designed after the original Ursuline Convent. Individual details were borrowed from the dormers and cupola of the Cabildo, from the grills and balustrades of other buildings of the Vieux Carré, and from the black and white marble checkerboard tiling of the St. Louis Cathedral floor. The seminary structure, formed like the letter E, is built around a central chapel erected to the deceased bishops and archbishops of New Orleans by the local clergy. The body of the building also contains the archbishop's suite, the presidents office, vaulted parlors, and a lobby. Attractive cloisters connect the wings, one of which houses lecture and recitation rooms, and the other the refectory and library. The basement contains a large auditorium and a recreation room for students.

Ecclesiastical furnishings include a $15,000 marble altar in the chapel given by E. J. Claire and his family, and two side altars donated by the Rev. Peter Pacquet of New Orleans in memory of his parents.

109. The *Waldo Burton Memorial Home*, 3320 Carrollton Ave., is an orphanage for boys conducted by the Society for Destitute Orphan Boys. The institution is non-sectarian and is more than 100 years old. Destitute boys of school age are taken care of, and either returned to their relatives or placed in permanent homes. About 70 inmates are being provided for at the present time.

R. from S. Carrollton Ave. on Washington Ave.

110. *Xavier University*, 3912 Pine St., corner Washington Ave. and Pine St., is the only Catholic institution of higher learning in the United States functioning solely for Negroes. Originated in 1915 by the Sisters of the Blessed Sacrament as a preparatory school for Negro youths, it rapidly expanded until 1925, when it became a full-fledged college. The school soon outgrew its original home on Magazine St. near Jefferson Ave., and moved in 1932 to its present site on Washington near Carrollton Ave.

The present campus contains four units: the college proper, a science hall, a faculty building, and a stadium. The three school buildings are designed in an adaptation of the English Gothic pattern and are built of Indiana limestone.

Like its counterpart, Dillard (*see Motor Tour* 1), Xavier University bestows academic degrees and prepares its students for entrance into professional and graduate schools. But in addition to its Colleges of Arts and Sciences, Pharmacy, Music, and Education, the university also has a Graduate School of Arts and Sciences and, most noteworthy of all, a School of Social Service that ranks with the foremost of its kind in the South.

Retrace Washington Ave.; (R.) on S. Carrollton Ave.

111. The *New Orleans Navigation Canal*, running parallel to Howard Ave., is still popularly known as the New Basin Canal, although it was built in 1832-35. Originally a drainage ditch, it was converted into a navigable waterway to meet the growing city's need for a water connection with Lake Pontchartrain.

112. *Heinemann Park*, corner Carrollton and Tulane Aves., is the home of the Pelicans, the baseball team representing New Orleans in the Southern Association. Both night and day games are held. Seating capacity of the park is 9500, with 2000 additional temporary seats available for the Dixie Series.

R. from S. Carrollton Ave. on Tulane Ave.

113. *The Criminal District Court Building and Parish Prison (free tours of inspection on appointment)*, 2700 Tulane Ave., corner Tulane Ave. and S. Broad St., were completed in 1931 at a cost of $1,775,000. Built of limestone and granite, the architecture of the buildings is a transition from classic to modern. A majestic colonnade supporting an entablature lends dignity and beauty to the main façade on Tulane Ave. The main entrance is also imposing because of the broad expanse of gradually sloping steps that ascend the height of the first story from the street. The Broad St. and White St. fronts are suggestive of an Egyptian motif. The corridor floors are of Tennessee marble, and the walls are decorated with marble pilasters.

Five courtrooms of the Criminal District Court of the Parish of Orleans, sections A-E, each a complete unit within itself with an entrance to the prison, occupy the upper floor. Two are finished in a modern style, two in Colonial, and one in Renaissance. Leather furnishings and lighting fixtures harmonize with the mahogany, black oak, and walnut woodwork. Police headquarters, the Identification Bureau, and the offices of the District Attorney, Criminal Sheriff, and Coroner are also located in the main buildings.

The Parish Prison, a five-story structure of wings and cell blocks adjoining the courthouse, is modern in every detail. Eight hundred prisoners can be accommodated, four to a room. A chapel, infirmary, exercise yards, kitchen, dining-rooms for attendants, and execution chamber are housed within the building. The sheriff very willingly conducts tours of inspection.

The *City Hospital for Mental Diseases (visiting hours 1-3)*, housed in a three-story brick building behind the prison, has accommodations for one hundred patients. It was erected in 1911 to provide for the mentally diseased, who in earlier days were confined without special care in city jails, and were inadequately cared for by the State after 1880.

114. *Hotel Dieu*, 2004 Tulane Ave. (*visiting hours 1-4.30, 6.30-8*), directed by the Catholic Order, Daughters of Charity of St. Vincent de Paul, commonly known as Sisters of Charity, is one of the oldest private hospitals in Louisiana. Founded in 1852 at Canal St. and Claiborne Ave. in a house owned by Dr. Warren Stone, it acquired its present name and site in 1858.

The hospital houses approximately 175 beds; it has about 110 nurses in training, and 6 resident interns in attendance.

115. *St. Joseph's Church* (Catholic), 1802 Tulane Ave., a building under construction for more than twenty-seven years, had its foundation laid December 8, 1871, two years after the first ground was broken. Twenty-one years later, when the edifice was dedicated, pews were not yet in place.

Designed by P. C. Keeley, prominent Brooklyn architect, and built under the supervision of D. M. Foley, Jr., St. Joseph's combines Gothic and Romanesque architecture. Of immense proportions, this structure has a frontage of no feet by 225 feet depth. Its height from foundation to main roof is 150 feet, and from ground floor to ceiling 95 feet. The front elevation presents a grand façade. Two towers, one at each corner, thrust, with their spires, 200 feet from base to summit. Placed above the entrance niches are busts of Pope Pius IX and Archbishop Perche. The lower front, forming an entrance to the vestibule, is finished with fine arches supported by four large columns of unpolished red Missouri granite. The central arch is surmounted by an iron cross approximately 25 feet high.

A large rose window of stained glass, 21 feet, 8 inches in diameter, adorns the center front wall of the building. This memorial window, portraying the Saviour and His twelve apostles, was made in Munich, Bavaria, at a cost of $1800. Running from the base of each tower, and arranged pyramidically above this central window, are nine niches containing statues of saints. Fourteen similar niches are set around the building.

At the main entrance to the vestibule, ceiled with grained vaulting and finished with moldings of marbelized Kentish cement, a flight of granite steps leads to a floor of vari-colored tiles. The three large doors opening upon the main entrance are of walnut wood, carved with figures and raised moldings. The circular transoms are fitted with colored lights. A double row of polished Missouri granite columns, whose arched interstices are capped with stucco and cement moldings, extends the entire length of the building. The semicircular nave is double-ceiled, and finished with inlaid panels of stained native hardwood. The arches are ornamented in rich mosaics, and the side walls garlanded with floral wreaths in stucco. The wainscoting is of oil-finished cypress.

The sanctuary, 57 by 102 feet, contains three beautiful altars. The entire wall to the rear of the great altar is devoted to a bas-relief of the Crucifixion. Rose windows illuminate the space above the vestries. The organ loft and choir gallery, 30 by 50 feet, carry out the grand and spacious design of this church, built to accommodate 1600 people.

116. *Charity Hospital*, 1532 Tulane Ave. (*visiting hours* 12.30-1.30,6.30-8), is operated by the State for the benefit of all indigent citizens of Louisiana. It is at present undergoing extensive rebuilding, which will make it one of the most complete institutions of its kind in the United States. Free hospitalization has been available to the poor people of New Orleans since the founding of the city, for when Bienville came from Biloxi in 1723 he brought with him the hospital equipment which had

been used there. In 1736 a sailor, Jean Louis, bequeathed to the city 10,000 livres for the construction of an institution to care for the sick. This is often considered the actual founding of the Charity Hospital. The present institution, however, is an outgrowth of the 'Hospital of St. Charles' constructed in 1782 by Don Andres Almonester y Roxas on a site on N. Rampart St., between Toulouse and St. Peter Sts. The building was destroyed by fire in 1809, and patients were cared for in a private home until 1814, when the State built a new hospital on Canal St., between Baronne and Dryades, which was opened in 1815. After a fire in 1828 had destroyed the Government House on Toulouse and Levee, the State took over the hospital buildings on Canal St. and converted them into a Statehouse, removing the hospital to its present site on Tulane Ave. in 1832. This structure, which formed the main building of the hospital group, remained in use until 1936.

Since the completion of the first building, many additions have been made to the institution. New buildings were added as the increased number of patients made extensions necessary, and twenty-six units were in operation at the beginning of the present reconstruction. No particular architectural style has been followed, most of the buildings representing the particular style in vogue at the time of erection.

The institution covers an area fronting on Tulane Ave. of three square blocks. In addition to the block behind the main group, there are a number of incidental buildings, while across from the main building on Tulane Ave., there are two structures used as repair shop and garage for ambulances, and as a dormitory for resident interns.

At the time rebuilding began in 1937, the hospital had 1800 patients, 160 nurses, 17 resident interns, and a large staff of full-time physicians and surgeons. Almost every doctor who practices in the city of New Orleans donates a portion of his time each week to the patients of the hospital. There are also a number of doctors practicing in the country parishes who come into the city and give regular hours to the clinics. A Women's Auxiliary meets weekly in the hospital to mend and make garments and gowns used in the hospital. The Catholic Order of the Sisters of Charity is in charge of the nursing and also supervises the household and diet departments.

Free clinics for both white and colored are maintained as well as an accident ward open at all hours for emergency cases. Outpatients may receive dental as well as medical treatment of every sort through the clinics, which are staffed by volunteer doctors and by senior students from the medical schools of Tulane and Louisiana State Universities.

Approximately $1,500,000 is required annually for the operation of the hospital, this amount being derived largely from State appropriations supplemented by numerous gifts and trust funds left to the institution.

117. The *Louisiana State University Medical School*, 1500 Tulane Ave., operates in conjunction with the Charity Hospital, on the grounds of which it is located. The school building was erected here in 1930 for the convenience of both State institutions. It is a ten-story structure of the modified skyscraper variety, with a plain stone-faced exterior, but elaborate bronze and chromium interior trimmings. Completely furnished with the most scientific equipment, the building has accommodations for every

department of medical research, and is a significant unit in the compact, well-organized medical center of New Orleans.

At 1556 Tulane Ave. is the *Pathological Museum* (*open to physicians, medical students, and interested persons by arrangement 9-4 weekdays*) of the L. S. U. Medical Center. It contains about 950 mounted specimens of the most common lesions of all of the anatomical systems of the body. Each specimen is accompanied by a mounted photomicrograph showing the characteristic changes. A complete abstract of the clinical history, physical examination, and postmortem findings in the other organs involved in the disease process is catalogued for reference.

118. The *Museum of the Department of Tropical Medicine*, Tulane University (*open to physicians only, 9-4 weekdays; Sat. 9-12*), is situated on the fifth floor of the Hutchinson Memorial Building, 1432 Tulane Ave. Headed by Col. Charles F. Craig, U.S. Army retired, Professor of Tropical Medicine, it is regarded as one of the finest in the United States.

Among the many interesting and important exhibits to be seen are those of malaria, leprosy, intestinal protozoa, plague, yellow fever, tropical diseases of the skin, venomous snakes, and disease-transmitting insects and worms.

In the first group are a number of interesting photographs of various parts of the human body at certain stages of malarial infection, accompanied by maps showing the distribution of malaria and black-water fever in various parts of the world. The exhibit also contains photo graphs of clinical malaria, as well as others depicting the life cycle of malarial plasmodia in the mosquito.

The second group consists of maps and photographs prepared by Dr. O. E. Denny of the Carville (Louisiana) Leprosorium, showing the distribution of leprosy in North America and throughout the world, and centers in the South from which patients have been received at the National Leprosorium at Carville. A number of highly interesting photographs, along with a very good specimen, convey a vivid idea of the ravages of this ancient disease, known since Biblical times.

The most interesting exhibit is that of the protozoan organisms living in the human intestines, the most important of which is the ameba responsible for amebic dysentery. The exhibit contains a map showing the distribution of amebic dysentery, photographs and drawings illustrating the organism and lesions produced by it, clinical charts, and specimens of drugs useful in the treatment of infection.

Another display deals with bubonic plague. Composing this group are specimens of various rodents to which the disease is peculiar, lithographed pictures of human organs and those of carriers at various stages of infection, and a map showing the geographical distribution of bubonic plague.

The yellow fever exhibit shows the epidemiology and transmission, and also the pathology of the disease. This group contains several good photographs, a few mosquito specimens of the species transmitting the fever, and clinical charts.

Tropical skin diseases have a very important place in the exhibits of the museum. A number of the commoner types are shown in a group of excellent etchings and photographs that composes a good part of the museum. These pictures are accompanied by maps giving the geographical distribution of the diseases. Common among these infections are molds, mildews, and fungi.

The display of venomous snakes includes the coral snakes and pit vipers of the Western Hemisphere, the pit vipers (without rattles) of Central and South America, and the rattlesnake group of Southwest United States, Mexico, and Brazil.

In the group of worms which produce diseases in man are tick worms, ground worms, flukes, etc. Most interesting are the models of a village and farms of South China, where the various diseases ascribed to flukes are contracted. Numerous specimens and photographs make up a large part of the exhibit.

Among the other exhibits to be found in the Museum are those of deficiency diseases, bacillary dysentery, cholera, tropical diseases of animal origin, diseases of domestic animals, and a number of excellent lantern slides showing some of the most important parasitic diseases.

The *Charles Edmund Kells Dental Library and Museum* is housed in the same building, the library on the second floor and the museum on the sixth. The library consists of approximately 1000 volumes dealing with dentistry, and the museum contains about 15 cases of dental instruments, teeth, plaster models of jaws and sets of teeth, skulls complete with teeth, and a display of dental office equipment. The library and museum were founded by the dentists of Louisiana, January 19, 1927, as the wall plaque states, 'in appreciation of the highly valued inventions and literary contributions to the science of dentistry rendered by Charles Edmund Kells, Jr.' (1856-1928).

119. The *Old Criminal Court Building*, corner Tulane Ave. and Saratoga St., now houses the First and Second Recorders Court, the Traffic Court, the Night Court, and the First Precinct Police Station. Considerable controversy and scandal developed over the construction of the building (1893-95), the contractor being charged with failure to comply with the terms of the contract as to material and dimensions, and the city officials with misuse of funds. The present condition of the building after forty years indicates that the material and workmanship were not of the best. When completed the Criminal Court Building presented the appearance of an early French Renaissance château, with its round towers, pointed spires, and tall clock. The material was red brick with soft, red sandstone trimmings. The structure was impractical and deterioration soon began. Only part of the building is now in use.

120. *Eye, Ear, Nose and Throat Hospital*, 166 Elk Pl. (visiting hours 8-8), occupies two adjoining buildings just across Tulane Ave. from the Old Criminal Court Building. One of these is two stories high, and was constructed in 1907 on the site of the famous Silver Dollar Saloon. The other, a five-story brick building, a gift of John Dibert, was erected in 1922. The hospital was established in 1889 to render service 'to those too poor to pay' by Dr. A. W. DeRoaldes. First located at 23 South Rampart St., the institution moved to a site at Custom House (Iberville) and North Rampart Sts. in 1891. During 1900 a festival was given and sufficient funds were raised to purchase the present grounds.

There are 70 beds in the hospital, a portion of them being used for 'pay patients'; the remainder take care of those admitted through free clinics. Funds for operating the hospital are received principally from a small subsidy from the City of New Orleans and the State of Louisiana. The remainder is derived from private patients and donations. The staff of the hospital is composed of doctors of the city who volunteer their services.

R. from Tulane Ave. on Saratoga St.; R. from Saratoga on Girod St.

121. *Girod Cemetery*, S. Liberty between Cypress and Perilliat Sts., is the oldest Protestant cemetery in the city. (*See Cemeteries.*)

122. The *City Yard*, located immediately behind the Girod St. Cemetery, occupies the site of one of the oldest prisons of New Orleans. In 1841, on ground purchased from the owners of the cemetery, then known as the Protestant Episcopal Burying-Ground, the city erected the Second Municipality Workhouse, of which only the outer walls and main gateway now remain. It was here that minor offenders were confined to work out their sentence, the more dangerous criminals being placed in the Parish Prison. Here also were kept unruly slaves, who repaired city streets in chain gangs under the alert eye of a guard. An interesting side-light on conditions of this era is that relating to Negro seamen; forbidden the freedom of the city by laws regarding slaves, they were confined here during their stay in port, or, as it was said, 'accommodated with an apartment in the Workhouse.'

The old walls, the only remnants of the jail, are constructed of brick and cement and are still in an excellent state of preservation. Buttressed and forbidding, they give all the appearance of an old stronghold, a fact probably responsible for the legend that the old prison was once a Spanish fortress. The stables and sheds within the walls are all of recent construction.

Return on Girod St.; L. from Girod on S. Rampart St.

South Rampart Street is the Harlem of New Orleans. For a distance of several blocks it teems with a great variety of shops catering largely to the Negro population. Countless cafés and refreshment stands are in evidence, and music-store phonographs supply the visitor with an introduction to local Negro melody. The street, which is seen to its best advantage on Saturday evenings, when it is crowded with shoppers and pleasure-seekers, has afforded material for numerous literary works, including stories by Roark Bradford and Octavus Roy Cohen.

123. A small *Chinese center*, consisting of several stores where native foods and supplies may be obtained, is to be found on Tulane Ave. just off S. Rampart St. to the left.

124. The *Semmes House*, 135 S. Rampart St., is a three-story, pressed-brick edifice, flush with the sidewalk and wedged in between buildings on either side. It extends through the narrow block from Rampart to Elk PL and was built some time before the Civil War by Mrs. Jones McCall, who later sold it to Thomas J. Semmes. The beauty of this mansion is its interior. There is probably no other home in New Orleans where more great men of all classes – cardinals, Presidents, artists, writers, and scholars – have been entertained. Mr. Semmes died in 1899.

Continue to Canal St.

MOTOR TOUR 4

IRISH CHANNEL and GARDEN DISTRICT, 6 m.

The following street-cars roughly parallel the tour route: Laurel car (for Irish Channel) from Canal and Tchoupitoulas Sts.; Magazine car (for return through Garden District) from Magazine St. and Louisiana Ave.

Up St. Charles St. from Canal; around Lee Circle and toward the river on Howard Ave. (For points of interest along St. Charles St., see Motor Tour 3.)

125. The *Sarpy House*, 534 Howard Ave., was built about 1764 and was one of the first buildings in the Faubourg Ste. Marie. Delord Sarpy, who first occupied the home, and for whom Howard Ave. was originally named Delord St., was one of the city's wealthiest and most popular citizens. Standing at the end of a long, oak-bordered drive leading from the river to the entrance, this building was one of the finest examples of the early plantation homes. Now, pitifully out of place, with one gallery gone and its wide entrance ways boarded up, the plantation home, at present a tenement house, stands surrounded by warehouses.

The building is typical of the early plantation, a house of brick and frame construction, with square brick pillars supporting the second floor and slender cypress colonettes supporting a hipped roof which is broken by delicately ornamented dormer windows. Only the side of the dwelling is visible from the street today.

R. from Howard Ave. on Annunciation St

Note: The route from the turn at Howard Ave. to the Mercy Hospital and again from Annunciation Square to the Kingsley House covers several blocks still paved with cobblestones, and the going is a little rough. Most of the vessels that came to New Orleans in the early 19th century carried cobble stones as salable ballast.

The area between Constance St. and the river extending from St. Joseph St. to Louisiana Ave. is known as the '*Irish Channel.*' The origin of the name is indefinite; it is said that sailors coming into port watched for a light kept burning all night in a saloon, and hailed the district as the Irish Channel because of the large number of Irish living in the section.

Almost from the beginning this district became known as one of the 'tougher spots' of New Orleans, and the reputation has clung to it until very recent times. At one time the 'Shot Tower Gang,' 'St. Mary's Market Gang,' and other bands of hoodlums dominated the political existence of this section, often making it dangerous for outsiders to enter it, even on entirely legitimate business. Rough characters sometimes set on strangers merely because they 'did not like their looks.' The saloons and brothels were the most boisterous and disorderly in the city. Lawlessness was often rampant, and robbery and other crimes originated in the rendezvous of some of the gangsters of this early period.

Today its most obvious peculiarity is that, while consisting of neighborhoods of many types, on the whole it has kept its character as the scene of the first great development in river traffic and port building. It is made up of a mixture of modern docks and port facilities. A few modern factories operate alongside of abandoned brick warehouses, empty cotton press yards, and other relics of former epochs in commerce and industry. They border streets roughly paved with cobblestones and Belgian blocks, interspersed with small, crowded, poorly built homes of the laboring classes. Here and there, shabby but still impressive houses recall the days when the American element was new to New Orleans and began to build homes above Canal St.

The Irish Channel came into existence with the influx of a new American as well as European element of population into New Orleans in the early part of the 19th century, when shipping and river trade began to push up the river-front above Canal St. One of the first centers of business in this district was St. Mary's Market, extending, when completed, between two short streets, N. Diamond and S. Diamond, from Tchoupitoulas St. to South Front St. It was established in 1836.

In 1840 many Irish immigrants arrived, and a number of Germans came several years later. With the increasing population and growing problems of its mixed population and rough-and-ready life, the Irish Channel began to attract the attention of those concerned with the social and moral welfare of New Orleans. Several groups of ministers and laymen started to work for the establishment of churches, missions, and schools.

The First Presbyterian Church established a mission in 1840 on Fulton St. between St. Andrew and Josephine Sts. The Redemptorists established St. Mary's Church for Germans in 1845 at the corner of Constance and Josephine Sts. St. Alphonsus Church, for English-speaking Roman Catholics, came into existence in 1848. Notre Dame, on Jackson Ave. between Constance and Laurel Sts., was the first Roman Catholic church for French in this portion of the city, and was established in 1858.

The mixed character of the population of the Irish Channel made social welfare work in the community difficult. It was not until the end of the century that effective measures in this direction were carried out. The Rev. Beverly E. Warner, rector of Trinity Episcopal Church, was the first to take definite steps toward organizing groups of young people. He was assisted by various members of his parish and the New Orleans Kindergarten Association, which had established a day nursery at Erato and Annunciation Sts. Clubs were formed for boys and girls, and plans made to inaugurate a system of education and entertainment. Two of the girls' clubs were housed in the kindergarten quarters, and a boys club was organized at Delord and Tchoupitoulas Sts. A number of New Orleans citizens, including members of the Tulane University faculty, gave valuable assistance in working out programs. Under the guidance of the first director, the late Miss Eleanor McMain, who was selected by Dr. Warner, the work increased in importance and popularity. It became known finally as the Kingsley House Association, which now has well-equipped quarters at 1600 Constance St. (*See below.*)

A few of the fine homes that distinguished some neighborhoods in this river-front district at an earlier period are still in use. In various stages of shabbiness and dilapidation, most of them are found in the vicinity of Annunciation Square. New Orleans families of importance lived at various times in these houses.

126. *Mercy (Soniat Memorial) Hospital*, 1321 Annunciation St. (*visiting hours 2-4, 6-8*) was founded in 1924 and is operated by the Sisters of Mercy. The main building is the old Saulet Plantation home, erected about 1816 on ground that was once part of the great Jesuit Plantation. The hospital has 118 beds, an average of 51 nurses in training, 4 resident internes, and a staff of 125 city doctors. A free clinic for white patients only is operated under the auspices of the Community Chest. An average of 17,000 persons is treated free of charge each year by the doctors on the hospital staff, who contribute their services.

127. *Missouri Pacific* and *Texas Pacific Terminal*, 1384 Annunciation St., is directly across the street from the Mercy Hospital.

128. *Annunciation Square*, bounded by Annunciation, Race, Chippewa, and Orange Sts., was formerly the center of one of the most select residential sections of the city. After the Civil War many of the old buildings were used as cotton warehouses, and it is said that certain clansmen frequenting the Irish Channel held meetings here. Today the square serves as a playground for children.

129. The *Kaul House*, 904 Orange St., uptown lake corner Annunciation and Orange Sts., was the boyhood home of Sir Henry Morton Stanley, explorer of Africa and roving correspondent, who as John Rowlands was adopted by the Stanley family and given the name of his foster-father, Henry Morton Stanley, then a prosperous New Orleans merchant. Scratched on one of the window panes in a small rear room of the house is the name 'Stanley,' resembling the signature of the famous explorer.

R. from Annunciation St. on Richard St.; L.from Richard on Constance St.

130. The *Kingsley House*, 1600 Constance St., corner of Market and Constance Sts. (*open daily*), is frequently called 'the Hull House of the South.' The Kingsley House Association was formed in 1902 under the direction of Miss Eleanor McMain, a native of Louisiana who took special training at the University of Chicago, Hull House, and the Chicago Commons. Before her death in 1934 the institution had grown to be one of the greatest of its kind in the South, with an annual enrolment of approximately 1000 adults and youths.

The institution is housed in two-story, red-brick buildings with white columns and green shuttered windows. They face a large courtyard and are interesting adaptations of Southern plantation styles. An old cotton press once occupied this spot, and some of the original walls remain. A great variety of clubs and classes are conducted for both instruction and recreational purposes. Among these are classes in cooking, sewing, weaving, pottery, craftwork, printing, dramatics, folk-dancing, calisthenics, and music. Recreational facilities include a large gymnasium, library, basketball court, swimming pools, and playgrounds. Small dues are collected annually from all members. Adults desiring membership are voted upon in the regular meetings of the members. Only those residents living within the area bounded by Gaiennie St., Washington Ave., Prytania St., and the river-front are eligible to participate in the activities offered. Children are allowed to join through invitation extended by the children's clubs. Regular attendance at club meetings and classes entitles each member to a 12-day vacation at Camp Onward, Bay St. Louis, Miss., which is conducted each summer under the auspices of the Kingsley House.

The institution is supported by the Community Chest, voluntary subscriptions, and a small revenue accruing from the sale of craftwork and pottery. A board of directors made up of New Orleans citizens assists in managing the institution; 8 full-time workers and 5 part-time helpers assist in class work. Visitors are always welcome, and are escorted over the grounds by a member of the staff.

R. from Constance St. on Felicity St.; L. from Felicity on Magazine St.; L. from Magazine on St. Mary St.; R. from St. Mary on Constance St.

131. The *Redemptorist Churches and Schools*, Constance St. from Josephine to St. Andrew, are noted for their fine examples of baroque brick architecture, popular in New Orleans during the middle of the 19th century. The group consists of two churches and four parochial schools offering courses extending from elementary through high-school grades.

St. Alphonsus, the main church of the group, was constructed after 1855 by lay brothers who toiled as artisans. It served the Irish and other English-speaking Catholics of the neighborhood.

Built at a cost of more than $100,000, the church is 145 feet long, 67 feet wide, and 55 feet high at its tower base. This Renaissance church, seating 1250, is covered with rough building brick but utilizes Greek architectural elements in its columns and its pilasters. The theme is repeated in the treatment of the still uncompleted towers of the upper story. The interior, not strictly basilican, is suggestive of a Roman church. The deeply coffered ceiling has enough curvature not to appear heavy; and the gallery, an innovation in church interiors, has been cut back from the columns at the forward end in order to preserve the effect originally designed. To the right of the sanctuary, taking the place of the right side altar, is the *Shrine of our Lady of Perpetual Help*. The mosaic representation of Our Lady of Perpetual Help was placed there by the Redemptorist Fathers in 1932. Perpetual novenas are offered every Tuesday, six services being held throughout the day.

St. Mary's Assumption was the first Catholic church to be established in Lafayette (the Fourth District), and marks the beginning of the work of the Redemptorists in New Orleans. A small frame church was built at the corner of

Josephine and Constance Sts. and dedicated Jan. 14, 1844, to serve the Germans of the neighborhood. The cornerstone of the present brick church was laid April 25, 1858. St. Mary's is an outstanding example of the splendid New Orleans brick masonry of the middle-19th century. Its baroque tower rises to a height of 142 feet, and the baroque architectural motif predominates in both the interior and exterior. The elaborate high altar and the stained-glass windows were imported from Munich, and the great bells were cast in France. The interior is notable for the pendentives which support the vaulting of the roof in place of central columns. The decorative designs are all in ornate German tradition.

R. from Constance St. on First St.

The area known as the *Garden District*, extending from Jackson to Louisiana Aves., between St. Charles Ave. and Magazine St., was originally the residential section of the American colony. In ante-bellum days the social center for the American aristocracy of New Orleans, the Garden District remains one of the most charming sections of the city. Here, half-hidden by palms, live oaks, and magnolias, stand dozens of massive structures. They were built near the middle of the 19th century, and are relics of a time when prosperity was at its peak in the South. Many of the houses, containing from twenty to thirty rooms, have been well preserved and are still in the possession of descendants of the original owners. Others, however, have been sold and converted into apartment houses or commercial buildings. The architecture of the homes is an odd fusion of classic styles with indications of Spanish, French, and English influence as well as the Greek Revival. A few are built on the typical Louisiana style, or the type known as the 'raised cottage.'

The owners of these homes spared no expense in decorating the interior of the buildings. In many instances artists were brought from abroad to paint murals or portraits. Bronze chandeliers, marble mantels, statuary, and curios of every description were common.

In the reception halls gathered the élite of New Orleans. There was a saying that a family must have lived in the Garden District at least twenty years before its members could be recognized as residents of this section.

The 'City of Gardens' still retains the dignity that characterized it three quarters of a century ago.

132. The *Forsyth House*, 1134 First St., deserves mention because in one of its rooms died Jefferson Davis, former President of the Confederacy. The home was formerly owned by Judge Charles Erasmus Fenner, an intimate friend of Jefferson Davis, with whom the Davis family visited in New Orleans. The house was built by J. N. Payne, father-in-law of Judge Fenner. The two-story cement-covered brick building was constructed in the early fifties by slaves brought from the Payne Plantation. Wide front galleries extend across both floors, supported by six columns of Ionic design.

In the guest room on the ground floor of the main building, the last room on the river side of the wide center hall, Jefferson Davis died. The house was recently bought and restored by Mr. William B. Forsyth.

L. from First St. on Camp St.; R.from Camp on Third St.

133. *General Hood's Home*, 1206 Third St., was erected shortly before the Civil War period. The architecture is something of a mixture. The building has a mansard roof, surmounted by an ornamental balustrade of grilled iron. It was here that Gen. Hood died, together with two members of his family, in the yellow-fever epidemic of 1878.

134. The *Hero House*, 1213 Third St., is one of the best examples of the school of architecture which flourished in New Orleans about the middle of the 19th century. The original owner was Archibald Montgomery, a native of Dublin, who employed James Gallier, Jr. to design and erect a residence for him. Maj. Andrew Hero bought the property some years after, and the home is still in the possession of his family. The garden surrounding the home, with its profusion of shrubs and flowers, and its flagged walk leading from the gate to the entrance of the house reminds one of a miniature park.

L. from Third St. on Chestnut St.

135. The *Baptist Bible Institute*, 1220 Washington Ave., a theological institution for men and women, organized in August, 1917, is supported by the Home Mission Board of the Southern Baptist Convention. Twenty-three buildings, including residences for students and faculty members, make up the institution. The property was purchased from the Board of Administrators of Tulane University in 1917. Previous to this date it had been occupied by the H. Sophie Newcomb College. There were 213 students enrolled in the 1935-36 sessions. The library contains some 40,000 volumes, mostly on religion.

The architecture of the Administration Building, originally the home of James Robb, wealthy banker and planter, is of Italian Renaissance design for which reason it was once known as the 'Italian Villa.' From the front an imposing marble stairway leads to a terrace extending across the building. Although a basement and two upper stories were originally planned, the second story, for financial reasons, was not constructed until 1890. James Freret of New Orleans was the architect, and Dominique Canova, nephew of Antonio Canova, was the decorator.

The library of this former residence now serves as an office for Mr. Sellers of the Institute faculty, and the old dining-room has become Dr. Denham's study. The main corridor, once an art gallery, connects with the original guest chambers, and with the interesting Mirror Room, designed to serve as a reception hall. This Mirror or 'Pompeian' Room is octagonal and is furnished with a mantelpiece of black onyx; the two doors are of hand-tooled Honduran mahogany. Five large silver-backed mirrors, decorated with an etched design in gold leaf, add richness; while two others, of oval shape, are so arranged as to afford an outlook in eight directions. Eight frescoed panels radiate from an octagonal ornament upon the ceiling, each worked out in a complicated design utilizing mythological themes. As the Robb Mansion, this house contained many handsome furnishings and works of art, among them being the 'Greek Slave' by the sculptor Hiram Powers, who presented it to James Robb in 1843.

This artistic tradition was continued by Newcomb College, which after purchasing the house and lot spent $30,000 for remodeling. At this time the present Religious Education Reading-Room was used as an art gallery, and its walls were hung with paintings. Prof. Ellsworth Woodward, of the Art Department of Newcomb College planned the gallery.

An interesting feature of the Baptist Bible Institute campus is a cluster of camphor trees, closely tangled together near the ground. These are offshoots of a giant parent, planted after Mr. Burnside had purchased the property in 1859. Before it was destroyed, this tree, said to have been the largest then growing in the United States, towered 30 feet above the main building.

R. from Chestnut St. on Eighth St.

136. *George Cable's Home*, 1313 Eighth St., originally a raised cottage painted in soft tones of red and olive, was built in 1874. Square brick columns supported the veranda, and a broad flight of railed steps led up to the living-quarters. On either side of the entrance stood large orange trees, and a luxuriant garden surrounded the house. Although the steps have now been removed and the house changed into a two-story dwelling, many aspects of the building remain the same. Set in the midst of modern houses, it has the appearance of an old plantation home. Only a small portion of the extensive gardens now remain with the building. The house was occupied during the winter of 1884-85, after Cable had left New Orleans, by Joaquin Miller, the California poet, who was in the city during the Cotton Exposition as special correspondent for several large newspapers. Flo Field, the New Orleans writer, occupies one of the apartments at present.

R. from Eighth St. on Coliseum St.; L. from Coliseum on Washington Ave.

137. *Lafayette Cemetery* 1, Washington Ave. and Coliseum St., is the oldest of the uptown cemeteries. (*See Cemeteries.*)

R. from Washington on Prytania St.; R. from Prytania on Fourth St.

138. The *Britten House*, 1450 Fourth St., is one of the largest and most interesting examples of the ante-bellum mansions in the Garden District. Built in 1859 by Colonel Robert H. Short, a native of Kentucky known as the 'Blue Grass Colonel,' the building, with its spacious garden, occupies almost an entire block. The structure, two stories in height, is built of cement-covered brick and is painted a rich mahogany brown. There are fifteen large rooms with lofty ceilings and massive antique furniture. On three sides of the house are verandas with wrought-iron railings and supports of the Spanish type. The home contains a wealth of statuary, pictures, and objects of art. The garden, filled with giant magnolias, elms, palms, and a network of vines and shrubs, is enclosed with a cast-iron fence of a cornstalk design. Another fence similar to this is found at a residence in the French Quarter at 915 Royal Street.

L. from Fourth St. on Coliseum St.

139. The *Eustis House*, 2627 Coliseum St., is a red-brick structure of Swiss and English design, originally built for James Eustis, Ambassador to France. The home was afterwards purchased by Julius Koch, who had designed and superintended its construction during the Reconstruction Period.

L. from Coliseum St. on Third St.

140. The *Pescud House*, 1415 Third St., was built by Walter Robinson, a Virginia gentleman, and was occupied by members of his family until it came into the possession of Peter F. Pescud, the present owner. The style of architecture is that of the later ante-bellum period, large and expansive, with wide galleries on both the first and second floors. The lower story is ornamented with Doric columns, the upper with Corinthian. The building is set several yards back in a beautifully kept lawn, surrounded with palms and shrubs. The garden was formerly noted for its rare plants and flowers, many of which had been brought from distant parts of the country. The interior is handsomely frescoed, and the carved mahogany stairway is one of the most beautiful in the city.

R. from Third St. on Prytania St.

141. The *Walmsley House*, 2507 Prytania St., is set well back from the street in a grove of oaks and palms, surrounded by a cast-iron fence. There are thirty rooms in the two-and-a-half-story building, with a handsome mahogany stairway leading from the first floor. The structure was erected shortly before the outbreak of the Civil War, but did not come into the possession of the Walmsley family until about fifty years ago. It is now occupied by the mother and brother of the city's former mayor, T. Semmes Walmsley.

142. The *James House*, 2405 Prytania St., was originally the residence of a Lewis family, but later came into the possession of Col. S. L. James, by whose name the home is usually known. The building is a two-and-a-half-story, plastered-brick structure, set far back in a garden filled with semitropical shrubs and flowers. The ironwork of the galleries is interesting. On the interior many fine paintings once adorned the walls

These were executed by European artists, one of whom painted a handsome oil portrait of the owner's daughter on the ceiling of the parlor. The building has recently been redecorated and converted into an apartment house.

143. *Louise S. McGehee School for Girls*, 2343 Prytania St., is a private school housed in the home built for Bradish Johnston in 1870 by James Freret. The building is a fine example of free Renaissance design. The wide front porch is supported by fluted Corinthian columns used in pairs across the front of the house. The floor of the entrance hall is of marble flags. The interior woodwork is Greek Revival, the staircase being particularly fine. In the garden is a magnolia tree pronounced by the late Charles Sprague Sargent, director of the Arnold Arboretum at Harvard, as the finest specimen of the Grandiflora variety in existence.

144. The *Westfeldt House*, 2340 Prytania St., is said to be the oldest building in the section, having been erected about 1830. The residence is a square white

structure, representing the raised cottage style of building typical of Louisiana. The original owner was Thomas Toby, manager of a large plantation, who came to Louisiana from Philadelphia in the early part of the 19th century. The residence was during those days the home of Toby's overseer, but after Toby's own home was destroyed by fire he moved into the building. At this time, the Toby plantation was at the end of the city bus line and the spot became known as 'Toby's Corner.' The building is surrounded by palms, magnolias, and live oaks, and is enclosed by a fence of white pickets. In the garden at the rear is one of the finest live oaks in the city, many artists having used it as a subject.

145. *Miss Sarah Henderson's House*, 2221 Prytania St. (*visitors admitted by appointment*), is a two-story plaster-brick building said to have been copied from an Italian villa. The original owner was a Mr. Grinnen, an Englishman who came to New Orleans before the middle of the 19th century and employed James Gallier to design and erect his home. Surrounding the residence are huge magnolias, palms, shrubs, and vines, and in the rear is one of the loveliest gardens in this section. The building is occupied by Miss Sarah Henderson.

R. from Prytania St. on Jackson Ave.

146. *Soulé College*, 1410 Jackson Ave. (*visitors welcome*), was formerly the home of Cartwright Eustis, a prominent citizen of New Orleans. This large rambling structure, surrounded by moss-hung oak, giant magnolia, sycamore, palmetto, palm, and banana trees, stands out as an excellent example of Louisiana architecture. The garden is enclosed within a cast-iron fence. The building is three and one-half stories high, and is surrounded by porches supported by Ionic columns. Cast-iron railings, popular during the middle of the 19th century, accentuate the depth of the porches. The building has now been converted into a commercial training school which is under the direction of Albert L. Soulé.

147. *Trinity Church*, 1329 Jackson Ave., often called 'the church which makes bishops,' is noted for the number of distinguished divines who have been its spiritual leaders. In 1855, Bishop Leonidas Polk was called to take charge of the Episcopal congregation organized in 1847. During the Civil War, Bishop Polk left his congregation to enter the Confederate service, and was killed in action June 14, 1864. In 1863 Dr. J. W. Backwith, afterward Bishop of Georgia, became rector. During his incumbency the church was extended and improved at a cost of $25,000. In 1868 Rev. J. N. Galleher, afterward Bishop of Louisiana, became rector. He was succeeded by Rev. S. S. Harris, afterward Bishop of Michigan. Dr. Hugh Miller Thompson, later Bishop of Mississippi, became the next rector.

Trinity Church was built in 1851 at a cost of $22,500. Of brick and stucco, in imitation of stonework construction, its exterior is now grayed and weathered. The design and decoration are the result of a Victorian conception of English Gothic architecture. The façade, approached by a steep flight of concrete steps facing Jackson Ave., has a central entrance, but the opening on Coliseum St. is the one generally used. A Sunday school occupies the wing on Coliseum St. To the rear of the church is the Howcott Memorial Parish House, erected in 1910.

The interior of this church is noted for its fine chancel and chancel window. An imposing stained-glass memorial, placed above and behind the carved altar, and dedicated to Leonidas Polk, first Bishop of Louisiana, represents three scenes from the life of Christ. A modern stained-glass window, representing the Last Supper, was dedicated to the memory of Bishop Hugh Miller Thompson in June, 1936.

L. from Jackson on Chestnut St.; R. from Chestnut on Felicity St.

148. The *Felicity Street Methodist Church*, 1218 Felicity St., has one of the oldest congregations in the city. The first church on this site was built in 1850 and dedicated on Christmas morning of that year. Thirty-seven years later the building was destroyed by fire, and a new building was erected in 1888. It was in this church that the first Southern branch of the Epworth League was organized, in 1891.

L. from Felicity St. on Camp St.

149. *Coliseum Square*, running from Melpomene to Race St., and bounded by Camp and Coliseum Sts., was laid out in the 1830's as a park, in which there was to be erected a university called the 'Prytaneum.' Greek art being much in vogue at the time, the streets of the section were given the names of the nine Muses. The university was never built, but for many years this was one of the fine residential sections of New Orleans.

The three following points of interest in the vicinity of Coliseum Square can be seen best on foot.

150. The *Caffery House*, 1228 Race St., facing the uptown side of Coliseum Square, is a three-story stucco-covered brick building, erected by John T. Moore during the Civil War. The foundation was laid by slave labor, and the house was partly paid for with Confederate money. The rooms have 16-foot ceilings, carved-marble mantels, beautiful chandeliers, and a mahogany spiral staircase. For a time the home was occupied by Donelson Caffery, a prominent New Orleans attorney.

151. *Grace King's House*, 1749 Coliseum St., was erected in 1830. The building, constructed of cement-covered brick, has two stories, an attic, and a classic façade. As the home of Grace King, well-known Louisiana author, it attracts much interest. The residence is in excellent condition, and the garden is well kept.

152. The *Thornhill House*, 1420 Euterpe St., lake side of Coliseum Square, which dates back to the early part of the 19th century, was purchased in 1845 by John Thornhill and occupied by his family until the Civil War, when Gen. Butler took possession and made it the headquarters for the Freedmen's Bureau. During the period in which it was occupied by the Federals, many of the valuable furnishings and objects of art stored here were destroyed.

Return to Camp St.

153. The *Coliseum Place Baptist Church*, 1376 Camp St., river side of Coliseum Square, is the oldest Baptist church in the city and has the second largest congregation. Built in 1854, it cost more than $50,000. The small group of members composing this first congregation struggled many years in paying for the building, final-

ly clearing the indebtedness sometime after the Civil War.

A red-brick structure of Gothic perpendicular design, the Coliseum Place Baptist Church closely resembles the Catholic St. Patrick's farther down the street. A square tower, aspiring to a low hexagonal steeple, dominates the rough, severe, and rather gloomy façade. Three arched Gothic door ways, one central and one at each side, lead into the entrance hall. One tall arched Gothic window surmounts the central entrance, and similar ones are cut into the sides of the structure.

The auditorium of the Coliseum Church, on the second floor, is rectangular in shape, with a circular balcony supported by flying wooden buttresses giving it a bowl-like effect. Walls and ceiling are plastered and painted a rich cream-yellow tone, blending with the dark mahogany color of the stained, polished, and age-mellowed cypress pews, furniture, and woodwork. The pipe organ, behind the central pulpit, is framed in a pointed arch and screened by a Gothic fretwork design in yellow plaster. Two graceful gilded Victorian chandeliers add to the charm of this interior. Centrally hung on the rear wall of the church room are three bronze plaques commemorating deceased deacons and pastors.

Continue on Camp St.

154. *Margaret Statue*, Camp and Prytania Sts., was one of the earliest memorials erected to women in this country. The statue of Margaret Haughery, the quaint little Irish woman who made philanthropy her lifework, stands in a triangular park bounded by Camp, Prytania, and Clio Sts., with a background of palms, old church steeples, and the façade of the Louise Home.

Born of Irish immigrant parents, Margaret, with her husband and child, came to New Orleans from Baltimore in search of health for her husband. Soon after arriving she lost both husband and child. In an effort to forget the tragedy, she attached herself to the Poydras Asylum and established a dairy and bakery, both of which expanded rapidly and brought in surprising profits. The greater part of her earnings flowed out immediately to the needy, to whose care she devoted the remainder of her life. At her death her life savings of $30,000 were left to charity.

Many glowing tributes were paid Margaret at her death, and within half an hour plans were made to erect a monument to her memory. Within two years sufficient funds – mostly five-cent contributions – had been raised. The statue was designed by Alexander Doyle and unveiled in July, 1884, with Governor Nicholls making the dedicatory speech.

The statue, which cost $6000, is of Carrara marble and rests on a 7-foot granite pedestal. The kindly old woman sits in a chair, dressed in her familiar calico gown, with an old shawl about her shoulders, looking down on a little child who leans against her chair. The monument bears the simple inscription 'Margaret.'

155. The *Louise Home*, Camp and Prytania Sts., facing Margaret Statue, was formerly the New Orleans Female Asylum, organized in 1850, an institution in which Margaret Haughery was interested. Today it is an inexpensive home for working girls.

156. The *Lighthouse for the Blind*, 734 Camp St. (*open daily except Sun.* 8-5), was established in 1919 to assist the blind of the city and to give them practical training. The Lighthouse is essentially self-supporting; the small yearly deficit is made up by the Community Chest. The chief industry carried on is the manufacture of brooms and mops. Training is also given in chair-caning, rug-weaving, wickerwork, and brush-making. The Braille and Point systems are also taught. About 50 workers report daily, some of whom are completely blind and others only partially blind. The building housing this institution is a neat stucco structure, with one corner built in the manner of a lighthouse.

157. *St. Patrick's Church*, 712 Camp St. A small wooden church was first erected here in the spring of 1833 to take care of the spiritual needs of the numerous Irish immigrants who had settled in the American section. The present church was erected in 1835-36, and is said to have been modeled after York Minster Church in England. The character of the ground presented a puzzling problem to the builders. In order to hold the soft ground the foundations were extended wide on both sides of the church and far out into Camp St. When nearly completed, the tower began to spread. James Gallier, Sr., was called in to the aid of Dakin, the contracting architect, and the great steel beams which he used to strengthen the walls can still be seen in the tower.

Father James Mullon, the first pastor, served the congregation from 1834 to 1866. An ardent Confederate, he had several 'difficulties' with Gen. Benjamin F. Butler. It was a daily custom to have the congregation unite in prayer after mass for the success of the Confederate cause. Butler sent word that the public prayers must cease. Father Mullon complied, but requested his congregation to pray in silence thereafter. At another time Gen. Butler sent for Father Mullon and accused him of having refused burial to a Union soldier, to which the good Father replied that he stood ready to bury the whole Union force, Gen. Butler included, when ever the occasion offered.

Originally a plain brick structure, the outside walls of the church have been covered with a rough coating of cement. Carved mahogany vestibule doors, a paneled wooden choir railing, decorated with copies of Fra Angelico's angels, oil paintings of the 'Crucifixion,' a copy of Murillo's 'Assumption of the Virgin,' a view of the town of Armagh above the side altar of St. Patrick, and a tiled floor have all been added by the present pastor, Father Raymond Carra. Several immense frescoes cover the wall surface of the sanctuary. In the center is a copy of Raphael's 'Transfiguration,' on one side 'Christ Walking on the Water,' and on the other 'St. Patrick Baptising the Kings and Queens of Ireland in Tara's Hall.' All three paintings are the work of Pomarede, a French artist. The statuary group of the 'Pietà' on the left-hand side altar came from the Chicago World's Fair of 1893.

158. The *Post Office*, 600 Camp St., facing Lafayette Square, stands on the site of St. Patrick's Hall, capitol under the Democratic administration of 1877. The present building, constructed at a cost of $1,157,000, was dedicated March 1, 1915. The architecture shows the Italian Renaissance influence. Deep horizontal lines space

the large marble blocks in the exterior wall, around which, upholding the overhanging tile roof, stand tall stately columns of monolithic stone. High windows, set back from a porch, extend from the second floor almost to the roof on the Camp St. side. Copper ornaments 25 feet in height, representing the world attended by female figures symbolic of history, the arts, industry, and commerce, cap the four corners of the roof. Santo Domingo mahogany and Georgia marble embellish the main lobby. Two Italian court yards occupy the center of the building. Besides the post office, the structure houses the Federal Courts, Department of Justice, Secret Service, Bureau of Narcotics, Interstate Commerce Commission, U.S. Marshal, Director of Naturalization, Bureau of Investigation, and the Weather Bureau.

For other points of interest in the vicinity of Lafayette Square see Motor Tour No. 3.

159. At 417 Camp St. is the site of the *American Theater*, built in 1822 by James Caldwell, a prominent actor and business man, originally from England, who fostered English drama in New Orleans. The building had a seating capacity of 1100 and was the first in Louisiana to be illuminated by gas. At that time the building stood in the open among truck gardens, on an almost impassable street.

Continue on Canal St.

ALGIERS TOUR: 14 m.

Cross river on Algiers ferry at foot of Canal St. Turn R., descend levee slope, and turn L. into Delaronde St.; R. from Delaronde St. on Valette St.; L. from Valette on Newton St. and General Meyer Ave.

THAT part of New Orleans on the west bank of the Mississippi River is so different from any other district of the city that its original identity as the town of Algiers has persisted unmistakably throughout the changes that have come to the city as a whole. Absence of a bridge has naturally done much to accentuate the contrast, and although the ferry trip across the river is made daily by thousands of Orleanians, and takes but a few minutes, there is less intercourse between the west and east bank districts of the city than between parts of New Orleans proper.

From the ferry landing Algiers stands out in the simplicity of its low, blocky buildings and open streets. Characteristics of the river town of an earlier epoch have not left it. Asphalt, concrete, and modern finish have concealed some of the details but have not changed the general appearance of the original community, which in the habits and customs of its citizens has retained consciousness of its separate existence. In almost every part of Algiers there are actual reminders as well as associations that recall its former separate identity. The visitor is more apt to think of it as one of the smaller towns in the bayou or upriver section above New Orleans than as the fifteenth ward comprising the fifth district of New Orleans.

Algiers extends along the Mississippi River for about 12 miles and is bounded on the upstream side by the town of Gretna in Jefferson Parish. The boundary line starts from the river at the foot of Socrates St. and runs in a southeasterly direction for 4 miles, beyond which point it be comes the dividing line between Orleans and Plaquemines Parishes along an irregular extension cutting back in a more easterly direction through Aurora, Belle Chasse, and other former plantation properties to the Mississippi River at the lower turn of Twelve-Mile Point.

In addition to the settled and industrial area, Algiers includes truck and dairy farms, portions of old plantations, and various Government establishments. A highway inside the levee runs along the river to the farming district in the lower part of the parish.

What is now Algiers formed part of the Crown property granted in 1717 to the Company of the West. Known as the 'Company's Plantation,' and after 1732, when it reverted to the Crown, as the 'King's Plantation,' the tract extended from the fort at Plaquemines Turn to the village of the Chitimachas (Donaldsonville). In 1770, after control of Louisiana had changed from French to Spanish hands, the Spanish Colonial Assembly authorized the sale of lands belonging to the Crown. Among such sales was one to Louis Bonrepo, which included all lands fronting the river between what became subsequently Verret St. and what became the boundary of McDonoghville, now part of Gretna, in Jefferson Parish. The tract passed to the ownership of Barthelmy Duverjé, August 9, 1805, and became the site of Algiers.

The true origin of the name Algiers is unknown, although it is explained in many ways. One story claims that the place was called Algiers because of the numerous slaves who worked there on King's Plantation; another credits the name simply to the similarity of the relative geographical positions of New Orleans and Algiers to France and Algiers on the Mediterranean; another to the fact that Lafitte made such regular use of the Verret Canal in his trips to and from Barataria that it was regarded as pirate territory, suggesting a comparison with the pirate country of the Mediterranean; another, that a New Orleans shipwright, after being released from his warehouse in Algiers by his unruly men upon his promise to stand treat for them all, remarked, 'This place deserves to be called Algiers, for you are all nothing but a lot of pirates.' Some old records refer to the place in the 1830's as Duverjéburg, but whatever its origin, the name became fixed to the locality early in New Orleans history. The community became a part of the Parish of Orleans in 1803 and was governed by a police jury until annexed by New Orleans March 14, 1870, as the fifth district of the municipality. Algiers, however, retained its own criminal courthouse and jail and a separate city court with jurisdiction over criminal cases. In the course of time it expanded both up and down the river from the Verret and LeBeuf Plantations. The Verret Canal, now a part of the drainage system, was dug in 1814 and connected the town with the Bayou Barataria district to the south. It is believed that the canal served as the principal route over wrhich Lafitte, Dominique You, and the other Barataria pirates transported their merchandise to New Orleans. McDonogh began his real estate development in 1818, and the hamlet of Tunisburg sprang up on the lower side.

With the development of steamboats, Algiers became a drydock and boat-building center. André Séguin established the first shipyard at the head of Seguin St. in 1819, thus beginning an industry in which Algiers has always had a leading part. The drydock industry began with the arrival of the first dock from Paducah, Kentucky, in 1837. The Opelousas Railroad (afterward Morgan's Louisiana & Texas R.R.) began the development of a railroad center in 1856. Connection was made with the New Orleans shore by ferryboat. By 1900 the Southern Pacific (successor to the Morgan Line) had an immense plant consisting of railroad shops, roundhouses, and depots in Algiers. Changing conditions, however, have-taken away the importance of Algiers as a river-shipping and railroad center.

While New Orleans has benefited by the largess of the river in accrued batture lands, Algiers has suffered by the corrosive action of the swift current. Algiers Point has been whittled away by successive floods, and much of the old town of McDonoghville, including the site of the McDonogh home, is now under the river. The greatest disaster occurred in 1844, when boathouses, stores, and a tannery slid off into nine fathoms of water in two cave-ins several hours apart. The present levees are strongly built, and there has been no trouble from the river in many years.

Algiers figured in Civil War history as the place from which Admiral Raphael Semmes sailed, flying the colors of the Confederacy for the first time on a vessel of war, April 22, 1861. Here also the Confederate flag was lowered from a war vessel for the last time when the 'Webb,' after descending the river and attempting to pass New Orleans in 1864, was burned and sunk by her own crew to prevent her falling into the hands of the Union forces. The old Marine Hospital at McDonoghville was destroyed by a powder explosion in December 1861.

207. The *U.S. Naval Station*, established 1849 and enlarged in 1894, borders the river between Behrman and Merrill Aves. and extends back to General Meyer Ave. The station covers 215 acres and includes about 55 buildings with a total value of about $4,000,000. It was officially closed in 1933, and is now conducted on a bare maintenance basis. The Inland Waterways Corporation and the U.S. Coast Guard use portions of the reserve. The U.S. Immigration Station and the Quarantine Station lie below the Naval Station.

R. from General Meyer Ave. on Florence Park.

208. The *Behrman Memorial Recreation Center* was built as a memorial to former Mayor Behrman, a life-long resident of Algiers. The plant includes various athletic fields, a Little Theater, and accommodations for the Children's Guild. The New Orleans Playground Commission controls the Center.

Return and continue on General Meyer Ave.

209. *Touro-Shakespeare Memorial Home*, 2650 General Meyer Ave., facing the Naval Station, maintained by the city with endowments left by Judah Touro and former Mayor Joseph Shakespeare, is a home for the aged. The present building was erected in 1933 and the inmates removed from the old building on Danneel St. between Nashville and Eleanore. The new building is set in attractive and spacious grounds. The façade is given a 'polka dot' or salt-and-pepper effect by the use of dark-faced brick, which contrasts with the lighter-colored brick and the concrete trim. Tall columns flank the main entrance.

L. from General Meyer Ave. on Merrill Ave.; R. along river road.

210. About a mile and a half down the river there stands an *Old Plantation House* slowly falling into ruins. From the *briqueté entre poteaux* construction (brick walls reinforced with timbers) it is likely that the house dates from the 18th century. The steep hip roof has dormer windows on four sides, and extends, with spindle columns supporting it, over the front and rear galleries. The brick foundation piers, with the space between them walled in to provide additional rooms, the cypress railings, and the outside stairway at the end of the gallery are all typical features of the early plantation home.

211. The *Aurora Plantation*, 1 mile farther down the river, set in beautiful landscaped grounds, has been considerably remodeled, but still retains evidence of

its age in the thick walls, dormer windows, and the peculiar roof construction, in which joists are pegged instead of nailed. The second building in the rear was formerly a houseboat that drifted on the plantation through a crevasse and was set upon foundations and made over into a dwelling. The earthworks of a redoubt used in the Battle of New Orleans can still be seen beside a tree-grown ditch, although most of the fortification has been leveled off.

Retrace route along river and General Meyer Ave.; L. from Newton St. (continuation of General Meyer Ave.) on Valette St. and its continuation, Hermosa St.

212. *McDonoghville Cemetery*, just across the Jefferson Parish Line, contains the tomb of one of the most interesting personalities in the history of New Orleans. John McDonogh, born in Baltimore, December 29, 1779, came to New Orleans on a business trip as a young man, and seeing the possibilities of making a fortune, returned and settled permanently in 1800. His chief interest was in real estate, and by skillful manipulations he soon acquired vast holdings in all the Gulf States. Always peculiar in manner, he remained a bachelor throughout his life and many romantic legends centered about his name. Removing to his plantation across the river from New Orleans in 1818, he came to be regarded as a miser and crank. He was actively interested in the welfare of the slaves, and in addition to being a promoter of the Liberia plan, he arranged a scheme of his own for the liberation of his slaves. At his death, October 26, 1850, he left a remarkable will which gave the bulk of his property to the cities of New Orleans and Baltimore to be used for educational purposes. Long and tangled litigation followed, and the cupidity and incompetence of politicians scaled down the original bequest; but both Baltimore and New Orleans received close to a million dollars each when final settlement was made. Baltimore used the money to endow a single fine institution for the education of boys which still flourishes, but New Orleans found it a welcome help in establishing the public school system, and thirty-six school buildings have been erected out of the fund.

His old plantation home on Homer St. slipped into the river long ago, and his remains were taken to Baltimore for burial, but a fine tomb stands in this cemetery in honor of McDonogh, who is further honored each year by the school children of New Orleans, who make a pilgrimage on the first Friday of May to his statue in Lafayette Square. The tomb is an oblong, white-stone sarcophagus standing in the center of the cemetery on a square lot paved with flagstones and surrounded by a heavy black iron fence. The four sides are inscribed in weatherbeaten gold lettering, with his birth and death dates, his own epitaph, and his 'Rules For My Guidance in Life – 1804.'

Return on Hermosa St. and take Verret St., the left-hand fork at Lamarque St.

213. *Holy Name of Mary Church*, in the 400 block on Verret St., is a fine brick church, the largest in Algiers, and was built in 1929 on the site of a church erected in 1871. It is designed in the English Gothic style and is surrounded by attractively landscaped grounds. The first Catholic Church in Algiers, old St. Bartholomew's, was built in 1849 opposite the old courthouse. Both church and courthouse have since disappeared.

The cement-walled interior of Holy Name of Mary is, for most part, undecorated. The nave is supported by large cement-covered columns arched between; the sanctuary finished in white marble, with marble altars and railings. The side altars are decorated with wooden tryptichs, instead of mural paintings or statues, painted with sacred subjects, except that of the altar of the Sacred Heart, which is decorated with a wood-carving of the Sacred Heart on the central panel.

There are several brilliant stained-glass windows in red and blue, but a number of the windows are still of plain blue glass.

L. from Verret St. on Pelican Ave.

214. *Martin Behrman's Home,* 228 Pelican Ave., is famous as the home of the man who served as mayor of New Orleans longer than any predecessor. He was born in New York, October 14, 1864, but came to New Orleans with his parents before he was a year old. His family settled in Algiers and Martin Behrman resided there until his death, January 12, 1926. Working his way up from a condition of poverty, he eventually became the outstanding politician of New Orleans and guided the city through an important period of development and industrial expansion. Elected mayor in 1904, he served for sixteen consecutive years, being re-elected every four years. In 1920 he was defeated by Andrew McShane, but won again in 1924. Death overtook him after he had served little more than a year. He was a successful and resourceful official and a master politician; although he made many enemies by his political activities, he always had a large following of personal as well as political friends. The modest cottage in which he lived, and in which his family still lives, is filled with mementos of his public life. Many famous visitors, including Gen. John J. Pershing, Eamon de Valera, and the late Cardinal Gibbons, were entertained there by Mayor Behrman. The Behrman home is a modest frame cottage one story in height, with a front gallery. The grounds are enclosed by an iron fence.

Turn L. around block and continue on Seguin St.; from Seguin St. on Morgan St. to ferry.

HERE AND THERE

Baptist Hospital (visiting hours 2-4 and 6.30-8), 2700 Napoleon Ave. *(St. Charles car from Canal and Baronne Sts.; transfer to northbound Napoleon car)*, a nine-story brick building housing 198 beds, was contructed in 1926. There is a two-story brick building directly behind the main hospital, which is used as a nurses' home. The hospital is operated under the supervision of the Southern Baptist Convention.

Beth Israel Synagogue, 1622 Carondelet St. *(St. Charles car from Canal and Baronne Sts. to Terpsichore; walk one block right)*, has the largest orthodox Jewish congregation in New Orleans. The Beth Israel Congregation was founded in New Orleans on October 25, 1903. The first rabbi was Moses H. Goldberg, now at the head of the Congregation Chevra Thilim.

The first synagogue, at 1616 Carondelet St., was completed and dedicated on April 1, 1906, and replaced in 1925 by a new brick building. The façade is of buff-colored brick decorated with cement and terra-cotta to represent stonework along the lower portion of the building. A flight of seven steps, extending almost the entire width of the front, leads up to an elaborate entrance of three sections, each section fitted with carved double wooden doors and flanked by two large round columns carrying heavy capitals of oriental design. A great five-paneled window surmounts the entrance. A seven-branched candlestick appears in relief above the central section of the entrance, and the tablets of the Ten Commandments occupy the highest point of the façade.

Adjoining the synagogue is the Menorah Institute (1631 Euterpe St.), also built in 1925, which is used as a social center and a day Hebrew school, and for Sunday School services.

The *First Unitarian Church*, 1806 Jefferson Ave. *(St. Charles car from Baronne and Canal Sts.)*, designed by Robert Soulé and built in 1901, is a small pressed-brick Gothic church with a front and rear gable. The congregation, ostensibly Unitarian from the time Dr. Theodore Clapp was ousted from the Presbyterian Church in the schism of 1833, incorporated in 1870 as the 'First Congregational Unitarian Church of New Orleans' and held its services in the Church of the Messiah, St. Charles Ave. and Julia St. Judah Touro, prominent Jewish philanthropist, aided the Unitarians materially in the construction of their first two churches.

Flint-Goodridge Hospital of Dillard University (visiting hours 2-4 daily; 7-8 Tues., Thur., and Sun.), 2425 Louisiana Ave. *(Freret car from Canal and St. Charles Sts. to Louisiana Ave.)*, is a private institution of 100 beds operated exclusively for Negroes. Opened in February 1932, the hospital is at present the newest in the city and is governed by Dillard University. The four-story main building, of buff brick and stone, faces Louisiana Ave.; behind it are two one-story structures used as a nurses' home and a power plant. The plant, including equipment, cost $365,000, all of which was contributed by colored and white citizens of the city.

French Hospital (visiting hours 10-11, 2-4, and 7-8.30), 1821 Orleans St. *(St. Bernard bus from Canal St. and Elk Place; walk two blocks north at Orleans)*, is a small private institution. It was first established as a refuge for French immigrants. The original home of the French Society, modified Italian Renaissance in architecture, and a new annex comprise the hospital buildings. The hospital began operating in 1913. There are 30 beds, with space for 13 more. The fine Sèvres vase standing in the main hallway was presented to the hospital by the French Government in recognition of the work of the institution among New Orleans French.

Good Shepherd Convent (visiting hours 5-9), 2601 Bienville St. *(West End or Cemeteries car from any place on Canal Street to Broad; walk two blocks downtown)*, is a Roman Catholic Institution for the care of delinquent girls between the ages of eight and twenty. Girls of any denomination are accepted at the request of parents, or on order of the Juvenile Court. Girls wishing to reform voluntarily occasionally take refuge at the convent. All inmates are kept in the institution until the nuns in charge feel that moral reformation has been accomplished. The Juvenile Court, however, ·has authority to remove girls who have been placed in the convent through its order. Many of the inmates choose to remain for the rest of their lives.

The girls in this institution are given training through the high-school grades, and those showing proficiency are given an additional two-year commercial course. They are also taught home economics, including fine sewing and hand embroidery, and have become well known for their excellent handwork. A laundry is operated by the older girls, the profits being used to assist in maintaining the institution. The balance of the funds necessary for the maintenance of the convent is obtained through city and Community Chest appropriations and voluntary subscriptions.

Grotto of Christ's Passion, Metairie Rd. and Bonnabel Blvd. *(West End or Cemeteries street-car from any place on Canal St.; transfer (left) to Metairie bus at City Park Ave.; open 9-5)*, was designed and erected by the Rev. Leo S. Jarysh. Although it occupies a portion of the front yard of the rectory of St. Catherine's Church, the shrine has no connection with the church; it was financed entirely from the personal funds of Father Jarysh and was built with the help of several of the parishioners, the material, in the form of broken concrete taken from city streets, having been obtained free from the city. Open to all creeds, the shrine serves as a place for meditation and for the edification of the faithful. Only partially constructed, it contains life-size statues of the Agony in the Garden, the Trial, the Crucifixion, and Our Lord in the Sepulcher. When completed, it will also contain the Stations of the Cross, the courtyard in which Peter denied Christ, and a large statue of the Risen Saviour.

Illinois Central Hospital (visiting hours 2-8), 800 Magnolia St. *(S. Claiborne car from Canal and St. Charles Sts. to Magnolia; walk three blocks downtown),* is operated for employees by the Hospital Department of the *Illinois Central Railroad;* 60 beds are maintained.

Inspiration Garden, 9 Neron Place *(S. Claiborne car at Canal and Carondelet Sts. to Carrollton and S. Claiborne; one block southwest to Short and Neron),* forms a part of the private garden at the home of Mrs. Raphael Ross. This unusual plot, literally writing 'sermons in stones, books in the running brooks,' is situated on the Short Street side of the property between the children's playgound and the back division fence, which supports a miniature mountain chain. Mrs. Ross' symbolic planting is designed to teach a graphic lesson concerning the value of humility and perseverance throughout the journey of life.

The *Knights of Columbus Bldg.,* 836 Carondelet St., is notable because of the fact that its façade, except for a number of alterations, once formed part of Christ Church, the first Protestant church in New Orleans, which stood at the downtown lake corner of Canal and Bourbon Streets. After the Christ Church congregation moved to a new location at Canal and Dauphine in 1847, the old building became Touro Synagogue. In 1859, because of the value of the site, the temple was taken down and rebuilt at the present address. The Knights of Columbus came into possession in 1907 and made extensive alterations.

The Ionic façade is one of the best remaining specimens of the elder Gallier's work. Six large fluted columns with Ionic capitals form a portico running across the entire front. A flight of steps, flanked by extensions of the portico floor, each platform surmounted by a tall, graceful lamppost, rises to three entrances. The side walls of the cement-covered brick building have two rows of double-arched windows. Rear wings, which have been added in recent years, are used as clubrooms.

Lafon's Old Folks' Home (Negro), 1121 N. Tonti St. *(Esplanade bus from Canal and Burgundy Sts. to N. Tonti St.; walk two blocks uptown),* was founded by the Sisters of the Holy Family in 1848 on St. Bernard Ave. near Villere St. The institution, which moved to Tonti St. in 1891, assumed its present name in 1895 in honor of Thomy Lafon, Negro philanthropist, from whom it received a sum of money. Approximately 80 persons may be cared for. All applicants are referred to the Department of Public Welfare before being admitted as inmates. Lafon's Old Folks Home is maintained at present by the Community Chest, the Department of Public Welfare, and the small Thomy Lafon endowment. The Sisters of the Holy Family still manage the institution.

The *Milne-Municipal Boys' Home* (*visitors admitted during school hours*), 5420 Franklin Ave. (*Gentilly car from Canal and Bourbon Sts. to end of line; walk one block toward lake*), called the 'Waifs' Home' until 1926, was established in 1909 as a detention home for delinquent boys; it was named for Alexander Milne, noted philanthropist. Both white and colored boys are committed to the institution by the Juvenile Court; others are brought by police officers, parents, social agencies, or schools. It is the policy of the home to parole boys, if possible, to responsible persons during the period they are awaiting trial. A complete case history is kept of each child, including details of his family and environment.

Education is provided the year round under the auspices of the Orleans Parish School Board, which provides 3 white and 3 colored teachers. The Touro Infirmary furnishes medical attention for the inmates; senior medical students of Tulane University render assistance in emergency cases. Swimming, ball games, and other forms of recreation are under the supervision of trained instructors.

The home is under the management of Robert L. McElree, who is assisted by a board of managers and a trained case worker. A budget allotment is made annually to the institution by the city of New Orleans. The establishment includes an administration building, two dormitories, two structures for classwork and manual training, and the cottage of the superintendent.

The *National Shrine of St. Ann*, Ursuline Ave. and N. Johnson St. (*City Park car to 2100 Dumaine St.; two blocks right to Ursuline Ave.*), the national headquarters of the Archconfraternity of St. Ann, is unique in that it is a composite shrine incorporating features of Lourdes, Calvary, the Scala Sancta, or Holy Stairway of Rome, and a shrine to St. Ann, all of which are combined in a reproduction of the famous grotto of Lourdes, which, set in a landscaped plot, rises as a miniature cave of pink artificial rock. To the right, in a niche, as at Lourdes, is a statue of the Immaculate Conception with the inscription 'Je suis l'Immaculée Conception.' Within the recession are an altar and a statue of St. Ann with the Blessed Virgin. A reproduction of the Holy Stairway in the church of S. Salvatore, near the Lateran in Rome, rises from the right of the interior. To gain indulgence granted by special concession, the stairway is to be ascended on one's knees, the Way of the Cross being made at stations at each second step of the twenty-eight. At the top of the structure, with the sky as its canopy, is the group of the Crucifixion – Mary, St. John, and Magdalen. At the bottom and to one side of the opposite stairway is a small room, the Cave of Many Shrines, wherein one may pray to the Sacred Heart, Mother of Perpetual Help, St. Joseph, St. Jude, and others. Petitions for spiritual and temporal favors to be prayed for during novenas may be deposited in a receptacle at the entrance of the grotto. An office for information, enrollment, and devotionals is situated below the Holy Stairway.

Weekly novenas are held, and a night procession, with participants holding lighted candles, is staged on Ursuline Avenue on the feast day of St. Ann, July 26, the culmination of a nine-day novena.

The *New Orleans Dispensary for Women and Children* (visiting hours 8-11, 2-4), 1823 Annunciation St. (*Laurel car from Canal and Tchoupitoulas Sts.*), occupies a group of frame buildings that once served as private residences. Founded in May 1905, the purpose of the hospital is to provide a place where women and children of small means may receive care. An average of 12,000 patients are treated each year, many of them free of charge.

The *Poydras Female Orphan Asylum* (*open daily*), 5334 Magazine St. (*Magazine car from Canal and Magazine Sts.*), was established in 1817, and named in honor of its benefactor, Julien Poydras. Orphaned or neglected children between the ages of three and eighteen years whose parents are unable to provide for them are accepted. The institution cares for approximately 90 children annually, offering training through the high-school grades, with additional commercial or industrial training when desired.

The Poydras Asylum is under the management of a board composed of twelve women. Support is derived chiefly from an endowment left to the institution by Julien Poydras, wealthy philanthropist. A small amount is received annually from the city, and small sums are received from the parents of those children who are not orphans.

The large three-story brick and concrete building was erected in 1855, and is an adaptation of Italian Renaissance architecture. The grounds cover two city blocks, part of which space is taken up with a lovely flower garden.

Roma Room, 724 St. Philip St. (*Gentilly car from Canal and Bourbon Sts. to St. Philip St.; one block toward river*), has a papal blessing because its owner prayed one hour daily for 1000 days. The Roma Room is fancifully decorated and adorned with lighted candles and fresh flowers. This shrine, located at the rear of an Italian delicatessen, is especially attractive on the evening of St. Joseph's Day, March 19, when people from the Vieux Carré, making the rounds of St. Joseph altars in the neighborhood, come to visit and receive 'lucky beans.'

St. John the Baptist Church, 1117 Dryades St. (*S. Claiborne car from Canal and St. Charles Sts. to Clio and S. Rampart; walk one block left*), is an excellent example of the splendid brick masonry characteristic of New Orleans in the middle of the nineteenth century. Its ornate baroque tower, 125 feet in height, is still a landmark in the neighborhood. The church, which has a seating capacity of 1200, is 45 feet in width and extends three-fourths of a block back from the street. The architectural style is modified Byzantine with baroque decorative features. The slate of the roof is imbedded in concrete, and the church tower is fitted with a four-faced Seth Thomas clock placed there years ago at considerable cost, and still a good timekeeper. Built when New Orleans terrain was an uncertain factor, the foundations of the church extend ten feet beyond the walls in all directions to insure a firm base. Cement-covered brick columns, twelve feet in diameter, support the roof of the nave. The fifteen stained-glass windows, representing the fifteen mysteries of the Rosary, are a product of Munich artists. The pews are solid mahogany, and the altar steps are marble.

Begun in 1864 to fill the needs of an Irish congregation that had built up the

Dryades Market section out of the swamps of Gormley's basin, St. John the Baptist Church was not completed until 1869. The approximate cost was $300,000. Fire gutted the building in 1907, and the roof fell in, but the tower and the walls remained standing. The church was rebuilt and withstood the hurricane of 1915.

St. John's once served a large and prosperous congregation, but the neighborhood has changed with the times, and this fine old church no longer enjoys the prominence it once had.

St. Raymond's Chapel, 3000 Melpomene Ave. (*S. Claiborne street-car from Canal and St. Charles Sts. to Melpomene; walk one block right; open 6.30 A.M. to 7.30 P.M.; services Tuesdays and Thursdays, 7.30 P.M.*), was founded in 1903 by Basil Bruno, a native of Contessa Entellina, Italy. The present building, a combination chapel and home, was erected in 1920. Although its founder is of the Catholic religion, this private chapel is open to all creeds. The only services are novenas, which are conducted by 'Brother Bruno.' The Tuesday services are in honor of St. Lucy, the patroness of the eyes; the Thursday services honor St. Raymond.

To the left of the entrance hall is a chapel which is filled with altars, statues of various saints, and hundreds of burning votive lights. To the rear is a glass case filled with plaster legs, arms, hearts, heads, and other pieces of anatomy – gifts of persons cured through novenas or prayers said at the chapel. The most prominent of these relics are plaster profiles of two brothers miraculously cured, through prayers said at St. Raymond's, of facial scalds inflicted when their still blew up while making liquor during Prohibition.

The main altar, Catholic in style, has a life-sized statue of St. Raymond in the center and statues of St. Lucy and St. Martha on either side. Below the altar is a figure of Our Lord in the Sepulcher. The archway in front of the altar is covered with angel busts made of wood, and cemented in the walls are 'thanks' plaques of every description. To the front of the rostrum, in two glass-inclosed boxes, are statues of Jesus of Prague and Marietta (young Virgin). In a niche to the left of the main altar is a small statue of St. Peter with hundreds of keys of every description hanging from its neck on varicolored ribbons. So many keys are brought to this shrine that some have to be placed in a case with the plaster casts every few weeks. Among the many interesting old keys in the collection are two made of gold.

There is an almost continuous stream of people, predominately Negro, who come to the chapel with petitions written on pieces of paper, either to burn votive lights and candles or seek spiritual advice. No fee is charged for advice, but donations are accepted. A small fee is charged for maintaining votive lights.

The *Scottish Rite Cathedral*, 619 Carondelet St., originally the First Methodist Church, or McGhee Church, as it was popularly known, was dedicated on May 14, 1853. While under construction the walls spread and collapsed as the roof was completed, and the church had to be rebuilt. The Masons took over the building in 1906, rededicating it as the Scottish Rite Cathedral.

A portico of Ionic columns, surmounted with a low wall fronting the hipped slate roof, extends across the façade and is set back about six feet in the central portion. Two flights of steps rise on either side of the street level entrance to two entrances on the portico floor. A large stained-glass window, with Masonic legend and insignia, occupies the space between the doorways.

Ursuline College, 2635 State Street (*South Claiborne car from Canal and St. Charles Sts. to State; walk three blocks left*), occupies a 12-acre tract bounded by State, Nashville, Claiborne, and Willow Sts. It is exclusively a girls' school, combining grammar, high-school, and college departments. Founded in 1727, under the auspices of Louis XV, King of France, and entrusted to the Ursuline nuns, the college is one of the oldest educational institutions for girls in the United States. The first convent, completed in 1734, housed the Ursuline nuns for ninety years, following which it served until a recent date as the residence of the bishops and archbishops of New Orleans. The building, located at 1114 Chartres Street, is still known as the 'old Archbishopric' (*see French Quarter Tour*). In 1824 the Ursulines moved to the lower limits of the city, remaining there for almost one hundred years, the convent being moved again, in 1912, to the present site. The founding of the Ursuline College of New Orleans in September 1927 commemorated the bicentennial of the first Ursuline nuns' arrival in New Orleans. Only a freshman course was taught in the college during its first year, but in succeeding years the other courses have been added.

The main building of Ursuline College is an impressive three-story edifice with a frontage of 600 feet on State Street. Tudor Gothic in design, it includes classrooms, living-rooms, dining-halls, and a culinary department. Next to the main hall stands the church. The high-school building, another three-story structure, stands behind the main building and is separated from it by a spacious courtyard, completing a quadrangle. A modern gymnasium, adjacent to the church, has recently been completed. Additional buildings will be erected as the need arises in the extensive grounds facing Claiborne Avenue. The present policy of the Ursulines calls for a broad extension of their facilities for advanced learning, and it is their intention to make the Ursuline College a counterpart of Loyola University.

Within the Ursuline College church is the *Shrine of Our Lady of Prompt Succor*, which is of unusual historic interest. The present shrine, erected to the Blessed Virgin as Our Lady of Prompt Succor by the Ursulines of New Orleans and their friends in January 1922, marks the culmination of a devotion begun by Mother St. Michel Gensoul of the French nuns of this order. Mother St. Michel, who was sent to Louisiana in 1810, is said to have prevented the destruction by fire of the first local convent in 1812, because she placed a statue of Our Lady of Prompt Succor in the window. Three years later, during the Battle of New Orleans, the statue of Our Lady of Prompt Succor was removed from the choir to the main altar, a mass was said, and Mother Mary Olivier de Vezin vowed that if the Americans won, a Mass of Thanksgiving in honor of the Benefactress would be sung annually at the Ursuline Chapel. This mass was not yet concluded when a courier entered the chapel with word of the American victory. Hence, for more than a hundred years an annual novena terminating with a high mass has been celebrated at the Ursuline Chapel each January 8.

At the shrine entrance, above massive doors of carved oak and between a magnificent oval window and the gable cross, is a large ornamented niche containing a Carrara marble statue of Our Lady of Prompt Succor. Across the base of the gable runs an inscription expressing the love and gratitude which prompted its erection: 'Maria Victrici' (To Mary the Victorious) – an allusion to General Andrew Jackson's victory over the British at the Battle of New Orleans, January 8, 1815, through the intercession of Our Lady of Prompt Succor.

Zatarain's Sanctuary of Christian Divine Healing, 925 Valmont St. (*Magazine street-car from Canal and Magazine Sts. to Bellecastle St.; walk one block right; open 7-6*), a private shrine built at his home by Mr. E. A. Zatarain, reproduces in miniature a number of famous places of the Old World connected with the history of religion. The owner, a prominent business man, constructed the shrine in the side yard of his residence, shortly after the death of his wife in 1929.

Within the shrine is a large wooden cross, at which several hundred keys have been left for St. Peter to 'open the way' for those who wish favors granted. Near the rear entrance is Elisha's Healing Well, decorated with numerous ornaments, illuminated by underwater electric lights, and containing 'holy goldfish.' In the garden the 'straight and narrow' and 'broad' paths are symbolized in the landscaping. Mr. Zatarain manufactures a root beer with which he is said to work cures.

Numerous crutches have been left at the shrine, attesting to the cures of various afflictions. Séances are held each Saturday night by a medium, and the 'spirits' said to have been summoned include those of the late Archbishop of New Orleans and the late Senator Huey Long.

PLANTATION TOUR

NEW ORLEANS, KENNER, NORCO, LAPLACE, RESERVE, LUTCHER, GEISMAR, BATON ROUGE. *Returning*: GONZALES, SORRENTO, LAPLACE, NEW ORLEANS, 200.3 *m.*, US 61, La 1, La 63, US 61.

Roads concrete, black-top, and gravel.

Restaurant and hotel accommodations at larger towns.

THIS tour follows the windings of the 'Old River Road' (La 1, La 63) to Baton Rouge, through one of Louisiana's earliest and finest plantation districts. It returns via the 'Airline' (US 61), which traverses for the most part uninhabited cypress swamplands. The round trip can be made conveniently in a day.

Follow S. Claiborne Ave. out of the city.

Protection Levee, 7.5 *m.*, marking at this point the eastern boundary of New Orleans, is one of a series of interior levees that were built to protect New Orleans from Mississippi River overflows or backwater from Lake Pontchartrain.

Camp Parapet Powder Magazine, 9.2 *m.* (L), visible about 150 yards from the road behind the Alto Tourist Camp, is a remnant of a Civil War fortification. The chimney-like projection at the top served as a ventilator. More recently the magazine was utilized as a temporary jail.

St. Agnes Church, 9.4 *m.* (L). This building formerly housed a night club and gambling house.

Huey P. Long Bridge, 10.9 *m.* (L) (*do not cross*), is Louisiana's only span over the Mississippi River. It was completed in 1935, at a cost of $13,000,000. The bridge proper consists of a steel cantilever accompanied by a series of truss spans and is supported by six dredged caissons and three pile piers. The approaches on both sides are supported by steel viaduct towers and plate girders. The bridge is a combination railroad and highway structure; the double tracks are flanked by two 18-foot concrete roadways, each with a 2-foot sidewalk. The height of the central pier is equal to that of a 36-story building, measuring 409 feet from the bottom of its foundation to the top of its superstructure.

At 11.9 *m.* (L) is a private road.

Left about 300 yards is *Elmwood*, an ante-bellum mansion standing near the foot of the levee. The thick walls and heavy columns of this house suggest a frontier stronghold, an impression deepened by barred windows and narrow gun slots which pierce the east wall of the ground floor. There is not an elm on or near the plantation, but thirty-two magnificent oaks, visible from the highway, form a triple square around the house, the only evidence that a dwelling stands there.

HARAHAN (alt. 11.5, pop. 892), 12.3 *m.*

Colonial Country Club, 12.9 *m.* (L). The clubhouse was originally the Soniat home, built in 1820. It is a large, two-story brick structure, with a high sloping roof broken by dormers; spacious galleries on all sides are supported by brick pillars.

KENNER (alt. 5.9, pop. 2440), 16.4 *m.*, is the shipping center for a vegetable-growing community. (The Airline and the River Road are connected here by Kenner's mile-long main street.) Continue (L) on La 1 (River Road).

ST. ROSE (alt. 15, pop. 1000), 21.9 *m.*, was, until the construction of the Cities Service Export Oil Co. plant, peopled mainly by Italian immigrants who engaged in truck-farming and dairying. Now the majority of the population is employed by the oil company.

At 22.3 *m.* (L) is the old *Pecan Grove Plantation Home*, the entire lower floor of which has been removed in recent years by treasure-hunters digging under its marble tiles.

DESTREHAN (pop. 500), 24.8 *m.*, is owned largely by the Pan-American Oil Co., the construction of whose plant brought the town into existence in 1914. The many small neat houses, with their trim gardens, make an attractive appearance, but the gleaming white house, visible from the road at 24.9 *m.* (R) is worthy of particular attention. This is *Destrehan* (open), built by Jean D'Etrehan in 1790 and recently restored. Deep porches on three sides are supported by heavy plain Doric columns that extend the height of the building. The line of the steeply sloping roof is broken by three small dormer windows. Until the middle of the 18th century the house was a square, one-story building ;jthen the wings and upper story were added, giving the house essentially its present appearance.

At 25 *m.* (R) is a cemetery that has been in existence for more than two hundred years.

At 25.3 *m.* (R) is *Ormond*, built by the Butler family some time before Destrehan was constructed. Wide galleries show clearly a Spanish influence. The wings at either end are later additions but detract little from the original effect.

GOOD HOPE (alt. 7.6, pop. 200), 28.8 *m.*, faces the highway within array of modern brick and stucco buildings built in the Spanish mission style. Extending the mile between Good Hope and Norco are refineries of the Pan-American Oil Co. and the Shell Petroleum Co.

NORCO (pop. 500), 29.8 *m.*, is another company-built town.

At 30 *m.* is a black-top road leading one half mile (R) to the Airline Highway

(US 61). It is necessary in very bad weather to detour around the Spillway to Laplace via the Airline.

At 30.1 *m.* is the *Bonnet Carré Spillway,* a huge dam designed to protect the city of New Orleans and adjacent territory from overflows of the Mississippi by diverting excess waters into the Gulf of Mexico through Lake Pontchartrain. The Spillway dam, which has nearly twice the flowage capacity of Niagara Falls, stands on a foundation of piling 70 feet deep. The project was completed in December 1935 at a cost exceeding $13,000,000.

LAPLACE (alt. 10, pop. 175), 36.8 *m.*, is a vegetable and sugar-cane center. There are three railroads, several general stores, automobile agencies, garages, and restaurant facilities. (Here Airline and River Road routes are separated by only a few blocks.)

The section of Louisiana traversed for the next 40 *m.* was originally settled by Germans, first of whom were John Law's Alsatians. These settled first on the west bank of the Mississippi River near the present village of Lucy, between 1719 and 1722. After 1728 the Germans extended their holdings to the east bank, as well as up and down the river for several miles. This gave rise to the term *Côte des Allemands* (Fr., 'German Coast'), applied to the land along both banks of the river in St. Charles and St. John the Baptist Parishes. Accessions of immigrants from Lorraine (1765) and French Acadians from Nova Scotia (1766) greatly extended settlement of the German coasts; they became the most prosperous sections of Louisiana – as much by reason of the industrious character of the settlers as because of the extremely fertile soil.

At 37.8 *m.* (L) is the *Ste. Jeanne D'Arc Church* (Roman Catholic), interesting in that a statue of Joan of Arc stands atop the central tower in place of the customary cross.

At 38.9 *m.* (R) is a rambling raised-cottage type building that is probably a century or more old.

At 40.8 *m.* (R) is the *Godchaux Belle Pointe Dairy (visitors welcome).*

At 42.8 *m.* (R) is the *Voisin Plantation Home,* reputedly built about 1785. Although quite unpretentious, the old building exudes an atmosphere of comfort and quiet dignity. It is of the earliest plantation home type of construction a raised cottage with spliced, mortised, and interlocked timbers between which is a filler of mud and moss (similar to adobe) covered with whitewashed plaster.

RESERVE (pop. 400), 43 *m.*, probably the most prosperous town between Baton Rouge and New Orleans, is the trading-center and shipping point for a very productive sugar-cane section. Interesting to note is *St. Peter's Church* (Roman Catholic) (R), unusual in that it contains a memorial to a Jewish planter and philanthropist – Edward Godchaux.

In Reserve is located the refinery of *Godchaux Sugars, Inc.* The daily capacity of granulated sugar is a half-million pounds. (*Visitors are welcome to visit the sugar plantation and refinery.*)

At 45.7 *m.* (R) is the *San Francisco Plantation Home*, built in 1850. Here a strange mixture of Spanish hacienda-like galleries, French ironwork, and German 'gingerbread' has produced a startling example of 'Steamboat Gothic.'

At 50 *m.* (R) is *Mount Airy*, an early 19-century raised plantation-type cottage whose ironwork outside stairs and gallery railings are worthy of particular attention; decorative details in wood and iron and tall shuttered windows contribute a distinctly French note. To the rear are several old outbuildings – *pigeonniers* (dovecotes), *garçonnières* (boys' quarters), carriage houses, servants' quarters, etc. *The Trackless Way*, by Adèle Le Bourgeois Chopin, paints an interesting picture of this and other near-by plantations, their owners, and slaves.

At *Grammercy*, 53.1 *m.*, the outskirts of Lutcher, is a plantation home (R) which was built about 1800. It is a two-story building with broad verandas on three sides and a high-pitched, dormer-windowed roof crowned by a balustrade.

LUTCHER (alt. 15, pop. 1481), 53.5 *m.*, is a sprawling village, characteristically Louisianian. There is an old plantation home or two, conjuring visions of a romantic past, and the usual cluster of small-town business houses. From the roadway one may catch glimpses of long rows of dusty cottages and a modern school building of red brick; oak trees and occasional palms lend dignity to the landscape. On the left the seemingly ubiquitous levee hugs the highway and conceals the willow-decked batture of the river.

Centering in and about Lutcher is a strip of land where Périque tobacco is grown; approximately one thousand acres devoted to this culture produce an annual crop of a quarter-million pounds. Périque was first grown in Louisiana by the Indians. Early in the history of Louisiana a Frenchman named Pierre Chenet, or 'Périque,' as he was nicknamed by the Creoles, became interested in the tobacco and was the first to grow it commercially. At the factory of the *Louisiana Périque Tobacco Company* visitors may look in on the actual processing. Périque requires three years for curing, and is one of the most expensive tobaccos grown; it is used almost exclusively in blending.

At 55.7 *m.* (R) is a group of frame buildings belonging to the *St. Elmo Plantation*, painted a dull red.

At 57.2 *m.* (R) is a double row of laborers' huts; suspended between two leaning posts is a plantation bell whose ringing notes awaken the country side to a day of work in the fields and at the end of the long day's labor invites it home to a supper of corn-pone, 'pot-likker,' ham hocks, molasses, yams, and other delectables. This is the old *Hester Plantation*, whose 'big house' was destroyed a quarter of a century ago by fire.

Along this stretch of road the river has for many years eaten farther and farther to the east. Where once stood elaborate mansions now swirls the turgid Mississippi; the road itself has been moved back several times. Now for several miles are many small fields of shallots (green onions); this particular section is eminently successful in growing shallots for shipment all over the world.

Welham Plantation, 58.8 *m.* (R), dates from 1835. This dignified and wellpre-served house, with its faded green shutters, sits close beside the roadside, bereft of front grounds by the river. Six massive columns rising two full stories support the roof, which is surmounted by a white balustrade. To the rear are a number of whitewashed outbuildings. The old sugar mill is now in ruins.

At 61.3 *m.* (R) is the *Zanor Trudeau Home*, built during the early 18th century; broad verandas and a background of oaks combined to offset an almost incon-gruously low, gabled, corrugated-iron roof.

Jefferson College, 61.4 *m.* (R), surrounded by a wooded park comprising a hun-dred acres, is one of the old-time landmarks of Louisiana. Magnificent oaks in long and imposing avenues and a symmetrical front lawn, once tastefully laid out with hedges and shrubs and rare flowers, impress visitors, especially as viewed from the crest of the levee (L).

Jefferson College was established in 1831, to take the place of the College of Orleans, at New Orleans. In 1842 it was partially destroyed by fire, and in 1845 the State withdrew its financial support. The college then struggled along until 1855, when bankruptcy temporarily closed its doors. The property was pur-chased at auction in 1859 by Valcour Aimé, a philanthropic sugar-planter, and presented to the Marist Fathers, who reopened the school. The college ceased to function in 1927; the property was subsequently purchased by the Jesuits, renamed 'Manresa House,' and transformed into a retreat for laymen.

CONVENT, 63.2 *m.*, is a village so named because of the near-by school described below. The church of *St. Michael* (Roman Catholic) is interesting not only for its fusion of Hispano-Moresque and French Renaissance architecture, but also for a grotto constructed of *bagasse* (residue of pressed sugar cane), a beautiful shell shrine, and an exquisite hand-carved altar brought from the Paris Exposition of 1867.

Academy of the Sacred Heart, 63.3 *m.* (R), for more than a hundred years attended by daughters of aristocratic Creole families, is now deserted. With its long central portion and peaked roof it resembles a French château. The façade is simple yet impressive; an upstairs gallery overlooks the river and the verdant levee.

Uncle Sam Plantation, 65.2 *m.* (R), with its buildings erected in 1836 by slave labor, is said to comprise one of the few complete plantation groups remaining in the State. The main buildings are arranged about a central two-story house; massive and almost classic simplicity is the keynote. Wide galleries, twenty-eight giant Doric columns, and a roof broken by dormer windows combine to make of the main struc-ture a pleasing whole. At the side and rear are *garçonnières*, *pigeonniers*, a kitchen, and other buildings, all conforming in architectural style to the main house.

ROMEVILLE, 67 *m.*, is a levee-side cluster of Negro shacks and stores.

At 68 *m.* (R), fronting flush on the roadway, is the *Colomb Home*, built about 1835.

Here and there in roadside pasture and grazing lots are open, bowl-shaped iron sugar kettles now serving as water troughs for stock. The open-kettle method of reducing cane juice to syrup was practiced by virtually every individual grower before the development of the sugar mill and is still used occasionally. Interesting to note is the use of discarded sugar-mill boilers for rain-water cisterns.

CENTRAL (pop. 200), 69.7 *m.*, is a village peopled almost entirely by Negroes.

UNION (pop. 200), 71.3 *m.*, is a settlement marked by towering pecan trees; it was once the center of a prosperous farming country.

At 71.9 *m.* (R) are several very old plantation buildings, interesting in that their construction is of the early *briqueté entre poteaux* type, i.e., soft bricks instead of sand and moss laid in between reinforcing timbers.

At 72.3 *m.* (R) is the *Union Plantation,* a cluster of plantation 'quarters' or laborers huts and old sugar-cane buildings.

At 73.3 *m.* is *Tezcuco,* the *Bringier Plantation Home,* a vine-covered raised cottage, set deep in a grove of moss-hung trees.

BURNSIDE (pop. 500), 75.3 *m.*, was once the site of an *Oumas* or *Houma* Indian village. Fronting on the river is *The Houmas,* a plantation house built about 1840. White-pillared, two and one half stories high, and surmounted by a belvedere, the house stands today in almost perfect condition. An avenue of magnificent oaks forms a fine setting for the main building and its two flanking hexagonal *garçon-nières* – the whole designed in the spirit of the Greek Revival.

At 79.5 *m.* is *The Hermitage,* one of the finest examples of columnar architecture in Louisiana. The present house is evidently a remodeling of an earlier dwelling built in 1812. It is a square brick structure, covered with smooth plaster stucco, and is entirely encircled with round, white columns, which enclose wooden galleries, upstairs and down.

DARROW (pop. 200), 81.3 *m.*

At 85.5 *m.* is *Belle Hélène,* built in 1843 by Duncan Kenner, sportsman, politician, and financier. Originally known as 'Ashland,' the main building is a charming brick-and-plaster structure set in a grove of oaks and willows.

GEISMAR (pop. 500), 88.8 *m.*

At CARVILLE (pop. 300), 93.5 *m.*, is the only lepers' home in the country, the 'Leprosorium' (officially U.S. Marine Hospital 66). It was founded by the State in 1894 and placed in charge of the Sisters of St. Vincent de Paul, a Roman Catholic order.

In 1921 the Leprosorium was taken over by the Federal Government. The present staff includes 4 physicians, a dentist, a Catholic priest, a Protestant minister, and 15 nurses; there are 360 patients, 10 per cent of whom may expect permanent cures.

At 96.3 *m.* is *St. Gabriel's Church,* which stands on a Spanish grant made in 1774 in favor of the 'parish church of Manchach.' Several earlier buildings were taken by the river, and the present church is of comparatively recent construction. There is a sidewalk leading from the church to the rectory that is paved with tombstones unclaimed by descendants of those buried in the old cemetery when the construction of a levee necessitated its abandonment. The steps of the rectory were also built of marble from abandoned tombs, and left-over slabs are piled in the rear cow-lot, probably destined to be used some day in an equally in genious way.

ST. GABRIEL (pop. 750), 96.8 *m.* Adjacent to the village is one of Louisiana's several penal farms, interesting in that it is practically self-supporting, as is the entire State penal system.

At 101.1 *m.*, the motorist may turn (R) on a short cut across a bend in the river, thereby saving 8 *m.*, or continue (L) on the river road (dirt) around Plaquemine Point. (*Ferry to Plaquemine.*)

At 118.2 *m.* is the *Cottage*, built in 1830. It is surrounded by live oaks and magnolias and has a lovely flower garden. The two-story house is of brick and cypress construction, with walls 2 feet thick; massive Doric columns enclose a bricked porch and support a wide second-story gallery.

At 121.7 *m.* (R) are the new buildings of *Louisiana State University Agricultural and Mechanical College.* Near the road are experimental farms of the Agricultural College, and beyond is the new stadium, seating 52,000. For a closer inspection take the gravel driveway (R) through the campus.

BATON ROUGE (alt. 60, pop. 30,729), 123 *m.*, is the capital of Louisiana.

Return to New Orleans via the 'Airline' (US 61).

HOPE VILLA (alt. 15, pop. 100), 132.3 *m.*, is a settlement on the south bank of Bayou Manchac, at one time an overflow outlet of the Mississippi River.

GONZALES (pop. 462), 137.8 *m.*, is the center of a rich cane- and vegetable-growing district.

For about 35 *m.* now, the route lies through heavily wooded swamps. The concrete roadway over which the motorist may now travel at almost any speed desired was built up from the surrounding country at a tremendous expense. Huge bucket dredges first built up an embankment 15 to 20 feet high and about 50 yards wide, thus creating deep roadside ditches whose waters soon became covered with water hyacinths; this, the sub-grade, was then allowed to settle for several years before the final layer of concrete was poured; the result is what might be termed a 'floating' highway.

SORRENTO (pop. 800), 144.8 *m.*, was at one time a thriving lumber town, but most of the timber has been cut away and only one small sawmill remains. Sorrento experienced something of a boom in 1928-29 with the discovery of oil in the near-by McElroy field, which later proved unproductive.

SAINT BERNARD – PLAQUEMINES TOUR

NEW ORLEANS, ARABI, POYDRAS, POINTE À LA HACHE, 48 *m.*, La 1.

Road concrete, black-top, and gravel.

Restaurant and hotel at English Turn.

THIS tour extends down the east bank of the Mississippi River through the St. Bernard and Plaquemines Delta, one of the earlier settled sections of Louisiana. Leave New Orleans via N. Rampart St. and St. Claude Ave. (La 1).

ARABI (alt. 6, pop. 280x2), 4.5 *m.*, is an unincorporated suburb of New Orleans. Angela Avenue marks the Orleans-St. Bernard Parish boundary.

> Right on Angela Ave. is the *Meraux Home*, 0.4 *m.* (*not open*), erected in 1808. It is an old plantation residence with square columns, upper and lower galleries, gabled roof, and dormer windows. The house was once known as the *Château des Fleurs*, because of its gardens, which are still beautiful. The almost dazzlingly white walls of the mansion, blanketed by a green-painted roof gleam through the verdant grounds. Continue down N. Peters St.
>
> At 0.8 *m.* (L) are *Jai Alai, Arabi*, and *Riverview* (*open* 6 P.M.-6 AM., *free*), large gambling resorts.
>
> At 0.9 *m.* (L) is an assembling plant of the *Ford Motor Company* (open weekdays 10 A.M.).
>
> At 1.1 *m.* (L) is the *American Sugar Refinery* (*open to visitors* 10 A.M. *daily except Sat. and Sun.; guide furnished free*).
>
> At 1.2 *m.* (L) is the *Three Oaks Plantation Home.*
>
> At 1.5 *m.* (R) is *Chalmette Slip*, a deep-water shipping terminal. The building used by Jackson as headquarters, the old Macarty Home, was destroyed to make room for the slip. Return up N. Peters St. to Friscoville Ave. (Jai Alai) and turn (R) to St. Claude Ave. (La 1).

At 5.2 *m.* (L) is the *St. Bernard Kennel Club*; dog races are held here nightly at 8 P.M. during the summer and early fall.

At 5.8 *m.* (R) is the *Chalmette Battlefield.*

> Right is a paved drive leading to *Chalmette Monument*, built in commemoration of the Battle of New Orleans (1815). The road here parallels *Jackson's Line* (about 50 yds. to the left) which ran from the river to a point a quater mile north of the present state highway. A slight depression and elevation, along which a row of moss-hung hackberry trees stands, is the only evdence of the breastwork that was thrown up at this point; the site was chosen because the old Rodriguez Canal

afforded an advantageous natural defense, and also because the distance between the cypress swamp and the river was the shortest line to be defended in that region. It is interesting to note that the Mississippi River has shifted its eastern bank to a great extent since the Battle of New Orleans, the present length of Jackson's line having been shortened by a 230-yard encroachment of the river. As a result, the sites of Batteries 1, 2, and 3 are now under water. Battery 3, which was captained by the Baratarians You and Béluche, is erroneously designated by a marker set up on a tree a short distance from the river. The position of two other markers pointing out Batteries 4 and 5 is approximately correct. The cypress swamp, which once extended well to the river side of La 1 and in which Coffee and his volunteers defended the left flank during the onslaught of the bulk of the British forces, is no longer in evidence.

Chalmette Monument (*see custodian on premises to gain admission to observatory*) marks the site of Jackson's position during the battle of January 8. The monument, a 110-foot marble obelisk modeled after the Washington Monument, was more than fifty years in building. Begun in 1855 with an appropriation from the State, construction reached a height of 60 feet when the Civil War intervened, and it was not until 1908 that the present shaft was completed by the U.S. War Department. The name is derived from the former owner of the plantation, Ignace de Lino de Chalmette. An iron spral staircase within the obelisk leads to an observatory, from which an excellent view of the battlefield may be had. Improvements are being made in the vicinity by the W.P.A., and a national park is being projected for the area.

Judge René Beauregard Home, a short distance to left of the monument, was designed and built by James Gallier, Sr., noted architect, in 1840. The old mansion embodies the Greek Revival style of architecture, of which Gallier was the most noted Southern exponent. Fronting wide upper and ground floor galleries, both front and rear, and supporting a low-pitched, dormer-windowed roof, are eight massive round columns. Return to La 1.

At 6 *m.* (R) is a gravel road.

Right on this road is *Fazendville*, 0.3 *m.*, a Negro settlement occupying the site of the former DeFazende Plantation. A marker 50 yards to the left of the Fazendville Road, about 300 yards in from La 1, marks the place where Gen. Pakenham was shot from his horse as he rallied his men to a second charge. Turn (on graveled river road.

The British position prior to the engagement of Jan. 8, 1815, was taken along the up-stream side of the cemetery situated 300 yards east of Fazendville Road, while on the downstream side were located the twenty-four field pieces that were silenced in the artillery duel of Jan. 1. Roughly paralleling this side of the cemetery may be seen the *Confederate Breastworks* erected in 1862 as a defense against a second invasion – that of Admiral Farragut and his Federal forces.

At 1.6 *m.* (L) is the *Colomb Home* (*visitors allowed*). To the rear are the *Four Oaks*, to which Pakenham was carried from the field of battle and under which he died. The century-old house is a raised cottage with a brick, basement-like ground story, above which is the white-painted cypress second floor; there is a wide veranda supported by massive square, brick columns. The remnants of an old slave jail are still standing. Return to La 1.

At 6.1 *m.* (R) is the *U.S. National Cemetery*, laid out in 1864; it contains the graves of more than 14,000 Union soldiers, more than half of whom are unknown.

At 7.3 *m.* (R) are the ruins of *Versailles*, the one-time plantation home of Pierre Denis de la Ronde III. Extending from the roadside ruins to the river is a magnificent avenue of giant, moss-festooned live oaks planted in 1762 and popularly known as *Pakenham Oaks*, through the erroneous supposition that the British leader died beneath them. Part of the bloody battle of December 23 was fought under these trees, and it was from this position that Jackson and his men retreated upstream.

At 7.5 *m.* is the junction of La 61 (L) *(paved)*.

> Left at 3.3 *m.* is *Bayou Bienvenue*, up which Pakenham brought his invading redcoats for the attack upon New Orleans after having anchored his fleet off the Chandeleur Islands, in the Gulf.

At 8.2 *m.* about 150 yards (R) a marker designates the point from which the schooner 'Carolina' poured a broadside into the British camp at 7.30 P.M. on December 23, thus giving the signal for a general attack. (It is interesting to note that the present bank of the Mississippi River is 600 yards south of this point, which in 1815 was close to the levee, thus making it necessary today to look away from the river to find the 'Carolina's' former position.) The British camp at the moment of attack was situated about 300 yards north of the marker.

> At 8.6 *m.* (L), about a half-mile from the highway amid a cluster of trees, is the 125-year-old *Lacoste Home*; the building was used by the British as headquarters for a battalion of infantry.

At 8.9 *m.* (L), several hundred yards back from the road, is the former overseer's house of *Conseil*, the plantation of Jacques Philippe de Villeré, first native-born Governor of Louisiana. Under a giant pecan tree, no longer standing, the viscera of Gen. Pakenham, British leader slain in the Battle of New Orleans, are said to have been buried. *(See History.)* Legend claims that the pecans of the tree ever afterwards were streaked with red. The remainder of his body is said to have been shipped to England preserved in a rum cask, the contents of which veterans of the campaign are supposed to have inadvertently drunk.

MERAUX (pop. 30), 11.4 *m.* Here is located the mile-square *Dockville Farm* (R) *(open Sun. morning; free)*, on which grow thousands of pear, plum, peach, orange, chestnut, and pecan trees.

VIOLET (alt. 5, pop. 50), 12.6 *m.*, is located at the Mississippi River end of the *Lake Borgne Canal*, a 7-mile channel which, when built (1901), saved smaller vessels 60 miles between New Orleans and the Gulf. Opening of the Industrial Canal at New Orleans (1923) resulted in the earlier waterway's virtual abandonment; it is today used principally by fish, oyster, and shrimp luggers.

At 13.1 *m.* (R) are six dilapidated brick buildings erected as slave quarters.

POYDRAS (alt. 8, pop. 50), 14.9 *m.*, was the scene of a serious levee break in 1922.

> Left from Poydras on La 32 is the region known in Louisiana's early days as *Terre-aux-Boeufs* (Fr., 'Land of Oxen'), supposedly because the early settlers

used oxen almost exclusively to till their farms. The inhabitants are descendants of the early French, Spanish, and Canary Island settlers; the last named were called *Isleños* (Sp., 'islanders'). The higher land is quite fertile, but there are great areas of uncultivable marsh and swampland adjacent to Lake Borgne, teeming with muskrats, otters, and wildfowl.

St. Bernard, 1.1 *m.*, is the seat of St. Bernard Parish and the location of Bernardo de Galvez's early home which once occupied the site of the present post office. The century-old *Turner Home* (R), to the rear of which is the family cemetery; the *Church*, 3 *m.* (L), on the site of the one originally built by Galvez in 1778; and the *Cemetery* (R) should be noted.

At 4.8 *m.* (L) is *Kenilworth*. The ground floor was built in 1759 and for a time used as a Spanish military post; the building was added to at later dates; it is now a private country home. With its massive brick columns, sloping shingled roof, and outside staircases, Kenilworth is typical of 18th-century Louisiana architecture. (*Visitors admitted by the owner.*)

CONTRERAS (alt. 5, pop. app. 50), 6.1 *m.*, is the birthplace of Gen. P. G. T. Beauregard, at whose command the first shot of the Civil War was fired.

At 8.8 *m.* is the junction with La 62 (gravel).

Right on this road is REGGIO, 0.8 *m.*, a sleepy village peopled by Spanish-speaking descendants of the Isleños.

At 2.1 *m.* La 62 bisects what was once the *Solis Plantation*, where, according to some accounts, sugar was first granulated in Louisiana.

DELACROIX ISLAND (alt. 3, pop. 50), 5.6 *m.*, is the center of a very productive trapping district. The 'island' was first settled by Isleños brought to Louisiana in 1778. The immigrants found hunting, trapping, and fishing more to their liking than farming, and were quite a disappointment to their importers. They suffered from hurricanes and floods on numerous occasions; perhaps these difficulties served to bind them closely together, for their descendants are clannish and related either by blood or marriage. During the trapping season (November-February) muskrat traps and drying-racks for pelts are much in evidence. Along Bayou Terre-aux-Boeufs, on whose banks the village is built, there are always numerous fishing boats and pirogues (dugouts). Crabbing here assumes the proportions of a major industry. Return to La 32.

YSCLOSKEY (alt. 4, pop. 50), 13.1 *m.*, bounded by Lake Borgne, Bayou Yscloskey, and Bayou La Loutre (Fr. 'otter'), is a hunting and fishing center, bothfor professionals and amateurs.

At 13.7 *m.* (L) behind the home of Captain Ritter are the remnants of an earlyIndian mound; excavation has unearthed pottery, arrowheads, and skeletons.

SHELL BEACH (alt. 4, pop. 50), 15.8 *m.*, situated on the shore of Lake Borgne, was once a very popular fishing and bathing resort. There are still bathhouse and restaurant facilities.

From Poydras southward to Pointe à la Hache are occasional great fields of sugarcane. During the cutting season – November to January – the fields teem with Negroes, men and women, colorfully clad in blue denim, varicolored ginghams, and red bandanas.

With a machete the stalks are cut and stripped of their long, knife-like leaves, then thrown upon a two-wheeled, mule-drawn cart to be hauled to a grinding mill, where the juice is extracted. The raw, grayish liquid is then sent to a refinery and transformed into the snow-white product known to all.

CAERNARVON (alt. 13, pop. app. 150), 16.1 *m.* The levee at this point was dynamited to relieve the flood danger at New Orleans, during the spring of 1927.

BRAITHWAITE (alt. 14, pop. app. 200), 18.3 *m.*, was until a few years ago a thriving industrial town (1930 pop. 1398), centering around a pulp paper mill.

> Right about 200 yards on a gravel road is *Orange Grove*, once a show place of the section. The mansion was built in 1850 by Thomas Morgan, railroad and steamship magnate.

ENGLISH TURN (alt. 7, pop. 100), 20.6 *m.*, marks the spot where Bienville, founder of New Orleans, succeeded through a ruse in turning back an English expedition in 1699, probably making secure France's claim to Louisiana. Bienville, who headed a very small party, told the English that the Mississippi River lay farther to the west and that the French had established a strong fort and several settlements to the north. Discouraged, the English turned about, leaving the French in undisputed possession.

At 24.9 *m.* (L) is the *Stella Plantation Home*, probably 135 years old; it is a simple raised cottage, set in a grove of fruit trees with live oaks in the rear. It is of a brick and cypress construction, with a hand-hewn shingle roof overhanging a front gallery.

PHOENIX (alt. 7, pop. 350), 38.9 *m.*, is the former site of a small fort, the first in Louisiana, constructed in 1700 by Iberville, French rediscoverer of the Mississippi River.

At 48.5 *m.* (R) is the Roman Catholic Church, built in 1820 and rebuilt a century later. The architecture is strongly suggestive of the Spanish Mission style. A lone oak, overhung with moss, stands near-by atop a small Indian mound; behind lies the little cemetery, containing many old tombs.

POINTE À LA HACHE (alt. 5, pop. 50), 49.5 *m.* According to one explanation of the name (Fr. 'point of the axe') the spot was in the early steamboat days used as a refueling station; seamen were compelled by officers to chop wood for their vessels, and, disliking the work, frequently deserted. The inhabitants are of the opinion that the name is derived from the axelike point made by the river.

NEW ORLEANS - COVINGTON TOUR
NEW ORLEANS, SLIDELL, MANDEVILLE, COVINGTON, 73.4 *m.*, US 90, La 2, US 190

Accommodations at larger towns.

Roads concrete and black-top.

THIS tour describes a semicircle about the eastern half of Lake Pontchartrain, whose shores, save on the north, are bordered by low marshes and swamplands, noted as hunting and fishing grounds. The area lying to the north of the lake, noticeably higher, with swamp flora giving way to pine forests, is known as the 'Ozone Belt,' and is dotted with recreational and health resorts.

Leaving New Orleans, US 90 (Gentilly Rd.) crosses the *Industrial Canal*, 6.2 *m.*, a deep-water channel opened in 1923, connecting Lake Pontchartrain with the Mississippi River.

At 13.6 *m.* (R) is an old chimney, all that remains of the Lafon sugar mill, a unit of the vast Lafon Plantation of the 19th century.

At 19.6 *m.* is the junction of a black-top road.

> Left on this road is the *Pontchartrain Bridge*, 6 *m.* (toll 50¢ one way, 60¢ round trip), spanning the eastern end of Lake Pontchartrain for a distance of 4½ miles. Use of the bridge effects a 10-mile saving.

At 22.6 *m.* (L) is *Bayou Sauvage*. To the right lie old plantation lands now largely fallow; general subsidence and consequent salt impregnation are said to be responsible.

Fort Macomb, 23A *m.* (R), now choked with underbrush and in ruins, was begun during the War of 1812 by General Andrew Jackson. The interior is a labyrinth of passageways and dungeon-like chambers. Surrounding the whole is a moat whose semi-stagnant, hyacinth-covered waters abound with crabs.

Chef Menteur Bridge, 23.6 *m.*, crosses Chef Menteur, one of two passes connecting Lakes Borgne and Pontchartrain. Owing to swift currents at ebb and flow of tide, swimming is dangerous. At both ends of the bridge, boats, bait, and guides may be obtained for fishing.

For the next 9 miles US 90 traverses *St. Catherine's Island*. Along the road are many sportsmen's camps, built on stilts above the low ground or water.

Fort Pike, 36.1 *m.*, occupies the site of a fortification built by Spanish Governor Carondelet, in 1793. The present fort was constructed under Andrew Jackson (1814) and later occupied by Confederates, but so far as is known no engagement ever took place here. Massive ramparts and winding passages lend a feudal atmosphere. Fort Pike was rehabilitated in 1935 and is now maintained as a State park.

Rigolets Bridge, 36.3 *m.*, spans the second and widest pass between Lakes Pontchartrain and Borgne. The Rigolets is noted as the habitat of tarpon and other game fish; dolphins are often visible. Boats, bait, and guides may be obtained.

At the northern end of the bridge US 90 leads straight ahead. Turn (L) on La 2.

At 39.1 *m.* is a gravel side road.

> Left about 400 yards is the old Rigolets ferry-landing and a good shell bathingbeach, bordered by oaks, trumpet vines, and Spanish daggers. (*No bathhouses.*)

SLIDELL (alt. 25, pop. 2807), 44.5 *m.*, is a town whose industries include shipbuilding, brick and tile manufacture, lumbering, and creosoting.

> Left from Slidell on La 1068 is *Bayou Liberty*, 1.5 *m.*, a stream noted for its bassfishing. Live oaks and water hyacinths lend beauty tothe spot, which is popular with picnickers.

Continue in a northwesterly direction from Slidell, on US 190.

At 48.5 *m.* is a side road.

> Left 0.6 *m*, is *Camp Salmen*, a Boy Scout camp occupying a 100-acre pine-forest tract. There are attractive cabins, tennis courts, a concrete swimming pool, and several artesian wells (not available to the public).

The route continues through the pinelands of the 'Ozone Belt' whose air is considered especially beneficial to tubercular patients.

LACOMBE, 56.2 *m.*, is located on Bayou Lacombe, formerly a busy avenue of boat and barge traffic.

> Just after crossing Bayou Lacombe, turn (R) to the *Huey P. Long Fish Hatchery*, 0.7 *m.* There are four large ponds where bass and other fish are spawned and raised.

Beyond Lacombe, the highway returns gradually toward the lake, through a forest of virgin pine.

MANDEVILLE (alt. u, pop. 1069), 65.4 *m.*, a popular summer resort, was founded in 1834 by Bernard Marigny de Mandeville, whose plantation, 'Fontainebleau,' extended nine miles along the lake. Because of the fishing, swimming, and boating to be enjoyed, many summer cottages are maintained here. There are good hotels and several boarding-houses; cottages may be rented. In the outskirts of Mandeville, US 190 crosses *Bayou Chinchuba* (Ind., 'alligator').

At 67.7 w. (R) is the former site of the Indian village of Chinchuba, now occupied by old buildings of the former Chinchuba Deaf Mute Institute. At this point also is the junction with La 122 (gravel).

> Left on La 122 is the *Penick Home*, 2.7 *m*. (R) (private), an interesting and authentic reproduction of an old plantation home that formerly occupied the site.

> MADISONVILLE (alt. 10, pop. 873), 4.8 *m*., situated near the mouth of the Chefuncte River, is noted for its game fish, especially tarpon. From Madisonville La 34 may be followed directly to Covington, 9.8 *m*. (cumulative); otherwise return to US 190.

At 69 *m*. US 190 crosses Bayou Tête L'Ours (Fr., 'Bear Head'), and continues through great forests of yellow pine. Two rivers flow through this region – the Chefuncte (Ind., 'deer') and the Bogue Falaya (Ind., 'Long River'), the town of Covington lying between them farther north.

At 72.8 *m*. is *Riverside Drive* (L), a beautiful suburban residential street.

> Left on Riverside Drive are *Villa de la Vergne*, 2.5 *m*., a 150-year-old plantation home, and the *Waldheim Azalea Gardens*, 3 *m*.

COVINGTON (alt. 35, pop. 3208), 73.4 *m*., the center of the Ozone Belt, is noted as a health resort; the town is also the trading and shipping center of an area productive of strawberries, Satsumas and other oranges, and pecans.

> East (R) of Covington on La 114 (black-top) is ABITA SPRINGS, 3 *m*., a resort noted for its mineral waters.

> Drive north from Covington on La 34 to junction with dirt road, 2.2 *m*. Turn (R) to SULPHUR SPRINGS, 3.7 *m*., a popular fishing, swimming, and picnicking resort attractively situated on the Bogue Falaya River.

PLAQUEMINES - DELTA TOUR

(*West Bank of the Mississippi*) NEW ORLEANS, BURAS, VENICE, 75.3 *m.*, La 31

Roads concrete, black-top, and gravel.

Hotel and restaurant accommodations at Buras.

Visitors may make arrangements with the New Orleans offices of the Freeport Sulphur Company to be taken by boat, free of charge, from Port Sulphur (see below) to the company's sulphur mine and plant on Lake Grand Ecaille.

THIS tour extends down the west bank of the Mississippi River, through one of Louisiana's most interesting sections, historically and otherwise – the Plaquemines Delta.

Cross the Mississippi River via the Canal Street ferry to ALGIERS (*see Algiers Tour*), that portion of New Orleans lying on the east bank of the river. From there proceed south on La 31.

BELLE CHASSE (alt. 4, pop. 20), 9.2 *m.*, is the location of the one-time home of Judah P. Benjamin, Secretary of War and State for the Confederacy. The white-painted, three-story house contains twenty spacious rooms, with 16-foot-wide hallways and correspondingly high ceilings. The rooms of the first floor have heavy cornices, typical of middle-19th century construction, as is the winding mahogany staircase ascending to the third floor from the lower hall. Upper and lower galleries surround the house, supported by square cypress columns. During Benjamin's residence the place was noted for its lavish interior decoration and furniture, and for its paintings and bronzes. The mansion (*open daily; free*) is to be restored to its original splendor as a Civil War museum.

At 10.5 *m.* (L) is the levee-side terminal of the *Seatrain*, an ocean-going car ferry plying between New Orleans and New York. To the right is the Alvin Callendar Airport, an emergency landing field.

From this point southward La 31 winds with the river. Along the levee (L) are usually great bucket-dredges and gangs of laborers working at the never-ending task of levee-building and maintenance. To the right occasional groups of magnolias and moss-laden oaks mark the former sites of palatial plantation homes. Plaquemines and St. Bernard Parishes in ante-bellum times supported huge sugarcane and rice plantations, but the abolition of slavery brought this and the planter aristocracy, that had arisen to an end.

JESUIT BEND (alt. 5, pop. 250), 18.5 *m.*, believed to be the first site settled by Jesuit missionaries in the early 18th century, is the center of an extensive vegetable-growing district.

At 28.8 *m.* (R) is a privately owned shell road.

> Right (*toll 20¢ per person*) 6.8 *m.*, through a beautiful virgin oak and cypress forest, is *Lake Hermitage.* The tract of land through which the road runs affords fine deer, rabbit, squirrel, and waterfowl hunting. At the lake is a camp where accommodations may be obtained.

At 29.5 *m.* (R) is a small 'bay' formed by a river crevasse in 1927, when an outbound 5000-ton molasses tanker rammed its prow through the levee. The adjacent country, largely uncultivated marshland, was soon inundated. The idea persists among the natives that the ship was intentionally run into the levee to relieve the flood danger at New Orleans.

At 34.8 *m.* (L) is a row of two-story brick structures built as slave quarters. The aged boxlike red buildings have almost unbelievably low ceilings and few windows. Along the corrugated-iron roofs juts a single chimney. A Negro occupant, 8o-year-old Abner Bean, remembers when 'Abraham Lincoln come up de river shootin'.' (The reference is probably to Union Admiral Farragut's triumphal upriver journey in 1862.)

Here is the beginning of a small district devoted in part to the cultivation of a species of lily known as the 'Creole Lily,' exemplifying the Louisiana tendency to apply the term 'Creole' to things as well as people; emphasis is placed upon the production of the bulbs.

At 38.3 *m.*, in a grove of orange trees (R) is the *Magnolia Plantation Home* (*private*), built about 1795. It differs from the usual Louisiana plantation home principally in its lack of the huge columns of the subsequently popular Greek Revival architecture. The unusually thick walls are of plaster-covered brick, made on the plantation. All labor on the building, even the fine interior woodcarving, was performed by slaves. Stability and comfort rather than adherence to architectural standards appear to have been the keynote. For many years the mansion was occupied by Reconstruction Governor Henry Clay Warmoth, famed for his lavish hospitality. Magnolia Plantation is now an immense orange orchard.

Extending from Magnolia to Venice, a distance of 37 miles, is the 'Orange Belt.' Here and there, especially beyond Buras, citrus groves line the roadway. Citrus-growing was begun here about 1750, but it was not until about 1917 that large-scale operations were undertaken; since then growth of the industry has been phenomenal. In the spring and early summer blossoming orchards perfume the atmosphere for miles around, and in the late fall and early winter the trees are heavily laden with golden fruit.

WEST POINTE À LA HACHE (alt. 7, pop. 20), 43.6 *m.* (A ferry crosses here to POINTE À LA HACHE; *see St. Bernard-Plaquemines Tour*).

PORT SULPHUR (alt. 8, pop. 500), 46.1 *m.*, is a modern town built by the Freeport Sulphur Co. in 1933; the sulphur mining and refining operations are carried on ten miles to the southwest, on Lake Grande Ecaille.

For several miles below Port Sulphur *crier* bushes (wax myrtle) grow in profusion. The production of wax from these plants to be used in candle-making was one of Louisiana's earliest industries. The marshlands here are excellent muskrat trapping grounds during the winter; in the summer many of the trappers hunt alligators for the hides.

EMPIRE (alt. 3, pop. 200), 55.9 *m.*, is a duck-hunting and fishing center, and the location of several small oyster canning plants.

BURAS (alt. 7, pop. 500), 60.9 *m.*, is the orange-producing center of the State. The population is a French, Spanish, Dalmatian, Slavonian, and Negro heterogeneity.

Voodooism is practiced generally in and about Buras, and 'remedie men' are often consulted in preference to qualified physicians. The treatment embodies primitive superstitions and ceremonials, and occasionally herbal medication.

In the vicinity of Buras are several oystermen's settlements built above the marshes on stilts; Dalmatians and Slavonians predominate.

> Across the Mississippi River from Buras, accessible by passenger ferry only, is OSTRICA, inhabited by fishermen, trappers, and oystermen. There is a semipublic fishing camp.

Oystering is a major industry of this lower delta section. For the most part the oysters are cultivated rather than wild. The 'farming' presents an interesting parallel to other, better-known farming operations.

TRIUMPH (alt. 5, pop. 300), 63.4 *m.*, is a slightly smaller edition of Buras; the manufacture of orange wine is the village industry.

At 66.4 *m.*, the road runs between the old (R) and the newer (L) portions of historic *Fort Jackson*. Construction was begun on the first unit in 1815; the later unit, which consists of massive concrete gun placements commanding the river from the crest of the levee, was built by the Confederates in 1861. The original star-shaped embattlement, with heavy brick casements, bombproofs, and a surrounding moat, is overgrown with grass, weeds, and trees; tourists are cautioned against snakes.

Fort Jackson, with its companion, *Fort St. Philip* (*see below*), across the river, figured prominently in one of the most important engagements of the Civil War. In 1862 a Federal fleet of 24 wooden gunboats and 19 mortar schooners engaged the Confederate forts in a 5-day bombardment that resulted in victory for the Federals, the occupation of New Orleans, and the ultimate splitting in two of the Confederacy.

> Fort St. Philip, directly across the river, accessible only by boat, was first constructed in 1795 under Spanish Governor Carondelet. It is also overgrown with underbrush and infested with snakes.

BOOTHVILLE, 70.8 *m.* is a picturesque settlement of fishermen, oystermen, and trappers. The village served as the locale of a recent best seller, *Green Margins*, by Pat O'Donnell (Houghton Mifmn, 1936).

VENICE, 75.3 *m.*, the southern terminus of La 31, is most commonly known, and appears on maps as 'The Jump,' because the river here once 'jumped' through to the Gulf. Game is abundant, particularly ducks and geese. There is a small hotel open only during the hunting season.

> OLGA, an island settlement across the river from Venice, accessible only by boat, is inhabited by the Slavonian fishermen and oystermen.

NEW ORLEANS - GRAND ISLE TOUR: 63 *m*.

(1) By boat: New Orleans, Harvey, Lafitte Village, Grand Isle – 63 *m*. Packet 'Chicago' leaves Harvey at 7.30 A.M. Tuesday and Friday, during winter; returning leaves Grand Isle 7.30 A.M. Wednesday and Saturday. *Summer*: leaves Harvey 7.30 A.M. Wednesday, and Grand Isle 7.30 A.M. Friday. (Schedule subject to change; advisable to telephone the New Orleans office of Grand Isle Chamber of Commerce.)

One-way trip consumes 10 to 12 hours. Round trip fare $4.

(2) Combining automobile and boat: New Orleans, Marrero, Lafitte Village (board 'Chicago' for Grand Isle) – 63 *m*. Cross Mississippi River from New Orleans via Napoleon Ave. ferry to Marrero; follow La 30 (gravel) to Lafitte Village; leave automobile and board Chicago on sailing days at 10 A.M. (see foregoing schedule). Round trip fare $3.

(3) Automobile only: New Orleans, Raceland, Golden Meadow, Leeville,Grand Isle; US 90, La 78, La 620 – 101 *m*. Roads concrete, black-top, and gravel.

Accommodations at two hotels on Grand Isle; rates (with meals) $2.50 per day and up.

The following route description, save for material on Grand Isle, applies only to (i) and (2).

THIS tour traverses the 'Lafitte Country' the portion of Louisiana whose many bayous, lagoons, and bays served as the rendezvous and sometimes sanctuary of the pirate-smuggler-soldier Jean Lafitte and his swashbuckling band of adventurers.

From the Wagner Bridge, 12 *m*., crossing Little Bayou Barataria, water and highway routes parallel each other as far as Lafitte Village, southern terminus of La 30.

LAFITTE POST OFFICE (alt. 5, pop. 50), 15 *m*.

Berthoud Cemetery, 15.3 *m*. (E. bank), is situated on an Indian shell mound upon whose peak are the graves of the Berthoud brothers, early settlers of the region, enclosed within a rusted iron fence; other graves are scattered about the foot of the mound, many of them marked by glass-fronted boxes containing wreaths of paper or bead flowers and statuettes of the Virgin Mary.

Isle Bonne, 15.5 *m*. (W. bank), is an oak-covered point jutting out into the waters where Bayou Villars (R) and Little Bayou Barataria unite to form Big Bayou Barataria. An annual event is a spring pirogue (dugout canoe) race, witnessed by thousands of enthusiastic bayou folk lining the course, which extends from Lafitte post office to Lafitte Village.

BARATARIA (alt. 5, pop. 600) (E. bank), 15.7 *m.*, is a scattered settlement stretching along the bayou for 2 or 3 miles, the home of a fleet of fishing vessels.

At 20 *m.* the *Lafitte Cemetery* (E. bank) nestles under sheltering oaks at the foot of a high-arched wooden bridge crossing Bayou des Oies (Fr. 'bayou of geese'). In the tiny cemetery, according to local legend, are buried the bodies of Jean Lafitte, John Paul Jones of naval fame, and Napoleon Bonaparte.

LAFITTE VILLAGE (alt. 5, pop. 200), 20.5 *m.*, was in the early 19th century the site of a pirate settlement frequented by Lafitte and his band, (*Leave automobiles here and board* 'Chicago.')

For the next 16 miles salt grass flats with oaks and cypresses in the background constitute the scenery. These unsubstantial and treacherous flats are known locally as 'trembling prairies,' after the old French term *prairie tremblante*.

At 27 *m.* (R) is the *Lafitte Oil Field*, where oil storage tanks, field buildings, and derricks are built on piling above the marsh, connected by elevated walkways or canals.

Several oaks on a windswept shell reef at 37 *m.* provide the only break in the monotonously flat landscape and seascape between Lafitte Village and Grand Isle.

MANILA VILLAGE (R) (pop. 200), 46 *m.*, is inhabited largely by Filipinos, with a sprinkling of Mexicans, Spaniards, and Chinese. It is typical of the several shrimp 'platforms' or settlements of the Barataria region. The dozen red-roofed, green-painted houses are built on stilts above the water. The sustaining industry is the sun-drying of shrimp which are brought to the platform by the fleet of fishing boats that has its headquarters here.

The route now lies through Barataria Bay, an inlet of the Gulf of Mexico; shrimp fishing has been carried on here commercially for half a century.

The 'Chicago' makes stops at several other shrimp platforms – *León Rojas, Bayou Cholas, Bayou Defon, Bayou Bruleau* – all similar to Manila Village, where cats, dogs, children, and adults swarm to meet the boat, their only contact with the outside world.

Bayou Rigaud, 59 *m.*, is Grand Isle's harbor, the headquarters for a large fishing and shrimping fleet.

Grand Isle, one of the several sea islands lying along the northern shore of the Gulf of Mexico, is 7 miles long and 1½ miles wide. Stately palms and oaks, dense jungles of palmetto, yaupon, and Spanish dagger, and the curving 7-mile beach present an almost idyllic, semi-tropical picture. The island's population of 400 is a mixture of French, Spanish, Portuguese, Filipinos, and Chinese nationalities; a French patois is the common language.

The principal occupations of the islanders – many of whom are descendants of Lafitte's pirates – are fishing and trapping. The waters surrounding the island teem with redfish, flounders, swordfish, shark, porpoise, and tarpon. A three-day 'tarpon rodeo' is held yearly, sportsmen from New Orleans and much more distant points participating.

An interesting characteristic of the island is its annual visitation by migratory fowl. Beginning in April, huge flocks of ducks, geese, and other birds that have wintered in the tropics make their way northward, their lines of flight apparently converging at Grand Isle. At the height of the migration period the island is alive with wildfowl that rest and feed before resuming the northward journey. The fall southward migration is less concentrated and of shorter duration.

The *Elinore Behre Field Laboratory*, a unit of Louisiana State University, conducts field courses and research in biology on the island.

Fort Livingston, located on Grand Terre Island, 1 mile across Barataria Pass from Grand Isle, can be reached by boat (*make arrangements at hotel, fare* $1-$3). This fort, named for Edward Livingston, Secretary of State in Andrew Jackson's cabinet, has an interesting but rather vague history. Some believe that the stronghold – of which today only ruins of brick walls and a few rusted cannon remain – was constructed by Lafitte's pirates; U.S. soldiers, known to have occupied the island after Lafitte's removal to Texas, are possibly due the credit for the building. The fort has been garrisoned several times, changing hands twice during the Civil War. After the great hurricane of 1893 partially destroyed it, the structure was abandoned.

The *Barataria Lighthouse* stands beside Fort Livingston. A brick tower built in 1857 housed the light for 40 years, but in 1897 was replaced by the present 76-foot wooden tower. Formerly the island had a number of inhabitants, but since the hurricane the only residents are the lighthouse-keeper and his family.

CHECKLIST OF SOME NOTED PERSONALITIES

ALMONESTER Y ROXAS, DON ANDRES (1725-98). Spanish grandee who provided funds for rebuilding St. Louis Cathedral after the great fire of 1788 and who built the Cabildo and sold it to the city.

AUDUBON, JEAN JACQUES FOUGERE (178?-1851). Ornithologist and artist whose *Birds of America* and *Ornithological Biography* are still highly regarded; the possibility of his having been the lost Dauphin of France was scouted for years.

BEAUREGARD, PIERRE GUSTAVE TOUTANT (1818-93). Creole Confederate general at whose command the first shot of the Civil War was fired (Fort Sumter, April 12, 1862).

BENJAMIN, JUDAH P. (1811-80). Confederate Secretary of War and State, who, after having been exiled, lived in England and gained international fame as a lawyer.

BIENVILLE, JEAN BAPTISTE LE MOYNE, *Sieur de* (1680-1768). French-Canadian explorer; three times Governor of Louisiana under French domination;founder of New Orleans; promulgator in Louisiana of celebrated 'Black Code.'

BORÉ, JEAN ÉTIENNE DE (1741-1820). Gave impetus to sugar industry by granulating sugar on a commercial scale; first mayor of New Orleans.

BURKE, EDWARD (1842-1928). Journalist-politician credited with having persuaded President Hayes to withdraw Federal troops from Louisiana; indicted while State treasurer for fraudulently negotiating State bonds, but escaped to Honduras and became a banana planter.

CABLE, GEORGE WASHINGTON (1844-1925). Gained international recognition as a novelist and short-story writer through works based on Louisiana; his uncomplimentary characterizations aroused the bitter animosity of Louisiana Creoles.

CALDWELL, JAMES H. (1793-1863). Instrumental in introducing English drama and gas illumination in New Orleans; built American and St. Charles Theaters and vied with Ludlow and Smith in making New Orleans the dramatic capital of the country.

CLAIBORNE, WILLIAM CHARLES COLE (1775-1817). Led Louisiana through a hectic decade as its first American Governor.

CLARK, DANIEL (1766-1813). Irish-American merchant and landowner who assisted Thomas Jefferson in negotiations leading to the Louisiana Purchase and who later wounded Governor Claiborne in a duel brought about by charges of his implication in the Aaron Burr conspiracy.

DELGADO, ISAAC (1839-1912). Philanthropist to whom New Orleans owes its art museum and boys trades school.

DIMITRY, ALEANDER (1805-83). Greek-American pioneer leader in public education; U.S. Minister to Central America and later Confederate postoffice official; befriender and reputed discoverer of Lafcadio Hearn.

FORTIER, ALCÉE (1856-1914). Teacher-historian noted for his Creole studies and historical works.

GAINES, MYRA CLARK (1805-85). Principal and ultimate victor of a sensational fifty-year lawsuit against the city of New Orleans for the estate of her wealthy father, Daniel Clark.

GALLIER, JAMES, SR. (1798-1866). Architect who designed the City Hall and many Garden District homes in New Orleans; exponent of the Greek Revival style of architecture.

GALLIER, JAMES, JR. (1827-68). Continued his father's architectural work in New Orleans; designer of French Opera House.

GALVEZ, BERNARDO DE (1746-86). As Spanish Governor of Louisiana he distinguished himself by wresting East and West Florida from the British (1780-83); later became Viceroy of Mexico.

GAYARRÉ, CHARLES ÉTIENNE (1805-95). Dabbled in politics while writing several histories of Louisiana and two novels, *Fernando de Lemos* and *Aubert Dubayet*; led Creoles in bitter controversy with George W. Cable.

GOTTSCHALK, LOUIS MOREAU (1829-69). Considered leading pianist-composer of his day; gave concerts throughout the world; *La Morte* and *Tremole Étude* best-known works.

HEARN, LAFCADIO (1850-1904). Cosmopolite from birth, he tarried long enough in New Orleans to launch his literary career.

JACKSON, ANDREW (1767-1845). 'Saviour of New Orleans' during War of 1812 and popular Louisiana hero for decades.

KENNER, DUNCAN FARRAR (1813-87). Active in behalf of Confederate cause and afterward instrumental in ridding the State of 'carpetbaggers' and 'scalawags.'

KING, GRACE ELIZABETH (1851-1932). Student of Creole life and manners whose *New Orleans, the Place and the People*, and *Creole Families of New Orleans* have enriched Louisiana literature.

LAFITTE, JEAN (1780?-1825). Famous smuggler and pirate who was pardoned because of his participation in behalf of the United States at the Battle of New Orleans.

LAFON, THOMY (1810-93). Colored philanthropist whose charities in New Orleans won him the distinction of having a public school named after him.

LAVEAU, MARIE (1783-1881). Mulattress 'Voodoo Queen,' leader of a strange sect and dealer in charms, remedies, and 'advice.'

LIVINGSTON, EDWARD (1764-1836). Represented both New York and Louisiana in Congress; Secretary of State under Andrew Jackson and later Minister to France.

LLULA, JOSÉ (1810?-88). One of the best swordsmen of his day; employed his art to advantage during a stormy life.

LONG, HUEY PIERCE (1893-1935). Virtual political dictator of Louisiana and leader of 'Share the Wealth' program; assumed a prominent place in national affairs as U.S. Senator and Presidential aspirant; assassinated at height of career.

LONGSTREET, JAMES (1821-1904). Brigadier general in the Confederate Army who after the war became a Republican, a resident of New Orleans, he became unpopular with the people of his State for his part in the politics of the Reconstruction period; appointed minister to Turkey by President Grant.

LOUIS, JEAN (1690?-1736). Humble sailor who left his life savings for the establishment of a hospital for the poor (the forerunner of Charity Hospital).

McDONOGH, JOHN (1779-1850). Wealthy but miserly merchant whose bequest formed the foundation for the New Orleans public-school system.

MENKEN, ADAH ISAACS (1835-68). New Orleans-born actress who led a sensational life and attained fame as an actress in Europe and America.

MONROE, JOHN T. (1823-71). Civil War and Reconstruction mayor of New Orleans; loyal but temperate advocate of the Confederate cause.

MORPHY, PAUL CHARLES (1837-84). Considered one of the greatest chess players of all time.

NEWCOMB, JOSEPHINE LOUISE LE MONNIER (1816-1901). Founded Sophie Newcomb College as a memorial to her daughter.

O'REILLY, ALEXANDER (1722-94). Sent to Louisiana in 1769 to take over the Colony after the insurrection against Spanish rule; called 'Bloody O'Reilly' after execution of five rebels.

PAUGER, ADRIEN DE (1670?-1726). Aided in plotting New Orleans; suggested construction of jetties to deepen channel at mouth of Mississippi River.

PETERS, SAMUEL JARVIS (1801-55). Business man and civic leader who played a prominent part in the development of the American Quarter over opposition of Creole element.

PINCHBACK, PINKEY BENTON STUART (1837-1921). Mulatto politician who be came Lieutenant Governor of Louisiana during Reconstruction.

POLLOCK, OLIVER (1737-1823). New Orleans merchant who rendered material assistance to the American cause during the Revolution.

PONTALBA, *Baroness* MICAELA (1795-1874). Daughter of Don Almonester y Roxas, whose civic works she carried on by donating to the city the Pontalba buildings and beautifying Jackson Square.

POYDRAS, JULIEN (1740-1824). Trader-philanthropist-poet; charitable works included establishment of dowry fund for impoverished Pointe Coupee and West Baton Rouge Parish maidens.

RICHARDSON, HENRY HOBSON (1838-86). Louisiana-born architect whose Romanesque designs won international recognition; examples of his work include the New York State Capitol and the Howard Memorial Library, New Orleans.

RIPLEY, ELIZA MOORE (1832-1912). Wrote entertainingly of life in New Orleans in the 1840's and '50's.

ROFFIGNAC, LOUIS PHILIPPE (1770-1846). As mayor of New Orleans (1820-28), he launched a program of civic improvement; remembered for the famous cocktail named in his honor.

ROUQUETTE, ADRIEN EMANUEL (1813-88). Creole priest and poet; lived with Choctaws as medicine-man; poetry reflects his religious philosophy and ascetic life.

ROUQUETTE, FRANÇOIS DOMINIQUE (1812-90). Vagabond-troubadour whose poetry and eccentricities made him a colorful New Orleans figure.

SEDELLA, ANTONIO DE (1748-1829). Expelled from Colony for attempting to set up Inquisition; returned and endeared himself as 'Père Antoine'; became involved in bitter religious controversy with ecclesiastical superiors.

SLIDELL, JOHN (1793-1871). Prominent in State and National affairs in 1850's; Minister to France under the Confederacy.

SOULÉ, GEORGE (1834-1926). Mathematician and educator; established first commercial college in New Orleans.

SOULÉ, PIERRE (1801-70). Came to New Orleans from France as a political refugee and became prominent as a criminal lawyer; entered politics and became leading exponent of 'States Rights.'

TAYLOR, RICHARD (1826-79). Soldier-author; led successful Civil War campaign against General Banks in West Louisiana; author of Destruction and Reconstruction.

TAYLOR, ZACHARY (1784-1850). Migrated from Kentucky to Louisiana, achieved fame in Mexican War, and became twelfth President of the United States.

TOURO, JUDAH (1775-1854). Gave liberally to numerous charities during his lifetime (Touro-Shakespeare Home, Touro Infirmary, and Touro Synagogue, New Orleans).

TULANE, PAUL (1801-87). Donated over a million dollars to the University of Louisiana (now Tulane University, New Orleans).

VAUDREUIL, PIERRE FRANÇOIS DE RIGAUD, Marquis de (1698-1765). Made New Orleans a miniature Versailles while French Governor of Louisiana.

WARMOTH, HENRY CLAY (1842-1931). Dominated carpetbag régime as Reconstruction Governor; author of War, Politics and Reconstruction.

WHITE, EDWARD DOUGLAS (1845-1921). Entered Confederate Army at eighteen; became associate justice of the Louisiana Supreme Court at thirtythree; later U.S. Senator, and finally Chief Justice of the United States.

WRIGHT, SOPHIE BELL (1866-1912). Teacher-humanitarian responsible for night schools and many social-service agencies in New Orleans.

YOU, DOMINIQUE (1775-1830). As a member of Lafitte's 'hellish banditti' he distinguished himself in the Battle of New Orleans, and settled down to become a law-abiding citizen.

CHRONOLOGY

1543   *July.* Luis Moscoso and the survivors of DeSoto's expedition, descending the river on their way to Mexico, are the first white men to view the site of the future city.

1682   *March* 31. La Salle and Tonti, on their trip from the Great Lakes to the Gulf, stop at an Indian village, at or near present-day New Orleans.
April 9. La Salle erects a cross three leagues above the mouth of the Mississippi and names the territory 'Louisiana' in honor of Louis XIV.

1699   *March* 6. Iberville and his scouting expedition stop at the present site of New Orleans, where a buffalo is killed, a cross erected, and some trees marked.

1718   *Spring.* Bienville, with the assistance of Pauger and de la Tour, lays out the streets and founds *La Nouvelle Orléans.*

1722   Under Governor Bienville, New Orleans becomes the capital of Louisiana.

1724   *March.* Bienville promulgates the *Code Noir* (Black Code) regulating slavery and religious worship.

1727   *August* 6. The Ursulines arrive and establish a convent school for girls.

1728   *December.* The first company of *Filles à la Cassette* (Casket Girls) arrive and are placed in the care of the Ursulines while being courted by the colonists, sadly in need of wives.

1729   *December.* Refugees bring news of the Indian massacre of Fort Rosalie (Natchez), and Governor Périer begins construction of first defense works (ditch and stockade) against a possible Indian attack.

1735   *November* 16. Jean Louis, a sailor, dies and leaves his savings to establish the first charity hospital in New Orleans.

1743   Under Governor Vaudreuil (1743-53) New Orleans becomes a gay social center.

1763   *February* 6. Louisiana is ceded to Spain by the Treaty of Paris.
July 9. The Jesuits are expelled from Louisiana by the French authorities and their property confiscated.

1768   *October.* Opposition to Spanish rule breaks into open rebellion and Governor Ulloa departs for Spain leaving the Colony without European government.

1769   *August* 18. General Alexander O'Reilly arrives with an armed force and takes possession of the city. Six leaders of the rebellion are eventually executed and seven others imprisoned. The Superior Council is abolished, the Cabildo established, and various changes made in government.

1777   Under Governor Galvez Americans are allowed to establish bases in New Orleans and send aid to the revolutionary forces. After war is declared between Spain and England, Galvez, in a series of campaigns, drives the English out of the Gulf Coast country (1779-82).

1788 *March* 21. Fire destroys over 800 houses and necessitates the re-building of a great part of the city.
December 5. Padre Antonio de Sedella, later known as 'Père Antoine,' is appointed Commissary of the Inquisition, and upon attempting to establish that tribunal (which had remained dormant since O'Reilly authorized it in 1770), is sent back to Spain by Governor Miro.

1791 Louis Tabary and his company of refugee players from Santo Domingo stage the first professional theatrical performances held in New Orleans.

1794 The first regular newspaper, *Le Moniteur de la Louisiane*, begins publication.
December 8. A second fire, almost as destructive as that of 1788, destroys a great part of the city. Rebuilding begins under the direction of Spanish architects.

1795 Carondelet Canal, connecting the city with Bayou St. John, is opened.
Autumn, Étienne de Boré succeeds in refining sugar in commercial quantities, thus giving impetus to the sugar industry.

1803 *November* 30. France takes formal possession of the Colony from Spain in the *Place d'Armes*.
December 20. William C. C. Claiborne and General James Wilkinson take possession in the name of the United States.

1805 The College of Orleans, the first institution of higher learning in the city, is established, but not opened until 1811.
February 22. The city of New Orleans is incorporated and the first municipal officials are elected shortly afterward.
April 19. The New Orleans Library Society is incorporated.
June 16. The Protestants of the city form their first church organization.

1812 *January* 10. The 'Orleans,' first steamboat to descend the Mississippi River, arrives from Pittsburgh.
April 30. Louisiana is admitted to the Union and New Orleans becomes the capital of the State.

1815 *January* 8. The American forces, under General Andrew Jackson, defeat the British in the final decisive action of the Battle of New Orleans.

1823 *May* 8. James H. Caldwell opens the first American Theater on Camp Street, introducing the use of illuminating gas.

1825 *April* 10. Lafayette arrives in New Orleans for a five-day visit.

1831 *April*. The Pontchartrain Railroad, first railroad west of the Alleghenies, offers freight and passenger service to Milneburg.

1835 *April* 2. The 'Medical College,' which eventually develops into the University of Louisiana (1847) and Tulane University (1884), is established.

1836 *March* 8. A new charter divides the city into three municipalities, each with its own board of aldermen, under one mayor, and a general council composed of the three municipal councils.

1837 *January* 25. The *Picayune*, now the *Times-Picayune*, begins publication.

1838 *Shrove Tuesday*. First Mardi Gras parade held.

1846- The *Picayune* 'scoops' the world on the Mexican War as George W. Kendall, first modern
1847   war correspondent, sends his copy by pony express.

1850   *October* 26. The New Orleans public school system is greatly enlarged from funds left to
       the city for that purpose by John McDonogh.

1853   Eleven thousand inhabitants perish in the most severe yellow-fever epidemic in the history
       of New Orleans.
       May 10. The City Hall, designed and built by James Gallier, Sr., is dedicated.

1859   *December* 1. The French Opera House opens its doors with the production of *Guillaume
       Tell*.

1860   *November* 19. Adelina Patti sings at the French Opera House in Donizetti's *Lucia di
       Lammermoor.*

1861   *January* 26. Louisiana adopts the Ordinance of Secession.

1862   *April* 30. The city surrenders to Admiral David E. Farragut and his Federal forces.
       May 1. General Benjamin F. Butler assumes command of the city.

1864   *May* 11. Constitution of Louisiana amended, abolishing slavery.

1866   *July* 30. A riot occurs at the Mechanics Institute in which a large number of Negroes and
       whites are killed and wounded.

1874   *September* 14. The White League forces defeat the Metropolitan Police in a pitched battle
       at the head of Canal Street.

1880   *August.* Captain James B. Eads completes the jetties at South Pass, thus deepening the
       channel at the mouth of the river and aiding shipping.

1884   Tulane University, endowed by Paul Tulane, takes over the buildings and equipment of the
       University of Louisiana.
       December 16. The Cotton Exposition is opened in Audubon Park and is continued, in part,
       the following year as the American Exposition
       (November 10, 1885, to March 31, 1886).

1886   *October* 11. Newcomb College is founded.

1891   *March* 14. Eleven Italian prisoners, alleged slayers of Chief of Police Hennessey, are taken
       from the Parish Prison by a mob of citizens and lynched.

1892   *September* 7. James J. Corbett defeats John L. Sullivan in a twenty-one round knockout
       victory under the auspices of the Olympic Athletic Club.

1902   *September* 27 – *October* 10. A street-car strike is productive of serious disorders.

1905   Last of yellow-fever epidemics occurs.

1911   Loyola University evolving from Loyola Academy, is established by the Jesuits.

1912   *August* 12. The commission form of city government is adopted.

1915   *September* 29. A severe tropical hurricane inflicts serious property damage throughout the city.

1934   *January* 1. The first Sugar Bowl football game is played by the Tulane and Temple elevens.

1935   *December* 16. The Huey P. Long Bridge across the Mississippi is completed and dedicated.
       September. Dillard University, a merger of several Negro colleges maintained in New
       Orleans under Protestant auspices since the Civil War, opens its doors.

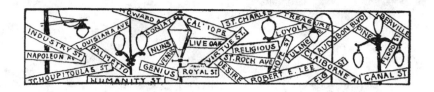

STREET NAMES IN NEW ORLEANS

THE visitor on a tour of New Orleans finds a great deal of interest and amusement in the endless list of odd names attached to the streets of the city. Those familiar with the five successive eras of government and the racial comminglings which have finally given the life and population of the city its cosmopolitan atmosphere will see in these names an epitome of the colorful history of New Orleans.

The French sought to perpetuate the memory of the reigning royal family of France by naming for its members several streets in the old French Quarter. Here one finds Royal, Dauphine, Toulouse, Bourbon, Dumaine, and Burgundy Streets. Bienville, Iberville, and many other personages connected with the early history of New Orleans are likewise honored. The nuns who became the first teachers and nurses in Louisiana established themselves on a street, the name of which was afterward changed to Ursuline in their honor.

The early French and Spanish settlers showed their religious inclinations in giving to streets such names as Conception, Ascension, Nuns, Religious, Annunciation, Piety, and Assumption. Scores of streets were named for their various saints, such as St. Louis, St. Peter, St. Ann, and St. Philip Streets. Other names which are somewhat unusual are Virtue, Genius, Pleasure, Desire, Humanity, Industry, and Mystery Streets.

The classical names of Greek mythology were not ignored when the city was being laid out. Among streets named for mythological characters are Calliope, Euterpe, Terpsichore, Melpomene, Polymnia, Erato, Clio, Urania, and Thalia. In addition to the Muses one finds such names as Homer, Socrates, Ptolemy, Coliseum, Dryades, and Olympia.

Several Governors of the State and mayors of the city, as well as prominent Louisiana planters, soon became included in New Orleans' street names. Among the many Governors thus honored were Nicholls, Galvez, and Claiborne; mayors whose names were attached to streets include Freret, Capdeville, Behrman, and Montegut. Outstanding citizens whose names are familiar through street names include Forstail, Marigny, McDonogh, Clouet, and Delord. National figures, such as General Pershing, Henry Clay, Lincoln, Andrew Jackson, Jefferson Davis, Robert E. Lee, and Beauregard, were also drawn into street nomenclature.

The aborigines who had first inhabited Louisiana and adjoining territory are also well represented. Tchoupitoulas, Opelousas, Choctaw, Apache, Chippewa, Chickasaw, Navajo, Teche, Cherokee, Natchez, and Seminole are among the names of tribes honored with street names. Some of the most fascinating chapters of early Louisiana history are bound up with the redskins who once flourished along the Louisiana shores.

The civic councils showed their literary bent, also, when new streets were being laid out and the city enlarged. Among those of great literary fame one finds Dante, Shakespeare, Milton, Rousseau, Poe, Hawthorne, and Spencer. Even astronomy was resorted to for Zenith Street, Mars Place, and Eclipse Alley.

One street is called 'Perdido,' since legend has it that this by-way once lost itself in a cypress swamp. Another was called Julia Street, and writers assure us that Julia was a 'free woman of color.' Other names which are typical of the State or section of the country are Magnolia, Pelican, Bayou Road, Redfish, and Iris.

PLACE NAMES
ORLEANS PARISH

Bayou Bienvenue, which begins at the Industrial Canal and empties into Lake Borgne, was so named because of the vast holdings of the Bienvenue family in that section. The English found their way into New Orleans by means of this bayou in 1814.

Lake Borgne is a large body of water lying between Lake Pontchartrain and theMississippi Sound, connected with the Lake by the Rigolets and the Chef. The name means 'one-eyed' and was given the lake by Iberville, probably because it had only one outlet into the Sound.

Chef Menteur, one of the outlets of Lake Pontchartrain into Lake Borgne, is named, according to tradition, for an Indian chief who was banished to its shores by his tribesmen because of his uncontrollable propensity for lying.

Micheaud is a local station on the Louisville and Nashville Railroad between theIndustrial Canal and Chef Menteur. The place was named for an old French family, descendants of whom still own most of the property surrounding the station. The place is popular as picnic grounds for New Orleanians, especially over the week-ends.

New Orleans, founded in 1718 by Bienville, was named in honor of the Regent of France, the Due d'Orléans, who had received his title from the old French city of Orléans, the home of Jeanne d'Arc. The name was originally *Nouvelle Orléans* (pronounced Noo-vel Or-lay-unh). The feminine form was adopted, probably for euphony, instead of *Nouveau Orléans*, although the alternate masculine form, *Nouvel Orléans*, would have been as satisfactory. As one early commentator wrote: 'Whether masculine or feminine, the custom is established, and custom rises above grammar.' When the French-Spanish city became a part of the United States in 1803, the English translation of the name came into common usage. Today in the outlying districts of the State, New Orleans (now correctly pronounced New Or'le uns or New Orl'yuns, not New Or leens') is usually called 'The City,' and that phrase means New Orleans and only New Orleans.

Lake Pontchartrain, the large lake lying north of New Orleans, was named by Iberville in honor of the Minister of Marine of France.

Rigolets is the main channel between Lake Pontchartrain and Lake Borgne. This name, given to the channel by the early French explorers of lower Louisiana, means 'narrows' or 'straits.'

GLOSSARY

Allée: A double row of trees leading from the road or river to a plantation house. (Fr. allée, an alley.)

Armoire: A cabinet closing with one or two doors, having rows of shelves, and used for keeping clothes. (Lat. *armarium*, from *arma*, arms.)

Arpent: A former land measure, of 100 perches, which were 22 feet square. (Lat. *arapennis* or *arepennis*.)

Bagasse: The residue of sugarcane after the juice has been pressed out. (Span. *bagazo*.)

Baire: A mosquito net or bar. (Fr., *barre*, cross-bar.)

Balcon: A balcony. (Fr. balcon, a Latin Case.)

Bamboula: A dance executed to the accompaniment of a bamboula drum. (Fr. bamboida, a primitive African drum.)

Banquette: A sidewalk, so called because the early wooden sidewalks were elevated above the muddy streets. (Fr. *banquette*, a low bench.)

Batture: The land built up by the silting action of a river. (Fr. *battre*, to beat.)

Bayou: A natural canal, having its rise in the overflow of a river, or draining of a marsh. (Choctaw *bayuk*, river or creek.)

Blanchisseuse: A washerwoman. (Fr. *blanchir*, to whiten, to clean.)

Blouse-volante: A mother-hubbard; a loose wrapper. (Fr. *voler*, to fly.)

Bouillabaisse: A stew of red snapper and redfish, with various kinds of vege tables, all highly seasoned with pepper and spices. (Prov. *bouia-baisso*, boiled down.)

Briqueté entre poteaux: A method of construction in vogue in the eighteenth century in which bricks were filled in between the spaces of a framework of cypress timbers. (Fr. bricked between posts.)

Cagou: Disgusted, disillusioned. (Fr. cagot, leprous, beggarly, indigent, pariah.)

Cajan: A French-speaking man or woman of the Bayou Country. (Corruption of *Acadian*, emigrants from Acadia, Nova Scotia.)

Carencro: The black vulture, *Coragyps urubu urubu*. (An Acadian corruption of 'carrion crow.')

Chacalata: The Creoles who remained among themselves, stubbornly refusing to accept new customs or ideas. A local term.

Chambre à brin: A screened enclosure on a corner of a 'gallery.' (Fr. *brin*, linen cloth. In Louisiana, *brin* is screen wire.)

Charivari: A serenade of 'rough music,' with kettles, pans, trays, and the like, given in derision of incongruous or unpopular marriages. (Picard *caribari*, Med. Lat. *carivarium*.)

Chenière: A mound, rising from a swamp, and covered with a grove of live oaks. (Fr. *chêne*, an oak.)

Cochon-dilaite: Negro-French for pill-bug. (Fr. *cochon de lait*, suckling pig.)

Compère: A term of affection or friendship. The Creole animal fables use it as a title of address for characters: *Compère Lapin* is equivalent to our Br'er Rabbit. (Fr. prefix *com*, with, and *père*, father.)

Congo: A very black Negro. Formerly it meant a Negro actually from the Congo nation.

Congo: The cotton-mouth moccasin, *Agkistrodon piscivorus*.

Congo Eel: A blue-black amphibian, *Amphiuma tridactylum*.

Courtbouillon: Redfish cooked with highly seasoned gravy. (Fr. *court-bouillon*, a sort of gravy consisting of white wine, salt, pepper, parsley, carrots, and onions, and in which fish or game may be cooked.)

Crayfish bisque: A rich soup made with crayfish, the heads being stuffed and-served in the soup. (Fr. *bisque*, thick soup, cullis.)

Creole: A white descendant of the French and Spanish settlers in Louisiana during the Colonial period (1699-1803). (Span, *criollo*, native to the locality. Believed to be a Colonial corruption of *criadillo*, dim. of *criado*, bred, brought up, reared, domestic; p. pple. of *criar*, to breed.)

Cyprière: Cypress forest or swamp. (Fr. *cyprès*, cypress.)

Fais-dodo: A country dance; from the *fais dodo*, 'go to sleep,' of children's speech. (Fr., *dormir*, to sleep.)

Free-Mulatto: A mulatto born free; that is, a person of color who was never a slave. (See *Mulatto*, below.)

F.W.C. or *F.M.C.*: These initials found in the old documents stand for 'Free Woman of Color' and 'Free Man of Color.'

Gabrielle: A loose wrapper worn in the house. Local term.

Gallery: A porch, balcony. (Fr. *galerie*, Lat. *galeria*, gallery.)

Garçonnière: Bachelor quarters, usually separate from the principal part of the house. (Fr. garçon, a boy, a bachelor.)

Gard-soleil: A sunbonnet. A local term coined from Fr. *garder*, to guard, and *soleil*, the sun.

Garde-de-frise: The spikes projecting from rails separating two adjoining balconies. (Probably a hybrid formation from Fr. *garde*, guard, and *cheval-de-frise*, spiked guard rail.)

Gaspergou: Local corruption of *Casse-burgau*, the fresh-water drum, *Aplodinotus grunniens*. It is so called because it feeds on large bivalves of the genus *turbo* (Fr. *burgau*), which it breaks (Fr. *casser*) with its teeth.

Gombo: See Gumbo.

Grasset: The kingbird, or bee-martin, *Tyrannus tyrannus*, or the vireo, *Vireo olivaceus*. (Fr. grasset, fatty.)

Griffe: The child of a Mulatto and a Negro; a person having three-fourths Negro blood. (Fr. *griffe*, origin uncertain.)

Gris-gris: Amulet, talisman, or charm, worn for luck or used to conjure evil on enemies by the Voodoo devotees. Presumably a word of African origin.

Grosbec: The night heron, *Nyctanassa violacea*. (Fr. *gros*, big, *bec*, beak.)

Gumbo: The okra plant, *Hibiscus esculentus*, or its pods. A soup thickened with the mucilaginous pods of this plant, and containing shrimp, crabs, and often chicken, oysters, or one of the better cuts of veal. (Negro-French *gumbo*, from Angolan *kingombo*.)

Gumbo-Filé: A condiment made by powdering leaves of the Red Bay, *Persea borbonia*, powdered sassafras root often being added. It is used in place of okra for thickening gumbo.

Gumbo-Zhèbes: Gumbo made of herbs instead of okra. (Negro-French Zhèbe, from Fr. *herbe*, herb.)

Ilet: A city square. (Fr. *îlet*, little island. So called because the ditches which drained the streets were always full of water.)

Jalousie: In Louisiana, the common two-battened outdoor blind. (Fr. *jalousie*, Venetian Wind.)

Jambalaya: A Spanish-Creole dish made with rice and some other important ingredient, such as shrimp, crabs, cowpeas, oysters, sausage, chicken, or game. No plausible origin can be found.

Lagniappe: A trifling gift presented to a customer by a merchant. (Span, *la*, the, *ñapa*, from Kechuan *yapa*, 'a present made to a customer.')

Latanier: The fan-palm or palmetto.

Levee: An embankment on the Mississippi or smaller stream to prevent inun dation. (Fr. *lever*, to raise.)

Make ménage: To clean house. A typical local translation of French *faire le ménage*, to clean house.

Mamaloi: The Voodoo priestess. (Probably from Fr. *maman*, mama, and roi, king.)

Mardi Gras: Shrove Tuesday, the last day of Carnival. (Fr., lit., Fat Tuesday.)

Maringouin: A mosquito. (S. American Tupi and Guarani.)

Marraine: A godmother. (Fr. *marraine*, from pop. Lat. *matrana*, from *mater*, mother.)

Minou: A cat. (Fr. *minet*, kitten.)

Moqueur: The mocking-bird, *Mimus polyglottos polyglottos*. The most famous songbird in Louisiana. (Fr. *moquer*, to mock.)

Mulatto: The offspring of a Negro and a Caucasian. (Span. *mulato*, young mule; hence one of mixed race.)

Nainaine: Creole diminutive of *marraine*, godmother.

Négrillon: Negro child, pickaninny. (Fr. diminutive of *négre*, Negro.)

Octoroon: The child of a quadroon and a Caucasian. (A non-etymological formation from Lat. *octo*, eight, after *quadroon*, in which the suffix is *-oon*.)

Pape: The painted bunting, *Passerina ciris*. (Fr. *pape*, pope.)

Papillotes: Curl-papers. (Fr. papillote, curl-paper, from papillon, butterfly.)

Papillotes: Buttered or oiled paper in which fish, especially pompano, is broiled, to retain the flavor.

Parish: In Louisiana, the equivalent of *county*. Parishes here were originally ecclesiastical, not civil divisions.

Parrain: Godfather. (Fr. *parrain*, from low Lat. *patrinus*, from *pater*, father.)

Perique: A unique kind of tobacco grown only in the Parish of St. James, said to have been the nickname of Pierre Chenet, an Acadian who first produced this variety of tobacco. Local term.

Perron: Porch. (Fr. *perron* from *pierre*, stone. A construction on a façade, before a door, consisting of a landing reached by several steps.)

Picaillon: Small, mean, paltry. (Provencal, *picaioun*, small copper coin of Piémont, worth about one centime.)

Picayune: Formerly the Spanish half-real, worth about $6\frac{1}{4}$ cents; now applied to the U.S. five-cent piece. (Provencal, *picaioun*.)

Pigeonnier: A pigeon-house, a dove-cote. (Fr. *pigeon*, pigeon.)

Pirogue: A small canoe-like boat, made by hollowing a log, used on the bayous. (Span, *piragua*, borrowed from the Carib.)

Porte-cochère: The gateway allowing vehicles to drive into a courtyard. (Fr. *porte*, gate, *coche*, coach.)

Praline: A bonbon made of pecans browned in sugar. (From Maréchal du Plessis Praslin, whose cook is said to have invented it.)

Quadroon: The child of a Mulatto and a Caucasian. A person having one-fourth Negro blood. (Span, cuarteron, a quadroon.)

Quartee: Half of a five-cent piece. Local term.

Soirée: An evening party. (Fr. *soir*, from Lat. *serum*, late afternoon.)

Sugar-house: A sugar-mill or factory. Local term.

Tignasse: Tangled hair. (Fr. *tignasse*.)

Tignon: A sort of turban made of a bright-colored Madras handkerchief, formerly worn by women of color. (Fr. *tignon*, or *chignon*, the nape of the neck, from Lat. *catena*, chain.)

Tisane: A tea made of orange leaves or soothing herbs and used as a specific in certain illnesses. (Lat. *ptisana*, an infusion of maple.)

Veillée: An evening spent in pleasant conversation. Also a wake. (Fr. veiller, from Lat. vigilare, to watch.)

Vieux Carré: The original walled city of New Orleans, bounded by Canal Street, North Rampart Street, Esplanade Avenue, and the Mississippi River. (Fr. lit., Old Square.)

Voodoo: An African cult imported into America by Negro slaves. (Dahomey, *vôdu*, a deity.)

Wanga: A spell. Presumably of African origin.

Zombi: Spirit. (Congo, *zambi*, a deity.)

BIBLIOGRAPHY

THE following bibliography is a brief selection from more than 2,500 books and articles consulted in the preparation of the *New Orleans City Guide*. Files of such newspapers as the *Times-Picayune*, the *New Orleans States*, the *New Orleans Item*, and the *Morning-Tribune* have likewise been consistently used. A list of New Orleans newspapers and periodicals, both extant and defunct, will be found in the essay on *Newspapers*. For fiction the essay on Literature should be consulted. Additional titles will also be found in the essay on the *Theater* and on *Cuisine*.

Allan, Wm., LL.D. *Life and Work of John McDonogh*. The Trustees, Baltimore, 1886. 105 p.

Arthur, Stanley Clisby, and Kernion, George C. H. de. *Old Families of Louisiana*. Harmanson, New Orleans, 1931. 432 p.

Arthur, Stanley Clisby. *Audubon, An Intimate Life of the American Woodsman*. Harmanson, New Orleans, 1937. 517 p.

Arthur, Stanley Clisby. *Old New Orleans*. Harmanson, New Orleans, 1936. 246 p.

Asbury, Herbert. *The French Quarter*. A. A. Knopf, New York, 1936. 455 p.

Audubon, John James. *Journal of John James Audubon's Trip to New Orleans*, 1820-1821. Edited by Howard Corning. Club of Odd Volumes, Boston, 1921. 234 p.

Augustin, George. *The History of Yellow Fever*. Searcy & Pfaff, New Orleans, 1907. 1194 p.

Barbé-Marbois, François, Marquis de. *History of Louisiana*. Translated by W. B. Lawrence. Carey & Lea, Philadelphia, 1838. 435 p.

Bartlett, Napier. *Military Records of Louisiana*. Graham & Co., New Orleans, 1875. 259 p.

Basso, Hamilton. *Beauregard, the Great Creole*. Charles Scribner's Sons, New York, 1933. 333 p.

Biever, Rev. Albert H. *The Jesuits in New Orleans and the Mississippi Valley*. Hauser Printing Company, New Orleans, 1924. 173 p.

Bikle, Lucy Lemngwell Cable. *George W. Cable, His Life and Letters*. Charles Scribner's Sons, New York, London, 1928. 299 p.

Bisland, Elizabeth. *The Life and Letters of Lafcadio Hearn*. Houghton Mifflin, Boston, 1006. 2 v.

Bremer, Fredrika. *Homes of the New World*. Translated by Mary Howitt. Harper & Brothers, New York, 1853. 2 v.

Bumstead, Gladys. *Louisiana Composers*. New Orleans, October, 1935. 24 p.

Butler, Gen. Benj. F. *Autobiography and Personal Reminiscences; Butler's Book*. A. M. Thayer & Co., Boston, 1892. 2 v.

Cable, George W. *The Creoles of Louisiana*. Charles Scribner's Sons, New York, 1884. 320 p.

Campbell, Thos. W. *Manual of the City of New Orleans*. No. pub. New Orleans, 1903. Contains concise history of various Mayoralty Administrations, 1860-1900.

Castellanos, Henry C. *New Orleans as It Was*. Graham & Son, New Orleans, 1895- 330 P.

Chambers, Henry Edward. *History of Louisiana*. American Historical Society, Chicago, 1925. 3 v.

Clapp, Theodore. *Autobiographical Sketches and Recollections During Thirty-Five Years Residence in New Orleans*. Phillips Samson & Company, Boston, 1857. 419 p.

Clemens, Samuel L. (Mark Twain). *Life on the Mississippi*. Harper & Brothers, New York, 1901. 465 p.

Cline, Isaac Monroe. *Art and Artists in New Orleans During the Last Century*. Biennial Report, Louisiana State Museum, New Orleans, 1922. 13 p.

Coleman, John P. 'Old New Orleans Homes.' *New Orleans States*. A series of newspaper articles published at irregular intervals from 1922-25. Collected into scrapbooks by Howard Library, New Orleans. Curtis, N. C. *New Orleans, Its Houses, Shops and Public Buildings*. J. B. Lippincott Company, Philadelphia, 1933. 250 p.

Didimus, Henry. *New Orleans as I Found It*. Harper & Brothers, New York, 1845. 125 p.

Falk, Bernard. *The Naked Lady or Storm Over Adah*. Hutchinson & Co., London, 1935. 295 p.

Fay, Edwin Whitefield. *History of Education in Louisiana*. Department of Interior, Bureau of Education, Washington, D.C., 1898. 264 p.

Ficklen, John Rose. *History of Reconstruction in Louisiana*. (Through 1868.} Johns Hopkins University Studies in Historical & Political Science. 28:1-234. Baltimore, 1910.

Fortier, Alcée. *History of Louisiana*. Manzi-Joyant Co., New York, 1904. 4 v.

Fortier, Alcée (Editor). *Louisiana*. Southern Historical Assn., Atlanta, 1909. 2 v.

Frémaux, Léon J. *New Orleans Characters*. 16 hand-colored plates. New Orleans, 1876.

French, Benjamin Franklin. *Historical Collections of Louisiana embracing many rare and valuable documents relating to the material, civil and political history of the State*, 1846-53. Wiley and Putnam, New York. 5 v.

French, Benjamin Franklin. *Historical Collections of Louisiana and Florida including translations of original manuscripts relating to their discovery and settlement, etc.* J. Sabin and Sons, New York, 1869. 362 p.

French, Benjamin Franklin. *Historical Collections of Louisiana and Florida, Second Series*. Albert Mason, New York, 1875. 300 p.

Furman, James J. *History of Louisiana*. New Orleans, 1817. 2 v.

Gallier, James, Sr. *Autobiography of James Gallier*, Architect. E. Briere, Paris, 1864. 150 p.

Gayarre, Charles Étienne Arthur. *The Creoles of History and the Creoles of Romance*. C. E. Hopkins, New Orleans, 1885. 32 p.

Gayarré, Charles Étienne Arthur. *History of Louisiana*. Hansell & Bros., New Orleans, 1903. 4 v.

Genthe, Arnold. *Impressions of New Orleans*. 101 Photographic Plates with a foreword by Grace E. King. George H. Doran, New York, 1926. 250 p.

Gould, E. W. *Fifty Years on the Mississippi*, or Gould's History of River Navigation. Nixon-Jones, St. Louis, 1889. 749 p.

Hall, Abraham Oakey. *The Manhattaner in New Orleans*. J. C. Morgan, New Orleans, 1851. 190 p.

Historic Sketch Book and Guide to New Orleans. W. H. Coleman, New York, 1885. 322 p.

Jewell, Edwin L. *Crescent City, Illustrated*. Edwin L. Jewell, New Orleans, 1873. 136 p.

Journeys of Sieur de La Salle. Edited by Isaac Joslin Cox. Barnes & Co., New York, 1905. 2 v.

Kendall, John S. *History of New Orleans*. Lewis Publishing Co., Chicago & New York, 1922. 3 v.

Kerr, Lewis. *An Exposition of the Criminal Laws of the Territory of Orleans*. The Practice of the Courts of Criminal Jurisdiction, the Duties of their officers, with a collection of forms for the use of Magistrates and others. The first criminal code of Louisiana under American rule. Printed in Spanish and English. Spanish translation by L. Moreau Lislet. Bradford and Anderson, and Jean Renard. New Orleans, 1806.

King, Grace E. and Ficklen, John R. *A History of Louisiana*. University Publishing Co., New York, 1900. 346 p.

King, Grace E. *Creole Families of New Orleans*. The Macmillan Company, New York, 1921. 435 p.

King, Grace E. *Jean Baptiste Le Moyne, Sieur de Bienville*. Dodd, Mead & Co., New York, 1892. 330 p.

King, Grace E. *New Orleans, the Place and the People*. The Macmillan Company, New York, 1895. 402 p.

Ku Klux Klan or The Carpet Bagger in New Orleans. Southern Baptist Publication Society, Memphis, 1877. 51 p.

Latrobe, Benjamin Henry. *The Journal of Latrobe; Being the Notes and Sketches of an Architect, Naturalist and Traveller in the U.S. from 1796-1820.* D. Appleton & Co., New York, 1905. 269 p.

Le Page du Pratz, Antoine S. *Historie de la Louisiana.* De Bure, Delaguette, and Lambert, Paris, 1758. 3 v.

Louisiana Historical Quarterlies. Louisiana Historical Society, New Orleans, 1917.

Louisiana Scrap Books. Howard Library, New Orleans. A large amount of miscellaneous material on New Orleans and Louisiana composed of news paper clippings; indexed.

McVoy, Lizzie C., and Campbell, Ruth B. *A Bibliography of Fiction by Louisianians and on Louisiana Subjects.* Louisiana State University Press, Baton Rouge, 1935. 87 p. Martin, François Xavier. *An Account of Louisiana.* Exhibiting a compendious sketch of its political and natural history and topography, with a copious appendix containing several important documents. Franklyn and Garrow, Newbern, N. Car., 1804. 272 p.

Martineau, Harriet. *Retrospect of Western Travel.* Saunders & Otley, London, 1838. 3 v.

Merrick, Mrs. Caroline Elizabeth. *Old Times in Dixie Land*, A Southern Matron's Memories. The Grafton Press, New York, 1901. 241 p.

Milton, Geo. Fort. *Eve of Conflict.* Houghton Mifflin Co., Boston, 1934.

Myers, W. E. *The Israelites of Louisiana.* W. E. Myers, New Orleans, n.d. 139 p.

Nolte, Vincent. *Fifty Years in Both Hemispheres, or Reminiscences of a Former Merchant.* Redfield, New York, 1854. 484 p.

Norman, Benjamin Moore. *Norman's New Orleans and Environs.* B. M. Norman, New Orleans, and D. Appleton, New York, 1845. 206 p.

O Connor, Thomas. *History of the Fire Department of New Orleans.* Thos. O'Connor, New Orleans, 1895. 566 p.

Official Letter Books of W. C. C. Claiborne, 1801-16. Edited by Dunbar Row land, State Department of Archives and History, Jackson, Miss., 1917. 6 v. Parton, James. *General Butler in New Orleans.* Houghton Mifflin Co., Boston, 1864. 174 p.

Picayune Guide to New Orleans. Pub. by Times-Picayune, New Orleans, 14 editions, 1890 to 1928.

Publications of the Louisiana Historical Society. Graham & Son, New Orleans, 1895-1917. 10 v.

Read, William Alexander. *Louisiana-French.* Louisiana State University Studies No. 5. Louisiana State University Press, Baton Rouge, 1931. 253 p.

Reynolds, George M. *Machine Politics in New Orleans, 1897-1926.* Columbia University Press, New York, 1936. 245 p.

Ripley, Mrs. Eliza Moore (Chinn) McHatton, 1832-1912. *Social Life in Old New Orleans.* D. Appleton & Co., New York & London, 1912. 331p.

Robertson, James Alexander. *Louisiana Under the Rule of Spain, France and the United States, 1685-1807*, as portrayed in hitherto unpublished contemporary ... or transcribed from the original manuscripts, edited, annotated, and with bibliography and index . . . maps and plans. Arthur H. Clark Co., Cleveland, 1911. 2 v.

Saxe-Weimar Eisenach, Bernhard, Duke of. *Travels Through North America, 1825-26.* Carey, Lea & Carey, Philadelphia, 1828. 2 v.

Saxon, Lyle. *Fabulous New Orleans.* Century Co., New York, 1928. 330 p.

Saxon, Lyle. *Father Mississippi.* Century Co., New York, 1927. 415 p.

Saxon, Lyle. *Lafitte the Pirate.* Century Co., New York, 1930. 387 p.

Saxon, Lyle. *Old Louisiana.* Century Co., New York, 1929. 388 p.

Scroggs, William Oscar. *Filibusters and Financiers; the Story of William Walker and his Associates.* The Macmillan Company, New York, 1916. 408 p.

Scroggs, William Oscar. *The Story of Louisiana*. Bobbs, Merrill Co., Indianap olis, 1924. 324 p.

Standard History of New Orleans. Edited by Henry Rightor. Lewis Publishing Co., Chicago, 1900. 729 p.

Thackeray, William Makepeace. *Roundabout Papers*. J. B. Lippincott Company, Philadelphia, 1879.

Tinker, Edward Laroque. Bibliography of French Newspapers and Periodicals of Louisiana. American Antiquarian Society, Worcester, Mass., 1933. 126p.

Trollope, Mrs. Frances (Milton), 1780-1863. *Domestic Manners of the Americans*. Whittaker, Treacher & Co., London, 1832. 2 v.

The Ursulines in New Orleans and Our Lady of Prompt Succor. A record of two centuries, 1727-1925. P. J. Kenedy & Sons, New York, 1925. 319 p.

Walker, Alexander. *Life of Andrew Jackson*. Derby and Jackson, New York, 1858. 414 p.

Warmoth, Henry Clay. *War Politics and Reconstruction*. The Macmillan Company, New York, 1930. 285 p.

Wharton, George M. 'Stahl.' *New Orleans Sketch Book*. T. B. Peterson & Bros., Philadelphia, 1852. 202 p.

Young, Perry. *The Mistick Krewe*. Chronicles of Comus and his Kin. With 30 plates. Carnival Press, New Orleans, 1931. 268 p.

Zacharie, James S. *New Orleans Guide*. F. F. Hansell & Bros., New Orleans, 1902. 323 p.

ABOUT THE AUTHORS

The **Federal Writers' Project** was established in 1935 as part of Federal #1, a program to provide work relief for artists and professionals under the Works Progress Administration. During the next eight years, the project produced over a thousand books and pamphlets on local history, folkways, and culture, in addition to the multi-volume American Guide Series. The Louisiana project, whose publications included books on both New Orleans and the whole state, was directed by novelist and historian Lyle Saxon, author of *Fabulous New Orleans* and *Children of Strangers*. He was one of only four state project directors to remain in office for the duration of the Federal Writers' Project itself.

Lawrence N. Powell is professor of history at Tulane University, where he has taught since 1978. His specialties are the Civil War and Reconstruction; Southern history; Louisiana history and politics; and the Holocaust. From 1998 to 2005 he was also the Director of Tulane's Campus Affiliates Program and the Tulane/Xavier National Center for the Urban Community. Among his publications are *Troubled Memory: Anne Levy, the Holocaust, and David Duke's Louisiana* (Chapel Hill: University of North Carolina Press, 2000), *New Masters: Northern Planters during the Civil War and Reconstruction* (New Haven: Yale University Press, 1980; Fordham University Press, 1999), editor of *Reconstructing Louisiana: Volume VI: Louisiana Purchase Bicentennial Series in Louisiana History* (University of Southern Louisiana Press, 2002), and co-editor with Richard N. Current et al. of *Encyclopedia of the Confederacy*, 4 Volumes (New York: Simon & Schuster, 1993). His latest book is *George Washington Cable's New Orleans* (Baton Rouge: LSU Press, 2008). His articles have been published in *Journal of American History*, *The American Scholar*, *Studies in American Political Development*, *The New Republic*, among many others.